Gendered Realities

Gendered Realities

Essays in Caribbean Feminist Thought

Edited by

Patricia Mohammed

UNIVERSITY OF THE WEST INDIES PRESS

Barbados • Jamaica • Trinidad and Tobago

and

CENTRE FOR GENDER AND DEVELOPMENT STUDIES

Mona, Jamaica

University of the West Indies Press
1A Aqueduct Flats   Mona
Kingston 7   Jamaica

06 05 04 03 02   5 4 3 2

CATALOGUING IN PUBLICATION DATA

Gendered realities: essays in Caribbean feminist thought / edited by
Patricia Mohammed

p. cm.
Includes bibliographical references.
ISBN: 976-640-112-8

1. Feminist theory – Caribbean Area. 2. Feminism – Caribbean Area. 3.
Women – Education – Jamaica. 4. Feminism and literature – Caribbean Area.
5. Sexual division of labour – Caribbean Area. 6. Sex role in mass media –
Caribbean Area. 7. Gender identity – Caribbean Area. I. Patricia Mohammed.

HQ1501.G46 2002   305.309729 -dc21

Cover illustration: Prudence Lovell, *Cor, Heart, Herte, Corazon, Hertz, Couer*
(Heart in Six Languages) (gouache on canvas).

Book and cover design by Robert Harris
roberth@cwjamaica.com
Set in Plantin Light 10/15 x 24
Printed on acid-free paper.
Printed in Canada.

Contents

PART I   NEW RUM IN OLD BARRELS: IDEAS IN FEMINIST THEORY AND METHODOLOGY

PART II   DECIPHERING THE SCRIPT: GENDER AND HISTORIOGRAPHY

PART V THE DOUBLE TAKE: GENDER
AND THE LITERARY IMAGINATION

PART VI SPEAKING THEIR PIECE: WOMEN,
GENDER AND THE MEDIA

Foreword

Some ten years ago the Women and Development Studies Project, carried out at the University of the West Indies, put out a benchmark publication entitled *Gender in Caribbean Development.* A number of papers presented at a 1986 inaugural seminar of the project, and edited by Patricia Mohammed and Catherine Shepherd, were pulled together in that publication. The production of this first reader in 1988 marked the genesis of an authentic but rudimentary Caribbean epistemology of women and of gender relations in Caribbean society. As noted in its introduction, the seminar

> aimed to begin developing the framework for a gender-aware approach for analysing social change in the region and to identify areas and issues for teaching, research and documentation in the programme of Women's Studies at the University. (p. xiii)

This process of teaching, research and documentation has not only continued between then and now; the intervening years have also allowed for the refinement of this framework and the acquisition of skills in gender analysis on the part of a number of persons. As a result, the Caribbean now boasts an increasing number of scholars and a burgeoning body of scholarship in gender studies. This is evidenced by the fact that the programme of Women and Development Studies, started in 1982, has now evolved into a widely accepted academic programme of Gender and Development Studies offered at both the undergraduate and graduate levels of the University of the West Indies.

This work, *Gendered Realities: An Anthology of Essays in Caribbean Feminist Thought,* is a project of the Mona Unit of the Centre for Gender and Development Studies. This is one of three major publications to come out of the Centre for Gender and Development Studies over the last two years, pointing to a sophistication and maturity that has been achieved in constructing a truly Caribbean perspective in gender studies. This volume collects twenty-nine papers which examine a range of Caribbean realities from a gender perspective.

The treatment and organization of the chapters seek to reflect the true epistemological nature of and methodological approaches to gender studies. Strict disciplinary boundaries of knowledge evident in earlier publications are less marked in this volume.

One chapter is an edited version of the inaugural professorial lecture given by Elsa Leo-Rhynie when she was appointed as the first professor in gender and development studies at the University of the West Indies in 1992. The paradigm shift from women and development studies (with its focus on issues that affect women), to gender and development studies (with its concern with relationships between the genders in all areas of life), is traced in this paper. This paper also explores ways in which gender studies in the academy has moved from the periphery to an integral and central area of study offered through the formal channels of the institution. This first paper therefore serves to situate the volume in its historical context, and provides readers with an appreciation of the evolution of gender studies in the academy.

As with other interdisciplinary readers emanating from the centre, this volume will, no doubt, add to the growing body of scholarship that seeks, through the application of a gender analysis, to find new ways of seeing, interpreting, understanding and reconstructing the dynamics of the Caribbean reality.

The financial contribution that supported this publication was made by the Project of Support in Teaching, Research and Outreach between the Government of the Netherlands through the Royal Netherlands Embassy in Jamaica. The Centre for Gender and Development Studies, University of the West Indies, gratefully acknowledges this assistance.

Special acknowledgment is also made of Dr Patricia Mohammed's contribution. She has been one of the pioneers in gender studies at the University of the West Indies and an outstanding scholar in feminist thought in the region. Not only has she followed through a full cycle of events, moving from being course director for the inaugural seminar of 1986 to being head of the Mona unit of the Centre for Gender and Development Studies, but she has also, after these many years, been instrumental in editing and producing a second volume of papers in gender studies. I am confident that this reader in Caribbean feminist thought will prove to be another significant benchmark in the life and history of the Centre for Gender and Development Studies, and will be an invaluable resource to scholars, students and the general reading public both within and outside of the region.

Barbara Bailey
Acting Regional Coordinator
Centre for Gender and Development Studies
University of the West Indies

Acknowledgments

This book has undergone several reincarnations and must acknowledge its debt to many people and institutions whose names or work may not be visible in the final product, but who have been instrumental and supportive in its making.

The major sources of funding for its preparation have been the University of the West Indies, Mona campus, Research and Publications Awards Committee and the Dutch Services Overseas, Royal Netherlands Embassy Project with the Centre for Gender and Development Studies.

In its earlier form several people were approached to read sections and write introductions. Among these were Mary Chamberlain, Don Robotham, Rosemary Hoefte and Kate Young. My thanks for their agreement, apologies that the initial ideas shifted course, and a reminder that books, like human beings, are also mercurial.

In the beginning there was no name. The book existed as a fledgling idea until it was dubbed "Gendered Realities" by Elsa Leo-Rhynie, given a fixed identity, and took on a definite form.

My sincere gratitude to Althea Perkins and Nazma Muller, both of whom assisted at various times with the editorial process. In the second-to-last lap before reaching the publisher, Hilary Nicholson's editorial assistance and insights were invaluable. This volume, however, owes its delivery to the organizational skills and efficiency of Shakira Maxwell, research assistant at the Mona Unit, Centre for Gender and Development Studies. For this as well as her goodwill in undertaking such projects of the Mona Unit, I thank her wholeheartedly.

The University of the West Indies Press has been supportive of this book since its inception. Both Linda Cameron and Pansy Benn have assisted and advised throughout its earlier stages. My sincere thanks to Linda Speth and Shivaun Hearne for seeing it through to the conclusion and for their continued encouragement of publication initiatives in gender.

To all the contributors who have both supported and reminded us of its impending existence, my warm thanks. I accept full responsibility for warts and blemishes you may find on your pages.

To those who have followed the fortunes of women and gender studies, it will be clear that the landscape of gender keeps changing with each decade. Such change must be measured against the first pioneers in this field in the region, some over two decades ago. That an institution such as the Centre for Gender and Development Studies exists today, from which a publication can take shape, is owed primarily to the women and men at the three campuses of the University of the West Indies who took on, many of them voluntarily, the often thankless task of institution building. The Mona Unit, Centre for Gender and Development Studies dedicates the book to the past members of the Women and Development Studies Groups on whose initiatives we now build.

Introduction
The Material of Gender

Patricia Mohammed

We are not born men and women, but we do become our gender. We each take our biological script and shape it into something we define as our gender and our sexuality. The essentialist contouring of gender, and its contingent sexuality, serves two purposes. On the one hand it provides institutions and the state with a normative framework by which to fit populations into "natural" slots for labour and social relations – both inside and outside the home. On the other, it ensures that there is a reference group with whom as individuals we can work out our similarities and differences and thus our capacities for survival. In most societies and among most peoples there are two genders which correspond more or less to the two sexes. But this is not always the case. Whether it upsets our equilibrium or not to admit this fact, the biological and social possibilities of gender and sexuality are perhaps not limitless, but certainly changeable and variable across, and within, space and time. This is a fundamental reality of gender, and at the same time it is one which we are least able to fully grasp.

The goal of the feminist agenda, as it has been shaped by the varied expressions of twentieth-century feminism, is to unearth the complexity of social and biological gender. "Gender" is used popularly to express the subordination of female to male, an order which for convenience is referred to as the patriarchal order. The gender system has recurrently relegated the activities and lives of men and women into two ideologically separate spheres: that of the male to a public realm and that of the female to a private or domestic domain. This division is not in itself particularly offensive, and it represents a certain aspect of the lived reality. But it poses a problem in that activities in the "public sphere" are assumed to be hierarchically superior to those carried out in the "private sphere". This has never been a true representation of the different and overlapping roles of gender in the development of human culture. The public and private lives of individuals are inextricably linked. In addition, a neat separation of gender in the past into a privileged public masculinity and a subordinate domestic femininity has assuredly never been an adequate description of the lives of men and women in the Caribbean. The colonial and postcolonial processes of settlement and migration have required equally the labour of both male and female. Culture has been dependent on the contribution of both women and men, sometimes in different areas of concentration. Yet in the forging of ethnic, community and national identities, women are frequently ascribed an adjunctive and less valued role.

By troubling the concept gender in its second and third waves, feminism attempts to address the problems both men and women experience as a result of fixed social ideas about sexual difference. There are several questions one might ask about this stirring of already muddy waters: Why have these issues surfaced in the twentieth century with such intensity? What purpose does it serve to further complicate an already complex "modern" existence in which multiple identities of class, caste, race, ethnicity, nationalism, religion and the like, compete with yet another identity, that of gender?

The answers, like the problems, are not as facile as they may appear to the uninitiated. The feminist movement cannot be reduced to a struggle by disaffected women to gain unmitigated female power to match that of an assumed always-powerful male. Expressions of power, in class relations for instance, may be more obvious to perceive or to challenge. Power in gender relations is not so easy to grasp except when it is physically demonstrated, as in the case of domestic violence or sexual abuse. It is disguised in gift-wrapped packages with notions of love and protection liberally etched on the paper. For example, until the last few decades it was convenient for societies to view women as the "weaker sex", or to interpret rape as a crime in which the victim was guilty of provocatively soliciting the act. These beliefs restricted female movement and curtailed female sexual expression. It was more convenient for a system of production, which depended on a labour supply uninterrupted by such inconvenient things as childbearing and child rearing, to restrict female education and assign women roles which were primarily to do with caring and nurturing. It was more convenient for the state to assume that this was what all women did, so that a family wage could be calculated for men, and women could provide an army of lower-paid surplus labour.

The explanations that kept such an order in place firmly for many centuries defied public confrontation in the past (except, as far as we know, in the actions and writings of very few individuals). They were justified on the basis of biology, religion, social customs and preference, and very resistant to change. Nonetheless, major challenges have emerged over the last few decades and with these challenges have come the scholarly investigations. Women and gender studies have begun and continue to unravel the scroll of gender, to rethink categories and reread old documents, to ask new questions of old adages and taken-for-granted beliefs. The old gender scripts have obscured another side of gender reality, presenting this as a fixed rather than dynamic process.

The study or understanding of gender should not be limited by the boundaries of the contemporary intellectual imagination. In the same way that our gendered identities are at some level fluid and malleable, so too should be the thought processes that allow us to explore the many dimensions of our gender and sexual identities. Still, the burden of naming remains a liability for gender, as if no suitable cap can be found to fit the many heads that work in this area. Is it women's studies, gender studies, or feminist studies? Is it a discipline in the making or a new interrogation of existing disciplines? The strength and potential of gender studies (and also a presumed weakness) lie in its interdisciplinarity, its unwillingness to confine knowledge within the boundaries of the existing paradigm, by constantly attempting to go "where no man has gone before" in finding new ways of seeing and constructing knowledge and experience. This is one way of reading the essays that rub shoulders in the different sections of this book. The different frameworks employed by the authors demonstrate that gender can be understood as a complex analytical construct, as part of our everyday lived experience, and can be read through the lens of a large number of disciplines.

Prudence Lovell's painting titled *Cor, Heart, Herte, Corazon, Hertz, Coeur (Heart in Six Languages),* used as the cover illustration of this book, is the first contribution in the text. Lovell, an English painter who lives and works in Jamaica, describes this painting as follows:

> This *Heart* painting is just one of many staging posts on a continuing line of enquiry which meanders this way and that. None of my paintings is conceived as a definitive or final statement at the time of its execution, although when you look at them in sequence later you sometimes see that a particular work has been a sort of summing up of a fairly discrete stage in my enquiry, a fairly well bounded train of my thought. I think I mostly postulate, "Could it be like this?"
>
> In recent works I have employed a sort of shallow space – a Pollockian space if you like –which does not use conventional devices to define it; it's just an all-over surface which advances and recedes in a small spatial depth. I like that surface to be seductive, so that is one aspect of what I am doing. With the painting in question, I was working with gouache, a liquid that acts like a solid. I like to work fast with this medium. Sometimes when you are exploring how paint works you need to respond rapidly to it and push and pull it around.
>
> When you're engaged in this process, you often just want a simple motif which you can return to and play with. In the *Heart* painting, I chose a simple shape that has a resonance for everyone: its potential for triteness was a challenge to move beyond it. More generally, as far as content is concerned, I find that I don't usually want to comment in any direct way on things that are happening in the country or the world. Nevertheless, they do impinge on me and they connect with my own internal imperatives to form alliances which ebb and flow and struggle to find an appropriate form.
>
> These are the things with which one deals in one's work. The challenge then is that one has to find some structural and haptic accommodation with those alliances. I find that if one's approach to this process is entirely rational then all the eddying that goes on at a subliminal level doesn't get a chance. I therefore try to suspend the rational mind up to a point. I do risk losing some critical awareness at the time of conception and execution, but that can be brought to bear later.

Lovell has also repeated this symbol in other paintings. The universality of the heart in any language or culture symbolizes certain elements that seem to underlie the condition of being human – love, courage, feeling and passion, the affective versus rationality. The process of thinking and writing about gender is in many ways similar to painting. It attempts to break down the artificial division of human beings along the divides of sex – an Apollonian rational logic versus a Dionysian preoccupation with the heart, spirit and romance, to move between the rational needs and the unconscious desires that shape those needs. Interlocked with the study of sexuality, the study of gender is also an attempt to arrive at another "truth of our being" (Foucault 1980).

The chapters in *Gendered Realities* engage in this ongoing academic exploration of masculinity and femininity using different media, disciplines and modes of expression. The five chapters in part 1, New Rum in Old Barrels: Ideas in Feminist Theory and Methodology, revisit some ideas in theory and methodology with the new insights of gender. How we perceive reality, how we shape our sexuality, our ideas and practices of gender in society are partly constructed by the institutional rules and regulations required for community and survival. They are also partly a result of our biological predispositions, which challenge the fixity of these rules. In other words, we negotiate the middle ground between the mind and the body, between reason and emotion, between social acceptability and ostracism, between gender norms and sexual identity.

Gender theory suggests that we actually live our lives by finding a rapprochement between the two poles of the social and the biological. Saskia Wieringa develops these ideas in her chapter "Essentialism versus Constructivism: Time for a Rapprochement?". Michelle Rowley "disrupts and reorders silenced spaces" by revitalizing overburdened depictions of woman around matrifocality, reputation and respectability, mothering, womanhood and marriage, and by allowing the "matrifolk", who have been quiet on the academic pages, to speak for themselves. Also examining this concept which has bedevilled "woman" in Caribbean society, Janet Momsen considers one of the major contradictions attached to its application – the double paradox inherent in the concept of matrifocality, the strength and resilience suggested by "mother centredness", coupled with the presence yet absence of patriarchy as the dominant ideological instrument which holds gender hierarchy in place.

The focus of gender inquiry in the region has tended in the previous decades to be on woman, with masculinity outside the women's room, opening the shutters little by little and peeping in. Keisha Lindsay's chapter, "Is the Caribbean Male an Endangered Species?", challenges the wholesale acceptance of yet another formulaic concept, that of "male marginalization", suggesting that we would be better employed as scholars to deconstruct such ideas both theoretically and methodologically and to cultivate home-grown alternative epistemologies.

The serious student of gender must take his or her first step by seeing these perennial concerns with new eyes, or as Maria Mies once phrased it, by "pouring new wine into old vessels". Odette Parry troubles the old debates in research methodology about positivism versus naturalism. She critically explores the process of research carried out on the education of boys and girls in the Caribbean region for the feminist insights which it reveals, commenting that there can be no one definitive feminist methodology. At the same time, she suggests a wise mixture of subjectivity and objectivity in any form of social research.

The re-presentation of history has a major role in the project of gender as seen in part 2, Deciphering the Script: Gender and Historiography. While the category "woman" has been expanding to include women of different ethnic groups, the identity of women of Indian descent as Caribbean settlers remains elusive, as Verene Shepherd observes. The sources for finding Indian women's voices and experiences in history are few, although they are clearly being addressed more and more in the historiography of the region. This recovery of diverse ethnic groups and classes of women and men, and the issues which affected them differently in the past, is still relatively virgin territory for the budding historian in this field. Bridget Brereton maps out some of the areas that need to be covered, both for the enhancement of Caribbean gender historiography and, ultimately, for a more inclusive historical understanding of racial and gendered categories as these have varied or recurred over time. These chapters invite students in particular to continue deciphering the historical documents and to rewrite the colonial script of our ancestral past in gender-sensitive ways.

In part 3, Unlocking the Doors: Gender in the Academy, Elsa Leo-Rhynie captures the birth pangs of gender studies at the tertiary level, providing a valuable record of its emergence and growth. She observes that the area is rich with possibilities for empowerment of the sexes and expansion of the academy itself. Leo-Rhynie also raises the many concerns that surfaced as women's studies has moved out of the periphery and into the open playing field of tertiary education. Barbara Bailey explores the realities of coeducation in the classrooms of secondary schools in Jamaica, questioning the claim of formal schooling that it is nondiscriminatory in allowing for the full development of both males and females. Peter Whiteley's findings on the underinvolvement of females in science education is a primary illustration of how sexual difference is deeply embedded in the choices made by boys and girls, and thus the way in which the perceptions of the rational male and irrational female personality and characteristics persist in society. Leo-Rhynie and Pencle continue, like Bailey and Whitely, to examine schooling as a space in which gender stereotypes are reinforced and maintained.

The study and revalorizing of women and their roles in society remain central to gender studies, as shown in the chapters in part 4, Housekeeping Matters: Women's Roles in Family, Economy and Society. The actual contributions and potential of woman as a sex, the symbols of strength and economic resilience on which a theory of gender has evolved in the region, and the material base from which the ideas of the Caribbean family and Caribbean womanhood have been constructed need to be revisited with clearer and more microscopic lenses, as Eudine Barriteau, Alissa Trotz and Joan Rawlins have done. From their vantage points, valuable insights and proposals emerge to continue shaping the directions of a feminist agenda for political and social change in the region. In a rethinking of women's economic marginality, Barriteau argues that women's contribution to economic development is undermined by stereotypic notions of femininity that hold women to be irrational as economic actors. In spite of, or perhaps because of, change, some ideas of sexual difference recur with remarkable consistency. Examining the situation of women in Guyana, Trotz warns that while we must question the implicit assumptions of universality as these attach to the experiences of gender, at the same time we must guard against the reification of *difference* amongst women of different ethnic groups in the region. Rawlins introduces a little-understood category of women, highlighting the valuable contributions which middle-aged and older women make to the society and the economy.

The literary imagination allows the writer to play with nuances of our multiple and competing identities. Conceptually, gender scholarship in the Caribbean has never limited itself to an examination of gender identity. There has been a consistent scrutiny and cross-examination of gender with the categories of race, ethnicity, class, age and regional difference by scholars of the region. In part 5, The Double Take: Gender and the Literary Imagination, David Williams, Anna Maria Bankay, Paulette Ramsay and Denise de Caires Narain draw on the fiction of selected male and female authors from Trinidad, Costa Rica, the Dominican Republic and Antigua, among others, to illustrate the interlocked nature of gender and race identities. Richard Clarke takes his point of departure from the film presentation of gender in *The Crying Game* to outline another bold way of seeing: that the conventional dualistic notions of gender must be interrogated. Such an approach may reveal that both gender and race are learned performances designed to secure an internal illusion to these social categories. Fiction, like film, permits this kind of exploration of gender and sexuality, as de Caires Narain has interpreted from Jamaica Kincaid's distinctive mapping of sexuality as a central construction of Caribbean womanhood

In part 6, Speaking Their Piece: Women, Gender and the Media, Hilary Nicholson suggests that the media should itself undergo interrogation and scrutiny towards producing a more gender-sensitive approach which balances male and female experience in society. Marjan de Bruin argues for women to be more involved in the control and management of media houses. One aspect of this re-visioning through the media may be to acknowledge, as Kathryn Shields-Brodber does in the next section, that we need to reconsider what is deviant for women. Drawing directly from the media world, two journalists, Kim Nicholas Johnson in "Saga of a Flagwoman" and Kathy-Ann Waterman in "Woman of the Shadows", have shown that the choices some women make are atypical rather than aberrant. Such pieces invite us to consider the ways in which media may be instrumental in shifting stereotypic notions of womanhood and manhood, granting dignity and humanity to those who have in the past been perceived as beyond the diameter of the respectable.

In the final section of this book, Made in the Caribbean: Constructing Gender, the regional stamp is evident in the stories, language, imagery, thoughts and propensities for stereotyping, which are not remote-controlled but are an outgrowth of a Caribbean cultural environment. The extract "Grandma's Estate", reprinted by permission of Sistren with Honor Ford-Smith, depicts, more incisively than can be captured in quantitative analyses, the way in which the individual sensibility leads to a self-conscious appraisal and understanding of multiple identities, particularly those of mixed race, in this part of the world. The legacy of Marxist scholarship and activism has left women who are more economically or socially privileged generally apologetic for the concerns they raise as female. Bread-and-butter issues of survival take pre-eminence over female subjectivity. Yet the very roots of feminist theory and a feminist vision were planted by the class of articulate, educated women who needed to transcend the limits of their socially expected roles. Like Prudence Lovell, Petrine Archer-Straw's "Diary Pages 1980–1990" allows us another kind of voice: the female artist, whose private expressions and self-conscious work processes paint different hues on our palette of gendered sensibilities.

Merle Hodge urges us with her usual directness to consider what has really constituted the Caribbean family and the different legitimate forms of familial organization that have evolved in the region. Hodge challenges the myopic and morally misinformed views which have constructed the notion of the Caribbean family as deviant, suggesting that a candid look at this institution will reveal its inherent strengths and the reasons for its weaknesses. In "Gender and Adult Sexuality", Barry Chevannes visits some popular expressions of male and female sexuality. He sets these in opposition to the private lived experiences of men and women, in an attempt to demystify some of the commonly held values which are symbolically preserved. Kathryn Shields-Brodber suggests that the talkative woman is not at all an aberration of some gender norm and that women in Jamaica, like men, have to hold the performance floor, particularly in the media, if they want to be heard.

The separation of gender into neatly opposed divisions of femininity and masculinity is a spurious one, as gender theorists have conceded. The condition of the Caribbean male and of Caribbean masculinity has, nonetheless, long prevailed as a subject of unfriendly discussions between the sexes. Linden Lewis, in the final and forward-looking chapter, "Envisioning a Politics of Change within Caribbean Gender Relations", bravely appeals to men to prepare more accommodating ground for negotiating gender and gender relations in the region.

While scholarship and programmes in gender are moving towards and increasingly incorporating the voices and concerns of men and masculinity, this trend is still relatively new, and perhaps necessarily so for the present, being centred around the recovery and visibility of women in relation to men, and for the present still creating a subject of the once objectified sex. Brereton, in her chapter here, points to the need for preserving the centrality of women's lives in our research and writing, emphasizing that it is "legitimate and useful because tremendous gaps in our knowledge still exist". This centring of women does not negate a gender approach, and it does not mean that gender studies will not expand organically in the future to shift and change positions or ideas in this way or that. Feminist theory and vision will no doubt be infused with new ideas and practices suggested by male scholars and a new generation of scholars and activists in the future, and this has already begun. Ultimately, a primary and sensible point of gender studies which we must keep constant is that the feminist goal is not to replace one central subject by another, not to reverse a hierarchy, but to arrive at a theoretical position in which neither sex is negatively objectified.

In the academy gender studies, compared to other long-standing disciplinary enquiries, is still in a fledgling state. The first courses in women's studies were taught in the region less than two decades ago. As we develop curricula and materials that break down the artificial barriers between disciplines, and the limits these impose on the new students who will engage in gender studies, we need to interrupt the traditional ways in which such knowledge is grouped and organized in the text itself, thus nurturing gender studies to fulfil its promise. As they are presented in this book, the chapters at times follow a transdisciplinary order to allow a preoccupation with the subject matter, the issues being raised, the new approaches to research being tried out and the different modes of presenting ideas, rather than be fenced in by artificial barriers. The reader is invited to explore the material differently. Public collides with private, institutional with individual, rational with intuitive, quantitative research with qualitative explorations. These essays were culled over a two-year period, works selected randomly from the main interests of each of the scholars and writers included here. In this sense they represent a candid view of how gender has preoccupied our thoughts in the Caribbean over the last twenty-five years.

References

Foucault, Michel. 1980. *The History of Sexuality*. Vol. 1, *An Introduction*. New York: Vintage Books.

New Rum in Old Barrels
Ideas in Feminist Theory and Methodology

1   Essentialism versus Constructivism
Time for a Rapprochement?

SASKIA WIERINGA

There have been two waves of feminism and two sexual revolutions since the beginning of the tewntieth century. The first one ended in and was drowned by the establishment of essentialism by the sexologists. The second one is still going on and has produced constructivism as the dominant paradigm by which to analyse sexuality.

The first wave of feminism is better known for its struggle for women's rights in the field of the vote, education and employment. That feminist women in those years also fought against what they saw as male sexual aggression is almost obliterated from memory. In Britain their campaigns were centred around the issue of "social purity", which included prostitution, traffic in women and abuse of girls. Male vice was seen to cause these problems, which resulted in what was at times dubbed "bodily slavery" of women. The sexologists, of whom Havelock Ellis was the best known, successfully deployed "natural sex" against feminism, by proclaiming the "scientific truth" of their findings.

There seems to be an unbridgeable rift between essentialism and constructivism or constructionism. If essentialism dominated the debate on "women's nature", human sexuality and human behaviour in general in the first sixty years of the twentieth century, present-day essentialists face heavy criticism. They are denounced as reactionary persons who attempt to continue women's subordination. When an argument is called "essentialist" no more discussion about the issue at stake is deemed necessary: doesn't essentialism mean that all women are seen as "natural" housewives and as masochists who delight in sexual humiliation?

No one wants to be regarded as such a backward person. Simone de Beauvoir's dictum that woman is made, not born, is generally regarded as the decisive blow against essentialism. And many more blows followed. Not women's nature but the construction of gender relations is the topic of the dominant type of research and debate. Yet, at the same time, specific rights for women are demanded. Women are seen as a distinct category, suffering from a special kind of subordination which requires specific policies and campaigns. Although feminists generally agree that there are wide differences between women in relation to class, race, ethnicity, sexual option and age, they still do talk about "women". What, then, *are* these "women"? What do women have in common? Only oppression? And what about their bodies, motherhood and sexuality?

The way sexuality has been conceptualized clearly demonstrates how far essentialism and constructivism diverge. Essentialist scientists have argued since the beginning of the twentieth century that women's sexual difference from men is the cause of women's oppression. Wittig takes an extreme constructivist position when she argues that oppression produces sexual difference.

In this chapter I explore the relations between these two positions. In so doing I suggest that we may need a *rapprochement* between the two. I argue that instead of resorting to an either/or position it may be most fruitful to find the interconnections between the two and where each of them can be most strategically deployed.

I first discuss essentialism, and stress that it arose partly in response to a strong feminist movement. Next I discuss the two major contributions to the unmasking of essentialist thought as it existed in the 1960s and 1970s: Foucault and the women's movement. In the conclusion I insist that although constructivism is a decisive step forward from essentialism, we should not completely denounce essentialism.

Essentialism

Essentialism arose in the first quarter of the twentieth century. The major theorists associated with this stream of thinking are Havelock Ellis, Kinsey, and Masters and Johnson. Although there are important differences between these three major sexologists, they are generally assumed to agree on the basic ideas of essentialism. They are presented as the ones who have liberated sexology from Victorian sexual repression. Admittedly, Victorian ideas about sexuality left a great deal to improve: a double morality (in which upper-class women, as opposed to men or working-class women, were seen as innocent beings who did not or at least should not know anything about sex), its class specificity and its legislative effects.[1] Essentialism is generally credited with "freeing" women as sexually active human beings.

But Havelock Ellis in particular, one of the major founding fathers of essentialism, waged his war not only against Victorian morality but also against the feminist movement of his day, with its strong critique of male domination. The feminists of his day were not only suffragists, they were also "spinsters", a term they carried proudly, rejecting and denouncing male sexual aggression. Around 1900 violent debates ensued against male violence, which, it was said, was used to control free women who refused these male ideas of sexuality. Sheila Jeffreys, in her excellent 1985 study of these debates, gives many examples of feminists who saw male sexuality as a weapon of male power. Elisabeth Wolstenholme Elmy, for instance, who worked alongside the radical suffragists Josephine Butler and Christabel Pankhurst and who founded her own Women's Emancipation Union in 1891, wrote in 1895, "[the Women's Emancipation Union] recognizes that the slavery of sex is the root of all slavery, and that injustice to womanhood, especially injustice within the family, is the perennial source of all other injustice . . ." (Wolstenholme Elmy in Jeffreys 1985: 28).

Wolstenholme Elmy was also very active in a campaign surrounding the Criminal Code Bill, which was introduced in 1880. This bill aimed to embody in statute law the fact that a man could not rape his wife. She denounced this provision as an attempt to reduce wives to "bodily slavery" (Jeffreys 1985: 31). In fact, the struggle for the vote was seen by both men and women to be for the right of women to control their bodies and against the right of men to freely exercise their bodily lusts on women. As Christabel Pankhurst stated:

The opposition argues thus: if women are to become politically free they will become spiritually strong and economically independent, and thus they will not any longer give or sell themselves to be the playthings for men. That, in a nutshell, is the case against votes for women. (Jeffreys 1985: 46)

Thus, feminists of the first wave did not see male sexual aggression as natural but as a weapon of male power.

In an attempt to counter these arguments, Ellis founded sexology as a science. Jackson, who has carefully studied Ellis's writings, concludes that he was seriously concerned about what he perceived to be the tendency of women to reject their maternal function and to "deny the laws of their own nature". Although he concedes that men were selfish and brutal lovers, he is confident that if they would engage in a more sophisticated "art of love", women would also get their own share of sexual pleasure. To this major task he vows to devote himself. He admits that this would be no mean task, with men behaving like "orangutan[s] playing the violin", yet he is confident of his success. He presents himself as the champion of women's erotic rights, for which he is regarded as adopting a progressive position (Jackson 1987: 56).

However, those erotic rights of women do not coincide with the ones that feminists like Wolstenholme Elmy advocated. As Jackson writes:

For Ellis, then, every act of heterosexual intercourse was essentially a re-enactment of primitive, animal courtship; the male sexual urge was essentially an urge to conquer, and the female sexual urge an urge to be conquered: "The sexual impulse in woman is fettered by an inhibition which has to be conquered . . . her wooer in every act of courtship has the enjoyment of conquering afresh an oft-won woman." Thus the close association between male sexuality, power and violence was a biological necessity and therefore inevitable: "to exert power . . . is one of our most primary impulses, and it always tends to be manifested in the attitude of a man towards the woman he loves". (1987: 57)

Jackson continues that Ellis tries to prove that "women 'really enjoy' being raped, beaten and sexually humiliated and brutalized. He concluded that in women pain and sexual pleasure were virtually indistinguishable" (Jackson 1987: 57).

It is no wonder, then, that feminists of the present wave of the women's movement denounced these ideas of a man who became the founding father of modern sex research and one of the major exponents of essentialism. The more so as Ellis clearly set his ideas up as the scientific proof to discredit feminist ideas of his time. Jackson again provides the relevant quotation:

I am well aware that in thus asserting a certain tendency in women to delight in suffering pain – however careful and qualified the position I have taken – many estimable people will cry out that I am degrading a whole sex and generally supporting the "subjection of women". But the day for academic discussion concerning the "subjection of women" has gone by. The tendency I have sought to make clear is too well established by the experience of normal and typical women – however numerous the exceptions may be – to be called into question. I would point out to those who would deprecate the influence of such facts in relation to social progress that nothing is gained by regarding women as simply men of smaller growth. They are not so: they have the laws of their own nature; their development must be along their own lines, and not along masculine lines. It is as true now as in Bacon's day that we only learn to command nature by obeying her . . . We can neither attain a sane view of life nor a sane social legislation of life unless we possess a just and accurate knowledge of the fundamental instincts upon which life is built. (Ellis in Jackson 1987: 57–58)

As Ellis and his followers apparently were not fully convinced that the "academically accurate laws of nature" that they had "discovered" were equally clear to women, they proceeded to produce sex manuals. One of the most influential marriage manuals was the one by Van de Velde, first published in English in 1928. It became enormously influential: by the late 1970s over a million copies had been sold. Based on Ellis's ideas, the book set out to "teach wives not only how to behave in coitus, but, above all, how and what to feel in this unique act" (Van de Velde in Jackson 1987: 59).

Sexual disharmony was seen as the root cause of marital discord, threatening the basis of modern society. In order to avert this evil, members of the medical profession, psychoanalysts, took it upon themselves to teach women and men the proper laws of nature. One of the major tasks to which they devoted themselves was to eroticize women's submission to men and to teach men how to give their women pleasure in this sexual order. The final reward would be sexual bliss. A last quote from Van de Velde:

woman is a harp who only yields her secrets of melody to the master who knows how to handle her . . . the husband must study the harp and the art of music . . . this is the book of rules for his earnest and reverend study . . . his reward comes when the harp itself is transformed into an artist in melody, entrancing the initiator. (Van de Velde in Jackson 1987: 62)

A far cry indeed from the autonomous sexuality, free from male domination, for which the feminists of those days fought. The sex manuals were particularly directed against the spectre of lesbianism. As another writer of a well-known sex manual wrote:

> If a married woman does this unnatural thing she may find a growing disappoint-
> ment in her husband and he may lose all natural power to play his proper part
> . . . No woman who values the peace of her home and the love of her husband
> should yield to the wiles of the lesbian whatever her temptation to do so. (Cited
> in Jeffreys 1985: 120)

Yet, despite the tremendous efforts to educate women to "yield their secrets of melody to the hands of the master", many refused to do so. The problem of the frigid woman was widely discussed and generally seen as a sign of resistance, generated by feminism.

Writing a few decades later, Kinsey and Masters and Johnson, although allowing a much greater space for women's sexual desires and the role of the clitoris, did not depart very far from the basics established by Ellis.

Characteristics and Limitations of Essentialism

Essentialism takes as its starting point a position that human behaviour is "natural", predetermined by genetic, biological and physiological mechanisms which are essentially the same in all humans and only need to be uncovered by science. These mechanisms are not subject to change.

Second, it posits a polarity between "female" and "male", which is seen as "natural". In this "natural" order man is the hunter and woman the hunted. Third, sexual desire is seen as a basic, biological drive, which demands satisfaction. If the dominant male sexual drive is denied outlet, men will resort to illegitimate methods such as rape and the abuse of girls. Thus, it is biology which urges men to become rapists. If, on the other hand, women are denied their "normal" sexual lives, they may become neurotic. Fourth, heterosexuality is seen as the only "natural" mode of sexuality; all other forms of sexuality are seen as perversions. An aggressive male model of sexuality is deemed to be the most "natural" way to behave sexually for human beings. Fifth, essentialism leads directly to biological determinism, the belief that biology is destiny. This line of thinking rests on the premise that women's subordination and masochism are "natural", as is male aggression, and that women are "naturally" better homemakers, peacekeepers and environmental managers, while men are better politicians, industrial producers and polluters.

Essentialism also feeds the assumption that forms of human behaviour which show some similarity are the same, the expressions of underlying biological drives or tendencies. This belief has fed many research projects into the "causes" of sexual behaviour. For instance, the following question is often asked: is it hormones, genes, or a variation in the human brain which causes human homosexuality? Thus, essentialist scientists are unable to account for cultural and transhistorical variations. In their explanations for sexual behaviour they always remain within the medicobiological debate. A consequence of this line of thinking is that sexual behaviour which was characterized as a sexual perversion (such as homosexuality) could eventually be cured, either medically or with psychiatric treatment. Or, alternatively, that it could be prevented (by teaching boys to become "real men" and girls to follow their "true nature").

Last of all, the only sexual act which essentialists regard as "natural" for both sexes is intercourse, copulation. Thus the primacy of the penis is established for both sexes. Even Kinsey and Masters and Johnson, who located the site of female pleasure in the clitoris, end up, in their final analysis, with the penis as the major sexual organ for both women and men. Masters and Johnson went to great pains to demonstrate that penile thrusting indirectly stimulates the clitoris. Miller and Fowlker point out that although Kinsey found higher orgasmic achievement among committed lesbians compared to married women, he nevertheless propagated heterosexuality for women: "Kinsey the zoologist told us that lesbianism was an attractive, adult alternative; Kinsey the moralist moved discussion to 'moral restraints' and magical phalluses" (Miller and Fowlker 1980: 268).

Yet, despite its limitations, I suggest that essentialism does have some positive points as well. If essentialism is stripped of its biological determinism and its heavily biased, sexist and racist moral statements, the following fundamental issues emerge. In the first place essentialism did open up the area of sexuality for scientific research. With the feminist movement (which it attacked so vehemently), it lifted the taboo on female sexuality which existed in the Victorian era in the West. Although Foucault (1978) demonstrated that sexuality, far from being simply repressed in the Victorian era (as the sexologists claimed), was sustained in a particular regime of power-knowledge-pleasure, bourgeois women especially were socialized to control their sexuality. Since the intervention of the sexologists valuable research has been carried out which should not be dismissed lightly. Biology and medical research do have important views to add to the debate on sexuality. Second, essentialism does have political weight. The finding that homosexuality is just one biological variation among others provides a strong argument against legal restrictions of homosexuality.[2] Likewise, the argument that women by their "nature" need special policies to give them "normal" rights is a strong feminist weapon which is heard in a wide variety of feminist settings. These were considered "special" as against male rights, which were viewed as the norm. I will return to these arguments after a discussion of constructivism.

Constructivism

Since the end of the 1960s essentialism and biological determinism have been heavily attacked from various sides. The French philosopher Foucault with his theories on power and discourse, the women's movement with its attack on patriarchy, and especially the black women's movement with its insistence on diversity, as well as the gay movement with its exposure of the medicalization of homosexuality, combined to discredit essentialism. A new body of theories arose which, in all its diversity, generally became known under the name of "constructivism".

This theoretical approach is characterized by the following insights. In the first place it does not conceptualize sexuality as a medicobiological phenomenon but stresses that it is mediated by historical and cultural factors. That is, constructivist theorists reject transhistorical and transcultural definitions of sexuality, and instead stress that sexual behaviour is the fluid and changeable product of human action in its historically determined forms. Thus, sexuality is seen not as the invariant result of the body, biology or an innate sex drive, but as the product of sociohistorical variables.

Second, the constructivist debate on sexuality and human behaviour no longer takes place within medicobiological circles but in the fields of social enquiry and linguistics. This paradigm shift has led to novel questions about differences between women and men and sexuality, challenging widely held assumptions about human behaviour.[3] The constructivist vocabulary has dumped the words "normal" and "natural" in relation to sexuality and relations between women and men.

In the last place, constructivism has an enormous political advantage. By showing how certain forms of behaviour, certain norms and certain institutions have been historically constituted, the constructivist analysis implicitly leads to debates on transformation. That which has been historically constructed can be politically deconstructed.

In the following paragraphs I will briefly chart some of the major contributions to constructivist thought, focusing on the contribution of the women's movement to the debate. As many feminist writings of the last decades have been influenced by Foucault, I will start by introducing some of the elements of his thinking which are relevant for this discussion.

Foucault's intention was to understand the discourses around certain themes, the "ritualized stories which entire societies have in common" and which shape or constitute human thought and behaviour.[4] Deconstructing the history of sexuality, he concludes that sexuality should not be seen as constituted by an uncontrollable biological urge or innate drive, but as a form of behaviour and thought which is malleable by power relations, which are employed in the interests of other ends than sexuality itself (Foucault 1978).

Using Foucault's own instruments against him, I have various problems with his theories, however fascinating and insightful they are. My major hesitation arises from the fact that Foucault only talks about the male body and male sexuality. Where does his androcentrism come from? If we see Foucault as a person who is also the product of his time and space, can we ask what his interest is in neglecting women?[5] Would it be possible for a female philosopher to so exclude women, and to so stress the social in relation to sexuality? It is striking indeed that in his analysis of the serologists he does not refer to their opposition against feminism as one of the motivations from which they worked. Why does he sociologize sexuality to such an extent that the biological dimension is virtually excluded from analysis? And then, by focusing on male sexuality, the power asymmetry between women and men – especially in the area of sexuality – is ignored. Yet, for women, this is a major issue for analysis and political action. Elsewhere (Wieringa 1999) I explored the notion of "desire" in Foucault's work. I decided that it is possible to understand the manifestations of "deviant desires" using Foucault's analysis.

The second wave of the women's movement gained momentum in the 1970s. Women realized that suffrage, and the other legal and educational reforms women had gained since the beginning of the twentieth century, were not enough to liberate women from their subordination. Adherents of the women's liberation movement engaged in debates on patriarchy and clearly pointed to sexuality as a major site of men's power over women. The sexologists were heavily attacked for legitimizing certain myths: that men rape women because of their uncontrollable sexual urge;[6] or that the vagina is the main site of sexual pleasure for women; or that heterosexual intercourse is the only "natural" model of sexual behaviour.

The first author who departed from biological determinism and essentialism was Simone de Beauvoir, with her thesis that "woman is made, not born". She demonstrated that women's "otherness" is historically constructed, and she advocated that women become subjects by speaking out on behalf of humanity and transcending their sex, their bodies.

The next theoretical step was made fifteen years later when Gayle Rubin introduced her concept of a "sex-gender system" in which biological sex is transformed into a sociocultural system of gender relations. Creatively combining elements of Freud, Marx and Lévi-Strauss, she argues that the sex-gender system is a power system that aims at concentrating material and symbolic capital in the hands of the fathers, the older men of a society. She conceptualizes the sex-gender system as a political economy, with the institution of heterosexuality supporting the dominant male homosocial bond. This position – the view that heterosexuality is an institution intended to support the prevailing sex-gender system in any given society – is directly opposed to that of Ellis, who saw heterosexuality as the only "normal" model of sexuality.

Since its introduction, the concept of gender as a major ideological and political system of power mechanisms, regulating individual, socioeconomic and political relations, has gained wide acceptance. Numerous feminist theoreticians have taken up the concept. I will highlight here just a few moments of what has become a substantial body of social theory.

Adrienne Rich attempted to deconstruct a subject which has long been considered "natural" for women: motherhood. She analysed motherhood as an institution, constructed as a normative enforcement of one model of sexual behaviour: reproductive heterosexuality. She differentiated between motherhood as an experience, which she views as enriching, and as an institution, when it becomes a means of oppression.

Another valuable contribution by Rich to constructivism is her observation that gender is not a unitary phenomenon experienced similarly by all women, but that it is intersected by a number of other experiences, such as race, class, age and sexual orientation. In this she was inspired by black feminism, to which I will return shortly. Haraway (1991) would later formulate the consequences of this insight in the following manner: we have to "situate" ourselves to know ourselves. But Rich retains more than a streak of essentialism when she writes:

> We need to imagine a world in which every woman is the presiding genius of her own body. In such a world women will truly create new life, bringing forth not only children (if and when we choose) but the visions, and the thinking, necessary to sustain, console and alter human existence – a new relationship to the universe. (Rich 1976: 285–86)

A major impetus to the women's movement was given by black feminist writers such as Lorde and Morrison and theoreticians such as Johnson-Odim (1991), Giddings (1984), and Hill Collins (1991). Although the roots of the women's movement in the United States can be traced back to the militant black consciousness-raising movement of the 1960s, those "black" roots were downplayed by the white middle-class women who dominated the women's movement from the late 1960s onwards. Both black women and poor white women denounced the "bourgeois whiteness" of the movement, and the homogenizing call for solidarity based on women's "common" experiences which white middle-class women insisted on. As Huggins expressed it: "black women, who have worked for necessity, are apt to view women's lib as a white middle-class battle irrelevant to their own often bitter struggle for survival" (Huggins 1991: 8). Giddings (1984) demonstrates how the participation of black women in gender struggles has been downplayed in the historiography of the women's movement so far.

Third World women, too, were disappointed by the minimal relevance of this kind of feminism to their own struggles. Johnson-Odim reminds her readers that there is a "widely accepted perception" among Third World women that the feminism emerging from white, middle-class Western women "narrowly confines itself to a struggle against gender discrimination" (Johnson-Odim 1991: 315). This "widely accepted perception" is due to a neglect of the history of early Third World feminism, rather than to the absence of struggles by Third World women against colonial exploitation and subordination (Wieringa 1988, 1995).

Yet many Third World feminists also realize that, in spite of so many differences, women all over the world do have certain experiences in common:

"we were wary of the tendency to generalize about women; although in their biological reproductive roles women experience a commonality of functions and responsibilities, they are less cohesive in their experiences of domesticity and the extent to which the double burden of nurturing and productivity come into daily conflict" (Afshar 1991: 3). If solidarity between Third World and Western women should become a reality, it would have to be constructed on the basis of both the commonalities and the specific experiences of women's oppression. This is borne out by the experiences in Beijing in 1995, where some forty thousand women from all over the world gathered for the Fourth World Women's Conference and the attending nongovernmental organization forum. One of the issues that came out most clearly is that the divide between women from the South and from the North seems to be becoming less striking. The differences between progressive and conservative women, which cut across religions, regions and countries, came much more to the foreground (Moghadam 1996). The critical intervention of black women was one of the major factors which blew up the myth of a homogenous women's identity. The realization that women's identities are multiple, constituted by intersecting, at times contradictory, variables, has been one of the most creative insights of the last decades in feminist theorizing.

Wittig (1991) takes the ultimate step of deconstructing womanhood altogether. She asks herself what is a woman? Does *woman* exist? Her answer is that a *woman* is just an ideological construct of male domination, that there is nothing real or essential about women, nor about men for that matter. In her view, there is no such thing as a biological reality of the two sexes, constructed as they are by patriarchy. This is a long way from de Beauvoir, who held on to the idea of two biological sexes. Wittig rejects this altogether, arguing that patriarchy, as the system of male domination, requires binary thinking, the division of the social and biological into two categories. As such, the gender system, the ideological construct of patriarchy, is imbued with masculine ideas. We cannot know it, but only politically deconstruct it. Woman is not, there are only human beings formed by the cultural and political system in which they are placed. But the problem remains from where patriarchy may have originated.

Although Wittig calls for the ultimate rejection of patriarchy and thus for concrete political action, her ideas have not easily been accepted by large parts of the women's movement. Her rejection of the commonality of women's experiences has the effect of disempowering the call for female solidarity by which many women are inspired. But new calls for "strategic alliances" may have come up (Dean 1996).

The approaches of Scott and de Lauretis have gained wider acceptance during the last decade. Scott (1988), drawing on poststructuralist analyses of power and discourse, conceptualizes gender as a network of power relations interacting with other power networks. This enables her to approach the initial question:

> We need theory that can analyze the workings of patriarchy in all its manifestations – ideological, institutional, organizational, subjective – accounting not only for continuities but also for change over time. We need theory that will let us think in terms of pluralities rather than of unities and universals. We need theory that will break the hold, at least, of those long traditions of (Western) philosophy that have systematically and repeatedly construed the world in terms of masculine universals and feminine specificities. We need theory that will enable us to articulate alternative ways of thinking about (and thus acting upon) gender without either simply reversing the old hierarchies or confirming them. And we need theory that will be useful and relevant for political practice. (Scott 1988: 33)

Two of the most important theoretical tools that recent poststructuralist theory has provided, in her view, are the concepts of difference and deconstruction. Difference, she writes, is related to "the notion . . . that meaning is made through implicit or explicit contrast, that a positive definition rests on the negation or repression of something represented as antithetical to it" (Scott 1988: 36–37). This establishment of contrast turns into hierarchical, fixed oppositions. Following Derrida, she stresses the need for feminist thinkers to deconstruct those oppositions: "Deconstruction involves analyzing the operations of difference in texts, the ways in which meanings are made to work . . . It shows them to be not natural but constructed oppositions, constructed for particular purposes in particular contexts" (Scott 1988: 37–38).

However, it is not difference as such that feminist analyses should oppose, but the hierarchical structures built upon it. Feminist political practice should be based on the careful assessment of differences and their operations. Thus, we should both deconstruct the differences upon which hierarchies are built and take them as the basis upon which to create solidarity: a solidarity based not on sameness, but on respect for the different locations in which we find ourselves. Scott again:

the critical feminist position must always involve two moves. The first is the systematic criticism of the operations of categorical difference; the exposure of the . . . hierarchies it constructs, and a refusal of their ultimate "truth". A refusal, however, not in the name of an equality that implies sameness or identity, but rather (and this is the second move) in the name of an equality that rests on differences – differences that confound, disrupt, and render ambiguous the meaning of any fixed binary opposition. (Scott 1988: 48)

Another important insight into the workings of gender is provided by Teresa de Lauretis. In her influential book *Technologies of Gender* (1987), she conceptualizes gender not only as a product of discourse (of the meanings produced in the power constellation that a discourse is), but also as itself a constructing process. Thus, one not only "receives" one's gender identity within a given discourse, but also, by assuming it, by enacting it, one creates the gender relations within such a discourse, producing and reproducing categories such as men, women, gays and lesbians. This is not an isolated process. As de Lauretis suggests, "the female subject is engendered across multiple representations of class, race, language and social relations" (de Lauretis 1986: 14). The intersecting normative variables of gender, race, class, ethnicity and age produce together the formidable construct of "normality".

Constructivist theorists thus conclude that there is no "true self", no inner essence of womanhood that can be uncovered. The feminist search for identity which had been carried out so vigorously in consciousness-raising groups, starting in the 1970s, led to the realization – which became especially acute after the intervention of black feminist thinkers – that there is no universal female identity. That, instead, women's identity is multiple, shifting, even contradictory at times. Feminist practice thus shifted from denouncing the definitions of the "normalcy" prescribed by Ellis and his successors, to denouncing and destabilizing the very category of "normalcy" itself.

Conclusion

Constructivism is a major departure from essentialism and biological determinism. It places sexuality on the social map and demonstrates that it is mediated by historical and cultural factors, that it is as fluid and changeable a product of human action and history as other forms of human behaviour.

The introduction of this concept of gender has opened new and intriguing avenues of research. In particular, the realization that gender as a cultural construction is a historical variable, intersected by and cross-cutting other variables, should be seen as one of the most innovative insights of the last decades. The insistence on flexibility and diversity of experiences has stimulated many creative research projects.

Politically too, constructivism has great relevance, as I indicated earlier. The realization that neither male dominance nor female subordination is "natural", but that both are instead the products of a long historical process, has swept aside the arguments of those conservatives, men and women alike, who are opposed to gender policies on the grounds that they would disrupt the "natural harmony of the sexes".

Yet constructivism does not convince as the all-encompassing paradigm some of its adherents claim it to be. My concern focuses on two problems. First of all, I am struck by the danger of sociologizing the body and the individual temperament of human beings. Second, I wonder whether it is at all possible to do away completely with essentialism – apart from the question of whether it would be politically desirable.

Although constructivists insist that discourses create their own counter-discourses, the mechanisms of this process remain vague. If, as Foucault and many of his followers attempt, sexuality is completely deconstructed, there is no or hardly any space left for individual choices. How then do we account for rebellion, for resistance, for the rejection of the dominant sexual or social model? To illustrate this point I will quote a few lines of a poem by Una Marson, an important Jamaican feminist and poet:

> I am afraid of that which lies within
> My very soul and like a smoldering fire
> Seems on the verge of bursting into flame
> And so consume my very being's might.
> I try to fathom what the urge may be,
> and sometimes it reveals its presence there
> Like fluttering of the tiny wings that grow
> Upon the fledgling and with which it soars
> To heights in later years.
>
> (in Ford-Smith n.d.)

Where does Marson's "smoldering fire" come from? How is it possible to relate that to the sociocultural conditions of her time? How is she able to translate that powerful "urge" into a "flame" with which she makes some impact upon her society? The dominant discourse she finds herself in un-doubtedly influences or even determines the content of her anger, but it is not the source of her "fire". This example makes clear that the relationship between "sex and society" is not solved once and for all by the constructivist insistence on the overall power of discourse.

In other words, what are the boundaries between the social and the individual, both in a psychological and in a sexual sense? It would be counterproductive to completely do away with sciences like biology and psychology, for several reasons. In the first place, important research is being carried out which is also directly relevant to women's lives. And in the second place, it is dangerous for feminists to completely ignore those sciences, as it would mean feminists renouncing the power to influence them. We cannot allow men only to carry out all research in genetic engineering, for instance.

A major question remains, where do we locate our bodily experiences, our desires, our moods? How can we insert the body, or the individual tempera-ment, into constructivist analysis without resorting to some elements of essentialism?

Another issue which points to the need for a careful rethinking of some essentialist premises is the possibility of certain sexual and social patterns which repeat themselves historically and cross-culturally (see also Blackwood and Wieringa 1999). Without the possibility of asking such questions we would be unable to engage in comparative research. Historical narration and description might take the place of analysis.

That essentialism and constructivism should not be seen as oppositional, that indeed many essentialist elements are contained in constructivist writing is demonstrated by Fuss (1989). She warns against the danger of constructing another binary opposition, the two elements of which are seen as incompatible with each other.

In conclusion I would like to stress that I view constructivism as a major step forward, both theoretically and politically, from essentialism. But we should not reduce essentialism to biological reductionism. From the very start essentialism has been abused for political purposes. The problem, however, is not so much the questions essentialism addresses, but the answers many of its adherents have provided, and the way it has been deployed politically. There are many essentialisms. Fuss even argues that constructivism operates as a more sophisticated form of essentialism. She rightly asks the question, how can we speak about the social if we reject the natural?

Grounding the social in a historicized natural, taking into account the way each element influences the other, may yield important new insights. Biologists such as Birke and Vines have pointed out that "nature" is not always "naturally given" either, that nature and culture are engaged in mutually transformative processes (Birke and Vines 1987). An approach like this may open up new avenues of research in which social scientists engage in fruitful debates with biologists or adherents of medical and psychological sciences about issues related to sexuality, the body and behaviour.

Apart from that, essentialism can also be highly valuable politically, if it is not based on the dominant group seeking a justification of its power, but on the subordinate groups who demand an end to their oppression. It is important that women of all races, classes and sexual orientations recapture our bodies, our diverging experiences, and deploy them for our own political strategies. Not because we *are* all the same, but because we all share certain experiences of oppression.

Notes

1. Although male homosexuality was prohibited, female homosexuality was not, for, as Queen Victoria is reported to have said: "What can the poor things do, anyway?"

2. Jeffreys (1985) points out that this issue carries less weight for lesbianism, as it was never punishable in Britain to start with. Instead, the sexologists succeeded in making the tradition of spinsterhood and female friendships which flourished in the last decades of the nineteenth and the first two decades of the twentieth century look very suspicious, as being tinged with lesbianism. Single women came to be seen as mannish and homogenic. See also Faderman 1981.

3. Notions that were challenged by constructivist analysis include, for instance, the assumption that "normal" men behave aggressively sexually, or that "normal" women like their men to be dominant, or are "naturally" more caring.

4. See Braidotti 1991, McNay 1992 or Bordo 1989 for an introduction of the major themes of the work of Foucault in relation to feminism.

5.   See the excellent biography by Miller (1994) for an exploration of certain
      themes in Foucault's life, such as his sadomasochism.
6.   Kathleen Barry (1981) called the dominant ideology a system of cultural
      sadism in which women were held in sexual slavery.

References

Afshar, Haleh. 1991. *Women, Development and Survival in the Third World.* Harlow:
    Longman.
Barry, Kathleen. 1981. *Female Sexual Slavery.* New York: Avon.
Birke, Lynda, and Gail Vines. 1987. "Beyond Nature Versus Nurture: Process and
    Biology in the Development of Gender". *Women's Studies International Forum*
    10, no. 6.
Blackwood, Evelyn, and Saskia E. Wieringa, eds. 1999. *Female Desires, Same-Sex
    Relations and Transgender Practices Across Cultures.* New York: Columbia
    University Press.
Bordo, Susan R. 1989. "The Body and the Reproduction of Femininity: A Feminist
    Appropriation of Foucault". In *Gender/Body/Knowledge, Feminist Reconstructions
    of Being and Knowing,* edited by A.M. Jaggar and S.R. Bordo. New Brunswick,
    NJ: Rutgers University Press.
Braidotti, Rosi. 1991. *Patterns of Dissonance: A Study of Women in Contemporary
    Philosophy.* Cambridge: Polity Press.
Dean, Jodi.1996. *Solidarity of Strangers: Feminism after Identity Politics.* Berkeley:
    University of California Press.
de Lauretis, Teresa, ed. 1986. *Feminist Studies/Critical Studies.* Bloomington:
    Indiana University Press.
_____. 1987. *Technologies of Gender: Essays on Theory, Film and Fiction.* London:
    Macmillan.
Faderman, Lilian. 1980. *Surpassing the Love of Men: Romantic Friendship and Love
    between Women from the Renaissance to the Present.* London: Junction Books.
Ford-Smith, Honor. N.d. "The Value of an Angry Woman: The Importance of
    Una Marson". Mimeo.
Foucault, Michel. 1978. *The History of Sexuality.* Vol. 1, *An Introduction.* New York:
    Pantheon.
Fuss, Diana. 1989. *Essentially Speaking: Feminism, Nature and Difference.* New York:
    Routledge.
Giddings, Paula. 1984. *When and Where I Enter: The Impact of Black Women on Race
    and Sex in America.* New York: Bantam Books.

Hill Collins, Patricia. 1991. *Black Feminist Thought: Knowledge, Consciousness and the Politics of Empowerment.* New York: Routledge.

Huggins, Jackie. 1991. "Black Women and Women's Liberation". In *A Reader in Feminist Knowledge,* edited by S. Gunew. London: Routledge.

Haraway, Donna J. 1991. *Simians, Cyborgs and Women: The Reinvention of Nature.* London: Free Association Books.

Jackson, Margaret. 1987. " 'Facts of Life' or the Eroticization of Women's Oppression? Sexology and the Social Construction of Heterosexuality". In *The Cultural Construction of Sexuality,* edited by P. Caplan. London: Tavistock.

Jeffreys, Sheila. 1985. *The Spinster and Her Enemies: Feminism and Sexuality, 1880–1930.* London: Pandora.

Johnson-Odim, Cheryl. 1991. "Common Themes, Different Contexts: Third World Women and Feminism". In *Third World Women and the Politics of Feminism,* edited by C.T. Mohanty, A. Russo and L. Torres. Bloomington: Indiana University Press.

Miller, James. 1994. *The Passion of Michel Foucault.* London: Flamingo.

Miller, Patricia J., and Martha R. Fowlker. 1980. "Social and Behavioural Constructions of Female Sexuality". In *Women, Sex and Sexuality,* edited by C.R. Stimpson and E.S. Pearson. Chicago: University of Chicago Press.

Moghadam, Valentine M. 1996. "Notes from the Field: The Fourth World Conference on Women – Dissension and Consensus". *Bulletin of Concerned Asian Scholars* 28, no 1.

Rich, Adrienne. 1976. *Of Woman Born: Motherhood as Experience and Institution.* New York: Norton.

Rubin, Gayle. 1975. "The Traffic in Women: Notes on the 'Political Economy' of Sex". In *Toward an Anthropology of Women,* edited by R.R. Reiter. New York: Monthly Review Press.

Scott, Joan W. 1988. "Deconstructing Equality-Versus-Difference: Or, the Uses of Poststructuralist Theory for Feminism". *Feminist Studies* 14, no. 1.

Shaffer, Elinor. 1980. "*The History of Sexuality,* vol. 1: *An Introduction*" (review essay). In *Women, Sex and Sexuality,* edited by C.R. Stimpson and E.S. Pearson. Chicago: University of Chicago Press.

Wieringa, Saskia, ed. 1988. *Women's Struggles and Strategies.* London: Gower Press.

———. 1995. *Subversive Women: Women's Movements in Africa, Asia, Latin America and the Caribbean.* New Delhi: Kali for Women.

Wittig, Monique. 1991. *The Straight Mind and Other Essays.* New York: Harvester Wheatsheaf.

2 Reconceptualizing Voice

The Role of Matrifocality in Shaping Theories and Caribbean Voices

MICHELLE ROWLEY

In yuh own way yuh have to find strength to move on from whatever mistakes yuh make.

    – Tobagonian woman interviewed

Introduction

The field of gender studies in the Caribbean has inherited the colonial anthropological bequest of the "strong Caribbean matriarch". This has been used to causally explain a series of phenomena such as "dysfunctional family structures"; "child delinquency"; "loose mating patterns" – all of which often stand unrelated to the concept (Mohammed 1988). Further, the concept of matriarchy has come to represent a homogeneous typeface of Caribbean womanhood, and in so doing silences the complex social, economic, ethnic, and inter- and intra-group activities which comprise matrifocal representations.

  The construction of matriarchy provides Caribbean feminist discourses with a burdensome paradox that disguises the subtle and meandering flows of patriarchal exercises of power. Patriarchy, when garbed in its state, institutional and ideological array, succeeds because it appears innocuous and lacking in coercion. I aim in this paper to begin a preliminary exploration of the theoretical and methodological implications of naming. This project is of particular relevance to feminist praxis, insofar as it has traditionally advocated the contested use of the category "woman", as a means of disrupting and reordering heretofore silenced spaces. The category woman is a fractured concept, and the permutations of this fracture are contextual and cannot be defined a priori. As such, representation becomes governed by the context of the research and the talk of that situation becomes the medium of translating that representation.[1]

The latter point presents us with a moment of anxiety, namely, the act of scribing or translating that identity into textually relevant sequences. Here, the researcher begins to navigate a tightrope of intersecting and cross-sectional identities. Where does the respondent end and the researcher begin? In what ways do my choice of words and selection of narratives reflect my own concerns rather than the issues of the subjects being interviewed? And, admittedly, how much neither I nor my reader will not know, indeed can never know, about these choices, as a result of the ever-present omissions and silent spaces that govern research. Indeed, any reflexively driven research becomes a moment of both co-construction and self-knowledge; further-more these processes are integrally linked to the issues of final documen-tation.[2]

This paper is part of a broader effort to examine the formation of subject identities by single mothers in the context of discursive constructions of matriarchy/matrifocality. It is guided by interviews done with three Tobago-nian women.

Matrifocality versus Matriarchy: The Nexus Revisited

"Matrifocality" and "matriarchy", though used somewhat loosely up to this point, cannot be taken as interchangeable concepts. While both concepts imply that women in a given society exercise some measure of power and control over their familial network, it is the impact of women's ability to act at the broader parameters of social, economic, political and ideological order which serves to differentiate the two concepts.[3] In this regard, anthropologist R.T. Smith has referred to the matrifocal family as "a social process in which there was a salience of women – in their role as mothers – within the domestic domain, correlated directly with the class position of the population involved, and focusing on the articulation of kinship and class" (Smith 1988: 8).[4]

"Matrifocality", therefore, implies a cultural and affective centrality of women within their kinship group. "Matriarchy", however, transcends notions of kinship, and addresses not only the familial centrality of women, but also a centrality that extends to the ideological and institutional ordering of social organization. The complexity of family structures and the household in the Caribbean is such that matrifocality can exist where males are present. Similarly, it is not to be automatically expected that female-headed households necessarily imply a matrifocal family structure. It is within these domestic/macrocosmic distinctions that I am suggesting that matrifocality be distinguished from matriarchy. Furthermore, what this distinction also suggests is the fact that the Caribbean has never been a matriarchal region, by virtue of its matrifocality.[5]

The centrality of women in their capacity as mothers within kinship structures does not necessarily translate into similar institutional or ideological centrality. I am inclined to suggest that somewhat of an inverted tension exists between the two levels of interaction with an unnamed and unproblematized subject negotiating the silenced spaces and fissures. My question here is what are the implications of such unnamed presence?

I take the liberty of naming these unnamed voices as the "matri-folk" of matrifocality.[6] I agree with R.T. Smith's rationale that the act of coining terms does not necessarily solve problems. The act of naming, however, can become a strategic means of positioning the issues, concerns, needs and struggles of this previously unnamed group firmly within the public domain. Naming therefore is not intended to locate identity within fixed parameters, neither is it aimed at convening a false sense of solidarity. It is rather a strategic process by which subject identity can be named and where this named category can begin to voice their demands for political and institutional resources.

Voicing Sameness/Voicing Difference: The Articulations of Agency

I use the term "voicing" to refer to the varying, articulated levels of consciousness and alienation, action and inaction which categories of Caribbean women experience. The term "voicing" stems from a need to reflect women's lived realities within our theoretical frames; it is a response to the challenge issued by Joycelin Massiah that women "speak for themselves, name their experiences and make their own connections" (Massiah, cited in Senior 1991). "Voicing" itself is significant, as a form of speech that is in the present continuous and therefore representing ongoing activity. The term possesses a subject that can, has been, and will voice. Finding the subject of this speech, however, presents us with the dilemma of the subject that has no name, again highlighting the need for a speaking "matrifolk" subject.

The act of voicing is one that also challenges dichotomous representations, in that it prompts the recognition that women's voices are not locked within social, ethnic, classist or ideological groups but that there is a continuous pendulum between discord and harmony, exclusion and inclusion. Voicing as an act of naming and representation is also a distinctly political and agentive process.

I am not suggesting that we can invoke the exercise of agency simply by the process of naming. I am drawing on Kamala Viswesaran's (1994) discussion on agency as performance, where she notes that while speech is important to the exercise of agency, the capacity to speak cannot be reducible to agency. This highlights the need to be constantly cognizant not only of what is said, but of the locales in which speech occurs. How does the interview process itself become a combined narrative of speech, whose silences, continuities and discontinuities are not only part of the interviewee's ability to construct and present versions of self, but simultaneously a reaction to a number of impacting, normalizing and countervailing discursive realities? In this context, therefore, how do we identify the agentive moment? Do we merely examine the text of the talk? What do we do with the experience of the text? Since respondents rarely, if ever, make the pronouncement ". . . and oh, I was exercising agency here!", the location of agency and interpretations of representation is the point that brings the hierarchical dimension of research sharply into focus, despite claims that attest to egalitarianism and democratic interactions.[7] In addition, because the exercise of agency is not coterminous to a freewheeling, autonomous subject, how then do we also locate the text of the matrifolk within the frame of the "unsaid" and "already said" intertextuality of all discursive interactions (Foucault 1972: 25)?

Historicizing the Matrifocal "Already Said"

Both the voiced and the silenced experiences of the matrifolk are crucial elements in historicizing the construction of the matrifocal identity and the embodiment of these discursive antecedents. By way of a quick overview, matrifocality needs first to be understood as an interaction with a colonial slave ideology, characterized by the pursuit of capital and the perpetuation of patriarchy. For example, historians such as Michael Craton (1991: 228) have observed that the " 'myth of matrifocality' stems from the planters' emphasis on motherhood because of their need to perpetuate slavery through the female line and their vain wish to breed rather than buy new slaves by granting slave mothers relatively easier conditions". At this point, issues of production reflected a seemingly coterminous relationship with issues of reproduction.

Similarly, the period of wage labour showed a continuum of women being placed in a socially and financially disadvantaged position. So evident was the shift in labour that H. Morsen (in a contemporary description of postemancipation changes in 1841) observed in 1838 that "mothers of families have retired from the field, to duties of the home" (cited in Momsen 1993). The difficult economic environment within which matrifocality was to exist as a result of unfavourable labour shifts was made even more difficult socially and politically by the sentiments of the Moyne Commission report.[8] In this regard, economic burden was even further intensified by the social "unacceptability" of the female single-headed family form. The report notes that where there was no father

> the whole financial responsibility [would] fall on the mother . . . In such circumstances cases of extreme poverty are inevitable, for the standard of living must be lower than it would be in a family group where even if both parents were not employed, more money would be available since the wages of men are normally higher than those given to women. (p. 40)

Rather than upgrade the structural and institutional needs available to matrifocal, single-headed family forms, the report, in dismissing the need for women to find gainful employment, advocated instead that girls were "to be companions for husbands" and would therefore need an adequate education for the achievement of such.

The adversarial construction of matrifocality in the Caribbean has in many ways impacted negatively upon women and their self-conceptualization. I draw on Barriteau's (1992: 7) assessment of the Women in the Caribbean Project Report conducted between 1979 and 1983. Here she states:

> Women emerge as economically vulnerable and insecure (Powell 1986; Barrow 1986); display alarming levels of female self-contempt (Clarke 1986); doubt their abilities to be effective leaders (Clarke 1986); and defer decision making to their male counterparts (Odie-Ali 1986) . . . "They recognise that they must accept male domination and a male dependent role" (Anderson 1986: 311).

This assessment is not homogeneous nor a universal position – as Barriteau herself notes – as Caribbean women were also found to have a strong sense of equity in relation to their male counterparts.

In addition to this constellation of sociohistorical discourses, there has been a decidedly misogynistic trend that has impacted forcibly on the formation of education policy in the Caribbean. It is in this vein that Errol Miller observes that

> [t]he matrifocal family and kinship institutions *characteristic of lower strata groups* in Caribbean society are neither African survivals nor merely the legacy of new world slavery. These matrifocal forms are the product of domination/subordination has [*sic*] been contested by men in Caribbean society and the liberation of Caribbean women in an *unintended consequence of this contest between men*. (Miller 1988; emphasis mine)

Miller's reading of matrifocality as "female liberation" is here a monolithic denial of the class, gender and ethnic differentials that operate in subject formation. Miller's assertion does not take cognizance of the fact that figuratively, matrifocality in the context of the Caribbean is much like an obstacle race being run on a course filled with weakening communal networks, decreasing social and state support services, low wages, inadequate workers' representation and working conditions for many of the matrifolk who work in low-income, feminized occupations (such as domestic workers and free zone employees).

Third, Miller needs to adopt a more sophisticated position on notions of power. What he refers to as the "promotion" of women does not automatically carry with it commensurate and proportional measures of power to act and effect change. The assumption that matrifocality exists primarily as a result of patriarchal contestations among men denies the fact that matrifocal forms are constructed within the dynamics of gendered inter- and intra-group relations, with institutional, ideological and social forces which are challenged and supported by *both men and women*. The perpetuation of these forms cannot be seen as an unintended consequence of intramale contestation. This denies the complex – and sometimes contradictory – interrelatedness of gender relations and the construction of our gendered identities.

Voicing as Bridge between Theory and Method

Nuancing the contradictory subtleties of matrifocality requires that we seek to identify variables of difference and to recognize that these variables can only be informed by asking new questions, alongside asking the old questions differently. Further to this is the need to bridge the gap that exists between the conceptual and operational, the experiential and material. I argue here that the tool that bridges these spaces is the *talk* of the narrative. In this assertion I am not making a purely linguistic turn, but rather suggesting that language becomes the means by which we can explore experience (Polkinghorne 1988: 22). My use of language is two-tiered, in that at one level I am referring to the performance of the talk, while at another, I refer to the content and intertextuality of the talk, to the multiple discursive elements that constitute *talk*.

The performance of talk is both an individual and collective activity. Equally important, however, is the social site of production as it conditions the content of the talk. On one end of the spectrum that sees talk as social discourse is David Edward's argument that

> [t]elling stories is discursive action doing discursive business. This certainly emerges when studying research interviews, but those essentially work against interaction considerations, because they tend to substitute, for the ordinary occasions on which stories might be told, got-up occasions for set-piece performances for interview. It is better to collect samples of natural talk, where possible, if we want to see how talk performs interactional work other than informing researchers who are interested in narratives, in family relations, in violence or social attitudes, or whatever. (Edwards 1996)

While the moment of talk is also a moment of co-construction, as well as being socially derived, the problematic assumption here is that we can actually identify something that constitutes "natural talk" or "unnatural talk". Admittedly, there may be differently produced talk in different sites of production, but it is questionable whether one talk can be seen as more legitimate or authentic than another. The interpretative moment should be guided by the context and situation of the talk, but not as means to produce notions of authenticity.

Similarly, talk not only projects experience, but also provides a vista into the impact that historically constituted discourses (as well as contemporary constructions and interactions) have on subject formation. Talk therefore enacts historical discursive formations (Scott 1992: 36). How do we then approach the talk in such a way that we are able to capture the experience; the collective, multiple and historical constructions of impacting discourses; and the interaction between these discourses and the individual? One means of approaching talk to achieve these aims is to look at the narrator's positioning in the talk. Does the narrator position herself as victim, perpetrator and so on? Second, how does the narrator position herself in relation to her audience/interviewer (for example, is there an attempt to convince or ally herself with the interviewer)? Third, what is the narrator's position in relation to other discursive realities intertwined in the local production of talk (for example, racism, sexism, and so on) (Bamberg 1988)?

The following is a preliminary and limited attempt to apply such an approach. The informing base is the mothering experiences of three Tobagonian women, between the ages of twenty-two and forty-seven. The women are all Afro-Tobagonian single heads of households, thereby limiting the extent to which cultural and ethnic differences can be explored. The three informants (by virtue of being Afro-Caribbean, low-income women) relocate the sample within the traditionally perceived ethnic and class parameters by which matriarchy and matrifocality have been studied. They all have female single-headed households with varying levels of financial assistance from the fathers of their children. These women are therefore unable to fully reflect the matrifocal experience within the context of a nuclear arrangement which, as a theoretical prescriptive, presents another dimension of the concept.

The spoken scripts, however, initiate a reexamination of matrifocality as it applies to those matrifolk (Afro-Caribbean, low-income, single female heads of households) who have traditionally dominated this discourse. The following, therefore, is an articulation of some of the issues that arose in the discussions surrounding their experiences of mothering.

Reputation and Respectability

*Ah know how Tobago parents like, I know wha we granparents like an' dey got some
taboo in dey head, and is no way in hell we could get dem to get rid ah dat eh. An I tink
more dan anyting else when it come to sex and making chilren, dey is de biggest set a
taboo. Dey is wha yuh does dig out and de primary concern is wha people go say dey
does'n care how yuh does feel.*

There are several moments in this passage which reflect the value of reputation
and respectability as primary influencing forces which manipulate and control
the construction of Tobagonian womanhood and notions of sexuality.[9] Both
the consciousness and being of the matrifolk (*"how yuh does feel"*) become
subsumed by concern for strictly enforced normative and generational (*"Tobago parents . . . granparents"*) codes of appropriate sexual behaviour. The
construction of the matrifolk, therefore, begins at a juncture where the self is
coerced into being marginalized from the experience and immediacy of the
context and redirected towards a community-based sanctioning of shame and
reproach.[10]

Two possible responses to this taboo on sexuality and reputation became
evident. First, there was the inclination to accept and internalize the collective
normative response as did one respondent who, despite the domestic support
and enthusiasm extended to her by her family, noted

*Well, ah thought dat . . . well, I have a very . . . Okay, at dat time I thought I had a
reputation to uphol. I was scared tinking dat people would not respect me much again.
De main ting was what people would say . . .*

The hesitance in the initial part of the statement is an interesting delay to the
rest of the text. At this point Lisa, the youngest of the respondents, makes a
marked time shift to "at dat time", somewhat suggesting that she has since
repositioned herself towards issues of reputation and respectability. Or even
further, possibly, that the act of having become pregnant out of wedlock no
longer gives her the "right" to lay claim to such issues. It also requires us to
ask what claims young single mothers "legitimately" see themselves as having.

The discussions revealed a second countervailing coping strategy which
pushed against the force of the community. Located within the women's
histories is an emotional numbness which becomes a means of confronting a
multiplicity of varying scenarios, such as being locked out of home, left without
food, or insulted publicly for having got pregnant. At one level this numbness

expressed itself in Agatha's (the oldest of the respondents) narrative in the following way:

> *Well, I doh really know, you see. Maybe dey use' to grumble, but it didn' matter much wit me at dat time. Yuh going through pressure so you eh care what people want to say at dat time. All yuh trying to do is to jus' get out.*

In another instance, and at a more extreme level, a similar response was shared in the interview, when Cheryl, who is twenty-five, commented:

> *I does tell my friends da' is why I doh cry anymore. I doh cry for anything. Yuh see if I watchin' TV an' ah sad picture going on, I go cry. If I reading my book an' I read ah sad part, I go cry. If someting happen yuh girl ehn shedding a tear. I cry so much . . . sometimes I could be so unfeeling towards tings . . . and people does wonder. It affect people different . . .*

and again towards the end of the interview

> *Yes, ah doh feel . . . because I remember how it does feel, is does be a kinda nakedness yuh does cyar cover with nothin no matter how hard yuh try, ah mean de people who yuh tink should love yuh an comfort yuh, an be with you . . . ah know ah do bad, but Oh God, is not as bad as it seems . . .*

At its most extreme, this numbness is articulated as possessing a conscious-ness-altering capacity ("*I does tell my friends da' is why I doh cry anymore. I doh cry for anything*"), as these women are faced with the task of coping with the onslaught of sanctions, having broken truce with definitions of female respect-ability. The metaphoric references in the above citation ought not to go unnoticed. The observation "*it does be a kinda nakedness yuh does cyar cover with nothin' no matter how hard yuh try*" points very much to the image of "original sin". The image again introduces the religious dictum and moral codes that drive the antagonism and sometimes violence that occurs between young mothers and immediate family members.

The consequences of breaking with traditions of respectability carries implications at the institutional level. The community and the sentiments of its members do not stand apart from a larger system of institutions and networks. As a result, notions of reputation and respectability gain currency because of the institutional force which support them. The discussions revealed institutional strength at two significant points: the education system and the medical services. These two institutions are significant, particularly when placed within the Caribbean context, where education has been a primary means of social and economic mobility for women.

With reference to the education system, Cheryl observed the following differentials between her experiences and those of her sister:

> . . . *she went back to school yes, but she . . . it had some teacher there ah doh know if de teacher did know dat she had a chile but she use to give she real pressure. So she tell me she couldn' make* [manage] *an' dat was she form mistress. So she say she couldn' make under dah lady ah tall. Because like me when I see the people in school who stan' up for me all dem was teachers who I did real hate, I didn' like non ah dem eh. One was Mrs A, she retired now . . . buh I didn' know dat the lady did like me* [laughter].

What becomes evident from this account is that in the absence of standardized legislation and policy, the implications of pregnancy for the life-chances of women and the children they bear become significantly exacerbated. Furthermore, the absence of institutional support compromises self-confidence and ability to achieve. We need therefore to continually ask ourselves about these women's coping strategies. What are the results at the end of their (often short-lived) academic careers? Equally significant are the outcomes for the children of these women and the ways in which institutional structures themselves come to reinforce cycles of poverty among the matrifolk.

The experience of childbirth in the absence of supportive institutional spaces comes at a point where both the matrifolk's feeling of self-worth and communal support are at their lowest, leaving the matrifolk alienated from herself, the community, and the experience of childbirth. Note for instance the differences in the above narrative between Cheryl's sister (who gave up on the system) and Cheryl's response to the support of teachers whom she thought were not supportive. The absence of support becomes additionally alienating, because of the perceived and actual interactions that these women faced as young, unmarried women in educational and medical institutions alike. This was reflected in the Lisa's concerns:

> **Lisa:** *To begin, when I went in the ward everybody was like, all the nurses so shocked. If is somebody big, or if is somebody small, or if you going crazy, I saw a nurse start digging in de papers for my age and den when she saw my date of birth she went oh! Then everybody was saying how old she is? How old she is? How old she is? I was twenty-one, no I was twenty.*
>
> **Int.:** *You looked so smalley?*

Lisa: *Den dey say okay, ah thought was a little person. Ah realize dat if I was younger I woulda really get bad-face like young people, teenagers who get themselves pregnant . . .*

Int.: *Because of the nurses' attitude you think?*

Lisa: *Yes because of their age. You not supposed to be having children as a teenager. I feel that was de reason for de bad treatment.*

The complicity of our institutions in marginalizing women and their life-chances is a developmental and theoretical issue: the intersecting point between the women and their institutional experiences often becomes disempowering for the women themselves.

The gendered nuances of these institutional responses are not lost in Lisa's statement, "*Ah realize dat if I was younger I woulda really get bad-face like young people, teenagers who get themselves pregnant.*" Assuming, if we may, that "*young people, teenagers who get themselves pregnant*" do not in fact get themselves pregnant, we can possibly consider the age-old adage of "you looked for it", which suggests that all other parties (such as men, families) are absolved of responsibility for the occurrence – and, by extension, absolved of responsibility to the female involved.

Sex, Sexuality and the Matrifolk

Within the existent social norms and sanctions, the women's narratives also articulate a decisive attempt to construct an autonomous and countervailing sense of their own sexuality in their immediate context. The experience of matrifocality becomes an attempt to pursue alternative and differing modes of expressing female sexuality. This process is neither deliberate nor linear in its construction, as various community structures and beliefs continually influence the way in which the women themselves conceive of their sexuality. Agatha, now forty-nine, was already on her fourth child when she came to the following level of consciousness:

> But you know you living in house with the man, you must have sex, you not using any protection so you get pregnant. But then you come and you bring yourself together, you have to put a stop to it, because if you don't put a stop you will just be going on. So you have to put a stop somewhere.

The script itself reveals a progression from feeling disempowered in controlling her sexuality and fertility in her relationships ("*But you know yuh living with the man . . ."*), to the point of recognition which repositions the locus of sexuality and reproductive control within the self (*"you have to put a stop to it because if you don't put a stop you will just be going on"*).

The scripts also show that there are no static means of framing and tracing alternatives modes of sexual construction. Analyses of difference and alternative representations call for contextualization of the lived experiences, age being one variable of impact on experience. While the older respondent was inclined to perceive her pregnancy as a result of a generational curse or misfortune having befallen her, the younger respondents related their pregnancies with a distinct exploration of their sexuality and womanhood:

> *I mean, all right, I was always curious about sex. I come and I get pregnant and all she used to be saying is what people would say, what people would tink, and what is this and bla, bla, bla.*

The youngest respondent similarly said, in answer to the question "Why did you get pregnant?":

> *This might sound strange but since I was seventeen I want to have a child to take care of.*

Int.: Why?

Resp.: *Because I like being ah mother. I always think that I would provide for my child in the best way possible, no matter what I have to do. If somebody say you have to walk down the street naked or else I'd kill the child, I would do it without thinking.*

In both excerpts, curiosity and exploration about one's sexuality and womanhood, coupled with a romanticized perception of mothering, appeared to have had a catalytic effect on the women's eventual pregnancy. Further to this was the role which pregnancy played in defining womanhood. Most importantly, the conceptualization of pregnancy/womanhood was also closely associated with struggle, hardship and sexual self-sacrifice (*"If somebody say you have to walk down the street naked . . ."*). Internal to the narrative however, is a seeming tension that exists between the desire for motherhood (". . . *since I was seventeen I want to have a child to take care of"*) and the tensions and sacrifice that the actual act entails (*"If somebody say you have to walk down the street naked or else"*). The relationship between these two positions and women's subjective positioning and decision-making capacity remains a major area for investigation.

Mothering, Womanhood, Marriage:
The Trajectory of Becoming

The women's narratives presented important insights on the construction of womanhood in the Caribbean. First, motherhood and marriage were voiced as mutually exclusive categories. Further to this, the two categories appeared in a hierarchical relationship with marriage being a stage which required training, as opposed to the perceived "naturalness" of mothering. The women knew "innately" how to be mothers, but not how to be wives (Senior 1991: 66). Their mothering skills, however, would have been derived from caring for younger siblings and kin or from observation. In contrast, the skills for marriage seemed to be derived from the experiences gained from the process of mothering and aging. Take, for instance, the following narrative given by the oldest respondent, Agatha:

> *Yes, I could marry in this age because I have a little experience so I would know how to address a situation. You went out there you had experience, you know a little, you learn the little good, de little bad, de little different. Ah tink ah could married now . . . Married life is serious ting. When you tinking about married you have to tink about commitment, you have to tink about understandin' de other individual. When you tink about marriage, you have to tink a lot of tings. You have a commitment, you wouldn't be able to go out as you want. Two become one, you have to ask your husban' questions. An' if is no well you have to stay home . . . . I jus happen to be a mudder and not a wife, and if I had to be a wife I don't know if my marriage would have been still together or apart.*

The above excerpt reveals contradictions on the question of autonomy and female agency. On one level marriage stands as both a desirable and achievable goal (*"Yes, I could marry in this age"*). For this respondent marriage reads as a "two become one"; what is significant though is that the husband becomes that one, with the female self being subsumed in that one (*"you have to ask your husban' questions"*). Accountability, therefore, becomes a project of deference as opposed to mutuality. It is not surprising, with this self-effacing perception of marriage, that it is relegated to one's waning years. Within this context the very act of remaining single can possibly be seen as an attempt by women to hold on to their personal identities.

The impossibility of simultaneously entertaining marriage and motherhood was vehemently expressed by the youngest mother interviewed:

To be wife and mother at the same time, that could drive you crazy. That would drive me crazy being a wife and mother at the same time. Because you want to do your best and you're not superwoman . . . you will end up paying for it and you become frustrated and you just want to quit. That's how I look at it, so I rather be one at a time, even if he say that when we get married he wants a child, the next one, I say no way.

The mother who stood in the middle of the age continuum, while rejecting marriage, voiced a more settled resolve at the prospect:

I didn' ever consider dat, ah mean sometime along de way we had spoken about it eh, but hear what happen at one point in time I tell him, ah say "M", leh we work together and save some money an' see if we find a piece of lan' to buil a house. Now dis kakahole man is going to tell me leh we buy a car. So I say, what de f— are you telling me about, we could live in car, we could mind chilren in car; and from dat day dere I just throw de whole idea out de window. 'Cause I cyar understan how big hard-back man go watch me in my face an' tell me, leh we buy a car when we eh ha door-post to put we self an we two chilren in?

Pregnancy therefore becomes central to the construction of womanhood in a way which marriage does not. In the following excerpt, to be "woman" comes to be defined as being with child:

Yuh know, ah felt more responsible and more . . . important. Yeah, dat was de mos' changes. Right! Yuh know, ah felt like ah was jus . . . big now [laugh]. Not like in tinking or size, for some reason ah felt like ah grow a little bit, I was bigger dan I was, not a child again.

To be "with child" holds within it the contradictions of social ostracism while simultaneously locating the female within the community as a participating member ("*ah felt more responsible and more . . . important*"). The need to feel important, therefore, within a social context, itself becomes a motivating factor for pregnancy.

This rite of passage is not and cannot always be enthusiastically embraced by the matrifolk themselves: there is a trauma associated with this particular entrance into womanhood. It is not an experience which is heralded for many of these women but one in which, like this respondent, they consider themselves to be

unfortunate . . . It have unfortunate ones and dat is just how it is. According to the people it have a saying dat say . . . dat dis is a kind of generation curse. So you have to get rid of dat, yuh know where you be making chilren, going on differen' men passing.

My mudder had all of us for different fathers also. So it come like we have a curse, so it come down yu understand. So I am jus' de unfortunate one to fall in that.

The process of "becoming woman", in a context which contains hostile and antithetical impulses to the women's experiences, relegates pregnancy – and, by extension, womanhood – to little more than a lot and burden to be carried through life. This fatalistic response presents an interesting contrast with Agatha's earlier statement:

But you know you living in house with man, you must have sex, you not using any protection so you get pregnant. But then you come and you bring yourself together, you have to put a stop to it.

This is not to suggest that one position is more agentive that the other – insofar as Agatha's appeal to a fatalistic cosmos can easily be seen as a means of absolving herself of responsibility for the "mistakes" made in her life.

Economics and Relaxation

With limited opportunities, due to being institutionally marginalized (for example by education and community), the women interviewed are minimum-wage workers in the labour force. In addition, domestic demands further limit the extent to which they are able to resist instances of exploitation on their time, earning capacity, bodies and so on.

Gal, me a-work for thirty-nine dollars a day, dere is no way in hell, ah could mine two children on dat. It was forty-two an' de other day de boss get vex, no other way ah could put it he get vex an give we a hatchet job braps. No explanation, no reason, no anything . . .

Unless yuh get some type ah good qualification or someting, dere is no way in hell yuh could move from one job to de next. As it is now, it have people who want jobs for boss people to be behaving like dat. 'Cause dem know dat we wouldn' do anything about it, right, because I does study, if I leave my wuk how my two dem go make out. Yuh understand?

Making ends meet therefore takes phenomenal effort on the part of the matrifolk. It is interesting, however, to observe how the need to generate income interacts with the psychological and physical well-being of the matrifolk by way of relaxation.

Yes. De little time I have the best relaxing place for me, it will sound so easy, is de toilet . . . Jus you alone, nobody could ever bother you in de toilet. You could jus' go to de toilet and sit down, you doh have to do anyting and you jus' sit and you may have someting to read.

Again,

Yes, I get time to relax, but I am a person dat don' like to relax. I feel if I sit down here and I have someting to do I mus' do it and go and sleep. Relaxin' is a ting I doesn' get much because when I go home like dis evening, I have to wash — we get water two days a week. When I finish wash I have to look for tings to prepare for the morning if God spare life. I get to bed early, sometimes I wake up all ten o'clock and I would stay up until after two. I read my Bible and sew, I sew my own clothes, and then I would say is time to get up now and to cool, iron.

Relaxation for these two women comes to be interpreted as the space to perform tasks which can still be seen as a necessary chore, yet is perceived as less laborious than their employment.

In the absence of additional financial support, the matrifolk are forced into low paying jobs, a situation which is further complicated by their short-lived educational careers. There is, however, tremendous determination to provide for children despite the personal levels of exploitation.

Int.: *What about your grandmudder, she wouldn' have nothing to do with dem?*

Resp.: *Oh no no no, your children you responsible, ah doh care how yuh do it. You responsible. An ah tink dat mek me go an look for a job too, an a day big argument ah cyar remember what de argument come up about an' she say "my money minding yuh children, and my house" an my, an my, an my. Dat grate on my nerves. Ah say eh-eh, an I went an look for a work. I tink was school open in September, October I did fine wuk an ah gone.*

Later within the same interview the respondent continues:

Ah does try, ah does try for dem sake. If it wasn't for dem ah wasn' working a shit. Ah was staying right here an' doing nothin. Yuh know, when yuh have dem yuh have to tink about dem. So ah mean yuh have to try yuh best for dem sake, an' as a lady tell me years ago, work ehn got no shame.

Similarly, the eldest respondent also observed:

Well, I will look for a work. I am not a lazy person, I would go around like at Christmas time and say, "Look you don't want your house to clean for Christmas?" Do the wares and they will give you a hundred dollars and then I would start to sell, I go for a food badge and start to make a few things, start to sell ice cream, paime, pone and that is how I got along. I build house . . .

Examining the categories of economics and relaxation focuses the ways in which motherhood and womanhood come to take on a tenor of self-sacrifice and self-denial. These experiences are the lived experiences of often repeated sentiments such as "Caribbean woman strong" or, similarly, "Caribbean woman could real take pressure". When these pronouncements are viewed within the economically stressed and psychologically precarious lived realities of these women, they are revealed to be no more than a means of absolving the social order of its responsibility to women.

Forging Caribbean Feminist Theory

A distinctive feminist body of literature in the Caribbean has mushroomed, challenging dominant structures and their inability to adequately engage with definitions of otherness. Significantly, this growing body of work has questioned notions of economics and development (Mohammed and Shepherd 1988; Hart 1986; Leo-Rhynie, Bailey and Barrow 1997); social history (Reddock 1984); anthropology and structures of class and ethnicity (Senior 1991). While these publications have successfully posed a challenge to broader paradigmatic concerns, there has also been a parallel feminist challenge which has allowed Caribbean women "to speak for themselves" (Massiah, cited in Senior 1991).

The potential for indigenous Caribbean feminist theorizing is limitless. At the point at which women are able to speak for themselves, to name their experiences, positions of difference will be articulated. Only at these points of difference can we accurately identify those variables that make for a distinctly Caribbean sense of feminist theory. Theoretically, therefore, the question that we must ask ourselves is: what are the variables which reflect an experiential difference between Caribbean women and women who occupy other geographical, political, economic, social and ideological spaces? Matrifocality represents only one such area of concern.

Acknowledgments

I wish to thank Lynette Joseph-Brown, Roy McCree and Patricia Joan Saunders for their comments, suggestions and thought-provoking discussions while reworking drafts of this paper.

Notes

1. I agree with Spivak's warning that we should question all presuppositions that aim to argue that women possess a "natural or narrative-historical solidarity". It becomes a difficult, if not impossible, project to suggest, as she does, that the translator/researcher completely surrenders herself to the text or talk of the moment. All engagement positions the researcher as a filter – and certainly not a transparent one – to the text.

2. See Yvonna S. Lincoln's discussion of the author as self, where she highlights that the author's own representation in the text is determined by her relationship both with an implied audience and with disciplinary parameters as well as with the subject-respondent's voice, and as such is the writing of multiple selves into text (1997: 37–55).

3. For an overview of these anthropological findings see Patricia Mohammed, "The Caribbean Family Revisited", in *Gender and Caribbean Development* (Mohammed and Shepherd 1988: 172–83).

4. I want to complicate Smith's relationship between kinship and class somewhat, in that while we can safely argue that female-headed households are disproportionately represented below the poverty line, we cannot assume that matrifocality is a working-class phenomenon. As such the intersections between matrifocality and other subject-formation components such as ethnicity, education, decision making and so on need to be brought more sharply into focus.

5. The Caribbean Sub-Regional Report compiled in preparation for the United Nations Fourth World Conference on Women has documented female-headed household averages which were as high as 32.9 percent in 1980; 30.2 percent in 1985; and 34.6 percent in 1992. Notably, the 1994 World Survey on the Role of Women in Development has indicated that the highest proportion of female-headed households in the developing world was to be found in sub-Saharan Africa, with an average of 31 percent. However, as reflected above, regional statistics on female-headed households have exceeded this amount (ECLAC/CDCC 1996: 2), thereby attesting to the integral positioning of women within Caribbean domesticity.

6.   The term "matrifocality" may be broadly seen as one that gives centrality to women. Nonetheless, its use conveys a gamut of nuanced meanings which calls for a measure of reexamination. Mohammed notes that "A major problem with hackneyed concepts is that very often they assume a generality which may be totally unsuited to the instance in which they are being applied . . ." She further suggests that in the constellation of possible meanings we need to ask if and what aspects may be assumed to exist in the Caribbean (Mohammed 1988: 174).

7.   An interesting discussion of this relationship can be found in Borland's " 'That's Not What I Said': Interpretive Conflict in Oral Narrative Research", which deals with the problems of interpretation and appropriation of the text, as well as the designation of agency in text. She observes that "Lest we as feminist scholars, unreflectively appropriate the words of our mothers for our own uses, we must attend to the multiple and sometimes conflicting meanings generated by our framing or contextualizing of their oral narratives in new ways" (1991: 73).

8.   The West India Royal Commission Report arose out of the 1930s labour disturbances in the Caribbean.

9.   Despite the use of Tobagonian specificity, there are still several continuities and similarities across the Caribbean region in the shaping of women's equality and womanhood. In this regard see Olive Senior's *Working Miracles*.

10.   The term "community" has been given a broader institutional frame of reference, insofar as the sentiments of domestic and community spheres of influence do tend to become co-opted within institutional frames and vice versa, because of the fluidity which operates between the two spaces.

References

Bamberg, Michael. 1997. "Is There Anything behind Discourse? Narrative and the Local Accomplishments of Identities". Paper presented at ISTP conference, Berlin, April.

Barriteau, Eudine. 1992. "The Construct of a Postmodern Feminist Theory for Caribbean Social Science Research". *Social and Economic Studies* 41, no. 2.

Beckles, Hillary. 1989. *Natural Rebels: A Social History of Enslaved Black Women in Barbados*. London: Zed Books.

Borland, Kathrine. 1991. " 'That's Not What I Said': Interpretative Conflict in Oral Narrative Research". In *Women's Words: The Feminist Practices of Oral History*, edited by S.B. Gluck and D. Patai. New York: Routledge.

Brathwaite, Edward Kamau. 1975. "Caribbean Man in Space and Time". *Savacou* 11 and 12.

Craton, Michael. 1978. *Searching for the Invisible Man: Slaves and Plantation Life in Jamaica*. Cambridge, Mass.: Harvard University Press.

_____. 1991. "Changing Patterns of Slave Families in the British West Indies". In *Caribbean Slave Society and Economy,* edited by H. Beckles and V. Shepherd. Kingston, Jamaica: Ian Randle Publishers.

Devault, Marjorie. "Talking and Listening from Women's Standpoint: Feminist Strategies for Interviewing and Analysis". *Social Problems* 37, no. 1.

ECLAC/CDCC (Economic Commission for Latin America and the Caribbean/Caribbean Development and Cooperation Committee). 1996 "Poverty Eradication and Female-Headed Households (FHH) in the Caribbean". Paper prepared for the Caribbean Ministerial Meeting on the Eradication of Poverty, 28 October–1 November, Port of Spain, Trinidad.

Edwards, David. 1996. *Discourse and Cognition*. London: Sage.

Fairclough, Norman. 1992. *Discourse and Social Change*. Cambridge: Polity Press.

Foucault, Michel. 1972. *The Archaeology of Knowledge and the Discourse on Language*. New York: Pantheon Books.

Harding, Sandra. 1992. *The Instability of the Analytical Categories of Feminist Theory. Knowing Women, Feminism and Knowledge*. London: Blackwell.

Hart, Richard, ed. 1986. *Women and the Sexual Division of Labour in the Caribbean*. Mona, Jamaica: Institute of Social and Economic Research, University of the West Indies.

Leo-Rhynie, Elsa, Barbara Bailey, and Christine Barrow, eds. 1997. *Gender: A Caribbean Multi-Disciplinary Perspective*. Kingston, Jamaica: Ian Randle Publishers.

Lincoln, Yvonna S. 1997. "Self, Subject, Audience, Text: Living at the Edge, Writing in the Margins". In *Representation and the Text: Reframing the Narrative Voice,* edited by William G. Tierney and Yvonna S. Lincoln. New York: State University of New York Press.

Mathurin, Lucille. 1986. *Women Field Workers in Jamaica during Slavery*. Mona, Jamaica: Department of History, University of the West Indies.

Miller, Errol. 1988. "The Rise of Matriarchy in the Caribbean". *Caribbean Quarterly* 34, nos. 3 and 4.

Mohammed, Patricia. 1988. "The Caribbean Family Revisited". In *Gender in Caribbean Development,* edited by P. Mohammed and C. Shepherd. St Augustine, Trinidad: Women and Development Studies Project, University of the West Indies.

Momsen, Janet. 1993. "Gender Roles in Caribbean Agricultural Labour". In *Caribbean Freedom, Economy and Society From Emancipation to the Present,* edited by H. Beckles and V. Shepherd. Kingston, Jamaica: Ian Randle Publishers.

Morrisey, Marietta. 1991. "Women's Work, Family Formation and Reproduction Among Caribbean Slaves". In *Caribbean Slave Society and Economy,* edited by H. Beckles and V. Shepherd. Kingston, Jamaica: Ian Randle Publishers.

Polkinghorne, Donald E. 1988. *Narrative Knowing and the Human Sciences.* New York: State University of New York Press.

Powell, Dorian. 1975. "Caribbean Women and Their Response to Familial Experiences". *Social and Economic Studies* 35, no. 2.

Reddock, Rhoda E. 1994. *Women, Labour and Politics in Trinidad and Tobago: A History.* Kingston, Jamaica: Ian Randle Publishers.

Scott, Joan. 1992. "Experience". In *Feminists Theorise the Political,* edited by J. Butler and J. Scott. New York: Routledge.

Senior, Olive. 1991. *Working Miracles: Women's Lives in the English-Speaking Caribbean.* Kingston, Jamaica: Ian Randle Publishers.

Smith, R.T. 1988. *Kinship and Class in the West Indies: A Genealogical Study of Jamaica and Guyana.* Cambridge: Cambridge University Press.

_____. 1996. *The Matrifocal Family: Power, Pluralism, and Politics.* London: Routledge.

Spivak, Gayatri. 1992. "The Politics of Translation". In *Destabilizing Theory: Contemporary Feminist Debates,* edited by Michele Barret and Anne Phillips. Stanford, Calif.: Stanford University Press.

Viswesaran, Kamala. 1994. *Fictions of Feminist Ethnography.* Minneapolis: University of Minnesota Press.

West India Royal Commission. 1945. *West India Royal Commission Report, 1938–39.* (Moyne Report.) London: His Majesty's Stationery Office.

3   The Double Paradox

Janet Momsen

The Caribbean was the locus of the world's first experiment in European colonialism. The indigenous Amerindian populations were virtually extermi-nated very soon after contact and so had little cultural impact on contemporary Caribbean society. The consequent demand for immigrant workers led to the development of a very complex and cosmopolitan society made up of people from many parts of the world, and to the institutionalization of migration, resulting in changes in the demographic gender balance that have affected gender roles and relations.

Small-scale subsistence agriculture was replaced by the archetypal com-mercial sugar plantation. A European plantocracy created some of the most profitable and advanced industrial enterprises of the seventeenth- and eight-eenth-century Western world, using African slave labour and later indentured workers from India, Indonesia and elsewhere. Even in those colonies where plantations were late in developing because of colonial rivalries (as in St Lucia), or lack of European interest in local agricultural exploitation (as in Cuba), sugar plantations came to dominate the economy in the nineteenth century. Where the environment was too dry to support successful sugar production, as in Caracas, the dominant regional influence of the sugar plantation allowed the Dutch to prosper by providing salt and technical and commercial skills to the plantocracy in other Caribbean territories (Abraham-Van der Mark 1993). This commonality of economic history and its associated social structures allows Hart (1989) to identify the region as the site of a precocious experiment in social engineering and a major crucible from which modern social organizations have evolved. Thus Caribbean society and its gender roles and relations are potentially of wide significance.

Within the Caribbean regional diversity of ethnicity, class, language and religion there is an ideological unity of patriarchy, of female subordination and dependence. Yet there is also a vibrant living tradition of female economic autonomy, of female-headed households and of a family structure in which men are often marginal and absentee. So Caribbean gender relations are a double paradox: of patriarchy within a system of matrifocal and matrilocal families; and of domestic and state patriarchy coexisting with the economic independence of women. The roots of this contemporary paradoxical situation lie in colonialism. This paper examines these contradictions within a framework of multiple European colonial legacies.

The Historical Context

The transshipment of men and women from Africa under slavery and the bonded or indentured migration of Asian workers offered women release from patriarchal control of individual men within their own households (Brereton 1988). Instead they were, like men, subordinated to the dictates of capital and the ruling class. Women slaves were seen as equal to men in the eyes of the slave owner as long as they worked as hard (Patterson 1967) although, in addition, women were expected to provide sexual services on demand. Also, their role in reproducing the workforce became more important after the end of the slave trade in the early nineteenth century. Women resisted slavery both by limiting their fertility (Bush 1990) and by active rebellion (Mair 1974).

Most women migrants came to the Caribbean to be plantation workers not housewives, as field workers, not household servants, and their labour contributed to the development of European industrial capitalism. Elite white women who came as wives and daughters of planters often found the freedom experienced on other colonial settlement frontiers. They were able to inherit land and farm in their own right (Momsen 1995). Paravisini-Gebert (1996) argues, using Caribbean women's novels, that female authority on the plantation was often used to undermine the patriarchal structure of the system but that such women were seen as unfeminine and, indeed, unnatural.[1] These experiences bestowed on Caribbean women a degree of social and economic independence which, in the postemancipation period, colonial and neocolonial agencies such as the church and the education system sought to destroy.

In the nineteenth century slavery was abolished and women were told that marriage was both prestigious and morally superior. Single women in towns were arrested for unbecoming behaviour. Yet many Caribbean women continued to resist formal marriage because of the familial patriarchal ideology which allowed domestic violence, loss of parental rights and a double standard of sexual freedom (Massiah 1986). Women's loss of independence was not compensated by economic support in a situation where employment was insecure for both men and women. Thus women often chose economic autonomy and personal freedom outside marriage. A mark of their freedom can be identified in the fact that many were punished for involvement in the anticolonial labour struggles of the early twentieth century (Rodney 1981; Reddock 1984).

Despite these pressures to conform to a Victorian ideology of "housewifization", Caribbean women's participation in the labour force continued to be very high. This ideological conflict is reflected in ambivalent attitudes towards women workers, for "while the planters criticized mothers for neglecting their offspring, they preferred to hire females, whom they considered more regular than males in their work habits" (Levy 1980: 113). Another indication was the postemancipation introduction of a gender-differentiated wage scale with lower rates for women, accompanied by higher labour participation rates for women than men in Barbados between 1890 and 1921 (Momsen 1993).

On the other hand, Safa (1995: 180) argues that in the Dominican Republic the poor (white) women in her sample felt more vulnerable in consensual unions and were more likely to subscribe to patriarchal norms than legally married women. She also notes the recent growth in female-headed households to about one-quarter of the total in Cuba, Puerto Rico and the Dominican Republic, and links this development to the post-1970 expansion of female employment.[2] However, Safa (1995: 48) also points out that the Latin American distinction of *casa/calle* (private/public space), used to restrict women's activities to the home, did not apply to Afro-Caribbean women in the Hispanic Caribbean. "Black slave women did not develop a tradition of dependency on men as did women of the white elite" (Safa 1995: 48); they were more likely than white women to live in consensual unions and so "[T]his helps explain why, from 1899 to 1920, Cuban labour force participation rates were three to five times higher among Afro-Cuban women than among white women, while among men, the percentages were almost equal" (Safa 1995: 49). As in Barbados, Cuban women's formal labour force participation fell during the depression of the 1930s, and after this period ethnic difference in female economic activity rates declined, although as recently as 1981 Afro-Cuban women had higher participation rates than white or mulatto women (Safa 1995: 55). Some of the earlier differences may have been more apparent than real, as many women worked in agriculture and prostitution and, in Puerto Rico, in home-based needlework, all sectors where underreporting is endemic. Class and racial biases probably encouraged such underreporting of white women workers especially, particularly in agriculture and home-working where the job could be seen as an extension of the domestic sphere.

In Trinidad, under indentureship, planters sought only male workers but the colonial government insisted on a small proportion of female indentured workers on the grounds that this would prevent immoral behaviour and prostitution (Tikasingh 1973). The contradiction between the planters' short-term preference for adult male labourers and their long-term need for a self-reproducing, cheap and plentiful labour force illustrates the paradoxes inherent in the perceptions of women's role in Caribbean society. Both Reddock (1985) and Emmer (1986) have shown (for Trinidad and Suriname, respectively), that the women who left India to work in the Caribbean were more independent than most of their compatriots. Indenture was an escape route for Brahmin widows and child-widows, offering the opportunity for both remarriage and economic improvement. Only about one-third of the women who arrived from India were accompanied by husbands. Indian women indentured workers did not easily accept the prevailing orthodox male colonial view of women as "housewives" or the Indian insistence on the seclusion of women of higher castes. During much of the indentureship period, the scarcity of Indian women enabled them to resist the subordination of traditional arranged marriages and to claim autonomy over their own lives. In 1880 in Trinidad, Hindu and Moslem Indian men, with the help of Presbyterian ministers, petitioned the colonial government to control the mobility of women and force them to return to their husbands. In this way, church and state combined to reconstruct the Indian patriarchal family.

Contemporary Context

A further paradox is that the contemporary patriarchy of Caribbean societies is often a patriarchy in absentia. This situation is linked to both matrilocal residential patterns and to gender-specific migration. Found in both urban (Brodber 1975) and rural (Clarke 1957; Pulsipher 1993) settings, the houseyard residential unit embodies a way of life that is several centuries old. The traditional settlement unit is now most common among rural Afro-Caribbean families. It is usually headed by a woman who has title to the land on which the yard is located and, in addition to the matriarch's house, it usually also contains the houses of adult children of the yard head.[3] Yards are primarily female spaces, and during the day women are overwhelmingly the main occupiers (Pulsipher 1993). They oversee and organize the various activities that support the social and economic reproduction of the yard and provide continuity from generation to generation. Young girls are encouraged to stay within the yard while boys are allowed to wander. As young males mature they spend less and less time within the yard but are still often the primary male role models for the children of their sisters and female cousins (Pulsipher 1993). Women are more likely than men to spend most of their life in one yard, and historically it has been common for young women to have their first child while living in their mother's yard (Olwig 1985). Today young single mothers are able to continue their education, find jobs in town or even migrate while leaving their children in the care of older female relatives in their maternal yard. Thus the female space of the yard facilitates both reproductive and productive activities of women without the long-term presence of biological fathers.

The peoples of the Caribbean have a migrant tradition resulting in today's international diaspora. At first, postemancipation migration mainly involved men going to Central America to build the Panama Canal and to work on banana plantations, to Brazil to build a railway through the Amazon, to Cuba as cane cutters and to Venezuela to work in the oil industry. After the Second World War, both sexes migrated separately and in families. The women who went to North America and Britain, mainly as nurses and domestic servants, usually left their children behind to be raised by grandmothers in the maternal houseyard. These migrant women commonly maintained closer links with their natal families and provided more consistent financial support than did male migrants, so reinforcing the matrifocal element of Caribbean society (Olwig 1993). Today every Caribbean territory is linked by complex movements of people, goods, money and information to settler communities in the industrialized countries of the north. Through this diaspora the influence of Caribbean social forms has spread widely. Although Caribbean nations may be tiny on a global scale, their peoples have cosmopolitan attitudes with spatial perceptions that extend their territorial boundaries to disjunct corners of the world. The development of large West Indian communities in such world cities as New York, Toronto, Paris, Amsterdam and London is especially important in maintaining transnational identities among Caribbean migrants.

The Caribbean as a Geographical Entity

Often the region is seen in terms of only one racial group, generally the poor, Afro-Caribbean sector of the population. Boserup, in her trailblazing study *Women's Role in Economic Development,* fell into this trap. She suggested that the Caribbean was a distinctive and anomalous region in terms of women's roles in agriculture, more like Africa than Latin America because of the dominance of a population of African origin. This explanation appears to contradict her basic materialist thesis in which gender roles are seen to be determined primarily by the system of production, through the working of the labour market and the level of technology. Others such as Safa (1995), basing their studies largely in the Hispanic Greater Antilles, see the Caribbean as a separate but undifferentiated extension of Latin America. Few people have attempted to explore these differences of class, race and language across the full spectrum of the Dutch, Spanish, French and anglophone Caribbean (Momsen 1993).

Caribbean feminist thought has been much influenced by that of both white middle-class feminism and black feminist thought from the United States. Mohammed (1994: 138) wisely points out the dangers of a literal transfer of these ideas onto Caribbean soil. Divisions of language resulting from colonization also encourage biases based on different theoretical approaches to gender in the metropolitan countries. Barriteau (1992) has sought to contribute to indigenous feminist theory building by foregrounding the differences within the region, in a postmodernist approach to understanding Caribbean gender structures. Development of such a theory is intrinsically difficult for, as Habermans indicates, "in studying the very different articulations of gender and subjectivity in societies formed by conquest and colonization, we confront a problem which has seldom been posed in modern theories of ideology – that is the violent incorporation of a population into 'forms of life' which they can never perceive as organic or natural" (Dews 1986: 209–10). Yet if the Caribbean region is to be seen as more than a geographical expression, we need to move from a focus on differences to explore the common ground for a feminist understanding of its culture and society.

Characteristics of Caribbean Women

Women in the Caribbean exhibit higher levels of economic autonomy than are found in most parts of the South. This has usually been explained in terms of the legacy of slavery reinforced by later male out-migration, leaving a female majority in the population. In the anglophone and Dutch-speaking Caribbean, women have long had equal rights to land ownership which has been an enabling factor in allowing women's rejection of patriarchal control and has provided the physical basis of the matrilocal settlement pattern. However, in the francophone and Hispanic Caribbean patriarchal inheritance laws have limited women's land rights (Poirier and Dagenais 1986; Safa 1995) yet women now constitute 40 percent of agricultural landowners in French Guiana, 22 percent in Martinique and 18 percent in Guadeloupe (Seager 1997: 76). Despite equality of rights to resource entitlements, women's farms in the English-speaking Caribbean are generally smaller, less accessible and on poorer soil than those of men (Henshall [Momsen] 1981).[4]

Throughout the Caribbean, women value education and often struggle to provide it for their children as the best means of ensuring upward economic mobility. As early as 1919, both Afro-Cuban and white Cuban women had higher literacy rates than men (Safa 1995: 49–50), and many of the region's universities now have more female than male students.[5] Where men have sought economic opportunity through migration, women have achieved it through education. This is especially noticeable in those islands such as

Montserrat and Nevis, where high male out-migration has enabled women to achieve an unusual dominance of the civil service and banking sectors (Momsen 1993).

During the 1980s real wages in the Caribbean fell and unemployment, especially for women, increased. Structural adjustment has undermined the myth of the male breadwinner in the Hispanic Caribbean (Safa 1995) and increased the need for the economic autonomy of women. This situation was further exacerbated in the 1990s. The end of the Cold War eliminated the political importance of the region to the super powers, leading to a sharp reduction in development aid, while the implementation of the North American Free Trade Agreement and the European Union trading blocs have removed the comparative advantage of many of the region's exports. Coping with these economic difficulties at the family level is seen as a task for women as men migrate or otherwise abandon their families. This has led to the paradoxical view of Caribbean women as overburdened superwomen, castrating and evicting men from the household (Dagenais 1988).[6]

Conclusion

Among major Caribbean social groups the paradox of patriarchal family values within a matrifocal and matrilocal society is most strongly developed within the lower-class Afro-Caribbean group, and least marked in East Indian communities. A further paradox is that the contemporary patriarchy of Caribbean societies is often patriarchy in absentia, arising from gender-specific patterns of social behaviour and high levels of independent migration by men and women. Furthermore, although Caribbean women are often better educated than men,[7] state patriarchal ideologies ensure that there have only been two women chief ministers.

A rejection of Eurocentric views of family structures and the causal links between industrialization, women's economic activity and the overthrow of female subordination may enable us to reach a true pan-Caribbean understanding of gender relations. We need to question the belief in the rigidity of the public/private dichotomy underlying gender roles, the emphasis on women and the family in Caribbean research, the interaction of race, class and gender differences, and the multiplicity of women's roles. A feminist critique, which privileges the subaltern voices of a people marginalized by both gender and race – in a region which itself is increasingly being marginalized in the global economy – may throw new light on the paradoxes of state and family patriarchy in matrifocal societies, where women are better educated than men and have labour participation rates and fertility rates similar to those of their sisters in the industrialized North.

Notes

1. Lizabeth Paravisini-Gebert, using eight representative Caribbean women's novels, suggests that these novels view women who exercise power as abnormal, and she provides examples such as the folk figure of Madame Grosdent of Trinidad who supposedly sold her soul to the devil and Annie Palmer, known as the White Witch of Rose Hall, in Jamaica. Such approaches are based on a Caribbean patriarchal tradition in which "*el poder y la autoridad son prerogativas masculinar que la mujer no puede ejercer con sabiduria y que sólo mujeres desnaturalizadas ansian*" (p. 197).
2. Throughout the region more than 20 percent of households are headed by women, with Barbados having the second highest proportion in the world (44 percent) after Botswana (Seager 1997: 20), and many women never marry.
3. See Pulsipher (1993) for a detailed description of such yards in Montserrat during the 1980s. She shows how such matrilocal settlement units enable child care and elder care to be shared by siblings, and brothers to participate in the upbringing of their sister's children.
4. According to the 1989 Agricultural Census of Barbados (Barbados 1991), 39 percent of farmers were women but they operated only 6 percent of the farmland.
5. For the Caribbean countries of St Lucia, St Vincent, Barbados, Jamaica, St Kitts-Nevis, the Bahamas and Cuba, women made up over 55 percent of university students in the mid-1990s (Seager 1997: 86).
6. Yet when the state provides financial support for single mothers it faces a male backlash, as men feel that such assistance makes women less dependent on them (Dagenais 1988).
7. In many Caribbean countries the illiteracy rate of men is higher than that of women, and Jamaica is the only country in the world where there are significantly more illiterate men (21 percent) than women (12 percent) (Seager 1997: 74).

References

Abraham-Van der Mark, Eva. 1993. "Marriage and Concubinage among the Sephardic Merchant Elite of Curaçao". In *Women and Change in the Caribbean,* edited by J.H. Momsen. Kingston, Jamaica: Ian Randle Publishers.

Barriteau-Foster, Eudine. 1992. "The Construct of a Post-Moderinist Feminist Theory for Caribbean Social Science Research". *Social and Economic Studies* 41, no. 2.

Brereton, Bridget. 1988. "General Problems and Issues in Studying the History of Women". In *Gender in Caribbean Development,* edited by P. Mohammed and C. Shepherd. St Augustine, Trinidad: Women and Development Studies Project, University of the West Indies.

Brodber, Erna. 1975. *A Study of Yards in the City of Kingston.* Working Paper no. 9. Mona, Jamaica: Institute of Social and Economic Research, University of the West Indies.

Boserup, Ester. 1970. *Women's Role in Economic Development.* London: George Allen and Unwin.

Bush, Barbara. 1990. *Slave Women in Caribbean Society, 1650–1838.* London: James Currey.

Clarke, Edith. 1957. *My Mother Who Fathered Me: A Study of the Family in Three Selected Communities in Jamaica.* London: George Allen and Unwin.

Dagenais, Huguette. 1988. "Du point du vue des dominants: Reflexions théorisés et méthodologiques à partir d'une recherche en Guadeloupe". In *Les rapports sociaux de sexe: Problématique, méthodologies champs d'analyse.* Proceedings of the International Round Table, 24–27 November 1987. Paris: CNRS Atelier/Production/Reproduction.

Deere, Carmen Diana [coordinator], with Peggy Antrobus et al. 1990. *In the Shadows of the Sun: Caribbean Development Alternatives and US Policy.* Boulder: Westview Press.

Dews, Peter, ed. 1986. *Habermas – Autonomy and Solidarity: Interviews with Jurgen Habermas.* London: Verso.

Emmer, M.R. 1986. "The Great Escape: The Migration of Female Indentured Servants from British India to Suriname, 1873–1916". In *Abolition and Its Aftermath: The Historical Context, 1790–1916,* edited by D. Richardson. London: Frank Cass.

Hart, Keith. 1989. Introduction to *Women and the Sexual Division of Labour,* edited by K. Hart. Mona, Jamaica: Consortium Graduate School of Social Sciences, University of the West Indies.

Henshall [Momsen], Janet D. 1981. "Women and Small-Scale Farming in the
Caribbean". In *Papers in Latin American Geography in Honor of Lucia C.
Harrison*. Muncie: CLAG.

Levy, C. 1980. *Emancipation, Sugar and Federalism: Barbados and the West Indies,
1833–1876*. Gainesville: University of Florida Press.

Mair, Lucille. 1974. "A Historical Study of Women in Jamaica, 1655–1844". PhD
thesis, University of the West Indies.

Mohammed, Patricia. 1994. "Nuancing the Feminist Discourse in the Caribbean".
Social and Economic Studies 43, no. 3.

Momsen, Janet H., ed. 1993. *Women and Change in the Caribbean*. Kingston,
Jamaica: Ian Randle Publishers.

——. 1993. "Development and Gender Divisions of Labour in the Rural Eastern
Caribbean". In *Women and Change in the Caribbean*, edited by J.H. Momsen.
Kingston, Jamaica: Ian Randle Publishers.

——. 1998. "Gender Ideology and Land". In *Caribbean Portraits: Essays on Gender
Ideologies and Identites*. Kingston, Jamaica: Ian Randle Publishers.

Olwig, Karen Fog. 1985. *Cultural Adaptation and Resistance on St John: Three
Centuries of Afro-Caribbean Life*. Gainesville: University of Florida Press.

——. 1993. "The Migration Experience: Nevisian Women at Home and Abroad". In
Women and Change in the Caribbean, edited by J.H. Momsen. Kingston, Jamaica:
Ian Randle Publishers.

Paravisini-Gebert, Lizabeth. 1996. "La mujer y el podor en la historiografia de la
plantación caribeña". *Revista mexicana del caribe*, no. 1.

Patterson, Orlando. 1967. *The Sociology of Slavery*. London: McGibbon and Kee.

Poirer, Jean, and Huguette Dagenais. 1986. "En Marge, la situation des femmes
dans l'agriculture en Guadelope: Situation actuelle, questions méthodologiques".
Environnement caraïbe.

Pulsipher, Lydia Mihelic. 1993. "Changing Roles in the Life Cycles of Women in
Traditional West Indian Houseyards". In *Women and Change in the Caribbean*,
edited by J.H. Momsen. Kingston, Jamaica: Ian Randle Publishers.

Reddock, Rhoda. 1984. "Women, Labour and Struggle in Twentieth Century
Trinidad and Tobago, 1891–1960". PhD thesis, University of Amsterdam.

——. 1985. "Freedoms Denied: Indian Women and Indentureship in Trinidad and
Tobago, 1845–1917". *Economic and Political Weekly* 20, no. 43 (26 October).

——. 1990. "The Caribbean Feminist Tradition". *Women Speak!* nos. 26/27.

Rodney, Walter. 1980. *History of the Guyanese Working People, 1881–1905*. London:
Johns Hopkins University Press.

Safa, Helen. 1995. *The Myth of the Male Breadwinner*. Boulder: Westview Press.

Seager, Joni. 1997. *The State of Women in the World Atlas*. London: Penguin.

Smith, R.T. 1956. *The Negro Family in British Guiana: Family Structure and Social Status in the Villages*. London: Routledge and Kegan Paul.

Tikasingh, G. 1973. "The Establishment of the Indians in Trinidad, 1870–1900". PhD thesis, University of the West Indies.

Wiltshire-Brodber, Rosina. 1988. "Gender, Race and Class in the Caribbean". In *Gender in Caribbean Development*, edited by P. Mohammed and C. Shepherd. St Augustine, Trinidad: Women and Development Studies Project, University of the West Indies.

4 Is the Caribbean Male an Endangered Species?*

Keisha Lindsay

Overview

From newspaper columnist Carl Wint's "Where Have All the Men Gone" (1989) to Professor Errol Miller's *Men at Risk* (1991b), the marginalization of the black male has emerged as key discourse. Central to this discourse is the notion that men are increasingly missing from the higher echelons of the family, the classroom and the labour force.

The marginalization thesis prompts a variety of understandings. On the one hand, the increased presence of Jamaican women in education, the labour force and as household heads suggests that the nation's traditional patriarchy is being reordered to produce a new female-dominated gender hierarchy. Reanalysis of the data surrounding women's participation in the family, the workplace and the classroom, on the other hand, casts doubt on both the extent and significance of women's participation in these arenas. Indeed, a close examination of the data surrounding Caribbean women's participation in these arenas indicates anything but increasing female dominance and converse

*This paper was previously published as *Working Paper I*, Centre for Gender and Development Studies, University of the West Indies, Mona, 1997.

male marginality. Instead, what appears as male marginalization stems not from any concrete material reality, but from a gender-biased methodological frame which recognizes some data sources and ignores or invalidates others.

The limitations of the marginalization thesis go beyond its narrow methodological approach to data and data collection. A core limitation of the thesis also lies in its epistemological frame; a frame premised not on the radical reordering, but on the fundamental reinscription, of masculine and feminine gender constructs. Far from advancing any fundamental reordering of gender constructs, the marginalization thesis arguably perpetuates the age-old patriarchal construct – that of woman as the "lesser", inferior being.

At the heart of the marginalization thesis is a presumption that women and women's advances are solely the by-product of *men's* endeavours. As Miller himself puts it, "the phenomenon we are investigating is that of men relaxing their patriarchal closure and permitting women meaningful education, employment and earnings comparable to men's" (Miller 1991b: 99).

The Marginalization Thesis Defined

Just as evidence of black male marginalization is to be found in men's diminished role in the family, school system and workplace, marginalization theorists contend, the cause of male marginalization can be located in the universal, patriarchal order; an order which oppresses men and women alike. Hence, Miller's description of Caribbean men's increasingly diminished role:

> in the family, role reversal in a small but increasing number of households, boys' declining participation and performance in the education system, the greater prospect of men inheriting the fathers' position in the social structure, the decline in the proportion of men in the highest-paying and most prestigious occupations and the decrease in men's earning power relative to women's, especially in white-collar occupations. (Miller 1991b: 93)

Proponents of marginalization concede that women have historically been made subordinate to men within the confines of the universal patriarchal order. Underlying this subordination has been the hierarchical sexual division of women's life-giving and men's life-taking powers; a division in which life-taking powers have proven to be more decisive than life-giving ones. For:

both birth and death "are once-in-a-lifetime events". One cannot be threatened with birth. Once born one can only be grateful for the privilege. The life-giving power therefore engenders only gratitude . . . Those with the power to take life [however] are usually feared. [Hence] men exercising the life-taking powers became the final authority . . . (Miller 1991b: 112)

Alien Men

For marginalization theorists, however, patriarchy concerns not only men dominating women, but men dominating "other men" (Miller 1991b: 134). Miller explains that the patriarchal order has historically been marked by a profound "inability to deal humanely and equitably with men of rival groups or communities which present a real challenge or constitute meaningful opposition to one's group" (Miller 1991b: 136). Early societies, Miller asserts, were premised on a respect for genealogical descent and social relationships between descendants of common ancestry. The growth of human society and the increase in contacts among groups of different descent, however, meant that social groups increasingly began to confront and ultimately conquer each other without the benefit of common culture and ancestry. Moreover, with the advent of wars of conquest, a new problem emerged for the patriarchy – what to do with conquered male groups. While there was some possibility of incorporating the women of the conquered lineage, given their still valuable life-giving powers, conquered men presented much less fruitful prospects. How could men be absorbed when they were imbued with life-taking powers implicitly detrimental to the conquering group (Miller 1991b)?

Today, while the units to which men belong and have primary allegiance may have changed from lineage, family or kin group to city, nation, class, religion, party or race, patriarchy's implicit problem – its inability to deal humanely with men of rival lineages – stands unchanged. As a result, those deemed "alien" men continue to be marginalized and subjugated, not through physically barbarous means, but via the "remote manipulation" of their "access to commodities, services, capital and symbols of material progress" (Miller 1991b: 166).

Ultimately, marginalization theorists conclude, it is within the context of men's own fight with other men for ascendancy to power, wealth and status and the resulting subordination and emasculation of those men who fail in their ascendancy to power, that the contemporary emasculation of the black male is to be understood (*Daily Gleaner,* 17 November 1991, 19C).

Liberated Women

If "alien" men have been the historical and contemporary losers in the patriarchal order, marginalization theorists assert, women have emerged as the clear victors (*Daily Gleaner,* 17 November 1991, 19C). While the patriarchal order has been clearly responsible for female subordination, marginalization theorists contend, the same patriarchal order has also created a significant "space" for female liberation. For:

> patriarchs, men of the dominant group, in defending their group's interest from challenges from the men of other groups in society, [ultimately] relax their patriarchal closure over education, employment and status symbols. Thus allowing their women and the women in the challenging groups most of the opportunities that would have gone to men of the challenging group. (Miller 1991b: 166)

Evidence of this patriarchal "relaxation" in the Caribbean, explains Miller, is clear. For instance, the evolution of primary school teaching and teacher education has

> shifted from being male dominated to being female dominated as a result of the intention of the ruling class to release black men from service type occupations to make them available for agricultural and industrial labour, and to stifle the possible emergence of militant black educated men who could possibly overthrow the power structure . . . The women who would benefit and the colleges for female teachers that would grow as a result . . . [did] nothing to cause the outcome. They were the only innocents in the matter. (Miller 1986: 68–73)

Women's liberation, in short, is the ultimate consequence of *men's* power struggles. Put more crudely, women have been "pawns manipulated by men locked in grievous conflicts . . . the pariahs of power in male conflicts . . ." (Miller 1991b: 168).

The consequences of female liberation are therefore multiple. As Miller explains, the "content of feminine socialization [caring, nurturance, patience]" would seem to have "much greater relevance and meaning in contemporary society than the patriarchal content of masculinity". In other words, while "men have taken humanity to the brink of destruction; it may be women that will take humanity permanently away from the brink" (Miller 1991b: 270).

At the same time, marginalization theorists caution, if men's marginalization and women's liberation continue unabated the very real possibility of a *female* patriarchy could arise – that is, "women could come to the conclusion that they can run the show better than men . . . the result could be feminine patriarchy [where] women new to power may . . . be tempted to imitate the best male practitioners they have known or learned about". In short, "while there could be a major change in the cast, the script would remain the same" (Miller 1991b: 281). The very threat of the "female patriarch" then lies in both her desire and her capacity to emulate her male predecessors.

The Empirical "Reality"

Marginalization theorists make reference to a concrete, easily identifiable empirical "reality" of black male marginalization.

The Family

Evidence of the systematic marginalization of the black male within the family, for instance, is to be found in a variety of landmark studies on the Caribbean family, including Clarke's finding (1957) that fewer than half of Jamaican children lived in homes with both their mother and father present (Miller 1991b: 69) and Massiah's finding (1970) that half the female-headed households in the Commonwealth Caribbean actually consist of resident male partners who have obviously "conceded headship or had it taken away from them" (Miller 1991: 69). Ortmayr (1992), too, in his discussion of family and illegitimacy in nineteenth-century Jamaica, asserts that

> Low wages, unsteady jobs and seasonal unemployment marginalize the lower class man. Those who are marginalized cannot fulfill their roles as breadwinners properly. Instead, they tend to remain dependent upon their family of descent, hesitate to take full responsibility over one family and prefer to live as temporary migrants, between mates, families and jobs. (Ortmayr 1992: 12)

Education

The educational advancement of Caribbean women is another area in which empirical evidence of black male marginalization is to be found. Indeed, the Caribbean is one of the few regions in the world where there are more literate adult women than men. At present, only 77 percent of Jamaican men are literate compared to 86.7 percent of Jamaican women (Miller 1991b: 75). The region is also one of the few in which the secondary school enrolment of girls exceeds that of boys. In the 1989/90 school year in Jamaica some 116,454 girls were enrolled in secondary school, compared to only 108,897 boys (STATIN 1991).

Enrolment figures at the University of the West Indies suggest a similar advance of females and converse marginalization of males at the tertiary level. In the 1960/61 academic year women constituted only 45.8 percent of the university population. By the 1986/87 academic year total female enrolment had increased to 55.3 percent, with the Faculties of Law and Arts recording female enrolment of over 60 percent (Miller 1991b: 76). By the end of the 1992 academic year 70 percent of all UWI graduates were female, while 65 percent of the forty-eight first-class honours graduates were women (*Daily Gleaner,* 3 December 1992, 1C).

Employment

The widespread changes taking place in the region's labour force provide further empirical evidence of the liberation of women and converse marginalization of men. In 1943 women constituted only 36.3 percent of Jamaica's working population. By 1988 the figure had increased to 46.6 percent. More importantly, the increased participation of women in the labour force has not been limited to low-status jobs. By 1984 only 16 percent of the female labour force was employed as domestics and only 4 percent as low-level agricultural workers (Miller 1991b: 82).

Caribbean women, moreover, have made seemingly significant gains in closing the income gap between males and females. Jamaican women now earn 77 percent to 92 percent of men's income; whereas in the United States and the former USSR the comparable figure is 67 percent to 82 percent (Miller 1991b: 87).

The Empirical "Reality" Reconsidered

What sense are we to make of Caribbean women's apparent dominance over men in education, employment and the family? The answer perhaps lies in recognizing the wealth of statistical data addressed neither by Miller nor by other proponents of the marginalization thesis.

Women and the Family – Caribbean Matrifocality Deconstructed

The Caribbean family has long been characterized by various researchers as matrifocal, as manifest in the number of female-headed households within the region (Miller 1991b). In pointing to the notion of a matrifocal Caribbean family, however, scholars often fail to recognize that there is no implicit correlation between female household headship and actual social and economic power within the family structure or in the wider society.

Indeed, headship status, in and of itself, is not economically empowering for Caribbean women. In fact, the opposite may be true. McLeod (1990), in her study of low-income households in the Kingston Metropolitan Area, found that although 41 percent of low-income households are headed by women, female-headed households were more likely than their male-headed counterparts to:

- spend a greater proportion of their income on shelter
- be caught in the high-priced rental market and thus have lower land ownership rates
- be sharing "yard" infrastructure – toilets, cooking facilities, and so on
- have never finished high school (due to early child-rearing/minding duties)
- be unemployed and thus more dependent on informal income generation
- have not invested in assets such as televisions, radios and other household appliances commonly used as collateral in accessing loans
- not be saving (some 60 percent of female household heads reporting no savings) (McLeod 1990)

While female household heads are "as equally involved in work as males . . . the pattern of their occupational distribution is markedly different" (Massiah 1984: 13). Across the region, some 20.9 percent of male heads of household are employed in productive enterprise, compared to 18.5 percent of female heads of household. Female household heads are concentrated instead in service industries far removed from the traditionally male-dominated technical fields (Massiah 1984).

Socioeconomic statistics aside, female household headship is more than "a simple demarcation between male and female autonomy". Instead, an "important consideration is the process by which decisions are made within the family" (Massiah 1993: 88). In other words, the status of many women as household heads may not correspond with the actual *social* and *psychological* power which women command regarding decision-making processes. Powell (1986), for instance, reports that within female-headed households in the Caribbean, decision making still revolves around conventional notions of masculine and feminine authority – with women exercising sole control over domestic tasks, while decisions concerning expenditure are determined either jointly or by men.

Ultimately, marginalization theorists' attempted reconstruction[1] of a matrifocal Caribbean family is undermined by their failure to fully conceptualize matrifocality itself. As Mohammed (1988) explains in her critique of conventional matrifocal analyses of the Caribbean family:

> Matrifocality may imply that the women in a society have a 'rather' good status generally, or that they have more control over income and expenditure; in another context it may refer to a situation where women are the primary earners in the household. Elsewhere it may refer to those societies where male absenteeism leads to a predominance of households headed by women. Which aspect of matrifocality can we assume exists in the Caribbean? (Mohammed 1988: 171)

Gender Ideology and Education

Marginalization theorists argue that Caribbean women have made significant educational strides over the last thirty years. The core of this advancement supposedly lies in the greater presence of females in all levels of the educational system – including primary and high schools, teachers' training colleges and the University of the West Indies (STATIN 1991; Miller 1991a).

In focusing entirely on enrolment levels of females relative to males in the educational system, however, marginalization theorists fail to recognize the perpetuation of patriarchal sex-role stereotyping at all levels of the region's educational system. Despite the significant inroads made by Caribbean women into traditionally "masculine fields", most women are still doing courses which limit them to professions and occupations that are essentially extensions of conventional "women's skills" (Mohammed 1982). Increased

Table 4.1   Technical and Vocational Schools: Students Enrolled by Subject and
Sex, 1986–87

Subject	Male Enrolment	Female Enrolment
Mechanical/Building Engineering	143	19
Mechanical/Production Engineering	318	45
Electrical Engineering	340	20

Source: Miller 1991: 265.

female enrolment does little to fundamentally challenge patriarchal notions of masculine and feminine.[2]

The region's secondary and vocational school systems represent two arenas in which high female enrolment figures obscure the still prevalent sex-role stereotyping of girls. In Trinidad and Tobago's vocational education programme, for instance, sex-role stereotyping by subject is prevalent. In the business education and management stream, for instance, females outnumber males 337 to 242 respectively. Similarly, in distributive education and management 160 females are enrolled, compared to 22 males. Conversely, it is the male students who predominate in the more technical fields of mechanical and building engineering, mechanical production engineering, and electrical engineering (see Table 4.1).

This gender bias in Trinidad and Tobago's vocational training system reinforces earlier findings by Mohammed (1982) in which male vocational students were shown to predominate in technical subject areas such as welding and mechanical engineering while female students were more likely to be enrolled in fields such as dressmaking and design, and shorthand and typing.

Leo-Rhynie reports similar trends in the Jamaican context, where "in new secondary, technical and comprehensive high schools, there is a clear distinction in terms of vocational subjects studied by boys and girls. Girls select secretarial and home economic courses, while boys concentrate on industrial offerings along with principles of business education" (Leo-Rhynie 1987: 9).

It is not only at the vocational level, however, where the sex-role stereotyping of females exists. As Morris explains, when girls do enter nontraditional fields their performance remains lower than that of boys:

> It is clear that more girls are sitting the CXC [Caribbean Examinations Council] examinations than boys. However a higher percentage of boys gain grades 1 and 2, indicating higher overall achievement . . . Girls obtain a larger number of grades 3, 4, and 5 which suggests that they are attaining a minimum level of competence but are failing to reach an acceptable standard for continuation of their study of science. (Morris 1989: 3)

Since "girls are in fact sitting these examinations in greater numbers than boys yet are not obtaining a higher proportion of grades 1 and 2", Morris concludes, "it would seem to suggest that teachers should examine their teaching styles, classroom interaction, feedback etc. to see whether girls are being prepared for the examination in the same manner of boys" (1989: 3).

Citing the majority female enrolment at the University of the West Indies, Miller suggests that men are being marginalized even at the tertiary level. Once again, however, he mistakenly concentrates on women's enrolment levels as opposed to the traditional subject areas in which they are to be found. While it is correct that women now constitute over 70 percent of the Faculty of Arts and 100 percent of nursing students, both subject areas have long been traditional "female" educational enclaves (UWI 1994). Given this, "domination" in either nursing or English literature does not fundamentally challenge conventional patriarchal notions of "women's work".

Many female students at the university remain underrepresented in the more traditionally masculine disciplines. For instance, women represent only 48 percent of undergraduates in the Faculty of Natural Sciences and 20 percent of undergraduates in the Faculty of Engineering (UWI 1994). At the postgraduate level the gender bias is similarly skewed, with women comprising 47 percent and 24 percent, respectively, of the students in agriculture and engineering (UWI 1994).

Underlying the gender-specific training or sex-role stereotyping of females at both the secondary and tertiary levels throughout the Caribbean is a deep-rooted gender ideology premised on the male as household head and breadwinner with financial responsibility for the family, and the "ideal" female as mother, housewife, frail, feminine, helpless and genteel (Ellis 1986). In other words, the very *process* of schooling in the region is guided by a prevailing gender ideology of dependent, domesticated woman, on the one hand, and public, independent man on the other. As King and Morrissey (1988) explain, Caribbean social science texts consistently deem women "invisible and voiceless" through practices such as: using "man" and "working man" to include women; grouping adult males in one category and women and children in another; and casting women in limited and/or submissive roles (mothers, prostitutes) when they do appear.

Women in the Workplace

Marginalization proponents cite the labour force as another arena in which women have emerged as the inadvertent victors in the patriarchal wars between dominant and "alien" men. This concern about the marginalization of working men extends beyond the academic sphere. As a letter to the editor from a "Worried Young Male" in Trinidad makes clear, the increased presence of women in the work force, and the implications thereof, is very much a popular concern:

> I am 22 years old, unemployed . . . on Tuesday, October 21 there is [a] headline which says: Women get 5,500 more jobs than men. Sir, are men now going to stay home and take care of the children, cook, wash and clean. Are men not qualified for the jobs given to women . . . what is the reason for this new trend? Are women's hands no longer the hands that rock the cradle? Are employees not aware of what is taking place in other parts of the English speaking world where this trend is in force. Would someone say by the year 2000 what would be the position with employment for men. (*Trinidad Guardian*, 10 November 1996: 10)

Sex Role Stereotyping

The presumption, however, that greater female participation in the labour force poses an implicit challenge to male domination in the workplace is fundamentally flawed. As Antrobus (1986) makes clear, a narrow emphasis on the high labour-force participation of women often conceals facts which demonstrate the broader unequal status of women in the workplace. The Caribbean is no exception. While women are participating in the labour force in greater numbers, their participation continues to be shaped by sex-role stereotyping.

First, a majority of the region's women remain in traditional female "service" occupations such as teaching, nursing, hairdressing and secretarial work (Ellis 1986). In Jamaica, for instance, the majority of men and women

Table 4.2   Industry by Gender: Jamaica, 1991

Industry/Occupation	Men ('000)	Women ('000)
Mining and Refining	6.4	0.8
Construction and Installation	57.2	1.8
Craftsmen	124.7	28.3
Agriculture, Forestry and Fishing	174.4	58.4
Commerce	95.4	49.2
Service Occupations	42.7	93.7
Professional, Executive, Management	28.5	41.8
Clerical/Sales Workers	40.1	66.4

Source: STATIN 1991.

remain in industries and occupations traditionally deemed as either "masculine" or "feminine" arenas, such as construction or clerical work, respectively (see Table 4.2).

Even the University of the West Indies has not escaped this pattern of gender-based occupational stereotyping. In the 1993/94 academic year, for instance, women represented 78 percent of the administrative and clerical staff, 52 percent of the ancillary staff but only 43 percent of the academic and senior administrative staff on the Mona campus (UWI 1994). What then are we to make of the claim that Caribbean women have begun to make significant inroads into formerly white-collar, masculine managerial and professional fields?

At first glance, the statistics suggest exactly this phenomenon. In Jamaica women now clearly outnumber men in the professional, executive, technical and managerial fields (see Table 4.2). Such figures are deceptive, however, because they obscure the fact that traditionally female occupations such as teaching and nursing account for the majority of female professionals (Massiah 1984). Moreover when the figures on women's participation in the Executive/Corporate arena are further disaggregated it becomes obvious that women once again predominate, not in the high-status executive officer positions, but in lower rung service-oriented roles. In Jamaica 83 percent of the data processing posts, 52 percent of the personnel posts and 98 percent of the administrative posts are filled by women. Conversely, only 10 percent of the chief executive officers or deputies are women (PIOJ 1994).

Unemployment

The marginalization thesis overlooks the fact that throughout the region "unemployment among women is everywhere higher than it is among men" (Antrobus 1986: 23). In Barbados, in particular, the unemployment rate for women has long been twice that of men (Antrobus 1986). Similarly in Jamaica, of the unemployed in 1993, 33.7 percent were women over twenty-five years; 31.1 percent women under twenty-five years; 15.9 percent men over twenty-five years and 19.2 percent men under twenty-five years (PIOJ 1994).

Occupational Status

Women's occupational status in the region is not only shaped by sex-role stereotyping and high unemployment but by their continued low ranking within most economic sectors. Mohammed explains that even "within the fields in which they are concentrated through increased educational opportunities and the expansion of certain economic sectors, women may still fill the lowest positions" (Mohammed 1982: 60).

In Barbados's agricultural sector, for instance, women and men are equally represented; yet women remain grossly underrepresented at the levels of manager and designated farmers. Only 1 percent of the Barbadian women in agriculture are farmers; only 0.5 percent are farm managers. Instead, 98 percent of women in agriculture function as low-ranking labourers. Meanwhile, of the Barbadian men involved in agriculture 4 percent are farmers; 5 percent are farm managers and 80 percent are common labourers (Massiah 1993).

Marginalization theorists are correct in their basic assertion that Caribbean women are decreasingly involved in agriculture (Miller 1991b). In citing the decline, however, they fail to acknowledge that male participation in agriculture is also on the decrease and, more importantly, that those women who remain in agriculture do so at levels below that of their male counterparts. The low status of women is not limited to agriculture alone. The heavily female free zones or industrial parks established by many regional governments are often little more than large factory shells in which women work in cramped conditions for low wages, few fringe benefits and few opportunities for advancement into management (Ellis 1986). Even Trinidad and Tobago's civil service was found to have "the highest proportion of female workers . . . in the range of Clerk I, while in the highest reaches of the civil service there were very few or no women" (Mohammed 1982: 60).

The Epistemological Challenge

What sense are we to make of the marginalization thesis? Does the inadequate data base on which it rests make it thoroughly invalid? Or do its limitations simply stem from inadequate data collection and analysis?

The solution lies in understanding that the thesis of marginalization of the black male is fundamentally flawed at an epistemological level – its limitations lie not just in an inadequate use and analysis of existing data, but in an epistemology or theory of knowledge which systematically invalidates women and women's experiences (Narayan 1989).

At the core of the thesis is an epistemological approach rooted in positivism – a philosophy which "proclaims the suitability of the scientific method to all forms of knowledge" (Bryman 1988: 22). Positivism presumes that "the logic and procedures of the natural sciences" provides the "epistemological yard-stick" against which all knowledge is measured.

Implicit in the positivist stance, and the quantitative research methods through which it is most often manifest, is the conviction that "human emotions and ability to communicate through language need not impede the implementation of the scientific method". Indeed, the scientific method itself presumes that it is "only those phenomenon which are observable, in the sense of being amenable to the sense", which "can be validly warranted as knowledge" (Bryman 1988: 14).

Miller's work is clearly rooted in this positivist presumption that "true" scientific research is that which is conducted through the accumulation of verifiable facts – facts which ultimately spawn "laws" or empirically established regularities (Nielsen 1990: 2). In discussing the progress of US, Soviet and Caribbean women in the workplace, for instance, Miller cites a number of what he himself terms "objective" sources of information – chief among them official government statistics concerning the percentage of women in the labour force; women's full-time earnings relative to men and the percentage of married women in the labour force. Miller, in fact, places a great deal of emphasis on the objectivity of his data. Hence his confident assertion (after a painstaking presentation of the statistical evidence needed to verify his thesis of the Jamaican male slide in education) that "the data is clear cut" (Miller 1986: 79).

How are we to interpret the positivist stance which underlies much of the marginalization thesis? Is objective "hard data" the only valid test or proof in social research, as the positivist school suggests? Or is the conventional positivist approach itself mired with its own brand of subjectivity and biases?

"Science" Deconstructed

Perhaps, as Bryman (1988) suggests, the answer lies in recognizing that the very ability of quantitative research design to "scientifically" link independent and dependent variables is questionable. In other words, the aim of quantitative, positivist analysis – to establish nomothetic or "law like findings which can be deemed to hold irrespective of time and place" – is arguably more of a theoretical quest than a practical endeavour. As Sharif explains:

> the standard research situation is loaded with opportunity for bias. The opportunity starts when a researcher decides what to study and it continues to widen during decisions about how to study the subject . . . The researcher decides, of course, often in highly arbitrary ways dictated by custom in previous research. What are to be included as the all-important independent variables? Which aspects of the individual's behaviour are to be noticed . . . The researcher makes all of these decisions, often forgetting at times that he or she is a human being who is part of the research situation too. (1987: 47)

Taking the critique even further, a number of feminist epistemologists assert that the positivist approach is not just biased, but is subjective in a manner which either "intentionally or unintentionally excludes the possibility that women could be "knowers" or "agents of knowledge" (Harding 1987a: 3). Feminist epistemologists contend that the positivist approach is not just value laden, but particularly biased with patriarchal value systems and assumptions (Nielsen 1990). Science, in other words – or the very quest for scientific knowledge – is grounded in the perpetuation of the patriarchal order. Hence the quest for "objectivity" is not just "a set of conversion rules . . . regarding the production of the written word", but a distinct "artifact with the sexual political system" (Stanley 1990).

The very data or statistical measures used in the construction and validation of scientific knowledge are no exception. Take, for instance, a conventional national accounting measure like the gross national product (GNP) which, despite its intention to simply "aggregate national income", has instead excluded informal and noncash output – the very economic sectors in which Third World women predominate (Rogers 1980). As Rogers explains, ultimately "the GNP and its variant are . . . a statistical illusion. It refers ostensibly to production"; yet "if women's productive work is not paid, [the work] has no place in real production" (1980: 64).

The work of many of the marginalization theorists is rooted in this very uncritical acceptance of supposedly "objective" data and statistical measures. For instance, marginalization theorists often incorrectly presume that female headship status automatically means that women command complete control over internal family decision-making processes such as the distribution of household income and the purchase of assets. This presumption is flawed, first because it ignores the persistence of male-dominated power relations even within many female-headed Caribbean households (Massiah 1993), and second because the preponderance of extended family structures throughout the region makes any presumption of "a fixed unit called a household" comprised of a mother, father, children and immediate family members, at best, a "figment of the statisticians' imagination" (Rogers 1980: 64).

"Masculine" and "Feminine" Hierarchy Reinscribed

Universal, Hierarchical Sex Opposition

A narrow "male reality" serves as not only the statistical but the theoretical focal point of much of the marginalization thesis. First, implicit in the thesis is a hierarchical sex opposition in which man serves as the "constructor" and woman as the passively "constructed". Woman is wholly the product or construct of man's actions. In Miller's own words, "it is the sponsorship of women by patriarchs in their contest with other men [which] provides the circumstances and the context of women's liberation from their historic marginalization under patriarchy" (Miller 1991b: 273). Women's advances then are the mere byproduct of *men's* conflicts, *men's* history. Women's contemporary progress, in short, is anything *but* the result of their own efforts (Jones 1992: 169).

Informing the marginalization theory's notion of constructed woman is a patriarchal, Cartesian rationality with established universal, hierarchical binary oppositions between masculine and feminine. As Best and Kellner explain:

> the humanist discourse of "Man" at once occludes important differences between men and women and covertly supports male domination of women. The humanist discourse postulates a universal essence as constituent of human beings which operates to enthrone socially constructed male traits and activities (such as reason, production, or the will to power) as essentially human. In such modern discourses, men are the paradigm of humanity, while women are the other, the subordinate sex. (1991: 50)

Within this binary opposition man is the rational, assertive, strong, public "constructor" of woman –the "lesser", irrational and emotional being. Woman is "that which is not man; she is minus male" (Hekman 1994: 50). Without her patriarchal male sponsor, woman is ultimately jeopardized – unable to progress and advance (Miller 1991b: 205).

Biological Determinism

At the heart of the constructing man/constructed woman paradigm is a fundamental subscription to biological determinism –the notion that "biological constraints fully determine the behaviour of the sexes" (Rosaldo and Lamphere 1974: 4). Biological determinism presumes that gender is rooted in biological sex difference. This ultimately fosters a sex-gender model which systematically limits the understanding and construction of woman. As Rosaldo and Lamphere (1974) explain:

> the facts of female biology, woman's domestic role, and the so-called "feminine personality" combine to encourage cultural definitions of the female that tend to be degrading. Women, who are excluded from cultural projects of transcendence, and limited to an existence largely dictated by their biology, come to be seen as more "natural" and less "cultural" than men . . . In other words, the ease of an association between woman and nonhuman nature provides a cultural rationale for female subordination; woman's biology, social role, and personality encourage

cultures to define her as "closer to nature" than man, hence to be subordinated, controlled, and manipulated in the service of "culture's" ends. (Rosaldo and Lamphere 1974: 8)

Some marginalization theorists do appear to acknowledge the limitations of biological determinism. Miller begins his work *Men at Risk* with the firm assertion that sex is biologically determined while gender is socially constructed (Miller 1991b: 1). Patriarchy, he admits, has shaped our very notions of masculinity and femininity. It has "ascribed roles and stereotypes for succeeding generations of men and women . . . conditioned mentalities and mystiques surrounding maleness and femaleness . . . delayed women's efforts to come out from under its yoke" (Miller 1991b: 202).

However, in acknowledging these patriarchal, "essentialist" notions of masculine and feminine, Miller fails to recognize that it is this same biological determinism which serves as the theoretical base of his own work – his own construct of masculine and feminine. First, underlying Miller's work and the marginalization thesis as a whole is the presumption that it is women's biologically determined capacity as life-givers which serves as the source of both their initial subordination and their ultimate liberation. On the one hand, women's *biological* capacity to give birth underlies their subordination: "Biology . . . pre-disposed that femininity . . . be defined as and females socialized in, behaviours and habits like caring, nurturing, gentleness, kindness, tenderness, cooperation, accommodation of differences, long-suffering, patience, acquiescence and passivity" (Miller 1991b: 114). At the same time, it is women's innate capacity for patience, passivity and nonaggression which ironically underlies their liberation, while it is their inability to challenge the patriarchy which underlies their use as pawns against "alien" men (Miller 1991b).

Second, the marginalization thesis assumes that it is not just women but men who are both liberated and oppressed as a result of their innate biological capabilities. On the one hand, man's greater biological capacity (relative to woman) to engage in life-taking and physical defence shapes his masculine traits – namely aggression, ruggedness, risk-taking and confrontation (Miller 1991b: 114). On the other hand, it is the presence of these same biologically determined traits among "alien" men which underlie their own marginalization and domination by the patriarchy. Biology, in short, inevitably shapes the destiny of "conquered" and "conquering" men alike.

Demonized Woman, Victimized Man

Like the very patriarchal order on which it rests, the biological determinism
implicit in the marginalization thesis obscures a number of important realities.
At the heart of its "essentialist" construction of masculine and feminine is a
failure to understand that for human beings, biology's importance lies mainly
in how it is "interpreted by the norms and expectations of human culture and
society" (Rosaldo and Lamphere 1974: 4). What is masculine and what is
feminine is culturally specific – interpreted and defined by the norms and
expectations of specific human cultures and societies.

The marginalization thesis's own notions of "masculine" and "feminine"
are no exception. In constructing a perspective which presumes masculinity
and femininity to be "primarily oppositional", the thesis serves to reinscribe
distinctly patriarchal Caribbean gender constructs –that of demonized woman
and victimized man. Mohammed explains that inherent in the traditional
Caribbean construct of masculine and feminine has been the largely uncritical
acceptance of biologically determined "opposition" or difference. Indeed,
within the region masculine and feminine have come to signify distinct
categories "describing characteristics of human expression and behaviour
between the sexes as immutable" (1996: 1).

On the one hand, a distinctly "mythologized" Caribbean masculinity has
emerged within the region – a masculinity marked by "the idea of man as
head of the family, provider and controller of female sexuality" (Mohammed 1996: 4). Any disruption in this ideal is not only seen as destroying
the foundation of a socially accepted idea of masculinity but as victimizing
the Caribbean male (Mohammed 1996). On the other hand, the quintes-
sentially Caribbean female has emerged as "an adaptable creature, adjust-
ing to the vagaries of life through pragmatic and devious means . . .
especially assiduous in her deployment of her sexuality to meet her ends"
(Mohammed 1996: 1–4). Though strong and resourceful, she possesses
an innate ability to deceive, overpower and make "marginal" her male
counterparts.

The marginalization thesis can clearly be located within this paradigm of
demonized woman/victimized man. First, underlying the thesis is a subscription to the mythologized Caribbean masculinity described by Mohammed
(1996) – that of man as the dominant head of the familial unit. Take, for

instance, Miller's heroic description of masculinity in the "pre-marginaliza-tion" era when "[f]athers were stewards of the power . . . the coercive effect of the threat of death . . . the magic and mystification of religious symbols . . . were all controlled, experienced or exercised by the male heads of families. Appropriately, the patriarch was labeled the protector/provider" (Miller 1991b: 149).

Second, the marginalization thesis presumes that masculinity has an im-plicit sexual charge – a charge that is ultimately taken away or victimized.[3] Hence, patriarchy's ultimate need to "emasculate" alien men – via a process of literal, and then figurative or material, castration. As Miller describes it, "punishment is inflicted through concealed and disguised means [whereby] the opportunities conceded by the victors are channelled to the females of the vanquished group. In time the men appear to have determined their own fate. The victim is ultimately blamed for the crime against himself . . ." (Miller 1991b: 199).

Finally, just as the masculine ideal of the marginalization thesis is that of the valiant yet victimized male, its construct of the feminine is firmly rooted in the stereotypical "deception and manipulation" described by Mohammed (1996). For to suggest, as does Miller, that black women have uncritically accepted their sponsorship by patriarchal males, is also to maintain that black women do in fact possess a basic level of complicity and deviousness – a deviousness which they have systematically directed against their black male counterparts (Miller 1994: 125).

Power Redefined

Do the patriarchal gender constructs which underlie the marginalization thesis thoroughly undermine its central tenet of a patriarchy in flux? Or does the "hard evidence" or empirical data on which it rests lend some credence to the notion of a systematic male marginalization?

The answer lies in understanding that *both* the empirical evidence and the theoretical constructs utilized by marginalization theorists rest on a very narrow conception of power. Implicit in the marginalization thesis is the presumption that power is wholly "concrete" or quantifiable – that power or the lack thereof can be measured according to aggregate statistics, be they literacy data or income levels. The thesis presumes power to be a fixed entity emanating from a series of specific points – specifically from the "institutions" of the family, the educational system, the workplace and labour force.

This dual notion of power as both fixed and quantitative is, however, flawed. To argue that women can overpower men simply on the basis of increased income or occupational status is to incorrectly presume that income or occupational dominance form the sole basis of men's control over women. Instead, there is a vast aspect of patriarchal power which is neither fixed nor quantifiable; an aspect which remains intact whether or not women increase their rates of literacy, university education or middle-class status relative to their male counterparts (Foucault 1980). In other words, women's institutional advances can and often do leave intact the "rest" of patriarchal power – a power which is "not an institution, and not a structure" (Foucault 1980: 93).

Alternative Epistemology and Method

A critical analysis of the thesis of the marginalization of the black male requires more than simply recognizing the rather limited understanding of power on which it rests. Indeed, the true value of the marginalization thesis lies in the impetus or rationale which it provides for the development of an alternative feminist epistemology and methodology.

Feminist Epistemology

The patriarchal bias implicit in traditional approaches to science or knowledge, like that of the marginalization thesis, mandates that a major part of the feminist project involve the establishment of an alternative epistemology. As Narayan asserts: "Our location in the world as women makes it possible for us to perceive and understand different aspects of both the world and human activities in ways that challenge the male bias of existing perspectives" (1989: 256). Feminist epistemologists suggest that women must seek to deconstruct the "objectivity" at the heart of positivism by openly declaring their own "subjectivity":

> Important strands in feminist epistemology hold the view that our concrete
> embodiments as members of a specific class, race and gender as well as our
> concrete historical situations necessarily play significant roles in our perspective

on the world; moreover, no point of view is "neutral" because no one exists unembedded in the world. Knowledge is seen as gained not by solitary individuals but by socially constituted members of groups that emerge and change through history. (Narayan 1989: 262)

The point is to move away from "integrating" women into an inherently flawed masculine concept of reason and rationality and towards "successor sciences" grounded in a distinctly feminine perspective (Hekman 1994).

One such "successor science" is standpoint epistemology – the notion that "women's experiences, informed by feminist theory, provide a potential grounding for more complete and less distorted knowledge claims than do men's". As Harding explains, since knowledge "is supposed to be based on experience", it follows that "feminist claims can [in fact] turn out to be more scientifically preferable [in] that they originate in, and are tested against, a more complete and less distorting kind of social experience" (1987b: 184).

Alternative Methods

The feminist project involves not only the development of alternative, "subjective" epistemological approaches, but the development and revalidation of alternative research methods and sources. The male, positivist paradigm has traditionally deemed surveys and other research methods which rely on the collection and processing of "hard data" as the only "true" methods of social research. In contrast, more subjective methods of research have been deemed untrustworthy because the "human memory on which [they are] based is malleable and susceptible to confusion and conflation" (Chamberlain 1995: 94).

An increasing number of feminist scholars, however, suggest that there is an inherent validity to be found within subjective research methods such as oral histories. Chamberlain in providing a rationale for the use of oral histories – particularly in exploring the social/historical reality of oppressed groups like women – explains that oral histories can provide not just individual accounts but a myriad of socially constructed images, priorities, languages and expectations. In other words, "although the voice may be individual, and differs from one to another, the form memory assumes, the ways in which it is collated and expressed, is collective, is culturally and socially constructed" (1995: 95).

Not only that, the subjectivity implicit in methods like oral history can provide clues to the private, personal and often unconscious "directives" with which women often negotiate. Indeed, when one considers that most official texts – be they newspapers, government statistics or periodicals – have historically been written by men, any garnering of women's perspectives must, of necessity, be premised on the analysis of texts produced by women themselves (Brereton 1995).

Conclusion

At one level, the marginalization thesis's flawed perception of the empirical reality of the role of Caribbean men and women in the family, workplace and classroom lies in its failure to thoroughly analyse the full dimensions of the available data. Hence the failure of the thesis to explore the ways in which head of household status is often economically *disempowering* to women; the continued occupational and educational sex-role stereotyping of girls and women in teaching, nursing, home economics and other arenas traditionally deemed as "women's work"; and the continued low occupational status of women vis-à-vis men in management, agriculture and other major economic sectors.

More fundamentally, at the heart of the marginalization thesis's misunderstanding of the empirical reality surrounding gender relations in education, the family and the labour force is its positivist epistemological orientation which presumes that "true" social research is that which is conducted via the accumulation of verifiable, objective facts; and its biologically determined theoretical base which systematically casts men as "constructors" and women as the "constructed".

The feminist epistemological and methodological project in the Caribbean is thus a three-pronged one. First, as the marginalization thesis suggests, there is a clear need for feminist interrogation of the epistemological frameworks which underlie much of gender discourse in the region to date. Second, with such interrogation comes the need for not criticism alone but the provision of viable, alternative epistemologies and methods. More broadly, efforts at Caribbean feminist epistemology must strive to be just that – Caribbean. Ultimately theories of knowledge which uncritically re-entrench imported concepts and norms contribute little to either feminist scholarship or the daily reality of women in the region.

Notes

1. In the manner established by M.G. Smith (1965), R.T. Smith (1956) and Edith Clarke (1957).
2. As Miller (1991) himself notes, conventional notions of masculine traits generally encompass aggression, valour and determination, while feminine traits are generally thought to include patience, understanding and nurturing.
3. Miller's emphasis on black male sexual emasculation is not unique. The "discourse of black resistance has almost always equated freedom with manhood, the economic and material domination of black men with castration, emasculation". These sexual metaphors reflect the "patriarchal belief that revolutionary struggle [is] really about the erect phallus, the ability of men to establish political dominance that could correspond to sexual dominance" (hooks 1990: 58).

References

Antrobus, Peggy. 1986. "Women and Employment". In *Women of the Caribbean*, edited by P. Ellis. London: Zed Books.

Best, Steven, and Douglas Kellner. 1991. *Postmodernism: Critical Interrogation*. London: Macmillan.

Bordo, Susan. 1986. "The Cartesian Masculinity of Thought". *Signs* 11, no. 3.

Brereton, Bridget. 1995. "Text, Testimony and Gender: An Examination of Some Texts by Women on the English-Speaking Caribbean, from the 1770s to the 1920s". In *Engendering History: Caribbean Women in Historical Perspective*, edited by V. Shepherd, B. Bailey, and B. Brereton. Kingston, Jamaica: Ian Randle Publishers.

Bryman, Alan. 1988. *Quantity and Quality in Social Research*. London: Unwin Hyman.

Chamberlain, Mary. 1995. "Gender and Memory: Oral History and Women's History". In *Engendering History: Caribbean Women in Historical Perspective*, edited by V. Shepherd, B. Bailey, and B. Brereton. Kingston, Jamaica: Ian Randle Publishers.

Chevannes, Barry. 1992. "*Men at Risk*". Review. *Caribbean Review of Books* 6.

Clarke, Edith. 1957. *My Mother Who Fathered Me: A Study of the Family in Three Selected Communities in Jamaica*. London: G. Allen and Unwin.

de Lauretis, Teresa. 1987. *Technologies of Gender*. London: Macmillan.

Ellis, Patricia. 1986. "Introduction: An Overview of Women in Caribbean Society". In *Women in the Caribbean*, edited by P. Ellis. London: Zed Books.

Farran, Denise. 1990. "Seeking Susan: Producing Statistical Information on Young People's Leisure". In *Feminist Praxis: Research, Theory and Epistemology in Feminist Sociology*, edited by L. Stanley. New York: Routledge.

Flax, Jane. 1990. "Postmodernism and Gender Relations in Feminist Theory". In *Feminism/Postmodernism*, edited by L. Nicholson. New York: Routledge.

Foucault, Michel. 1980. *The History of Sexuality*. Vol. 1, *An Introduction*. New York: Vintage Books.

Harding, Sandra. 1987a. "Conclusion: Epistemological Questions". In *Feminism and Methodology*, edited by S. Harding. Bloomington: Indiana University Press.

_____. 1987b. "Introduction: Is There a Feminist Method?" In *Feminism and Methodology*, edited by S. Harding. Bloomington: Indiana University Press.

Hekman, Susan. 1994. "The Feminist Critique of Rationality". *The Polity Reader in Gender Studies*. London: Polity Press.

hooks, bell. 1990. *Yearning: Race, Gender and Cultural Politics*. Boston: South End Press.

Jones, Adam. 1992. "*Men at Risk*". Review. *Caribbean Studies* 25, nos. 1 and 2.

King, Ruby, and Mike Morrissey. 1990. *Images in Print: Bias and Prejudices in Caribbean Textbooks*. Mona, Jamaica: Institute of Social and Economic Research, University of the West Indies.

Leo-Rhynie, E.A. 1987. "Educational Opportunities for Jamaican Female Students: A Contemporary Perspective". Paper presented at First Interdisciplinary Seminar on Women and Development Studies, University of the West Indies, Kingston, Jamaica, 17 June.

"Male Non-Performance Causing Concern". 1992. *Daily Gleaner*, 3 December.

Massiah, Joycelin. 1982. "Female-headed Households and Employment". *Women's Studies International* 2.

_____. 1984. "Indicators of Women in Development: A Preliminary Framework for the Caribbean". In *Women, Work and Development*, edited by M. Gill and J. Massiah. Women in the Caribbean Project, Research Papers, Phase 1. Cave Hill, Barbados: Institute of Social and Economic Research, University of the West Indies.

_____, ed. 1993. *Women in Developing Economies: Making Visible the Invisible*. Oxford: Berg Publishers.

McLeod, R. 1990. *Daughters of Sisyphus: A Study of Gender Related Differences in the Search for Shelter Among Low-Income Heads of Household in Kingston, Jamaica.* Nairobi: UNCHS Habitat.

"*Men at Risk*: A Fascinating, Daring Study". 1991. *Daily Gleaner,* 17 November.

"Men's Worth Needs to be Recognized". 1993. *Daily Gleaner,* 26 January.

Miller, Errol, 1986. *The Marginalization of the Black Male: Insights from the Development of the Teaching Profession.* Mona, Jamaica: Institute of Social and Economic Research, University of the West Indies.

———, ed. 1991a. *Education and Society in the Commonwealth Caribbean.* Mona, Jamaica: Institute of Social and Economic Research, University of the West Indies.

———. 1991b. *Men at Risk.* Kingston, Jamaica: Jamaica Publishing House.

Mohammed, Patricia. 1982. "Educational Attainment of Women in the English-Speaking Caribbean, 1835–1945". *Women and Education.* Mona, Jamaica: Institute of Social and Economic Research.

———. 1988. "The Caribbean Family Revisited". In *Gender in Caribbean Development,* edited by P. Mohammed and C. Shepherd. St Augustine, Trinidad: Women and Development Studies Project, University of the West Indies.

———. 1991. "Studies in Education and Society: A Review of Educational Research in Trinidad and Tobago". In *Education and Society in the Commonwealth Caribbean,* edited by E. Miller. Mona, Jamaica: Institute of Social and Economic Research, University of the West Indies.

———. 1996. "Unmasking Masculinity". Paper presented at First Annual Caribbean Conference on Masculinity, University of the West Indies, St Augustine, Trinidad, January.

Morris, Jeannette. 1989. "Gender Difference in Science and Mathematics in CXC Examinations". Paper presented at Gender and Education Third Disciplinary Seminar, Mona, Jamaica, University of the West Indies.

Narayan, Uma. 1989. "The Project of Feminist Epistemology: Perspectives from a Non-Western Feminist". In *Gender Body and Knowledge,* edited by A. Jaggar and S. Bordo. New Brunswick, NJ: Rutgers University Press.

Nielsen, Joyce. 1990. *Feminist Research Methods.* San Francisco: Westview Press.

"No Jobs for Men". 1992. *Trinidad Guardian,* 10 November.

Ortmayr, Norbert. 1992. "Family and Illegitimacy in Highland Austria and Jamaica (Nineteenth and Twentieth Centuries)". Typescript.

Planning Institute of Jamaica (PIOJ). 1994. "Executive Salaries within the Jamaican Labour Market". *Labour Market Information Newsletter of Jamaica,* no. 14.

Powell, Dorian. 1986. "Caribbean Women and the Response to Familial
    Experiences". *Social and Economic Studies* 35, no. 2.
Rogers, Barbara. 1980. *The Domestication of Women: Discrimination in Developing
    Societies*. London: Routledge.
Rosaldo, Michelle, and Louise Lamphere. 1974. Introduction. *Woman, Culture and
    Society,* edited by M. Rosaldo and L. Lamphere. Stanford, Calif.: Stanford
    University Press.
Sharif, Carolyn Wood. 1987. "Bias in Psychology". In *Feminism and Methodology,*
    edited by S. Harding. Bloomington: Indiana University Press.
Smith, M.G. 1965. *The Plural Society in the British West Indies*. Berkeley: University
    of California Press.
Smith, R.T. 1956. *The Negro Family in British Guiana: Family Structure and Social
    Status in Three Villages*. London: Routledge and Kegan Paul.
Statistical Institute of Jamaica (STATIN). 1991. *Men and Women in Jamaica*.
    Kingston, Jamaica: STATIN.
University of the West Indies (UWI). 1994. *Official Statistics*. Kingston, Jamaica:
    UWI.
"Where Have All the Men Gone". 1989. *Daily Gleaner,* 15 August.

5 Gendered Methodologies and Feminist Awakenings

ODETTE PARRY

This paper, which explores my introduction and conversion to feminist research methodologies, is informed by my research experiences at the Institute of Social and Economic Research, University of the West Indies, Mona campus, between 1993 and 1996. I joined the Institute of Social and Economic Research from the United Kingdom as research fellow and specialist in education. My discipline of origin is sociology, but within that, fifteen years as a contract researcher have made me eclectic; I have worked in the sociology of medicine, science and education in criminology, architecture, and in gender. My greatest interests lie with the sociology of education and specifically in gender and education.

My theoretical roots can be traced to symbolic interactionism, and within sociology of education my earliest affinities lay with the work of the Chicago school. This interactionist and interpretive theoretical framework has informed the naturalistic, inductive and qualitative research paradigm from within which I prefer to work.[1] Although I have developed and moved on from these early beginnings, it was upon joining the University of the West Indies, through my contact with the Centre for Gender and Development Studies and the research which I carried out while there, that I was alerted to, influenced by and later became an ardent supporter of feminist research. Like many sociologists of my generation, I had grown up with and rejected the privileged research position of positivism, I was female and I considered myself a feminist. But although I carried out work on gender within many of the research areas in which I worked, largely researched women, and employed what I thought were appropriate qualitative tools, I had not seriously taken on board a feminist epistemological position or political programme. This is an account of the way in which researching gender in secondary education in the Caribbean began to change all that.

Choice of Topic

As research specialist in education at the Institute of Social and Economic Research, I was expected to identify a topical education issue, write research proposals and attract funding to carry out the research. As a newcomer to the institution and the culture, and ignorant of those academic networks which at home sustained my research interests and activities, the prospect was daunting. It required a lot of networking and reading, about the region generally, and about Caribbean education in particular. Given my long-term interests in gender, particularly female gender, this seemed a good place to start.

The topic which I identified was an obvious choice. The literature, academics, specialists in the field, and educators were consumed with the issue of gender and education, specifically and surprisingly with that of male educational achievement which was grabbing the headlines. For several reasons, which will become clear later, the study for which I wrote proposals and which was eventually funded focused on the educational underachievement of Caribbean males.

That my research led directly to an interest in feminist methodology may at first seem to be at odds with the study of males. There were several reasons why this focus was selected, some pragmatic, others more convoluted. The choice of topic reflected both regional and international concern that males are becoming vulnerable, marginalized and at risk. The vulnerability of males, and black males in particular, was currently at the centre of a discourse in popular culture which had entered into the vernacular of social science. Within this discourse the Jamaican male, for example, was constructed as socially marginalized and excluded, having lost power and authority over domestic, educational and occupational spheres. In popular discourse he was "in crisis". A growing sympathy and support for the Jamaican male emerged both through media demands of "leave our men alone" and "let's stop the male bashing" and through attempts to reconstruct a more positive image of Jamaican men as model parents and husbands (*Daily Gleaner,* June 1996).

In the academy, the concept of male marginalization has provoked a mixed response. Pedro Noguera (1996) has taken issue with the use of terms such as "crisis", "at risk", "marginal" and "endangered" to describe the plight of black males in America, Britain and the anglophone Caribbean. While not disputing the broad array of social and economic indicators which may locate many black males in lower socioeconomic categories, black women, he argues, are thereby rendered invisible. He asks, "What does this mean for black women? – and aren't they in crisis too?" Furthermore, as Noguera points out, the term "crisis" suggests a short-term urgency, a temporary and recent state. He disputes whether the problems facing black men are any greater than in the past, or that there are any signs of improvement. On the contrary, both in America and the Caribbean, available figures suggest that first, things are worsening for black men and second, they are facing no more hardships than those facing black women. Noguera also points out how the construction of marginalized man makes an implicit assumption that black males share the same experiences and problems as white males and also that all black men share identical problems.

My own research study developed around this topic because education is one area in which Caribbean males were felt to be particularly vulnerable. The importance with which this problem was imbued was apparent from its success in attracting research funding. The study on male educational underachievement was funded by UNICEF who had previously demonstrated commitment to the study of males by funding a large study of masculinity in the region (Brown 1995). It is worthy of comment that the interest and concern expressed about the plight of males at that time had never before, to the same extent, been expressed in relation to the position of females in education, either in the region or internationally. Concerns about women have never been mainstream in the research community. As far as research goes, the most obvious way of differentiating between mainstream and peripheral is to examine how much funding there is and to whom it is being allocated.

Concern about educational performances of males in the Caribbean had been fuelled by Caribbean Examination Council examination results, which suggested some changes to previous gender performance patterns. World Bank figures showed that the majority of Caribbean Examination passes were claimed by females, although subject choices still followed a traditional pattern, with girls highly visible in arts and boys in science (Whiteley 1994). In 1993 in Jamaica (one of the three territories in my research) 54.3 percent of the entries were from females and 45.7 percent were males. Of the total Grade I results, 36.4 percent went to males and 54.3 percent went to females. Comparing English to physics grade results, 81.4 percent of the Grade I English results were taken by females and 60.7 percent of the Grade I physics results went to males.

Figures available for Barbados and St Vincent (the other two territories in the research) showed similar trends. In Barbados 59.6 percent of passes in English language went to females, as did 63.9 percent of the passes in biology. In physics males did marginally better than the females, taking 55.5 percent of passes. In St Vincent 58.1 percent of English language passes went to females and 58.7 percent of passes in biology. In physics, gender differences in performance were negligible, with males claiming 50.7 percent of the passes. Overall in Barbados, for all subjects, females secured 60.4 percent of the passes and in St Vincent 61.1 percent. These trends were mirrored by educational performance in developed countries to the extent that the "problem" of male underachievement is now being conceived as an international phenomenon (Stockard and Wood 1984; Klein 1985). Females were and are still achieving equally with, or surpassing, males (Klein 1985; Stockard 1985; Stockard and Wood 1984; Mickleson 1992; Saltzman 1994), despite the fact that they continue to face unequal opportunities in the occupational structure upon leaving school (Mickleson 1992).

These percentages and the findings which they represent in the Caribbean are historically very interesting, in that they indicate a reversal of educational trends in the last century. For example, Department of Education figures for Jamaica show that in 1988, 41.4 percent of high school enrolment was male, compared with 58.5 percent female entry. This contrasts with corresponding figures for 1899 where 72.9 percent of high school enrolment was male, compared to only 27.1 percent female. These early figures reflect restricted educational opportunities for females compared to males, and social attitudes which encompassed the notion that education was inappropriate for women. Where education was thought to be appropriate for females it was highly selective and channelled females into areas deemed necessary for their domestic and child-rearing duties.

Today, the legacy of beliefs which structured educational opportunities for males and females in the last centuries is still felt. While examination results indicate that females are now performing overall at a higher level than previously, the statistics need to be treated with caution for a number of reasons. First, girls are still clustered primarily in subject areas which have traditionally been seen as female. So, for example, females do better than males in English but males are still more visible, and do better than females, in physics (Whiteley 1994). Second, although females seem to utilize education as an agent of social mobility more successfully than males, there remain glaring inequalities in the occupational structure once they leave school. Social mobility studies have indicated (Gordon 1986, 1989) that females are more socially mobile than males in the Caribbean, in that their socioeconomic status of destination is more likely to be different from their socioeconomic status of origin. However, while education constitutes an important agent of social mobility in the Caribbean, patterns of employment remain a function of gender inequality (Barrow 1988). Taking into account the class composition of the labour force, women, who are more likely to be in the middle strata, are heavily concentrated in the lower-status and lower-paid occupations. Furthermore, within the professions it is men who monopolize higher and better-paid positions. For example, although women dominate the teaching profession they are significantly underrepresented in headships. This disparity becomes more noticeable further up the academic scale, and particularly within the university structure (Drayton 1991).

American and British research suggests that groups of pupils who are aware that they face a job ceiling or that they will be denied equal access to professional jobs shape and channel their educational output accordingly (Mickelson 1992; Ogbu 1978; Willis 1977). However, whilst previous research suggests that both race and class can affect motivation, the same is not true of gender. On the contrary, poor occupational return on educational investment does not appear to depress either school performance or willingness to earn advanced degrees (Mickelson 1992). This raises two questions: why is it that when Caribbean males appear to have many advantages in the occupational structure, they perform badly in school? Conversely, why is it that when they face many disadvantages in the occupational structure, Caribbean girls continue to strive to do well in education?

In the Caribbean, male educational failure and female educational success have been understood in zero-sum terms. That is, followers of the "male marginalization" thesis in education (developed by Miller 1986, 1989, 1991) feel that they represent two sides of the same equation. Built into this equation is a causal function, so that males are thought to be doing badly precisely because females are doing well. When the problem is conceived in this way it appears that there is a definitive amount of "success" to be had, and if females have it males cannot.

This thinking underpins educational policy, which addresses male underachievement by discriminating against females at the first level of educational testing, the common entrance examination. In some territories, females have to score higher on the test than males to get a high school place. The policy has been justified on the grounds that females mature earlier than males and are therefore at an advantage when the test is administered. Rather than the test being seen as the problem, its validity has for a long time gone unchallenged.

The research I devised set out to explore the experiences of both males and females in secondary education and to challenge the assumption, at the same time exploding the myth, that male educational failure resulted from female educational advances. This was the first piece of research that I had embarked upon which I felt could truly reflect a feminist political programme.

Research Paradigms

At one level, research methods can be described as the way we set about collecting and analysing data. However, they also reflect philosophical, theoretical and epistemological positions from which we experience and understand the social world in which we live. It is through these positions that understandings are reached about the social realities which we inhabit. A striking example of the way in which methodologies reflect theoretical paradigms can be found in the very different – and sometimes antagonistic – methodological traditions of positivism and naturalism. While positivism and naturalism are described here as two distinct research traditions, in fact, social scientists rarely adhere exclusively to either category (Hammersley and Atkinson 1983).

Positivism, which reached its climax in the "logical positivism" of the 1930s and 1940s, has a long philosophical history, stretching as far back as Aristotle. Its impact upon social science has been considerable, lending itself to a distinct methodological tradition which promoted the methods of the natural sciences for the study of society. The basic tenets of positivism as they are translated into the study of the social world are briefly outlined below. First, physical science celebrates the type of logic characterized by the scientific experiment, where quantitatively measured variables are manipulated in order to establish relationships between them. Second, events are interpreted in a deductive fashion with recourse to universal laws which must obtain across all circumstances. Priority is given to phenomena that are objectively observable, tested by appeal to the real world and beyond doubt. A central tenet of positivism is that the social science method is modelled on the method of the natural sciences. The most important feature of scientific theories is that they are open to and subjected to testing and that they can be confirmed, or at least falsified. This testing involves comparing what the theory says should happen and what actually does happen. Empirical facts are collected by neutral (or objective) methods and all attempts are made to eliminate contamination of the data by the researcher.

In retaliation to the natural science approach advocated by positivistic social scientists, an alternative research paradigm called naturalism developed. This approach advocates that social life should be examined in its natural state, not in artificial settings like the experiment, and as much as possible undisturbed by the researcher. In naturalistic research the researcher develops an attitude of respect towards participants and is sensitive to the setting. Here deductive logic is replaced by inductive method. Theories are developed through data collection, rather than by recourse to universal laws, hypotheses are built up rather than knocked down. Before looking at some of the theoretical paradigms which these two distinct methodological traditions reflect, I want to briefly visit two early philosophers to whom some of these very different approaches can be traced.

The first of these was Plato, follower of Socrates, who became absorbed in what he described as the reality which lay behind the material world. For Plato this was the world of ideas which constituted eternal and immutable patterns which were behind natural phenomena. Plato believed that the only thing we can have true knowledge of is that which we understand by our reason. Everything else belongs to the material world which we only have access to via our senses. The natural or material world for Plato merely constituted shadows of eternal ideas. It is also worth mentioning here that Plato believed women to have identical reasoning powers to men, provided they were exposed to the same training and were exempt from child rearing and domestic responsibilities (Gaarder 1995). The relevance of this will become clearer later on.

In contrast, Aristotle, who was a pupil of Plato's Academy, was interested in natural processes. Whereas Plato emphasized the importance of reason, Aristotle emphasized the importance of both reason and senses. It was Aristotle who made a major impact upon the science of today by developing the language of science, the logic of deductive reasoning and rationality. Whereas the highest degree of reality in Plato's theory was that which we think with our reason, for Aristotle it was that which we perceive with our senses. Aristotle's view of women was less enlightened than that of Plato. Aristotle saw women as unfinished men who were incomplete. In reproduction, Aristotle described women as passive and men as active; man the form, woman the substance (Gaarder 1995). It is particularly lamentable that Aristotle's philosophical beliefs became the pivot of positivism and dominated our understanding of scientific inquiry for the succeeding few thousand years.

Although it is only in the last sixty years or so that naturalistic and positivistic traditions have generated distinct research disciplines, the very different philosophical standpoints of Plato and Aristotle are apparent, reflected by the current dichotomy between naturalism and positivism. Social scientists with positivistic allegiances continuously look for causal relationships between phenomena which will reflect underlying universal laws. They draw on a range of sociological and psychological ideas including behavioural psychology, functionalist sociology, Marxist and structuralist ideas. While the dissimilarities in these approaches outweigh any similarities in common with each other, they both make recourse to grand theories. Methodologically they are realized in hypothesis testing, deductive reasoning and quantitative data collection strategies, such as the social experiment and survey research.

The antithesis of positivism is naturalism. Followers of naturalism view social phenomena as very different from natural phenomena. Social scientists who adhere to naturalistic principles draw on a different range of sociological ideas, including symbolic interactionism, phenomenology, hermeneutics, linguistic philosophy and ethnomethodology. From different starting points, these perspectives agree that the social world cannot be understood in terms of causal relationships or by the subsumption of social events under universal laws. According to interactionists, people interpret stimuli, and these interpretations are continuously under revision as events unfold and shape actions. The same stimulus can mean different things to different people and indeed to the same people at different times. Because of this the search for universal laws is abandoned in favour of detailed descriptions of concrete experiences of life within particular cultures and of patterns which constitute life. Any attempts to go beyond this are discouraged (Hammersley and Atkinson 1983).

Feminist Methodologies

Because methodological approaches reflect theoretical paradigms and underlying philosophical standpoints, there can be no one definitive feminist methodology. Different feminist positions, such as liberal feminism, radical feminism and socialist feminism, approach the study of women in society differently. However, despite differences in feminisms and feminist methodologies, they all share a common objective, namely, to change power relations between women and men in society.

The starting point of feminist analyses is patriarchal society, although different ways of perceiving patriarchy have led to liberal, separatist and socialist feminist politics. Liberal feminists aim to achieve full equality with men in all spheres of life without radically transforming social and political systems. In contrast, radical feminism aims for a new social order in which women are not subordinated to men, and femaleness and femininity are not debased. The way in which radical feminists assert autonomy from men and recover their true and natural femininity is by separation from men and patriarchal society. For socialist feminists patriarchy is inseparable from class and race oppression and can only be abolished through transformation of the social system. Socialist feminism sees gender as socially produced and historically shifting.

Feminism is not just political, it is also theoretical. Theories about patriarchy include radical feminist, socialist feminist and psychoanalytical feminist theory. However the women's liberation movement has been characterized by an active hostility towards theory. This hostility has been particularly extended to those theories such as liberalism and Marxism which attempt to add women on to existing theoretical paradigms. Another criticism lodged against theory is that it is a way of removing control from the lives of women and telling them what to think. In this respect some radical feminist writers (such as Daly 1979 and Griffin 1984) reject theory as a masculine form of discourse and as the pillar of patriarchy. Powerful discourses are understood as ways of constituting knowledge, together with social practices, power relations and forms of subjectivity embodied by knowledge. On one hand, powerful discourses in society are rooted in institutions (such as law, medicine and education), and on the other they govern the body, the mind and the emotions of individuals.

In rejecting theory, some feminists assume women's experience, unburdened by unnecessary theorizing, is both the source of knowledge and the base for women's politics. This approach is founded on the assumption that subjectivity is an authentic interpretation of reality. This approach also rejects rationality as a masculine construction which marginalizes feminine forms. Chris Weedon (1988) argues, in her account of poststructuralist feminist theory, that rather than turning our backs on theory and taking refuge in experience alone, we should attempt to transform the social relations of knowledge production and the type of knowledge produced. She argues that we must focus upon how and where knowledge is produced and by whom, and what counts as knowledge. For example, if experience is different for men and women we need to understand the essential, social or psychoanalytic nature of this difference. In the constitution and reconstitution of the meaning of femininity and biological difference, which is prerequisite for political change, Weedon argues that we will need to develop new forms of rationality. In other words, feminist theory should comprise both subjective experience and rationality – although, as she acknowledges, this would involve the development of a new, nonpatriarchal rationality which would operate in the interests of women's liberation.

Some feminists reflect a similarly hostile attitude to the idea of a feminist methodology. The criticisms are strikingly similar. The first is that a feminist methodology should not simply take existing methodology and tack women's "problems" on to it. The second is that preoccupation with methods removes the women's control over their experiences and mystifies the most interesting aspects of feminist research (Harding 1987). This position reflects the feminist programme of celebrating the subjective experience of women and the rejection of rationality as an agent or pillar of patriarchy.

The dichotomy between subjective experience and rationality was evident in the different philosophical approaches of Plato and Aristotle, which today still characterize the antagonistic traditions of naturalistic and positivistic research traditions. Furthermore, this has led feminist researchers to reject positivism (and the quantitative methodology which it celebrates) in favour of more naturalistic methodologies and qualitative research techniques. However, while embracing naturalistic research methodologies, I treat with caution the demands to reject rationality on the grounds that it is a patriarchal construction, for two reasons. The first is that in order to achieve the dialectical combination of sensory perception and rational construction, which is arguably a prerequisite for political change, it may prove inadvisable to take rationality out of the equation (rather like throwing the baby out with the bathwater). Second, and related to this, just because rationality has been fashioned as an agent of patriarchy does not necessarily mean that it may not be reconstructed for the purpose of feminist political change. This, however, could be the subject for another chapter.

Gender Identities

Drawing on ideas from both theories and methodologies discussed above, this research study was based on the premise that activity in classrooms is not given, but the outcome of a process of interaction, interpretation and negotiation. At the same time it was recognized that classroom interaction does not occur in a vacuum but is influenced by a range of other considerations including history, ethnicity, biology, socioeconomics and environment. It is also very important, therefore, to locate what happens in classrooms in the context of schools, cultural expectations and wider societal structures which operate as mediators of power and social control. In looking further than the classroom, the research distanced itself from simplistic explanations which hold teachers solely responsible for the production and reproduction of gender divisions. It attempted, as urged by Stanworth (1983), to explore classroom interaction as a reflection of, or embedded in, the much wider societal experiences and expectations in which it is situated.

Starting from the understanding that schooling is different for male and female pupils, the research focused on the relationships between experience of schooling and gender identities for both males and females. It is compatible with an interactionist tradition that gender identities are not interpreted as the manifestation of inner essences but are understood as socially constructed as well as historically shifting (Kimmel 1996). Furthermore, there are in existence any number of masculinities, only one of which gains ascendancy at any particular historical juncture. Connell (1995) (borrowing Antonio Gramsci's use of hegemony from his analysis of class relations) describes the ascendant masculinity as hegemonic masculinity. For both Gramsci and Connell, "hegemony" refers to a cultural dynamic by which a group claims and sustains a leading position in social relationships.

Hegemony, however natural in appearance, is arrived at via the social processes of competition, domination, subordination and resistance. From within this struggle, hegemonic masculinity emerges as the configuration of gender practices. The important point here is that hegemonic masculinity currently legitimates patriarchy and guarantees a dominant position for men alongside the subordination of women.

It is also important that the relationship between hegemonic and other masculinities is not oversimplified in the analysis, and that we recognize how masculinities which are not tolerated or condoned within the school nevertheless exist and have implications for educational outcomes. Caribbean historian Hilary Beckles (1996) describes the historical dimension of black Caribbean masculinities by locating them within the hegemonic white patriarchal institution of chattel slavery. Beckles suggests that hegemonic white masculinity in the West Indies is associated with the possession of power, profits, glory and pleasure, all of which articulated as core elements of a white masculine ideology in which historically black masculinity was negated and relegated to "otherness".

In the quest for control over masculinity, white slave owners employed two key strategies; the denial to black men of the right of patriarchal status, and the sexual appropriation of black females. Both strategies, exercised through violent regimes, effectively deprived black males of domestic authority as either husbands or fathers. In relegating black males to a state of "otherness", Beckles notes that in slave-owner literature, infantilization was linked closely with feminization in the conceptualization of both male slaves and white and black women. The black man, by virtue of being denied masculine roles or access to institutionalized support systems on which to construct counter-concepts, was conceived to have degenerated into preconsciousness, a condition which Beckles associates with nothingness, innocence and femininity.

The historical impact of white hegemonic masculinity of slave owners arguably has implications for the importance which Caribbean males attach to the exercise of power and control over women (Johnson 1996). Recent ethnographic research carried out in Jamaican, Dominican and Guyanese communities suggests that "manhood" is attested by sexual prowess, usually measured in terms of numbers of serial or concurrent female sexual partners. Secondary proof of "manhood" resides in numbers of offspring whether inside or outside of a steady relationship. Furthermore the women's liberation movement, harsh economic realities and foreign media are seen as contributors to the erosion of men's authority in the home and to power struggles between men and women. These struggles, apparent in group discussions in all the communities researched, seemed related most often to the growing economic independence of women (Brown 1995).

The shift in occupational roles and the capacity of women to be providers and breadwinners have challenged notions of Caribbean masculinity while allowing women to extend concepts of femininity. Mohammed (1996) suggests that this may lie at the root of male fear that they are losing ground and privilege, that their manhood is threatened when they cannot fulfil what they see as the "God given and natural role of men". This fear is the source of Caribbean black "male marginalization" described by Miller (1986, 1989, 1991). Miller's work on the marginalization of the black male has resonances with the "emasculation thesis" in which men are again victims of the dominant colonial order. The problem with this is that Miller works within a paradigm of male dominance, assuming that this ideology is a natural one which must obtain in society. He places the burden once again on the backs of women for emasculating men (Mohammed 1996). While Miller accurately observes that Jamaican women have taken advantage of educational opportunities and achieved greater mobility than men (Mohammed 1996), unfortunately he does not question the notion of manhood itself and the way in which this may be at variance with the requirements of the changing education system. Lewis (1996) similarly argues that male marginalization, which is mediated by factors of race, class, age and sexual orientation, is the product of changing socioeconomic and political considerations and not a wilful attempt (by women) to penalize men.

The construction of hegemonic male identities cannot be understood in isolation outside of the dynamic relationship between male and female gender identities. In his contribution to *Engendering History* (Shepherd, Brereton and Bailey 1995), Beckles suggests that how slave women's position, at the bottom of the slave order power pyramid, was secured essentially by sex and gender representation. This was, he suggests, a politically imposed position where the demands of both (biological) reproduction and (economic) production converged. The black woman's experience, identity and consciousness structurally represented characteristic features of the slave mode of production.

Changes in constructions of male gender identities have implications for constructions of femininity and for male/female gender dynamics. Furthermore, the way in which femininities are constructed in the Caribbean must reflect the unique experiences of Caribbean women. It is important not to make assumptions or base any analysis of Caribbean women on extrapolations from our understandings of the experiences of women elsewhere. Research in both America and Britain highlights the dissimilarities between constructions of black female gender identity and mainstream white female constructions of femininity (Dill 1987; Mirza 1992). Examination of these differences helps us to understand the unique situations which different women experience in different societies.

In stressing the uniqueness of the experience of Afro-Caribbean women, British and American studies argue that research should critically appraise accounts of women's situation in every race, class and culture (Dill 1987). More simplistic explanations have led to the misrepresentation of black women, whose attitudes, behaviours and interpersonal relationships are, arguably, adaptations to a range of factors. These include harsh environmental factors, Afro-American images of womanhood, and conflicting values and norms of wider society. Mirza (1992) in Britain makes a similar claim that the reproduction of white gender disadvantage is inappropriate in a black context because cultural constructions of femininity among Afro-Caribbean women are fundamentally different from the forms of femininity among their white peers. Black women in Mirza's study expressed an ideology that emphasized the relative autonomy of both male and female roles and which Mirza attributes to the external imposition of oppression and brutality. The young black Afro-Caribbean women in Britain, whom Mirza studied, had not adopted the dominant Eurocentric ideology in which gender is regarded as the basis for the opposition of roles and values. They also had different concepts from their white peers of masculinity and femininity. One striking difference was the few distinctions which the young women made between male and female abilities and attributes with regard to work and the labour market. Sutton and Makiesky-Barrow (1977) in their classic study in Barbados suggested why this particular definition of masculinity and femininity should result in greater female participation in the labour market. They argued that distinct qualities of masculine and feminine sexual and reproductive abilities are not viewed by either sex as a basis for different male and female capacities. This is quite removed from the self-limiting and negative sexual identities Euro-American women have had to struggle with.

Furthermore, it is crucial that our understandings of any social realities are historically situated. It is interesting that historical research has traditionally aligned itself to positivism, hence rendering the accounts produced more "scientifically" credible. This is ironic, in that all historical accounts are socially produced and cannot be divorced either from those who produce them or from the interests which they serve. Attempts by women (and some men) have more recently set about reconstructing events by writing women back into history; a notable Caribbean example of which is *Engendering History* (Shepherd, Brereton and Bailey 1995). In providing a gender dimension to Caribbean history, through both "texts" and "testimonies" of Caribbean women, the accounts distance themselves from the documentary evidence largely generated by men through so-called scientific inquiry (Brereton 1995).

Marginal Identities

Both Beckles (1996) and Noguera (1996) write about the importance of non-hegemonic masculinities. In this respect it is interesting to note a Caribbean (and Jamaican, in particular) cultural tendency to condemn nonheterosexual identities. This social policing of sexualities implies the importance with which agents of social control imbue control over sexualities. The very different gender experiences of patriarchal society suggest that the power invested in the social construction of sexualities and their relationship to gender experience is a crucial area for feminist research. Foucault's analysis of the ways in which social power relations are produced and sustained in the discursive production of historically specific sexuality is particularly useful here. By opening up sexuality to history and change, and by resisting single explanations, Foucault's analysis avoids simplifying the social implications of sexuality. Rather, he argues that discourses surrounding sexuality are tactical elements which operate in a field of force relations that function to disguise the interests they serve. At the same time Foucault recognizes how alternative or nonhegemonic discourses are able, through resistance, to affect and transform hegemonic forms. This point can be illustrated by the ways in which female Afro-Caribbean gender identities have transformed mainstream white female gender identities in the United Kingdom (Mirza 1996).

In Classrooms

One of the main questions which the research addressed was "How is the nature of femininity and masculinity conducted in Caribbean classrooms?" In common sense and other discourses abounding at any one time, we are offered subject positions which assume how it is to be a woman or a man. These discourses seek to construct femininity and masculinity and offer "gender-appropriate" ways of being and behaving (Weedon 1987). Ethnographic research in British schools has suggested (Mac An Ghaill 1994; Haywood and Mac An Ghaill 1996; Weekes et al. 1996) a mismatch in the orientation of education and the way in which masculinities are perceived, and the implications of this for male educational achievement. Unfortunately this work says little about femininities because much of it has excluded females (for examples, see Willis 1977; Mac An Ghaill 1994; Benyon 1989).

The main body of the research comprised an ethnographic study which was carried out in a purposeful sample of high schools in Jamaica, Barbados and St Vincent. Here I want to concentrate specifically upon this qualitative work; discussion of the overall sample and design can be found elsewhere (Parry 1996, 1997). Data collection was comprised of observation (observer as a participant) in high school classes and unstructured interviews with teachers (who were mainly women) of those classes. Data was collected by myself in all schools which took part in the study and I had research assistance in Jamaica and Barbados. In Jamaica, Florence Pearson worked as research assistant, doing observation and interviewing alongside me in schools; and in Barbados I was assisted by Nicky MacDonald. Both brought quite different interests and experiences to the project. Florence is a black Jamaican woman and the cultural and gender-specific experiences which she brought to the project were very important. She was able to develop more spontaneous and easier relationships with the respondents with whom she shared a range of cultural understandings. It was apparent that some respondents talked to Florence in a way that they could not talk to me as a white, European, female outsider. At the same time there were conversations which occurred between myself and respondents which happened precisely because I was seen as different, foreign and "temporary". These characteristics made me less "threatening" or "important", and hence topics were raised which would have seemed dangerous to share with a Jamaican researcher.

In Barbados, Nicky, a Canadian woman, carried out observation and interviewing alongside me in schools. Nicky is an experienced teacher, having taught in Canada and the West Indies, and this experience was an enormous asset to the research. Drawing on her teaching experiences, she was able to develop very good rapport with teachers who took part. Furthermore, her knowledge of curriculum and pedagogy informed our discussions, the issues which were raised and the analysis of data which we collected. I also found that, as with the experience in Jamaica, there were some topics which partici-pants felt happier to discuss with Nicky and some with me. While some teachers were clearly pleased to be interviewed by a teacher, who understood teaching, others found it threatening and were wary of implied criticism of the methods they used.

The relationship between respondent and researcher is central to feminist methodologies. Positivistic methodologies claim that objects of study exist independently from both the agents and tools of research and thus have the capacity to resist incorrect or inappropriate methods. In contrast, feminist methodologies are derived from the epistemological position that data does not exist independently, but is constructed through the process of research and through the relationship between researcher and respondent. Alternative positions which argue that data is discovered rather than constructed are dismissed as naively realist. Feminist research thus takes issue with the mythology of "hygiene" research and accompanying mystification of the researcher as an objective instrument. Oakley argues that this must be replaced with the recognition that personal involvement is more than a dangerous bias. It is, she suggests, "the condition under which people come to know each other and to admit others into their lives" (1981: 58).

This is a position which challenges the positivistic practice of objectifying research subjects or, in other words, of making the distinction upon which most social science research rests, between the researcher as knowing subject and the respondent as knowable object (Lal 1996). In particular, feminist methodologies see social science research as a social interaction in its own right, and therefore encapsulating or reflecting the social world in which it is situated. Hence if the social world being studied is sexist and hierarchical, the processes of research will be sexist and hierarchical as well. For feminist researchers the most central research dilemma is power and the unequal hierarchies or levels of control that are often maintained, perpetuated, created and recreated during and after fieldwork (Wolf 1996). To address this dilemma it becomes necessary to acknowledge the respondents' agency and to treat the researched as subjects with whom the researcher engages in a mutual, though unequal, power-charged social relationship (Haraway 1988). The researcher/subject dynamic is one which characterizes the research encounter but which also informs analysis of the data and the end products of research. This constitutes a rejection of a positivistic view of science which encourages distance and noninvolvement between researcher and researched, and assumes that the researcher can objectively see, judge and interpret the life and meanings of his or her subjects. These are methodologies which can be described as empowering, because they challenge notions of epistemological privilege and attempt to locate self as a political and historical subject and as part of the forces that shape the research subjects.

In this paper I set out with the purpose of suggesting the many ways in which research that I carried out while at the University of the West Indies led to the development of my understanding and commitment to the principles of feminist methodologies. It was the experience of living in a "foreign" culture, and attempting to explore cultural experiences, many of which I could not share, that led to this "awakening". Growing awareness of my own cultural incompetency and how this might have affected my relationship with participants, the data which I collected, and the finished research products which I wrote led me to be much more critical of the interview process. While I acknowledge that being an outsider did afford me privileged access to some areas of some women's lives, it compensated poorly for what was lost through the fact that I had little experience in common with the participants.

Since carrying out the research, which I acknowledge to be the most rewarding that I have been involved in to date, I have reflected upon the issues and problems that the experience raised. In particular I have reflected upon the political, epistemological, theoretical, methodological and personal position from which we interviewed participants in the study and the different positions from which respondents came. Awareness of the process of research and the construction of data through reflexivity has, for me, flagged the necessity of clarifying where we come from (socially, culturally, politically, personally and theoretically) and what we bring into the research encounter. It has also brought home the need to understand subjects not as a homogenous group but as individuals who differ in terms of ethnic identities, gender, age and able-bodiedness. Furthermore, it accentuated the principle that the topic we study and the way we study must be historically located and specific. Where the multiple dimensions of subjects and researchers meet, at specific times in specific locations, the research exercise must be itself understood, even while it amplifies our understanding.

Note

1. Although not exclusively.

References

Barrow, C. 1988. "Anthropology, the Family and Women in the Caribbean". In *Gender in Caribbean Development,* edited by P. Mohammed and C. Shepherd. St Augustine, Trinidad: Women and Development Studies Project, University of the West Indies.

Beckles, H. 1996. "Black Masculinity in Caribbean Slavery". Paper presented at the conference The Construction of Caribbean Masculinity: Towards a Research Agenda, Centre for Gender and Development Studies, St Augustine, Trinidad, 11–13 January.

Beynon, J. 1989. "A School for Men: An Ethnographic Case Study of Routine Violence in Schooling". In *Politics and the Processes of Schooling,* edited by S. Walker and L. Barton. Milton Keynes: Open University Press.

Brown, J. 1995. "Findings of the Gender Socialization Project". Paper presented at the annual UNICEF Global Seminar, Achieving Gender Equality in Families: The Roles of Males. Caribbean Child Development Centre, University of the West Indies.

Cockburn, C.K. 1987. *Two-Track Training: Sex Inequalities and the YTS*. London: Macmillan.

Connell, R.W. 1985. *Teachers Work*. London: Allen and Unwin.

_____. 1995. *Masculinities*. Cambridge: Polity Press.

Daly, M. 1979. *Gyn/Ecology*. London: The Women's Press.

Dann, G. 1987. *The Barbadian Male*. London: Macmillan.

Dill, B. 1987. "The Dialectics of Black Womanhood". In *Feminism and Methodology*, edited by S. Harding. Bloomington: Indiana University Press.

Drayton, K. 1991. *Gender Bias in Education*. WAND Occasional Papers no. 2.

Gaarder, J. 1995. *Sophie's World*. London: Phoenix House.

Gordon, D. 1986. *Occupational Segregation and Inter-Generational Mobility in Jamaica*. Sociological Research Unit Working Paper. Cardiff: College of Cardiff, University of Wales.

Gordon, D. 1989. *Class Status and Social Mobility in Jamaica. Population, Mobility and Development Studies*. Mona, Jamaica: Institute of Social and Economic Research, University of the West Indies.

Griffin, S. 1984. *Women and Nature: The Roaring Inside Her*. London: The Women's Press.

Hammersley, M., and P. Atkinson. 1983. *Ethnography: Principles in Practice*. London: Tavistock.

Haraway, D. 1998. "Situated Knowledges: The Science Question in Feminism and the Privilege of Partial Perspective". *Feminist Studies* 14, no. 3.

Harding, S. 1987. *Feminism and Methodology*. Bloomington: Indiana University Press.

Haywood, C., and M. Mac An Ghaill. 1996. "Schooling Masculinities". In *Understanding Masculinities*, edited by M. Mac An Ghaill and M. Buckingham. London: Open University Press.

Johnson, U. 1996. "The Reconstruction of Masculinity: Breaking the Link Between Maleness and Violence". Paper presented at the conference The Construction of Caribbean Masculinity: Towards a Research Agenda, Centre for Gender and Development Studies, St Augustine, Trinidad, 11–13 January.

Kaufman, M. 1996. "A Theoretical Framework for the Study of Men and Masculinities". Paper presented at the conference The Construction of

Caribbean Masculinity: Towards a Research Agenda, Centre for Gender and Development Studies, St Augustine, Trinidad, 11–13 January.

Kimmel, M. 1996. "Masculinity as Homophobia: Fear, Shame and Silence in the Construction of Gender Identity". Paper presented at the conference The Construction of Caribbean Masculinity: Towards a Research Agenda, Centre for Gender and Development Studies, St Augustine, Trinidad, 11–13 January.

Klein, S., ed. 1985. *Handbook for Achieving Sex Equity Through Education*. Baltimore: Johns Hopkins University Press.

Lal, J. 1996. "Situations Locations and 'Other' in Living and Writing the Text". In *Feminist Dilemmas in Fieldwork*. edited by D. Wolf. Boulder: Westview.

Lewis, L. 1996. "Caribbean Masculinity at the *Fin de Siècle*". Paper presented at the conference The Construction of Caribbean Masculinity: Towards a Research Agenda, Centre for Gender and Development Studies, St Augustine, Trinidad, 11–13 January.

Lewis, R., and Lovegrove, M. 1987. "The Teacher as Disciplinarian: How Do Students Feel". *Australian Journal of Education* 31.

Mac An Ghaill, M. 1994. *The Making of Men*. Buckingham: Open University Press.

Mickelson, R.A. 1992. "Why Does Jane Read and Write So Well? The Anomaly of Women's Achievement". In *Education and Gender Equality*, edited by J. Wrigley. London: Falmer Press.

Miller, E. 1987. *Marginalization of the Black Male*. Mona, Jamaica: Institute of Social and Economic Research, University of the West Indies.

_____. 1989. "Gender Composition of the Primary School Teaching Force: A Result of Personal Choice?" Paper presented at Gender and Education Third Disciplinary Seminar, Mona, Jamaica, University of the West Indies.

_____. 1991. *Men at Risk*. Kingston, Jamaica: Jamaica Publishing House.

Mirza, H. 1992. *Young Female and Black*. London: Routledge.

Mohammed, P. 1996. "Unmasking Masculinity and Deconstructing Patriarchy: Problems and Possibilities within Feminist Epistemology". Paper presented at the conference The Construction of Caribbean Masculinity: Towards a Research Agenda, Centre for Gender and Development Studies, St Augustine, Trinidad, 11–13 January.

Noguera, P. 1996. "The Crisis of the Black Male in Comparative Perspective". Paper presented at the conference The Construction of Caribbean Masculinity: Towards a Research Agenda, Centre for Gender and Development Studies, St Augustine, Trinidad, 11–13 January.

Oakley, A. 1981. "Interviewing Women". In *Doing Feminist Research*, edited by H. Roberts. London: Routledge.

Ogbu, J.U. 1978. *Minority Education and Caste*. New York: Academic Press.

Parry, O. 1996. "Equality, Gender and the Caribbean Classroom". *Twenty-first Century Policy Review Special Issue: Institutional Development in the Caribbean: Acting Upon Changing Structures* 3, no. 12.

_____. 1996. "In One Ear and Out the Other: Unmasking Masculinities in the Caribbean Classroom". *Sociological Research On Line* [UK electronic journal] 1, no. 2.

Saltzman, A. 1994. "Schooled in Failure". *US News and World Report,* 7 November.

Shepherd, V., B. Brereton, and B. Bailey, eds. 1995. *Engendering History: Caribbean Women in Historical Perspective*. Kingston, Jamaica: Ian Randle Publishers.

Stanworth, M. 1983. *Gender and Schooling: Study of Social Divisions in the Classroom*. London: Hutchinson.

Stockard, J. 1985. "Education and Gender Equality: A Critical View". *Research in Sociology of Education and Socialization* 5.

Stockard, J., and J.W. Wood. 1984. "The Myth of Female Underachievement: A Re-examination of Sex Differences in Academic Underachievement". *American Educational Research Journal* 21, no. 40.

Sutton, C., and S. Makiesky-Barrow. 1977. "Social Inequality and Sexual Status in Barbados". In *Sexual Stratification: A Cross-Cultural View,* edited by A. Schlegel. New York: Columbia University Press.

Weedon, C. 1996. *Feminist Practice and Poststructuralist Practice*. Cambridge: Blackwell.

Weekes, D., et al. 1996. "Masculinised Discourses Within Education and the Construction of Black Male Identities Amongst African Caribbean Youth". Paper presented to the Annual British Sociological Association Conference, University of Reading.

Whiteley, P. 1994. "Equal Opportunity? Gender and Participation in Science Education in Jamaica". Working paper, Department of Education, University of the West Indies, Mona, Jamaica.

Willis, P. 1977. "Learning to Labour: How Working Class Kids Get Working Class Jobs". *Household Abuse and Neglect* 6. Aldershot: Saxon House.

Wilson, F.C. 1982. "A Look at Corporal Punishment and Some of the Implications of Its Use". *Child Abuse and Neglect* 6.

Wolf, D. 1996. *Feminist Dilemmas in Fieldwork*. Boulder: Westview Press.

World Bank. 1993. "Access Quality and Efficiency in Education". World Bank Country Study, Washington, DC.

SECTION

II

Deciphering the Script
Gender and Historiography

6 Constructing Visibility

Indian Women in the Jamaican Segment of the Indian Diaspora

VERENE A. SHEPHERD

The migration to, and settlement of, thousands of Indian women in the Caribbean, the result of a continuing postslavery imperialist project, has altered the epistemological foundations of the history of the region. Scholars have been forced more and more to take into account the differential experiences of women in the Caribbean according to legal status [bonded or free] and ethnicity, and not only according to "race", class and colour. The task of uncovering the historical experiences of Indian women is not an easy one, for colonialist historiography has tended to mute the voices of exploited people, and the subaltern, as female, was even more invisible. This paper engages with the problem of creating a space for indentured women in the discourse of migration. More specifically it raises the question of the extent to which Indian diaspora women's experiences have been constructed by themselves as opposed to the representations that claim to speak for them. In other words, as Gayatri Spivak asks, "Can the subaltern speak? How does one begin to valorize the concrete experiences of the oppressed? Who spoke for the historically muted subject of the subaltern woman?" (Spivak 1993: 66). What sources exist to enable one to find the Indian woman's voice and experience?

The Sources and Their Limitations

In seeking to probe the history of Indian women in the Caribbean, one is largely dependent on the official records. These include census reports, reports of visiting Indian officials, annual departmental reports from the immigration and emigration offices, correspondence between the protector of immigrants/emigrants and the governor or colonial secretary; correspondence between the colonial governors and the Colonial Office; and correspondence between the Colonial Office and the India Office. Deeds, wills and plat books (which record land grants made to the Indians) represent another category of records. Yet another category consists of church records, primarily the records of the Scottish Presbyterians and the Quakers. There are also the ships' papers kept by the captains of the various ships which carried and returned Indians and which include the surgeon-major's reports. Other records are the documents generated by the plantations, various Indian communal organizations, oral history testimonies and immigrants' letters. Of the range of sources identified, only the reports of visiting officials (where they took evidence from women), oral history testimonies and letters have the potential to give a voice to Indian women and to allow them to represent their own history. However, even this potential is limited: most of the visiting officials took evidence from plantation officials or, after 1930, from the male-run Indian communal associations. The population of first- and second-generation immigrants was largely nonexistent at the time research was conducted in the early 1980s; and the batch of letters deposited in the Jamaica Archives (and to which I refer loosely as "Immigrants' Letters"), though tantalizing in terms of the possibility they hold for learning about the actual experiences of Indian women, contains very few letters written by or about women.

The historians' task of uncovering the experiences of Indian women in the diaspora in the light of the paucity of sources actually generated by women, therefore, remains a difficult one. An examination of the following eight aspects of the immigrants' experiences will demonstrate clearly the degree to which the Indian woman's voice was muted in the discourse of migration, and the way in which much of what is "known" about their experiences was represented by others. An examination of these areas will also show the way in which much of the discourse of migration was "gender-neutral", making it difficult to consistently distinguish the experiences of men and women. The areas to be explored are:

1. The local anti-immigration discourse
2. Anti-emigration and push factors of emigration in India
3. Proprietors' attitudes towards the importation of immigrants
4. The "crossing"
5. Plantation labour and indentureship
6. Repatriation
7. The debate over the continuation of indentured labour migration after the First World War
8. The socioeconomic experiences of postmigrant Indians

While acknowledging the gender-neutral nature of much of the sources and the absence of women's voices, however, the article will try to indicate that the records on immigration still yield a commendable amount of material on Indian women; and my ongoing research is likely to yield even more data – perhaps even filling gaps identified here.

The Local Anti-Immigration Discourse

The anti-immigration discourse was examined to see if it shed any light on how the host society viewed the impending arrival of Indian women as opposed to Indian men, for there was much anti-immigration discourse in Jamaica when the importation of additional labourers was posited as the antidote to emancipation. However, I have found nothing in this discourse that was gender specific. Opposition came mainly from the missionaries and the antislavery society, who feared a revival of slavery and the effects of Hindus and Muslims on the Christian population. The African-Jamaicans feared competition for work and wages. The nonsugar proprietors, able to command local labourers, opposed being taxed to import labourers they would not need (Shepherd 1994: 30–33).

Anti-Emigration and Push Factors of Emigration in India

The recruitment of women was made part of the arrangement between the British government and the interest groups in Indian immigration. Quotas changed from time to time, but the female-to-male ratio never fell below

25:100. The rationale for recruiting and exporting women was tied less to their labour potential and more to social reasons, primarily the alleviation of the high incidence of wife murder in the colonies – due to the serious disparity in the relative populations of men and women.

We know very little about how Indian women felt about leaving India for distant shores, or about the gender specificity of push factors in India. The records simply make vague statements about a general preference of immigrants for Trinidad and Guyana where wages were higher and the Indian populations larger. Jamaica seems not to have been a preferred destination. There is also some hint that there were local conditions in India which could have acted as a catalyst for the emigration of women as opposed to the emigration of men. One outstanding example was the impact of the industrial revolution on the textile industry in India. The introduction of the railway facilitated the wide marketing of British cloth in the remotest parts of India, permanently altering the domestic market and handicraft industry production patterns and throwing millions of people back into agriculture at a time when that industry was under transition. Women, the majority of weavers, were severely affected by the removal of a primary source of income. Other factors specific to women relate to widows, who felt tyrannized by the traditions and expectations of the traditional household, and women who wished to escape domestic marriage arrangements. There was also some opposition on the grounds that Indian women were being pressed into prostitution in the colonies; and there was certainly a generalized objection to the element of coercion evident in the pattern of recruitment. Ken Parmasad has shown that recruitment did not take place unproblematically, as there was clear evidence that Indians resisted the recruiters' net, but the records are mostly silent on gender-specific resistance strategies (Parmasad 1988). Officials in Bengal also opposed the requirement to increase the numbers of women shipped, on the basis that this would necessitate the recruitment of "a low and immoral class of women" (Mangru 1987: 97), since high-caste women had fewer incentives to emigrate. When family emigration was discouraged (initially on the grounds that large numbers of children would increase the possibility of epidemics and delay the ship's departure from India), many women refused to leave India without their children.

Public opinion in India over the emigration of women for contract labour overseas is quite well documented for the twentieth century, and particularly for the period after the First World War when debates surfaced over whether or not emigration to the colonies should resume after its temporary cessation during the war. Much of the anti-emigration discourse in the post-1914 period focused on the condition of indentured women on the grounds that Indian women were being pressed into prostitution in the colonies. Mass meetings were being held all over India by 1917; and various interest groups, some part of the decolonization movement, passed resolutions against the continuation of Indian emigration and petitioned government officials. Among these were petitions concerning the emigration of Indian women. A telegram sent by the superintendent of the Widows' Home in Cawnpore in 1917 stated, for example, that at a recent protest meeting, those gathered opposed "further continuation of the system of indentured labor which dishonours womanhood and has been officially admitted to be pernicious and degrading" (Public Record Office 1917). The perspective of potential migrants still remains skewed, however, as the petitions were generated mostly by literate, middle-class women.

The records are also clear about how migrant men felt about their wives opting for migration and about the treatment of women prior to embarkation for the colonies. Married men were reportedly reluctant to have their wives emigrate because they did not like the fact that male doctors had to examine the women before declaring them fit for emigration. Suggestions were made that female doctors should be employed.

The records are much fuller in relation to how Caribbean (and specifically Jamaican) planters felt about importing Indian women rather than men as contract labourers. I have seen no evidence about how the women felt about the planters' views on their labour potential.

Proprietors' Attitudes towards Female Migrant Labourers

The tendency in the mid-nineteenth century to dichotomize work and family, public and private, determined the landholders' attitude to the recruitment of Indian women. It is clear that they initially regarded the importation of women as uneconomical. In the first place, planters did not regard Indian women as capable agricultural workers. They believed that Indian men worked more efficiently and productively. Their view, as expressed by the acting protector of immigrants, was that "indentured women as a rule are not nearly the equal of the men as agricultural labourers", and in the early twentieth century, when efforts were being made to increase the numbers of women shipped, planters objected to being obliged to pay to import women who they claimed were "not as good" as male agricultural workers (Colonial Office 1913). Second, unlike during slavery when black women had the potential to reproduce the labour force (though fertility rates were generally low), the progeny of Indian females could not automatically be indentured; so Indian women were not initially highly valued for their reproductive capacity. Indian children could only be indentured at age sixteen, though in practice many were used in the fields from age six, receiving wages of three to six pence per day. But this was only with their parents' consent. Furthermore, proprietors were obliged to provide rations for immigrants' children, whether such children had been imported from India or born in the colony. In some cases, they also had to stand the cost of hiring nurses and establishing creches to look after immigrants' young children (Colonial Office 1913). Third, landholders were not too concerned, initially, about the social life of the immigrants; so the imbalanced male-female ratio and its implications for the stability of family life did not preoccupy them. Indeed, the requirement to provide immigrants with return passages at the end of their contracts made it less critical to be concerned about the Indian family and the impact of a shortage of women.

Proprietors therefore maintained an importation policy which favoured men, and recruiters in India mostly carried out the instructions of the Jamaican planters regarding the composition of recruits. Records up to 1882 show, surprisingly, that recruiters were paid less for each female emigrant recruited for Jamaica. The recruitment rate paid was six annas per head for females and eight annas for males (India Office Library). Thereafter, rates for women exceeded those for men to encourage female emigration. On the ship *Blundell*, which in 1845 carried the first group of Indian indentured workers to Jamaica, women comprised just 11 percent of the total of 261. When the number of girls under age ten is added to this figure, then the percentage of females increases to 15 percent. On the *Hyderabad* in 1846, women made up 12 percent of the total shipment of 319, with total females comprising 15 percent, as on the *Blundell*. On the *Success* in 1847, women comprised 10 percent of the shipment of 223 adults (Jamaica Archives Ships' Papers; Protector of Immigrants 1845–1916). Jamaican planters relented and adjusted the unfavourable female-male ratio only in the face of governmental pressure to conform to a 40:100 female-male ratio for immigrants over age ten.

The result of the pressure to increase the numbers of females imported to the colonies was reflected in the sex ratio of immigrants by the late nineteenth and early twentieth century. On the *Chetah* in 1880, there were 112 females (30 percent of the total) and 256 males. Females comprised 31 percent of the total number shipped on the *Hereford* in 1885 and 30 percent on the *Volga* in 1893–94. Of the 2,130 imported on the *Moy, Erne* and *Belgravia* in 1891, females totalled 689 or 32 per cent. On the *Belgravia,* which imported 1,050 in all, females numbered 360 compared with 690 males. On some shipments in the nineteenth century, the proportion of women landed in Jamaica even exceeded the stipulated female-male ratio of 40:100. For example, in the 1876 shipment the female-male ratio was 46:100 and it was 43:100 in 1877–78. Between 1905 and 1916, the percentage of women on each ship which arrived ranged from 22 to 30 percent (Jamaica Archives Ships' Papers; Protector of Immigrants 1845–1916; India Office Library).

Recruiters were not only encouraged to obtain more women, but more women "of a respectable class", preferably as part of families. This meant excluding single, unaccompanied women. This was because there had developed a notion in India that single women were forced into prostitution in the colonies. Indeed some visitors to Jamaica seem to have shared this belief. One H. Roberts, a noted opponent of immigration, claimed in 1847 that "the utter disproportion of females in each locality tends greatly to the increase of vice and immorality" (Colonial Office 1847). Chimman Lal and James McNeil later agreed with this view, although they disagreed that prostitution was widespread. According to their report, "of the unmarried women, a few live as prostitutes whether nominally under the protection of a man or not. The majority remain with the man with whom they form an irregular union" (Lal and McNeil 1915). They attributed this to the fact that some women were "constantly tempted into 'abnormal' sexual behaviour by single men with money": "But they [the women] are open to temptation as on all estates there are single men who have more money than they need to spend on themselves alone" (1915). The acting protector of immigrants in Jamaica also claimed that prostitution was noted among some Indian women in the island. Thus, while agreeing that more women should be recruited, he warned that these should be of a "better class": "it is no use increasing the proportion of women if they are to be picked up off the streets. They will only lead to further trouble as these women go from man to man and are ceaseless cause of jealousy and quarrels" (Lal and McNeil 1915).

It was in an attempt to induce women of a "better class" to emigrate that landholders tried to reduce the period of indenture for women to three years, in the belief that a shorter indenture and the promise of domestic life thereafter would attract women and their husbands. However, not only were indentured men unable to afford the cost of maintaining their wives, on account of the low wages they received, but Indian women demonstrated a preference for wage labour over uncompensated labour in the home.

Planters were very concerned about the tensions which developed among Indian men over scarce Indian women, and the resulting violence against Indian women; for Indian men did not at first respond to the scarcity of female Indian partners by cohabiting with African-Jamaican women. There were frequent reports from men that Indian women were displaying a great degree of sexual freedom and independence. Some single Indian women reportedly changed partners frequently and seemed unwilling to marry. This behaviour resulted in suicide and wounding of Indian women by jealous Indian men. Chimman Lal and James McNeil (1915) expressed the view that "perhaps the best guarantee against infidelity to regular or irregular unions is the birth of children". However, the birth rate among indentured women remained low for the entire period of indentureship.

In 1913 the acting protector of immigrants in Jamaica, in a letter to the colonial secretary, supported an increase in the numbers of females shipped to the island as a remedy for the growing incidence of abusive behaviour towards Indian women:

> increasing the proportion of women would most likely reduce the number of cases of wounding and murder on account of jealousy, and be an excellent arrangement from the male immigrants' point of view as there would not be such a dearth of East Indian women as there is now on a good many estates. (Colonial Office 1913)

Despite the attempts to increase the numbers of women in the island, the female Indian population in Jamaica was outnumbered by the male Indian population for the period of indentureship. Up to the end of indentureship in 1921, Indian women were still less than 50 percent of the total Indian population, though the proportion had improved from 31.5 percent in 1871 to 45.2 percent in 1921.

National Library of Jamaica

Figure 6.1   Indian woman in nineteenth-century Jamaica

The Crossing: The Journey to the Caribbean

The physical conditions under which emigrants were transported to the Caribbean were constantly being criticized and reviewed in London and India. Of concern was the need to minimize the mortality rate and prevent the charge of a revived middle passage. Gender-specific data relating to conditions on board the ships and the gender differences in the mortality rate on ships to Jamaica are not abundant. Not all of the reports of the ships' surgeons have survived, and while those that do give valuable insight on the conditions of the emigrants, the sample is not large enough to enable researchers to make firm conclusions about the gender differences in the experiences of emigrants on board the ships. No definitive answers can be supplied to questions like: Did women survive the crossing better than men? Were women given preferential treatment? Were they subjected to wide-scale sexual abuse despite the laws prohibiting sexual contacts aboard emigrant ships? Were the illnesses affecting women different from those affecting the general emigrating population? How did pregnant women fare? Nevertheless, the surviving reports, which include statistical data, indicate that the mortality rate was highest among infants; that higher death rates were recorded on sailing as opposed to steam ships; that the switch to steam ships caused the mortality rate on ships to Jamaica to range between 4 percent and 1 percent after the 1890s; and that the mortality rate on ships leaving from Madras was lower than on those leaving from Calcutta (Mangru 1987: 10; McDonald and Schlomowitz 1992: 212).

The ships' papers indicate that men and women were accommodated in different sections of the ships, single women being placed aft and single men forward. Married couples were separated from single people. The extent of sexual abuse of emigrants is unclear, though there were occasional reports that despite efforts to prevent social mixing between crew and emigrants, complaints about sexual abuse of Indian women by white male crew members surfaced. The data provided on deaths are not always gender specific, except in the case of suicide and deaths associated with childbirth. Reports are that pregnant women suffered from seasickness which at times caused them to lose their babies, and that men rather than women tended to commit suicide. Beyond that, deaths were caused from dysentery, mumps, diarrhoea, pneumonia, phthisis and bronchitis. The ships' surgeon suggested that in some instances infants died from "maternal neglect" and that some women did not seem keen on their babies' survival. The report on the voyage of the ship *Silhet* in 1878 indicated that a nine-month-old girl was "ill before embarkation and [was] very carelessly nursed by [her] mother", and eventually died from dysentery. The same report stated that a five-month-old baby boy, Beharee, also died from dysentery, but added: "mother appeared to wish for death" (Colonial Office 1878).

Attempts were made to make men and women comfortable by attention to their medical care, accommodation and entertainment, with musical instruments allowed on board. They were provided with combs, rum mixed with lime, and chillum pipes. It is unclear if these were provided equally for males and females.

Plantation Labour

Even though the intention behind increased female immigration was to expand the pool of potential wives in the island, the majority of Indian women did not play a primarily domestic role in the nineteenth and early twentieth centuries. They were important as agricultural labourers on various properties in the island. Most females available for emigration were single women who, like their male counterparts, were recruited primarily as indentured workers. Information on the female experience of the indenture system comes mainly from official and planter documents and hardly from the voices of the women.

As a consistent feature of colonial and imperial organization of migrant labour, the indenture or contract system provided a means of retaining labour in the short and medium term, and facilitated the further movement of labour in the postslavery period. At the inception of labour migration, contracts were for only one year, with the option to renew. The period of contract for men and women was later extended to three years. By 1870, immigrants were given five-year contracts with repatriation due only after a further five years of continuous residence in the island.

Archival records yield more data on issues relating to fertility, the sexual disparity in migration schemes and male-female social relations than on the gender differences in the working condition of immigrants – specifically the extent to which they were subjected to sex-typing of jobs and gender discrimination in wages for equal work. But from the data available, it is clear that female Indians were subjected only to a limited form of the sex-typing of jobs, according to which women were confined to service industries and men to agricultural field or factory positions. This sex-typing of jobs under capitalism was one of the forms of the sexual division of labour which European colonizers attempted to replicate in the Caribbean. It was traditionally created by the interaction in capitalist society between the family and public economic life. But as Indian women could not be confined to the private sphere as wives of indentured men, and as there were insufficient openings for domestic servants in the scaled-down planter households of the postslavery period, landholders were forced to use them in the fields. The proprietors, however, still maintained a gender division of labour in nonfield occupations. Thus, while Indian women were confined to field labour and domestic service (much as enslaved women had been), they were not given the factory jobs or the skilled artisan positions which were deemed suitable only for men.

The few surviving plantation records indicate that indentured women had a narrower range of tasks on the sugar estates and banana plantations which were the principal users of their labour; and they were subject to discrimination in wages. They came to Jamaica during the operation of a system where men began to be paid more than women, and, despite the experience of slavery, women survived the plantation system better than their male counterparts. The contracts signed in the nineteenth century indicate that women were paid nine pence for a nine-hour day and men one shilling for the same number of hours, though not always for the same types of tasks. The acceptance of a differential rate of pay seemed to have been part of the patriarchal thinking of the period, predicated on the assumption that women's work was not as valuable as men's. Thus the wage differential was made an integral part of the indenture contract even before any tasks were allocated – and remained in place up to 1909. In that year the protector of immigrants, Charles Doorly, informed Governor Sydney Olivier that "during the first three months of their residence in Jamaica, immigrants are paid a daily wage of –men 1/- and women 9d. (a day of 9 hours); 2/6d per week deducted for rations in the first three months" (Jamaica Archives 1909). At the end of three months, theoretically, immigrants could ask to go on task work at rates of pay approved by the protector. In any event, it was stipulated that the rates for task work should allow immigrants to earn at least the minimum rates of one shilling for men and nine pence for women. In many cases, the tasks given to female workers were less remunerative than tasks given to men. The only exception was "heading bananas", which paid four to five shillings per hundred bunches to both men and women. It is not clear from the sources whether men carried fewer or more bunches of bananas on their heads from the fields to the railway siding or the wharf.

On banana plantations, which by the early twentieth century were the principal employers of female immigrants, the most remunerative tasks, apart from "heading bananas", recorded in work allocation books were: forking, trenching, ploughing, lining, circling and cutting. "Trenching" paid two to three shillings per day and "forking" two shillings an acre; but not all of these

Figure 6.2   Banana carriers

tasks were made available to women. Some men could earn up to ten shillings per week from some of these tasks. Picking cocoa, typically a woman's job, paid two pence for every hundred pods picked (Sanderson Committee 1909).

On sugar estates, as long as Afro-Jamaicans were available, they were given the more remunerative tasks. Less remunerative tasks were given to Indian men and the least remunerative to Indian women.

But there is not much evidence that, even where task work was chosen, female immigrants increased their wages significantly. For example, a report on wage rates in 1919 showed that women earned an average of 6s.11¼d. per week while men earned an average of 9s.10½d. In 1920 men earned an average of 12s. and women 8s.6d. per week. The protector of immigrants, from time to time, identified outstanding immigrants who earned above this average. Three women – Dulri, Inderi and Jaipali – all earned above 12s. per week in 1920; but in every case, the wages of the outstanding male workers (16s.–18s. per week) exceeded those of the outstanding women (Protector of Immigrants 1919–20). In addition to earning lower wages, the records show that, but do not explain why, female workers were faced with higher expenses than their male counterparts. At a conservative estimate, based on rough statistics supplied by Chimman Lal and James McNeil, it would seem that the annual expenditure for females was 76 percent of annual wages compared with 57 percent for males (Colonial Office 1916).

Women with young children experienced further problems that affected the number of hours they worked and the wages they received. Where neither nurses nor creches were provided, indentured women often had to carry their infant children to the fields. This could affect their productivity and therefore their earnings, and was the complaint of women on some of the estates visited by the acting protector of immigrants in 1913. He stated that "recently when I visited a certain estate the indentured women complained to me that it was impossible for them to do a good day's work if they had to take their children to the fields and look after them there" (Colonial Office 1913). A nurse was employed to relieve the mothers of child care responsibilities during working hours after the protector appealed to the manager on behalf of the women. On another estate where similar complaints were made by the female workers, the manager agreed to build a creche and employ a nurse. The acting protector expressed his wish that "all employers of a large number of indentured immigrants ought to be willing to do something of the kind as a great deal more of the time of the women who have children would be available for work" (Colonial Office 1913). However, not many estates adopted this practice, arguing that it was too much of an added expense for proprietors.

The Fate of Indentured Labour Migration after the War

Concerns over a possible labour shortage if labour migration ceased also caused the early twentieth-century immigration rhetoric to reflect a greater pronatalist stance – and to reveal a certain gender specificity. Thus, just as the situation of enslaved women featured prominently in the emancipatory rhetoric of the 1820s and 1830s, and just as the improvement of their conditions was enshrined in the amelioration proposals to stem the tide of antislavery resistance (as well as improve their fertility rate), so gender considerations were critical in the debate over the system of Indian labour which was to replace indentureship.

The discussions about replacing Indian indentureship surfaced in the years after the First World War. It was suggested that the emigrants' agreement should be in the form of a civil contract, rather than an indenture contract, and that the term of contract should be reduced to three years. But the conditions of servitude for women were placed at the centre of the debate. Suggestions were now made for women labourers with three children under five years to be exempted from work, subject to the approval of the protector of immigrants. It was also proposed that

> any woman labourer may receive an exemption from work for any particular period either by agreement between the employer and the woman and subject to the approval of the protector of immigrants or on the Certificate of the Immigration Department. During advanced pregnancy and after childbirth, a woman may be exempted from work for a period not exceeding six months. Immediate steps should be taken to require the issue of free rations to pregnant and nursing women for a period not less than six months. (Colonial Office 1916)

The inducements to be held out to male labourers, though, were linked to efforts to improve their economic welfare. It was suggested that any new scheme of Indian labour after the First World War should include provisions to make land available to male labourers. The recommendation was that all possible steps should be taken to require employers to provide small garden plots of one-tenth of an acre of land for each male labourer and facilities for labourers keeping cows. A larger acreage – a third of an acre – should be given to male labourers who were more industrious than the rest. This land was to be given after the first six months of labour in the island (Colonial Office 1916). No such considerations were given to Indian females, who in fact were to be encouraged to focus more on family – their "proper role in life" – rather than on work outside of the home.

Repatriation

Unlike enslaved Africans and most other immigrants in the Caribbean, Indians were guaranteed either free or assisted repatriation to India at the end of their contract and period of compulsory residence. We know that roughly twelve thousand of those who arrived returned to India, but the precise male-female proportion remains in doubt. Surviving records of return ships do indicate that fewer women than men returned to India; perhaps a reflection of the sexual disparity in the Indian population. We also know that when free passages were abolished after 1895 (except for children and the indigent), women were required to contribute less than men towards their passage. Men who arrived in the island between 1895 and 1898 were required to pay one-quarter of the total cost of repatriation; women, one-sixth. Those who arrived after 1898 had to pay a half and one-third, for men and women respectively. In 1930 state-sponsored repatriation from Jamaica was discontinued. All those who wished to return to India had to do so at their own expense. This decision was greeted with much opposition from the Indian and Indian-Jamaican populations, and many petitions were sent to the government. However, repatriation petitions, numerous in the 1930s and 1940s, came from Indian communal associations rather than from individuals. The individual requests for repatriation viewed came from Indian men.

Finally, the records do not allow for a clear analysis of the gender differences in the experiences of repatriates. Isolated accounts, some anecdotal, do reveal that both men and women took back accumulated savings to India; that on the whole, men took back larger sums; and that after 1879, wives' and husbands' accounts were separated in order to protect women's financial interests, for there were husbands who allegedly abandoned their wives on arrival in India. By 1917 opposition emerged in India among such influential people as Mahatma Gandhi, to the continued repatriation of Indians – many of whom were destitute, ill and disabled and unable to readjust to life in India; but that debate appears to have been gender neutral.

Socioeconomic Conditions of Postmigrant Indians

The system of indentureship confined Indian women to agricultural and domestic occupations in rural Jamaica and provided them with limited opportunities for upward social mobility. The influence of the gender division of labour under indentureship as well as the limited educational opportunities for immigrants – in particular for female immigrants – caused more men than women to pursue nonagricultural occupations at the end of their contracts.

The censuses, J.D. Tyson's report and the "Immigrants' Letters" provide the only detailed accounts of the occupations and socioeconomic experiences of the female Indian population in the immediate postindentureship period.

Occupations

The censuses show clearly that Indian women had a narrower range of occupations than their male counterparts. Indian women were confined to the lowest-paid occupations and were underrepresented in the commercial and professional areas. As under indenture, there continued to be a gender division of labour in the skilled and supervisory positions even within the agricultural sector; and women were overrepresented in certain jobs such as laundering, care giving and domestic service. According to the 1911 census (as well as previous censuses), the majority of Indian females worked as agricultural labourers mostly in the banana and sugar industries. On the all-island level, there were 49,116 females in agricultural labour: Indian women comprised 3,461. They also worked on livestock farms/pens and in rice cultivation. A significant proportion worked as domestic servants. On the all-island level, there were 35,701 domestic servants of whom women made up 30,316. Of 188 Indian domestic servants, 134 were women; an additional 10 Indian women worked in other domestic/personal service.

In the 1921 census, only one Indian woman was represented among the 144 rangers and supervisors on agricultural properties in the island. Among

Table 6.1   Summary of Occupations of Indians in Jamaica: Male/Female, 1911

	Males	Females	Main Categories
Professional	35	11	Students, nurses, teachers
Domestics	91	152	Indoor house servants
Commercial	386	204	Barkeepers, peddlers, shopkeepers, store servers
Agricultural	6,649	3,373	Wage earners on plantations
Industrial	165	78	Skilled trades, e.g. milliners, washers
Indefinite and unproductive	2,602	3,273	

* Included women working at home

Source: Jamaica Census 1911.

the peasant farmers, male Indians dominated. Of 188 Indian banana farmers returned in the 1921 census, there were only 31 females. There were 13 females out of 62 Indian cane farmers; 2 out of 13 cocoa farmers; 107 out of 399 provision farmers; 40 out of 110 rice farmers, and 7 out of 30 tobacco farmers (even though more females than males worked on tobacco farms).

Employment Opportunities and Socioeconomic Conditions after Indentureship

Employment was not guaranteed for Indian women who were not under indentureship or who had not opted to renew their indentureship contract under the system of reindentureship. Employment opportunities for free women increased only marginally as a result of male emigration from the 1880s. The migration wave was dominated by African-Jamaican men and the gap created by the emigration of African-Jamaican men was increasingly filled by Indian men, with African-Jamaican and Indian women getting work where male labour was not available. Even so, any such new employment opportunities were available mostly in agriculture. J.D. Tyson reported that after 1930, employment opportunities for Indian women were severely limited. The 1930s represented a period of economic crises, return migration and labour uprisings. There was much competition for jobs between Indian agricultural labourers and African-Jamaican workers, many repatriated from Cuba and Panama. As employers evinced a preference for male labourers, women were severely affected by the lack of employment in the 1930s. Many Indian women could only get one or two days' work on the estates per week (Tyson 1939).

Lack of educational opportunities and the sex-typing of subjects in schools further served to limit Indian women's occupational choices. Those wishing to move out of agricultural jobs found job openings mainly in domestic and service industries and were late to enter the professional and commercial arenas. Their poor socioeconomic conditions in the twentieth century were reflected in "their" letters to the protector of immigrants.

Indian Women "Speak"?

The hundreds of letters from and about Indians stored as part of the protectors of immigrants' files in the Jamaica Archives represent a potentially rich source for listening to the voice of Indian women. The 1,858 letters used, spanning the period from the 1930 to 1949, are essentially correspondence between the various protectors and Indians, or between the protectors and government institutions or Indian communal organizations. For the most part, they represent the concerns of the rural and urban poor, and could have provided an opportunity to learn about the experiences of a marginalized group from the perspective of that group. However, the high level of illiteracy (in English) among the Indian population up to the 1950s meant that many of them could not write the letters themselves; they simply marked an "X" after the letter was written for them or scrawled a barely recognizable signature. Nevertheless, these letters come the closest to being sources generated by the Indians themselves. The letters deal with a wide range of concerns: marriage, divorce, settlement of estates of deceased Indians, verification of age, requests for passports, requests for information about relatives who had emigrated to Cuba and Panama, sports facilities, poor relief, relief work, medical care, unemployment, repatriation and land grants. Pressing problems reflected in the letters were poor employer/employee relations, poor working conditions, child maintenance, orphaned children, domestic disputes, police harassment and racial discrimination.

Of the 1,858 letters selected for analysis, 77 percent were written by, to or on behalf of men; 14 percent concerned female immigrants and settlers specifically, while the remainder related to children and groups of Indians (as, for example, letters containing petitions and signed by several people). The concerns of Indians living in Kingston and St Andrew predominated, accounting for 67 percent of the letters compared to 25 percent relating to Indians in rural Jamaica; yet only 19 percent of the total Indian population resided in Kingston and St Andrew. A minority of the letters concerned Indians who emigrated to Cuba and Panama, but who were in destitute circumstances and wished to return to Jamaica or be repatriated to India.

The letters enable us to learn about the ways in which Indian women made a living, particularly those in urban centres. The major complaint of Indian women in Kingston was about police harassment as they sought to peddle their vegetables door-to-door – an activity banned by the Kingston and St Andrew Corporation in 1940.

Women were also among those complaining of lack of employment and inability to access poor relief. In a letter to the protector written for her in

December 1937, Lis Tarfie complained: "I have been sick for nearly one year and cannot do any work. I am appealing to you for some sort of help . . . If you cannot then I would be glad if you could get me on the pauper roll" (CGF 1B/9/126). Some women complained that even when the protector recommended poor relief for them, the inspectors of poor in the parishes did not always treat such requests favourably. Latchmina from Trinity Estate in St Mary wrote to the protector in 1939, informing him, "I carry it [letter requesting poor relief] to the inspector of poor as you told me to do but he drove me like a dog; he say he don't count coolie as a people . . . so for that cause I write you again . . . Remember I am a stranger in this land" (CGF 1B/9/129, 12 February 1939).

Letters dealing with domestic disputes and conflicts invariably came from women who had been chased out of their homes by jealous men. One women wrote to the protector in 1935 stating that her partner had "run me from 'is yard" and had "take away all my Banggle". She appealed to the protector to talk to the man and make him take her back into his home as "I have no were to go" (CGF 1B/9/124, 11 November 1935).

There were also letters from women who implored the protector to ensure that husbands were prevented from emigrating, as such husbands had made no financial provisions for their families. Letters relating to child maintenance were often written by or on behalf of women. Those who had not registered their Indian marriages also found themselves in financial difficulties, as Jamaican law did not recognize unregistered Indian marriages and made it difficult for women and children to inherit property left by deceased Indian husbands.

The limited attempt at using the oral history technique (in 1983) to get information on Indian women's experience of migration, indentureship and settlement in Jamaica was not particularly fruitful. Of seventy-five interviewees, only a minority were women. The men seemed more willing to grant interviews and were generally older and therefore thought by the community to have more to pass on; but there was not much that was gender specific in the information made accessible to me. We await the publication of the results of interviews conducted by Dr Ajai Mansingh just over ten years earlier than my efforts, when the population of first- and second-generation Indians available for interview was larger.

Conclusion

In the end, therefore, knowledge about the experiences of Indian women in the Jamaican section of the Indian diaspora is largely dependent on what others have said about them, not on what they said about themselves. The essentially "official" view of migration has to be contested; but in the absence of reliable alternative sources generated by migrant women themselves, the "official view" of the Indian female experience will remain dominant, though problematic, for some time.

References

India Office Library (London). India Office Records, V/24/1210.

Jamaica. Jamaica Archives. Ships' Papers.

_____. Jamaica Archives. Central Government Files [CGF] 1B/9/86, 103, 111, 118–48, 154–66.

_____. Jamaica Archives. 1909. 4/60/10A/29, Charles Doorly to Governor Olivier, enclosure in Despatch no. 13, 25 March.

Lal, Chimman, and James McNeil. 1915. Report. *Jamaica Times*, 8 May.

Mangru, B. 1987. *Benevolent Neutrality: Indian Government Policy and Labour Migration to British Guiana 1854–1884*. London: Hansib.

McDonald J., and Ralph Schlomowitz. 1992. "Mortality on Chinese and Indian Voyages to the West Indies and South America, 1847–1874". *Social and Economic Studies* 41, no. 2.

Parmasad, K. 1998. "Resisting the Recruiter's Net: The Attitude of India's Poor to Indentureship Recruitment Practices". Paper presented at Thirtieth Annual Conference of the Association of Caribbean Historians, Suriname, 17–22 April.

Sanderson Committee. 1909. Report on Emigration from India. Evidence of Sir Arthur Blake, 6 May.

Shepherd, V. 1994. *Transients to Settlers: The Experience of Indians in Jamaica 1845–1950*. Warwick: Peepal Tree Press/University of Warwick.

_____. 1998. "The Politics of Migration". In *Before and After 1865*, edited by B. Moore and S. Wilmot. Kingston, Jamaica: Ian Randle Publishers.

Spivak, G. 1993. "Can the Subaltern Speak"? In *Colonial Discourse and Post-Colonial Theory: A Reader*, edited by P. Williams and L. Chrisman. London: Harvester Wheatsheaf.

Tyson, J.D. 1939. *Report on the Conditions of Indians in Jamaica, British Guiana and Trinidad 1938–39*. Simlar: N.p.

United Kingdom. 1845–1916. Protector of Immigrants Reports.

_____. 1847. CO 318/173. "Analysis of Observations . . . amongst the 'Collies of Jamaica' ", 19 October.

_____. 1878. CO 384/118. Surgeon's Superintendent's Report.

_____. 1913. CO 571/1. Acting Protector of Immigrants to the Hon. Colonial Secretary, 13 December.

_____. 1916. CO 571/4. "Report of the delegates appointed by the governments of British Guiana, Trinidad and Jamaica to consider . . . the future policy to be adopted . . . in regard to immigration from India . . .". Enclosure in British Guiana Despatch no. 226, 9 August.

_____. 1916. CO 571/6. "Note on Indian Emigration", December.

_____. Public Records Office. 1917. CO 571/5, Minute Paper 27270, 23 March.

_____. 1919–20. Protector of Immigrants Reports. Report F.N. Isaacs.

7 Gender and the Historiography of the English-Speaking Caribbean

BRIDGET BRERETON

Introduction

In 1974 Lucille Mathurin Mair completed her doctoral dissertation at the University of the West Indies Mona, "A Historical Study of Women in Jamaica, 1655–1844", the first full-length work on Caribbean women's historical experience; in 1993, Verene Shepherd organized a successful international symposium (also at UWI Mona) out of which emerged the collection of essays published in 1995, *Engendering History: Caribbean Women in Historical Perspective* (Shepherd, Brereton and Bailey 1995).[1] These two events symbolize the development, over the last twenty or twenty-five years, of a significant body of work on women and gender in the history of the English-speaking Caribbean. In this article, I wish to indicate some of the main lines this work has taken, and the major issues it has raised.

Readers of this anthology will be aware of how "women's history" emerged as a distinct sub-field, receiving its impetus from organized Western feminism in the 1960s and 1970s, but also responding to international trends within the discipline, especially the "new" social history which provided a hospitable place for research on women and gender in past societies. Readers will also be aware of the distinction made between "women's history" and "gender history", reflecting two different – though usually closely related – approaches. The first tries to recover information about women in past society, it concentrates on their special historical experiences, it insists on their centrality to the research (her story). The second tries to analyse significant differences in the historical experiences of men and women in a given society and chronological period, it focuses on gender roles and ideologies and how they develop and change over time.

We often speak of a progression from women's history to gender history, and in fact there has been a tendency, chronologically: a move from the former to the latter approach over the last twenty years. But I am not sure that we should assume that gender history is *superior*. It certainly is the broader approach, because it stresses the relations between men and women and is not limited to women's historical experiences; "the construction of masculinity in the postemancipation Caribbean" would be a good example of a research topic in gender history. But the women's history approach, with its insistence on the centrality of women's lives to its research, is still, in my view, legitimate and useful, especially since such an approach today is always combined with gender analysis. I think it is legitimate and useful because tremendous gaps in our knowledge still exist, and because mainstream Caribbean history is far from fully recognizing the need to engender history itself. Both approaches are potentially valuable, and in any case, in practice, they often blur together.

Several scholars have written on the theoretical and methodological issues surrounding women's history and gender history in the Caribbean context. There is a considerable range of approaches. Rosalyn Terborg-Penn (1995) advocates an Afrocentric perspective, viewing Caribbean women's historical experience essentially as part of a wider diaspora with gender ideologies derived from mainly African origins – a position which certainly presents some problems, especially for the southern Caribbean, where very large sections of the population are of Indian descent. Patricia Mohammed develops the concepts of "gender negotiations" and "bargaining with patriarchy" at many different levels in society, a concept fruitfully applied by her to gender relations in the Indo-Trinidadian community in the first half of the twentieth century (Mohammed 1994, 1995). Others have thought about problems of methods and sources, always at the heart of the historical project. In fact, three recent Elsa Goveia Memorial Lectures at Mona have engaged with these problems.[2]

In 1989, Blanca Silvestrini pointed out that women's lives were often ignored in the archival sources and their voices could rarely be heard in the documents. She urged us to utilize the oral history method, not merely to obtain information, but so that the voices and the life histories could help *shape* the historian's discourse and interpretation. In an interesting article in *Engendering History,* Mary Chamberlain (1995) discusses some of the issues in the use of oral evidence in gender history. She suggests that women's spoken testimony and narratives of their lives may follow distinctly different patterns to those by men, patterns the historian must recognize and respect even if they seem at times "illogical" or preoccupied with "trivialities" such as "feelings" or appearances. Now, it is one thing to state a commitment to the oral history method as a tool for engendering history, quite another actually to practise it; so now one notes with admiration three scholars who have done so. Erna Brodber (1986, 1991) based her ambitious study of rural Jamaicans born around the end of the nineteenth century on one hundred life history interviews (by no means limited to gender aspects). Rhoda Reddock (1994) used oral history extensively in her important work on Trinidad and Tobago women in the twentieth century. And Patricia Mohammed (1994, 1995) creatively integrated data from about sixty oral history interviews with written sources in her study of gender relations in the twentieth-century Indo-Trinidadian community, "privileging" the voices of her informants (male and female) in the way that Silvestrini had advocated.

Valuable though it is, of course, oral testimony is only one type of historical source, and one which is only usable for fairly recent periods. Elizabeth Fox-Genovese (who had published in 1983 a seminal article on "placing women's history in history") used her 1992 Goveia Lecture to raise the possibility of using creative writing as a source for probing the "inner dimensions" of slave women's lives. She particularly had Toni Morrison's *Beloved* (1987) in mind. And in my 1994 lecture, I drew attention to writings by Caribbean women – diaries and journals, memoirs and autobiographical writings, private letters – as a fruitful source of "gendered testimony", though unfortunately these are not abundantly available.

In general, I think that the women's history approach predominates in Caribbean historiography over the last twenty years, reflecting our relatively late start, and the tremendous invisibility problem which needed to be addressed. More recently, there are signs of a shift to gender history, although there is a great deal of overlap, and a consistent need for studies taking both approaches. I shall now analyse some of the issues which have been raised in the literature, dividing the analysis between the slavery and the postemancipation eras.

The Slavery Era

This era has been the major focus of research on women's history and gender history, reflecting general trends in Caribbean historiography. The pioneer, we saw, was Lucille Mathurin Mair with her unpublished 1974 doctoral dissertation, her popular but useful little book *Rebel Women* (1975) and her 1986 Goveia Lecture entitled "Women Field Workers in Jamaica during Slavery". She was the first to explicitly raise issues about slavery and gender, and to ask if female slaves' historical experiences might have been significantly different from those men; her thesis was the first full-length study in women's history on a Caribbean country. A solid contribution was made by demographic and medical historians, especially Barry Higman, Michael Craton and Richard Sheridan; their research elucidated the basic parameters of the enslaved woman's existence: births and deaths, fertility and reproduction, infant and child mortality, health, disease and diet, and family forms. A few articles were published on family patterns among Caribbean slaves, responding in part to a dynamic branch of their "new" social history, family history. (Higman 1973, 1975, 1976, 1978, 1984; Craton 1978, 1979; Sheridan 1985) By the late 1980s the groundwork had been laid for more ambitious studies of enslaved Caribbean women.

The first full-length published work was on the French Antilles, Arlene Gautier's *Les Soeurs de Solitude* (1985), a study of female slaves in the French Caribbean from the seventeenth century to emancipation. Then three books on the British Caribbean appeared in 1989–90, those by Hilary Beckles (1989), Barbara Bush (1990) and Marietta Morissey (1990).[3] They took different approaches, though addressing very similar issues. Beckles's work has the narrowest focus (Barbados), but it is the richest of the three in original research and empirical data, solidly grounded in the primary sources (despite their paucity and biases), a model of a single-island study. Morissey did virtually no archival research, but she gives a brilliant synthesis of a vast amount of scholarly literature, is strongly comparative (the English, French and Spanish Caribbean, the United States, Spanish America and Brazil), and very good on theory and key issues in the historiography. Bush did some archival research on the last decades of British Caribbean slavery, but relies mainly on eighteenth- and nineteenth-century published accounts. Despite her title, she deals almost entirely with the British Caribbean, with a focus on Jamaica, but she discusses nearly every aspect of slave women's lives. Together these books, along with a number of articles and unpublished papers, have given us a solid picture of the historical experience of enslaved British Caribbean women, especially in the later decades of slavery.

Several important issues seem to be central to the historiography of gender and slavery in the Caribbean. One cluster of questions addresses the work regime on the sugar plantation. Was plantation slavery "gender blind", were men and women "equal under the whip"? Did the work regime have a levelling effect, by which men and women were equally treated as units of labour, so that gender played little role in the allocation of tasks? Trying to deal with these questions, our historians have investigated male-female ratios in the slave trade and on the plantations at different periods, the sexual division of labour and work regimes; the occupational opportunities open to men and women; the situation of the slave domestics; the occupations of urban slave women; the females' participation in nonplantation food production and, more generally, in what Morrissey calls the slaves' "household economy"(1990). The consensus seems to be that the plantation regime was largely gender blind with respect to field labour. The gang system used men and women indifferently and, indeed, by the 1820s the latter outnumbered the former in the field labour force of most British Caribbean sugar estates. The regime was perhaps also gender blind with respect to punishment, but it discriminated against female slaves in all other areas, notably in their exclusion from virtually all supervisory, skilled, "prestige" occupations.

A second cluster of issues focuses on sexual relations, fertility and reproduction, motherhood and family forms; here, of course, the work of the demographic historians has been critical. How did slavery affect slaves' family lives, sexual relations and experience of motherhood and fatherhood? We have long abandoned the older notion that there was *no* family life under slavery, but how precisely did the slave regime distort and shape family forms?[4] How did gender differentiate male and female experiences in the "private" sphere?

What was the balance, in the enslaved women's lives, between "producer" and "reproducer", at different periods in the history of Caribbean slavery? What sort of gender norms developed among the slaves? How far did male authority exist in the slave community; did women conform to African gender norms in their "free time", in the spaces away from plantation control?

It has long been recognized that one of the striking features of Caribbean slavery is that the slave populations nearly everywhere failed to reproduce themselves naturally, unlike that in the United States. Appallingly high infant and child mortality was a major reason, but the demographic historians have also established that fertility rates were very low. How far was low fertility due to factors beyond the slaves' control – punishing gang labour for women in their reproductive years, poor diet, disease and ill health, unstable unions? How far could, and did, women control their own fertility through abstinence, contraception, abortion and infanticide? Was some kind of "gynaecological strike" (phrase from Bush 1990) going on? These issues are hard to deal with, for the evidence is, almost inevitably, scanty, tainted and difficult to interpret, but our historians, in particular Morrissey (1990), provide detailed and often finely nuanced analyses.

Finally, a third set of issues addresses resistance. Were women much less inclined to oppose slavery than men, were they accommodators more often than resisters, betrayers of slave plots more often than rebel heroines? Why do they figure less prominently than men as leaders of rebellions and conspiracies? Did they run away like men, and were they involved in Maroon communities? Were women "natural rebels" who led the day-to-day resistance, the campaigns of noncooperation and sabotage which did so much to undermine the slave system? Were there gender-specific forms of resistance, including the notion of a gynaecological strike? As mothers and caregivers, did women inculcate a spirit of defiance and Afrocentric cultural traditions in their children, at the same time as they tried to pass on the skills necessary to survive slavery?

The Postslavery Era (to 1960s)

On the whole, the historiography for this period is less developed than for the slavery era, but there is a rapidly growing body of work, scattered widely in one or two books, and many articles, conference or seminar papers, and theses.

Some useful articles on the postslavery period appear in *Engendering History.*[5] Up to the time of writing, however, we lack general studies attempting a synthesis comparable to the trio of books on slavery. This body of work has focused on several issues or themes.

Logically, we should start with emancipation itself. What did the end of slavery mean, specifically for the African-Caribbean women? It meant the end of the most flagrant abuses of slavery: physical punishment; coerced gang labour even when a woman was ill, pregnant, nursing an infant, or anxious to care for small children; and automatic vulnerability to sexual abuses. It meant the possibility of opting out of regular gang labour, especially for wives and mothers. It effected a transformation in women's health and fertility, a "demographic revolution" for African-Caribbean women, so that birth rates rose significantly after 1838, though death rates remained high well into the twentieth century. It made more stable family life possible and allowed for family strategies to ensure survival without total dependence on the plantation. A few historians have considered the withdrawal of many (perhaps most) ex-slave women who were wives and mothers from regular plantation labour after August 1838: how far was this withdrawal the result of family strategies to secure the welfare and safety of all family members, how far was it imposed by ex-slave men who preferred to keep their women at home, or even by planters opting for a mainly male, full-time labour force? And what were the consequences of the withdrawal, for the women and for their kin? (Wilmot 1985; Brereton 1996).

After the end of slavery, policy makers in London and magistrates, officials and clergy in the Caribbean shared the common aim of imposing European gender norms on the ex-slaves: fathers/husbands who were "heads of families" and breadwinners, mothers/wives who were full-time, dependent housewives and child raisers. But was this project successful? Did ex-slave women and their female descendants become "housewives" once they had left the full-time wage labour force? Historians have examined the occupations and employment patterns of Caribbean women after 1838, and into the middle of the twentieth century, using census returns, other kinds of written documentation, and oral testimony as their sources. Attention has been directed to the shifts in female participation in the wage labour force; the absorption of many women into peasant production (family farms, marketing, domestic production of charcoal, food and drink, livestock raising); urban women's occupations, especially domestic service, seamstressing, vending; the economic role of women of the former "free coloured" sector; and the "housewification" of the middle stratum. Most of this work has been on Jamaica (Brodber 1988; Lobdell and Higman 1983; Kerr 1985; Joseph 1993) and on Trinidad and Tobago (Reddock 1990).

Another set of issues has to do with the family forms emerging among African-Caribbean populations after 1838. What was the role of family patterns and gender ideologies deriving from West Africa? What was the legacy of slavery in shaping postemancipation developments? The findings of the demographic historians that nuclear families were not uncommon in the decades before 1838 and that slave husbands/fathers often played an important role have made the answer to this question not nearly as clear as it used to seem. What was the impact of migration, poverty, depressed sugar industries, female withdrawal from wage earnings and male unemployment, on family patterns? What kind of gender norms characterized African-Caribbean communities during the "long" nineteenth century? Did women, and men, *choose* loose family structures, often female-headed, often with no permanently resident adults? Did African-Caribbean women see legal, Christian marriage very differently from the official European-based ideology as propagated by churches, schools and governments? Were wider kin ties, and networks of neighbours, more important than conjugal ties? As we enter the 1940s and 1950s, the work of the anthropologists and the sociologists overlaps with that of the historians, and is often very valuable to the latter, though it needs to be approached with caution, granted its preoccupation with "deviant" African-Caribbean family forms (see Barrow 1996).

The history of postemancipation immigrant women, especially Indo-Caribbean women, is another focus of research. Important contributions have been made by Verene Shepherd for Jamaica, Rhoda Reddock and Patricia Mohammed for Trinidad, and Brian Moore for Guyana. They have investigated the women's immigration experience; the role of gender in the indenture system and on the plantations during the era of indenture (to 1920); women's lives in the postindenture peasant villages of Trinidad and Guyana; and the situation of Indo-Caribbean females in the traditional Asian family forms which were partially recreated in post-1880 rural settlements. Most of this growing body of work focuses on the era of immigration (1838–1917), but an important exception is Mohammed's work on gender relations in the Indo-

Trinidadian community after 1917 (see Shepherd 1995; Reddock 1986; Mohammed 1994, 1995; Moore 1995; Barrow 1996).[6]

Several other issues have been taken up by historians, though they have certainly not received the kind of attention they deserve. One is the role of women and gender in Caribbean religions, especially the various Christian churches, the African-influenced ones as well as the more orthodox bodies (see Warner-Lewis 1977; Rowe 1980; Lake 1994). The historians of education have begun to consider the impact of schooling girls, and the emergence of secondary education and teaching as channels for female mobility (see Mayers 1995; Campbell 1996). Women's involvement in crime and criminality, and the lifestyle of women in the urban "underworlds" of Kingston or Port of Spain, for example, have received some attention (see Trotman 1984). Finally, a little work has been done on attitudes towards women as reflected in the regional press, textbooks, religious literature and fiction (see Brodber 1982); such studies should help us to probe the impact of Victorian gender ideology on Caribbean women of different class and ethnic strata.

As we move chronologically into the middle decades of the twentieth century, the work tends to focus on women's participation in the political and labour struggles of the period. Rhoda Reddock's *Women, Labour and Politics in Trinidad and Tobago* is the only full-length published study and a very important contribution to the field (Reddock 1987, 1988, 1996). Useful work has also been done on Jamaica, by Linnette Vassell (1993a, 1993b, 1995), Joan French (1988), Joy Lumsden (1993) and others, and by Linda Peake (1993), Neville Duncan (1983), Honor Ford-Smith (1994) and Roberta Kilkenny (1984) on Guyana. These scholars have looked at the organizations of middle-class women, often connected to black nationalist groups or other progressive political bodies, which campaigned both for civil rights and legal equality for females, and for improvements in the lives of the poor; they were led by women like Audrey Jeffers in Trinidad and Una Marson and Amy Bailey in Jamaica. They have documented the involvement of women in the labour unrest of the 1930s, and their (limited) role in postwar trade unions and political parties, as well as the positions taken by the parties and unions in the era of decolonization and early independence on gender issues and female political activism. On the whole, we know more about the 1930s–1950s than we do about the 1830s–1930s, but this situation is changing; and some general studies of the latter period, such as those by Brian Moore on Guyana and Patrick Bryan on Jamaica, are useful sources of data on women and gender (Moore 1995; Bryan 1991; Brereton 1979).

Conclusion

There are periods of Caribbean history regarding which little research on women or gender has so far been attempted, and, as we might expect, this is especially true of the earlier periods, reflecting in part the problem of inadequate sources. We know little about how gender operated in the precontact Amerindian societies – or, for that matter, in the postcontact indigenous communities which survived past the sixteenth centuries (the Lesser Antilles, into the seventeenth or even eighteenth centuries; Trinidad, to around 1790; Dominica, Guyana and Belize, to the present day). What we do know (or think) rests mainly on accounts by Spanish chronicles, starting with Columbus's famous log of 1492–1493, and French observers, especially priests, of the 1600s. Some of these were keen observers who provided much rich ethnographic description, especially of the Island Caribs of the Lesser Antilles in the seventeenth century. There are also nineteenth- and twentieth-century anthropological accounts of Amerindians in Dominica, Guyana and Belize, from which we can try to extrapolate backwards to the earlier years. Yet all these writings were, of course, part of the colonial discourse; they are both ethnocentric and androcentric; we see Amerindian women (when we see them at all) in the "male gaze", in the eyes of male Europeans (see Loven 1935; Hulme 1986; Lafleur 1993; Gonzalez 1980).

Nor do we have much research on gender and women in the early colonial era, the period of conquest, colonization and settlement, before slave society had matured. Conquest and colonization were a profoundly masculine enterprise, and the early, frontier phase was characterized by mainly male colonial populations, both white and African. Though a great deal of relevant data can be extracted from general studies such as those by Richard Dunn, Richard Sheridan and the Bridenbaughs, there has been little research on the period specifically focused on women or gender, though Trevor Burnard's studies on early colonial Jamaica are a welcome exception (see Dunn 1973; Sheridan 1974; C. and R. Bridenbaugh 1972; Burnard 1991, 1992). Even the work on the slavery era deals in the main with the decades after 1770, reflecting the greater availability of sources for the late slave period. Nor have we had much research on white women in slave society (though Hilary Beckles and Mary Butler have made a start), or on the free coloured and free black women, except in Jamaica (Beckles 1993; Butler 1987, 1993; Boa 1993; Kerr 1993).

There are significant gaps in our understanding of women's lives and gender systems in the postemancipation nineteenth and twentieth centuries. More work is needed on the situation of women of the old free coloured sector after 1838, and on the emergence of middle-class, educated women of all ethnicities. We know very little about the historical experience of women in the smaller immigrant communities, the Chinese, Portuguese, Syrian/Lebanese and Jewish groups. We need more research on Indo-Caribbean women, especially after 1917; on education and religion and their role in female social mobility; on women's involvement in popular culture such as Jonkonnu and Carnival; on the "housewife ideology" and its impact in the nineteenth and twentieth centuries among the various class and ethnic groups. Reflecting the historiography of the region as a whole, most of the research to date has focused on Jamaica, Barbados and Trinidad; there is relatively little on Guyana, Belize or the smaller islands from a specific women's history or gender history perspective.

Nevertheless, the slow accumulation of knowledge, insights, analysis and theoretical perspectives on the role of gender and the situation of women in the region's past has helped and will continue to help us to reconstruct Caribbean history in a way which is both more nuanced and more holistic, furthering our project of engendering Caribbean history.

Notes

1. This work is dedicated to Lucille Mathurin Mair, and to the memory of the late Elsa Goveia. After a lecture delivered by the author in November 1995, Mathurin Mair stated that although she had encountered some opposition from senior Mona historians for her choice of dissertation topic, Goveia consistently supported and encouraged her.

2. The Elsa Goveia Memorial Lectures, organized by the Department of History of the University of the West Indies at Mona, Jamaica, are delivered annually by distinguished historians in memory of Elsa Goveia, an eminent Guyanese historian who was a pioneering member of the Mona department and who died in 1980.

3.   For a comparative review of the last three, see Brereton 1992.

4.   Chapter 5 of Barrow 1996 gives a good summary of these issues, and includes short readings on the topic from the work of O. Patterson, S. Mintz and R. Price, M. Craton, B. Higman, and H. Beckles.

5.   Those relating to the British Caribbean are by P. Mohammed, C. Hall, G. Robertson, P. Kerr, V. Satchell, V. Shepherd, J. Mayers, S. Wilmot and L. Vassell.

6.   Chapter 6 of Barrow 1996 deals with Indo-Caribbean family patterns, reproducing four anthropological studies published between 1959 and 1980, all on Trinidad.

References

Barrow, C. 1996. *Family in the Caribbean: Themes and Perspectives*. Kingston, Jamaica: Ian Randle Publishers.

Beckles, H. 1989. *Natural Rebels: A Social History of Enslaved Black Women in Barbados*. London: Zed Books.

————. 1993. "White Women and Slavery in the Caribbean". *History Workshop Journal* 36.

———. 1995. "Sex and Gender in the Historiography of Caribbean Slavery". In *Engendering History: Caribbean Women in Historical Perspective*, edited by V. Shepherd, B. Brereton and B. Bailey. Kingston, Jamaica: Ian Randle Publishers.

Boa, S. 1993. "Urban Free Black and Coloured Women: Jamaica 1760–1834". *Jamaican Historical Review* 28.

Brereton, B. 1979. *Race Relations in Colonial Trinidad, 1870–1900*. Cambridge: Cambridge University Press.

———. 1992. "Searching for the Invisible Woman: A Review Essay". *Slavery and Abolition* 13, no. 2 (August).

———. 1994. *Gendered Testimony: Autobiographies, Diaries and Letters by Women as Sources of Caribbean History*. Mona, Jamaica: Department of History, University of the West Indies.

———. 1995. "Text, Testimony and Gender: An Examination of Some Texts by Women on the English-speaking Caribbean from the 1770s to the 1920s". In *Engendering History: Caribbean Women in Historical Perspective*, edited by V. Shepherd, B. Brereton and B. Bailey. Kingston, Jamaica: Ian Randle Publishers.

———. 1996. "Family Strategies, Gender, and the Shift to Wage Labour in the British Caribbean". Paper presented at Conference on the Atlantic World: From Slavery to Emancipation, Tulane University, New Orleans.

Bridenbaugh, C., and R. Bridenbaugh. 1991. *No Peace Beyond the Line*. New York: Oxford University Press.

Brodber, E. 1982. *Perceptions of Caribbean Women*. Cave Hill, Barbados: Institute of Social and Economic Research, University of the West Indies.

_____. 1986. "Afro-Jamaican Women at the Turn of the Century". *Social and Economic Studies* 35 (September).

_____. 1991. "Finding the Ruins: The Study of the Second Generation of Free People in Jamaica". Paper presented at Twenty-third Conference of Caribbean Historians, Santo Domingo.

Bryan, P. 1991. *The Jamaican People, 1880–1902*. London: Macmillan.

Burnard, T. 1991. "Inheritance and Independence: Women's Status in Early Colonial Jamaica". *William and Mary Quarterly* 48.

_____. 1992. "Family Continuity and Female Independence in Jamaica, 1665–1734". *Continuity and Change* 7, no. 2.

Bush, B. 1990. *Slave Women in Caribbean Society, 1650–1838*. London: Heinemann.

Butler, M. 1987. "Female Creditors and Plantation Owners in Barbados, 1823–1843". Paper presented at Nineteenth Conference of Caribbean Historians, Martinique.

_____. 1993. "White Women and Property in Early Nineteenth Century Barbados". Paper presented at the symposium Engendering History, Mona, Jamaica.

Campbell, C.C. 1996. *The Young Colonials: A Social History of Education in Trinidad and Tobago, 1834–1939*. Kingston, Jamaica: The Press, University of the West Indies.

Chamberlain, M. 1995. "Gender and Memory: Oral History and Women's History". In *Engendering History: Caribbean Women in Historical Perspective*, edited by V. Shepherd, B. Brereton and B. Bailey. Kingston, Jamaica: Ian Randle Publishers.

Craton, M. 1978. *Searching for the Invisible Man: Slaves and Plantation Life in Jamaica*. Cambridge, Mass.: Harvard University Press.

_____. 1979. "Changing Patterns of Slave Families in the British West Indies". *Journal of Interdisciplinary History* 10, no. 1.

Duncan, N. 1983. *Women and Politics in Barbados, 1948–1980*. Cave Hill, Barbados: Institute of Social and Economic Research, University of the West Indies.

Dunn, R. 1973. *Sugar and Slaves*. London: Jonathan Cape.

Ford-Smith, H. 1994. "Una Marson: Black Nationalist and Feminist Writer". *Caribbean Quarterly* 43, nos. 3 and 4.

Fox-Genovese, E. 1983. "Placing Women's History in History". *Past and Present* 101 (November).

_____. 1992. *Unspeakable Things Unspoken: Ghosts and Memories in the Narratives of African-American Women*. Mona, Jamaica: Department of History, University of the West Indies.

French, J. 1988. "Colonial Policy towards Women after the 1939 Uprising: the Case of Jamaica". *Caribbean Quarterly* 34, nos. 3 and 4.

Gautier, A. 1985. *Les soeurs de solitude: La condition feminine dans l'esclavage aux Antilles de XVIIe au XIXe siècle*. Paris: Editions Caribéennes.

Gonzalez, N.L. 1988. *Sojourners of the Caribbean*. Urbana: University of Illinois Press.

Higman, B.W. 1973. "Household Structure and Fertility on Jamaican Slave Plantations: A Nineteenth-Century Example". *Population Studies* 27, no. 3.

_____. 1975. "The Slave Family and Household in the British West Indies 1800–1834". *Journal of Interdisciplinary History* 6.

_____. 1976. *Slave Population and Economy in Jamaica, 1807–1834*. Cambridge: Cambridge University Press.

_____. 1978. "African and Creole Slave Family Patterns in Trinidad". *Journal of Family History* 3.

_____. 1983. "Domestic Service in Jamaica since 1750". In *Trade, Government and Society in Caribbean History, 1700–1920*, edited by B.W. Higman. Kingston, Jamaica: Heinemann.

_____. 1984. *Slave Populations of the British Caribbean, 1807–1834*. Baltimore: Johns Hopkins University Press.

Hulme, P. 1986. *The Colonial Encounter*. London: Methuen.

Hulme, P., and N. Whitehead, eds. 1992. *Wild Majesty*. New York: Oxford University Press.

Josephs, A. 1993. "Gender and Occupation in Labour Force Statistics". Paper presented at Twenty-fifth Conference of Caribbean Historians, Mona.

Kerr, P. 1993. "Jamaica Female Lodginghouse Keepers in the Nineteenth Century" *Jamaican Historical Review* 28.

_____. 1995. "Victims or Strategists? Female Lodging-House Keepers in Jamaica". In *Engendering History: Caribbean Women in Historical Perspective*, edited by V. Shepherd, B. Brereton and B. Bailey. Kingston, Jamaica: Ian Randle Publishers.

Kilkenny, R. 1984. "Women in Social and Political Struggle: British Guiana, 1946–1953". Paper presented at Sixteenth Conference of Caribbean Historians, Barbados.

Lafleur, G. 1993. "La femme et les Caraïbes dans la periode historique". Paper presented at Twenty-Fifth Conference of Caribbean Historians, Mona, Jamaica.

Lake, O. 1994. "The Many Voices of Rastafarian Women". *New West Indian Guide* 68, nos. 3 and 4.

Lobdell, R. 1988. "Women in the Jamaican Labour Force 1881–1921". *Social and Economic Studies* 37 (March–June).

Loven, S. 1935. *Origins of Taino Culture*. Goteborg: Elanders Boktrycken Akfiebolag.

Lumsden, J. 1993. "Women's Participation in Political Activities in Jamaica between 1884 and 1914: A Preliminary Survey". Paper presented at the symposium Engendering History. Mona, Jamaica.

Mathurin Mair, L. 1975. *The Rebel Women in the British West Indies during Slavery*. Kingston, Jamaica: Institute of Jamaica Publications.

_____. 1987. *Women Field Workers in Jamaica during Slavery*. Mona, Jamaica: Department of History, University of the West Indies.

Mayers, J. 1995. "Access to Secondary Education for Girls in Barbados, 1907–43: A Preliminary Analysis". In *Engendering History: Caribbean Women in Historical Perspective*, edited by V. Shepherd, B. Brereton and B. Bailey. Kingston, Jamaica: Ian Randle Publishers.

Mohammed, P. 1994. "A Social History of Post-Migrant Indians in Trinidad from 1917 to 1947: A Gender Perspective". PhD diss., Institute of Social Studies, The Hague.

_____. 1995. "Writing Gender into History: The Negotiations of Gender Relations among Indian Men and Women in Post-Indenture Trinidad Society, 1917–47". In *Engendering History: Caribbean Women in Historical Perspective*, edited by V. Shepherd, B. Brereton and B. Bailey. Kingston, Jamaica: Ian Randle Publishers.

Moore, B. 1995. *Cultural Power, Resistance and Pluralism: Colonial Guyana 1838–1900*. Kingston, Jamaica: The Press, University of the West Indies.

Morrissey, M. 1990. *Slave Women in the New World*. Lawrence: Kansas University Press.

Peake, L. 1993. "The Development and Role of Women's Political Organisations in Guyana". In *Women and Change in the Caribbean*, edited by J. Momsen. London: Macmillan.

Reddock, R. 1986. "Indian Women and Indentureship in Trinidad and Tobago, 1845–1917: Freedom Denied". *Caribbean Quarterly* 32 (September–December).

_____. 1987. "Women in Revolt: Women and the Radical Workers' Movement in Trinidad, 1934–1937". In *The Trinidad Labour Riots of 1937*, edited by R. Thomas. St Augustine, Trinidad: Extra-Mural Department, University of the West Indies.

_____. 1988. *The Life of Elma Francois*. London: New Beacon Books.

_____. 1990. "Women and Garment Production in Trinidad and Tobago, 1900–1960". *Social and Economic Studies* 39 (March).

_____. 1994. *Women, Labour and Politics in Trinidad and Tobago*. Kingston, Jamaica: Ian Randle Publishers.

Rouse, I. 1992. *The Tainos*. New Haven: Yale University Press.

Rowe, M. 1980. "The Women in Rastafari". *Caribbean Quarterly* 26 (December).

Shepherd, V., B. Brereton, and B. Bailey. *Engendering History: Caribbean Women in Historical Perspective*. Kingston, Jamaica: Ian Randle Publishers.

Shepherd, V. 1995. "Gender, Migration and Settlement: The Indentureship and Post-Indentureship Experience of Indian Females in Jamaica, 1845–1943". In *Engendering History: Caribbean Women in Historical Perspective,* edited by V. Shepherd, B. Brereton and B. Bailey. Kingston, Jamaica: Ian Randle Publishers.

Sheridan, R. 1974. *Sugar and Slavery*. Eagle Hall, Barbados: Caribbean Universities Press.

_____. 1985. *Doctors and Slaves*. Cambridge: Cambridge University Press.

Silvestrini, B. 1989. *Women and Resistance: Herstory in Contemporary Caribbean History*. Mona, Jamaica: Department of History, University of the West Indies.

Terborg-Penn, R. 1995. "Through an African Feminist Theoretical Lens: Viewing Caribbean Women's History Cross-Culturally". In *Engendering History: Caribbean Women in Historical Perspective,* edited by V. Shepherd, B. Brereton and B. Bailey. Kingston, Jamaica: Ian Randle Publishers.

Trotman, D. 1984. "Women and Crime in Late Nineteenth-Century Trinidad". *Caribbean Quarterly* 30 (September–December).

Vassell, L. 1993. "The Jamaica Federation of Women and Politics 1944–50". Paper presented at Twenty-third Conference of Caribbean Historians, Mona, Jamaica.

Vassell, L., comp. 1993. *Voices of Women in Jamaica, 1898–1939*. Mona, Jamaica: Department of History, University of the West Indies.

_____. 1995. "Women of the Masses: Daphne Campbell and 'Left' Politics in Jamaica in the 1950s". In *Engendering History: Caribbean Women in Historical Perspective,* edited by V. Shepherd, B. Brereton and B. Bailey. Kingston, Jamaica: Ian Randle Publishers.

Warner Lewis, M. 1977. "The Nkuyu: Spirit Messengers of the Kumina". *Savacou* 13.

Wilmot, S. 1995. "Females of Abandoned Character? Women and Protest in Jamaica, 1838–65". In *Engendering History: Caribbean Women in Historical Perspective,* edited by V. Shepherd, B. Brereton and B. Bailey. Kingston, Jamaica: Ian Randle Publishers.

III

Unlocking the Doors
Gender in the Academy

8 Women and Development Studies

Moving from the Periphery

Elsa Leo-Rhynie

Introduction

In March 1992 the University of the West Indies (UWI) appointed a professor and regional coordinator for Women and Development Studies (WDS). This appointment marked the tenth anniversary of the first meeting, in March 1982, of a group of individuals based on the three campuses of the university who were involved in teaching, outreach and/or researching women's issues. This meeting was convened to discuss the possibility of the introduction of a Women's Studies programme at the university. The vision, energy and activity which typified the work of those early years were fully and carefully documented by Joycelin Massiah in 1986. Following a decade in which a number of women worked tirelessly, with limited resources, to raise funds, as well as establish and manage a project in WDS on the three campuses of the university, the UWI in 1992 signalled to the academic community in the Caribbean and elsewhere that this institution had committed itself to teaching, research and outreach in this area of study. This commitment to moving WDS from the periphery of the university's concerns is significant, as it represents an advance on "cautious acceptance".[1]

Caution is still evident, however, and the acceptance is moot. Several members of the Caribbean community, academic and nonacademic, male and female, have expressed curiosity, scepticism, reserve and downright denial of the validity, relevance and necessity for WDS in the UWI. Their comments reveal attitudes which suggest that WDS cannot be taken seriously as an academic discipline as it is inherently biased, that such studies are not sufficiently important for Caribbean governments to spend scarce resources on them; the more flippant ask, "What about men's studies?" Such responses betray a lack of awareness of the fact that feminist research and theory have been the most dynamic area of scholarship in academia over the past twenty years, and of the rich contribution which feminist methodology has made to research and teaching during that period. Winkler, writing in the *Chronicle of Higher Education,* made the observation that "the growth of Women's Studies is one of the success stories of American Higher Education" (1988: A4–A7), and similar growth has been recorded in Europe, Australia and New Zealand. In the developing world, the growth has been accompanied by research and social action which address issues of poverty, unemployment and inequality which adversely affect the lives of women in these settings.

Feminist theory has advanced in twenty years, from being a relatively simple analysis of male domination to complex, critical analyses of discrimination, exploitation, domination and oppression, based not only on gender, but also on class, race and age. This evolution has resulted from

- a questioning of historically accepted theories and explanations about human beings in general and women in particular;
- the identification of new areas for investigation and new methods for carrying out such investigation;
- the formulation of concepts and development of terminology which inform the methods of analysis;
- a heightened awareness of the diversity and complexity of the study of women.

Unfortunately, radical definitions and interpretations of the term "feminist" have been highly publicized, sensationalized and influenced perceptions of the women and men who describe themselves in this way, and who dedicate their careers and lives to work in this area. Such interpretations translate "feminist" to mean "man-hating", "aggressive", "strident", "power-hungry", "lesbian", and "members of a lunatic fringe". These commonly held stereotypes alienate both women and men, hindering their understanding of the concept of feminism and the work of feminists.

Rhoda Reddock defines feminism as "the awareness of the oppression, exploitation and/or subordination of women within the society, and the conscious action to change and transform this situation" (1988: 53). This definition embraces an ideology, a methodology, and a range of behaviours which typify the human beings for whom feminism is a goal. Addelson and Potter (1991) identify four categories of feminists as follows:

1. Political: individuals who are members of an activist women's organization.
2. Professional: academics who carry out gender research within or across disciplines and/or persons who work in professional organizations on women's issues.
3. Theoretical: self-conscious members of the group of women living in male-dominated societies.
4. Practical: individuals who assist women who are victims of rape, domestic violence, discriminatory or exploitative practices.

Many feminists can place themselves in more than one of these categories.

Feminist scholarship and women's studies had their origins in the women's movement which was part of the upheaval decade of the 1960s, when issues of racial and social equality were in the forefront of political and social concerns. Feminist scholarship sought to identify the origins of power differences between the two sexes, and the division of human characteristics along gender lines; arrive at an understanding of the world which takes women, their perceptions, their lives and achievements into account; formulate effective change strategies which would result in an acceptance of individuals as "human". This acceptance would be independent of gender and would reduce the power difference along gender lines.

Groups of feminists differ in their views on the method by which these change processes should be achieved, and much controversy surrounds the validity of the approach of each group. Liberal feminists feel that the gender distinctions will end once equal opportunity is created for women to compete with men within the existing system, and so they target those behaviours and structures which keep women in positions of disadvantage – the legal, social and economic factors which limit women's potential. Their basic objective is to assist women to assume roles which men now hold within society. Denial of this opportunity to women is waste of a valuable human resource. Radical feminists consider the lower status of women and their oppression to be an integral part of a patriarchal, hierarchical societal structure, and are of the view that equality for women within the existing system is impossible. The objectives of this group, therefore, are the radical restructuring of society and the elimination of hierarchical structure, to be achieved by some by establishing communities consisting solely of women. Marxist and socialist feminists also feel that a complete restructuring of society is needed to change the oppression of women. Their view is that the economic and social institutions in different societies, and the roles which women are forced to perform in these societies, create significant barriers to change.

Black feminists challenge the exclusion, by other feminists, of experiences which contribute to the cultural mosaic of multiracial societies such as the United Kingdom and the United States of America. They feel that existing theories do not adequately address the special, complex nature of the discrimination, oppression and exploitation experienced by black women. Thus black feminism constitutes a separate voice seeking to redress the imbalance created by early work on women. Many of the concerns of black feminists are also those of Caribbean and other Third World feminists who are critical of the assumption of homogeneity among women, and of a lack of recognition of differences and interactions based on culture, race, class as well as sex, and who emphasize that gender is not the sole determinant of a woman's role in life. Eudine Barriteau (1992) points to the failure of existing theories to account for the diversity of women and their experiences, and builds on the tenets of postmodernist thought to construct a postmodernist feminist theory for use by Caribbean social science researchers. This theory acknowledges and supports the exploration of diversity and difference among women based on race, class and sexual identity, and also examines the ways in which "gendered woman", that is, biological woman socially constructed, affects and is affected by these variables differently at different times and in different situations.

Within feminism there is a wide variety of opinions, and each feminist can (and often does) disagree with some of what is presented as feminist views. We differ, yes, but we all have confidence in, and are supportive of, the integrity of women's studies as an academic discipline, and have stopped being deferential and near apologetic in the face of doubt and scepticism about the programme offered. The varying feminist viewpoints have greatly enriched programmes and activities geared towards women. Liberal feminism has focused on the elimination of sexism in the curriculum, attention to changing legal and social barriers to women's achievements and the demand for greater participation of qualified women in national government and organizational management, as well as in university policy making and administration. Radical feminists focus on women's strengths and women's lives, as well as power in personal and sexual relationships. Their idea of a separate women's culture has been controversial, but has been of immense support to many women. The Marxist and socialist feminists have stimulated an examination of the economic and social roles as well as the relationships of women's oppression to that of other groups, and suggested ways of changing these. All groups stress the need to change women's sense of themselves as oppressed, to build women's self-image and sense of self-worth, and by doing this, to help them create new options in terms of their personal lives and societal roles.

Centring Woman's Studies

In recognition of its power in any process of change, education was identified as a central strategy in bringing about the necessary transformation, and women's studies was identified as the vehicle through which this education would take place. Women's studies is thus committed to the objectives of feminist scholarship and is a programme of research and teaching which is interdisciplinary, and which is involved in developing and using new interdisciplinary methodologies for the production of knowledge. Women's studies programmes, therefore, are designed to assess, analyse and challenge existing disciplines and traditional methods of acquiring and disseminating knowledge; to establish curricula to address issues of gender and analyses based on gender; and to establish and maintain a strong link with the community and with organizations addressing women's concerns.

As Chhachhi noted, "Women's Studies does not just mean 'add women and stir' but rather requires a reformulation of disciplinary concepts and a new approach to social reality" (1988: 79). Several controversial issues surround WDS, its activities and its movement from the periphery of the university. Three of these issues which I would like to examine briefly are the multifaceted nature of WDS; the role of men in women's studies; and women's studies versus gender studies.

The Multifaceted Nature of WDS

The ultimate purpose of WDS is to improve women's lives. There is compelling need to design, develop, offer and support programmes and projects which reach nonacademic women and women whose lives are on the periphery of society. Marginal women are not only found in Third World countries, and Chhachhi (1988) uses this fact to criticize the liberal feminist analysis of equal sex roles. She points to satisfaction of a number of the demands of liberal feminists in advanced industrial countries by way of legal sanctions against sex discrimination, improvement of the legal status of women, and movement of women into leadership positions, even political leadership of countries. Despite this, however, women in such countries continue to be employed in low paying, sex-segregated occupations, to perform unstimulating and repetitive tasks, to be primarily responsible for housework and child care, and to increasingly experience domestic violence. She asserts that the active, outreach origin of the women's movement must not be forgotten as women move into academia, that it needs to be maintained as a focus so that research and teaching address the betterment of women's lives. In the Caribbean, the need is more vital in a situation where global recession and structural adjustment have had negative effects on the health, education, employment and lifestyles of men, women and children, with the most serious consequences being experienced by women and children.

One of the four principles established as a basis for WDS activity was that the programme should integrate research, teaching and action. The emphasis on action, and recognition of the vital importance of gearing research and teaching towards production and dissemination of information which can be used to guide policy makers (both governmental and nongovernmental), has been central to the WDS agenda in the Caribbean. WDS must, directly or indirectly, assist in formulating strategies to help women suffering from economic, political and domestic hardship, and must also promote women's autonomy and their acquisition of the means to control their own political, social, economic and personal lives.

The Women and Development Unit (WAND)[2] has, over the years, served as a trailblazer in designing and delivering training programmes, and in providing technical assistance for the betterment of women in the region, and has been very involved in international activities geared towards reducing the vulnerability of women worldwide. As part of its task of responding to the activities of the Decade for Women (1975–85), it also served as catalyst, in 1982, for the formation of the WDS groups and the introduction of WDS at the UWI. Its catalytic role was greatly enhanced by the collaborative research work on the Women in the Caribbean project undertaken by the Eastern Caribbean branch of the Institute of Social and Economic Research of the university; thus were established, from the outset, the very strong bonds between research, outreach and the academic programme which are the basis of the WDS agenda. It also set the stage for the ongoing links with the Women's Bureau and other agencies whose activities are complementary to those of WDS.[3]

Another important outcome of these initiatives was recognition of the interdisciplinarity which would typify work in this area. The commitment to interdisciplinary curricula, programmes and analyses presents serious practical problems which have already been experienced by WDS: problems of fitting into the university's academic structure, of staffing, funding and examining. The importance of working through these problems and ensuring that the interdisciplinary approach is not lost is emphasized by the experiences of writers such as Ruth (1990), who points to the artificiality of intellectual boundaries, the need to appreciate knowledge globally, and to explore the multiple perspectives which provide insights into various components of women's lives and the way in which these lives have affected human growth and development. These perspectives do not fit neatly into academic disciplines but range across fields of anthropology, sociology, history, biology, psychology, economics, law and education. Ruth uses the term "counterdisciplinary" to describe this rejection of disciplinary boundaries. Magarey (1983) uses another term, "transdisciplinary", to describe a similar approach which both uses and transcends the range of existing disciplines to investigate issues originating in the women's movement. This approach is an eclectic one, permitting the development of theories based in the cultural environment, and it emphasizes, as WDS in the UWI does, the need to work closely, in a collaborative learning mode, with women's organizations with close connections to women, their problems and needs.

The Role of Men in Women's Studies

During the rapid growth of women's studies within the academic community, a number of men have demonstrated an interest in this area, and have conducted research, taught and been supportive of women's issues. This has been viewed by a number of women as a sign of progress, of attitude change, of "winning over the enemy", and they have been appreciative of the male support. This view has been criticized by radical feminists, who accuse such women of using men's involvement as evidence that they are "doing things right". The radical feminists are suspicious of men's involvement, seeing this as an example of men identifying a situation which is fertile with opportunities for research, publications and academic advancement, and using it to further their careers. Warnings that the men, if allowed participation, will quickly take over, have also been issued. Radical feminists view women's studies as a place where only women's voices are heard, where they make their own statements, where their concerns are not de-emphasized, where they no longer exist at the periphery, but are totally centred.

Belinda Kremer (1990) supports the view that feminist research should be research done by women for women, whereas others such as Sandra Harding (1987) argue that men cannot be excluded from feminist research or a feminist perspective on the basis of gender. The issue of men producing knowledge about women challenges the concept of women determining the methodology and perspectives which are brought to bear on feminist knowledge production and dissemination. Kremer (1990) refers to methodological guidelines for feminist research developed by Maria Mies (1981) and argues that men cannot share the same "critical plane"[4] as women since they do not have the double consciousness of the female researcher both as woman and as researcher; they cannot share woman's view of themselves and of men "from below", nor can they be part of research carried out by objects of oppression ("conscientization" [Mies 1981]) as they never experience the normal life of a woman ("collectivization" [Mies 1981]). Women do not, the radical feminists claim, have the problem in researching men's issues that men have in dealing with women's issues. Kremer notes "Because the dominant culture is forcibly lived by all, while the lived reality of subordinate or oppressed cultures is unique to the subordinate or oppressed . . . each of us is daily forced to inhabit male reality" (1990: 465).

The issue/standard/criterion of a shared critical plane cannot be limited to gender, to a question of whether women, rather than men, should teach women's studies, or whether it is preferable to have a gender-sensitive man teach women's studies than a non-gender-sensitive woman. It must also be addressed from race, class and culture perspectives: knowledge and experiences differ across these dimensions as well as gender – would it not be more acceptable to have a Jamaican male researching the living conditions and life experiences of rural Jamaican women than to have a non-Jamaican female researcher carry out this assignment? Which critical plane is it more critical that researcher and subject share?

One of the guiding principles of WDS stated in 1982 was the need to follow the tradition of Caribbean women's style of operation, rather than follow foreign modes of functioning. This principle was expanded upon by Massiah (1986), who noted the history of Caribbean women working alongside their men for the betterment of their communities, and pointed to the unanimity with which it was agreed that WDS programmes would establish and build close links and networks with interested women and men in faculties, departments and institutes within the university. WDS recognizes the value of having male and female perspectives on certain situations, as each makes different but important contributions to feminist analysis. Reiteration of this principle at this time is important in light of the debates in women's studies circles, and the uncertainty expressed among male students and colleagues as to the role they can play in WDS. I know that I run the risk of being dubbed a "feminist apologist" in assuring men of the rejection by WDS of the separatist view, and of WDS's recognition of the value of the involvement and contributions of our male colleagues. I concur with Sandra Harding's view that "feminists should find it inappropriate both to criticize male scholarship and research for ignoring women and gender and also to insist that they are incapable of conducting research which satisfies feminist requirements" (1987: 12).

Gender versus Women's Studies

The issue of men's involvement in women's studies is closely associated with the third issue, that of whether we should be involved in developing a programme of "gender and development studies" rather than "women and development studies". Increasingly in universities overseas, "gender studies" is replacing "women's studies" in the curriculum.

The term "gender" has been used loosely as a synonym for the biological sex category. Gender, however, is a more complex concept: it has been described by Kate Young as "a shorthand term which encodes a very crucial point: that our basic social identities as men and women are socially constructed rather than based on fixed biological characteristics" (1988: 98). These socially constructed categories are of particular importance in the socialist feminist analysis which favours a holistic examination of economic, social and political influences on the expectations and the roles and responsibilities assumed by women and men in both their private and public spheres of life. The object of their analysis is not only women, but includes the relationships between men and women as well as between women and women. The analysis also recognizes that the social relations of women and men, men and men, and women and women are intersected by other social relations based on race and class.

There is strong feminist opinion, however, that the movement away from women's studies to gender studies is a yielding of the study of sexual inequality and the social subordination of women to the mere study of differences between the sexes. The term "gender", it is argued, implies a certain neutrality which is not acceptable, as it does not highlight the asymmetry which exists in the power relationships between men and women in society. University programmes which identify with gender rather than women's issues have been accused of trying to be noncontroversial, of allowing men to be part of this area of study, of needing to be seen as "objective" and "nonpolitical" and of adopting a socially convenient term which has greater appeal and would be more easily accepted as part of the central concerns of academia than women's studies. The desire to maintain a focus on women's issues, but also address gender concerns, has created centres in universities overseas with interesting designations such as women and gender studies.

WDS needs to consider carefully its objectives in developing and offering programmes of study within the university. If, as we noted earlier, this objective is to establish curricula to address issues of gender and analysis based on gender; if these issues are discrimination, domination, subordination, exploitation, oppression of one gender by another; if these situations could come about because of the nature of roles assumed and the interactions between the gender in specific cultures, races and classes, then the study of one group with the objective of changing these relationships and situations, seems impossible without reference to and comparisons with the other. Our gender identities have been built through our membership and participation in domestic, educational, economic, cultural and community groups and/or institutions which have contributed to what Sandra Bem (1993) calls gender polarizing lenses through which we view ourselves and gender roles in our close relationships, in societies and the world. The ways in which differences based on power have evolved and been perpetuated in society must be considered, by examining the interrelationships of both groups as well as those factors which significantly affect these relationships. If the objectives of WDS are to address power relationships between women and men, and to create respect and a sense of human worth between the groups, then to focus on woman only is to imply that this creation is her responsibility. If we agree with bell hooks that "reconstruction and transformation [of] behaviours of masculinity, is a necessary and essential part of feminist revolution" (1988: 127), then we have to reject the radical feminist view of male exclusion and must actively involve men in the process. "Gender studies" seems to better describe the concerns of UWI's WDS groups which include and emphasize, but are not exclusively, women's studies.

Out of the Periphery

WDS affirms its commitment to an interdisciplinary programme of teaching, research and outreach activities, of focus on feminist scholarship, women's issues and gender concerns, involving women and men who are committed to this area of work. We stand ready to move from the periphery of the university's activities. A home of our own, funding support from our governments and resources to develop and mount a strong, viable programme are, to us, important indicators of such movement. WDS notes, with gratification, the assertion made by the UWI in its document *Into the Twenty-First Century* that "the university plans to increase and institutionalize its commitment to this area of study [that is, WDS] by providing a complement of academic staff as well as the proper facilities and equipment necessary to foster development" (n.d.: 17). Such development, the document states, will take the form of "increasing financial support, extending research, and developing more courses in order to make WDS an integrative [*sic*] part of the university's structure".

This integration is not easy. Thus far, the majority of WDS courses have been sited in the Faculty of Arts and General Studies, and courses are also offered in the Faculties of Education, Social Sciences and Agriculture, as well as the Consortium Graduate School of the Social Sciences. Several courses also include modules which address gender concerns. Students have responded enthusiastically to these offerings, and a number of requests have been received for additions and for complete degree programmes in WDS at both undergraduate and graduate levels. The question of whether courses on gender should be integrated into existing offerings has been strongly debated. Radical feminists, whose ideas of feminist scholarship are the most revolutionary, fear that integration will compromise this scholarship if it becomes part of the academy's mainstream (which they have dubbed the "male stream"). Integration, it is felt, will provide an opportunity for the more revolutionary aspects of feminist scholarship to be omitted, thus losing complete bodies of thought which provide alternative responses and solutions to the gender question. The retention of autonomy and a separate independent interdisciplinary field of research and teaching is considered to be important so that connection, communication and support among persons who share certain common objectives can be maintained. Integration will require the development of new courses, and the expansion of existing syllabuses to address gender issues within the many disciplines which are already part of the university's mainstream. This process calls for a critical examination of existing course content, and the inclusion of gender perspectives as well as gender analyses of the issues and concepts therein. Implicit in this is the requirement that individuals offering these courses possess gender sensitivity, and are able to bring a feminist perspective to bear on the discourse so that the curriculum is transformed to reflect the understanding that the perspectives and experiences of women have helped to create history, society and culture.

Integration of gender cannot be limited to course offerings within the departments; it must be reflected in the entire university community. If the institutionalization of WDS is merely a token gesture to keep up with current trends in academia, or to satisfy requirements of funding agencies, then gender issues will remain peripheral to the life of the university. In the same way that an institution which prepares teachers should ensure that its educators demonstrate the highest standards of pedagogy, and management education institutions should be models of good management practice, the university which voices a commitment to gender issues must reflect this in its institutional structure and climate as well as in its course offerings.

At UWI, the structure is strongly male dominated: the chancellor, vice chancellor, campus principals and all but one pro vice chancellor are male. The first female pro vice chancellor was appointed in 1991 and the first female university registrar in 1992. There are only two female deans: in Arts and General Studies, and Education, the "female" faculties. Women make up only 29 percent of the full-time academic and administrative staff, and the status of these women within the university is interesting. There are 89 male and 7 female professors, 11 male and 2 female readers, 219 male and 71 female senior lecturers, 289 male and 168 female lecturers, 10 male and 10 female assistant lecturers (UWI 1991). Women are found in greatest numbers in the lower categories of the academic hierarchy. The overwhelming majority of the decision-making, strategic-planning and policy-making bodies of the university is male. The appointment of two women in senior managerial positions is welcome, and it is expected that they will bring a female perspective and view to the examination of issues and the decision-making process, and also serve as role models for other women who may be starting out on academic and other professional careers.

Research has identified a number of factors which act as barriers to women's advancement within organizations, and one of these is the existence of an organizational climate which is not hostile, not unfriendly, but also not encouraging to women. Within the university community we need also to build a climate which is encouraging to women, to guard against what Sandler and Hall (1986) call micro-inequities – subtle, everyday types of discrimination – actions which single out, ignore or in some way devalue women, their ideas or their work on the basis of sex. The cumulative effect of these seemingly trivial, minor annoyances is reflected in the climate of the institution, and strongly influences expectations and behaviour.

As WDS moves from the periphery it plans to establish, within the university, a Centre for Gender and Development Studies which will develop independent, autonomous interdisciplinary teaching programmes, and also work with faculties to promote the integration of gender and gender perspectives into existing disciplinary programmes.[5] In the Caribbean, the interaction of gender, race and class creates a complex picture for the analysis and study of human experience, and so presents rich opportunities for research. This research must, however, inform both teaching and outreach, and issues arising from outreach activities must generate further research so that these aspects can be part of the cycle of activities which will ensure the continued validity and relevance of the Centre for Gender and Development Studies.

Great confidence is being placed in the university's commitment to move WDS from the periphery. We hope that this commitment will not be evaluated in the way that the West Indian Commission assessed the commitment of governments in the region to women and development. The West Indian Commission states "Commitment to women and development remains token and under-resourced. The setting up of a Bureau of Women's Affairs within a government ministry, for example, serves only to acknowledge that adjustments are necessary, but without the necessary resources does little or nothing to effectively address the needs" (1992: 335).

The Centre for Gender and Development Studies wants to address effectively the many needs it has identified in research, in teaching, in reaching out to noncampus territories, to teacher's colleges, to adult community education centres, to policy makers and other people and organizations. We hope that our movement from the periphery will be achieved, and that the support of the university, governments, funding agencies and private sector interests will assist us in this movement. The exciting opportunities which exist for the development of a dynamic, vibrant area of scholarship which can only enrich the knowledge base of the university, and the involvement of all in exploring, in greater depth, the human conditions, should not be missed. We invite the academy to join us in this exploration – to move with us.

Notes

1. The phrase "cautious acceptance" was used by Joycelin Massiah to describe the UWI's response to and support of the initial activities of the Women and Development Studies groups.
2. WAND is the acronym for the Women and Development Studies Unit, which was established in 1978 by the University of the West Indies School of

Continuing Studies. WAND's mission is to contribute to building the human and institutional capacity of the Caribbean region and to document the process. The unit is committed to a model of development which is equitable, integrative, participatory, self-reliant and sustainable.

3. In 1988 Peggy Antrobus, coordinator/tutor of WAND, expressed satisfaction that the Caribbean had avoided the distinction between women in development and women's studies which was made in the United States and some Third World countries. WDS, as planned, would create a synthesis between concepts of feminism and development, geared specifically towards Caribbean development.

4. Sandra Harding (1987) used the term "critical plane" to describe the combination of perspectives of women and men as they carry out research. These "critical planes" differ because of the different experiences which women and men have, and thus will affect the nature and outcomes of any research conducted.

5. The Centre for Gender and Development Studies was officially established in September 1993. This paper is derived from an inaugural lecture marking the tenth anniversary of the WDS in December 1992, and provides a valuable record of the emergence and growth of gender studies in tertiary level education.

References

Addelson, Kathryn Payne, and Elizabeth Potter. 1991. "Making Knowledge". In *(En)Gendering Knowledge: Feminists in Academe,* edited by J.E. Haitman and E. Messer-Davidow. Knoxville: University of Tennessee Press.

Andersen, M.L. 1987. "Changing the Curriculum in Higher Education". *Signs* 12.

Antrobus, Peggy. 1988. "Women in Development Programmes: The Caribbean Experience, 1975–1985". In *Gender in Caribbean Development,* edited by P. Mohammed and C. Shepherd. St Augustine, Trinidad: Women and Development Studies Project, University of the West Indies.

Barriteau, Eudine. 1992. "The Construct of a Postmodernist Feminist Theory for Caribbean Social Science Research". *Social and Economic Studies* 41, no. 2.

Bem, Sandra Lipsitz. 1993. *The Lenses of Gender: Transforming the Debate on Sexual Inequality.* New Haven: Yale University Press.

Chhachhi, Amrita. 1988. "Concepts in Feminist Theory: Consensus and Controversy". In *Gender in Caribbean Development,* edited by P. Mohammed and

C. Shepherd. St Augustine, Trinidad: Women and Development Studies Project, University of the West Indies.

Evans, Mary. 1990. "The Problem of Gender for Women's Studies". *Women's Studies International Forum* 13, no. 5.

Harding, Sandra. 1987. "Introduction: Is There a Feminist Method?" In *Feminism and Methodology: Social Science Issues,* edited by S. Harding. Bloomington: Indiana University Press.

hooks, bell. 1988. *Talking Back: Thinking Feminist, Thinking Black.* Toronto: Between the Lines.

Kremer, Belinda. 1990. "Learning to Say No: Keeping Feminist Research for Ourselves". *Women's Studies International Forum* 13, no. 5.

Lowe, Marian, and Margaret Lowe Benston. 1991. "The Uneasy Alliance of Feminism and Academia". In *A Reader in Feminist Knowledge,* edited by S. Gunew. London: Routledge.

Magarey, Susan. 1983. "Women's Studies in Australia: Towards Transdisciplinary Learning?" *Journal of Educational Thought* 17.

Massiah, Joycelin. 1986. "Establishing a Programme of Women and Development Studies in the University of the West Indies". *Social and Economic Studies* 35, no. 1.

Mies, Maria. 1981. "Towards a Methodology for Feminist Research". In *Theories of Women's Studies II,* edited by G. Bowles and R. Duelli Klein. Berkeley: University of California Press.

Reddock, Rhoda. 1988. "Feminism and Feminist Thought: An Historical Overview". In *Gender in Caribbean Development,* edited by P. Mohammed and C. Shepherd. St Augustine, Trinidad: Women and Development Studies Project, University of the West Indies.

Ruth, Sheila. 1990. *Issues in Feminism,* 2d ed. Mountain View, Calif.: Mayfield Publishing.

Sandler, B.R., and R.M. Hall. 1986. "The Campus Climate Revisited: Chilly for Women Faculty, Administrators, and Graduate Students". Project on the Status and Education of Women, Washington DC.

Sheridan, Susan. 1991. "From Margin to Mainstream: Situating Women's Studies". In *A Reader in Feminist Knowledge,* edited by S. Gunew. London and New York: Routledge.

The West Indian Commission. 1992. *Time for Action.* Christ Church, Barbados: West Indian Commission.

University of the West Indies (UWI). N.d. *Into the Twenty-first Century.* Kingston, Jamaica: Vee Kay Communication.

_____. 1991. *Statistics 1990/1991.*

Weiler, Kathleen. 1991. "Freire and a Feminist Pedagogy of Difference". *Harvard Educational Review* 61, no. 4.

Winkler, Karen J. 1988. "Women's Studies after Two Decades: Debates over Politics, New Directions for Research". *Chronicle of Higher Education.*

Young, Kate. 1988. "Notes on the Social Relations of Gender". In *Gender in Caribbean Development,* edited by P. Mohammed and C. Shepherd. St Augustine, Trinidad: Women and Development Studies Project, University of the West Indies.

9   Gendered Realities: Fact or Fiction?

The Realities in a Secondary Level
Coeducational Classroom

BARBARA BAILEY

Introduction

Provision of opportunities for formal education is pivotal to the development
of the human resources of every nation. In developing countries the secondary
cycle is particularly important in this respect since, for the majority, this stage
is terminal and prepares individuals for entry into the adult world of work.
With their typical patterned activities and hierarchical relations, schools mirror
the social order of the societies in which they are located. As happens in social
systems, schools are subject to a number of forces which create social, racial
and sexual inequalities and inequities. The extent to which formal schooling
is nondiscriminatory and allows for the full development of males and females
is therefore questioned by feminist educators. The discourse developed by
these scholars suggests that biological sex provides the most pervasive basis
for differentiation throughout school life, and that schooling is a major
mechanism for reproducing the sexual inequalities and gendered relationships
that are evident in life outside of school. Schools, as sites of this reproduction,
can therefore be regarded as microcosms of the wider society in which they
are located and in which they function.

This paper is based on primary research carried out in a coeducational classroom at the secondary level of the Jamaican education system. It focuses on the delineation of patterns based on sex differences in curriculum participation, and the sexual politics of the interactions between teachers and students, and students and students. This exploratory pilot study aimed to identify and report on the gendered realities in a mixed-sex setting to determine the extent to which traditional gender codes were evident and transmitted through pedagogical and social processes.

Alternative Theoretical Frameworks

Educational Inequalities: Classical Sociological Perspectives

Much of the work done on inequalities in schooling during the decades of the 1950s and 1960s focused on social class inequalities and the generation of theories to explain these inequalities. The dominant classical functionalist perspective, advanced by educational sociologists such as Durkheim and Parsons, examines the role of the school in social stratification and social mobility within its functionalist role of providing a literate and adaptable workforce seen as necessary for the survival of advanced industrial societies such as Britain and the United States (Burgess 1986).

In the view of the Functionalists, schooling is meritocratic and success depends primarily on the motivation and intellectual ability of the individual. Although it was acknowledged by this group that schools function as agents of socialization and allocation, in the process stratifying society, it was also argued that they do so on the basis of merit (Stromquist 1990). Functionalism therefore sought to examine the relationship between education and the economy, between education and selective mechanisms in the education system, as well as to provide an analysis of the role of the school in the transmission of the dominant value system of society.

Educational sociologists of the 1970s sought alternative explanations for educational inequalities, and moved from the more superficial concerns of the functions of the school in socialization and allocation to a more detailed examination of classrooms processes, and to a focus on epistomological and pedagogical issues. Young (1974), for example, was concerned with how knowledge is selected, organized and assessed in educational institutions, and argued that this reflected both how power is distributed and principles of social control. An important aspect of Young's work, therefore, centred on the social organization and stratification of knowledge and how the availability of some dominant categories of knowledge to some groups enables them to assert power and control over others. Bernstein's (1970) work, on the other hand, was concerned with the different conceptual schemes, related to social class assignment, that students bring to the pedagogical process. These class-regulated codes are reflected in differing language and cognitive abilities which, he argues, could explain observed educational inequalities.

The later neo-Marxist perspective reverts to an analysis of the importance of economic and political forces on education. Adherents of this view argue that schools, particularly in capitalist society, assist in the reproduction of the society. The work of Bowles and Gintis (1978) which focuses on differential socialization of individuals by the school into dominant and dominated groups is well known in this regard. Burgess contends:

> Central to their analysis is the view that there is a high degree of correspondence between school and work, as they argue that the educational system helps to integrate young people into the economic system. (1986: 16)

Educational sociologists who work in this paradigm therefore set themselves the task of revealing how domination and oppression are produced through the various mechanisms of schooling.

Educational Inequalities: Feminist Perspectives

Theories proposed by the above-cited educational sociologists have been criticized by feminist educators and others for their shortcomings and limited usefulness in terms of questioning the gender order in society and offering explanations of sexual inequalities in education. It is argued that these theories take social class as the main variable of analysis but fail to deal with gender as a major social construct (Stromquist 1990).

Barriteau (forthcoming) postulates that in societies, including Caribbean society, a definite gender system is identifiable which is comprised of a network of asymmetrical power relations with two identifiable dimensions: one material and the other ideological. An analysis of the material dimension reveals unequal access to material and nonmaterial resources and unequal allocation of power and status between the sexes. On the other hand, an analysis of the ideological dimension reveals how a society constructs and maintains notions of femininity and masculinity.

It is now acknowledged that the school and the educational process are very important in determining one's position and experience within this gender system. More recent work on the sociology of education therefore highlights the fact that the education of individuals is differentiated on the basis of three major hierarchical structures of inequality, and a combination of social relations and interactions based on social class, race and sex. Feminist educators, in their analysis of educational inequalities, focus on sex as their main variable of interest and have proposed a number of theories to explain sexual inequalities in the educational process, and how schooling contributes to the reproduction of not only "classed" societies but also "gendered" societies.

The theories on sexual inequalities in education emanating from feminist research and the corresponding discourse fit into two broad categories: the cultural and the political economy perspectives. According to Arnot (1994), the cultural perspective focuses on the patterns of sex-role socialization and processes internal to the school that shape the formation of gender identities, while the political economy perspective focuses on factors external to the school and examines the relationship of schools to the economy, to dominant class interests and to the hierarchical structure of economic and cultural power. The work of liberal and radical feminist educators fits into the cultural perspective, while that of the socialist and postmodernist feminists can be subsumed under the political economy perspective.

Early frameworks supplied by liberal feminists to explain sexual inequalities in education are based on a sex-role theory in which it is contended that girls, *inter alia,* are socialized to "fear success" in certain areas of educational endeavour. This, they argue, results in girls being found concentrated in certain curriculum areas and certain school activities. Additionally, Stromquist (1990) purports that they are also socialized to accept traditional reproductive roles related to homemaking and child care, and so have lower levels of aspiration – and therefore lower levels of educational achievement.

In the Caribbean the reverse pattern is observed, where the gender gap in enrolment and achievement is in favour of females. At least one explanation can be advanced for this reversal of what seems to be the norm in many other societies. Stromquist's (1990) explanation based on the "inferiority theory" can be applied to Caribbean society. She suggests that because of the widely held view and existing ideology that women are the inferior sex, women have to obtain more education and competence than men in order to compete on an equal footing. This is confirmed by a study carried out by the UN Economic Commission for Latin America and the Caribbean which found that women need to have more years of schooling than men in order to compete for similar levels of remuneration in the labour force (ECLAC/UNIFEM 1995).

Individuals in these societies are therefore socialized to accept that men need less education to succeed in society than do women, who need to have higher aspirations if they are to be competitive in the marketplace. What is of significance, however, is that these higher levels of attainment do not translate into women having equal social status to men in Caribbean society. Women as a group are still in a subordinate position to men in the labour force, in decision-making positions and in terms of access to the means of production (Bailey 1997a).

The major solutions and strategies recommended by liberal feminists to redress the typical sex imbalances in education range from awareness raising; the removal of barriers to women's full participation (Weiner 1990); altering socialization practices; changing attitudes and, where necessary, the use of legal processes to ensure equal access for women (Acker 1994). Radical feminist educators, in keeping with the cultural perspective, contend that sexual inequalities in education stem from the patriarchal system that defines men as being superior to women. Patriarchy is maintained through an intricate system of beliefs, norms, laws and institutions – the school being one such institution. These beliefs reinforce the division of labour between the sexes which relegates women to the private sphere and men to the public sphere. Schools reproduce this division of labour through the sex-segregation of the curriculum, where girls are concentrated in the domestic crafts and boys in the technical crafts. Where women use these skills outside of the home in the public domain, they are concentrated in areas which require service and nurturing skills. Stromquist agrees that

> the concentration of females in certain curriculum areas is explained in terms of the influence of the patriarchal system that inculcates in women the value of domestic responsibilities with the consequence that they choose careers that tend to be extensions of domestic roles or that will not conflict with them. (1990: 145)

Borrowing from Bernstein's analysis of the underlying structure of message systems operating in schools in relation to curriculum, pedagogy and evaluation, McDonald (1980) suggests that schools transmit a gender code with "strong classification", which reproduces the power relations of a male/female hierarchy, and "strong framing", where teachers play a significant role in determining definitions of femininity, masculinity and patterns of control. Diamond (1991) explains that strong classification obtains in schools where quite separate behaviours and appearances are designated as being appropriate to each gender, and strong framing exists where teachers and students have very little control over the selection and organization of the categories of femininities and masculinities and when these categories are manifested. Socialist/Marxist feminist educators go beyond the sex-role and reproduction theories to advance yet another theory of sexual inequalitiy in education that corresponds to the political economy viewpoint. They argue that any explanation of inequality must take into account the interconnection between ideological and economic forces through which patriarchy and capitalism reinforce each other (Stromquist 1990). They argue that the picture is therefore even more complex than has been suggested, and they focus on an analysis of gender relations and their interconnections to social class.

Arnot therefore proposes that what is required in an analysis of educational inequalities is the bringing together of theories of two different structures of inequality, social class and gender, and the ways in which gender reproduction is inherent in and not independent of the patterns of social class reproduction, class control and class struggles. Arnot argues that

> both class and gender relations constitute hierarchies in which material and symbolic power are based. Inside these hierarchies, the dialectics of class and gender struggles are waged. If we want to research the role of schools as one social "site" in which the reproduction of sociosexual division of labour occurs, then it is necessary to be aware of the nature of these two forms of social struggle, the different stakes involved, and how such struggles are "lived through" by individuals who negotiate terms within these power relations and who construct for themselves specific class and gender identities. (1994: 85)

Socialist/Marxist feminist educators therefore seek to analyse educational practices and policy in terms of the relationship of school to the economy, dominant class interests and the hierarchical structures of economic and cultural power.

Transformational feminist educators, like the socialist/Marxist group, contend that existing social and political structures support the oppression of particular groups, including women, and that women's experiences have been ignored in looking at these situations. They agitate for a transformation of the male-oriented curriculum to one which brings women into educational thought and also incorporates female values, skills and ways of relating (Noddings 1992).

The Study

Much of the educational research in the Caribbean region on sexual inequalities in education has focused on factors that fit into the sex-role socialization paradigm and therefore on sex-role stereotyping, inequalities in access, differentiated patterns of curriculum participation, imbalances in achievement, career choice and the pursuance of related training options. An exception is Parry (1996), who has done work on the relationship between male gender identity, cultural expectations and educational responses in high school classrooms in Jamaica. Beyond this little has been done on how patriarchal forces operate in schools, the power hierarchies in classrooms and the role played by sexuality in the oppression of girls, and the effect of these factors on the teaching/learning environment.

The importance of these factors in classrooms and their impact on the life experiences of women, however, is widely recognized and acknowledged. Arnot contends that

> women have become colonized within a male-dominated world through a wide variety of "educational moments" that seen separately may appear inconsequential, but which together comprise a pattern of female experience that is qualitatively different from that of men. (1994: 84)

In this exploratory study, a naturalistic approach was used to observe some of these "educational moments" in a coeducational classroom at the secondary level of the school system in Jamaica, in an attempt to identify aspects of the gender regime operating in that specific setting. Kessler et al. use the term "gender regime" to describe "the pattern of practices that constructs various kinds of masculinity and femininity among staff and students, orders them in terms of prestige and power and constructs a sexual division of labour within the institution" (1985: 45).

An unobtrusive observer studied 207 Grade 11 students (104 females and 103 males) who had already exercised subject choice options and were preparing for the Caribbean Examinations Council school-leaving examinations. Observations were made across three curriculum areas: physics, a traditionally male-dominated area; English literature, traditionally a female domain; and mathematics, an area in which boys are expected to out-perform girls. These classes were observed in terms of the gendered patterns of participation in these curriculum areas, the pedagogical practices in these classrooms and the sexual politics of teacher-student and student-student interactions.

Observations were made over a two-week period and were used as the basis for follow-up ethnographic focus group discussions with female and male students and teachers of the observed classes. Discussions were unstructured and were used as the means of tapping students' and teachers' interpretations and understandings of how power and control were exerted and negotiated in the classroom setting and the role that sexuality played in the observed interactions. The account that is presented is based on an analysis of the teaching episodes that were observed, as well as the follow-up discussions.

The major limitation of this pilot study was that it was not possible to observe and analyse the way in which social class mediated the observed gender interactions and relations. In order to do this, observations would have to have been made of classrooms in contrasting social class contexts. This would have allowed for a comparative analysis which would point to differences in the gender codes operating in these different social settings. The school in which classes were observed serves a lower middle-class clientele, and one can only assume that the reported observations were mediated by and constructed through the social class subjectivities and realities of those observed.

Analysis and Discussion of the Findings

Curriculum Participation

Even where the sexes are taught in a mixed-sex classroom setting, the methodology, the learning materials and the attitudes of teachers lead students to believe that some subjects are more sex-appropriate than others. Subject choice is therefore a fundamentally important aspect of secondary schooling, particularly in the Jamaican context. As soon as students enter secondary school they learn to associate subject with careers as well as with gender differentiation, and the choices they make at this level have a direct effect on future careers, employment opportunities and adult social roles (Cuffie 1989).

The typical sex-differentiated pattern of participation was evident in the curriculum areas of the coeducational school which was studied. Physics was male dominated, with approximately a 3:1 ratio of males to females, while the reverse was the case for English literature, where the ratio of females to males was 10:3. For mathematics there was a 7:12 ratio in favour of females. Further probing would be required to explain this discrepancy since, in most schools, mathematics is regarded as a core subject that all students must pursue. One possible explanation could be absenteeism on the part of boys on the days that observations were made. The pattern of sex-segregation of the curriculum is so pervasive that it often extends beyond students to the sex of the teacher associated with the respective subject areas. In the case in point, physics and mathematics were taught by male teachers while the English literature teacher was female.

The observed pattern of subject choice is not only shaped by traditional socialization practices on the part of parents and teachers but also by school factors such as cross-timetabling and selection processes. Prerequisites for some subjects also serve as a gender-related barrier. Peer pressure and the fear of a girl being thought of as "masculine and tough" or a boy as being "soft and effeminate" also affect students' choice of subjects – and, ultimately, careers – not considered appropriate to their sex. This, as a matter of course, is very prevalent in mixed school settings where teachers and guidance counsellors may steer students into making "safe" (traditional) subject and career choices (Parry 1996). Generally, therefore, schools replicate the sexist nature of the wider society and make it difficult for the sexes to make unbiased, nontraditional choices of subjects and careers (Bailey 1997b).

Research carried out by Leo-Rhynie (1987) shows that the phenomenon of sex-linked subject choice is most marked in coeducational settings. In single-sex settings girls are more likely to choose subjects that are regarded as "male" than their counterparts in coeducational schools. She attributed this to the positive ways in which girls in single-sex schools are treated in the absence of boys. The same thing, she argues, holds for boys, who are more likely to choose traditional female subjects within the single-sex setting.

Explanations of this observed segregation of the curriculum are often based on arguments of expectations of differing sex-based cognitive abilities. Linn and Peterson (1985) report on research findings on cognitive sex differences and point out that many of the studies have attempted to establish male/female differences on verbal and spatial abilities, but the results have not been uniform so that no definitive conclusions have been reached. What happens, however, is that implicit messages of differential expectations from a number of sources are conveyed to male and female students, who then conform to expectations.

Inequality between males and females in the educational process is so ingrained in the psyche of both students and teachers that it extends even to aspects of classroom life such as the physical location of the two sexes in the classroom and the nature and level of physical contact between the two. In classes taught by male teachers where the seating arrangement was organized by the teacher, the girls were made to sit either at the very back of the room or to the far side. In other classes where the seating arrangement was student organized, the teachers, particularly the male teachers, tended to stand closer to the boys. The latter occurred in five of six observed classes where the teacher was male. According to Stanworth (1981) these classroom encounters, although subtle, contribute to the generation of a sexual hierarchy of worth in which boys emerge as the "naturally" dominant sex.

Classroom Interactions

The pedagogical strategies employed by the teachers reflected distinct gender differences in the terms of the power system operating in the classrooms. In the physics and mathematics classes the male teachers utilized the traditional didactic, authoritarian mode where limited student interaction was accommodated and, where it was allowed, the boys dominated the interactions. The preferred approach was to dispense information from a frontal position and to use male exemplars to illustrate concepts. The female teacher, on the other hand, attempted to use a discussion approach and to allow for greater student participation which is more in keeping with a feminist pedagogical style. In this case girls were more inclined to dominate the discussion, while some of the boys showed total disinterest in these lessons.

One manifestation of the sexual politics of everyday life in school alluded to by radical feminists is that of teachers' attention being unequally divided between the sexes, to the advantage of boys (Acker 1994). Both sexes therefore have an experience of the classroom where boys are the focus of activity and attention. Houston (1994) believes that studies on teacher-student interactions indicate that in coeducational classrooms teachers, regardless of sex, interact more with boys and give boys more attention, and that this intensifies at the secondary level. Patterns observed in the classrooms that were studied suggest that these vary with the curriculum area and the corresponding sex of the teacher.

In the physics classes more questions were asked of and answered by boys. In cases where boys to whom the questions were directed could not respond, the questions were redirected to other boys. More use was also made of ideas initiated by male students. Where girls attempted to participate, their efforts were often drowned out by male voices.

Houston (1994) reports on studies that show that student interactions with one another appear to dampen female participation in mixed-sex classes, and believes that part of the explanation of these classroom inequities may be that the everyday linguistic patterns of how men and women talk in mixed-sex groupings is carried over into the classroom. These studies indicate that generally, in mixed-sex groupings, men talk more than women, for longer periods of time, take more turns at speaking, exert more control over the conversation and interrupt women more than women interrupt men. Men also introduce trivial or inappropriate personal comments that bring a woman's discussion to an end or change its form. In Houston's view the danger of perpetuating this pattern of interaction is twofold. First, male ways of thinking and speaking become equated with intelligence and authority, and second, such a gendered valuation of classroom talk poses special problems for girls who seek to take on ways of talking associated with this assumed intelligence and authority.

In the physics classes, praise and encouragement were directed in more instances to male students, and where one female student was complemented for doing well on a physics test, she was sarcastically referred to as "Miss Genius". No corresponding comment was made to male students, suggesting that girls are not expected to perform creditably in physics, and if they do, this must be a deviation from the norm.

The opinions of boys about the competence of the girls to cope with physics varied. Generally, it was observed that the girls attempted to record information given by the physics teacher whereas the boys did not. When the boys were asked to explain why no record was kept of what transpired in the class, varying explanations were advanced. One boy indicated that on weekends he borrowed a notebook from one of the girls to copy the notes, while another indicated that at the time for a "test" he could get notes from one of the girls. All boys, however, did not hold the girls in such high esteem; some viewed note-taking differently. One boy felt that "some of the girls are sort of slow so that they have to take down every word while the bright boys listen and make sure that nothing is missed". This notion of male cognitive superiority was generally held by the male students, who suggested that they (the boys) were more educated than the girls – and this they based on the fact they could get by without "living" in their books.

As was the case in the physics classes, blatant instances of gender bias and sex-typing were displayed by the mathematics teacher, who expressed great surprise at the good performance of two girls who were ridiculed for their achievement on a piece of work done in class. In respect of this the following statement was made by the teacher to the class: "These girls have never got anything right before and if these two can get it right, this means that everybody else must also have it right. I don't need to look at any more books!" On the other hand, one apparently "slow" boy who had the correct answer for the same problem was praised for trying and for showing improvement. Girls were sarcastically referred to as "budding artists" when diagrams were properly drawn and as "elementary babies" when they were not able to cope with the problems. When a girl admitted to not understanding a concept, the teacher's comment to the class was "What must I do with this joker?" However, when a boy asked a question which reflected that he also did not understand, he was asked if he could hear clearly from where he was sitting and was invited to come closer to the front of the room.

When a question related to the subject matter was initiated by a female student, instead of dealing with it as a serious concern, the teacher used this as an opportunity to openly ridicule her by saying: "Please note class, little Pam Pam has finally asked a question." He then approached the student and placed the back of his hand on her cheek as if checking for a temperature and further commented: "Are you sure that you are feeling alright, my dear? Please don't stress yourself out now!" This intimidation of the girls and open display of sexism by the male teacher was challenged by one of the girls in the class who, after being ridiculed by the teacher, defended herself by saying: "That's why I don't like this class. Whenever I come to class and participate you make it look as if I'm not trying. Sir, you know that I'm not 'bright' in maths and you just keep ridiculing me." This comment was supported by other girls in the class, who obviously shared her view and who muttered in undertones that she was telling the truth.

This stereotyping of female students in terms of their capacity to cope with mathematics is not only a teacher-related behaviour. Findings of studies reported by Stage et al. (1985) show that for mathematics both parents and teachers have higher achievement expectations for high school and college males than for comparable females. Further, it has also been shown that these stereotypes affect students' attitudes and their consideration of math-related options. The overall effect of this stereotyping of girls is that it creates strong negative feelings about the subject that are increasingly difficult to overcome and lead to what has been described as "math anxiety", not only about the subject matter but also about the classroom environment in which the subject is taught. As a result there is now the feeling that women at the college level should be segregated for instruction in these areas and special classes developed to address problems women face in this area of study.

Many of the interactions observed between the male teachers and female students went beyond exchanges related to the subject matter and could be categorized as acts of sexual harassment. Larkin (1994) suggests that for most females, crude language and other forms of sexually harassing behaviour are part of the fabric of daily life. Writers such as Shilling (1996) point to the fact that the school is very much a part of this fabric and a site of harassment for girls. These acts of harassment in school are legitimized on the basis of widely held views of patriarchal norms and attitudes and, according to Larkin, are often given little attention because they have come to be accepted as part and parcel of typical male-female interactions.

In one of the mathematics lessons observed, there was constant bantering between the male teacher and a male student at the expense of a particular girl who controlled her irritation by laughing on most occasions. At two different times, however, the girl asked, "Sir, why don't you leave me alone?" Another girl was constantly referred to as "Girl X", "X" being the name of one of the boys. Remarks were made by the teacher about this girl's size (she is a big-bodied girl) and veiled comments were made about her physique, her breasts and her hairstyle. In the same class, terms such as "sweetheart", "honey" and "dear" were used in responding to girls, whereas boys were consistently referred to as "gentlemen" or "boys".

There was mutual touching between the boy "X" and two female students. The teacher condoned and encouraged this behaviour, as is reflected in the comment made by him: "X, I see you are having great fun. I have no problem with that, but are you sure that you want to have fun for all of us to see? Outside of class may be more private and successful." The girls generally resented this type of behaviour, and in a discussion with the observer they expressed the opinion that "the boys in the class are too friendly". When asked to explain this statement they claimed that "they touch your things, they trouble you, they squeeze you. They touch your hand and call you names like monkey and skettel" (a derogatory term). The female students received no support from the teacher in their attempts to resist this type of behaviour, because when complaints were made about such unwelcome attention they were told that "Only two bears behave like that when they love each other – by pawing and clawing each other." The girls, however, were quite aware of the dynamics of male hegemony operating in the classroom, and assessed the attempts of the male students to exert dominance and control in the following way: "These boys are immature, irresponsible and disgusting. They are male chauvinists, living in a man's world expecting that we should follow whatever they say just because they are men."

Although the girls attempted to resist and contest the system of power and control operating in the classroom environment, not only were these behaviours condoned by the male teacher but, as a member of the patriarchal classroom system, he actively contributed to the situation in a significant way. Larkin (1994) contends that where the sexual harassment that girls experience in schools is tolerated, educators are in fact contributing to the reproduction of a patriarchal society where women are devalued, reviled and mistreated, and where men use violence to express their social domination over women. The outcome is the nurturing of misogynist attitudes and the breeding of a new generation of men who are abusers.

Parry, therefore, is of the opinion that "hegemony, however natural in appearance, is arrived at via the social processes of competition, domination, subordination and resistance. From within this struggle hegemonic masculin-ity emerges as the configuration of gender practice which legitimates patriar-chy and guarantees a dominant position for men alongside the subordination of women" (1996: 78).

The display of hegemonic masculinity was not as evident in the English literature classes as that observed in the physics and mathematics classes. This was no doubt due to the fact that the interactions in these classes were mediated through a female teacher who, as in the typical teacher-student pedagogical relationship, held the dominant power position in the classroom. The teacher admitted that she paid more attention to the boys, who were invariably the lower performers, and justified this on the basis that the girls were generally more prepared and therefore understood the story plots more readily. On the other hand, she bemoaned the fact that she had to constantly help the boys to achieve a level of comprehension of the story line and plot.

Parry (1996) found in her study that skills such as reading, which were not traditionally seen as masculine or "macho", were not coveted by male students, and that this had far-reaching implications for the performance of male students. This is confirmed by the fact that the boys themselves admitted that they did very little reading. One boy commented, "It is not that boys can't read, they just don't like to read." As a result, they were often unable to respond to questions posed by the teacher – but when they were unable to respond, girls whose hands were raised were bypassed and the question redirected to another boy. Boys in these classes, as in the others, were therefore given more attention and encouragement than were the girls, so that even in cases where girls are the dominant group in terms of numbers and ability, the boys are still given more time and attention, both directly and indirectly.

The boys in this study of a coeducational classroom argued that the ways in which they expressed their masculinity were due, in part, to cultural expectations as well as to the attitude displayed towards them by female students and teachers. In the group discussion they contended that "the girls bring down the boys too much and let the boys feel discouraged and the boys therefore think that it makes little sense to bother to try". When asked to explain the meaning of "bringing down the boys" they advanced the following explanation: "They [the girls] tell the boys they are disgusting so why bother to change. If they have us down as disgusting why not just be disgusting. They really don't appreciate us and its not only the girls that say this. Teachers say it. Everybody says it. It is the normal thing for men – men are disgusting and irresponsible. Men are down there. Men are dogs."

This, they claimed, was experienced more in English literature than in science, and they contended that they felt this way in classes where discussion was used as the main pedagogical strategy but that they were more relaxed in classes with a "practical" orientation.

Conclusion

This account of the nature of curriculum participation and classroom interactions in a mixed-sex, secondary level Jamaican classroom clearly illustrates the ways in which gender struggles are waged and lived out in the educational setting as well as how gender identity and masculinity and femininity are negotiated, constructed and maintained in the social context of classrooms. It also points to the contra positions taken by the sexes in these negotiations in contrasting epistemological discourses.

The "educational moments" which are presented indicate a clearly defined gender regime with strong classification and framing operating in the observed classrooms. The manifestations of femininity and masculinity, however, varied within this regime, depending on the specific context in which the observations were made. The observed patterns of interaction were therefore not static but depended on the particular "educational moment" under scrutiny.

In the traditionally male-dominated areas of physics and mathematics, the typical male/female hierarchy was evident, with the boys displaying the expected "macho" type masculinity and the girls, more often than not, being the subject of open acts of harassment, and occupying the typical subordinate position within the pedagogical relationships. In these classes sexuality therefore played a significant role in shaping the relationships.

In the context of the literature classes, the converse was the case with the boys being less "macho", being less openly antagonistic towards the girls but presenting themselves as "victims" who, instead of taking responsibility for their behaviour, claimed that it was precipitated by the attitude of females towards them. This represents a typical male response to a situation in which it is perceived that their position of power is being usurped and is at risk.

Alternative masculinities and femininities were evident from one time of making observations to another and were dependent on the particular "educational moment" being observed. It is evident that the particular form of masculinity and femininity displayed at any given time were mediated by a nexus of interrelated factors, including the nature of the discourse, the sex of the teacher, the pedagogical strategies employed and the pedagogical relationships between teacher and student and student and student.

These findings corroborate findings by other researchers. Ghaill (1996: 11) examines schooling as a masculinizing agency in the British context and points to the centrality of the official curriculum in making available different versions of masculinity – and, I would argue, different versions of femininity – that students can inhabit. He postulates that feminist deconstructionist theory has been important in moving beyond social reproduction models that assume that teachers and students are unitary subjects occupying predictable power positions. Ghaill (1996: 11) refers to the work of Walderdine (1990), who describes how teachers and students "are not unitary subjects uniquely positioned, but are produced as a nexus of subjectivities in relations of power which are constantly shifting, rendering them at one moment powerful and at another powerless". On this basis Ghaill argues that there is a range of positions that may be occupied within different contradictory discourses, which is useful in understanding the contextual specificity of young heterosexual males (and females) learning to be men (and women) within a school arena.

The gender regime operating in a school setting is not static, but shifts in accordance with a number of frame factors that are themselves dynamic. Any study of how the school functions in constructing and maintaining gender ideologies and gender relations is not as clear-cut as much of the existing discourse would lead one to believe. Studying this phenomenon is therefore theoretically as well as methodologically complex and demands an approach to research design and theorizing which allows for the pluralities of the situation to be taken into account.

References

Acker, S. 1994. *Gendered Education: Sociological Reflections on Women, Teaching and Feminism.* Toronto: Ontario Institute for Studies in Education.

Arnot, Madeline. 1994. "Male Hegemony, Social Class and Women's Education". In *The Education Feminism Reader,* edited by L. Stone. London: Routledge.

Ashenden, D., R.W. Connell, and G.W. Dowsett. 1995. "Gender Relations in Secondary Schooling". *Sociology of Education* 58.

Bailey, Barbara. 1997a. "Women's Education: the Caribbean Situation". Paper presented at CARICOM/ECLAC/UNIFEM Caribbean Sub-regional Ministerial Conference, Georgetown, Guyana, in preparation for the Seventh Regional Conference on the Integration of Women into the Economic and Social Development of Latin America and the Caribbean.

_____. 1997b. "Sexist Patterns of Formal and Non-Formal Education Programmes: The Case of Jamaica". In *Gender: A Caribbean Multidisciplinary Perspective,* edited by E. Leo-Rhynie, B. Bailey, and C. Barrow. Kingston, Jamaica: Ian Randle Publishers.

Barriteau, Eudine. Forthcoming. "Theorizing Gender Systems and the Project of Modernity in the Twentieth-Century Caribbean". In *The Culture of Gender and Sexuality in the Caribbean,* edited by L. Lewis. Michigan: University of Michigan Press.

Bernstein, Basil. 1970. "Elaborated and Restricted Codes: Their Social Origins and Some Consequences". In *Readings in Child Socialisation,* edited by K. Danziger. Oxford: Pergamon.

Bowles, S., and H. Gintis. 1976. *Schooling in Capitalist America.* London: Routledge and Kegan Paul.

Burgess, Robert G. 1986. *Sociology, Education and Schools.* London: B.T. Batsford.

Cuffie, J. 1989. "Gender and Subject Choice in Secondary Schools". Paper presented at a gender and education seminar, Women and Development Studies and Faculty of Education, University of the West Indies, Mona.

Diamond, Anne. 1991. "Gender and Education: Public Policy and Pedagogic Practice". *British Journal of Sociology of Education* 12, no. 2.

Economic Commission for Latin America and the Caribbean/United Nations Development Fund for Women (ECLAC/UNIFEM). 1995. *Regional Programme of Action for Women of Latin America and the Caribbean, 1995–2001.* Santiago: United Nations.

Ghaill, Mairtin. 1996. *The Making of Men: Masculinities, Sexualities and Schooling.* London: Open University Press.

Houston, Barbara. 1994. "Should Public Education Be Gender Free?" In *The Education Feminism Reader,* edited by L. Stone. New York: Routledge.

Kessler et al. 1985. "Gender Relations in Secondary Schooling". *Sociology of Education* 58.

Larkin, June. 1994. "Walking through Walls: The Sexual Harassment of High School Girls". *Gender and Education* 6, no. 3.

Leo-Rhynie, Elsa. 1987. "Educational Opportunities for Jamaican Female Students: A Contemporary Perspective". Paper presented at a gender and education seminar, Women and Development Studies and Faculty of Education, University of the West Indies, Mona.

Linn, M.C., and A.C. Peterson. 1985. "Facts and Assumptions about the Nature of Sex Differences". In *Handbook of Achieving Sex Equity through Education,* edited by S.S. Klein. Baltimore: Johns Hopkins University Press.

Noddings, Nellie. 1992. "Gender and the Curriculum". In *Handbook of Research on Curriculum,* edited by R. Jackson. London: Macmillan.

Parry, Odette. 1996. "Sex and Gender Constructions in the Jamaican Classroom". *Social and Economic Studies* 45, no. 4.

Shilling, Chris. 1991. "Social Space, Gender Inequalities and Educational Differentiation". *British Journal of Sociology of Education* 12, no. 1.

Stage, E.K., et al. 1985. "Increasing the Participation and Achievement of Girls and Women in Mathematics, Science and Engineering". In *Handbook for Achieving Sex Equity through Education,* edited by S.S. Klein. Baltimore: Johns Hopkins University Press.

Stanworth, M. 1981. *Gender and Schooling: A Study of Sexual Divisions in the Classroom.* London: Unwin Hyman.

Stromquist, Nellie P. 1990. "Gender Inequality in Education: Accounting for Women's Subordination". *British Journal of Sociology of Education* 11, no. 2.

Young, Michael F.D. 1971. "An Approach to the Study of Curricula as Socially Organised Knowledge". In *Knowledge and Control: New Directions for the Sociology of Education,* edited by M. Young. London: Collier Macmillan.

Weiner, G. 1994. *Feminisms in Education: An Introduction.* Buckingham: Open University Press.

10 Gender Issues in Science Education

PETER WHITELEY

Introduction

Many now argue that science and science education are not as gender neutral as popularly believed. This paper presents data that suggests the existence of gender-related inequalities in science education in the Caribbean. Relevant research into factors that may be contributing to these inequalities, both from the region and elsewhere, is then surveyed.

Kelly (1987) has suggested that science can be seen as masculine in at least four distinct ways. First, in terms of numbers: in the numbers who study science, who teach it, who are recognized as scientists and who practise science professionally or have careers in the applied sciences such as in engineering. Second, in terms of the way in which science is presented in resource materials, in the examples cited and the applications included. Third, in the classroom behaviours and interactions, which tend to confirm stereotypes previously developed and accepted in the culture outside of the classroom. Finally, Kelly (1987) puts forward an epistemological argument that thought in science embodies an intrinsically masculine world view. Given the "constructivist" nature of knowledge, all the foregoing leads science itself to be masculine.

These issues are important, as the gender stereotypes associated with science place restrictions on individuals. All gender stereotypes can be damaging, and if the choices made by male or female students are limited by what the students (or others) consider "suitable" then the individual's potential is unlikely to be developed to the full. Stereotyping may keep boys out of French, biology and home economics and girls out of engineering and plumbing. Stereotyping therefore reduces liberty, and both the individual and society lose from such a restriction of talent.

Girls' and women's underinvolvement in science is of particular concern. A knowledge of science and the possession of science-related qualifications allow individuals to obtain jobs which are often secure, well paid and with higher than average status. Such jobs may further lead to greater power and influence in a society (Kelly 1987).

Not all who obtain science qualifications will use these directly in their jobs. Science is an important component of general education, and people are disadvantaged by being excluded. Science education can give a sense of control rather than a feeling of being at the mercy of the technology. Further, technology is a powerful force in our societies and its use and development is presently controlled by men. Women's voices need to be heard to a greater degree in scientific and technological discussions – such participation needs to be informed by knowledge of the science and technology involved.

Morris (1991) notes that cross-national research has consistently demonstrated the higher attainment of boys than girls in the physical sciences. In her research Morris used Caribbean examination data for the period 1987–89. She found significant differences, in favour of the male candidates, between the performance of male and female candidates for the biology and physics examinations of the Caribbean Examinations Council (CXC), with small differences in chemistry. She noted the very different entry patterns of the males and the females, with considerably greater numbers of males than females entering for physics, the reverse being true for biology, and approximately equal numbers of each entering for chemistry.

This paper presents data on the results of science examinations in the Caribbean at both the secondary and tertiary levels. It is only in recent years that data arranged according to gender have consistently become available, either from the examination boards that serve the Caribbean or from other regional institutions. Lack of complete data prevented the tracing of a particular cohort from, say, Grade 10 (fourth form) through to introductory courses at university. The decision was made to adopt a cross-sectional approach, and it is hoped that the picture that emerges might guide further investigation.

Science Examinations in the Caribbean

Barbados, Jamaica, and Trinidad and Tobago are the territories for which data was obtained. They all used to be colonies of Britain and obtained their independence in the 1960s. Their education systems are derived from a British model in which high school students are entered for examinations, external to the schools, at the end of both Grade 11 (fifth form) and Grade 13 (upper sixth form). Students in Grades 10 and 11 in secondary schools in the region now follow syllabi published by the CXC[1] and then sit examinations, at the end of Grade 11, which are set and marked by the CXC. Much smaller numbers progress to the two-year Advanced (A) level courses of the Cambridge (England) examination board and then sit the A level examinations at the end of Grade 13. Most of the students who are successful in the A level examinations enter the University of the West Indies (UWI).

The participation in and results for the 1994 CXC examinations are considered for the three selected territories; between them they provide about 80 percent of the total entry for each of the CXC biology, chemistry and physics examinations each year. Data for the A level sciences are also presented, along with data on the introductory courses in science at UWI. Data on the numbers of students graduating from science- and technology-related faculties of UWI are then considered. Information was obtained from the Registry on the Mona campus of the UWI, the Cambridge Local Examinations Syndicate and the CXC. The data utilized were for 1994 for secondary schools and for the 1993–94 academic year for UWI.

CXC Examinations

Most secondary schools in the Caribbean enter students for the CXC examinations for the separate sciences, physics, chemistry and biology. At the time this study was undertaken, Grade I and II were designed to represent a standard sufficient to allow further study of the discipline, and these grades were generally considered to be "passes". Recently the grading system was modified so that Grade III is now also considered a pass. Tables 10.1, 10.2 and 10.3 present the 1994 results for biology, chemistry and physics, respectively.

There are similarities among the territories in the percentage of pass rates, which are lowest in biology and highest in physics. In Jamaica this appears to

Table 10.1   CXC Biology Examination Results, 1994, by Territory and Gender

		Entries	Grades I/II
Barbados	Male	297	86 (29.0%)
	Female	441	166 (37.6%)
Jamaica	Male	908	270 (29.7%)
	Female	1,651	457 (27.7%)
Trinidad and Tobago	Male	2,144	818 (38.2%)
	Female	2,694	1,109 (41.2%)

Table 10.2   CXC Chemistry Examination Results, 1994, by Territory and Gender

		Entries	Grades I/II
Barbados	Male	271	115 (42.4%)
	Female	318	135 (42.5%)
Jamaica	Male	906	342 (37.7%)
	Female	899	317 (35.3%)
Trinidad and Tobago	Male	1,805	789 (43.7%)
	Female	1,656	785 (47.4%)

Table 10.3   CXC Physics Examination Results, 1994, by Territory and Gender

		Entries	Grades I/II
Barbados	Male	251	162 (64.5%)
	Female	225	136 (60.4%)
Jamaica	Male	1,043	462 (44.3%)
	Female	530	258 (48.7%)
Trinidad and Tobago	Male	1,732	941 (54.3%)
	Female	980	532 (54.3%)

result in part from a policy of entering the less able students for biology in the (mistaken) belief that it is "easier" than physics or chemistry. Differences in the size and nature of the candidate population in the three subjects would, however, need to be known and considered to make valid comparisons among them.

There are also considerable differences in the size of the age cohort in Barbados, Jamaica, and Trinidad and Tobago which need to be taken into account for comparisons among the territories to be useful and valid; the age cohorts in the three territories are approximately 4,200, 58,000 and 22,000, respectively. Using this data it can be shown that the pass rate as a proportion of the age cohort is similar in Barbados and Trinidad and Tobago but far lower in Jamaica. For example, in physics, about one in eighty obtain a Grade I or II in Jamaica, one in fourteen reach this standard in Barbados and one in fifteen in Trinidad and Tobago. Some students in Jamaican schools are still entered for the British Ordinary (O) level science examinations – when the students passing these examinations are added into the figures for Jamaica the pass rate in the age cohort becomes one in sixty-five in Jamaica. This has been analysed in detail by Whiteley (1993).

Gender differences in participation in the three sciences by high school students are clear; overall, chemistry appears to be equally attractive and accessible to both genders, whereas biology is a "girls' subject" and physics a "boys' subject". This is better appreciated by determining the male to female ratios for the entry and pass numbers. These are presented in Table 10.4.

Table 10.4   Male/Female Ratio, Entry/Pass Numbers, by Territory and Discipline, 1994

	Biology	Chemistry	Physics
Barbados			
Entry	0.67	0.85	1.12
Pass	0.52	0.85	1.19
Jamaica			
Entry	0.55	1.01	1.97
Pass	0.59	1.08	1.79
Trinidad and Tobago			
Entry	0.80	1.09	1.77
Pass	0.74	1.01	1.77

Although it can be seen that in Jamaica the polarization in biology and physics is somewhat greater than either of the other two territories, and in Barbados physics is close to a "neutral" subject, there is reasonable similarity among the three territories.

If one accepts that career opportunities are likely to be restricted for individuals who choose, for whatever reason, not to pursue certain subjects, then the imbalance in participation rates in both physics and biology is cause for concern. The lack of a qualification in physics, in particular, may result in greater difficulties, as this denies entry into a range of technological and engineering careers. The lack of the equivalent qualification in biology does not appear to be similarly restricting: medically related programmes, such as nursing, often allow entry with a science other than biology.

Advanced Level Examinations

A similar pattern to that at the CXC level is found in the A level science examination results. The relevant data for Jamaica is presented in Table 10.5.

In Table 10.5 the ratios are higher than the equivalent ratios at CXC in all cases, suggesting that the A level sciences are particularly "male-friendly" in the Caribbean. In Britain, Goldstein and Thomas (1996) have shown that males make more progress than females while enrolled in A level courses. The fact that the male-to-female pass ratio for physics is lower in Table 10.5 than the entry ratio indicates that the female entry is obtaining a higher percentage pass rate. This has also been found elsewhere (Elwood and Comber 1996), and it has been suggested that this effect may be understood as a consequence of the female students in the A level classes being of higher average ability and motivation than the male students.

Table 10.5:   Male/Female Ratios for Entries and Pass Numbers, Jamaica, 1993–1994

	Biology	Chemistry	Physics
Entries	0.69	1.27	2.72
Passes	0.79	1.42	1.85

UWI Examinations

All three campuses of UWI award degrees in the natural sciences and medical sciences whereas only the St Augustine campus, in Trinidad, awards engineering degrees. Although the students on each campus come mainly from the territory in which the campus is situated, a student may register on a campus other than that of his or her country of origin. Thus, in the following analysis the country of origin of the student is used rather than reference being made to the "campus" results. Table 10.6 presents the number of first degrees awarded in 1994 in natural sciences, medical sciences and engineering to students from Barbados, Jamaica, and Trinidad and Tobago, with the data being collated from the three campuses.

The overwhelming numerical male dominance in engineering is immediately obvious and, in this writer's view, is an issue that needs to be addressed. The greater numbers of female graduates than male graduates in the natural sciences, for both Jamaican and Trinidadian students, is interesting. The female Jamaican students obtained degrees majoring mainly in the biological sciences or chemistry; the male Jamaican students majored in electronics or pure physics for the most part. As a reasonable proportion of UWI graduates find employment in the secondary school system, this distribution of graduates leads to most physics teachers in Jamaica being male and most biology teachers being female. This may be one factor which influences the students' perception of the "gender" of the discipline.

There are significantly greater proportions of male medical graduates than female medical graduates in both the Barbadian and Trinidadian groups. The

Table 10.6:   First Degrees in Natural Sciences, Medical Sciences, Engineering by Origin of Student and Gender, 1994

	Natural Sciences		Medical Sciences		Engineering	
	Male	Female	Male	Female	Male	Female
Barbados	38	24	11	4	11	3
Jamaica	90	121	36	38	46	8
Trinidad and Tobago	68	99	52	30	97	21

Table 10.7:   Introductory Science Courses, University of the West Indies, Mona, 1993–1994

		Entries	Passes
Biology	Male	53	34 (64%)
	Female	66	54 (82%)
Chemistry	Male	141	94 (67%)
	Female	163	113 (69%)
Physics	Male	148	83 (56%)
	Female	50	29 (58%)

students from these territories generally enter the medical faculty from A level, which is one factor that leads to this higher number of males. There is, however, a gender equality in the numbers of Jamaican students graduating from the Faculty of Medical Sciences. Transfers from the Faculty of Natural Sciences after completing the introductory courses contribute to this. Women are as likely to transfer from the Faculty of Natural Sciences as be admitted directly after the A level examinations. The registrations in these courses at the Mona campus of UWI in 1993–94 are displayed in Table 10.7.

The higher number of registrations in chemistry than biology or physics is a consequence of the fact that a good grade in chemistry is compulsory for transfer to the Faculty of Medical Sciences. Chemistry also has a higher number of female students registering and being successful than male students. The Department of Physics is the only department on the Mona campus of UWI in which male students are in the majority.

Discussion

The data presented above shows that the participation and performance of students of science in the Caribbean are linked to the gender of the student and are similar to the data obtained elsewhere (Kelly 1987; Bazler and Simonis 1991). These differences may be interpreted as implying a "gender bias". It is useful to note two possible meanings that have been attached to this term. Stobart, Elward and Quinlan (1992) point out that an absence of bias may be judged in terms of equality of access or equality of outcome. Flew supports the former understanding: "The equality which justice demands is not a substantial equality of outcome, either for individuals or for sets, but rather a formal equality of treatment for all relevantly like cases" (1986: 16).

An alternative perspective assumes that the distribution of talent is random in the population, and in different groups within it, leading to the expectation that equality of opportunity would be indicated by the different groups achieving equal success rates (Gillborn 1990).

Research has looked for reasons for the underparticipation or performance of girls in science education and for the lower numbers of females that choose science and science-related careers. An early focus was on individual attitudes and personality traits; sometimes there was a tendency to blame the victim – the conclusion would be that the girls had to change!

Now other reasons are being explored in the belief that causes lie within science, schools or society at large. Consideration may be given to the students' or teachers' behaviour, both inside and outside the classroom, or analysis made of curricula, assessment practices, textual materials and so on. Some of the results of such research in the Caribbean and elsewhere are now outlined and discussed. While it is recognized that this is an area of research that may be strongly culture-specific, it is hoped that the results of work outside the region may help to illuminate the situation in the Caribbean and suggest lines for research here.

Examinations

Perhaps the most obvious site of possible bias is in the examinations themselves. Murphy (1988) suggests that it is now generally accepted that gender differences in examination performance should represent real differences in educational achievement. Any differences should not be a consequence of bias in the items or the format of the examinations. For example, the style of assessment has been shown to affect the relative performance of males and females. Research in several disciplines suggests that boys do better on multiple-choice items (Murphy 1982; Bolger and Kellaghan 1990) and practical tests (Murphy 1988) while girls perform relatively better on free-response items (Bolger and Kellaghan 1990) and coursework (Fawcett Society n.d.; Cresswell 1990), although the type of coursework may be an important factor (Quinlan 1991). Thus it might be possible to affect gender differences in examination performance by varying the format of the examination, but such variation would then raise questions as to the validity of the examination. Stobart, Elwood and Quinlan (1992) argue against the manipulation of assessment schemes in order to obtain a gender equality of outcome, but recommend the active investigation of the demands made by syllabi and modes of assessment in relation to gender differences.

Other research has investigated and compared procedures that may be used to identify gender differences or bias in specific items on science examinations (Sudweeks and Tolman 1993). It appears that possible gender bias in examinations could be a fruitful area for investigation in the Caribbean.

Schools and Science Classrooms

Whiteley (1995) has investigated the performance of physics students in Jamaica and Trinidad and Tobago. A pattern has emerged that is similar to that identified by Hamilton (1985); boys and girls in single-sex schools do better than their counterparts in coeducational schools, and boys do better than girls in coeducational schools. The reasons for these findings are complex. It has been argued that being in a single-sex school in itself may contribute to a greater proportion of the girls pursuing the sciences, particularly physics, and to the higher level of performance in those subjects (Hamilton 1985). An alternative explanation may be the fact that single-sex schools in the Caribbean often have a higher status than coeducational schools. Thus they may attract the more able students from homes with a higher socioeconomic level, as well as being able to attract and retain better qualified teachers; Whiteley's (1995) data supports these inferences.

Work outside the Caribbean has centred on science classrooms and the attitudes and behaviour of the teachers towards boys and girls in their classes. Shephardson and Pizzini (1992) used a sample of forty-two female elementary (primary) teachers in Iowa and found a gender bias in the perception of the scientific ability of students. Boys were perceived to possess more cognitive scientific skills than girls. Shephardson and Pizzini (1992) suggest that this may result in a differential educational treatment of boys and girls, and that such a bias may result in the communication of a negative message to girls concerning their scientific ability. It should be noted that their sample of teachers was exclusively female – perhaps male teachers possess different perceptions – but given the relatively small numbers of male primary teachers in much of the Caribbean these results may point to an issue that needs investigation here.

The Assessment of Performance Unit in Britain (APU 1981–84) found no significant differences in the knowledge that boys and girls bring to secondary school science from the primary school. On the other hand, significant differences were found in the attitudes and interests of students leaving primary school, which appeared to predispose boys towards the physical sciences and the girls towards the biological sciences later in their school lives. There is also evidence that girls at the primary level may experience fewer scientific activities in school than boys, although they have similar levels of interest at that age (Kahle and Lakes 1983). Coulthard (1990) notes that the expectations of the boys seem to lead to an assumed dominance wherever tools or electrical equipment are being used. In mixed groups in primary schools, this may lead to the girls missing out on many experiences.

Crossman (1987) used a modified form of the Flanders's Interaction Instrument (Flanders 1970) in a study of third-year biology and physics classes in a British secondary school. She found that, overall, there was one and a half times as much communication between the boys and the teachers than between the girls and the teachers. Hildebrand is reported to have found a similar pattern (Kahle 1988). The global picture, however, conceals the fact that the imbalance in communication found by Crossman was greater for female teachers than male teachers and greater in physics classes than in biology classes. In addition, the boys were found to talk and answer more questions than the girls as well as obtaining higher achievement scores. Crossman notes that one does not know whether the boys' talking more causes greater achievement, or a higher level of achievement leads to more talk. She suggests that the difference between biology and physics teachers' behaviour may be one factor that influences the subject choices made and the level of achievement attained. An interesting point that emerged from this work was that the female teachers who actually favoured the boys stated that they either made a special effort to include and encourage the girls or made no distinction. Generally the teachers seemed unaware of any imbalance in their communication patterns. Work in Jamaica (Soyibo and Whiteley 1994) has suggested the existence of gender-related differences in teachers' behaviour towards the boys and girls in high school science classes.

Kahle (1988: 257) notes research which has shown boys "dominating discussions" and "hogging resources" in science classes. Boys are reported to be asked more higher-order questions than are girls (Tobin and Gallagher 1987), and boys are more likely to be encouraged to "try harder" when unsuccessful (Kahle 1988).

Teachers may use examples of applied science that are of greater interest to boys than to girls. Jones and Kirk (1990) have shown that considerable differences may exist between the interests of male and female students. Sjoberg (1989) reports similar differences in interest, which increase with age. Perhaps teachers unwittingly deter girls from pursuing physics by their choice of exemplars.

Goddard-Spear's (1987) work has shown that some teachers award significantly higher marks, on a range of criteria, for written work that is believed to be the work of a boy than for identical work which is believed to be from a girl. The teachers also possessed higher expectations for boys than for girls. Gipps and Murphy (1994) point to the possibility of assessor (that is, the teacher) bias in the marking of coursework.

Returning to work conducted in the Caribbean, Hamilton (1984) investigated the attitudes of Jamaican fifth-form students towards "women in science". Girls in single-sex schools reported a more favourable view of women in science than girls in coeducational schools. By contrast, boys in single-sex schools had much more negative attitudes towards women in science than all the girls. No significant gender-related difference was found between the attitudes of boys and girls in coeducational schools. Hamilton suggests that the school type may influence attitudes of both boys and girls towards the sciences, and speculates whether the girls' exposure to appropriate role models is greater in all-girls schools. In other work, Hamilton (1982) highlighted the important role that a positive attitude towards science may play in the examination performance of female students.

A small pilot study in Jamaica (Bailey and Leo-Rhynie 1994) investigated the factors affecting the option choices of Jamaican high school students. They reported that the boys seemed to have had a freer choice than the girls, that parents were the greatest influence on the choices and that the perceived mathematical component of the sciences tended to deter students, and girls in particular, from choosing the sciences. In recent work, Lightbody and Durndell (1996) discuss the complex interactions among the sex-stereotyping of occupational roles, self-concept and self-stereotyping. They suggest that the sex-stereotyping of science and technology may be a symptom of the lack of female participation rather than the cause. They further argue that female school leavers may know exactly what they want and that careers in the physical sciences and technology do not meet their requirements and thus are not chosen. This argument would have significant implications for any approach taken to increase the numbers of females in science and technology.

Images of Science

Elsewhere much work has been reported that has investigated gender bias in science textbooks (see, for example, Potter and Rosser 1992; Bazler and Simonis 1991; Powell and Garcia 1985; Taylor 1979). Potter and Rosser claim, however, that although overt sexism has largely been eliminated, more subtle forms of sexism may still be detected. Whiteley (1995) has found a "male bias" in the integrated science textbooks used in the lower forms of Caribbean secondary schools and a similar bias in CXC physics textbooks (Whiteley 1996). These findings along with the results of the work, at the primary level, of Douglas-Smith (1995) suggest that Jamaican and other Caribbean students are exposed to a gender bias in their science textbooks throughout their school careers. Given the greater sensitivity to these issues that now exists amongst authors and publishers it is to be hoped that as new textbooks are published or new editions produced, the text and illustrations will reflect a better gender balance, as well as perhaps helping to challenge some of the gender-related stereotypes that now exist. Due to the relatively small market, however, textbooks in the Caribbean are not frequently revised.

The focus of other research has been the image of science and scientists in broader contexts. Kahle cites the verbal descriptions of scientists by students as including "a man in white coat, with bald head and glasses", "he does appear in some way crazy", "[scientists] don't care about appearance [or] . . . meals", "They just seem to care about their science work" (1988: 249–50). Research in which subjects are asked to draw scientists has also repeatedly indicated an image of a white male with laboratory coat and glasses (Schibeci 1986; Chambers 1983; as well as Mason 1986 and Gardner 1986, both cited in

Kahle 1988), although in recent work Matthews (1996) presents data that suggest that boys and girls in Britain are moving towards less stereotypical views of scientists. Little research has been reported in the Caribbean in this area, although exploratory work by education students at the UWI in Trinidad and Tobago in 1994 suggests that the findings might be similar if such work were carried out.

Societal Expectations and Cultural Stereotypes

Stereotypical images may be the cumulative result of several influences such as fiction books, television series, mass media, cartoons and, within schools, the science teacher's gender, behaviour and personality, along with the influence of textbooks used (Sjoberg 1989). Sjoberg also notes the image of a "humane biologist" and an "inhumane physicist". Secondary school students considered a biologist as caring and open while a physicist was selfish and closed (as well as boring and unartistic – biologists were considered "neutral" on these traits). Such images may well influence the choices made by these students.

Girls are said to view science careers as masculine and, therefore, to avoid them (Matyas 1985). The traditional "female" qualities of gentleness, quietness, tenderness, subjectivity and emotionality are not associated with scientists. Men are associated with aggressiveness, dominance, rationality, independence, unemotionality and objectivity – and some of these characteristics are associated with scientists. It may be that when girls are choosing science courses in coeducational schools, they are viewed as (relative) nonconformists. Levin, Sabar and Libman (1991) cite strong evidence of culture stereotyping of the female role and career orientation which guides choices. Further, in Jamaica and elsewhere in the Caribbean, perhaps it is not easy for girls to cope as a small minority in a physics class. Matyas (1985) also points to the dearth of role models for girls in the scientific and technological community in the United States; a similar situation appears to exist in the Caribbean.

Differences in attitudes and expectations between girls and boys may be generated partly by different extracurricular and home experiences. Levin, Sabar and Libman (1991) note research that attributes girls' lower performance in sciences to lower parental expectations and encouragement, which leads to fewer opportunities to explore scientific phenomena at home. Matyas (1985) has shown that American girls participate less in extracurricular science activities and Sjoberg (1989) found similar differences between Norwegian boys' and girls' participation; both these authors noted that the differences increased with age.

These culturally based stereotypes and expectations are hard to change; perhaps a first step is to sensitize educators, at all levels, to the issues. That there is far to go in the Caribbean may be inferred from the comments of the dean of the Faculty of Natural Sciences at the opening of the Gender, Science and Technology seminar held at UWI (Mona) in February 1994. The dean held that there was "no problem" in his faculty because, overall, the registrations were approximately equally male and female. His views are reportedly shared by most of the faculty members in the Mona campus Department of Physics (all male); it is also noteworthy that, in 1993–94, sixty-seven of the eighty faculty members in the Faculty of Natural Sciences in Jamaica were male.

Note

1.   The Caribbean Examinations Council is a regional examination board that sets examinations for Grade 11 high school students in sixteen territories across the Caribbean.

References

Assessment of Performance Unit (APU). 1981–84. *Age 11: Reports 1, 2, 3 and 4.* London: Her Majesty's Stationery Office.

Bailey, B., and E. Leo-Rhynie. 1994. "Factors Affecting the Choice of Science Subjects by High School Students: A Pilot Study". Paper presented at the seminar Gender, Science and Technology, University of the West Indies, Mona, Jamaica.

Bazler, J.A., and D.A. Simonis. 1991. "Are High School Chemistry Textbooks Gender Fair?" *Journal of Research in Science Teaching* 28.

Bolger, N., and T. Kellaghan. 1990. "Method of Measurement and Gender Differences in Scholastic Achievement". *Journal of Educational Measurement* 27.

Chambers, D.W. 1983. "Stereotypic Images of the Scientist: The Draw-a-Scientist Test". *Science Education* 67.

Coulthard, J. 1990. "What's Stopping the Girls?" *Primary Science Review* 13.

Cresswell, M. 1990. "Gender Effects in GCSE: Some Initial Analyses". Paper presented to a Nuffield Seminar, Institute of Education, University of London.

Crossman, M. 1987. "Teachers' Interactions with Girls and Boys in Science Lessons". In *Science for Girls?* edited by A. Kelly. Milton Keynes: Open University Press.

Douglas-Smith, J. 1995. "An Analysis of Selected Primary School Science Texts to Determine Their Level of Suitability". Master's thesis, University of the West Indies, Mona.

Elwood, J., and C. Comber. 1996. "Gender Differences in 'A' Level Examinations: New Complexities or Old Stereotypes?" *British Journal of Curriculum Assessment* 6, no. 2.

Fawcett Society. N.d. *Exams for the Boys.* London: Fawcett Society.

Flanders, N. 1970. *Analysing Teaching Behavior.* New York: Addison Wesley.

Flew, A. 1986. "Clarifying the Concepts". In *Anti-Racism: An Assault on Education and Value,* edited by F. Palmer. London: Sherwood Press.

Gillborn, D. 1990. *Race, Ethnicity and Education: Teaching and Learning in Multi-ethnic Schools.* London: Unwin Hyman.

Gipps, C., and P. Murphy. 1994. *A Fair Test?* Buckingham: Open University Press.

Goddard-Spear, M. 1987. "The Biasing Influence of Pupil Sex in a Science Marking Exercise". In *Science for Girls?* edited by A. Kelly. Milton Keynes: Open University Press.

Goldstein, G., and S. Thomas. 1982. "Using Examination Results as Indicators of School and College Performances". *Journal of the Royal Statistical Society* 159.

Hamilton, M. 1982. "Jamaican Students' Attitudes to Science as it Relates to Achievement in External Examinations". *Science Education* 66.

_____. 1984. "The Attitudes of Older Jamaican Adolescents to Women in Science". *Journal of Education in Science for Trinidad and Tobago* 11, no. 3.

_____. 1985. "Performance Levels in Science and Other Subjects for Jamaican Adolescents Attending Single-Sex and Co-Educational High Schools". *Science Education* 69.

Jones, A.T., and C.M. Kirk. 1990. "Gender Differences in Students' Interests in Applications of School Physics". *Physics Education* 25.

Kahle, J.B. 1988. "Gender and Science Education II". In *Development and Dilemmas in Science Education,* edited by P. Fensham. Lewes: Falmer Press.

Kahle, J.B., and M.K. Lakes. 1993. "The Myth of Equality in Science Classrooms". *Journal of Research in Science Teaching* 20.

Kelly, A., ed. 1987. *Science for Girls.* Milton Keynes: Open University Press.

Levin, T., N. Sabar, and Z. Libman. 1991. "Achievements and Attitudinal Patterns of Boys and Girls in Science". *Journal of Research in Science Teaching* 28.

Lightbody, P., and A. Durndell. 1996. "Gendered Career Choice: Is Sex-Stereotyping the Cause or the Consequence?" *Educational Studies* 22.

Matthews, B. 1996. "Drawing Scientists". *Gender and Education* 8.

Matyas, M.L. 1985. "Factors Affecting Female Achievement and Interest in Science and Scientific Careers". In *Women in Science: A Report from the Field,* edited by J.B. Kahle. Philadelphia: Falmer Press.

Morris, J. 1991. "Gender Differences in Educational Achievement". In *Proceedings of the Cross-Campus Conference on Education,* complied by E. Brandon and P. Nissen. Kingston, Jamaica: University of the West Indies.

Murphy, R. 1982. "Sex Differences in Objective Test Performance". *British Journal of Educational Psychology* 52.

_____. 1988. "Gender and Assessment". *Curriculum* 9.

Potter, E.F., and S.V. Rosser. 1992. "Factors in Life Science Textbooks that May Deter Girls' Interest in Science". *Journal of Research in Science Teaching* 29.

Powell, R.R., and J. Garcia. 1985. "The Portrayal of Minorities and Women in Selected Elementary Science Series". *Journal of Research in Science Teaching* 22.

Quinlan, M. 1991. "Gender Differences in Examination Performance". Typescript, ULSEB/LEAG.

Schibeci, R.A. 1986. "Images of Science and Scientists and Science Education". *Science Education* 70.

Shephardson, D.P., and E.L. Pizzini. 1992. "Gender Bias in Female Elementary Teachers' Perceptions of the Scientific Ability of Students". *Science Education* 76.

Sjoberg, S. 1989. "Gender and the Image of Science". In *Adolescent Development and School Science,* edited by P. Adey. Lewes: Falmer Press.

Soyibo, K., and P. Whiteley. 1994. "Gender Differences in Students' Perceptions of the Democratization of Science Classes". Paper presented at Third Cross-Campus Conference of the Faculty of Education, University of the West Indies, Cave Hill, Barbados.

Stobart, G., J. Elwood, and M. Quinlan. 1992. "Gender Bias in Examinations: How Equal Are the Opportunities?" *British Educational Research Journal* 18.

Sudweeks, R.R., and R.R. Tolman. 1993. "Empirical Versus Subjective Procedures for Identifying Gender Differences in Science Test Items". *Journal of Research in Science Teaching* 30.

Taylor, J. 1979. "Sexist Bias in Physics Textbooks". *Physics Education* 14.

Tobin, K., and J.J. Gallagher. 1987. "The Role of Target Students in Science Classrooms". *Journal of Research in Science Teaching* 24.

Whiteley, P. 1993. "Science Examinations' Results in Barbados, Jamaica and Trinidad and Tobago, 1982–1991". *Caribbean Curriculum* 3, no. 2.

———. 1994. "Equal Opportunities? Gender and Participation in Science Education in Jamaica". Paper presented at Third Cross-Campus Conference of the Faculty of Education, University of the West Indies, Cave Hill, Barbados.

———. 1995. "Gender Issues in Caribbean Science Education". *Science Education International* 6, no. 1.

———. 1996. "The Gender Balance of Physics Textbooks: Caribbean and British Books, 1985–91". *Physics Education* 31.

11 Gender Stereotypes

Perceptions and Awareness of a
Sample of Jamaican Adolescents

ELSA LEO-RHYNIE AND
CARMEN PENCLE

Introduction

Gender is a term which has come to have a distinctive meaning in psychology as well as in feminist literature. It refers to a range of behaviours, roles and positions which are socially and culturally attributed to men and women. Gender is constantly being shaped through social and cultural experiences which are expressed through the attitudes, values and behaviours characteristic of interpersonal interaction. The "gendering" process is a complex one, beginning at birth and constantly reinforced throughout life. The attitudes, values and behaviours demonstrated by gender groups in the society have implications for the gender identities which adolescents develop, and determine, to a large extent, the careers and lifestyles which they select, and the roles they see themselves and others performing in the future, in public as well as in private spheres.

Several theories have been proposed to explain the development of gender identity by individuals. Identification theories of sex role acquisition base their assumptions on Freudian as well as Lacanian concepts, which equate being female with an awareness of woman's inferior anatomy, and an inability to form a separate and definitive identity because of her continued attachment to her same-sex parent who nurtures her. This results in the development of character traits which are defined by their human-relatedness; traits such as caring, empathy, and nurturing – which are less valued and perceived in a less favourable light by society than the aggressive, dominant traits which are deemed typical of masculine behaviour.

The theoretical position taken by social learning theorists is that all behaviour is learned behaviour, and sex role learning occurs through a process of imitation and modelling of sex-appropriate behaviour observed first in the home, then in the wider environment. The observational and imitation learning is reinforced by social and physical rewards for sex-appropriate behaviour, as well as punishment for sex-inappropriate behaviour (Frieze et al. 1978; Archer and Lloyd 1982; Bandura 1989; Bussey and Bandura 1992). Parents are considered to be particularly important models, because young children depend on these powerful adults to provide them with physical and emotional security. Rohrbaugh (1979) and Bandura (1989) also point to the strong influence of warm, nurturing same-sex parents in stimulating imitation of sex-typed behaviours. This theory has been criticized by Maccoby and Jacklin (1974) and Constantinople (1979), who contend that parents do not reward their children differently according to sex to the extent proposed by social learning theorists, and that children do not model exactly the behaviours they observe. They consider that the child plays an active part in developing their sex role behaviour by selecting from the behaviours observed and combining these in unique ways.

The active role of the child in the development of a gender identity is an important consideration of cognitive development theorists who are of the view that it is the child's conceptualization of both biology and society that determines the development of gender characteristics. Maccoby and Jacklin call this the self-socialization theory. The gender identity of the child serves as a "basic organizer of attitudes", determining which sex-appropriate objects and behaviours are to be valued (Kohlberg 1966). Although this identity starts to emerge by age three, and gender may be used as a classification cue at this time, it is not until the child is five or six years old that the permanence of a gender identity is established, and this identity can be used as a cognitive organizer. Martin and Halverson (1981) consider that the child uses the behaviour patterns observed in the environment, and provided by cultural structures, to develop cognitive schema about acceptable and appropriate male and female behaviours in society. Bem (1981) proposed the development in children of gender schema which respond to the bipolar gender distinctions in society, and which guide the development of other schema, as well as the extent to which children, as they grow, function socially in gender-appropriate ways. These schemata provide children with a framework for interpreting their own behaviour. They come to value objects, attitudes and behaviours associated with their own sex, they model sex-appropriate behaviours, and avoid those that are inappropriate (Bigler and Liben 1990). The sex role concepts are initially imperfect because of the child's level of cognitive development, but they are gradually refined as age advances and intellectual development improves. Sex role behaviour, therefore, is not just made up of acts of imitation, but is based on generalized, organized concepts which develop as the child's experience increases and behaviour is matched to such experience. Acceptable behaviour is rewarded and reinforced by the home, school and society as the child grows.

Within each society, certain norms of gender behaviour and stereotypes of male and female behaviour become established and culturally accepted, and there are sanctions for persons whose behaviours do not conform to the societal norm for their gender group. Despite the fact that research studies have shown that men and women, when placed in the same situation with clearly defined expectations and demands, respond in remarkably similar ways (Rohrbaugh 1979), women have been the object of widespread stereotyping, which is accompanied by a low valuation of those behaviours and tasks assessed to be stereotypically feminine. When this value persists, and activities at home and school support this conclusion, young women gradually develop a loss of pride and self-esteem, and growing feelings of inferiority.

The school serves as an important agent of socialization in the society. There, behaviours considered to be "appropriate" for both sexes are made explicit through rules and regulations or are implicit in terms of the expectations communicated to, and the reinforcement provided for, students. Teachers, therefore, become "significant others" in the lives of students, not only exerting a direct effect on their behaviour through the acceptance of socially appropriate actions and rejection of those which are socially inappropriate, but also serving as role models for these students in the development of a gender identity. The school environment also provides examples of gender stereotyping which are observed by students, and help to form the opinions and attitudes which they develop. The traditional concept of women as domestic managers, for example, persists in many classrooms. Mahony (1988), observing classrooms in British schools, noted that girls in these classrooms had already begun to practise the supporting, secretarial role for their male counterparts, as they are expected by the boys to be an infinite source of erasers, rulers, sharpeners and writing materials. In one classroom observed, a boy left his seat and walked halfway across the room to have his bandage fixed by a girl. Mahony's view is that mixed-sex classes "provide an excellent training ground for both boys and girls; for boys to practise behaving to women in such a way as to assert their right to dominate; for girls to find unobtrusive strategies for resistance" (Mahoney 1988: 89).

Pencle (1994) notes that socialization into the sexual division of labour is evident at the primary level of the Jamaican school system, where girls are usually assigned the indoor tasks of sweeping and dusting, while the boys are expected to run errands, lift furniture and tend the school garden. Observation of the sexual division of labour in the home, and a continuation of this observation in the school, results in the production of men who experience great difficulty in acknowledging and accepting the potential of women to make valuable and meaningful contributions in the public sphere, as well as women who consider that the essence of their nature is to nurture and be nurtured.

Sex role stereotyping is also found in textbooks, and this stereotyping often provides an inaccurate view of society to young people, a view which devalues the role of women. Honor Ford-Smith (1986) points out that Caribbean women have a tradition of female leadership and that, prior to emancipation, they worked alongside men in some of the toughest jobs. She notes that the majority of the workers in the cane fields at the time of emancipation were women, and is critical of the fact that the role of women in social change in the Caribbean has been "repeatedly underestimated, and sometimes ignored altogether by both historians and politicians". This is vividly demonstrated by King and Morrissey (1988), who examined a sample of contemporary texts in history, geography and social studies used in the preparation of students to sit the Caribbean Examinations Council examinations and concluded that these books reinforce traditional views of societies as being male dominated. The use of language in these books excludes women, who, when portrayed, play passive, subordinate and menial roles. No acknowledgment is made of the contribution of women to Caribbean development. Whiteley (1994), in analysing integrated science textbooks used in the lower grades of Jamaican high schools, found considerable male bias in these texts and speculated on the influence of such texts on girls' choice of science for study in the higher grades.

Students usually base their subject choices in Grades 10 and 11 (Forms 4 and 5) on a variety of factors, chief among them being interest, perceived competence in the subject and vocational choice (Bailey and Leo-Rhynie 1994). Local research evidence points to the greater involvement of girls in arts-based subjects and boys in science-based subjects (Leo-Rhynie 1989), and this has implications for the courses of study which they pursue at tertiary level, the careers they select and for which they qualify themselves. The subject choices and programmes of study pursued by girls reveal an obvious attraction to the "helping" professions such as teaching, nursing and clerical/secretarial work, which are considered to be appropriate career choices for them. These professions, though performing a valuable service role, are among the lower-paid professional jobs in the society, and do not command high status or prestige. Teachers' colleges in Jamaica have had a female enrolment in excess of 80 percent since 1976. The University of the West Indies (UWI) has had, since the 1982–83 academic year, a larger female than male population and in the academic year 1993–94 there were 8,742 female students (58.5 percent) registered compared to 6,197 male students (41.5 percent). Most of these female students are found in the Faculties of Arts and General Studies (81 percent female) and Education (77 percent female), which are arts-based faculties. In the Faculty of Natural Sciences, where the percentage of female students is 49 percent, the majority of women are to be found studying the biological sciences, with relatively few pursuing the physical sciences. Very few women are enrolled in the Faculty of Engineering (18 percent) while in Agriculture the percentage of women enrolled is 35 percent (UWI Statistics 1993–94). At the College of Arts, Science and Technology (CAST) – now the University of Technology (UTech) – similar patterns are reported by Pencle (1994) for the 1991–92 academic year, with a large majority of women in hospitality and food science (89 percent), technical education (69 percent), as well as in science, which includes pharmacy, medical technology and health records (68 percent), and commerce (66 percent); and very few women pursuing engineering (5 percent). The figures reported for women in building and architecture are 22 percent and 38 percent respectively.

Research has shown that one factor which may influence the attitudes which girls and boys develop about their competencies is whether they are taught in single-sex or mixed-sex groups. From the point of view of academic achievement, single-sex groups seem to be more facilitating for both girls and boys (McMillan 1982; Williams 1981; Salmon 1986). Hamilton (1984) compared the attitudes of students attending single-sex and coeducational schools to women in science. The most favourable attitudes were held by girls in single-sex schools, these attitudes being significantly higher than those held by girls in coeducational schools. Boys attending boys' schools expressed the most negative attitudes, significantly lower than those of girls attending either coeducational or girls' schools. No significant differences emerged in the attitudes of boys and girls attending coeducational schools.

Changes in the roles of both sexes have been taking place rapidly not only in the advanced industrial areas of the world but also in the Caribbean. These changes have been largely generated by the activities of the women's movement worldwide, which has raised issues about the gender inequity found in most countries of the world, and demonstrated in the burdensome workload and unequal access to resources faced by women. The United Nations Convention for the Elimination of All Forms of Discrimination against Women, which was framed in response to calls made to the United Nations prior to and during International Women's Year (1975), has challenged societies and international agencies to work towards redressing this imbalance. These initiatives have brought about a great deal of change in the status and expectations of women, and the roles they can play in society. The young people who will assume their adult roles in a society where such change is occurring are, in many instances, developing gender identities which have been modelled on, and influenced by, significant others of another generation. The extent to which they hold traditional, stereotypical views about their own sex roles, and also about the roles which women will play in the society of the future, is, therefore, of interest and importance.

Research Objectives

This research investigation set out to determine the extent to which students

1. Observe the sexual division of labour in their homes.

2. Perceive occupations in terms of "gender suitability".
3. Perceive women's roles in the year 2000 in traditional gender stereotypical terms.
4. Accept traditional sex role stereotypes.
5. Differ in response to 1–4 according to sex, stage of schooling and school type.

Methodology

Instruments were designed to measure students' response to the variables identified for study, as follows:

1. Observed sexual division of labour in the home

The extent to which students were exposed to a sexual division of labour in their households was explored by this variable. The instrument used in its measurement presented students with a list of thirty-one common household tasks, and they were asked to indicate whether each one was done more often by mother, father, by both parents equally or by neither parent. Examples of the tasks identified were:

- changing a light bulb
- caring for the student when ill
- attending parent-teacher meetings
- fixing a broken window

A score of 3 was given to a response which indicated that the task was carried out by both parents equally; a score of 2 represented a response which identified one or other parent as being the individual who carried out the task most often; while a score of 1 was allotted when neither parent was involved. A high score was indicative of very little observation of a sexual division of labour between parents in the home.

2. Perception of occupations in gender suitability terms

This variable sought to tap students' perceptions of the suitability of certain occupations for women and men. Thirty-eight occupations were listed and students were asked to indicate, for each one, whether they thought it was more suited to women, to men or whether the sex of the individual would not make a difference. Examples of the occupations presented were:

- plumber
- nurse
- doctor
- computer analyst
- veterinarian

Responses which made no distinction between the sexes in terms of who should be involved in the occupations listed were given a score of 2; those which declared a preference for one sex group over the other received a score of 1. A high score on this scale, therefore, indicated that the student was not governed by stereotypes in relation to occupations.

3. Perceptions of women's roles in the year 2000

This variable assessed students' perceptions of women's capacities, goals and responsibilities, relative to those of men, as these would be at the turn of the century. Eighteen items were used to measure this variable. Students were presented with a selection of "nontraditional" female and male roles, both domestic and occupational, and were asked to express their level of agreement or disagreement with the possibility of these occurring in the year 2000. Examples of the items used were:

- a woman being head of the army
- women being principals of all-boys' schools
- men staying at home to look after babies and children while women go out to work
- men and women sharing jobs such as washing and ironing

A five-point Likert scale was used to assess the responses of students, with the high score representing nonstereotypical views, ones which accept the capability of women and men to function in nontraditional roles.

4. Level of acceptance of traditional sex role stereotypes

This variable tapped the extent of students' agreement with traditional opinions on the roles of the sexes. A list of twenty-six such opinions was presented and students were required to use a five-point Likert scale to express their level of agreement or disagreement with each one. The items included the following:

- Important decisions on any issue should only be made by a man.

- It is wrong for men to do jobs such as cooking and cleaning in the home.
- Jobs which take one travelling away from home should never be given to a woman.
- A husband should always earn more money than his wife.

High scores on this scale would be given to students who disagreed with these statements, and who, therefore, were rejecting traditional sex role stereotypes.

The other variables examined were sex of student, stage of schooling (that is, whether Grade 8, 10 or 12 – Form 2, 4 or 6) and school type (girls', boys', or coeducational).

Sample

The sample was a stratified random one, and was constituted as shown in Table 11.1.

Students making up the sample were drawn from three secondary high schools in the Kingston and St Andrew Metropolitan area; one single-sex girls' school, one single-sex boys' school, and a coeducational school. The selection of students from three levels – Grades 8, 10 and 12 (Forms 2, 4 and 6) allowed for a cross-sectional analysis of views on the variables being examined.

Table 11.1   Composition of the Sample

Grade	Male		Female		Total
	Coed	Single-Sex	Coed	Single-Sex	
Grade 8/ Form 2	15	30	15	30	90
Grade 10/ Form 4	15	30	15	30	90
Grade 12/ Sixth Form	10	20	10	20	60
Total	40	80	40	80	240

Findings

Table 11.2 presents data on the performance of the students making up the sample on the four variables being measured. The range of scores on each variable, the mid-point of the range, as well as the sample mean and standard deviation, allow for an analysis of students' performance on these variables.

In all instances, the sample scored above the mid-point of the range of scores for the particular variable, although this was more pronounced in the case of Perceptions of Women's Roles in the Year 2000 and Acceptance of Traditional Sex Role Stereotypes. The scores suggest, therefore, that respondents did observe some sexual division of labour in their households, but not to a very great degree, and whereas they did not readily accept traditional sex role stereotypes, and were ready to predict a certain degree of change in women's roles by the year 2000, they still held fast to the concepts of certain occupations being more suited to one sex or the other.

Male/female differences in performance on the variables were explored using the Student's "t" test. The results are shown in Table 11.3.

Significant sex differences are observed for three of the variables, and in all instances, male students demonstrated more traditional opinions in respect

Table 11.2   Performance of the Sample on the Variables Being Examined

Variable	Score Range	Mid-point of Range	Sample Mean	Standard Deviation
Sexual division of labour observed in the home	31–93	62.0	68.0	8.78
Perceptions of gender suitability of occupations	38–76	57.0	59.73	8.20
Perceptions of women's roles in the year 2000	18–90	54.0	62.24	13.31
Acceptance of traditional sex role stereotypes	26–130	78.0	92.74	16.23

Table 11.3   Results of the Student's "t" Analysis of Sex Differences in the Scores on the Selected Variables

Variable	Male		Female		"t"	Prob.	Sig
	Mean	SD	Mean	SD			
Sexual division of labour observed in the home	66.99	9.20	68.90	8.31	1.7	0.09	NS
Perceptions of gender suitability of occupations	57.28	7.51	61.87	8.18	4.5	0.00	S
Perceptions of women's roles in the year 2000	56.88	11.39	66.93	13.14	6.3	0.00	S
Acceptance of traditional sex role stereotypes	85.85	14.31	98.77	15.43	6.7	0.00	S

df = degrees of freedom

of the issues presented. The girls were less likely than the boys to sex-type occupations, or to accept traditional sex role stereotypes. Significantly more girls than boys also perceived women's roles in the year 2000 as moving away from the stereotypes which currently prevail. There was no significant sex difference in terms of students' observations of the sexual division of labour in the home.

The extent to which different views were expressed by students at different stages of their schooling was explored using one-way analysis of variance (ANOVA), followed by Scheffe's post-hoc test to identify significant between-group differences. The ANOVA identified significant differences on three

Significant Differences Identified by the Scheffe Test:	
Perceptions of gender suitability of occupations	Form 6>2; 6>4
Perceptions of women's roles in the year 2000	Form 6>2
Acceptance of traditional sex role stereotypes	Form 6>2; 6>4

Table 11.4:   Results of the One-Way ANOVA and Scheffe Tests Assessing Difference in Views of Students According to Their Stage of Schooling

Grade		Mean	SD	"F" Value	Prob.
Perceptions of gender suitability of occupations					
Grade 8/Form 2	N = 90	58.50	8.21	9.50	.0001
Grade 10/Form 4	N = 90	58.38	7.72	–	–
Sixth Form	N = 90	63.58	7.78	–	–
Perceptions of women's roles in the year 2000					
Grade 8/Form 2	N = 90	60.09	14.89	3.96	0.02
Grade 10/Form 4	N = 90	61.77	10.84	–	–
Sixth Form	N = 60	66.18	10.84	–	–
Acceptance of traditional sex role stereotypes					
Grade 8/Form 2	N = 90	89.67	14.09	8.55	.0003
Grade 10/Form 4	N = 90	91.01	16.70	–	–
Sixth Form	N = 60	99.95	16.59	–	–

variables only – Perception of Gender Suitability of Occupations, Perceptions of Women's Roles in the Year 2000, and Acceptance of Traditional Sex-Role Stereotypes. The results are presented in Table 11.4.

The older, more mature sixth-form students were less bound by stereotypes than their younger schoolmates, differing significantly from Form 2 (Grade 8) and Form 4 (Grade 10) students on the Perceptions of Gender Suitability of Occupations, and Acceptance of Traditional Sex Role Stereotypes. Although the Form 4 (Grade 10) subsample did not differ significantly from either the Form 2 or the sixth form group in their projections of women's roles in the future, their mean score on this variable, which was much closer in value to that of the Form 2 sample, indicates that their responses were more conservative than those of their older colleagues.

Table 11.5: Results of the One-Way ANOVA and Scheffe Tests Assessing Difference in the Views of Students According to Their School Type: Single Sex (SS) or Coeducational (Coed)

School Type		Mean	SD	"F" Value	Prob.
Perceptions of gender suitability of occupations					
Coed Girls	N = 40	64.72	8.08	8.47	.0000
Coed Boys	N = 40	59.00	8.06		
SS Girls	N = 80	60.15	7.66		
SS Boys	N = 80	57.16	7.78		
Perceptions of women's roles in the year 2000					
Coed Girls	N = 40	73.10	11.42	20.34	.0000
Coed Boys	N = 40	59.45	11.46		
SS Girls	N = 80	64.58	12.41		
SS Boys	N = 80	55.88	11.96		
Acceptance of traditional sex role stereotypes					
Coed Girls	N = 40	108.85	11.87	27.37	.0000
Coed Boys	N = 40	88.50	18.10		
SS Girls	N = 80	94.61	12.69		
SS Boys	N = 80	84.94	14.10		

The opinions of students attending coeducational schools were compared with those at single-sex schools. One-way ANOVA again revealed significant differences on only three of the variables, and the Scheffe post-hoc test identified significant between-group differences. These are shown in Table 11.5.

These results show that the least traditional of all the subgroups in terms of gender stereotypes was the sample of girls from the coeducational school,

Significant Differences Identified by the Scheffe Test:

Perceptions of gender suitability of occupations	Coed Girls > SS Boys
Perceptions of women's roles in the year 2000	Coed Girls > SS Girls
	Coed Girls > Coed Boys
	Coed Girls > SS Boys
	SS Girls > SS Boys
Acceptance of traditional sex role stereotypes	Coed Girls > SS Boys
	SS Girls > SS Boys

while the most traditional were boys attending boys' schools. The girls from coeducational schools differed significantly from this group in terms of their opinions on the sex-typing of occupations, and their acceptance of traditional sex role stereotypes. The girls from single-sex schools also differed significantly from the single-sex boys on this latter variable, showing less acceptance of these traditional stereotypes than did the boys. When predictions for the future roles of women were examined, a significant difference emerged between the female subgroups, with the girls from the single-sex school being more inclined to predict that women's roles would remain traditional and sex-typed than were their same sex group from the coeducational school. Both subsamples of girls, however, were significantly more progressive in their opinions of the future roles of women than were the boys from the single-sex school, with the girls from the coeducational school differing significantly from their male school mates in terms of this variable.

Discussion: Boys Hold More Traditional Views than Girls

The findings of this investigation reveal that male/female differences – in perceptions of the gender suitability of occupations, acceptance of traditional sex role stereotypes and perceptions of women's roles in the future – all point to more traditional views being held by male than female students. These views are modified somewhat by the level of schooling of the respondents and the gender composition of the school population.

Most of the changes which have been agitated for over the past thirty years in terms of gender roles and functions have focused on women's roles, so it is not surprising that girls appear to be less accepting than boys of traditional domestic as well as occupational roles in terms of their futures. The fact that they, more than boys, anticipate significant change in stereotypical roles by the end of the century suggests that they are aware of and subscribe to these changes, despite the fact that such change may not be evident in the sexual division of labour in their homes. The implications of these gender role expectations are interesting, as where female adults expect these changes but their male counterparts do not, conflict – both in domestic and professional situations – could arise.

Younger students expressed significantly more traditional views than their older schoolmates. This may reflect a tendency for younger adolescents to base their opinions on what is familiar to them, as they may not yet have reached the stage where they are able to conceive of possibilities for which they have no, or few, concrete examples. Such examples would be provided by the gender relationships observed in the home, which the study found to be fairly traditional. This has implications, particularly in the Jamaican and Caribbean setting, where students are required to make subject choices prior to entering Form 4 (Grade 10); choices which can have a significant effect on the occupations they prepare for and pursue. The selection of science versus arts versus business subjects at this stage, for example, can make a change later on extremely difficult, and so virtually rules out career possibilities in the categories not selected. This limits choice, and could frustrate career goals at the stage where the students' views may have become less tied to traditional gender role expectations.

The coeducational/single-sex difference probably reflects the effect of close association and observation by the sexes of each other when they are allowed to share a learning environment, which is a controlled one in classrooms, and also less formal in out-of-class exchanges and activities. Girls and boys, through this association in coeducational schools, develop a clearer perspective and understanding of their capabilities, possibilities and limitations vis-à-vis those of the opposite sex. Such an assessment is almost impossible for students at single-sex schools, who are therefore more likely to hold fast to the stereotypes they are exposed to on a day-to-day basis; and even when there is change, it is less likely that this change will move too far away from what is comfortable and familiar. Interestingly, however, the boys at the coeducational schools who have opportunities to make such assessments still anticipate that girls will continue to follow sex-typed, traditional female roles. These boys are more progressive in their views than those from single-sex schools, but, in general, male expectations of domestic and occupational roles remain traditional.

The gender gap in expectations, which is evident in this investigation, must be addressed in order to reduce the potential for male/female misunderstanding and conflict which is already evident in society. Educational policy must focus on gender issues such as these if educational institutions are going to be able to play the vital role they must in order to ensure gender equity in society. The Reform of Secondary Education (ROSE) project currently underway in Jamaica has recognized that gender is an important variable to be considered in terms of providing instruction and practical training. The integration of gender issues in the school curriculum, however, has not been recommended for implementation at this time, despite the fact that open discussion of topics such as the sexual division of labour, which allow for questioning of traditional roles, valuing unwaged work and changes in gender roles over the years, can provide a framework for discussion and opinion formation in students who may not have exposure to such issues in other settings. When policy measures do not provide guidance on such matters, implementation is left up to the initiative of individual teachers.

These needs demand that teacher educators be prepared, not only to integrate gender in the courses which they use in the preparation of teacher trainees, but also to assist them in developing gender awareness among their pupils, from kindergarten to university. This preparation of teacher educators is urgent, so that their knowledge and awareness of the pivotal role they have to play in the socialization of students can be translated into action in the classrooms of colleges as well as schools islandwide. Recent publications which supply information on women's roles in history (Shepherd, Brereton and Bailey 1995) provide a rich source of material which can support and expand instruction in such a way that students develop an awareness of the contributions and potential of both sexes in nation building. Careful use of textbooks which portray stereotypes, and critical assessment of these portrayals, encourages the development of the cognitive skills of analysis and evaluation and also creates an openness to issues of this nature in the society. The need for young men, in particular, to be made aware of social change in the area of sex role stereotyping, and its impact on their lives, is crucial.

The creation of gender awareness and gender sensitivity among teachers and students is a first step in the complex process of "engendering" the educational system, and preparing graduates of that system to understand and appreciate the changing world of the future, and their place in that world.

References

Archer, J., and B. Lloyd. 1982. *Sex and Gender*. Harmondsworth: Penguin.

Bailey, Barbara, and Elsa Leo-Rhynie. 1994. "Factors Affecting Choice of Science Subjects by High School Students". Paper presented at the seminar Gender, Science and Technology, University of the West Indies, Mona, Jamaica.

Bandura, A. 1989. "Social Cognitive Theory". In *Annals of Child Development: Vol 6. Six Theories of Child Development*, edited by R. Vasta. Greenwich, Conn.: JAI.

Bem, S.L. 1981. "Gender-schema Theory: a Cognitive Account of Sex Typing". *Psychological Review* 88.

Bigler, R.S., and L.S. Liben. 1990. "The Role of Attitudes and Interventions in Gender Schematic Processing". *Child Development* 61.

Bussey, K., and A. Bandura. 1992. "Self Regulatory Mechanisms Governing Gender Development". *Child Development* 63.

Constantinople, A. 1979. "Sex-role Acquisition: in Search of the Elephant". *Sex Roles* 5.

Ford-Smith, Honor. 1986. "Caribbean Women and Social Change – Some Aspects of History". In *A Caribbean Reader on Development*, edited by J. Wedderburn. Kingston, Jamaica: Friedrich Ebert Siftung.

Freize, I.H., J.E. Parson, P.D. Johnson, D.N. Ruble, and G.L. Zellman. 1978. *Women and Sex Roles*. New York: W.W. Norton.

Hamilton, Marlene. 1984. "The Attitudes of Older Jamaican Adolescents to Women in Science". *Journal of Education in Science for Trinidad and Tobago* 11, no. 3.

Hamilton, Marlene, and Elsa Leo-Rhynie. 1984. "Sex Roles and Secondary Education in Jamaica". In *Women and Education: World Yearbook of Education 1984*, edited by S. Acker et al. New York and London: Nichols.

King, Ruby, and Michael Morrissey. 1988. *Images in Print*. Mona, Jamaica: Institute of Social and Economic Research, University of the West Indies.

Kohlberg, L.A. 1966. "A Cognitive-Developmental Analysis of Children's Sex Role Concepts and Attitudes". In *The Development of Sex Differences,* edited by E.E. Maccoby. Stanford, Calif.: Stanford University Press.

Leo-Rhynie, Elsa. 1989. "Gender Issues in Education and Implications for Labour Force Participation". In *Women and the Sexual Division of Labour in the Caribbean,* edited by K. Hart. Mona, Jamaica: Consortium Graduate School of Social Sciences, University of the West Indies.

Maccoby, E.E., and C.N. Jacklin. 1974. *The Psychology of Sex Differences.* Stanford, Calif.: Stanford University Press.

Mahoney, Pat. 1988. "How Alice's Chin Really Came to Be Pressed Against Her Foot: Sexist Processes of Instruction in Mixed-Sex Classrooms". In *Frameworks for Teaching,* edited by R. Dale, R. Fergusson, and A. Robinson. London: Open University.

Martin, C.L., and C.F. Halverson. 1981. "A Schematic Processing Model of Sex Typing and Stereotyping in Children". *Child Development* 52.

McMillan, Veta. 1982. "Academic Motivation of Adolescent Jamaican Girls in Selected Single-Sex and Co-Educational Schools". MEd Thesis, University of the West Indies, Kingston, Jamaica.

Pencle, Carmen. 1994. "Students' Perceptions of Women's Roles Now and in the Future". MA Ed. Thesis, University of the West Indies, Kingston, Jamaica.

Richardson, Mary. 1980. "Identity in the Jamaican Context: Its Measurement and Relationship to Certain Biographical, Environmental, Personality and Attitudinal Variables". PhD diss., University of the West Indies, Kingston, Jamaica.

Rohrbaugh, J.B. 1979. *Women: Psychology's Puzzle.* New York: Basic Books.

Salmon, Hazel. 1986. "Factors in Achievement and Attrition in Spanish at Grade 9 in Jamaican High Schools". PhD diss., University of the West Indies, Kingston, Jamaica.

Shepherd, Verene, Bridget Brereton, and Barbara Bailey, eds. 1995. *Engendering History: Caribbean Women in Historical Perspective.* Kingston, Jamaica: Ian Randle Publishers.

University of the West Indies. 1994. *Statistics 1993/1994.*

Whiteley, Peter. 1994. "Science Textbooks in Jamaican High Schools: Gender Fair?" Paper presented at the seminar Gender, Science and Technology, University of the West Indies, Mona, Jamaica.

Williams, Claudette. 1981. "The Relationship Between Achievement Motivation, Academic Performance and Certain Selected Variables in a Sample of Fifth Form Jamaican Students". BEd study, University of the West Indies.

Housekeeping Matters
Women's Roles in Family, Economy and Society

12 Women Entrepreneurs and Economic Marginality

Rethinking Caribbean Women's Economic Relations

Eudine Barriteau

Being black and being a woman is a disadvantage. Some men and some narrow minded women feel that women should be housekeepers. Because of that we have to strive three times as hard and could never relax.

– Woman interviewed in the Survey of Female Entrepreneurs

Introduction

In this article I examine Caribbean women's economic relations from the perspective of gendered social relations. I start from the premise that a particular gendered construct of Caribbean women exists based on closure and exclusion. I investigate the experiences of women who own productive capital, who operate within the formal, capitalist sphere of the economy and who appear to be socially and economically privileged. I argue that if these women are marginalized in the discourses and operations of the state and its institutions, then the perceived visibility given to the activities of working-class or other women is suspect, and requires reinvestigation. I seek to destabilize our understanding of Caribbean women's lives as overly determined by the social relations of class and the ubiquitous classification as victims. I am suspicious of the particular attentions given to the experiences of working-class women and the generalizations created by this narrow vision. I am equally sceptical of the created marginalization of women operating in the formal, capitalist economy and the assumption that there are women whose economic and social activities can occur in some gender-neutral public space.

I use gender to refer to a system of social relations through which women and men are constituted and through which they gain differential access and are unequally allocated status, power and material resources within a society (Barriteau 1994). I theorize a gender system as having two principal dimensions, one ideological and the other material. The material dimension reveals how women and men access and are allocated status, power and resources within a society. The ideological dimension indicates how a given society's notions of masculinity and femininity are constructed and maintained. Gender ideologies reveal what is appropriate or expected of the socially constituted beings "women" and "men" and establish the sexually differentiated, socially constructed boundaries for "males" and "females" (Barriteau 1997). I demonstrate how gender ideologies held by government and development officials may influence women's access to status, power and resources, and are so pervasive that women's agency as economic actors is often distorted or ignored.

Women in Entrepreneurship in Caribbean Countries

Women's entrepreneurial activities are significantly absent from the literature on women in the anglophone Caribbean. Preindependence studies focused on family life and the kinship patterns of "lower income black families" (Smith 1956; Clark 1957; Braithwaite 1957). Women were not the central subjects for analyses until the late 1970s. Given women's central positions in family structures, the early studies do provide a systematic analysis of colonial social institutions and practices affecting Caribbean women in familial organizations (Barriteau 1994). Still, from the 1950s to the 1970s, there has been an unexplained lapse between the early studies of West Indian or Caribbean family structures and the later multidisciplinary approaches used by the Women in the Caribbean Project (Barriteau 1994).

The earlier focus eventually yielded to research that targeted informal economic activities, sexual aspects of women's lives, male images of women, education, organizational and political participation, and agricultural work (Massiah 1986a). The Women in the Caribbean Project also sought to recognize the nature and importance of women's economic roles in economic development. The findings yielded an analysis of strategies pursued by Caribbean women to ensure economic survival, and provided a survey and examination of Caribbean women's contribution to economic activity (Gill 1982; Barrow 1986).

These studies illuminate and establish the centrality of women's economic activities in development in the Caribbean. The research provides a preliminary insight into the experiences of self-employed women, some of whom own businesses (Massiah 1986b; Barbados 1978: 213). It provides a brief discussion of the women's access to and use of commercial credit facilities. None of these studies, however, scrutinizes the relations between entrepreneurs and economic development planning, or yields insights into the activities of women as entrepreneurs or as owners of productive capital (Barriteau 1994).

Although studies on entrepreneurship in the anglophone Caribbean have grown in the last two decades, they have had a particular focus. Some of these studies concentrate on the racial composition of the business elite, their corporate interrelationships, and their practices to maintain white or near-white dominance of economic activity (Reid 1977; Karch 1982; Barrow 1983; Beckles 1989). Other studies analyse the development of the small business sector, its role in economic development and the constraints these businesses face (Barrow and Greene 1979; Downes 1988). None of the earlier research examines the experiences of women in the anglophone Caribbean as a component of an entrepreneurial class, nor did the researchers attempt any gender analysis (Barriteau 1994).

Several researchers, policy makers and activists investigate women's productive and reproductive activities in the Caribbean (Duarte 1989; Massiah 1995; Downing 1991; Deere 1990; Barrow 1986; Gill and Massiah 1982). These researchers are sensitive to the importance yet persistent marginalization of women's contributions to macroeconomic activity, social continuity and survival. Their attempts to centralize women's contributions fail because the analyses do not interrogate the economic theories underlying women's exclusion. The resulting analyses and prescriptions for transforming this situation are descriptive and well meaning, but leave the core problem intact. I use gender analysis to reveal the disjunctures between the experiences and activities of the women on one hand, and officials' and researchers' interpretations of these economic relations. On the other, I employ findings to reveal the agency and economic leadership of women, and argue for rethinking and destabilizing some of the common assumptions about women and economic activity.

Methodology

The quantitative and qualitative data presented comes from a survey of thirty-two women entrepreneurs in Barbados between 1991 and 1993. These are supplemented with interviews of nine officials from government and nongovernmental organizations and the commercial banking sector.[1]

My research grew out of a desire to accomplish several things. I wanted to grapple with the multiple experiences of Caribbean women which were not being addressed in ongoing research and the "women in development" discourse. I also wanted to juxtapose the experiences of these women with the officials' understandings of what women in business do. I wanted to discover if the officials' perception of women's entrepreneurial activities matched what women were actually experiencing or doing. The interviews with the officials and the women were two independent activities. The questions for the women were designed to capture their experiences, their assessments of their economic roles, their frustrations if any with economic policy, and their goals. My intent was to include women involved in as wide a range of entrepreneurial activities as possible.

I selected the thirty-two women interviewed from a list of ninety-two women in business compiled in 1991. The women in the initial list met the first criterion of selection: ownership of an enterprise classified as a small business by the Barbados government. The categories and definitions for the small business sector appear in Table 12.1. This list was put together from the registrar of public companies, publications of the Barbados Manufacturer's Association, perusal of the yellow pages and government statistical publications. The businesses selected are all listed in the yellow and white pages of the telephone directory.

Table 12.1   Definitions for the Small Business Sector in Barbados

---

1. Manufacturing (must not exceed any two of the following)

Capital Investment	$500,000
Annual Sales	$750,000
Employment	36 persons

---

2. Commerce, Services, Construction (must not exceed any two of the following)

Capital Investment	$300,000
Annual Sales	$750,000
Employment	25 persons

---

3. Small Hotels and Guest Houses (must not exceed any two of the following)

Capital Investment	$600,000
Annual Sales	$300,000
Employment	25 persons

---

4. Agricultural Enterprise (must not exceed any two of the following)

Acreage	25 acres
Capital Investment	$100,000
Annual Sales	$300,000
Employment	25 persons

---

5. Transportation (must not exceed any of the following)

Vehicles	$250,000
Annual Sales	$300,000

---

6. Medical, Health or Educational Services (must not exceed any of the following)

Capital Investment	$100,000
Annual Sales	$300,000

---

7. Professional Services (must not exceed the following)

Annual Sales	$200,000

Source: Barbados n.d.

I selected the interviewees from the population of women who operate in the formal economy who own and manage their businesses. Their businesses represent the major industrial classifications used in Barbados and correspond with those used by the International Standards Classification of the International Labour Organization.

The entrepreneurs have registered businesses with the division of Corporate Affairs of the Ministry of Finance and Planning. They employ others who are not family members. They pay national insurance (social security) contributions on behalf of workers, and grant paid holidays and maternity leave. They maintain accounts which are audited by certified, public accounting firms and (even though most had difficulty in securing loans) they use the commercial banking sector for business operations. With the exception of one, all the women maintain business establishments physically separated from their homes with commercial signs advertising the business.[2] In other words, these women are not in the informal economy. Their businesses are not back-door, one-shop, family-operated enterprises. The government is officially aware of their existence, even if on a daily basis they receive no attention from policy makers. The key characteristics of informal economic activity of self-employment, very small enterprises, and statistical underreporting do not apply to these ventures (Bromley 1978: 1033).

My research departs from certain basic requirements of empiricist investigations in that I am sceptical about the capacity of these techniques to isolate and capture some objective reality hitherto unknown. I do not believe my research can capture an objective reality that may be accessed by the right application of statistical and scientific techniques.

The interviews and conversations with female entrepreneurs were intended first to give voice to their particular experiences and to increase the visibility and relevance of these experiences. To paraphrase bell hooks (1990: 128), I wanted to reveal the multiple identities and varied experiences of women in the Caribbean.

I value the methodology used to reveal the observations of the women who speak because it enables offering their perspectives, their truths, however fragmentary these are. This focus allows an investigation of why women entrepreneurs have been excluded from studies of women in developing countries, and challenges us to rethink the issues surrounding their marginalization as economic agents. The privileging of the subjectivities of the women is necessary and relevant. I want to destabilize the stereotypical, essentialist view of Caribbean women and recognize the multiple experiences constituting our lives.

Women and the Cult(ure) of Entrepreneurship

In the interviews with officials in the public, private and nongovernmental sectors, a particular negative view of women's entrepreneurial activities kept reoccurring when I spoke with the officials who formulate policy. These officials either make or influence the decisions that allocate the resources of the state, regional organizations and international development agencies. Their perceptions of women's economic behaviour can have a direct effect on women's access to public or nongovernmental resources.

In our conversations they asked me to investigate what they described as several disturbing features of the way women do business.[3] Underlying their request was a concern that women were not handling the business environment optimally. Most recognized that the women worked very hard. However they implied that women did not understand the rules or did not inculcate the values of an entrepreneurial culture. Many of the untested assumptions about the ways in which women operate in business originate in five of the areas I have chosen to explore. These are:

- Nature of the business endeavour
- Perceptions on size of operations
- Employment profile
- Sources of start-up capital
- Level of support

To the officials each of these areas signalled a different cause for concern. Rather than showing interest in what would emerge in the research, they asked me to examine women's

- concentration in female-type business endeavours;
- fear of expansion and fear of partnership;
- overemphasis on the employment of family members or female employees;
- risk aversion or fear of risk taking;
- work/home role conflict.

Table 12.2   Issues of Female Entrepreneurship

Areas of Investigation	Officials' Views
Nature of the business endeavour	Concentration in female-type businesses
Perceptions on size of operations	Fear of expansion, fear of partnerships
Employment profile	Overemphasis on the employment of family members and female employees
Sources of start-up capital	Risk aversion or fear of risk taking
Levels of support	Work/home role conflict

When each of the areas of business operations is matched with the officials' perceptions of women's activities a different reality emerges. Table 12.2 presents the issues I investigated and the "official" interpretation of each.

The Nature of Women's Business Endeavours (The Feminine Trade)[4]

Of the thirty-two women in the sample, 40.6 percent are concentrated in the industrial sector, social and personal services, while another 15 percent are in wholesale and retail trade. Manufacturing represents another 25 percent of the sample, as Table 12.3 shows.

Table 12.3   Nature of Business Ventures

Industrial Sector	Number of Women	Percentage
Manufacturing	8	25.0
Agricultural/livestock production	2	6.3
Social and personal services	13	40.6
Wholesale and retail trade	5	15.6
Business services	3	9.4
Other	1	3.1
Total	32	100.0

The entrepreneurial literature describes these concentrations as traditional areas of businesses for women. In the sample the classification "social and personal services" includes beauty salons, child care centres, nursery schools, catering services and a bridal salon. The manufacturing businesses the women own include manufacture of: condiments; clothing; baskets and small household furnishings; and cakes, pastries and other food and catering services. Manufacturing and social and personal services make up 66 percent of all the businesses. An official of the Barbados Development Bank concludes: "Women are mostly involved in hairdressing, mobile canteens, day care centres, the garment industry, a few are in trucking, and one has a boat. They are concentrated in feminine trade. It is part of our culture."[5] However, the preponderance of women in the so-called feminine trade is not peculiar to Caribbean culture. It is what researchers on entrepreneurship might refer to as women's culture. This profile corresponds with research findings in the United States. In a study of 138 women entrepreneurs in Roanoke, Virginia Standard Metropolitan Statistical Area, investigators found a concentration in the following areas:

- apparel and accessories
- food services
- general merchandise
- home furnishings
- personal services

(See Pellegrino and Reece 1982: 16–17.)

In another study, the authors note that although the ventures vary widely, traditionally female areas such as travel agencies or clothing design predominate (Hisrich and Brush 1984: 33). Hisrich also found over 90 percent of the businesses begun by women are service oriented, 7 percent are in manufacturing and 3 percent in finance (1989: 1). While Clark and James (1992: 25) contend that most businesses owned by women are small and situated in retailing and services.

In Barbados one official of the development bank states that "women tend to go into areas where they can control the show, where they are certain of the skills involved".[6] A deputy executive director of the National Development Foundation interprets the concentration of women in traditional female areas as laziness: "Hairdressing is the most popular. They want the easy way out.

They do not want the headaches of big business. They look for areas traditional to women."[7]

Hisrich (1989: 11) insisted that the high number of service-oriented businesses reflects the educational and occupational background of many women entrepreneurs, and in many cases, the advice of guidance counsellors and friends who discouraged women from entering male-dominated fields. This observation does not hold for female entrepreneurs in Barbados. Table 12.4 shows that 59.4 percent of the women had completed only a secondary level of education in high schools in which there would have been no guidance counsellors at the time. This level of educational attainment is equivalent to graduating from high school. Six women gained university degrees and another six studied or trained at institutions equivalent to community colleges. In comparison with the population as a whole, while the percentage of women with a secondary education is below the population average, their educational attainment for tertiary level is noticeably higher than averages for the general population, as Table 12.4 reveals.

The residual suggestion of this particular analysis is that women only succeed as entrepreneurs, or their entrepreneurship should only be taken seriously, when they operate in male-dominated fields. Why are women's business ventures described as traditionally female? What is implied by this terminology? Why are officials worried that women are overrepresented here? The persistent claim that the ventures women engage in are "traditionally female" suggests implicitly that they are inferior. The women are portrayed as deficient in entrepreneurial skills. This gendered evaluation of women's

Table 12.4   Educational Attainment

	Number	Percentage	Percentage in population
Secondary	19	59.4	61.7
Tertiary	6	18.2	5.6
Other Tertiary*	6	18.8	10.0
Other	1	3.1	1.5
Total	32	100.0	

*The equivalent of community colleges.
Source: Survey of Female Entrepreneurs; Barbados 1992.

economic behaviour is an effect of asymmetrical social relations of gender. The negative evaluation of women's ventures provides a glimpse of a gender system in which ideological assessments of women's economic behaviour do not correspond with the material consequences of their activities or with the women's assessment of their achievements and performance. The majority of the women, 87.5 percent, are satisfied with their achievements. Their satisfaction centres on offering a good product or service and a general feeling of being successful and the reputation they have earned. Of the four who are dissatisfied, three are displeased with slow growth and one gave an unspecified response.

In assessing the performance of their businesses 31.3 percent (ten) rate their ventures as very successful, 28.1 percent (nine) as successful and 34.4 percent (eleven) state they are performing satisfactorily. This gives a total of 93.8 percent who assess their businesses as viable. Only two women (6.3 percent) state their concerns are not performing as well as they could. While the women measure successful performance by sales and profits, they also believe good customer relations, hard work, and offering a good product or service are necessary for successful businesses.

Despite the viability of their businesses, these women entrepreneurs are deemed by officials to have poor economic judgement for operating in these sectors. The analysis offered by researchers who do not question the dominant epistemological frame sets up a dichotomy between what is acceptable, rational, economic decision-making and what is irrational and traditionally female. Women's economic activities are compared to men's and deemed inadequate, reinforcing the gender bias that economic decision making is the responsibility of men. This focus re-echoes the deeply embedded, recurring ideology of liberalism that women are excluded from, and are insignificant in, the public sphere of production. Fundamental to this analysis is an epistemological frame in which man is the specific, dominant – and, at times, sole – actor in the economy. This epistemological frame insists on perceiving and interpreting women's entrepreneurial activities through androcentric, patriarchal lens and results in a continued unwillingness by research officials to examine the factors, goals and values that women decide are meaningful to informing their economic activity.

One of the outcomes of economic relations of subordination is that ultimately they contrive to rob women of the power of choice. Once women's concerns, projects and ventures do not fit male entrepreneurial patterns, they are marginalized. The recurring hierarchical dichotomies of liberal political and economic ideology such as male/female, superior/inferior are reinforced – to the material and psychological disadvantage of women.

Clark and James's conclusion captures this dismissal of women's business ventures: "We conclude that there is little economic rationale for intense, new public efforts to stimulate or support women-owned businesses, but that the federal government must continue to promote equal opportunity within businesses at large" (1992: 25). This statement illustrates how an ideological position – *the belief that there is little economic rationale for public efforts to stimulate or support women-owned businesses* – can produce material conse-quences.[8] Governments following the authors' advice would see no need to channel financial and other resources to these businesses, and would continue to pursue the enduring myth of liberal ideology that there is equality of opportunity.

No researcher asks what is inherently wrong, economically or socially, with providing services used primarily by women or for which women are the main suppliers. Neither do they question who would provide these services, should women entrepreneurs move out of these areas *en masse* into nontypical female ventures. The entrepreneurial profiles of men are held up as the norm. Research indicates that motivational factors, departure points, sources of funds, occupational background and support groups differ for women and men (Hisrich 1989: 205; Pellegrino and Reece 1982: 204; Lee-Gosselin and Grise 1990: 423–33; Clarke and James 1992: 25–40). Yet the different types of ventures women create are questioned or dismissed.

Perceptions on Size of Operations (Fear of Expansion and Fear of Partnership)

Officials of the National Development Foundation, the Barbados Manufac-turer's Association, the Barbados Development Bank, Women in Develop-ment, and the Small Enterprise Assistance Project all maintain that women are reluctant to expand the size of their operations. Table 12.5 shows that the majority of the ventures are indeed individually owned.

Twenty-two of the women, 68.7 percent, own single proprietorships and make all the investment and managerial decisions. Seven women, 22 percent,

Table 12.5   Type of Business Owned

	Number of Women	Percentage
Single Proprietorship	22	68.7
Partnership	7	21.9
Family Owned	2	6.3
Limited Liability Co.	1	3.1
Total	32	100.0

Source: Survey of Female Entrepreneurs.

are involved in partnerships, and two women, 6.3 percent, own the businesses with other family members. One woman and her husband are the controlling directors of a limited liability company. Of the seven women who have partnerships, four have only one other partner and three have two partners.

Twenty-eight women, 87.5 percent, are willing to expand the size and volume of their operations. This does not support the assumption that women are reluctant to expand. Two are not interested in expansion and the remaining were uncertain. Of the twenty-eight wanting to expand, 14.2 percent want to do so to increase their profits. Another 21.4 percent want to satisfy the existing demands for their goods and services. They believe they could cater to a larger clientele and realize the potential of their businesses. Another 14.2 percent want to gain recognition and become the biggest enterprise within that industrial sector. Of the twenty-two women who are the sole owners of their ventures (see Table 12.6), six, 27.2 percent, would enter a partnership to double their operations while fourteen, 63.3 percent, would not. Two of them are uncertain.

The women in the survey have no fear of growing larger. Twenty-eight women, 87.5 percent of the sample, want to expand but they do not wish to do so by entering into partnerships. They regard partnerships as a loss of autonomy. Maintaining control over the businesses they start is of fundamental importance to these women, many of whom state this aspect as the reason they started the business. They want some aspect of their lives to be under their control.

Popular opinion, officials and the literature assume that an unwillingness to expand through partnerships represents a fear of growing larger rather than a reluctance to grow by that means.[9] Twenty-eight of the women entrepreneurs want to expand through an influx of capital. They view partnerships as fraught with difficulties:

> Partnerships are problematic. It would have to be a sleeping partner, someone who invests money but not involved in the day to day operations like me.

> I have seen partnerships that haven't worked out. Partnerships hardly ever work out.

> I just don't like partnerships. I like my own decisions, I don't like reporting to anyone. My philosophy is to sink or swim on my own.

> It is a personal thing because on a personal level I like to be in control of my own business. One of the reasons I am here is to be in control and I do not want to share that control.

"Unwillingness to expand" is frequently interpreted as a fear of risk or a fear of expansion. That is incorrect. The majority of the women would expand if they could get an influx of capital other than through third parties buying into the ownership structure. While their decisions may not be the most feasible financially, women rate work satisfaction, peace of mind and autonomy as critical to their performance. These noneconomic factors cannot be dismissed: what women rate as important must first be understood before any attempt is made to change or discard it. Researchers and officials operating within an androcentric frame fail to value or legitimize the differing goals women set themselves in entrepreneurship. Clark and James state:

> Many women apparently manage their business to yield a profit, but not to grow substantially. Small enterprises offer income, independence, autonomy, and control of their owners, yet can be consistent with other career responsibilities. Rapid growth, in particular, is seen by some women to be disruptive and to jeopardize family and other commitments. (1992: 34)

Employment Profile (Overemphasis on the Employment of Family Members or Female Employees)

These ventures have small work forces, as Table 12.6 shows. Seven businesses have two employees, four have four employees and four others hire seven workers. Although the majority (twenty-three businesses) have four or fewer workers, one establishment has twenty-two employees, another has fourteen, and two employ thirteen each. These thirty-two businesses generate employment for 192 workers.

Table 12.6   Number of Employees

Number of Employees	Number of Businesses	Percentage
1	4	2.5
2	7	21.9
3	1	3.1
4	4	12.5
5	2	6.3
6	1	6.3
7	4	12.5
8	1	3.1
10	3	9.4
11	1	3.1
13	2	6.3
14	1	3.1
22	1	3.1
Total 192	32	100.0

Source: Survey of Female Entrepreneurs.

While findings on the hiring of full-time employees are inconclusive, perhaps the most significant finding related to employees is that twenty-three women, 71.9 percent, employ no family members.[10] There is a widespread belief that women seek safety and primarily hire members of their own family. Downing reports:

> To lower internal transaction costs, women tend to limit the hiring of employees to a small number of trusted relatives or close friends. In Jamaica, for example female informal commercial importers, despite their strong growth orientation, relied almost completely on real or fictional kin to assist them in their businesses.[11] (1991: 9)

The findings of the survey do not support this notion. Of the 192 employees, 154 are women and 38 are men. Can one conclude that women prefer female employees? The high number of female employees has to be placed in the context of the preponderance of services and products catering to women. Men are not usually employed in child care, hairdressing and preschool occupations. For example, the 1990 census reveals the following data on occupations for the population aged fifteen years and over (Barbados 1992):

	Total
Other sales and services occupations	
Female	7,990
Male	3,954
Drivers and mobile machinery operators	
Female	69
Male	4,577
Shop assistants and market traders	
Female	3,586
Male	1,423
Teaching professionals	
Female	2,587
Male	1,458

Men are heavily concentrated in occupations such as skilled agricultural and fishery workers, extraction and building trade workers, and legislators and administrators.

Sources of Start-up Capital (Fear of Risk Taking)

The assumption that women possess a genetic fear of taking risks saturates the research on female entrepreneurship. Far too many researchers assume that women do not take risks or are afraid to do so. The assumption is based on the fact that many women finance the start of their businesses with their own capital. I found that 65.6 percent of the women did start their businesses with their own capital, but the majority had applied for, and had been refused, loans from commercial or development agencies.

The women raised the capital they needed in unorthodox ways for businesses, but traditional ways for women. Hisrich notes, for instance, that "start up financing is another area where male and female entrepreneurs differ. Males often list investors, bank loans, or personal loans along with personal funds as sources of start-up capital; women usually rely solely on personal assets or savings" (Hisrich 1989). They used their own savings, and borrowed from family and friends. Table 12.7 indicates their sources of start-up capital.

Table 12.7   Main Source of Start-up Capital

	Number of Women	Percentage
Family	5	15.6
Friends	2	6.3
Own savings	14	43.8
Commercial bank	6	18.8
Nongovernmental development institution	4	12.5
Other	1	3.1
Total	32	100.0

Source: Survey of Female Entrepreneurs.

Fourteen women, 43.8 percent, used their savings to establish their ventures. In all, twenty-one women, 65.6 percent of the sample, started these businesses without the assistance of commercial banks or nongovernmental development institutions.

In a detailed review of the literature on women entrepreneurs in the United States, Hisrich concludes, "In general women entrepreneurs have a conservative risk taking posture in terms of product or service ideas" (1989: 30). Sexton and Bowman-Upton report on a study of bank loan officers' perceptions of male and female entrepreneurs, in which it was found that women were perceived as less entrepreneurial than men. Their study concluded that "female entrepreneurs were evaluated significantly lower on dimensions related to leadership, autonomy, risk-taking propensity, readiness for change, endurance (energy level), and low need for support (succorance)" (1990: 30).

Reporting on several studies, Downing offers one of the reasons why it is believed women are afraid of risk. It is argued that the goal of women is to feed and educate their children, while men, free of the burden of family responsibilities, "are able to pursue individual interests and to take business risks in search of profits" (1991: 5). I was asked by a nongovernmental official to investigate why women do not like to take risks. He stated, "they pay their loans well but they are afraid to expand and they are afraid of risks".[12] Another official adds: "Two characteristics of the female client are reluctance to borrow money and an aversion to risk. They are reluctant to expand. They need to be more receptive to training and they need to think big."[13]

Twenty-one women speculated with their savings and those invested in them by family and friends rather than be dissuaded by lack of commercial credit. The fact that women are willing to risk their own assets does not mean they are reluctant to borrow. Some women complained about the unwillingness of banks to lend them money. Some said this was frustrating after they had prepared proposals or feasibility studies:

> The financial side is the most problem. The lending facilities for small businesses are limited. Faith in small business people, especially females is very cloudy.

> The biggest problem is not having the loans before I started off in business. I could have attracted a better type of clientele from the beginning.

> Always finance, to get money to get going, at twenty-one [years] you cannot have much security, but I have never been refused a loan. My first loan application was to the BDB [Barbados Development Bank], four years operating and I never had a reply from them yet. I went through a feasibility study, a prospectus and I never got a reply.

The last woman quoted could not resist giving a sarcastic twist to her comment. She had never been refused a loan – because the bank never bothered to reply. The willingness of the women to use their own money should be read as a measure of their determination and entrepreneurial spirit, rather than a fear of risk. For most women it was only after being refused loans that they resorted to using their savings. Examples of orthodox risk-taking behaviour are reconstructed as a fear of risks:

> Women as borrowers will pay far better than men. On average they are slightly more conservative not quite as aggressive, but I am telling you when a woman cannot pay very often she cannot feed her kids.

> Women generally are more thorough as well. They will stick to it. They will work harder and make a greater effort to make the business a success. They are willing to put in longer hours. Women will put in all the security required. They have faith in the project. They will agree to a salary reduction. Men are not as willing. They (women) are willing to risk their personal possessions to secure a loan.[14]

There is a need to rethink the concept of risk taking as it now exists to include the ways in which women speculate with all their assets and personal savings to finance a business venture. It is ultimately much more risky and challenging (in even the conventional meanings of the term) to finance a business with one's own savings than with money obtained commercially. If the business financed from personal savings fails then the women lose their ventures *and* all the assets. In some cases this is everything they own. A failed business started with a loan from a commercial bank immediately becomes a liability to that financial institution.

To conclude that women fear taking risks because they are determined to finance their businesses indicates one of the instances in which researchers and the concepts of entrepreneurship totally misread the factors women prioritize in their decision making.

Sources of Support (Work/Home Role Conflict)

The literature on female entrepreneurship and popular opinion reveal a preoccupation with sources of emotional support for business women: "In addition to family size, the degree of family support appears to be an important factor affecting work-home role conflict" (Stoner, Hartman and Arora 1990: 31). One of the areas I was very interested in examining was the support women received from their spouses and children. I wanted to know to what extent family support was a determining factor. Government officials, academics and members of regional organizations with whom I spoke had a similar interest, although they had differing expectations for the outcome of this question. They repeatedly requested that I investigate the level of support women received from their families, especially their men, in establishing and running their ventures.[15]

In reply to the question "When you started this business whose encouragement was the most important to you?", twelve women (37.5 percent) mentioned their husbands or common-law partners, while ten women, 31.3 percent, stated that no one encouraged them. Of the latter ten women, three are single, one is married, five are divorced and one is separated.

In a related question I probed the reaction of their partners to the start of the businesses. Nineteen women reported that their husbands or partners were supportive at the start; one said her husband was indifferent, and five stated that their partners disapproved. Seven women did not answer the question. Of the nineteen, nine are married, six are single, and four are divorced. A cross-tabulation of sources of support with marital status reveals that for seven of the eleven married women their husbands provided the strongest encouragement at the start of the venture.

In assessing whether the initial embrace of the women's entrepreneurial activity changed, marital status was cross-tabulated with reaction of spouses and partners at the time of the interview. Support remained consistent, but the level diminished slightly. Seventeen women, 53.1 percent, stated that their partners are still supportive, one did not know, and three gave other responses. Married women comprise ten of the seventeen. Four women are single. Ten women did not answer, including seven who are divorced. Most women continue to receive the support of their spouses and partners for their business operations.

Of the fourteen women whose children reacted to their entrepreneurial activities, nine gained approval; two were greeted with indifference; the child of one disapproved and two experienced other negative reactions. The women report that their children's attitudes improved between the start of the enterprise and the time of the interview. Nineteen women now receive the support of their offspring.

On the whole, therefore, the women state that they have the support of their partners and children. Unfortunately, I did not probe the form this support takes. Caribbean women have a long tradition of self-reliance and self-sacrifice (Sutton and Makiesky-Barrow 1981: 469–98; Barrow 1986: 131–76) that is at times romanticized. Many would be satisfied with verbal assurances of support. The autonomy and independence of Caribbean women is an area that needs reinvestigating. Their resourcefulness can lead others to depend on their survival mechanisms. The state and family members benefit from this dependence on women, and in return the woman receives the empty accolades of the myth of the miracle worker.

That women need support is evident, in that some women suffer work/home role conflicts as a result of the multiple demands made by business and family responsibilities on their time (Williams 1982). Officials and researchers assume that the degree of support women receive alleviates the strains of this conflict. Alternatively, its absence can compound conflict: "Family support for female entrepreneurs maybe limited, husbands are often non-supportive and may be obstructive to the careers of their entrepreneurial wives" (Stoner, Hartman and Arora 1990: 31). The opinion that women need more emotional support than men stems from the portrayal of female entrepreneurs in the literature. Female entrepreneurs are viewed as either traditional, or first-generation, or as modern (Moore 1990: 276; Gregg 1985: 10–18). The characteristic orientation of the traditional female entrepreneur is to home and family, as opposed to the career orientation of the modern, second-generation female entrepreneur (Moore 1990: 276).

This preoccupation with sources of support for women stems from researchers wanting to determine how women meet the conflicting demands of home, family and business enterprises while accepting their primary responsibility to home and family. I argue that the real source of the "work/home role conflict" is the oppressive nature of existing gender relations, which implicitly convey to women that any new responsibilities they undertake in the public sphere of production cannot be at the expense of their assigned responsibilities in the private sphere of the household. It becomes unimportant for researchers to ask whether *male* entrepreneurs receive emotional support or whether work/home role conflicts exist for them. Neither would officials in development institutions be concerned with whether a woman's support might motivate a man to enter into entrepreneurship. Gender ideologies assume that support for men is natural and merits discussion only in its absence. On the other hand, most women internalize the belief that they are supposed to cope with these conflicting and stressful demands.

Conclusion

The experiences of women entrepreneurs in the Caribbean require that feminist researchers reevaluate the conventional interpretations of women's economic behaviour. We should discard the conceptual tools and epistemological framework provided by standard economic analysis, and devise alternative economic analyses grounded in gender analysis. This analysis should recognize that gender relations constrain women's access to material and psychological resources. These relations are asymmetrical relations of domination and power.

Women as entrepreneurs contribute to economic development and generate employment. They display economic leadership in ways that are misinterpreted. Women can perform better in business if their needs are understood and their ways of operations in business are recognized. Concepts of what constitutes entrepreneurial behaviour should be inclusive of women's economic agency and should validate the possible ways in which different women do business.

Contrary to the views of officials, women understand the constraints they face and make decisions accordingly. Women are risk takers and are not reluctant to expand the size of their operations, although they are generally unwilling to do so through partnerships. Control and agency are paramount for these women, just as they are to the vast majority of male entrepreneurs. The problematic relationship between women and power, and the particular and differing factors that influence women's economic behaviour, should be examined before policy is designed to assist them. Governments should understand how gender relations complicate women's economic and political agency as a prerequisite to developing gender-sensitive economic policy.

The problem of validating how women take risks is compounded because risk taking is defined as an integral element of entrepreneurial behaviour. Brockhaus (1987: 1) notes that Mills was one of the first political economists to use the term "entrepreneur". Mills regarded direction, supervision, control and risk taking as the primary functions of the entrepreneur. He singled out risk taking as the main distinguishing feature between the manager and the entrepreneur. Risk taking has come to symbolize mastery of entrepreneurship. The reluctance to grant this quality to women supports the gendered notion that women cannot do business (as well as men).

We need more research in the Caribbean on the economic agency of women across class, income and racial structures. For too long our experiences have been forced to fit into explanatory frameworks whose assumptions do not mirror the conditions of our lives. Our multiple experiences have been cut and pasted, thus denying complexities and contradictions.

Practices such as the denial of loans to women should be interrogated to determine whether there is a deliberate policy to shift to women the responsibility for financing their ventures. When women are constantly denied access to credit – even though they meet the formal requirements of obtaining it – then financial institutions and governments are shifting to women the costs of operating in the public domain of the economy. I suggest that the hierarchies and inferior ranking of women implied by the private/public dichotomy follow them into entrepreneurship. Because women are seen as "naturally" belonging in the private sphere, there is a tendency to view their thrust into entrepreneurship as also privatized. If women using personal financing for start-up costs fail, then governments need to examine the social and economic consequences of having both a business investment and personal assets wiped out. Financial losses for women have material and psychological consequences for families, communities and the economy.

The experiences of women entrepreneurs and the perceptions of their activities as illustrated in my survey indicate the androcentric biases of neoclassical economic theory. These biases have material, lived consequences. The activities and experiences of female entrepreneurs are misunderstood, because many of the factors that influence how women make economic decisions are discarded. Part of the difficulty in conceptualizing the economic agency of women originates in economic theories defining development and entrepreneurial behaviour. Neoclassical economic theory informs development policy in the Commonwealth Caribbean (Barriteau 1996). The theory is embedded with the notion that the central economic actor is a rational autonomous agent (England 1993; Strassman 1993; Nelson 1993). This rational actor operates in a polity envisioned "as a public, rational community of heads of households" (Nelson 1993: 1).

Feminist political theorists and economists have problematized this reading of economic agency and the public sphere. Through research on household economies and decision making, feminist economists are rethinking how economic decisions are made. They reject the assumed rationality and autonomy of economic actors. Instead they identify androcentric biases in the theoretical structure and core assumptions of neoclassical economics (England 1993; Strassman 1993). The challenges feminist economists pose to the assumptions central to neoclassical economic theory should now be applied specifically to unravelling the misinformation surrounding women's economic agency.

By clinging to concepts that make women's economic agency marginal, we are robbed of understanding how women's entrepreneurial activities contribute to economic development. When officials continue to perpetuate a view of women as uncertain of their business environment, the culture of female entrepreneurship is distorted. More significantly, these views become powerful policy tools for arguing that it is not necessary to design programmes to assist women. Reworking these concepts to include the ways in which women do business benefits women's economic activity, and enriches our understanding of entrepreneurial culture.

Notes

1. The research was funded by a terminal fellowship from the Graduate School of Arts and Sciences, Howard University, and the Women and Development Studies Group of the University of the West Indies, Cave Hill.

2. The one woman whose business and dwelling place share the same structure has a bridal salon in a self-contained spacious shop with a separate entrance, large sign and separate commercial and residential directory listing. One cannot enter her home via the salon or vice versa.

3. I told the officials I was doing a study of women in business and wanted to talk with them about what they saw as the challenges women faced. They were not shown the interview schedule nor asked to frame any questions. My emphasis in talking with them was to learn what they thought about women entrepreneurs.

4. Note that for each heading discussed here, the left part of the topic presents what I investigated, the bracketed right side how the officials interpreted the topic to be investigated.

5. Interview with the manager of research and planning, Barbados Development Bank, 7 June 1991, Bridgetown, Barbados.

6. Interview with the manager of research and planning, Barbados Development Bank, 7 June 1991, Bridgetown, Barbados.

7. Interview with deputy executive director, National Development Foundation, 7 June 1991, Bridgetown, Barbados.

8. I am not trying to suggest that the researchers pulled their conclusion out of thin air. Rather I am attempting to illustrate how an opinion – whatever its origins – can affect the (non) allocation of resources.

9. Please note that these enterprises are part of the formal economy, and the criterion for remaining in the small business sector has to do with meeting two of the three specifications set out in Table 12.1. None of the women exceeded the limit for number of employees nor were they concerned with this as a constraint.

10. There is a wide distribution among the concerns that hire full-time employees. Nine businesses have one full-time worker while four have three full-time workers, although three women each hire twenty, thirteen and twelve workers. Three women employ two full-time workers, another three, five workers and a final three employ seven workers. There is a total of five businesses with ten or more full-time employees. Seventeen businesses have no part-time employees. Seven have one, and three each hire four, five, and six part-time workers.

11.   Downing draws heavily on the work of Elsie Le Franc to reach that conclusion. However, Le Franc researched only women in the informal economy. The women in this study are deliberately drawn from the formal economy. See Le Franc 1989: 99–132.

12.   Interview with regional coordinator, Small Enterprise Assistance Project, Caribbean Association of Industry and Commerce, 14 June 1991, Bridgetown, Barbados.

13.   Interview with deputy executive director, the National Development Foundation of Barbados, 7 June 1991, Bridgetown, Barbados.

14.   Interview with the assistant vice president, Credit, Caribbean Commercial Bank, 20 July 1993, transcript, author's file, Barbados.

15.   Series of interviews and discussions with officials, 22 May–16 August 1991, Bridgetown, Barbados.

References

Barbados. N.d. "Final Report Small Business Development Committee". Ministry of Trade.

_____. 1978. "Women and Employment". In *The Report of the National Commission on the Status of Women in Barbados*. Vol. 1. Bridgetown: Government Printing Department.

_____. 1992. *The 1990 Population and Housing Census*. Vol. 1. Bridgetown: Government Printing Office.

Barriteau, Eudine. 1994. "Gender and Development Planning in the Post-Colonial Caribbean: Female Entrepreneurs and the Barbadian State". PhD diss., Howard University.

_____. 1998. "Theorising Gender Systems and the Project of Modernity in the Twentieth Century Caribbean". *Feminist Review*, no. 59.

Barrow, Christine. 1983. "Ownership and Control of Resources in Barbados 1834 to the Present". *Social and Economic Studies* 32, no. 3.

_____. 1986. "Finding the Support: Strategies for Survival". *Social and Economic Studies* 35, no. 2.

Barrow, Christine, and J.E. Greene. 1979. *Small Business in Barbados: A Case of Survival*. Cave Hill, Barbados: Institute of Social and Economic Research, University of the West Indies.

Beckles, Hilary. 1989. *Corporate Power in Barbados. A Mutual Affair: Economic Injustice in Political Democracy*. Bridgetown, Barbados: Lighthouse Publications.

Bourque, Susan C., and Kay B. Warren. 1987. "Technology, Gender and Development". In *Learning About Women: Gender, Politics, and Power,* edited by J.K. Conway, S.C. Bourque and J.W. Scott. Ann Arbor: University of Michigan Press.

Braithwaite, Lloyd E. 1957. "Sociology and Demographic Research in the British Caribbean". *Social and Economic Studies* 6, no. 4.

Brockhaus, Robert. 1987. "Entrepreneurial Folklore". *Journal of Small Business Management* 25, no. 3.

Bromley, Ray. 1978. "Introduction – The Urban Informal Sector: Why Is It Worth Discussing?" *World Development* 6, nos. 9 and 10.

Clark, Thomas A., and Franklin J. James. 1992. "Women Owned Businesses: Dimensions and Policy Issues". *Economic Development Quarterly* 6, no. 1.

Clarke, Edith. 1957. *My Mother Who Fathered Me.* London: Allen and Unwin.

Deere, Carmen, et al. 1990. *In the Shadows of the Sun: Caribbean Development Alternatives and US Policy. A PACCA Book.* Boulder: Westview Press.

Downes, Andrew. 1988. "The Development of Small Business in Barbados". Paper presented at Emancipation Lecture Series 4, Barbados.

Downing, Jeanne. 1991. "Gender and the Growth of Micro-enterprises". *Small Enterprise Development* 2, no. 1.

Duarte, Isis. 1989. "Household Workers in the Dominican Republic: A Question for the Feminist Movement". In *Muchachas No More,* edited by E.M. Chaney and M. Garcia Castro. Philadelphia: Temple University Press.

England, Paula. 1993. "The Separative Self: Androcentric Bias in Neoclassical Assumptions". In *Beyond Economic Man: Feminist Theory and Economics,* edited by M.A. Ferber and J.A. Nelson. Chicago: University of Chicago Press.

Gill, Margaret. 1982. "Women, Work and Development: Barbados 1946–1970". In *Women, Work and Development,* edited by M. Gill and J. Massiah. Cave Hill, Barbados: Institute of Social and Economic Research, University of the West Indies.

Gill, Margaret, and Joycelin Massiah. 1982. *Women, Work and Development.* Cave Hill, Barbados: Institute of Social and Economic Research, University of the West Indies.

Gregg, Gail. 1985. "Women Entrepreneurs: The Second Generation" *Across the Board* 2, no. 1.

Hisrich, Robert D. 1989. "Women Entrepreneurs: Problems and Prescriptions for Success in the Future". In *Women-Owned Businesses,* edited by O. Hagan, C. Rivchun and D. Sexton. New York: Praeger.

Hisrich, Robert D., and Candida Brush. 1984. "The Woman Entrepreneur: Management Skills and Business Problems". *Journal of Small Business Management* 24, no. 1.

Hooks, Bell. 1990. *Yearning: Race, Gender and Cultural Politics*. Boston: South End Press.

Karch, Cecilia. 1982. "The Growth of the Corporate Economy in Barbados: Class and Race Factors 1890–1977". In *Contemporary Caribbean: A Sociological Reader*, edited by S. Craig. Vol. 1. St Augustine, Trinidad: C. Karch.

Lee-Gosselin, H., and J. Grise. 1990. "Are Women Owner-Managers Challenging Our Definitions of Entrepreneurship? An In-Depth Survey". *Journal of Business Ethics* 9.

Le Franc, Elsie. 1989. "Petty Trading and Labour Mobility: Higglers in the Kingston Metropolitan Area". In *Women and the Sexual Division of Labour*, edited by K. Hart. Mona, Jamaica: Consortium Graduate School of Social Sciences, University of the West Indies.

Massiah, Joycelin. 1986a. "Women in the Caribbean Project: An Overview". *Social and Economic Studies* 35, no. 2.

_____. 1986b. "Work in the Lives of Caribbean Women". *Social and Economic Studies* 35, no. 2.

_____. 1995. "Weathering Economic Crises: Economic Recession and Barbadian Women in Manufacturing 1970–1989". In *The Human Cost of Women's Poverty: Perspectives from Latin America and the Caribbean*, edited by UNIFEM. Mexico City: UNIFEM.

Nelson, Julie. 1993. "A Feminist Perspective on Economic Justice". Paper presented at Conference on Feminist Economics.

Pellegrino, Eric T., and Barry L. Reece. 1982. "Perceived Formative and Operational Problems Encountered by Female Entrepreneurs in Retail and Service Firms". *Journal of Small Business Management* 20, no. 2.

Reid, Stanley. 1977. "An Introductory Approach to the Concentration of Power in the Jamaican Corporate Economy and Notes on its Origin". In *Essays on Power and Change in Jamaica*, edited by C. Stone and A. Brown. Kingston, Jamaica: Jamaica Publishing House.

Sexton. Donald L. 1989. "Research on Women-Owned Businesses: Current Status and Future Directions". In *Women-Owned Businesses*, edited by O. Hagan, C. Rivchun and D. Sexton. New York: Praeger.

Sexton, Donald L., and Nancy Bowman-Upton. 1990. "Female and Male Entrepreneurs: Psychological Characteristics and Their Role in Gender-Related Discrimination". *Journal of Business Venturing* 5, no. 1.

Sexton, Donald L., and Calvin A. Kent. 1981. "Female Executives versus Female Entrepreneurs". In *Frontiers of Entrepreneurial Research*, edited by K. Vespers. Wellesley: Boston College.

Smith, Raymond T. 1956. *The Negro Family in British Guiana: Family Structure and Social Status in the Villages*. London: Routledge.

Stoner, Charles R., Richard I. Hartman, and Ray Arora. 1990. "Work-Home Role Conflict in Female Owners of Small Businesses: An Exploratory Study". *Journal of Small Business Management* 28, no. 1.

Strassmann, Diana. 1993. "Not a Free Market: The Rhetoric of Disciplinary Authority in Economics". In *Beyond Economic Man: Feminist Theory and Economics*, edited by M.A. Ferber and J.A. Nelson. Chicago: University of Chicago Press.

Sutton, Constance, and Susan Makiesky-Barrow. 1981. "Social Inequality and Sexual Status in Barbados". In *The Black Woman Cross Culturally*, edited by F.C. Steady. Cambridge, Mass.: Schenkman.

Tinker, Irene. 1976. "The Adverse Impact of Development on Women". In *Women and World Development*, edited by I. Tinker and M.B. Bramsen. Washington, DC: Overseas Development Council.

Williams, Constance H. 1982. *The Women's Project: Philadelphia Small Business Development Center*. Philadelphia: University of Pennsylvania Press.

13 Gender, Ethnicity and Familial Ideology in Georgetown, Guyana

*Household Structure and Female Labour Force Participation Reconsidered**

Alissa Trotz

Introduction

The feminist and gender development literature have demonstrated in a variety of settings that "supply" factors constitute critical constraints on female labour force participation. Although not the first to identify the relationship between the household and female employment, what distinguishes feminist analyses is their problematization of what was previously seen as a natural and utility-maximizing domestic strategy, and their depiction of the household as a locus of political activity. The relevance of household structure to this discussion has been the feature of a plethora of more recent studies. In fact, it is now axiomatic that the person or persons a woman lives with will have a significant effect on her relationship to the labour market, and sometimes even on the location of her income-earning activities.

This article aims to take this discussion further by questioning some of the assumptions behind the projected relationship between the domestic domain and female employment. Drawing on a case study of black and Indian women in Guyana, it examines how ethnicity intercedes in household organization

*First published in *European Journal of Development Research* 8, no. 1 (1996): 177–99.

and women's labour market behaviour. It argues that analyses of patriarchy which prioritize gender at the expense of other social constructs through which women's experiences are refracted are ultimately unable to offer an explanatory framework that can adequately account for the production of similarities and differences among women.

The Household and Female Labour Supply

Delineating the linkages between who women live with (household structure) and what women do has been a critical aspect of much recent theorizing on female employment. Underlying these analyses tends to be an assumption that a specific constellation of patriarchal norms circumscribes women's activities when they live with a man. In this regard, a significant finding has been that women who head their own households display greater levels of involvement in the labour force than those in coresidential units.

This derives from three factors. First, economic necessity compels female heads to seek employment to support their homes. Second, such women are free from the possible prohibitions placed upon them by a breadwinning spouse. Finally, female-headed households are structurally more conducive to women's entrance into the workforce, since the incorporation of other women into the domestic domain facilitates help with household chores and in particular with young children, where the woman in question is a single mother (Bolles 1981; Massiah 1982 on the Caribbean; Chant 1985 on Latin America; Lesser Blumberg 1977 in general).

Another important contribution has been the recognition that discussion of the household cannot be abstracted from the external environment. Some of the most interesting analyses in this regard have emerged from a systematic consideration of the pervasiveness of gender divisions in the household *and* in the labour market; indeed in some cases the two have been spatially indistinguishable. Research has demonstrated how gendered labour markets bolster male breadwinner models, along with the difficulties of sustaining such divisions of labour in conditions of economic immiseration, male unemployment or expanding opportunities for female employment (Beneria and Feldman 1992; Chant 1991; Safa 1995). Additionally, accounts of changing divisions of labour suggest that the household's internal dynamics should be treated as a process whose outcome is not only influenced by broader structural constraints, but is equally contingent on patterns of conflict and negotiation among members.

While undoubtedly these findings have been shown to be relevant to a variety of cross-cultural settings, they have relied, for the most part, on largely aggregate figures or homogenous samples of women. Yet it is precisely because gender is made the primary variable to be investigated that the bulk of the available material fails to address ethnic differentiation or to locate the underlying basis of such variations when they emerge. Are they to be explained away as deviations? Where other dimensions of female experience are not incorporated into the analytic frame, several of the extrapolations leave themselves open to the charge of universalizing/stereotyping a particular type of household relationship. Without a consideration of ethnicity-diverse family patterns, can we rely on general presumptions that women who live with men will face constraints on their activities? If we do, are we not perhaps making an assumption that there is a *standard* version of patriarchal relations which, while modified by economic change or household structure, remains the common point of departure? In short, how does the existing paradigm explain varying household types among different ethnic groups, or households which may be structurally similar yet radically diverse in function? Further, how do we relate these findings to the labour market, when gender divisions have been made the principal focus of academic interest?

There is now a rapidly growing body of work, primarily on the experiences of migrant and ethnic minority women in the United Kingdom and the United States, contrasting female labour force participation rates across ethnic groups (Afshar and Maynard 1994; Amott and Matthaei 1991; Bruegel 1989). Much of the research so far has been devoted to examining the hierarchical structure of the labour market, with relatively little detailed inquiry into intrahousehold patterns: gender ideologies, domestic divisions of labour and women's perceptions of and reasons for entering the labour market. Undoubtedly (and understandably), these are critical correctives to the ethnic studies tradition which tended towards volitional models based on the cultural choices of ethnic groups. These have been discredited for reducing ethnicity to cultural differences, for their exclusive, inward-looking emphasis, and particularly for not engaging with racism as manifested in the systematization of inequalities in the labour market and the institutions of the state (Parmar 1982; Brah 1994).

Locating ethnic inequalities in the workplace does not invalidate an investigation of whether and how households are internally stratified. (In other words, it is sterile to conclude that racism cancels out gender divisions in the household for women from ethnic minority groups.) It does, however, underline the need to seek out the interactions between both levels of analysis. Discussions which isolate one or the other, at the expense of elucidating the dynamic interface between the two, limit our understanding of the ways in which gender and ethnicity mediate the relationship between the household and female labour supply (Brah 1994; McIllwaine 1993).

Finally, this article's principal concern is to undermine the stereotyping of the household–labour force nexus by illustrating how ethnicity differentiates experiences of gender. Yet "difference" itself needs to be closely interrogated, lest the explanation reproduce an unproblematic division, in this case between ethnic groups. Avoiding this tautological trap requires us to be sensitive to three issues: the historical conditions creating ethnically specific familial ideologies and practices; the manner in which these are sustained or transformed in the contemporary situation; and cross-cutting social relations which underline the porousness of ethnic boundaries. As this case study will attempt to show, women respond to the challenges they face in ways which do not reflect ethnic absolutes but which have been shaped by the specific and intersecting histories of their relationships to Guyanese society.

Women in Guyana: An Overview

Guyana's social structure is far more complex than that of those Caribbean societies which did not experience a vast influx of immigrants in the post-slavery era. The Amerindian population (Guyana's original inhabitants) was largely destroyed by the colonial encounter in the sixteenth century. In the seventeenth century, the requirements of the sugar plantations led to the large-scale importation of slave labour from Africa. Following the abolition of slavery in 1838, alternative labour supplies were brought in on indentured contracts from Portugal, China and eventually on a massive scale from India. Today Indo-Guyanese account for some 51 percent of the population and Afro- and mixed-Guyanese constitute around 42 percent. Indo-Guyanese are concentrated in the rural areas, although growing numbers in urban centres, particularly in Georgetown, are fast altering the demographic profile of areas once predominantly Afro-Guyanese in composition.

This plurality – particularly in relation to the two dominant groups – is an important dimension of contemporary society. The most salient indicator resides in the political arena, with the two major political parties being polarized along ethnic lines. Guyana has recently emerged from twenty-five years of authoritarian rule under the People's National Congress, an Afro-Guyanese-dominated party. The return to political democracy in 1992 brought to power the Indo-Guyanese supported party, the People's Progressive Party, in an election which demonstrated that ethnic identification remains central to Guyanese politics.

The racialization of power at the national level can easily be read as a reflection of pluralism in Guyanese society and its political institutionalization.[1] Yet it needs to be emphasized that structural explanations exist for what are portrayed as irreducible ethnic (read cultural) differences – residential segregation, for example. Additionally, these differences are more often ideological productions and less an adequate description of each group's relationship to the labour market, to the state and to each other. Undoubtedly cultural differences exist – most notably at the level of the family, as this article will discuss – although the boundaries are far less marked and more obviously fluid today. Despite a growing convergence in many areas of their lives, the fact that Indo- and Afro-Guyanese continue to portray themselves in many ways as fundamentally different groups, while simultaneously asserting their authenticity as Guyanese with a claim to an equal share in the benefits of nationhood (Williams 1991), can only be properly understood when placed in the context of the politicization of ethnicity in Guyana (Jaywardena 1980).

Economically, from the mid-1970s Guyana has been in a state of crisis whose origins are both regional and internal. The former pertains to the colonial legacy in the Caribbean which has produced mainly primary export economies, all of which were adversely affected by the world recessions of the early 1970s and 1980s. In Guyana the key exports are bauxite, sugar and rice; manufacturing constitutes only 12 percent of gross domestic product (Strachan 1989). The internal dynamics of the crisis refer to the consolidation of authoritarian power in the postindependence era. Under the slogan of feeding, housing and clothing the nation, the government embarked on a programme of cooperative socialism in 1970; by the end of the decade over

80 percent of the economy had come under government ownership. In reality, however, cooperative socialism stood for the regime's lack of legitimacy; its self-perpetuation through fraudulent means; the use of the state sector for political patronage and as a channel of accumulation for the political elite; massive and unsustainable state expansion and public expenditure; and economic mismanagement (Thomas 1988).

A glance at some macroeconomic indicators reveals the extent of the country's decline. Real gross domestic product, which averaged an annual growth rate of 3.6 percent during the 1960s, fell to 0.9 percent in the 1970s and negative growth rates of -3.3 percent were registered in the 1980s (Thomas 1993: 12). The visible trade balance moved from a position of surplus in 1971 to a deficit in 1981, and the external debt mushroomed from US$364 million in 1980 to US$769 million or 168.8 percent of gross domestic product in 1985 (Ferguson 1995: 34). Following a series of negotiated and suspended agreements, in 1985 the International Monetary Fund declared Guyana ineligible for assistance (Ferguson 1995: 1). By the mid-1980s the country was characterized by rampant domestic shortages, infrastructural collapse, bankrupt social services, inflation and growing levels of unemployment. Economic disintegration also spilled over into the social sphere, manifested in growing crime levels and endemic corruption (UNICEF 1993: 18).

The situation forced an abandonment of the cooperative agenda following the death of the president in 1985. Under new leadership, the government embarked on talks with the International Monetary Fund, resulting in the adoption of a structural adjustment programme in 1990, involving standard divestment procedures, restructuring of the public sector and economic liberalization measures. Liberalization in the political sphere resulted in a change of government in 1992; the structural adjustment programme has continued unabated under the new administration.

The terms of the structural adjustment programme have meant greater economic immiseration for a population already hard hit in previous years, while adding formerly protected categories of workers to the ranks of the poor (UNICEF 1993: 15). Between 1985 and 1991, the cost of living index spiralled a thousandfold while the minimum wage in US dollars was reduced by some 65 percent (UNICEF 1993: 16). It is estimated that well over 60 percent of the population live below the poverty line, with some putting the figure as high as 75 percent (Ferguson 1995: 109). Available social indicators attest to the crisis in living standards. Life expectancy declined from 70 to 65 years between 1985 and 1991, while maternal and infant malnutrition and mortality rates are now among the highest in the English-speaking Caribbean (Boyd 1989: 10–12; UNICEF 1993: 16). Social expenditure on health, education and housing accounts for a declining proportion of gross domestic product (Ferguson 1995: 108). There is evidence of increasing homelessness and the proliferation of squatter settlement, with nonexistent or rudimentary drainage, sewage and water supply systems (Peake 1997).

Faced with such immense constraints, one can identify numerous popular responses, but two in particular have become firmly imprinted on the Guyanese landscape. The first is the massive informalization of the economy that began in the 1970s with the expansion of illicit trading in response to scarcities, the imposition of bans on a number of imported items and bureaucratic constraints on entrepreneurial activity. Previously confined to mainly agricultural and local produce, trading has been transformed into an international movement of people and goods of unparalleled proportions in the country's history. Other avenues of informal employment followed the loss of jobs and drop in real wages occasioned by the decline of the economy. While goods are now readily available following liberalization, the cost of living, coupled with low wage rates in the formal sector, has made self-employment and microenterprises far more viable alternatives for women and men (Holder 1988).

The virtual explosion in the scale of emigration since the 1970s denotes the other significant response to the crisis. While outward migration is an integral aspect of the fabric of Caribbean societies in general, none has witnessed such a haemorrhaging of its human resources as Guyana. Faced with declining standards of living and the systematic repression of opposition by the state, vast sections of the population fled the country: annual population growth fell from 2.5 percent in the 1960s to 0.4 percent in the 1970s. In the 1980s negative population growth rates of –0.1 percent were recorded (Thomas 1993: 12). Preliminary projections for 1992 show numbers well below the 1980 census estimates.[2]

Women in particular have been profoundly affected by the crisis. Despite a progressive legal framework in regional terms (following a 1976 state paper on equality, the principle of gender equality was enshrined in the 1980 constitution and addressed in a 1990 Equal Rights (Amendment) Act), women occupy a relatively disadvantaged position in Guyanese society. This is the combined result of socioeconomic conditions and politico-ideological factors. The association of women with the domestic sphere was reinforced by gender-stereotyped and welfarist policy initiatives (Peake 1993: 122), largely dictated in the pre–1992 era by political allegiance to the ruling party. Gender equity in the workplace has been limited by the absence of comprehensive and enforceable employment legislation, and the grossly inadequate provisions for daycare (Andaiye 1993; UNICEF 1993). Other critical issues, most notably domestic violence, remain unaddressed by existing legislation.[3]

Consequently, in a context in which households are increasingly pressed to substitute for limited and nonexistent state services, it is women – over half of the population – who have shouldered the greatest burden of adjustment over the last two decades, a process which has intensified in recent years under the structural adjustment programme (Trotz 1995: 71–75). This is reflected in women's growing visibility in the workforce, although as we shall see later, this has in the main meant access to the lowest-paid and worst jobs. Additionally, women have demonstrated a greater propensity to emigrate, often in search of incomes to shore up households and families. As much of this migration tends to be illegal, families are often reunited only after several years, if at all (Andaiye 1993: 4). These dramatic changes have affected women across ethnic lines, reconfiguring gender and ethnic identities in ways that underline their fluidity.

To be sure, these "survival strategies" – the contemporary catchword in the development literature – are poignant testimony to the resilience and creativity of the Guyanese population. Yet they should not distract us from the violence of the conditions under which women have been forced to make their lives. Nor should they blind us to the reality that many households are barely coping and some are simply *not* surviving; they are, after all, not infinitely adaptable to poverty.

Methodology

Most of the fieldwork that forms the basis of this article was carried out between October 1992 and May 1993 in a low-income urban area in Georgetown, the country's capital. With a population of around eight thousand persons in 1980, one-third of whom were of Indian origin (Central Housing and Planning Authority 1982), the community was a particularly suitable location for fruitful comparative research.

Both quantitative and qualitative research methods were used in the study area. A short structured survey of a random sample of residents was carried out. The sampling frame used was obtained from the visitation records of the 1991 census. Given the specific aims of the research, households consisting of a single male or a man and small children were eliminated from the survey. Two lists of residents were drawn up – one for Afro-Guyanese and another for Indo-Guyanese – and equal numbers of households randomly selected from each. All of the women interviewed were similarly positioned within the household, as household head or partner of the male head. In all a total of 184 women were interviewed, 89 Indian and 95 black respondents. A second qualitative round was carried out with twenty women at various stages in the life cycle, in different types of relationships and with varying employment histories. A small snowball survey was also carried out of eleven employers and an official from the government's central recruiting agency.

Household Characteristics

Even the briefest of glances at kinship structures of Afro- and Indo-Caribbean populations alerts us to the danger of reifying household types. The broad contrasts between the two groups have been amply documented. Ethnographies of Indo-Caribbean populations have shown the basic unit of the Indian kinship system to the "nuclear" family based on marriage, linked through a system of reciprocal familial obligations to the extended family and ideally represented in the wider community by the male head (Jaywardena 1962; Vertovec 1992). Women's sexual relations with men are confined to marriage, which includes legal ceremonies as well as weddings conducted according to customary religious rites, which may or may not be legalized; for present purposes both will be treated as marriages. Marriage is part of a woman's standard process of maturation into adulthood, completed when she bears her first child.

A radically different picture is presented by Afro-Caribbean family patterns. Although motherhood is similarly considered the hallmark of womanhood, it is not necessarily linked to marriage or even coresidential relationships. Common-law (consensual) and visiting (nonresidential) unions are common. This accounts for high numbers of female-headed households, kinship networks in which consanguineal kin and especially women play a central supporting role, and the primacy of the mother-child bond, all of which have led to the characterization of Afro-Caribbean households as matrifocal. More recent sociodemographic analyses of fertility and family structures in Guyana's urban centres demonstrate that, despite greater levels of interaction, household and marital patterns between these two groups remain distinct (Balkaran 1983: 115; Wilson 1989: 150).

These patterns were corroborated by the survey findings (see Tables 13.1 and 13.2). The majority of the Indian women (74 percent) had been or remained married, while nonmarried women constituted the largest propor-

Table 13.1   Marital Status by Ethnicity

	Indo-Guyanese		Afro-Guyanese	
Marital status	No.	Percent	No.	Percent
Married	40	44.9	17	17.9
Divorced	5	5.6	2	2.1
Separated	9	10.1	14	14.7
Widowed	12	13.5	12	12.6
Never Married	23	25.8	50	52.6
Total	89	100.0	95	100.0

Source: Respondent survey, Georgetown, 1992–93.

Table 13.2   Union Status by Ethnicity

	Indo-Guyanese		Afro-Guyanese	
Marital Status	No.	Percent	No.	Percent
Married	40	44.9	17	17.9
Common-law	30	33.7	28	29.5
Visiting	30	33.7	19	20.0
Single	16	18.0	31	32.6
Total	89	100.0	95	100.0

Source: Respondent survey, Georgetown, 1992–93.

tion of the black respondents (53 percent). Turning to consider the types of relationships in which the respondents were involved at the time of the interviews, only 47 percent of the black women lived with a man, with 20 percent in a visiting relationship; the corresponding figures for the Indian respondents were 79 percent and 3 percent.

Not surprisingly, there were identifiable ethnic differences in household structure. Male partners were present in three-quarters of the Indo-Guyanese households, with the largest proportions of the respondents residing in a unit consisting of a woman, man and children only (46 percent). In contrast, only 46 percent of the Afro-Guyanese respondents reported a resident male.

The contrast was even starker when households with young children (aged six and under) were isolated. While in both cases the largest percentage fell within the coresidential category, the likelihood of children being raised in a household in which a man was present appeared to be far greater among the Indo-Guyanese population (93 percent as against 54 percent for black women).

Further interesting contrasts emerged from a comparison of the marital status of female household heads. Widows comprised the largest category amongst Indian women (43 percent). The majority of Afro-Guyanese female heads were unmarried (51 percent), while only 19 percent of the Indian heads were in a similar situation. This suggests that while it is fairly common for black women to set up their own households *prior to* or *instead of* marriage, Indian female-headed households are more often the consequence of marital disruption or widowhood.

There were also notable similarities, particularly in relation to female-headed households. For both groups, women living with men tended to be younger than female heads of household. A large percentage of all households were extended, comprising persons in addition to the respondent, her partner (where applicable) and children. However, there was a much greater proportion of female-headed households in this category (64 percent as against 29 percent of coresidential units). Women living without a partner also tended to incorporate other women to a much greater extent than where the respondent's partner was resident; one can perhaps characterize their households as being constituted of confederations of female kin. This arrangement was found to have significant implications for the domestic division of labour (Trotz 1995: 261–301).

Household Structure and Female Labour Force Participation

Following on the position sketched in the opening sections of this article, the divergent household patterns should result in varying levels of involvement in the workforce. Specifically, we should expect Afro-Guyanese women to display higher activity rates, given their disproportionate representation among the female-headed population and the higher numbers of single mothers.

The definition of employment used in this survey was influenced by the massive informalization of the Guyanese economy. The tendency of official data to equate employment with regular, formal-sector work renders invisible many of the activities in which women are involved. Already undercounted, the deepening casualization of work opportunities threatens to underestimate women even further. Thus, employment was broadly interpreted to cover any activity that was income generating, *regardless of where it was carried out or the regularity of the respondent's involvement.* Both women who were working at the time of the survey and those seeking a job were regarded as economically active.

Not surprisingly, the majority of the respondents were economically active (63 percent), reflecting the broad impact of recession and adjustment on low-income households. The majority of the women in the labour force were black (61 percent), while nonworking women were predominantly Indian (65 percent). The survey results showed that a woman living with a man was indeed less likely to work (57 percent) than a female household head (72 percent). Fewer female heads in extended households worked than women living with children only, for whom the highest activity rates were registered. The former tended to be older women living with and depending on other adults. However, when the data were disaggregated by ethnicity, only among the Indian respondents did female heads show a greater tendency to work (71 percent) than women with working partners (44 percent). In marked contrast, black female heads and women in coresidential unions displayed roughly similar levels of labour force involvement (73 percent and 77 percent, respectively; see Table 13.3).

As we saw earlier, while most Indian women with infants resided with men, a significant percentage of their black counterparts lived in female-headed households. Given that the presence of infants may act as a dissuasive

Table 13.3   Household Structure by Employment Status and Ethnicity

Household Structures	Afro-Guyanese Women				Indo-Guyanese Women			
	Working		Not Working		Working		Not Working	
	No.	Percent	No.	Percent	No.	Percent	No.	Percent
Households with man*	34	77.2	10	22.7	30	44.1	38	55.9
Households without man	37	72.5	14	27.4	15	71.4	6	28.5
Total	71	74.7	24	25.3	45	50.5	44	49.4

*Refers to respondent's partner
Source: Respondent survey, Georgetown, 1992–93.

influence on women's entry into the labour market, is it possible that the higher labour force participation rates of black women in coresidential unions can be accounted for by the lower incidence of young children in such households?[4] Again the evidence showed that the activity rates of black women remained more or less unaffected – 74 percent worked when children were present and 75 percent when they were not, with relatively minimal adjustment when a partner was resident. A far lower proportion of Indian women with children were working (36 percent) than those with no infants in the home (64 percent).

Other sociodemographic variables (education, age, transfers, marital status) also had little consequence for the Afro-Guyanese respondents, or displayed marked variations when the figures were disaggregated ethnically. For example, income data on women's partners made it possible to explore whether they were lower among Afro-Guyanese households, making the need for extra earnings imperative. While in both cases the highest levels of female labour force participation occurred in the lowest categories of earnings (where the bulk of the respondents were located), the *proportion* of Indian women working at each income level was consistently below the levels recorded for the black respondents (Trotz 1995: 192–223).

In short, the presence of a man and the experience of motherhood did not appear to define black women's relationships to employment in the way that they did for the Indian respondents. Only when the latter group headed their own households did their work rates approach parity with their black counterparts.

These findings, particularly those relating to black women, cannot be tidily contained within a general paradigm of the household structure/labour market relationship. While the variations allude to functional differences in gender relations for the two groups, an adequate explanation can only be provided through an analysis of intrahousehold dynamics.

"Inside" the Household: Gender, Ethnicity and Familial Ideologies

The evidence presented so far points to the changing and varying relationship between gender norms (the cultural context which shapes behaviour) and demographic variables commonly seen as significantly influencing the female labour supply. In fact, the evidence suggests that gender ideology, far from being yet another in a list of possible factors affecting women's workforce involvement, may play a role in *constructing* sociodemographic variables themselves. For example, the effect of fertility on women's work rates depends not only on the different types of demands for female labour, but also on how mothering is perceived by and organized for different women at specific historical moments, so that no general relationship can be unproblematically projected. Instead, the household itself needs to be reconsidered from the vantage point of specific experiences. I begin by exploring perceptions of motherhood and employment prevailing in the respondents' households.

All of the women felt that childbearing signified adult feminine status. However, definitions of what motherhood entailed and the conditions under which it was permitted differed sharply. The Indian respondents across age groups indicated that sexual relations and motherhood were permissible only in the context of a marital relationship, expressed in the comments of one respondent as "all women should have children, yes, children good. But you got to first be a wife and then a mother." This contrasted with Afro-Guyanese women, who indicated that sexual relations and motherhood outside of marriage were not only acceptable, but often preferable, a view succinctly expressed in the comment that "marriage, common-law, visiting, it don't make a difference . . . is according to how the individual really treats you, that you would know how to do things".

Similar distinctions characterized perceptions of the extent to which women's activities could legitimately extend into income earning. Among the Afro-Guyanese respondents, motherhood and employment were not seen as mutually exclusive; on the contrary, participation in income-earning activities was an inextricable aspect of women's mothering obligations. Employment was also singled out as one way of ensuring access to an independent source of income. Linked to an awareness of male dominance, it was identified as a critical means of achieving more egalitarian gender relations in the home.

Perceptions of acceptable female activity for Indian women, on the other hand, denoted a clear conceptual distinction between the private and public spheres, as revealed in the comment of one woman who defined herself as "a wife and a mother. A wife and a mother is actually the same thing. A worker sound so out of bounds." Men were the ones responsible for the economic upkeep of the household and women for domestic management, which included their involvement in a family business as unpaid labour. Some respondents stated that a woman could work if her husband died, reneged on his familial obligations or was unable to support the home.

Gendered Norms, the Household and Female Employment

One would, however, be mistaken to assume that norms are necessarily reflective of social practices (Scott 1990: 198–201). To avoid this simplistic elision, we must specify how cultural constructions articulate with the material reality of women's lives (and, it follows, identify the processes through which disjunctures occur).

Three main points stood out with regard to the Afro-Guyanese respondents.[5] First, residential histories were complex and involved numerous household changes, many of which resulted from the termination or initiation of relationships. Second, there was no consistent link between childbearing and coresidentiality or marriage. Finally, employment histories were generally continuous and demonstrated strong linkages to childbearing and male-female relationships; in fact, motherhood often acted as the catalyst for entry into the labour market.

At one level, employment trajectories were related to the temporary nature of the relationships some women formed with men. Consequently, coresidential arrangements were often quite transitory. In such cases, households consisted of a core unit revolving around the female head and her children, with close linkages with wider consanguineal networks. Given the temporary nature of these unions, employment was one of a number of strategies whereby women maintained their homes and families.

This was reinforced by patterns of childbearing. Multiple childbearing unions and residence of children with their mother or her family were regularly cited as significant factors behind women's employment, regardless of male presence. One respondent, naming five fathers for her six children, explained why she continued to work after getting married as follows: "We had a basic problem, you see I have children that were not his. It was my obligation to look [after] them." To be sure, the overemphasis on male marginality within the Afro-Caribbean domestic domain has overlooked the existence of enduring male-female relationships (Roberts and Sinclair 1978). Yet regardless of the stability of relationships, work histories were also relatively continuous.

This paradox was resolved by shifting the focus to childbearing and household formation patterns. All case study respondents had children while still resident in their maternal homes. As adult residents, and especially having introduced further children, young mothers were often expected to contribute, with older women assuming childcare responsibilities. In short, providing for one's child was both structurally and ideologically compatible with motherhood. This frequent separation between childbearing and coresidence means that women who then began to live with a man had had the experience of providing for their families. They generally continued to work, relying on extended networks of female kin to assist with housework.

Among the Indo-Guyanese case study respondents, employment histories were far more contingent on conjugality and childbearing. All of the women who worked prior to marriage left their jobs once they got married, while those with no employment experience transferred their financial dependency from parents to husbands.

This was partly the result of the types of households in which Indian women with young children were found. In contrast to the Afro-Guyanese patterns, where it was not uncommon for women to regularly support their children *prior* to moving in with a man, motherhood for the Indian women was primarily experienced through a marital or coresidential relationship. The basic residential unit consisted of the husband, wife and child/ren; three women had moved in with parents-in-law for a short period of time before establishing separate residences.[6] Given the allocation of domestic responsibilities, household structure presented a material hindrance to Indian women's ability to work after marriage.

Additionally, the exit of the Indian respondents from the workforce after marriage was the outcome of proscriptions on their employment; all of the respondents reported that their partners did not expect them to work after marriage, save in a family-run business.

The issue was far more complex than the apparent practical obstacle of finding child care suggested. All of the women had stopped working *prior* to having children, and some of the respondents had female relatives who could have assisted with household maintenance. Indian women were also more restricted from engaging in home-based income-earning activities, which have been characterized elsewhere as partially resolving the conflict between paid employment and domestic responsibilities (Beneria and Roldan 1987). That female kin may actually *reinforce* limitations on women's activities draws our attention to the household's interaction with the wider kinship system in the construction and reproduction of familial ideologies. In the case of the Afro-Guyanese women, kin greatly facilitated their involvement in the workforce. These points also highlight men's reluctance to allow women to transgress the boundaries of acceptable female activity. Several respondents reported that their husbands believed that working was a man's obligation, or that it would undermine their sexual and financial control if women were allowed to seek employment.

Recognition of the household-level factors which placed prohibitions on the employment of Indian women does not mean that these gender codes were insuperable in the face of individual and systematic contradictions, particularly in the face of the economic crisis. A few of the older women had experienced such difficulties, but today there is far more widespread imperative to augment male income. A number of the respondents had recently re-entered the labour force, attributing this development to low wages of their partners.

That male objections to female employment can be overcome by economic constraints does not simply reflect a survival strategy that operates independently of the existing configuration of gender relations (Lessinger 1989:

111). In this case, women's employment was justified as a necessary extension of their domestic responsibilities, with respondents describing their involvement in the workforce as fulfilling their commitment to being good (Indian) wives and mothers. By defining employment in these terms it was, on the face of it, rendered more easily accommodated without appearing to provoke tensions resulting from perceived challenges to gender hierarchies. Yet whatever the rationalization offered, the growing entry of Indian women in the labour force is certainly reshaping gender relations and identities within an increasing number of households although, as in the case of black women, female autonomy remains limited by women's subordinate position in the labour market (Trotz 1995: 261–301).

Beyond Essentialism: The Household in Historical Perspective

So far, I have pointed out the dangers of reifying how household structure affects women's labour force participation. Yet focusing on diverse experiences of gender creates the dilemma that one form of essentialism is now exchanged for another, this time in the form of ethnic/cultural absolutism. Avoiding this requires two things. First, that we trace the historical processes through which households and their accompanying ideologies are constituted. Further, that such an analysis necessarily involves a discussion of the wider and cross-cutting social relations into which households are inserted.

This is starkly illustrated in the situation of unfree labour which existed in the colonial Caribbean setting. Whatever their familial ideologies may have been prior to their violent transplantation into New World societies, families and households played *no* role in mediating the release of women into the workforce for African slaves and Indian indentured labourers *alike*.

The postslavery and postindentureship periods were critical junctures insofar as the emergence of differences was concerned, the result of specific dynamics of labour/capital relations. Space does not allow for detailed analysis of these developments, but some critical points should be noted.

The abolition of slavery in 1834 saw efforts by ex-slaves to procure lands which would afford them greater autonomy from the sugar plantations. Guyana, with one of the lowest population densities in the Caribbean, experienced the most comprehensive village movement in the region (Farley

1954). There was also, at least in the initial stage, a withdrawal of many women, children and the elderly from the estate workforce to work on newly acquired lands. To preserve the monopoly previously enjoyed by the planters in the labour market, the colonial government passed a series of restrictive ordinances relating to land sale and maintenance (Mandle 1973: 22). Sustained efforts to reimpose hegemonic control over the labour force reached their apogee with the large-scale importation of Indian indentured labour from the mid-nineteenth century.

The effect of these measures was the gradual displacement of African labour from the estates, with profound implications for the viability of the villages after 1850 as villagers left to seek their livelihoods elsewhere. Women and men migrated to the urban areas, with men also moving into the emerging mining and timber industries of the hinterland regions (Rodney 1981: 90–102). In the villages, male outmigration and frequent loss of life contributed to the high incidence of female-headed households, intensifying the need for women to remain in or re-enter the labour force.

Patterns of female employment were also shifting. From the mid-nineteenth century, the formal agricultural sector occupied a declining share of total female employment. This was due in part to the substitution of Indian for African female labour, but also increasingly the result of technological modifications in the sugar industry which affected female employment as a whole. By 1960 domestic service formed the largest category of female employment (Peake 1993: 121). In the urban areas the opportunities for women were primarily as domestics, street vendors, washerwomen and garment factory workers (Rodney 1981: 205–10). Some women later went on to occupy positions in the lower rungs of the civil service, albeit in jobs considered typically feminine pursuits.

In the urban areas, female-headed households were also common, suggesting not only that women moved to the city on their own, but also that some access to employment provided them with a degree of flexibility to define their lives in relation to men. Women appeared to be accustomed to supporting their households, although their economic position frequently made it difficult for them to survive without some form of male support (Rodney 1981: 207). In short, the evidence suggests that the pattern of black women caring for their children both within and outside of marriage, and regardless of the availability of male support, was a defining feature of the postslavery era.

Plantation work was a critical aspect of the lives of Indian women, like the slaves whom they succeeded. In particular, the fact that women were wage earners had manifold repercussions for gender relations amongst the indentured workers (see Reddock 1985 on Trinidad; Trotz 1995: 110–16). However, the postindentured Indian community faced a very different situation from that which had confronted Afro-Guyanese in the postabolition era, and one which led to a significant curtailment of wage earning opportunities for Indian women. The restrictive land laws were lifted as an enticement to ex-indentured immigrants to remain in the colony (Mandle 1973: 36–37), a move that encouraged the relocation of Indian women's labour to the domestic unit where it came to form the base of subsistence and commercial farming by the 1960s. This was consolidated by technological introductions in sugar cultivation which progressively eliminated several labour-intensive jobs in which the bulk of the female labour force had been concentrated. These changing requirements necessitated a shift in gender-specific definitions of labour. One can trace the emergence of a colonial project aimed at the "restoration" of family life amongst the Indian community, which was principally dependent on the domestication of Indian woman (Mohapatra n.d.).[7] Additionally, the household division of labour was actively shaped by efforts to reconstitute an Indian ethnic identity, with considerable implications for women as custodians of the domestic space.

Despite these ideological and structural inhibitions, Indian female withdrawal was not complete. Some women continued to work in the estate gangs; money was also earned by retailing produce in rural communities and urban marketplaces. In the urban areas, some women worked as vendors, domestics and garment employees. Nonetheless, Indian women were relatively marginalized from paid employment, reinforced by the paltry provision of educational facilities, alternative job opportunities and the earlier access of Afro-Guyanese women to urban-based occupations.

Contemporary Patterns, Economic Crisis and Household Change

The structure of women's employment in Guyana has undergone considerable changes over the last twenty-five years. The bulk of formal sector employment opportunities for women (in service and light industries) are now located in Georgetown. Women's activities have become more diversified, with the commercial and service industries replacing the agricultural sector as the principal employers of female labour. Despite these changes, women have not been integrated into the economic sectors as broadly as men, being concentrated in the sales/clerical and service sectors. Although female representation in the professions has clearly grown, women are channelled into a narrow range of "caring and serving" occupations.

Preliminary figures for 1992 indicate that a considerably smaller proportion of Indian women are in the workforce than black women, and that they continue to be less represented in the higher echelons.[8] Some differences were also exhibited across industrial sectors, with greater percentages of Indian women in agriculture, commerce and manufacturing, and larger proportions of black women in public administration and other community services (Guyana Statistical Bureau 1992: Tables 1.5.1, 1.8.1 and 1.7.1). Three factors appear to be responsible for these disparities. Female job opportunities in the rural environs continue to be extremely limited. The overall lower level of education of Indian women is also reflected in their relative position in professional and managerial occupations. Finally, historical trends of exclusion from the public sector have been further affected by the distribution of patronage along ethnic lines in the postindependence context (Debiprashad and Budhram 1987).

Unfortunately, it is not possible to trace how broad changes in the labour market have affected black and Indian women over time, since employment data for the last three censuses (1960, 1970, 1980) were not disaggregated by ethnicity. Yet I would suggest that the economic restructuring of the last two decades has produced increasingly similar tendencies among the two groups. Women have been heavily pressed to seek employment; between 1970 and 1992, female participation rates rose from 20 percent to 39 percent of the documented female workforce. Given the decline in the productive sectors of the economy and scaling down of the public service by the late 1970s, this increase is more an indicator of households in crisis than of a growing demand for female labour. In fact, while women constituted 34 percent of the total labour force in 1992, they accounted for 53 percent of the unemployed in the same year (Government of Guyana 1970; Guyana Statistical Bureau 1992: Table 1.5.2). There have been sharp drops in public sector employment – where Afro-Guyanese women predominate – accompanied by an exponential increase in the number of women engaged in own-account work, especially in the commercial sector (Trotz 1995: 141–49).

These observations were borne out by the survey data. Although most of the interviewees had relatives who had migrated, in none of the households were remittances regular or anywhere near sufficient to meet domestic needs; this was equally true of help acquired through extended family networks. In the absence of adequate transfers, adult members were under increasing pressure to find employment. While children were increasingly relied on to assume housework and childcare duties, in only about two instances were they involved in income-earning activities.

Pauperization has made it increasingly difficult for households to reproduce themselves on a division of labour based on female noninvolvement in the labour force. As a result there is a growing resemblance in the labour-market behaviour of black and Indian women. Pauperization is not only reinforcing the centrality of income earning in black women's lives, but also making wage earning increasingly unavoidable – and, in many cases, acceptable – for Indian women in households with men, as seen in Table 13.3.[9]

The paucity of female employment opportunities, particularly for poor women, was also evident from the sample surveys. Both black and Indian women interviewed stressed the limited options available to them, regardless of whether they wanted to or were available for work; neither group appeared to have a distinct advantage or better employment prospects. Although men were not interviewed, information was collected on respondents' partners where available, and the data used as the basis for comparisons. While most men were in production-related jobs, women were concentrated in sales and service occupations that were socially devalued and enjoyed far lower levels of return.

Not surprisingly, almost half the respondents (47 percent) were self-employed and earned the highest levels of income. Even here, men were listed as having three times as many occupations as women, who were predominantly seamstresses, laundresses and petty vendors; only two women were small overseas traders. Most work principally from their homes, and the area outside their homes is normally bustling with activity in the mid to late afternoons as women set up their stalls to attract residents returning from work elsewhere. During the day, time is spent on household duties or, where necessary, on procuring and preparing items for sale. Gender differences are extremely visible. In one typical example, the woman earned money by selling ice and cold drinks (a particularly fruitful enterprise as hers was one of the few households with a refrigerator), while her partner operated an auto repair shop. Women's confinement to a narrower and less well remunerated range of activities was the result of differential access to credit, clients and apprenticeships, as well as the constraints imposed by domestic responsibilities on the mobility, regularity and scale of operations (Trotz 1995: 185–91). Daycare was a perennial problem, exacerbated by the attrition of informal support networks as more and more women were pressured into seeking employment. In addition, the scope for both black and Indian women to negotiate more equitable relations with their partners – involvement in decision making, allocation of housework – remained highly circumscribed, particularly by the levels of female remuneration.

Conclusions

This article set out to reexamine the relationship between household structure and female labour force participation. The assumptions that female heads are more likely to work than women who live with men, and that the household itself is a critical player in the determination of the female labour supply, are widely accepted tenets in the literature. Yet the evidence from this study warrants qualifications to these conclusions on two counts. From a comparative perspective, differences between ethnic groups alert us to the dangers of reifying the ways in which the domestic unit affects women's income-earning activities. Second, data pertaining to the Afro-Guyanese women studied here suggest that household structure does not *necessarily* have any explanatory force in accounts of women's participation in the labour market (a suggestion that may well extend to their Indian counterparts if current economic trends continue); indeed, structurally similar units have been shown to function in distinct ways. The relationship between household structure and female labour force participation, therefore, cannot be taken for granted *prior* to analytical investigation. Failing this, we must argue that the Afro-Caribbean case (and, it follows, that of any other group which displays such characteristics) is exceptional, which is clearly an untenable position.

By recognizing the shortcomings of an academic overemphasis on gender at the expense of other social relations we do not mean to say that the household is irrelevant; the main intention of this article has simply been to problematize certain lines of enquiry. The question is why household structure appears to matter more for some women than for others. In short, why do such variations occur? I argue in the above case that variations can only be satisfactorily addressed by examining how ethnicity shapes gender roles and relations within the household – and, more particularly, how these intersect with broader gender *and ethnic* hierarchies within the labour market in historically specific contexts.

Finally, this article has questioned implicit assumptions about the universality of specific experiences of gender. Yet it also warns *against* the reification of difference – representing black and Indian women's lives as responses to irrevocably separate patriarchal scripts. Beginning with the point of their arrival in the Caribbean, it is clear that neither African nor Indian households mediated the release of women into the workforce. Ending with the survey data presented here, it is equally obvious that household adjustments are leading to greater similarities in the labour market practices of low-income women. These observations *alone* should underscore the historical, contingent and overlapping nature of gender and ethnic identities. I have argued for a close examination of the interrelationship between household structure, familial ideologies and the labour market, and against the assumption of a functional relationship between these different analytical levels. Only then will we be able to provide a more sensitive reading, not only for ways in which ethnic differences become salient and are reproduced at the level of the household, but also of the manner in which they themselves are undermined and transformed.

Notes

1. For a discussion of the variants of pluralism, see M.G. Smith 1960.
2. The estimated population size for 1992 was 730,000 persons; in 1980 it was 758,619 persons (Government of Guyana 1980; Guyana Statistical Bureau 1992).
3. Mainly as a result of the work of women's organizations, a domestic violence bill is soon to be tabled in Parliament.
4. For discussions of the effect of the household's development cycle on female labour force participation rates, see Standing 1981 and Stichter and Parpart 1990.

5.   This section is based on twenty case study interviews.

6.   Among the Indo-Caribbean population, joint families – whereby young couples live with the husbands' parents – represent the normative ideal. Although they are far less prevalent today, this is not to say that underlying aspects of Indian family life are abandoned. In the present sample there were few joint units, and little evidence of ethnic differentiation on structural grounds with respect to extended households.

7.   Interestingly, this was taking place at a time when female headship and employment among Afro-Guyanese women was explicitly recognized, if not fully endorsed, in commission reports.

8.   Clearly these figures need to be treated with caution, especially since Indo-Guyanese are predominantly rural, where women's work, often carried out within the context of a family unit, is vastly undercounted (Odie-Ali 1986).

9.   Education is another factor which may obviate the negative evaluation of women's work, although its effect in the present study was not clear as most women interviewed had not gone beyond primary-level schooling.

References

Afshar, Haleh, and Mary Maynard, eds. 1994. *The Dynamics of "Race" and Gender: Some Feminist Interventions*. London: Taylor and Francis.

Andaiye. 1993. "Women and Poverty in Guyana". Paper presented at the seminar Poverty in Guyana: Finding Solutions, Institute of Development Studies, 18–19 March.

Amott, Teresa, and Julie Matthaei, eds. 1991. *Race, Gender and Work*. Boston: Southend Press.

Balkaran, Sundat. 1983. "Patterns of Marital Unions, Their Stability and Fertility: A Study of Indians and Non-Indians in Guyana". PhD thesis, London School of Economics.

Beneria, Lourdes, and Martha Roldan. 1987. *The Crossroads of Class and Gender: Industrial Homework, Subcontracting and Household Dynamics in Mexico City*. Chicago: University of Chicago Press.

Beneria, Lourdes, and Sally Feldman, eds. 1992. *Unequal Burden, Economic Crises: Persistent Poverty and Women's Work*. Boulder: Westview Press.

Bolles, Lynn. 1981. "Household Economic Strategies in Kingston Jamaica". In *Women and World Change: Equity Issues in Development*, edited by N. Black and A. Cottrell. Newbury Park, Calif.: Sage.

Boyd, D. 1989. "Macroeconomics Consultant Report on the Social and Economic Impact of Guyana's Economic Performance and ERP". Inter-American Development Bank, Washington, DC.

Brah, Avtar. 1994. " 'Race' and 'Culture' in Gendering of Labour Markets: South Asian Young Muslim Women and the Labour Market". In *The Dynamics of "Race" and Gender: Some Feminist Interventions,* edited by H. Afshar and M. Maynard. London: Taylor and Francis.

Bruegel, Irene. 1989. "Sex and Race in the Labour Market". *Feminist Review,* no. 32.

Central Housing and Planning Authority. 1982. *Georgetown Planning Area: Development Plan, Year 2000.* Vols. 1–3. Georgetown, Guyana: Central Housing and Planning Authority.

Chant, Sylvia. 1985. "Single-Parent Families: Choice or Constraint? The Formation of Female-Headed Households in Mexican Shantytowns". *Development and Change* 16.

_____. 1991. *Women and Survival in Mexican Cities: Perspectives on Gender, Labour Markets and Low-Income Households.* Manchester: Manchester University Press.

Debiprashad, S., and D. Budhram. 1987. "Participation of East Indians in the Transformation of Guyanese Society 1966–79". In *India in the Caribbean,* edited by D. Dabydeen and B. Samaroo. London: Hansib Publishing.

Farley, R. 1955. "Rise of a Peasantry in British Guiana". *Social and Economic Studies* 2.

Ferguson, Tyrone. 1995. *Structural Adjustment and Good Governance: The Case of Guyana.* Georgetown, Guyana: Public Affairs Consulting Enterprise.

Government of Guyana. 1970. *Population Census, 1970.*

_____. 1980. *Population Census, 1980–81.*

Holder, Yvonne. 1988. *Women Traders in Guyana.* Santiago: Economic Commission for Latin America and the Caribbean/Caribbean Development Co-operation Committee.

Jaywardena, C. 1962. "Family Organization in Plantations in British Guiana". *International Journal of Comparative Sociology* 3.

_____. 1980. "Culture and Ethnicity in Guyana and Fiji". *Man (NS).*

Lesser Blumberg, Rae, and Maria Garcia. 1977. "The Political Economy of the Mother-Child Family: A Cross-Societal View". In *Beyond the Nuclear Family Model: Cross Cultural Perspectives,* edited by L. Lenero-Otero. London: Sage.

Lessinger, J. 1989. "Petty Trading and the Ideology of Gender Segregation in Urban South India". In *Women, Poverty and Ideology in Asia: Contradictory Pressures, Uneasy Resolutions,* edited by H. Afshar and B. Agarwal. London: Macmillan.

McIllwaine, C.J. 1993. "Gender, Ethnicity and the Local Labour Market in Limon, Costa Rica". PhD thesis, London School of Economics.

Mandle, J.R. 1973. *The Plantation Economy: Population and Economic Change in Guyana, 1838–1960*. Philadelphia: Temple University Press.

Massiah, J. 1982. "Women Who Head Households". In *Women in the Caribbean Project*. Vol. 2. Cave Hill, Barbados: Institute for Social and Economic Research, University of the West Indies.

Mohapatra, P. N.d. "Restoring the Family: Wife Murders and the Making of a Sexual Contract for Indian Immigrant Labour in the British Caribbean Colonies, 1860–1920". Manuscript.

Odie-Ali, Stella. 1986. "Women in Agriculture: The Case of Guyana". *Social and Economic Studies* 35.

Parmar, P. 1982. "Gender, Race and Class: Asian Women in Resistance". In *The Empire Strikes Back: Race and Racism in 70's Britain,* edited by the Centre for Contemporary Cultural Studies. London: Hutchinson.

Peake, Linda. 1993. "The Development and Role of Women's Political Organizations in Guyana". In *Women and Change in the Caribbean,* edited by J. Henshell Momsen. London: James Currey.

_____. 1997. "From Co-operative Socialism to a Social Housing Policy? Declines and Revivals in Policy in Guyana". In *Self-Help Housing, the Poor and the State: Pan-Caribbean Perspectives,* edited by D. Conway and R. Potter. Knoxville: University of Tennessee Press.

Reddock, Rhoda. 1985. "Freedom Denied: Indian Women and Indentureship in Trinidad and Tobago, 1845–1917". *Cimarron* 1.

Roberts, G.W., and S. Sinclair. 1978. *Women in Jamaica: Patterns of Reproduction and Family*. New York: KTO Press.

Rodney, Walter. 1981. *A History of the Guyanese Working People, 1881–1905*. London: Heinemann.

Safa, Helen. 1995. "Economic Restructuring and Gender Subordination". *Latin American Perspectives* 22.

Scott, A.M. 1990. "Patterns of Patriarchy in the Peruvian Working Class". In *Women, Employment and the Family in the International Division of Labour,* edited by J. Parpart and S. Sticher. London: Macmillan.

Smith, M.G. 1960. "Social and Cultural Pluralism". In *Social and Cultural Pluralism in the Caribbean,* edited by V. Rubin. New York: Annals of the New York Academy of Sciences.

Standing, Guy. 1981. *Unemployment and Female Labour: A Study of Labour Supply in Kingston, Jamaica*. London: Macmillan.

Statistical Bureau of Guyana. 1986. *Guyana Retrospective Demographic Survey.* Georgetown, Guyana: Economic Commission for Latin America and the Caribbean/Statistical Bureau.

_____. 1992. *Preliminary Results of the Household and Income Expenditure Survey.* Georgetown, Guyana: Statistical Bureau.

Stitcher, S., and J. Parpart. 1990. *Women, Employment and Family in the International Division of Labour.* London: Macmillan.

Strachan, Alan. 1989. "Guyana". In *Urbanization, Planning and Development in the Caribbean,* edited by R.B. Potter. London: Mansell Publishing.

Thomas, C.Y. 1988. *The Poor and the Powerless: Economic Policy and Change in the Caribbean.* London: Latin American Bureau.

_____. 1993. "The State of Poverty and Poverty Studies in Guyana". Paper presented at the seminar on Poverty in Guyana: Finding Solutions, Institute of Development Studies, 18–19 March.

Trotz, D.A. 1995. "Gender, Ethnicity and Familial Ideology: Household Structure and Female Labour Force Participation in Guyana". PhD thesis, Cambridge University.

UNICEF. 1993. *Analysis of the Situation of Women and Children in Guyana.* Georgetown: UNICEF/UNDP.

Vertovec, Steven. 1992. *Hindu Trinidad: Religion, Ethnicity and Socio-Economic Change.* London: Macmillan.

Williams, Brackette. 1991. *Stains on My Name, War in My Veins: Guyana and the Politics of Cultural Struggle.* Durham: Duke University Press.

Wilson, Leon. 1989. "Family Structure and Dynamics in the Caribbean: An Examination of Residential and Relational Matrifocality in Guyana". PhD diss., University of Michigan.

14 Middle-Aged and Older Women in Jamaica

Joan M. Rawlins

Introduction

Even before the Women in the Caribbean Project[1] was undertaken, a fair amount of exploration had been done indirectly into the lives of women in the Caribbean, through extensive research on the Caribbean family conducted by sociologists and anthropologists. These investigations include the work of Smith 1962, Smith 1970, Barrow 1988 and Massiah 1983, to cite only a few. In all of the work which had been done on family and women, very little considered older women, and even less, middle-aged women. Those which touch on the lives of older women include Eldemire 1989 and 1993, Braithwaite 1990 and Senior 1991. The main work which explores the lives of middle-aged women is Sennott-Miller 1989.

Middle-aged and older women have traditionally been important to Jamaican and indeed to Caribbean families. They are sometimes referred to as the "backbone" of their families, especially those older women who do one round of childminding then, years later, have to take up another round for their grandchildren or for other relatives of that age group. There is no denying that there has been some recognition of middle-aged and older women especially in relation to their familial caregiving role. In what ways, however, do middle-aged women and older women contribute to family in Jamaica? How significant is their contribution to the economy? What is the state of their health and are they treated as a special group by the health service? What do they do in the event of widowhood? What are some of their concerns about the future and their relationships with their children? How do the migratory patterns of Caribbean life impact on their lives? This paper attempts to answer these and other questions.

For the purposes of this paper, middle-aged will refer to those women who are between fifty and fifty-nine and older women to those who are sixty to seventy-four years old.

Methodology

The data from which this paper is written comes from a research project (Rawlins 1996) in which two hundred women were studied. The women were drawn from two communities, one working class and the other middle class. Of the women interviewed in the surveyed communities, twenty-five were chosen for in-depth follow-up interviews, to provide more detailed case studies. In addition, a perception questionnaire was also administered to fifty family and community members. This questionnaire sought to determine how middle-aged and older women were perceived by family and society.

Middle-Aged and Older Women: The Feminist Discourse

Rawlins (1996) employed Michel Foucault's ideas on discourse and power to explain the lives and coping strategies of middle-aged and older women in Jamaican society given the changing economy and their familial obligations. Discourses are culturally structured ways of knowing. Through the existence of dominant discourses we arrive at conclusions about how best our lives should be lived. Discourses are not merely linguistic; they influence our thinking and our behaviour, producing what becomes knowledge and truth. In the dominant discourse, despite the vitality and lived experiences of middle-aged and older women, they are taken somewhat for granted because they are not perceived as important and as "economically significant". Wherever there is discursive power, however, there will be resistance. Resistance takes the form of counter-discourses, which present new knowledges and new truths.

The Main Findings

Women of this age group were very important to their family and their family to them. They were guided in their relationships with family by the societal expectations about what they should be and should do, and the relationships which they should have with others. They were also influenced by other forces which included employment and/or unemployment, migration and the health of their relatives and themselves. The data showed that although women brought income into the homes, family members did not see these women as productive income earners, but primarily as care givers. (Some acknowledgment was given grudgingly to their economic role.)

Despite the class differences, women of both groups had many similarities in relation to their family life. For example, those who worked outside the home also had responsibilities within the home. In both groups some were aided in their domestic tasks by family members, who preferred to be selective about the tasks with which they assisted.

Some of the working-class women saw their children as a resource for the future, while others did not. There was more ambivalence in respect of children as investments for the future among the working-class women than there was among middle-class women, who did not see their children as such. Almost equal numbers of women in both groups, 37 percent for the working class and 42 percent for the middle class, had adopted or fostered children. This suggests that both groups of women valued taking responsibility for children other than their own.

The dominant discourse on the family life of women of this age group suggests that women will continue to "do" for children, even in their old age, and the data confirms this. It was not always one-sided, as there were at times reciprocal benefits, such as gift sharing and health care on one another's behalf. The most apparent act of interdependence was that of house sharing: 31 percent of the working-class women and 55 percent of the middle class had at least one adult offspring still in residence. House sharing took place in an environment in which rents were especially high and mortgages astronomical. House sharing provided companionship and fostered greater savings. However, interdependence through house sharing was not always beneficial to these women (Rawlins 1996), as privileges were abused by live-in relatives. Some women allowed their daughters, even overtly negligent ones, to share their homes, because they hoped to grow emotionally closer to them, and so have improved chances of care in their old age.

Another similarity among the two groups was the importance of daughters to these women. The data showed that women of both groups were emotionally closer to their daughters than to other relatives, and anticipated care from these daughters when they grew too old to care for themselves. No such hope was held out for sons. Working-class women admitted that the group they felt closest to (next to their daughters) were other female relatives. Middle-class women felt next closest to their spouses and then to their other female relatives. Middle-class women, although primarily expressing closeness to daughters, perhaps experienced life through the dominant discourse (which idealizes marriage) and therefore reported closeness to the spouse next. It would seem that the working-class women rejected this discourse vehemently, and gladly admitted that their greatest closeness was with their female relatives.

Across both classes, women of these age groups – although they presented themselves as independent women – were reluctant to make decisions without consulting family members. Only 5 percent of the working-class women and 15 percent of the middle-class women would go ahead with decisions with which their relatives had not agreed. This suggests that although these women seemed independent, and often were economic providers, they so cherished the relationship with close relatives that at times they would inconvenience themselves rather than offend others.

With regard to their sexuality, middle-aged and older women had to be cautious, especially if they no longer resided with their spouses, or if they were widowed. These women deliberately subdued aspects of their sexuality because of their fear of being in conflict with their grown offspring, church and wider society. Their expression of their sexuality was bound up with the dominant discourses about what is "proper behaviour" for women of these age groups.

The data showed working-class women as more reserved with regard to discussions about their sexuality. They tended to be more overtly religious, and belonged to evangelical denominations, which were likely to be more controlling in matters of social behaviour for their members. They were also more likely to state that the society did not expect women of their age group to be sexually active. But women of these age groups are sexually active (Rawlins 1996). The women in the fifty to fifty-nine-year group were almost all sexually active. The older women, it would seem, were unable to create an alternative perception of their sexuality; working-class women, in particular, were most vulnerable to society's attempts to control their sexuality.

Large numbers of middle-class women, more so than working-class women, had relatives abroad. These included close relatives such as sons and daughters. They did not give the impression that they saw this as a great advantage to themselves, although it was clearly important. They were in contact with such relatives, and received occasional gifts and remittances from them. A few of these women, along with relatives such as sons and daughters, had already worked out domestic arrangements for the time when they were too old to take care of themselves. In some instances, among the middle class, daughters living abroad in North America had suggested that the mothers migrate to live in the daughter's home. Having relatives abroad, for some women, therefore determined what would happen in the future. Concerns about the future were as important for middle-class women as for working-class women: the main concerns expressed were loneliness first, followed by economic security, a general concern for old age, and ill health. The women should not have feared loneliness as much as they did for, as previously discussed, the research revealed a high degree of house sharing and relatives living with them. Some might have expressed their fear of loneliness because they felt they would be on their own in their old age, especially if they owned their own home. With the depressed economic crisis and high interest rate it was unlikely that young adults would be acquiring residences for themselves. The main concerns expressed by the working-class women for the future were, however, economic ones.

Undoubtedly, middle-aged and older women undertook many roles for family and community, yet in many ways they were taken for granted. The women responded to demands which were made on them ranging from the unpaid minding of children, to sharing their homes, without receiving any financial assistance. Many of these women undertook these challenges to make life easier and better for their relatives, and to improve their relationships with them.

Work

The data in this study suggested that middle-aged and older women worked for an income but did not see themselves as being productive. The majority of the women in this study (64 percent) were in paid employment, and only those women who were in ill health (about 10 percent of the sample) were not engaged in an activity which might be called work.

The data demonstrated that these women were very busy, working both as housewives and outside the home. In the area of paid employment there were some real differences noted between the women of the two communities. The middle-class women were paid much better salaries than the working-class women. The former had a significantly higher level of education. All had completed secondary education and some had attended colleges, universities and other places of tertiary education. Some working-class women worked at two jobs – and even then their wages were not significantly improved compared to the salaries of the middle-class women.

The work in which they were engaged was very important to the women as well as to their family. Despite the common belief that women of this age group are "taken care of by their relatives", this was not really the case. The data revealed that their relatives were at least as dependent on them as they were on their relatives, and of those who were in paid employment, 73 percent of the working-class and 72 percent of the middle-class women stated that they contributed to the financial maintenance of their household. The women worked because they needed to maintain their relative independence and because the economic circumstances of their family demanded this.

The working-class women were in twenty-five main occupations, primarily domestic work, cleaning and "selling-type" jobs. The middle-class women had a wider range of occupations which included teaching, nursing and administration, but which were conventionally thought of as "female" occupations. Not only did the younger group of women age fifty to fifty-nine work but 29 percent of those also in paid employment were in the sixty to seventy-four age group.

Middle- and older-aged women provided an invaluable service to family. Through their paid employment and all the services rendered to family members, to community through a range of activities, and in their involvement in community organizations, they aided the state by providing services for which the state would otherwise have to take responsibility.

Health

The research here shows that the Jamaican health care system does not treat women of this age group as a special group, or provide adequately for them, although there is much that they have to do and so they need to be in the best possible health. Resources are said to be limited and priority is given to other sectors, such as maternal and child health sectors.

Despite the low priority accorded to "older" women's health, some women saw their group as special because of the unique needs which they know they have as women at a particular point in the life cycle. Some women, however, tended to understate the extent of health problems and were reluctant to admit that they had anything wrong with them.

Generally the women were in good health. Approximately 25 percent of the women of each group had no health problem at the time of the survey. This is a reflection of their understanding of preventive health care, and the fact that they had enjoyed better health care in Jamaica in their younger years than that which was available in 1991.

The main illnesses which the women experienced were hypertension, diabetes and arthritis. A total of fifty-four of the two hundred women in the study were hypertensive. This was one area in which there was a real difference between the two groups of women: 37 percent of the working-class women were hypertensive as opposed to 17 percent of the middle-class women. There are many factors which contribute to hypertension in the individual (Waldron et al. 1982 and Dressler 1992) and the higher percentage of hypertensives in the working-class group was perhaps caused by a variety of reasons related to their overall socioeconomic situation, including diet.

Middle-aged and older women recognized that they were provided with less than ideal health care, and had several suggestions for an improved service. They felt that more could be done to educate older women about the benefits of preventive health care and that more doctors should be specially trained in the needs of an older population. The latter, they stated, was very important, as there was so much to understand about older people, and that "regular, everyday doctors were not able to understand it all". These women also complained that the high cost of medication resulted in their not always being able to take their medicines as prescribed. Much of what these women knew and hoped for in relation to their health care was part of a repressed discourse which did not gain the attention of the necessary state authorities.

In the overall financial allocation for the various sectors of the economy, health was always neglected (Levitt 1991), and insufficient resources were allocated to the special needs of these age groups. It was discovered in this study that the knowledge and ideas of these women about their own health had not been communicated to the relevant decision makers. They were aware that there were insufficient resources to dramatically improve state health care provisions, not only for themselves, but for the entire nation.

In addition to their concerns about their own health, middle-aged and older women also had responsibility for the health of others in their family and their community. Women of this age group are seen as appropriate caregivers and time-givers, because they are not viewed as centrally important economic contributors to the society.

Widowhood

The issue of widowhood was a particularly important area of concern to women in these age groups. Twenty-five percent of the women in the study were widows.

Widowhood is described in the literature on the subject as an event which causes great disruption and disorganization in women's lives. This was the experience of the women studied, primarily in the early years of widowhood. Nonetheless, the responses of the majority of widows surveyed were not in accord with the dominant ideas. The women did not seem overwhelmed by widowhood as might have been expected. One explanation of this is that these women had been reasonably independent women in their husbands' lifetimes, and so had relevant "survival experiences" (Rawlins 1996). The fact that most of them had been employed during significant parts of their adult years would have contributed to their being able to fend for themselves, and thus not experience greater feelings of loss. Tremendous feelings of loss are identified in the widowhood literature for some North American widows (Lopata 1986; Zick and Smith 1986). Working-class women in particular did not dwell on the loss. Widowhood did cause problems, but the economic loss was not stressed as the husband's meagre income, or that part of his income which would have been available to working-class women, did not make that great a difference. Nor did they complain of being lonely, as they had other people living in their homes. This was an area of real difference between the women of the two communities. The middle-class women were more likely to complain about being lonely, as more of them had been living with husbands alone up to the time of the men's death. Even this group of women did not make many complaints, and both groups spoke of the new freedoms which they had: freedom to use their time in new ways and to come and go as they pleased.

Despite the difficulties of being widowed, the majority were adamant that they desired to remain in their new single state, in contrast to what might have been expected. It could be argued that new intimate relations might have helped them to overcome feelings of loneliness, the dominant discourse about women in the society suggesting that "women without men" are at a disadvantage. The reasons women gave for not wanting to establish new relationships were that they did not feel that they could find "good and trustworthy men", a reluctance to share their material resources with these men, and suspicions that offers of marriage and friendship might have been motivated by the desire of unscrupulous men to benefit from material resources left by their husbands, or from those acquired by their own resourcefulness. Women were also concerned that such new relationships might cause them to lose the respect of their children, especially sons. The working-class women were more vehement in presenting the reasons for remaining single, but some of the reservations, especially those relating to financial resources, were also outlined by the middle-class women.

The study sought to determine the support which was available to widows. Women received emotional support from friends, relatives and the church community, especially in the early period of their widowhood. Not all women received such support. Eight percent of the working-class widows and 22 percent of the middle-class widows stated that they received no assistance from relatives. Women who were eligible for widows' benefits and pensions in their own right received these benefits. But these widows complained that the benefits were unrealistic and meagre given the high and increasing cost of living in Jamaica. Forty-eight percent of this combined group of widows (mainly middle class) received state benefits. Women who had not been in pensionable jobs or whose husbands had not been in jobs which contributed to the National Insurance Scheme which administers the widows' benefits were not eligible for such benefits. Many felt that the state could do much better for these women in the provision of financial assistance to all widows, with improved benefits to those who had contributed to the National Insurance Scheme.[2]

Widowhood was not a situation which women desired, but most of the women were able to rise above the difficulties occasioned by their widowhood and continued to lead useful and fulfilling lives, in ways which it would seem their North American and European counterparts, referred to in the widowhood literature, are unable to do. Some Jamaican widows declared that they had grown more resourceful in a number of ways since their husbands had died.

Conclusion

The data showed that middle-aged and older women were expected to be primarily caregivers, and that they fulfilled these expectations. However, there were situations in which they were reluctant to undertake the expected caregiving roles, such as free childminding and chores for their daughters. Even in this area of caregiving which has been determinedly allocated to midlife and older women, some women sought occasionally to reject the dominant discourse which influences the allocation of roles. But this role rejection was not nearly as frequent as the converse. Women provided a variety of services for relatives and community, even in situations where relatives at home and abroad did not provide the remuneration promised. Community members also did not reimburse these categories of women for expenses incurred in providing services. Thus we see that middle-aged and older women provide useful and necessary services but are persistently taken for granted by family, community and state.

This paper and the study from which it was derived has drawn attention to the lives of Jamaican women aged fifty to seventy-four. Some of the findings were anticipated and in accord with the dominant discourses on older women. However, more interestingly, the study also reveals new findings which challenge the assumed repression of some aspects of women's lives. The most important repressed areas were those of sexuality, health and widowhood. These women viewed themselves as active sexual agents in society. In relation to their health, they saw themselves as a special group, requiring special attention to their needs. As widows, they were especially resourceful and pragmatic about their potentials and possibilities for future partnerships with men.

Notes

1. The Women in the Caribbean Project was executed by the Institute of Social and Economic Research, University of the West Indies, Cave Hill, Barbados, under the leadership of Joycelin Massiah. The principle objectives of the project were to establish a Caribbean data base for teaching, research and planning purposes, and to sensitize policy makers to women's needs in order to influence planning.
2. This might well be possible if funds collected by the National Insurance Scheme were more creatively invested.

References

Barrow, C. 1988. "The Family and Women". In *Gender in Caribbean Development*, edited by P. Mohammed and C. Shepherd. St Augustine, Trinidad: Women and Development Studies Project, University of the West Indies.

Brathwaite, F. "The Elderly in Barbados". *Bulletin of PAHO* 24, no. 3.

Brodber, Erna. 1982. *Perceptions of Caribbean Women*. Cave Hill, Barbados: Institute of Social and Economic Research, University of the West Indies.

Dressler, W., et al. 1992. "Social Factors Mediating Social-Class Differences in Blood Pressure in a Jamaican Community". *Social Science and Medicine* 35, no. 10.

Durant-Gonzalez, V. 1980. "Role and Status of Rural Jamaican Women: Higglering and Mothering". PhD diss., University of California.

Eldemire, D. 1989. "Medical Care for the Elderly: A Study in Kingston Jamaica". In *Midlife and Older Women in Latin America and the Caribbean*. Washington DC: Pan American Health Organization and the American Association of Retired Persons.

Foucault, M. 1980. *Power/Knowledge: Selected Interviews and Other Writings 1972–77*, edited by C. Gordon. Brighton: Harvester Press.

_____. 1984. *The History of Sexuality*. Vol. 1, *An Introduction*. London: Penguin.

Fraser, N. 1989. *Unruly Practices, Power Discourse and Gender in Contemporary Social Theory*. London: Polity Press.

Levitt, K. 1991. *The Origins and Consequences of Jamaica's Debt Crisis 1970–1990*. Mona, Jamaica: Consortium Graduate School of Social Sciences, University of the West Indies.

Lopata, H.Z. 1986. *Dissolution through Widowhood*. Chicago: Loyola University Press.

Massiah, J. 1983. *Women as Heads of Households in the Caribbean: Family Structure and Feminine Status*. London: UNESCO.

Rawlins, J. 1989. "Widowhood: The Social and Economic Consequences in the Caribbean". In *Midlife and Older Women in Latin America and the Caribbean*. Washington DC: Pan American Health Organization and American Association of Retired Persons.

_____. 1996. "Women from Midlife: Coping in Jamaica – A Study of Power in the Lives of Women Aged 50–74". PhD diss., Institute of Social Studies, The Hague.

Sanchez, D. 1989. "Informal Support Systems of Widows over Sixty in Puerto Rico". In *Midlife and Older Women in Latin America and the Caribbean*. Washington DC: Pan American Health Organization and American Association of Retired Persons.

Senior, O. 1991. *Working Miracles*. London: James Currey.

Sennott-Miller, L. 1989. "The Health and Socio-Economic Situation of Midlife and Older Women in Latin America and the Caribbean". In *Midlife and Older Women in Latin America and the Caribbean*. Washington DC: Pan American Health Organization and American Association of Retired Persons.

Smith, M.G. 1962. *West Indian Family Structure*. Seattle: University of Washington Press.

Smith, R.T. 1970. "The Nuclear Family in Afro-American Kinship". *Journal of Comparative Family Studies* 1.

Waldron, I., et al. 1982. "Cross-Cultural Variation in Blood Pressure: a Quantitative Analysis of the Relationship of Blood Pressure to Cultural Characteristics, Salt Consumption and Body Weight". *Social Science and Medicine* 16.

Zick, C.D., and K. Smith. 1986. "Intermediate and Delayed Effects of Widowhood on Poverty". *Gerontology* 26.

SECTION

V

The Double Take
Gender and the
Literary Imagination

15 Rereading Our Classics
In the Castle of My Skin *and*
The Lonely Londoners

DAVID WILLIAMS

Feminist criticism in the Caribbean, for practical as well as ideological reasons, has to address itself to the works of the male writers who have thus far dominated the literature. The canon of anglophone West Indian literature is too firmly established, and the output of women writers too small, for the activities of rereading and reassessment to remain on the periphery of feminist concern. The status of such activities is the subject of intense debate among feminist critics. For people who have undertaken to question the basic assumptions of literary theory and history, the rereading of works enshrined in the approval of academia might seem an irrelevance. The mission of feminist criticism in our region is no less urgent, but there is a great deal to be said for attempting to influence the perceptions of reality communicated in "classic" West Indian novels. An alert reading of the world of this fiction should, at the very least, facilitate a more sensitive writing of the body of female experience in the Caribbean.

A defence of the label here attached to these novels should not be necessary. Separately and collectively, these texts anatomize the experience of being West Indian, at home or abroad; more than anything else produced by the region, they explain why West Indianness is a state of mind, a sense of being at home in exile. The surefootedness of the exploration undertaken in each of these works should not prevent us from noting just how sustained is the control exercised by each narrative. Autobiographical impulse in Lamming's novel, the casual insistence of the storyteller in *The Lonely Londoners* – each mode is a different kind of narrative authority which channels our response into an acceptance of the text as an artifact shaped to a predesigned plan. Each novel is carefully curved into a closure that demonstrates the control of the creative mind that made it. Each text, in other words, exists in what a feminist critic would describe as a "filial relationship" to its author (Gilbert and Gubar 1979: 4–6). In reading the text we acquiesce in this process of control.

The very awareness of this process, however, can make for an alternative way of reading, one that displaces the authority of the narrative by looking more closely and from a different angle at the contours of the experience recorded therein. To do so with regard to *In the Castle of My Skin* is to immediately notice how consistently the women in the novel are used to evoke the "sleep" that Lamming presents as the negative condition from which Creighton Village must awaken. Ma and her husband Pa, the village's oldest inhabitants, are the repository of the community's memory; but Ma's staunch religious faith is indivisible from her loyalty to a feudal structure which she regards as ordained by God. In contrast, Pa is conscious of how exploitation and betrayal have dominated the region's history. Miss Foster, like Ma, is caught in the dreaming sleep of traditional submissiveness: she is tremendously gratified when Mr Creighton fleetingly recognizes her existence by offering her a cup of tea and sixty cents. Behind both women is the figure that functions as an icon of female existence in the novel: the derelict old woman who staggers through the wood that separates the landlord's house from the village, her head "awhirl with the intoxication of nothingness" (Lamming 1970: 27). She is the nightmare in the village's sleep. To thus allow her presence its full force involves a readjustment of focus, one that opens up a field of meaning larger than that encompassed by the cycle initiated by the protagonist's ninth birthday. The subtext of *In the Castle of My Skin* becomes available for our attention.

It is this subtext that Edward Baugh examines in the course of his analysis of what he describes as "the emotional climax of the novel", the scene which recounts the last meal cooked for G by his mother before his departure for Trinidad (1977: 23–33). Baugh emphasizes the authority and grace which infuse this woman in the ritual of preparing the food. What is just as noteworthy, perhaps, is the way in which the entire scene reinforces our sense of this woman as imprisoned, like all the other women in the novel, in a maze composed of habit, learned prejudices and an inarticulate frustration. The "personal pride in craftsmanship and achievement" (1977: 29) which Baugh here detects in her is significant precisely because it marks the only real opportunity provided in the narrative to demonstrate a creative consciousness comparable to her son's. It is in keeping with the general tone of the novel, moreover, that even here the individuality of the woman preparing this meal should be progressively superseded by the narrator's preoccupation with collecting the evidence of another cultural artefact. The woman disappears behind the ritual.

G's relationship with his mother is characterized by such constant sense of strain that his need to leave the village eventually becomes inseparable from his need to break away from her. Creighton Village, with its domesticated, neat topography, is associated in his mind with the feminized contours of a conquered territory governed by the colonizing will: significantly, the epic figure of the fisherman can exist only *outside* this tidy world, secure in his contempt for those who accept its authority. For G, even his awareness of the weight of colonial authority becomes negatively linked with his perception of the female: school may be reminiscent of military drill, but behind it all is the idea of Mother Country and Queen Victoria. Power and authority, on the one hand, mark out the limits of his life as a colonial, expressing themselves in female images; on the other hand, the psychic "sleep" that is imposed by such power is most clearly imaged in the women of the novel. Above all, the ambivalence of G's relationship with his mother is at least partially rooted in his sense of her as being *both* authoritarian *and* powerless.

To read *In the Castle of My Skin* in this way does not contract the novel's range of possibilities. A feminist refusal to accept the novel's narrative control represents an opening up of the text. A similar – though just as necessary – approach to *The Lonely Londoners* may be more difficult. The sheer affability of the narrator's voice here is a disarming device which has the effect of lessening some of the uneasiness which this novel's depiction of women might arouse. The narrator's use of generalized observations that carry a proverbial force, moreover, seems to call into question some of the negative perceptions that arise from the particular incidents he recounts. When he observes, for instance, that "sometimes you does have to start thinking all over again when you feel you have things down the right way" (Selvon 1991: 45), it is difficult not to apply this to his comments about women. The insinuating camaraderie of the narrator's voice is really a rhetoric of seduction, and it is employed to ensure our acquiescence in a deliberately restricted vision of human relationships, a vision that never becomes the focus of sustained irony.

The Lonely Londoners, to begin with, suggests that human responses necessarily become reduced to the most basic urges in a situation of extremity; food, shelter, warmth and sex are the needs which have to be satisfied. This is the context within which the novel's unapologetic characterization of women as objects has to been seen. The woman as sexual quarry is the most obvious version of this trait: "Cap with woman left and right – he have a way, he does pick up something and take it home when he finish and she ask for money, throw she out on the streets" (Selvon 1991: 44–45). This is interesting for its linguistic shift: the impersonal pronoun gives way to the personal *after* the act of sex is completed. To ask for money is to demand recognition of a sort.

But the depersonalization of women ("Bags of pussy in London") is itself part of an equally obvious tendency to present women as stereotypes, in a novel which almost defiantly attempts to rejuvenate the stereotype as a valid basis for characterization. Like Charles Dickens, however (whom he resembles in this single feature), Selvon takes much less care with his female characters in this respect than with his male. Even Tanty, the most interesting woman in the novel, remains confined to type. Her introduction of the credit system into the neighbourhood grocery is of a piece with her taking care of Tolroy when he was a boy; Tanty is the woman as universal aunt, always looking after others. She is the nonsexual version of the stereotype that Selvon uses in *The Lonely Londoners.* His women are either sexual targets or mother/aunt figures.

Assessment of Selvon's novel becomes more interesting, however, when one goes beyond these obvious features and considers some of the narrative's implicit assumptions. One such is that sexuality is as dangerous as it is essential to the lives of these men, adrift in a city which exerts a siren-like fascination on them. The conflation of these two ideas leads the narrator to suggest repeatedly that these men "go wild" when they arrive in London. Cap, Lewis, Galahad: the pattern repeats itself. Infatuated with London, they become sexual predators, as if the act of possessing a white woman is a way of claiming the city as theirs. But the practice of sexuality is almost always portrayed in *The Lonely Londoners* as harmful to the male – just as remaining in London involves, for most of them, a steady deterioration. The novel portrays male existence as consisting, in large part, of an obsession with a female essence, and a compulsive and basically unrequited search for it. The story of Bart's search for his Beatrice is, in this respect, the most significant episode in the novel.

One of the most intriguing suggestions in the novel has to do with the existence of a world of all-male camaraderie defined mainly by language rituals, by the ability to "run a ballad". At the centre of this world is Moses, the one who has learned how to live with sexuality as a controlled appetite ("Take it easy"), the one who has come to terms with his ambivalence about London, the one whose voice might well be that telling the story. It is a world in which the ability to "talk good talk" is valued because it is part of one's survival kit: Cap's voice "would melt butter in the winter, and he does speak like a gentleman" (Selvon 1991: 32–33); Galahad, afflicted by a stammer when upset, has to learn to handle "big talk" properly; and Moses, the veteran, is a master of "old talk". But the skill of "talking good talk" is important also because it allows for the assertion of identity in a city which refuses to acknowledge them even as it fascinates them.

That Selvon should so consistently characterize women as talking too much, talking out of turn, nagging, gossiping ("Tanty with she big mouth", p. 66) is perhaps the most telling comment that feminist criticism could make about *The Lonely Londoners*. Women are repeatedly associated with "bad talk"; they are effectively barred from the world of friendship and communal warmth which provides the only sustenance to these castaways in the city. And in a narrative that is itself a "ballad", they become at best objects in somebody else's story, at worst unacknowledged presences. In a company of exiles, they are doubly exiled.

References

Baugh, Edward. 1977. "Cuckoo and Culture: *In the Castle of My Skin*". *Ariel* 8, no. 3 (July).

Gilbert, Sandra, and Susan Gubar. 1979. *The Madwoman in the Attic*. New Haven: Yale University Press.

Lamming, George. 1970. *In the Castle of My Skin*. London: Longman Caribbean.

Selvon, Samuel. 1991. *The Lonely Londoners*. London: Longman Caribbean.

16 Androgyny and Miscegenation in *The Crying Game*
The Case for a Performative Model of Gender and Race

RICHARD L.W. CLARKE

Androgyny

Conventional dualistic notions of gender are interrogated in the film *The Crying Game*. Fergus, a member of the Irish Republican Army, is forced to flee for his life from Belfast as a result of having bungled the kidnapping of a not uncunning British soldier named Jody. Fergus bungles the kidnapping because he unwisely strikes up a close relationship with his hostage, as a result of which he finds himself in a quandary when the time comes to execute him. At the crucial moment Jody runs away, banking on the fact that his abductor will not be able to shoot him in the back, only to be knocked down by a British army Saracen. Not all of Fergus's companions escape with their lives from the ensuing conflagration. Once in London, Fergus makes good a promise to his former prisoner to seek out the latter's "girlfriend" Dill. After meeting "her", Fergus, now going by the name of Jimmy, finds himself falling in love with a "woman" who, to all intents and appearances, is set up as the object of male sexual desire.

There is one scene in particular where the boundaries demarcating the genders are radically blurred. I am referring to that startling moment when, as they start to make love, Fergus removes Dill's dressing gown to reveal not a vagina but a penis. Fergus immediately takes refuge in the bathroom where he proceeds to vomit; a reaction, I would contend, with which many heterosexual male spectators would sympathize. Some have ascribed the intensity of the public response to *The Crying Game* (the title song of which is sung, appropriately, by the transvestite Boy George) to the degree to which it caters to a lurid fascination with the bizarre. I would argue that the excitement and controversy stirred up by the film are related to the problems that an androgynous figure poses for those binary models of sexual difference. The consternation of the heterosexual male, both on-screen and off, measures the degree to which comfortable expectations of what is "natural" have been rudely upset.

Laura Mulvey's seminal "Visual Pleasure and Narrative Cinema" asserts that mainstream films are addressed largely to men and reflect, reveal and play on the "straight, socially established interpretation of sexual difference which controls images, erotic ways of looking and spectacle" (1991: 432). They skilfully manipulate the male spectator's sexual and ego libido in such a way that the "alienated subject, torn in his imaginary memory by a sense of loss, by the terror of potential lack in fantasy" (1991: 433) which the eroticized figure of the leading lady reminds him of, simultaneously finds substitutive satisfaction in identifying with the leading male.[1] The appearance of the female star is always visually coded for strong erotic impact upon the male spectator. The latter's sexual attraction necessarily coexists, however, with a certain degree of horror precisely because the female's body connotes castration and hence "unpleasure":

> Ultimately, the meaning of woman is sexual difference, the visually ascertainable absence of the penis, the material evidence on which is based the castration complex essential for the organization of entrance to the symbolic order and the law of the father . . . [T]he woman as icon, displayed for the gaze and enjoyment of men, the active controllers of the look, always threatens to evoke the anxiety it originally signified. The male unconscious has two avenues of escape from this castration anxiety: preoccupation with the re-enactment of the original trauma (investigating the woman, demystifying the mystery), counterbalanced by the devaluation, punishment or saving of the guilty object . . . or else complete

disavowal of castration by *the substitution of a fetish object* or *turning the represented figure into a fetish* so that it becomes reassuring rather than dangerous (hence overvaluation, the cult of the female star). (Mulvey 1991: 438; emphasis mine)

Mulvey points out that cinema, however, has "structures of fascination strong enough to allow temporary loss of ego while simultaneously reinforcing it" (1991: 435). As a form of compensation, films encourage the male spectator to identify with their male stars via a process which Mulvey interprets in terms of the Lacanian mirror stage:

> As the spectator identifies with the main male protagonist, he projects his look onto that of his like, his screen surrogate, so that the power of the male protagonist as he controls events coincides with the active power of the erotic look, both giving a satisfying sense of omnipotence. A male movie star's glamorous characteristics are thus not those of the erotic object of the gaze, but those of the more perfect, more complete, more powerful ideal ego conceived in the original moment of recognition in front of the mirror. (Mulvey 1991: 437)

Significantly, Mulvey asserts that the male figure cannot bear the burden of sexual objectification, as a result of which the male spectator is reluctant to gaze at himself.

Consequently, it is not difficult to theorize with regard to *The Crying Game* the startling impact on the heterosexual male spectator of a film that disrupts precisely this scheme of things. The consequences of a penis being where a vagina "must" be, a presence where, judging by the other anatomical clues, there "ought" to be an absence, are radically disruptive. Expectations concerning sexual difference are upset because androgyny blurs the boundaries between rigidly discrete gender categories. Perhaps most importantly, the play of difference indicated by androgyny, that is, the co-presence of both masculine and feminine physical characteristics in one body as a result of which it is impossible for the onlooker to firmly decide upon the gender, may serve to undermine the attribution of a fixed gendered core to any human being purely on the basis of anatomy. Moreover, in inviting the male spectator to identify with a bewildered Fergus, uncertain from the very beginning about his personal qualifications for the job of "terrorist" and unsure right to the very end about having a relationship with a so-called she-male, *The Crying Game* simultaneously dislocates the compensatory regime of imaginary identifications.

Miscegenation

Some theorists argue that the perception of skin colour plays a role analogous to that of the sexual organs in the course of the psychic maturation of the subject. Gwen Bergner, for example, states that questions of "racial difference pry open a system of representation that seems closed when women, exclusively, are equated with lack" (1995: 85). Mary Ann Doane observes, similarly, that blackness and femininity are "intersecting marginalities" that share the same space in the European imaginary: the "force of the category of race in the constitution of Otherness within psychoanalysis should not be underestimated. When Freud needs a trope for the unknowability of female sexuality, the dark continent is close at hand" (cited in Bergner 1995: 86). Jean Walton contends, in a similar vein, that

> early psychoanalysts would have argued that a male/female binary is a much more "universal" one than a black/white binary insofar as all humans are assumed to grow up in a context where they are distinguished from one another by gender, and where one is constituted [solely] by one's identification within and desire across that binary division. (1995: 779)

However, Walton insists correctly, "maturity also implies the full assumption of a heterosexualized *raced* adulthood; according to this model, one must be fully "white" (or perhaps fully one's "race", however that might locally be constructed) in order fully to become a subject" (1995: 779). Her point is that, despite the silence of mainstream psychoanalysis in this regard, "racialized binaries were and continue to be a reality in the world inhabited by Freud's patients and the patients of other psychoanalysts for as long as the institution has existed" (1995: 779). This is as true, she stresses, for the racist history of the United States as it is for Europeans, "whose fantasmatic life is permeated by the Orientalist and Africanist ideologies that underwrite and justify what, by the time psychoanalysis was in its nascent stages, had become a long and vexed history of European colonialist expansion and decline" (1995: 780).

Frantz Fanon's seminal *Black Skin, White Masks* represents, of course, the first attempt to rethink psychoanalysis in terms of the fundamental determination enacted upon the subject by his or her race. The particular significance of Fanon's theory resides in his attempt to argue that what he views as the Negro's "pathological condition" is equatable with a form of neurosis that is the consequence of being black and non-European in a racist, Eurocentric sociocultural order. The inevitable product of processes of acculturation is a split psyche: the Negro internalizes, to the detriment of his mental health, the privileges accorded to whiteness as well as the denigrations of blackness that historically form such an undeniable part of European culture. This results in the formation of a curiously hybrid creature who, although endowed with black skin, nevertheless partakes of an undeniably Eurocentric collective unconscious in what is, from an existentialist viewpoint, an act of self-denial and *mauvaise foi*.

Influenced by both Freud's model of the personal unconscious and by Carl Jung's notion of the collective unconscious, Fanon argues that the black West Indian in particular and the Negro in general is shaped by the Eurocentric world in which *he* grows up and is educated, where *he* lives, moves and has his being.[2] Self-division is the consequence of "*l'imposition culturelle irréfléchie*" (1952: 154): "We read white books and we assimilate little by little all the prejudices, the myths, the folklore which come to us from Europe" (1952: 155).[3] It is in this manner that the Antillean "has appropriated all the archetypes of the European" (1967: 154), a particularly harmful process for the Negro precisely because "in Europe, Evil is represented by the colour black" (p. 152). Fanon stresses that

> the West Indian has recognized himself as black, but, via a shift in the moral meaning, he has perceived (the collective unconscious) that one is Negro to the extent that one is bad, blind, wicked, instinctual . . . In the collective unconscious, black ugly, sinful, shadowy, immoral. In other words, to be black is to be someone immoral. (1952: 155)

The internalization of such stereotypes makes for the fragmentation of the Negro's psyche, of which there are two symptomatic indices. First, the phenomenon of "projection" (Fanon 1967: 165):

> To the extent that I discover in myself something unusual, something reprehensible, for me only one solution remains: I have to get rid of it, to attribute its paternity to another. In so doing, I put an end to a circuit of tension which threatened to upset my equilibrium. (1967: 154)

In "Remembering Fanon", Homi Bhabha quotes Fanon, to similar effect: "I had to meet the white man's eyes. An unfamiliar weight burdened me . . . I was battered down by tom-toms, cannibalism, intellectual deficiency, fetishism, racial defects . . . I took myself far off from my own presence" (1983:

115). Second, internalization induces "transitivism": a breaching of the boundaries of self to the point where self identifies itself almost entirely with other. The consequence of all this for the Negro is that irreconcilable self-division which Fanon's title so neatly encapsulates: the rejection of most that is black and the embrace of most things white.

Bhabha's point in "Remembering Fanon: Self, Psyche and the Colonial Condition" is that the subjectification of both colonizer and colonized must be reconceptualized in terms of the Lacanian imaginary. In so arguing, Bhabha ends up calling into question the rigid demarcations between self and other, white and black which, for Fanon, structure an essentially Manichaean colonial situation.[4] Bhabha's view in this regard is undoubtedly related to Fanon's brief allusion to Lacan, to wit, his suggestion that Lacan's notion of the mirror stage might prove useful for analysing the colonial situation. Fanon writes that it

> would be interesting, on the basis of Lacan's theory of the mirror period, to investigate the extent to which the image of his fellow built up in the young white at the usual age would undergo an imaginary aggression with the appearance of the Negro. When one has grasped the mechanism described by Lacan, one can have no further doubt that the real Other for the white man is and will continue to be the black man. And conversely. Only for the white man The Other is perceived on the level of the body image, absolutely as the not-self – that is, the unidentifiable, the unassimilable. (Fanon 1967: 161)

Fanon's allusion, however, betrays a misunderstanding of Lacan which it is Bhabha's duty, seemingly, to rectify.

Bhabha seems to suggest that what Fanon would have said, had he fully understood the significance of Lacan's notion of the Imaginary, is that the "ambivalent identification of the racist world . . . turns on the idea of Man *as* his alienated image, not Self and Other but the 'Otherness' of the self" (1993: 116). It is "not the Colonialist Self nor the Colonized Other, but the disturbing distance in between that constitutes the figure of colonial otherness" (p. 117) and thus the "liminal problem of colonial identity" (p. 117). For Bhabha, the colonial subject is in effect not, caught in a no (wo)man's land, being neither self nor other, neither Negro nor white, but forever suspended in the gap between. Bhabha offers, in this regard, a useful summary of the exotopic nature of the split colonial subject in particular, and of the subject in general. He points out that the "very place of identification, caught in the tension of demand and desire, is a place of splitting" (p. 117) precisely because "to exist is to be called into relation to an Otherness, *its look or locus*" (p. 117). Identity at the imaginary level is, thus,

> never an *a priori,* nor a finished product; it is only ever the problematic process of access to an "image" of totality . . . For the image as point of identification marks the site of an ambivalence. Its representation is always spatially split, it makes present something that is *absent* – and temporally deferred . . . The image is only ever an *appurtenance* to authority and identity; it must never be read mimetically as the "appearance" of a "reality". (p. 118)

Identification, in short, is "always the return of an image of identity which bears the mark of splitting in that "Other" place from which it comes" (p. 117) that produces a liminal state of "alienation within identity" (p. 116).

Moreover, at the level of the Symbolic, through a racialized scene analogous to the castration complex, the subject is socially positioned relative to the *perceived* possession of a particular skin colour which, as a signifier of power and social privilege, plays a role analogous to the phallus. The subject, both white and nonwhite, is subordinated to a symbolic order ("langue") that actively privileges whiteness and denigrates nonwhiteness, the racist demarcations of which she or he then ventriloquizes in the "parole" of his or her everyday existence. The non-European is inserted into a symbolic order in which, as a result of his or her lack of whiteness, she or he has historically also been an object of exchange and thus relegated to a position of servitude, subservience and inferiority. As a result, the non-European turns away from itself and its race, as Bhabha points out in "The Other Question", in order to totally identify with the "positivity of whiteness which is at once colour and no colour" (1983: 28). Thereby, in an act of "disavowal and fixation the colonial subject is returned to the narcissism of the Imaginary and its identification of an ideal ego that is white and whole" (p. 28). Evidently, if the nonwhite male finds himself in a position of marginalization akin to that of the white female (where she is marginalized by her lack of a penis, he is marginalized by his lack of a white skin), the nonwhite female is, from this point of view, doubly marginalized.

However, from the perspective of the European, the non-European, like the European female, signals "castration" and thus threatens lack (of whiteness). The European, accordingly, in this scheme of things experiences the horror of loss at the sight of nonwhite skin. As Bhabha suggests in "The Other

Question", the racist stereotype functions in a manner analogous to that of the fetish in order to disavow the horror of loss attendant upon the sight of nonwhite skin. Hence, to adapt Mulvey, the substitution of comforting fetish objects such as the gollywog that are tantamount, in fact, to a calcified description of the non-European or the turning of the non-European into a fetish (the eroticized Negro conflated with his or her sexuality, for example).

It is possible, in the light of the foregoing, to adapt Mulvey's account of the cinematic experience of the *male* spectator in order to theorize the *white* spectator's response to the figure of the nonwhite on screen. Mainstream films cater (comfortingly, I would suggest) to the white spectator's unconscious expectations as to the Negro's "natural" subservience and inferiority and his or her historical role as object of exchange between whites. These expectations, while comforting to the white European's sense of his or her own primacy and superiority, are, however, tinged by the horror of loss that nonwhite skin signifies. Hence the fetishistic substitution of racist stereotypes (Hollywood's "dancing Negro", for example) and/or the eroticization of the Negro. Hence, as well, compensatory imaginary identifications with the figures of white costars.

It is from this point of view that I would argue that the fact that Dill is of racially mixed heritage is as important as his/her ambiguous gender and sexuality in *The Crying Game*. This is a film pervaded by a subtle refusal of discrete categories. Jody, for example, is anomalous as much on sexual as on racial grounds. First, he is not homosexual per se in the common acceptance of the word. He is evidently something even more disturbing within the masculine imaginary: a bisexual. He is to some degree attracted to women, but is more fond of so-called drag queens who are themselves neither "men" nor "women". Hence the significance of his initially cryptic comment to Fergus that the "tart" that seduced him to his doom is not really his "type". Second, as a man of African descent, whose history is more than likely one of enforced transplantation, slavery and colonialism, Jody serves as an English soldier in an operation long described by Irish nationalists as a colonialist occupation conducted by a hegemonic power.[5] Moreover he serves amongst a people known to describe themselves as the "niggers of Europe" in a "colony" located, however, in England's own "backyard".

From the outset, the spectre of miscegenation – as well as the accompanying dialectic of desire and revulsion – hangs over events. The opening scene depicts the process by which the black soldier Jody is lured to his demise by the prospect of a "quickie" with a young white woman in a short skirt. She is later quick to refer to him scornfully as an "animal" who was "all over" her. It is difficult to say, however, which is the greater source of her disgust, the fact that he is black or that he is English. The Metro pub which Dill patronizes is the setting for the performances, both musical and otherwise, of the drag queens, some of whom seem to be racially "impure", as well as for mixed race couples. One wonders to what extent Dill's abusive but rather childlike white boyfriend is attracted to "her" penis and to what extent he is drawn to the imprecision of "her" exotic brown skin. It may indeed be the latter which initially attracts Fergus himself.

Moreover, Dill's insecurity and even neuroticism (revealed in "her" constant questioning of Jimmy as to whether he loves "her" and will take care of "her") is perhaps related as much to "her" racial "impurity" as to "her" ambiguous gender. Faced with her reflection in a mirror, Dill cries out, "I don't recognize myself." Her lament is a function, I would suggest, of a protean physical appearance that defeats, on racial as much as on gendered grounds, the possibility of a fixed imaginary identification. I would suggest that Dill's mixed race provokes in the viewer confusion rather than horror (of loss). The ease with which s/he seems to be accepted within an essentially white society as an equal, while remaining undeniably a sexual object of exchange among white males, confounds the unconscious expectations of the white spectator. Her beige skin dislocates concomitant fetishistic strategies of disavowal that would seek either to make her conform to racist stereotypes or to turn "her" into an eroticized object. The latter is, of course, complicated by the dialectic of attraction and repulsion that attends her androgyny.

At the same time, Fergus himself does not offer the spectator a compensatory imaginary identification on the grounds of either his gender or his race. Ethnically speaking, Fergus is a hybrid. After being forced to "emigrate" to London he finds himself, as an Irishman, involved in several experiences analogous to those faced by the ex-colonized nonwhites who in large droves sought to colonize the United Kingdom in reverse after the Second World War. Under an assumed identity, Fergus/Jimmy is forced to work as a manual labourer in order to support himself. He eventually becomes embroiled in an ethnic conflict with his wealthy English employer who, filled with a seemingly unjustified dislike for him, scornfully hurls the derogatory epithet "Paddy" at him, makes fun of his accent and delights in extracting money from his wages for accidents on the job.

In a symbolic order predicated upon exclusion, the difficulty in precisely pinpointing what a racial/cultural "half-breed" is *not* renders miscegenation an anomalous prospect of the same order as androgyny. The result of this is a confusion, within particular individuals and groups, of signifiers of degeneracy, savagery, and/or inferiority, on the one hand, with those of moral priority, civilization and effective superiority, on the other. In a manner analogous to androgyny, miscegenation gestures to the infinite deferral of the presence of a substantial raced core to any human being, as much as it denies the idea of a "pure" cultural identity to any social formation.

Gender and Race as "Performances"

The consternation and anxiety that characterize the white male's reaction to racial and gender hybridity solicit certain remedial strategies. The patriarchal, racist symbolic order of European civilization deliberately distinguishes (and thus privileges) both masculinity from femininity and the white from the nonwhite by forcibly fixating the play of difference/deferral between the sexes and the races. This is Elizabeth Grosz's precise point with regard to the function of the phallus in Freudian psychoanalysis and, by extension, the patriarchal order of Western society in general: the

> two sexes come to occupy the positive and negative positions not for arbitrary reasons, or with arbitrary effects. It is motivated by the already existing structure of patriarchal power, and its effects guarantee the reproduction of this particular form of social organization and no other. They are distinguished not on the basis of (Saussurian [*sic*] "pure") difference, but in terms of dichotomous opposition or distinction; not that is, as contraries ("A" and "B"), but as contradictories ("A" and "not-A"). In relations governed by pure difference, each term is defined by all the others; there can be no privileged term which somehow dispenses with its (constitutive) structuring and value in relation to other terms. Distinctions, binary oppositions, are relations based on one rather than many terms, the one term generating a nonreciprocal definition of the other as its negative. (1990: 124)

Biddy Martin argues similarly that the "phallocentric meanings and truths of our culture have repressed multiplicity, and the possibility of actual difference, by appropriating difference, naming it opposition, and subsuming it under the 'Identity of Man' " (1988: 13). In other words, phallocentrism functions to erect distinctions at points of the deepest resemblance, that is, where the play of difference lurks. That is, phallocentrism functions to reinscribe boundaries between categories which are always already inherently in danger of being elided.

The fetish plays an indispensable role in reinscribing the genders. Alluding to the classic essay "Fetishism" where Freud argues that the sexual fetish functions to disavow the horror of loss attendant upon the sight of castration, Bhabha's point in "The Other Question" is that the fetish is always the index of the yearning for an original presence now lost. The fetish is also, more importantly, the means by which this presence is ostensibly restored: it represses similitude and forcibly fixates the play of difference (without positive presence) between male and female. Bhabha points out that the "recognition of sexual difference – as the precondition for the circulation of the chain of absence and presence in the realm of the Symbolic – is disavowed by the fixation on an object that masks the difference and restores an original presence" (1983: 27).

Bhabha suggests that the racist stereotype functions, especially within the colonial context, in a manner analogous to that of the fetish, in order to disavow the horror of loss attendant upon the sight of nonwhite skin. He contends that the racist stereotype also hinges around the "myth of historical origination – racial purity, cultural priority" (1983: 26) and expresses, as such, the desire for an "originality . . . threatened by the differences of race, colour and culture" (p. 27). The racist stereotype also functions to delimit the play of difference between the races. Accordingly, the racist stereotype is not a simplification because it is a false representation of reality. It is a simplification because, rather, it is an "arrested, fixated form of representation" (p. 27) that, significantly, denies the "play of difference (that the negation through the Other permits)" (p. 27). The racist stereotype functions, in short, to reinscribe distinctions between races where boundaries are inherently in danger of being elided.

As a necessary supplement to the psychoanalytic "narrativized myth of *origins*" (Butler 1990: 332; emphasis mine) according to which an "originally undifferentiated state of the sexes suffers the process of differentiation and hierarchization through the advent of a *repressive* law" (p. 330), Judith Butler proffers a Foucauldian account of the "*exclusionary* practices" (pp. 330–32;

emphasis mine) which *function* to *produce* gendered identity.[6] Butler's point is that the masculine subject deliberately marks off the feminine through exclusion, a process which instantiates gender specificity and subsequently organizes identity. As a result, "identifications exist in a mutually exclusive binary matrix conditioned by the cultural necessity of occupying one position to the exclusion of the other" (p. 333). Gender is, in short, the "disciplinary production of the figures of gender fantasy through the play of presence and absence in the body's surface, the construction of the gendered body through a series of exclusions and denials, signifying absences" (p. 335).

Butler's point is that the "male" has discursively produced the "female" in an exclusionary process based on imaginary value judgements without any basis in reality. The ultimate goal in so doing is his self-consolidation. Woman, as Mulvey points out,

> stands in patriarchal culture as a signifier for the male other, bound by a symbolic order in which man can live out his fantasies and obsessions through linguistic command by imposing them on the silent image of woman still tied to her place as bearer, not maker, of meaning. (Mulvey 1991: 433)

The construction of lack unconsciously imposed upon the vagina has thence been translated into the production of a whole system of conscious "truths" concerning all the other ways in which women have been entirely "lacking" by reference to men. All this serves to obscure the fact that the self-definition of the male is inextricably linked to these constructions imposed upon the female. The masculine imaginary

> depends on the image of the castrated woman to give order and meaning to its world. An idea of woman stands as lynchpin to the system: it is her lack that produces the phallus as a symbolic presence, it is her desire to make good the lack that the phallus signifies. (Mulvey 1991: 432)

Femininity, clearly, is a category constructed in and through discourse.

From a Foucauldian perspective, the non-European is also the discursive product of the regime of colonial "truth", a point that Bhabha is at pains to emphasize in "The Other Question". The play of difference between races and cultures is arrested in a Procrustean fashion and the white European forcibly distinguished from and privileged over his nonwhite others. Bhabha's major influence in this respect is undoubtedly Edward Said's classic *Orientalism* (1993). It is here that Said discusses the process by which Europe discursively constructed its racial and cultural Others. As he makes clear, the "Orient is not an inert fact of nature" (p. 132). It is, rather, an "idea that has a history and a tradition of thought, imagery and vocabulary that has given it reality and presence for the West" (p. 132). Orientalism is a "system of truths" (p. 142), the deliberate "distillation of essential ideas about the Orient – its sensuality, its tendency to despotism, its aberrant mentality, its habits of inaccuracy, its backwardness –into a separate and unchallenged coherence" (p. 144) enshrouded in an appearance of objectivity. Significantly, the discursive construction of the Oriental serves a specific, vital purpose: it is complicit in the binary process by which the "idea of European identity as superior to all the non-European peoples and cultures" (p. 133) is promulgated, that is, the "idea of Europe, a collective notion identifying 'us' Europeans as against all those non-Europeans" (p. 134). The Orient functions, as such, to confirm the "unchallenged centrality" (p. 134) of a "sovereign Western consciousness" (1993: 134).

The exclusionary process by which self is distinguished from other represents only one half of the coin. The other half is the process of subjectification by which each individual internalizes and rehearses those characteristics deemed appropriate to a given category. For example, Butler's point is that each biological male and female is made both to ingest and to regurgitate in his or her everyday acts and gestures the regulatory prescriptions concerning what it means to be "masculine" or "feminine". Gender is, from this point of view, less the innate expression of anatomy than tantamount to a performance whose traits are acquired. Butler's "performative" model of gender stands in stark contrast to the conventional "expressive" model according to which gender is understood to be an attribute that expresses the substance of anatomical sex. It is worth quoting at length her notion of the "performativity" of gender. She argues that

> acts, gestures, and desire produce the effect of an internal core or substance, but produce this on the surface of the body, through the play of signifying absences that suggest, but never reveal, the organizing principle of identity as a cause. Such acts, gestures, enactments, generally construed, are performative in the sense that the essence of the identity that they otherwise purport to express becomes a fabrication manufactured and sustained through corporeal signs and other discursive means. That the gendered body is performative suggests that it has no ontological status apart from the various acts which constitute its reality, and if

that reality is fabricated as an interior essence, that very interiority is the function of a decidedly public and social discourse, the public regulation of fantasy through the surface politics of the body. In other words, acts and gestures articulate and enacted desires create the illusion of an interior and organizing gender core, an illusion discursively maintained for the purposes of the regulation of sexuality within the obligatory frame of reproductive heterosexuality. (Butler 1990: 336–37)

In short, Butler argues, gender is a learned performance and the "inner truth" of gender a fantasy inscribed on the surface of bodies. "Pure" genders are fabricated, "produced as the truth effects of a discourse of primary and stable identity" (p. 337).

From this point of view, "race" may also be a learned performance which functions to retroactively assign an illusion of an internal raced core to the subject. Each individual learns to regurgitate in his or her everyday acts and gestures the regulatory prescriptions concerning what it means to be "white" or "black". Race is, from this point of view, perhaps less the innate expression of anatomy than tantamount to a performance whose traits are socially acquired. Moreover, the idea of a *pure* race may also be a truth-effect, in this case of what Bhabha characterizes as the discourse of historical originality and unity. The "expressive" model by which race might be understood as that set of attributes that express one's genetic heritage may be the effect of the yearning for clearly demarcated races and the consequent anxious distrust of miscegenation that this generates. The notion of a given "race" can perhaps exist, like gender, only within a binary framework, that is, when predicated upon negation and exclusion and when potential intermixture is disavowed. Perhaps, in the final analysis, racial identity is, like gender in Butler's schema, ultimately tantamount to a masquerade, a performance by bodies compelled to signify as their inmost essence, style and necessity the cultural unease with hybridity and, consequently, the unconscious taboo on interracial intercourse.

Notes

1.   Subsequent film theorists such as Mary Ann Doane have sought to extend Mulvey's insights in this regard by theorizing the experience of the female spectator.
2.   See his *Wretched of the Earth.*
3.   See Nicholas Canny, for example, among others.
4.   Foucault coined the phrase the "economics of untruth" in "Two Lectures" to denote Marxism's continued preoccupation with the economic determination of ideology qua false consciousness, that is, the distortion of the real conditions of existence in the service of the economic and political domination of a given social class. Opposed to the emphasis implicit within Marxism on the *repression* of *the* truth, Foucault preferred to emphasize instead the *production* of *truths,* to be precise, knowledge qua a conscious will to "truth" in itself neither true nor false; hence, his preferred focus being on what he called the "politics of truth". Foucault's point is that power functions not by hiding the "truth" from individuals left to exist in a state of false consciousness but by encouraging individuals to produce particular discourses which form the very objects of which they speak and which then function to prescribe the "truth" for all who imbibe those discourses.

References

Bergner, Gwen. 1998. "Who Is That Masked Woman? Or, The Role of Gender in Fanon's *Black Skin, White Masks*". *PMLA* 10, no. 1.

Bhabha, Homi K. 1983. "The Other Question . . . Homi K. Bhabha Reconsiders the Stereotype and Colonial Discourse". *Screen* 24, no. 6.

_____. 1993. "Remembering Fanon: Self, Psyche and the Colonial Condition". *Colonial Discourse and Post-Colonial Theory,* edited by P. Williams and L. Chrisman. New York: Harvester Wheatsheaf.

Butler, Judith. 1990. *Gender Trouble: Feminism and the Subversion of Identity.* New York: Routledge.

Canny, Nicholas. 1976. *The Elizabethan Conquest of Ireland: A Pattern Established, 1565–76.* Hassocks: Harvester.

The Crying Game. 1993. Produced and directed by Neil Jordan. London: Palace and Channel Four Films.

Derrida, Jacques. 1986. "Différance". In *Critical Theory since 1965,* edited by Hazard Adams and Leroy Searle. Tallahassee: University of Florida Press.

de Saussure, Ferdinand. 1986. "From *Course in General Linguistics*". In *Critical Theory since 1965*, edited by H. Adams and L. Searle. Tallahassee: University of Florida Press.

Doane, Mary Ann. 1991. "Dark Continents: Epistemologies of Racial and Sexual Difference in Psychoanalysis and the Cinema". In *Femmes Fatales: Feminism, Film Theory, Psychoanalysis*. New York: Routledge.

Fanon, Frantz. 1952. *Peau Noire Masques Blancs*. Paris: Seuil.

_____. 1967a. *Black Skin, White Masks*, translated by Charles Lam Markmann. New York: Grove.

_____. 1967b. *The Wretched of the Earth*, translated by Constance Farrington. Harmondsworth: Penguin.

Foucault, Michel. 1980. "Two Lectures". In *Power/Knowledge: Selected Interviews and Other Writings 1972–1977*, edited by Colin Gordon. Brighton: Harvester.

_____. 1984. *The Foucault Reader*, edited by Paul Rabinow. New York: Pantheon.

Freud, Sigmund. 1957a. *Fetishism*. Vol. 5 of *Collected Papers*. London: Hogarth.

_____. 1957b. *The Splitting of the Ego in the Defensive Process*. Vol. 5 of *Collected Papers*. London: Hogarth.

_____. 1974a. *The Dissolution of the Oedipus Complex*. Vol. 19 of *The Standard Edition of the Complete Psychological Works of Sigmund Freud*, edited by James Strachey, London: Hogarth.

_____. 1974b. *Five Lectures on Psychoanalysis*. Vol. 11 of *The Standard Edition of the Complete Psychological Works of Sigmund Freud*, edited by James Strachey, London: Hogarth.

Grosz, Elizabeth. 1990. *Jacques Lacan: A Feminist Introduction*. London: Routledge.

Irigaray, Luce. 1991. "Another 'Cause': Castration". *Feminisms*, edited by R.R. Warhol and D.P. Herndl. New Brunswick, NJ: Rutgers University Press.

Jung, C.G. 1983. *The Essential Jung*, edited by A. Storr. Princeton, NJ: Princeton University Press.

Lacan, Jacques. 1977. *Ecrits: A Selection*, translated by Alan Sheridan. New York: Norton.

_____. 1986. "The Mirror Stage as Formative of the Function of the I". In *Critical Theory since 1965*, edited by H. Adams and L. Searle. Tallahassee: University of Florida Press.

Martin, Biddy. 1988. "Feminism, Criticism and Foucault". In *Feminism and Foucault: Reflections on Resistance*, edited by I. Diamond and L. Quinby. Boston: Northeastern University Press.

Mulvey, Laura. 1987. "Visual Pleasure and Narrative Cinema". In *Feminisms*, edited by R.R. Warhol and D.P. Herndl. New Brunswick, NJ: Rutgers University Press.

Parry, Benita. 1987. "Problems in Current Theories of Colonial Discourse". *Oxford Literary Review* 9, nos. 1 and 2.

Riviere, Joan. 1991. "Womanliness as Masquerade". In *The Inner World and Joan Riviere: Collected Papers: 1920–1958,* edited by Athol Hughes. London: Karnac.

Rubin, Gayle. 1975. "The Traffic in Women". In *Toward an Anthropology of Women,* edited by R.R. Reiter. New York: Monthly Review Press.

Said, Edward. 1993. "From *Orientalism*". In *Colonial Discourse and Post-Colonial Theory,* edited by P. Williams and L. Chrisman. New York: Harvester Wheatsheaf.

Walton, Jean. 1995. "Re-Placing Race in (White) Psychoanalytic Discourse: Founding Narratives of Feminism". *Critical Inquiry* 21, no. 4.

Young, Robert C. 1995. *Colonial Desire: Hybridity in Theory, Culture and Race.* London: Routledge.

17 From Object to Subject

*The Affirmation of Female Subjectivity in
Quince Duncan's* La Paz del Pueblo
and Kimbo

PAULETTE A. RAMSAY

Quince Duncan is one of four Afro–Costa Rican writers who interpret the Afro–Costa Rican experience for us in their creative writing. Duncan's literary works are wide ranging and include considerations of sociohistorical situations such as slavery and colonial West Indian society. His literary treatment of gender and gender roles frequently suggests that he is aware of feminist theories and is interested in satisfying a feminist agenda. This article will focus on the author's treatment of gender in the novels *La Paz del Pueblo* and *Kimbo*.

One of the basic premises of feminism is that the relations between men and women are essentially relations of power in which women have less power than men (Young 1988: 99). This feminist position embraces Simone de Beauvoir's development of Sartre's thesis that each being establishes itself as Subject or Self by defining other beings as Object or Other. De Beauvoir argues that it is man, the male, who views himself as fundamentally different from the female and has relegated woman to the position of Other in order to establish himself as Subject or Self:

> Just as for the ancients there was an absolute vertical with reference to which the oblique was defined, so there is an absolute human type, the masculine . . . Thus humanity is male and man defines woman not in herself but as relative to him,

she is not regarded as an autonomous being . . . She is defined and differentiated with reference to man and not he with reference to her, she is the incidental, the inessential as opposed to the essential. He is the Subject, he is the Absolute, she is the Other. (de Beauvoir 1974: 101)

In this article, we will examine the literary manipulation of two male/female relationships by Quince Duncan, and his response to this feminist notion of male supremacy and its manifestations. We will begin with the author's narrativization of the sexual relationship between the slave master and the slave woman. This analysis allows us to explore the author's approach to a well-established paradigm of power relationships: how he views the notion of the female's lack of agency within male/female relationships.

Traditionally, the dominant image of the slave woman is that of the passive, helpless victim of racism, sexism and classism. This image was established from the time abolitionists argued that the slave woman was the "innocent victim of the unholy lust of callous and brutal white men" (Bush 1990: 11). The slave master is presented predominantly as the lustful, lascivious white male who unscrupulously decides that one of the roles of the slave woman is to perform sexual duties.

Contemporary feminist scholars such as Angela Davis and bell hooks denounce this relationship, although not merely on the basis of abolitionist moral principles. For Davis, the relationship underscores the fact that the black slave woman's oppression was based on gender as well as race, given her dual role as slave and mistress to the white slave master (Davis 1971). bell hooks is of the view that the sexual exploitation of black female slaves was more demoralizing and dehumanizing than racist exploitation (hooks 1981: 25).

Without doubt, the sexual subordination of slave women represented a natural extension of the general power of white over black. Moreover, the sexual relationship between white master and black female slave illustrates the extent to which the social construction of gender parallels the racial situation. The female was, as Davis argues, marginalized and exploited on the basis of race and gender.

La Paz del Pueblo

The sexual relationship between the slave master and the slave woman appears in the secondary narrative strand of the novel *La Paz del Pueblo*. The historical setting is early postemancipation Jamaican society. The slave woman/slave master relationship is portrayed primarily through flashbacks in which different characters recall this aspect of plantation life during slavery.

In keeping with the historical reality, difference in the novel is narrated in gendered and racial terms. The slave master is depicted, stereotypically, as adulterous and unscrupulous. He continues his father's tradition of indulging in a sexual relationship with the slave woman, exploiting his dominant position as master. He is racist, as is demonstrated by his insistence that despite Mamy's refinement she is still "*una negra*" (Duncan 1986: 47). The condescending tone in which he says this emphasizes his perception of Mamy's social, racial and gendered Otherness. Mamy has spent her life performing dual roles as slave/servant and concubine to two generations of the Moody family. Mamy has therefore been property and the source of sexual fulfilment to the Moody men – and, for a while, has served simultaneously as concubine to father and son.

The relationship unfolds on two levels, both of which imply that the exploitation of the female slave is more complicated than is normally believed. On the first level the author focuses on Mamy's undeniable victimhood as well as on her responsibility in the situation. The implication that Mamy is not merely a passive victim in the situation is first conveyed by her conversation with another servant:

> . . . *desde niña tuvo la fineza de apartarme . . .*
> ¿ *Te apartó de qué?*
> *De los otros esclavos, porque yo era demasiado linda para andar así entre tantos brutos.* (Duncan 1986: 138)

> When I was a little girl he had the decency to separate me . . .
> He separated you from what?
> From the other slaves because I was too pretty to walk among so many brutes.

Indeed, there is no indication that Mamy objected to being separated from her own people. Instead there is a suggestion that she enjoyed this preferential treatment, especially in light of her use of the term "brutos" to describe the other slaves. Moreover, the term "fineza" implies a feeling of approval of the actions of her master as well as what seems to be her sense of pride in her beauty.

The idea that Mamy is not merely a victim in the relationship is further intimated by a combination of narrated monologue and Mamy's own speech:

lo había mimado aun antes de la muerte de la señora, haciendo de él un hombre entre rato
y rato cuando lograba escapar de sus ocupaciones en la casa y su romance con el amo.

Les fui fiel a los dos . . . (Duncan 1986: 138)

she had pampered him even before his wife's death, making of him a man from time to time when she managed to escape from her household chores and her romance with the master.

I was faithful to both of them.

It seems therefore that while we cannot deny that Mamy has been sexually exploited, we can also infer from her perception of her relationships with father and son ("*Les fui fiel a los dos*") that there is complicity on her part.

Kingsman Moody's description of the scene in which he discovers his father and Mamy locked in a passionate embrace also suggests that Mamy is an active participant in the relationship with her white master. The scene which he recalls conjures up a picture of Mamy which contests the notion that the relationship was always solely one of white oppressor and black victim:

los dos con los ojos cerrados, como si estar así, desnudos, les hubiese causado una felicidad
indescifrable . . . (Duncan 1986: 127)

the two with their eyes closed, as if being in that state, naked, had brought them inexplicable happiness.

The relationship between Mamy and Kingsman Moody may almost be regarded as incestuous because Mamy nurtured and reared the young Moody as a boy. The following excerpt highlights the initial stage of Mamy's development from being just a maternal figure in Kingsman Moody's life:

Mamy . . .

Sí señorito . . . ¿qué desea?

¿Puedo poner mi cabeza aquí?

Hubo un largo silencio y una tensión infinita porque desde niño él ponía su cabeza
allí y nunca había solicitado permiso. Si ella no se equivocaba, era el primer brote de la
masculinidad definitiva, y él se sentía morir . . . ¿Qué dirá su padre? – preguntó ella
con malicia y crueldad . . . Está bien, Mamy . . . era sólo una pregunta. Lo tomó en sus
brazos, mi pobre muchachito, acomodándole la cabeza en sus regazos con ternura
infinita, le acarició los cabellos con incomensurable ternura, y lo besó. (Duncan 1986:
47–48)

Mamy . . .

Yes my little master . . . What do you want?

May I put my head here?

There was a long silence and an interminable tension, because ever since he was a boy he would put his head there and he had never asked for permission. If she

> were not mistaken, it was the first surge of definite masculinity, and he felt like he was going to die . . .
>
> What will your father say? she asked maliciously and cruelly.
>
> It's okay, Mamy, it was only a question.
>
> She took him in her arms, my poor little boy, adjusting his head on her lap with immeasurable tenderness, and she kissed him.

This portrayal of Mamy as an accomplice confirms the power she has in her complicity. Here, she is aware of their "mother/son" relationship, but is willing to accept what she regards as a cue to his readiness for sexual initiation, and takes him under her tutelage.

The author simultaneously develops the relationship to another level by focusing our attention on Mamy's motives for playing such an active part in this relationship. While the young Moody focuses on his youthful inexperience, "*su juventud inexperta*", Mamy is preoccupied with thoughts of revenge, "*su venganza total sobre la casa Moody*" (Duncan 1986: 48). We now recognize that Mamy has all along been fully conscious of the framework of triple oppression in which she operates and consequently, has carefully resorted to complicity as a strategy for survival. Her seeming affection has been cunningly used for her own purposes, as she has outwardly conformed to the sexual demands of the slave master while exploiting the situation to avenge the cruelties and ignominies she has suffered as a woman, as a slave and as a black person.

Mamy has been driven by her belief that by playing the roles of sexual initiator and mistress to the white men she exercises power over them. The delight with which she exults in her victory is expressed in metaphors where tasting, savouring and chewing represent her pleasure and satisfaction:

> *Estaba en su cuarto pensando en él, masticando su triunfo sobre la vida, saboreando su victoria.* (Duncan 1986: 48)
>
> She was in her room thinking about him, chewing on her triumph over life, savouring her victory.

The words "*triunfo*", "*victoria*", and "*venganza*" reveal that she has been on a quest for vengeance. Her plan to seek revenge has been carefully calculated to undermine and dismantle the powerless/powerful binary dynamic in which she is caught as slave woman. She has set the terms of her complicity because she recognizes that she has no other access to revenge except within the sexual exchange. Complicity is a way of establishing her subjectivity.

Hence, while the author does not dismiss the fact of Mamy's victim-hood, he suggests that she is not a passive victim, nor is she a completely passive objectified Other, but has affirmed her subjectivity in the situation. In her microcosm, her agency means power – more power than ordinary slaves have.

The strategies used by Mamy in her quest to cross boundaries and reject her status as Object to become Subject subvert the view taken by some historians that the slave woman complied with the sexual demands of the slave master out of a desire for economic gain. They speak, instead, to some of the subtle mechanisms of resistance or marronage which some slave women employed to undermine the patriarchal system of slavery. Moreover, this focus on the slave woman's cunning resort to marronage not only addresses the problem of voicelessness of the female slave, but also implies the author's criticism and rejection of the wider oppression of blacks under the system of Caribbean slavery.

Kimbo

The production of gender in the work *Kimbo* seems to be informed by a desire to subvert the concept of Subject as male. The female is initially depicted as being completely under the domination of her male partner, El Barrigón, who has established himself as master of her life. She is insecure and bored from having nothing to do but serve a decorative function in the home. She is totally submissive to her dominant husband and meekly complies with his every wish. This female character is nameless, symbolizing her subordination and Other-ness. In short, she is imaged as a shadowy, "zombified" Other.

The male character, El Barrigón (the potbellied man), is not only powerful in physical stature, as his name suggests, but also in terms of how he dominates and controls the life of his wife. In his view his role is to mould and shape her into the meek, subservient wife which he holds as the ideal. Moreover, he refuses to accept that she has matured beyond the eighteen-year-old he married, to become an adult, capable of making responsible decisions as well as meaningful contributions to the operations of the family business. Hence, matters relating to the business are never discussed with her as he maintains that she is incapable of comprehending the complexity of these – which, in his view, belong to the masculine domain.

The method of employing the reflections and interior monologues of El Barrigón as one of the main narrative modes by which the female character is presented underscores the extent to which she lacks agency and power:

> *Recogí a esta pobre mujer cuando más necesitaba de mí. Estaba confundida, golpeada por la vida, y la llevé a conocer el mundo conmigo. La hice codearse con las damas elegantes de la ciudad. Se ganó el respeto simplemente porque era mi esposa.* (Duncan 1989: 60)

> I picked up this woman when she needed me most. She was confused, beaten by life and I took her to explore the world with me. I made her rub shoulders with the elegant ladies of the city. She gained respect simply because she was my wife.

The fact that the reader's attention is focused on El Barrigón's assessment of his role as agent of the female character's development highlights his dominance and her alterity. Moreover, phrases such as "*la llevé*" and "*la hice*" underline the extent to which he perceives her as an object which is totally in his control.

The author rejects the patriarchal assumptions upon which the relationship is based by allowing the female character to develop an awareness of her position as Other and of how her meek compliance has contributed to her own "zombification".[1] The first indication that she is dissatisfied with her life of powerlessness and emptiness is her decision to seek medical assistance for what she perceives to be her physical limitations, in order to be able to have a child. This is a clear act of defiance against the wishes of a husband who, though sterile, has hypocritically ruled that their marriage should be a childless one. She is eventually seduced by her doctor who takes advantage of her obsession with childbearing, and she becomes pregnant with his child. The birth of the child reveals El Barrigón's obsession with protecting his supremacy. He will, at all costs, continue to define himself as the one who is always in control:

> *el niño nació y su marido dijo que era parecido a un tío suyo y era verdad porque el médico era primo de su marido. Pero el marido lo sabía. Sabía que era estéril y nunca lo dijo. Y se fue conformando porque de todos modos descubrió que era lindo decir éste es mi hijo y la gente lo respetaba por eso.* (Duncan 1989: 68)

> The child was born and her husband said that he resembled an uncle of his and it was true because the doctor was her husband's cousin . . . But her husband knew. He knew he was sterile and never disclosed it. And so he decided to conform,

because at any rate he discovered that it was nice to be able to say "this is my son" and people respected him for that.

The shift in the narrative mode, from the monologue of El Barrigón to the omniscient third-person narrator, is a strategy which the author employs to indicate that El Barrigón's status as Subject is being challenged. The reader no longer focuses on the biased voice of El Barrigón but on that of an impersonal narrator who effectively exposes the ulterior motives behind El Barrigón's seeming acceptance of the child. El Barrigón really wants everyone to continue to believe the lie about his fertility.

The second situation, which registers the female's developing awareness of her position as subaltern, occurs when she is faced with the difficult task of trying to arrange for her husband's release from kidnappers. She suddenly realizes her inability to function in the outside world. Her bewilderment when faced with this challenge forces her to admit that she has led a life of total dependence and incompleteness. The author focuses on her internal monologue to convey her struggles to assert herself:

> *Tengo indominables deseos de rebelarme. Tengo ganas de mandarlo todo al diablo . . . Te espero aquí reclamando la posiblidad de ser lo que quiero ser . . . mujer pero no decorativamente . . . Ser yo. Libre. Mujer pero yo. Mujer yo. Persona yo. Mujer-persona, yo . . . Te espero aquí, pensando por primera vez en mi vida que puedo hacer el viaje . . . sólo he sabido lo que es. Todas las cuentas a tu nombre. Todo el dinero a tu nombre. No sé cuanto tienes ni dónde lo tienes. No sé nada de las finanzas porque eso es función masculina, eternamente vedada a mí.* (Duncan 1989: 96–97)

> I have overwhelming desires to rebel. I feel like sending him to hell . . . I am waiting here for you, holding on to the possibility of being what I want to be . . . a woman but not an ornamental one . . . To be me. Free. Woman but myself. I a woman. I a person. I a female-person . . . I am waiting here for you. For the first time in my life thinking that I could make it by myself . . . only I have known what it is . . . All the accounts [bank accounts] in your name. All the money in your name. I don't know how much you have or where you have it. I know nothing about the finances because that is a masculine function, forever hidden from me.

Despite the use of "thesis language" rather than realistic literary discourse, the internal monologue reveals the character's thoughts and emotions as well as her awakening consciousness and emergent spirit of rebellion. The word "*vedada*" graphically reveals her exclusion from the "male" domain of financial matters, while the repetition of the phrases "*mujer yo*" and "*persona yo*" is a compelling affirmation of self and subjectivity.

Interestingly, the author later utilizes the male character himself to acknowledge the transformation that is taking place in the female character. This is achieved through the use of flashbacks in which El Barrigón reveals the previous subservient attitude of the female:

> *Nos llevamos bien al principio. Era muy servicial, muy obediente, dedicada a mí en la misma forma en que la Santa Iglesia está dedicada a Cristo. Me servía fielmente. No me alzaba la voz ni me pedía nada.* (Duncan 1989: 60)

> We got along very well at the beginning. She was very subservient, very obedient, dedicated to me in the same way that the Holy Church is devoted to Christ. She served me faithfully. She never raised her voice at me or asked me for anything.

The adjectives "*servicial*", "*obediente*" and "*dedicada*" point to the manner in which those who endorse patriarchy encourage women to accept their subordination by validating qualities such as obedience, meekness and humility.

The author, however, rejects El Barrigón's chauvinistic attitude by highlighting the female character's ultimate rejection of his sexist expectations. Her decision to establish her status as subject is no longer a mere thought but is now articulated in her own voice as she rejects alterity. Her defiance is explosive and violent:

> *Ándate al carajo, Barrigón, porque tendrás que hacer tu café de ahora en adelante, o pagar para que te lo hagan. Porque yo voy a salir por esa puerta mañana. Es más, voy a salir por esa puerta ahora mismo. Y te lo juro por Él, que ésta será la última vez que yo pase por este dintel.* (Duncan 1989: 144)

> To hell with you, Barrigón because you will have to make your own coffee from now onwards, or pay someone to make it for you! Because I'm going to leave through that door tomorrow. In fact, I am going to leave by that door right now! And I swear that this will be the last time that I cross this threshold.

The repetition of "*voy a salir*" indicates a rejection of her passivity and the active decision to begin to chart the course of her life. Her defiance is an act of self-liberation and self-assertion: it dramatizes de Beauvoir's argument that "If woman is to become a self, a subject, she must, like man, transcend the definition, labels, and essences limiting her existence. She must make herself be whatever she wants to be" (de Beauvoir 1974: 95).

Conclusion

The preceding analyses suggest that Quince Duncan is addressing a feminist agenda. Duncan selects two different contexts in which to "engineer female subjectivity".[2] In *La Paz del Pueblo* he rewrites the relationship between the slave master and the slave woman in an attempt to redefine or represent the slave woman as one who has power in her situation.

Moving out of this specific and binding historical context, in *Kimbo* the author subverts the patriarchal assumptions upon which the fictional relationship is established. However, whereas the slave woman rejects alterity by undermining the slave master's power through her strategic compliance, in *Kimbo,* the female is at best described as taking the first bold steps in crossing the boundaries from "zombification" to personhood.

Quince Duncan's preoccupation with the affirmation of female subjectivity not only bespeaks his consciousness of a general feminist discourse but also serves to situate him within the broader ideological framework of Caribbean literature. It has been noted by critics of Caribbean literature, such as Michael Dash, that the literature exhibits a longstanding engagement with the "quest for self-formation". Dash asserts:

> Active self-formation or subjectification, a major concern of modern critical theory . . . is a phenomenon which occurs with obsessive frequency in Caribbean writing. Establishing a new authority or authorship is one of those vital continuities in Caribbean literature that has created the possibility of a redistribution of discourse, of re-presenting self. (Dash 1989: 18)

Indeed, Duncan's concern with female "self-formation" may be viewed as an integral and necessary part of his creative response to wider issues. These issues involve the threat of submersion or domination, the problem of self-definition and struggles with feelings of alienation which are experienced by minority groups in multicultural societies such as Costa Rica and by groups which have been marginalized by colonial and neocolonial hegemony in the wider Caribbean region. Through the portrayal of female agency, Duncan brings into focus the need to challenge the Eurocentric and imperialistic attitudes of that sector of Caribbean society which insists on imposing itself as the dominant, the "sovereign self"; and he calls for the "assertion of a self-assured subject free to confer meaning on his [or her] world" (Dash 1989: 18).

Notes

1.   Evelyn O'Callaghan defines zombification as "flesh that takes directions from someone, results from the trauma of being forcibly rewritten by imperial discourse, and then attempting the futile task of living as a subject in relation to one's scripted Otherness" (1993: 71). (The first part of O'Callaghan's definition is taken from the novel *Myal* [Brodber 1998: 108].)

2.   This phrase is borrowed from O'Callaghan 1993: 68.

References

Bush, Barbara. 1990. *Slave Women in Caribbean Society 1650–1838*. Kingston, Jamaica: Heinemann.

Dash, Michael. 1989. "In Search of the Lost Body: Re-defining the Subject in Caribbean Literature". *Kunapipi* 11.

Davis, Angela. 1971. "Reflections on the Black Woman's Role in the Community of Slaves". *Black Scholar* 3 and 4, no. 13.

de Beauvoir, Simone. 1974. *The Second Sex,* translated and edited by H.M. Parshley. New York: Vintage Books.

Duncan, Quince. 1986. *La paz del pueblo*. San José: Editorial Costa Rica.

_____. 1989. *Kimbo*. San José: Editorial Costa Rica.

hooks, bell. 1981. *Ain't I a Woman: Black Women and Feminism*. Boston: South East Press.

O'Callaghan, Evelyn. 1993. *Woman Version: Theoretical Approaches to West Indian Fiction by Women*. London: Macmillan.

Young, Kate. 1988. "The Social Relations of Gender". In *Gender in Caribbean Development,* edited by P. Mohammed and C. Shepherd. St Augustine, Trinidad: Women and Development Studies Project, University of the West Indies.

18 Crossing Boundaries

Race, Gender, Identity in Short
Narrative Fiction by Women Writers
of the Dominican Republic

ANNE MARIA BANKAY

The literary production of women writers in the Caribbean cannot be easily labelled. Terms such as "feminist" seem inadequate. Although there are similarities which may be due to the writers' experiences as members of a group marginalized because of gender, the similarities may, in fact, be due to a variety of other reasons: common historical experiences or social conditions which typify Third World countries. The marginalization experienced by Caribbean women writers has resulted in a double barrier. First, women writers did not seem to produce enough over the last few decades of the twentieth century. Second, what was actually produced was often not accepted for publication – and what was published received scant critical attention. These barriers (boundaries if you will), have posed a challenge to women writers from the different linguistic zones in the Caribbean region, and to cross these boundaries, women writers have had to make their voices heard, using appropriate aesthetic vehicles for their expressions.

Elaine Fido and Carole Boyce Davies speak to this issue in *Out of the Kumbla,* pointing out that women writers of the Caribbean have been silent and silenced for many years but that in recent years they have begun to express themselves in writing – not only establishing a voice but seeking new forms of expression consonant with the issues and ideas with which they deal (1990: 1). A case in point is Ana Lydia Vega's short story "Pollito Chicken", in *Vírgines y mártires,* which has been described as linguistically aggressive (1981: 75–79). Vega has combined English and Spanish as a metaphor for her protagonist's cultural confusion. Suzie Bermiúdez faces an identity crisis as she aspires to being white, but her Puerto Rican roots surface in emotional crises. Vega captures this conflict in Suzie's speech.

Over the last twenty years women writers of the Caribbean have been producing literature which has been considered worthy of being published. Thus Evelyn O'Callaghan in *Woman Version* refers to the noticeable increase in published work by women in the anglophone Caribbean since the 1970s (1993: 1–2). This is equally true of the Hispanic Caribbean. With regard to critical commentary on women's writing in the Caribbean, there has been a dearth. Recent reactions by women critics to work published by women have tended to rely on one of the various feminist critical approaches. Many of these approaches are restricting and often have resulted in monofocal analyses of texts. O'Callaghan comments on one critical approach which sees textual conflict in terms of binary opposites. The text is often viewed in terms of the hegemony of the powerful and the victimization of the powerless (1993: 9). Such an approach is too limiting: instead we need to be able to accommodate multiple perspectives and possibilities in our analyses. O'Callaghan has proposed a paradigm which allows for the acceptance of different "versions" of a text or of language. This paradigm may be worth exploring as an analytical approach to Caribbean women's writing although, with the "anything and everything goes" approach, there is the danger of a total absence of standards (1993: 11).

Hispanic women writers, like women writers from other linguistic areas in the Caribbean, are still engaged in the struggle to give expression to their voice and to find suitable aesthetic vehicles for communicating their ideas and views. In the Dominican Republic the genre of narrative fiction has not had a long tradition, but women writers are producing more and are experimenting with a variety of literary devices. Emelda Ramos speaks to this crossing of a boundary in her seminal article *"Hacia una narrativa femenina en la literatura dominicana"* (1992). She comments:

> *se ve que las mujeres narradores dominicanas comparten las mismas preocupaciones*
> *temático–formales que su otredad. Carecen, como los hombres, de una tradición*
> *narrativa fuerte y definida, pero buscan también nuevas formas de expresión ajustables,*

respresentativas de nuestra realidad social, que conduzcan nuestra narrativa hacia un
espacio importante dentro de la actual narrativa latinoamericana. (1992: 422)

It is clear that Dominican women who write fiction share the same concerns with
regard to themes and techniques as their male counterparts. They lack, as do the
men, a strong and well-defined narrative tradition but they are also seeking new
and suitable forms of expression which are representative of our social reality and
which can take our narrative to an important position within the present body of
Latin American fiction.

In an effort to establish themselves firmly in the genre of narrative fiction in
Latin America, women writers in the Dominican Republic have been encouraged and promoted recently by women's literary groups created for this
purpose. So literary activity is extending from the capital, Santo Domingo, to
other areas such as Salcedo and Puerto Plata, the impetus coming with the
establishment of the *Sociedad Renovación* (Vicioso 1992: 410). Chiqui Vicioso
has confirmed that there now exists a stronger feeling of solidarity among
women writers in the Dominican Republic. For her, the catalyst has been
feminist thought, although not in its traditional form. It is a particular
interpretation of feminism, a Dominican Republic version if you will, based
on solidarity and shared experiences:

En República Dominicana me atrevo a sugerir que el Movimiento cultural importante
de conjunto . . . ha sido el Feminismo, entendiéndose como tal . . . la solidaridad básica
entre las mujeres como hermanas en sufrimiento, en deber, en propósito, como miembros
de la humanidad con análogos problemas vitales. (Vicioso 1992: 409)

I would venture to suggest that in the Dominican Republic, the important cultural
movement of the group has been feminism, understanding by this, the basic
solidarity among women as sisters in suffering, sisters in their duty, in their
purpose, as members of humanity with similar fundamental problems.

This paper focuses on short stories written by women from the Dominican
Republic. We find in their work themes such as the search for identity,
sociopolitical concerns, issues which affect them specifically as women. They
deal with topics ranging from dictatorship and US influence, to parenthood
or the experience of lesbianism in patriarchal society. Many of the stories are
traditional in structure, with linear narration, but there is an increasing
tendency to experiment with new techniques, and often the line is blurred
between empirical reality and illusion as the writers explore the psychological
dimension of their characters.

Three issues which tend to predominate in the narrative fiction of women writers will be examined: race, gender and identity. Indeed, the issue of identity is one which still haunts the literature of the entire Caribbean – not surprising, given the ravaging effects on the psyche caused by colonial and neocolonial influences. In the Dominican Republic, miscegenation as well as invasion and domination by Spain, the United States and Haiti have caused the people to question who they really are, to adopt a hispanophile attitude and concomitantly to despise and reject the Negro presence in their lives.

Aida Cartagena Portalatín foregrounds the problem of race in the story "La llamaban Aurora, pasión por Donna Summer" (1992). Colita, the protagonist, has had her name changed to Aurora by Señorita Sarah while being registered in school. Colita/Aurora wants to accept her Negro heritage and black culture but she is constantly ridiculed by Señorita Sarah and by others, who call her "Negra fea". Portalatín uses Donna Summer's music as a leitmotif throughout the story, and the music itself underscores the attitude of whites to blacks. Colita/Aurora sees herself as a black woman and is moved emotionally by Summer's music. She sees music as one way in which black people can express themselves in the struggle for justice. Donna Summer's music evokes in Colita/Aurora memories of blacks in South Africa who fight against injustices, who protest killings in Soweto and Johannesburg or the murder of Steve Biko. But white people see black cultural expressions as entertainment and nothing more:

> . . . *los negros con su jazz y su ritmo, los negros alegran el mundo . . . algo deben hacer los negros que está bien que diviertan a los blancos.* (Portalatín 1992: 133)

> . . . Negroes with their jazz and their rhythm . . . Negroes make the world a happy place . . . Negroes should do something so it is good that they entertain whites.

In these short stories women writers not only address concerns of women but increasingly we find stories told from a male perspective or by a male narrator. Homosexuality – female as well as male – is a narrative subject. Hilma Contreras explores the problems faced by lesbians, their ideas and feelings, in "La espera" from the collection *Entre dos silencios* (1987a). Contreras's technique is to provide a stereotypical description of one woman, Lucía, who has "*formas hombrunas*" (p. 46), masculine features and attributes. This stereotypical presentation of Lucía is juxtaposed and sharply contrasts with that of Josefina, who is a more complex figure, struggling with internal conflicts. Josefina is aware of society's attitude to lesbians and is afraid of being discovered. She is not yet fully committed to this sexual option, and as she works through her conflicts she goes through the gamut of sexual experiences including autoeroticism and narcissistic pleasure in her young body:

> *Al cabo de unos segundos de contemplación sonrió jubilosamente a la turgente juventud de su pecho reflejado en el espejo.* (Contreras 1987a: 48)

> After a few seconds of reflection, she smiled happily at the turgid youthfulness of her breasts which were reflected in the mirror.

Lesbianism, until recently, was considered taboo in literature, but women writers are extending the limits of literature and addressing sensitive issues which are specific to their gender.

Women writers in the Dominican Republic delve deep into the psyche of women and expose the feelings of women when faced with spinsterhood and old age. Constanza Colmenares gives us a protagonist, in "Sueños de naftalina", who is unmarried. Rebeca is unable to face her present reality, as society expects women to get married and become mothers. Spinsterhood is an aberration. She therefore locks herself in her room and creates imaginary worlds, with music boxes, clocks and old letters being the catalysts for her mental flight. Rebeca's sense of inadequacy and alienation are captured in her desire to become small enough to fit into the music boxes:

> *Entonces siente unas ganas enormes de convertirse en un ser minúsculo para poder penetrar en el interior de las cajitas.* (1992: 338)

> Then she feels a tremendous desire to become a minute being so as to be able to get into the music boxes.

In "Mire, mamita" Hilma Contreras, using italics to highlight her protagonist's thought processes, depicts a woman who is brought face to face with the fact that she is growing old. Teresita criticizes other women of her generation for being old and feels pity for them. She cannot accept her own aging:

> *Manuela, Estebanía, Carmela y las otras, las que evité ver de cerca, viejas todas, pero yo . . . yo.* (1987b: 97)

> Manuela, Estebanía, Carmela and the others, those whom I avoided looking at close up, all of them old, but I . . . I.

Teresita's shock comes when she is addressed as *"Mamita"* by the bus conductor. After an agonizing process of self-examination she refers to *"la súbita revelación de los años olvidados*" ("the sudden revelation of forgotten years") and concludes "*sin ínfulas ya, penetré penosamente en el sendero gris del invierno de mi vida*" ("without pretensions now, I started out painfully along the grey path of the winter of my life") (Contreras 1987b: 17).

Different types of relationships between/among females appear in the short stories under study. Female bonding between two friends is examined in three stories by Ángela Hernández in which Ana is the protagonist. The author's device is to cloud the line between empirical reality and illusion-dream-spirit as she presents a friendship that defies death. Ana visits her friend although in objective reality she is far away, dying in a hospital bed, unable to move (Hernández 1992: 159–73).

The mother-daughter relationship, and its inherent difficulties, is put under the microscope by Julia Álvarez in "El verano del futuro". The mother cannot speak openly about female issues such as menstruation and uses euphemisms such as "*cosas de señoritas*" ("ladies matters") and "*allá abajo*" ("down there") to refer to "*cualquier parte del cuerpo debajo de la cintura*" ("any part of the body below the waist").

Structurally, the story is sophisticated in the way that Álvarez delineates the physical development of two sisters from the Dominican Republic who reside in the United States. Paralleling their journey into womanhood is the development of their social consciousness, awakened not only because of political events in the Dominican Republic itself but also because of the aggressive, violent behaviour of the North American girls towards them.

To examine the issue of identity the women writers from the Dominican Republic use female protagonists. When women feel they lack an identity they tend to retreat from reality and are often considered "mad". Evelyn O'Callaghan speaks to the preoccupation of women writers with "mad" protagonists: "Women who withdraw into worlds of fantasy or seek refuge in suicide or symbolic self-annihilation" (1993: 37). She cites Marie-Denise Shelton, who explains this condition as resulting from the "inability to find a place in their societies, their feelings of abnormality, an existential disease of belonging nowhere, of being deprived of identity" (O'Callaghan 1993: 37). This phenomenon is present in the story "Sueños de naftalina", where Rebecca's behaviour is considered abnormal. Because she lacks a traditional identity as wife and mother, she withdraws into worlds of fantasy and seeks self-annihilation.

National identity is an ubiquitous theme in stories from the Caribbean region. In the Dominican Republic, attitudes to race often create identity problems – as we see occurring with Colita/Aurora in "La llamaban Aurora", where the change of names signals the intention to erase the old identity and impose a new one, one devoid of Negro traces. In "La fuerza aniquilada", Aida Cartagena Portalatín reveals the crippling effects of the influence of North American culture. Prebisteria Sánchez, to ease her absorption into North American culture, has had to anglicize her name to Prebis. In like fashion to Suzie Bermiúdez in Ana Lydia Vega's "Pollito Chicken", Prebis arrives from New York with all the trappings that she believes will make her American – an alien in her own country – including a blonde wig. Portalatín uses humour to criticize Prebis's attitudes and behaviour, particularly her resolve not to return to her country until the Americans are in control:

> La Prebis resolvió no volver, en su país tenían que poner orden los americanos, tenían que dirigirlo todo los americanos.

> Prebis decided not to return, in her country the Americans had to take charge, the Americans had to run everything.

The tragedy is that Prebis's unresolved cultural conflict affects her mentally. Having worked in and for the benefit of America, she is sent back to the Dominican Republic after she becomes depressed and has had a nervous collapse. Prebis is left alienated, without an authentic identity, having embraced an alien culture at the expense of her own.

Issues related to gender, race and identity have found their way into the writing of women of the Dominican Republic. Not only is narrative discourse a relatively new literary activity for these women, but, having made strides in poetry, they are now creating a space and a voice for themselves in another area (see Bankay 1993). Their experiments with form – as much as the inclusion of sensitive or controversial topics – speak of a determination to break out of the traditional mould, to cross barriers.

Daisy Cocco de Filippis has done much to call attention to the narrative work being produced by contemporary women writers in the Dominican Republic, with the publication of an anthology of short stories. The efforts being made to encourage these writers should result not only in an increase in the quantity of literary production, but also in a honing of their literary skills. When Daisy Cocco de Filippis describes her colleagues as "*combatidas, combativas y combatientes*" (women who have been fought against, who have a fighting spirit, who are fighters) her explanation is:

> *Es decir, que las mujeres que escriben deben esperar el ataque, estar listas para defenderse y en última instancia, estar preparadas para entrar en pleno combate.* (Vicioso 1992: 11)

> This means that women who write must expect an attack, they must be ready to defend themselves and as a last resort be prepared to enter fully into combat.

This confrontational attitude is evident in the short stories by the women writers under study, and it is clear that they are prepared to do battle to achieve their literary goals.

References

Álvarez, Julia. 1992. *Combatidas, combativas y combatientes: antología de cuentos escritos por mujeres dominicanas,* edited by D. Cocco de Filippis. Santo Domingo: Editora Taller.

Bankay, Anne Maria. 1993. "Contemporary Women Poets of the Dominican Republic: Perspectives on Race and Other Social Issues". *Afro Hispanic Review* 12, no. 1.

Colmenares, Constanza. 1992. "Sueños de naftalina". In *Combatidas, combativas y combatientes: antología de cuentos escritos por mujeres dominicanas,* edited by D. Cocco de Filippis. Santo Domingo: Editora Taller.

Contreras, Hilma. 1987a. "La espera". In *Entre dos silencios.* Santo Domingo: Ediciones de Taller.

_____. 1987b. "Mire, mamita". In *Entre dos silencios.* Santo Domingo: Ediciones de Taller.

Hernández, Ángela. 1992. " 'La ilusión de Ana'; 'El amor de Ana'; 'La otra Ana' ". In *Combatidas, combativas y combatientes: antología de cuentos escritos por mujeres dominicanas,* edited by D. Cocco de Filippis. Santo Domingo: Editora Taller.

O'Callaghan, Evelyn. 1993. *Woman Version: Theoretical Approaches to West Indian Fiction by Women.* London: Macmillan.

Portalatín, Aida Cartagena. 1992a. "La llamaban Aurora, pasión por Donna Summer". In *Combatidas, combativas y combatientes: antología de cuentos escritos por mujeres dominicanas,* edited by D. Cocco de Filippis. Santo Domingo: Editora Taller.

_____. 1992b. "La fuerza aniquilada". In *Combatidas, combativas y combatientes: antología de cuentos escritos por mujeres dominicanas,* edited by D. Cocco de Filippis. Santo Domingo: Editora Taller.

Ramos, Emelda. 1992. "Hacia una narrativa femenina en la literatura dominicana". In *Combatidas, combativas y combatientes: antología de cuentos escritos por mujeres dominicanas,* edited by D. Cocco de Filippis. Santo Domingo: Editora Taller.

Savory Fido, Elaine, and Carole Boyce Davies, eds. 1990. *Out of the Kumbla: Caribbean Women and Literature.* Trenton, NJ: Africa World Press.

Vega, Ana Lydia. 1981. "Pollito Chicken". In *Vírgenes y mártires.* Río Piedras: Editorial Antillana.

Vicioso, Chiqui. 1992. "Los caminos de la solidaridad entre mujer es escritoras". In *Combatidas, combativas y combatientes: antología de cuentos escritos por mujeres dominicanas,* edited by D. Cocco de Filippis. Santo Domingo: Editora Taller.

19 Standing in the Place of Love

Sex, Love and Loss in Jamaica Kincaid's Writing

DENISE DE CAIRES NARAIN

Introduction

This chapter offers a reading of Jamaica Kincaid's fiction which foregrounds the treatment of sex in her work and places her in relation to other women writers of the region. I argue that Kincaid's writing is distinctive in mapping sexuality as central in constructions of Caribbean womanhood. She insists on sexuality as the site of both limitation *and* possibility for her protagonists and, in the process, refuses the alternative seductions of an escape into "the folk" and collectively articulated Caribbean identities.

Representations of explicitly sexual material are scarce in the literary output of Caribbean women writers. In male-authored texts, women's sexual power is often invoked as the cause of the male protagonist's downfall or, harnessed to a nationalist ideology, as a vehicle for his upliftment; either way, she functions as a sexual object rather than sexual agent. Since the 1980s Caribbean women writers have increasingly recognized the ways in which female sexuality has been socially coded to signify limitation and shame, and they have offered a range of responses to this in their writings. Jean Rhys, for example, consistently presents woman as victim because of her sex. She outlines the very limited parameters within which women can "trade" with their bodies, and often highlights the fate of older women in patriarchal culture, rendered worthless at a "certain age".

More contemporary writers, such as Merle Collins, Olive Senior, Erna Brodber and Merle Hodge, have pinpointed puberty and the onset of adult female sexuality as the most intense moment of crisis in the assertion of selfhood for their young female protagonists; this is the moment at which identity formation is presented as most vulnerable to manipulation. Both Collins (in *Angel*) and Hodge (in *Crick Crack Monkey*) suggest that the way out of the alienation resulting from an internalization of racist/sexist European cultural values, disseminated via colonial education systems, is a revaluation of and reconnection with creole culture and the values of the community. Brodber suggests a similar kind of solution (in *Jane and Louisa Will Soon Come Home* and in the later novels, *Myal* and *Louisiana*), as does Olive Senior (in *Summer Lightning* and *The Snake Woman and Other Stories*). All of these writers, in their different styles of writing, imply in their texts that positive individual identities can only be realized via a more collectively mobilized notion of identity. In this sense, Mordecai and Wilson are right in their introduction to their anthology of Caribbean women's writing, *Her True-True Name* (1989), when they argue:

> the women have lined up solidly behind the poet and folklorist, Louise Bennett's point of view, for historically Bennett's work, while it is painfully (sometimes gleefully) aware of her society's pretensions, foibles, failings and fragmentations, *has always affirmed the island place, its language and culture*. (1989: 17–18; my emphasis)

What Hodge, Senior, Brodber and Collins share with Bennett is both a belief in the strength and value of creole culture and a desire to use writing to "realistically" represent and thereby validate that culture. In the novels and short stories referred to above, these women writers have not only encoded creole culture positively at the level of theme in their texts but they have attempted, via a range of writing strategies, to "creolize" their writing practice as well. The most obvious strategy used is for large portions of the text to be given over to the spoken word, with various attempts being made to position the reader as listener. In *Crick Crack Monkey*, for example, Hodge plays Tantie's expressive and succinct creole speech off against the stilted fakery of Aunt Beatrice's use of "speeky-spokey" English. Senior frequently makes use of a creole-speaking narrative voice in her stories, as does Collins who punctuates her novel *Angel* with Grenadian proverbs and folk wisdom; Brodber's hybridized, polyvocal texts are the most formally complex of the writers mentioned so far, making use of a dense network of voice. But, again, her protagonists all come to realize that their construction of a "workable" identity is only possible if constituted via creole community and culture. While Hodge, Senior, Collins and Brodber all outline the fear and shame surrounding their female protagonists at puberty when the full weight of their prospective gender roles hits them, the texts tend to foreground a resolution which hinges much more strongly on notions of national/cultural identity than on sexual identity. The moral imperative in these texts to provide some sort of satisfactory closure on the issue of Caribbean cultural identity makes the accommodation of the figure of an adult, sexually active woman impossible. In other words, female sexuality appears not to be easily reconcilable within a nationalist project.

Carolyn Cooper has attempted to remedy this situation at the level of theory. In her book, *Noises in the Blood,* she argues that "Upward social mobility in Jamaica requires the shedding of the old skin of early socialization: mother tongue, mother culture, mother wit – the feminised discourse of voice, identity and native knowledge" (1993: 2–3). Cooper's strategy for overturning this hierarchy involves a celebration of creole culture, particularly the "slackness" and subversive irreverence and hybridity which she aligns with popular Jamaican cultural forms. This is a critical manoeuvre which is in tune with current concerns in postcolonial discourse in which "orature" is increasingly pitted against the "uptight" closure of the "scribal" Eurocentric word. While I am sympathetic to these critical interventions, they hinge upon a rather static model of both European *and* creole cultures, and often elide the gendered contradictions which mark creole culture. Perhaps the very contradictory ways in which sex is viewed in the Caribbean context makes any overarching theoretical grid impossible; attitudes to sexuality shuttle between a frank and raucous explicitness about sex and an almost Victorian prudery and decorousness. Clearly class is a deciding factor in the location one can occupy in this continuum; but across all classes, men unquestionably have a greater degree of sexual mobility and agency. Nevertheless, I think Cooper's celebration of creole as a "native, feminized discourse" is useful in the context of this paper, for it is an ideology which underpins the texts of many of the Caribbean women writers referred to above. This, however, is not an association which Kincaid's texts suggest.

Kincaid's three novels, *Annie John* (1985), *Lucy* (1991) and *The Autobiography of My Mother* (1996), outline and persistently dwell on the devaluation of the girl child in the Caribbean context and the limited spheres in which women can exercise power in their adult lives. In a short story, "Girl", from her collection *At the Bottom of the River* (1984), Kincaid offers a definition of what it means to be a girl which, in the staccato list of prohibitions and prescriptions issuing from the mother, suggests that becoming a "lady" – as opposed to becoming a "slut" – involves a precarious balancing act in which the child must constantly police her sexuality and learn to service the needs of men. This story is punctuated by variations on the mother's warning against falling into "sluthood": "[O]n Sundays try to walk like a lady and not like the slut you are so bent on becoming" (1984: 3). Kincaid concludes this story with the following exchange (one of only two moments in this very short short story) in which the daughter manages to voice a question in the interstices of her mother's monologue:

> this is how to make ends meet; always squeeze bread to make sure it's fresh; *but what if the baker won't let me feel his bread?*; you mean to say that after all you are really going to be the kind of woman who the baker won't let near the bread? (1984: 5)

Here, Kincaid succinctly captures the contradictory combination of subservience and feistiness expected of a woman who has to make ends meet in tough circumstances and command respect from men while, at the same time, keeping up appearances as a "lady".

Annie John

The centrality of sexuality in the construction of adult female identity is developed further in *Annie John*. Here, the paradisaical union with the mother is violently ruptured when Annie reaches puberty, at which point the mother prohibits the easy identificatory bonds that had previously shaped their relationship and insists that Annie take on the burden of her gendered role. This "ladyhood business", as Annie refers to it, entails not just the rupture between mother and daughter but also involves a range of activities which attempt to groom the young girl into English norms of genteel ladyhood and to reject the values associated with the indigenous "mother-culture". Annie makes use of a range of strategies, in the early stages of puberty, to resist the "ladyhood business", when her mother sends her to "someone who knew all about manners" (1985: 27). She insists on farting whenever she curtsies and her English piano teacher asks her not to come back because she eats the cherries placed "for show" on the piano; she plays marbles and hangs out with the wild, tomboyish "red girl". At this age and stage in her development, Annie can resist the restraints of ladyhood by assuming the role of "tomboy", a role which is not an option as she gets older and her body physically changes. Later on in the text, the subversion of her gender role takes on wider significance when she inscribes her mother's words beneath the picture of "Columbus in chains" – the mother's voice and words are ventriloquized and enscripted by Annie, pitting the female body against the pomposity and distortions of his/story.

However, while Annie's mother's words may provide an "indigenous base" (or, in Cooper's terms, "a feminized, nativist discourse") from which Annie can launch a challenge to patriarchal, European culture as described in the "Columbus in Chains" chapter, the mother's simultaneous insistence on colonially inherited prescriptions of the feminine systematically renders ambivalent the mother's role as *uniformly* subversive of colonial values. Instead, the mother's warnings about her burgeoning sexuality operate to distort and damage Annie's sense of her physical self:

> Behind a closed door, I stood naked in front of a mirror and looked at myself from head to toe . . . I tried to push my unruly hair down against my head so that it would lie flat, but as soon as I let it go it bounced up again. I could see the small tufts of hair under my arms. And then I got a good look at my nose. It had suddenly spread across my face, almost blotting out my cheeks, taking up my whole face, so that if I didn't know I was me standing there I would have wondered about that strange girl – and to think that only recently my nose had been a small thing, the size of a rosebud. But what could I do? I thought of begging my mother to ask my father if he could build for me a set of clamps into which I could screw myself at night before I went to sleep and which would surely cut back on my growing. (1985: 26–27)

As in the short story "Girl", the mother's warnings in *Annie John* against a fall from the innocence of childhood into sluthood renders the female body and female sexuality the source of shame and pain. So, when the mother catches sight of Annie merely talking to a group of boys on the street, she accuses

Annie of thwarting all her efforts to teach her "proper conduct" and calls her a slut:

> The word "slut" (in patois) was repeated over and over, until suddenly I felt as if I were drowning in a well but instead of the well being filled with water it was filled with the word "slut", and it was pouring in through my eyes, my ears, my nostrils, my mouth. (1985: 102)

Unable to recognize herself in the dangerous role of "slut", Annie takes refuge in identifying with the fictional heroines of her favourite books, increasingly occupying a dream world in which she can enact roles, unhampered by the danger which her female sex poses in the "real" world. The conflict between stereotyped female roles and Annie's distress at the loss of her old, close relationship with her mother eventually precipitates a kind of nervous break-down. That this illness is generated by anxiety about her sexed identity is economically captured in the image of Annie washing and scrubbing the photographs in her room so that she erases her mother and father "from the waist down" (1985: 120), and all that remains of a picture of herself on her confirmation day is her shoes. The chapter describing Annie's breakdown is immediately followed by the concluding chapter, "A Walk to the Jetty", in which Annie leaves the island for England, a move which is suggestive of a narrative impasse – a familiar one in Caribbean-authored texts where the protagonist's quest for a less alienated identity is left suspended or projected into another geographical space away from the motherland (Lamming's *In the Castle of My Skin* and Hodge's *Crick Crack Monkey* immediately spring to mind). Reconciliation of the "lady" versus "slut" dilemma is foreclosed by the novel's end: Annie lies on her berth aboard ship surrounded by water, an ending that suggests both a "beginning" back in her mother's womb and that Annie is – literally – at sea.

Lucy

In many ways, Kincaid's second novel, *Lucy*, takes up the story where *Annie John* leaves off, though Lucy is in America. In *Lucy*, geographical distance away from the biological mother and the "mother culture" allows the protagonist to experiment with female identity in ways not possible for Annie in *Annie John*. The young woman, Lucy, who travels to America to work as an au pair, looking after Mariah and Lewis's three children, uses her experiences away from the constraints of her island home to question the role model prescribed for her by her mother and to test it against the model of "liberated woman" projected by Mariah. Lucy's gaze throughout this text is a coolly appraising one as she assesses and questions the happy family romance which Mariah, Lewis and their middle-class lifestyle represent.

In *Lucy* the loss of the mother's love and the powerful sense of betrayal which accompanies this loss is recognized as crucially formative for Lucy's ability to sustain any other kind of loving relationship: "My life was something at once more simple and more complicated than that: for ten of my twenty years, half of my life, I had been mourning the end of a love affair, perhaps the only true love in my whole life I would ever know" (1991: 132).

This assertion comes after a "heart to heart" conversation in which Lucy tells Mariah of the way in which she (Lucy) comes to realize how little her parents value her by comparison to the pride and ambition they feel for the three sons, born after Lucy was nine years old. It is the loss of being made to feel special and uniquely valued which Lucy mourns and which, coupled with her sense of strangeness as a "poor visitor" in an alien landscape and culture, forces her into a defensively fierce self-reliance and to embrace the pleasures of the body.

If in *Annie John* Kincaid dramatizes the young girl's fall from the grace of her mother's love into the dangerous and frightening knowledge of her sexuality, in *Lucy,* the protagonist embraces this danger and aligns herself with the world of Lucifer (whom her mother says Lucy was named after) and embarks, with a curiosity verging on the clinical, on a series of sexual encounters. All of these affairs are recounted in ways which assert Lucy's control over the sexual situation itself as well as over the *telling* of the situation. The cool frankness of Lucy's attitude to sexuality is indicated early on in the text, in the chapter "The Tongue", in which she describes herself at fourteen, "sucking on poor Tanner's tongue as if it were an old Frozen Joy with all its flavour run out and nothing left but the ice" (1991: 43–44). Later in the text, she describes a brief encounter with the man in the camera shop, Roland, whom she sleeps with because he reminds her of her father, and whose bed she leaves only because she is expected by her "regular" lover, Paul, later that night. "At the door I planted a kiss on Paul's mouth with an uncontrollable ardor that I actually did feel – a kiss of treachery, for I could still taste the other man in my mouth" (1991: 117).

The power generated by being desired gives Lucy a sense of control which she exploits fully, disengaging herself from any of the emotions, such as love, with which women are conventionally meant to (over)invest sex. This control is tested earlier in the novel when Lucy has a brief but intense relationship with Hugh; a relationship which she acknowledges makes her happy. But it is a happiness which the narrator keeps under surveillance, for Lucy's commentary on this love affair reveals her clear-eyed assessment of it:

> He kissed me on my face and ears and neck and in my mouth. If I enjoyed myself beyond anything I had known so far, it must have been because such a long time had passed since I had been touched in that way by anyone; *it must have been because I was so far away from home. I was not in love.* (1991: 66–67; my emphasis)

The insistent tone of the narrative voice here is revealing, for it suggests an attempt by the speaker to convince herself of her own version of the narrative; a version which *denies* love rather than risk losing it. In the chapter "Cold Heart", Lucy tells the story of her affair with the artist Paul; it is an affair she launches into with clear eyes and a "cold heart", acknowledging straightaway that all she wants is to be "alone in a room with him and naked" (1991: 100). The sight of Paul's hands in the fish tank precipitates the memory of another pair of hands – those of a fisherman at home – and a story in which the young Lucy envies her friend, Myrna, who would regularly receive money for allowing Mr Thomas to put his finger inside her vagina. Being the object of sexual desire gives Myrna a kind of power and a dangerous "specialness" which the young Lucy envies:

> I, of course, had many feelings about this amazing story – all the predictable ones – but then one feeling came to dominate the others: I was almost overcome with jealousy. Why had such an extraordinary thing happened to her and not to me? . . . This would have become the experience of my life, the one all others would have to live up to. What a waste! It meant nothing to Myrna. (1991: 105)

Despite it not having happened to *her*, Lucy manages to make this incident her own by inviting parallels, however implicit, between the arrangement between Mr Thomas and Myrna and her own arrangement with Paul ("It was understood that when everyone left, I would not leave with them" [1991: 100]). There is a cool recognition of the way in which sexual relationships often hinge upon "trade" of some sort, and it is also telling that what strikes Lucy about Myrna's story is the potential for self-dramatization which it offers (and which Myrna stupidly "wastes"); there is no indication that this incident might represent an *exploitative* transaction. As is often the case in Kincaid's writing, the reader is not given any cosy moral "take" on events by the narrator – she alludes to having "predictable" feelings in response to Myrna's story, but these are not stated. Instead, sexual relationships are presented as purely instrumental transactions, devoid of any emotional cost, and the reader is left to guess at just how convincing Lucy's sexual bravado is in relation to the sense of loss and bereftness which activates such bravado.

The sense of emotional detachment which such sexual encounters imply – and the manner of their recounting – is compounded by the sense that these affairs are part of a strategy for defying the mother, despite the fact that they simultaneously damage the daughter. After receiving news that her father has died, Lucy eventually writes to her mother – "a cold letter" – putting the record straight:

> I said that she had acted like a saint, but that since I was living in this real world I had really wanted just a mother. I reminded her that my whole upbringing had been devoted to preventing me from becoming a slut; I then gave a brief description of my personal life, offering each detail as evidence that my upbringing had been a failure and that, in fact, life as a slut was quite enjoyable, thank you very much. (1991: 126–27)

Despite her physical absence, then, the mother continues to exercise control over Lucy's attempts to reinvent herself, so that opposing the norms of femininity drilled into her by her mother becomes a source of direction and energy. When Lucy looks to alternative sources for role models, she finds them lacking too. Thus, although Mariah becomes a kind of mother-substitute (whom Lucy alternately loves and hates), her confidence (and complacence) in offering Lucy a feminist framework does not speak to Lucy's sense of herself as "marginal" on several counts: "I was not a man; I was a young woman from the fringes of the world, and when I left my home I had wrapped around my shoulders the mantle of a servant" (1991: 95).

Lucy's decision to embrace "sluthood" is a rejection of the models of femininity offered by her mother (ladyhood) and by Mariah (feminism); instead Lucy cultivates an oppositional identity as the only plausible one for survival. Early on in the novel, there is a telling description of Mariah:

> Mariah, with her pale-yellow skin and yellow hair, stood still in this almost celestial light, and she looked blessed, no blemish or mark of any kind on her cheek or

anywhere else . . . The smell of Mariah was pleasant. Just that – pleasant. And I thought, But that's the trouble with Mariah – she smells pleasant. By then I already knew that I wanted to have a powerful odor and would not care if it gave offense. (1991: 27)

The Autobiography of My Mother

It is this insistence on embracing rather than rejecting the female body which Kincaid develops further in *The Autobiography of My Mother*. In *Lucy*, despite the many assertions of confidence in the body and in female sexuality, the novel is littered with reminders of the overwhelming loneliness and isolation which force Lucy to take refuge in her body and to rely solely on her own resources. The text concludes with Lucy alone in her apartment (symbol of her independent life away from home, mother and Mariah), busying herself with a variety of "little things"; her best friend, Peggy, is out with her lover, Paul – a twin betrayal which the narrator claims she does not care about: "I only hoped they would not get angry and disrupt my life when they realized I did not care" (1996: 163). The concluding paragraph of the novel is narrated by Lucy lying alone in bed with the notebook Mariah gave her open – and empty – in front of her, and she writes the words: " 'I wish I could love someone so much that I would die from it.' And then as I looked at this sentence a great wave of shame came over me and I wept and wept so much that the tears fell on the page and caused all the words to become one great blur" (1996: 163–64).

What is disturbing about this scene is not Lucy's lack of interest in being betrayed (one is convinced that neither Peggy nor Paul deserves much interest) but that the control she exercises over people with whom she has relationships is also extended to herself, so that she views her momentary "lapse" into an emotional response ("I wish I could love someone so much that I would die from it") as sentimental and shameful. The novel ends, rather like the ending of *Annie John*, with an image of Lucy dissolving in a blur of tears, an image which lingers and forces a double take on the commanding control which Lucy appears to exercise throughout the body of the text. Sexual conquests can only *partially* alleviate her emotional maroonage in America. This notion of ambivalent heroism is fine tuned in Kincaid's *Autobiography of My Mother* which, like *Lucy*, recognizes the devalued status of women in

Caribbean society and suggests that female sexuality can be harnessed to productive – rather than purely *reproductive* – ends. However, Kincaid's canvas in *The Autobiography of My Mother* is much broader – almost epic – in scale, not only because the narration covers seventy years of the narrator's life but also because explicit links are made between the personal and the political with regard to the exercise of power and the experience of love and loss. In this novel, Kincaid's treatment of female sexuality allows for interesting developments with regard to the representation of female sexuality and the role of the sexed body in projecting "the" Caribbean woman's identity. Kincaid offers a radical alternative to the dominant models of the Caribbean woman as grounded, exuberant "Tantie" or elevated spiritual Mother.

The Autobiography of My Mother charts the seventy years of the life of the protagonist/narrator, Xuela Claudette Richardson. Starting from her formative years when she is packed off – along with the bundle of her father's dirty washing – to a wet nurse/washerwoman (Ma Eunice) – who looks after her, the novel traces her relationship with her father and her stepmother as well as a succession of sexual relationships which culminate with her marriage to Philip, an English doctor. The novel opens with a stark assertion of a cataclysmic loss: "My mother died at the moment I was born, and so for my whole life there was nothing standing between myself and eternity; at my back was always a bleak, black wind" (1996: 3).

This is a loss which shapes Xuela's life at every point but which also resonates with significances for the entire Caribbean as a region predicated upon trauma and loss. The statement of this loss is also used to punctuate the novel, for it is reiterated as a haunting refrain throughout the text.

Kincaid presents both Xuela's parents as orphaned in some way; her father's father, a red-haired Scots man, abandons his family, leaving his son (her father) clinging to his copper skin ("the color of corruption: copper, gold, ore" [1996: 181]) for upward mobility. But, as Xuela remarks, "I did not have red hair, I was not a man" (1996: 183), so her social status is much more closely aligned with that of her dead mother who was abandoned as a baby outside the gates of a convent and whose Carib ancestry Xuela has inherited. Throughout the text, we are reminded of Xuela's status as disinherited on several counts – her class, her race, her gender – and the rage she feels at such marginality finds expression in the carefully controlled anger of the repeated statement: "I, Xuela, am not in a position to make my feeling have any meaning" (1996: 137). Treated like a bundle by her father (she questions whether he distinguishes between the two bundles deposited at the wet nurse/washer), and acutely aware of the broader contexts of disregard and lovelessness within which she is located, Xuela narrativizes her life as a series of rejections and short-lived, compromised sexual encounters. The final sentence in the penultimate paragraph of the book is evocative of the frustration and desolation which characterizes her life:

> In me is the voice I never heard, the face I never saw, the being I came from. In me are the voices that should have come out of me, the faces I never allowed to form, the eyes I never allowed to see me. This account is an account of the person who was never allowed to be and an account of the person I did not allow myself to become. (1996: 227–28)

The suggestion here is that the narrator interprets her own severely circumscribed life as representative of the lives of many others who are, like her, "of the vanquished people, [. . .] of the defeated people" (p. 215), but this connection to community is one which is *not* a two-way flow. Where Collins, Brodber, Hodge and Senior (however rigorous they are in pointing up the limitations of being in/of a "small place") suggest in their texts that the community provides a plethora of culturally rich possibilities through which their protagonists can construct a more confidently Caribbean identity, in Kincaid's *Autobiography*, "the community" provides no such solace. There is a strong sense in all of Kincaid's texts that, in important ways, every woman is an island, so that to take refuge in collectively articulated identities is to escape the responsibilities *and* possibilities of self-definition. Surveying her life at the end of the novel, Xuela says: "My impulse is to the good, my good is to serve myself. *I am not a people, I am not a nation.* I only wish from time to time to make my actions be the actions of a people, to make my actions be the actions of a nation" (1996: 126; my emphasis).

Kincaid's construction of the narrator as embattled and *alone* invites parallels with Walcott's notion of the poet as castaway and his rejection (particularly in the essay "What the Twilight Says") of any easy, ideologically driven, Caribbean identity – what he calls in that essay, "fake folk". But perhaps gender (and genre) makes a telling difference here because, unlike the possibilities for an Adamic naming role which Walcott's poet/castaway envisions, Kincaid's narrator talks of her life beginning with a "wide panorama of possibilities"; the pages of her life *should* have been filled with volumes of adventure and expansive action. Instead, surveying the "panorama" of her life, Xuela talks bitterly of possibilities denied, of circumscription and limitation. The image of her seventy-year-old body is presented to suggest the ageing process but, more importantly, to suggest the sense of a *shrinking into* the body which such restrictive circumstances force:

> My body now is still; when it moves, it moves inward, shrinking into itself, withering like fruit dying on a vine, not rotting like fruit that has been picked and lies uneaten on a dirty plate . . . I refused to belong to a race, I refused to accept a nation. I wanted only, and still do want, to observe the people who do so. The crime of these identities, which I know now more than ever, I do not have the courage to bear. (1996: 225–26)

The image of the body as shrivelled, having lost its child-bearing fecundity, is suggestive of an *implosive* dynamic. This sense of a withering into the body comes as the poignant "last word" at the end of a text in which the narrator has repeatedly insisted on testifying to the power and beauty of her body and its centrality as the only – and limited – source and site of resistance.

Throughout the text, the narrator regularly reminds the reader of her physical strength and beauty. This insistence on loving the body takes shape early on in the novel when Xuela goes to live with her father and his new wife. The stepmother's dislike of her is quickly registered by Xuela: "She did not like me. She did not love me. I could see it in her face. My spirit rose to meet this challenge. No love: I could live in a place like this. I knew this atmosphere all too well. Love would have defeated me" (1996: 29). Later, when the stepmother is showing her how to wash herself, her dislike is explicit: "It was not done with kindness. My human form and odour were an opportunity to heap scorn on me" (1996: 32). In order to survive this systematic attempt to denigrate her, Xuela begins to worship her own body:

> I loved the smell of thin dirt behind my ears, the smell of my unwashed mouth, the smell that came from between my legs, the smell in the pit of my arm, the smell of my unwashed feet. Whatever about me caused offense, whatever was native to me, whatever I could not help and was not a moral failing – these things about me I loved with the fervor of the devoted. (1996: 32–33)

This fascination with her own body – with "funk", to use Toni Morrison's formulation in *The Bluest Eye* – is savoured in private while hidden under the mantle of piety which she adopts at school:

> To my teachers I seemed quiet and studious; I was modest, which is to say, I did
> not seem to them to have any interest in the world of my body or anyone else's
> body. This wearying demand was only one of many demands made on me simply
> because I was female. (1996: 41–42)

Xuela caresses her own body, secure in the knowledge that *she* knows who she
is, even if others are fooled by her deception. The chapter ends with Xuela
alone in bed, imagining the fear and suffering outside in the wider world and
comforting herself by masturbating. All of the sexual relationships with men
which follow (except for that with Roland) are preceded by a description of
Xuela fondling herself, a recurring image of her self-reliance *and* vulnerability.

The cultivation of a love of her body is not disrupted by puberty; where
Annie John wants her father to build her a frame to curb her growth, Xuela,
like Lucy, revels in the secretions and smells of the postpubescent female body:

> The sight of my changing self did not frighten me, I only wondered how I would
> look eventually; I never doubted that I would like completely whatever stared back
> at me. And so, too, the smell of my underarms and between my legs changed, and
> this change pleased me. In those places the smell became pungent, sharp, as if
> something was in the process of fermenting, slowly; in private, then as now, my
> hands almost never left those places, and when I was in public, these same hands
> were always not far from my nose, I so enjoyed the way I smelled, then and now.
> (1996: 58–59)

This revelling in the pleasures of the corporeal is both a powerful rejection of
the pristine asexuality expected of a lady and an indication of Xuela's
embattled isolation *within* the body. This isolation is not explained solely by
the lack of love within the immediate familial context, for the novel is
punctuated with reminders of the historical legacy of a violently exploitative
and humiliating colonial past which has left the entire community in a state of
defeat, and mistrustful of each other:

> The people we should naturally have mistrusted were beyond our influence
> completely; what we needed to defeat them, to rid ourselves of them, was
> something far more powerful than mistrust. To mistrust each other was just one
> of the many feelings we had for each other, all of them opposite of love, all of them
> standing in the place of love . . . for love might give someone else the advantage.
> (1996: 48; my emphasis)

An example of the kind of cruelty which Kincaid points to as resulting from
this colonial history is charted very early on in the novel when the four-year-

old Xuela is punished for breaking one of Ma Eunice's plates. The punishment consists of Xuela having to kneel on the stone heap in the hot sun with her hands raised above her head, holding a large stone in each hand, until she is prepared to apologize – which she refuses to do. Kincaid makes explicit the link between this "small", personal act of cruelty and the exercise of larger cruelties: "redolent as it was in every way of the relationship between captor and captive, master and slave, with its motif of the big and the small, the powerful and the powerless, the strong and the weak . . ." (1996: 10).

But the enactment of such cruelty is seen as a self-perpetuating cycle in a series of interlinked episodes which follow: while being punished on the stone heap, Xuela notices some land turtles which she subsequently captures in an enclosure, but when they refuse to come out of their shells, she punishes them by blocking their neck openings with mud and burying them. They all die. This image of entrapment is first paralleled in the way Philip traps – in order to "study" – various insects and reptiles in boxed sheets of glass where they die, and in the narrator's description of how she comes to control Philip's life:

> He now lived in a world in which he could not speak the language. I mediated for him, I translated for him. I did not always tell him the truth, I did not always tell him everything. *I blocked his entrance to the world in which he lived; eventually I blocked his entrance into all the worlds he had come to know.* (1996: 224; my emphasis)

In examples such as these Kincaid skilfully foregrounds the ways in which the broader political context impacts upon the personal. Nowhere is this dynamic more in evidence than in the accounts of the sexual relationships which Xuela is involved in.

The first "relationship" she has, aged fifteen, is with the friend of her father with whom she is sent to stay in Roseau (ironically, because her father is anxious about the influence of her male friends in Mahaut). Xuela does household chores in return for her board and keep with Monsieur and Madame La Batte; she quickly befriends *her* while engaging in sex with *him*. The scene of Xuela's first "seduction" is rife with ironies and ambivalences. Sitting amongst the flowers in the garden at twilight, Xuela (who has taken to not wearing underwear) is touching herself – "sometimes absentmindedly, sometimes with a purpose in mind" – when Monsieur LaBatte appears: "He did not move away in embarrassment and I, too, did not run away in embarrassment. We held each other's gaze. I removed my fingers from between my legs and brought them up to my face, I wanted to smell myself. It was the end of the day, my odour was quite powerful" (1996: 70).

When he asks her to take her clothes off: "I said, quite sure of myself, knowing what it was I wanted, that it was too dark, I could not see" (1996: 70). They have sex in the room in which he counts his money, but this dense image of patriarchal power is undermined by the coolly appraising way in which Xuela sees through his acquisitiveness, and is further diminished by the clear sense she has of the role of her own imagination in *constructing* him as desirable: "I was surprised at how unbeautiful he was all by himself, just standing there; it was anticipation that was the thrill, it was anticipation that kept me enthralled" (1996: 71).

Similarly, there is a sense in which her reconstruction and reliving of sex with Monsieur LaBatte is as crucial as "the event" itself: "It was through all the parts of my body that ached that I relived the deep pleasure I had just experienced" (1996: 72). This is not to say that sex with men is described as without pleasure for Xuela but that she is an active agent in mobilizing this pleasure, in *taking* such pleasure, and that pleasure of this kind precludes her from the kinds of roles her peers would be aspiring to and is, therefore, an attempt to subvert her ascribed gender role. Indeed, she acknowledges that "To become a schoolgirl again was not possible, only I did not know this right away . . . I could not like what it [colonial education] would lead to: a humiliation so permanent that it would replace your own skin" (1996: 78–79).

Xuela falls pregnant by Monsieur LaBatte, a development welcomed by his wife who is desperate for a child, but whose interest in sex has long been exhausted. Just as the marriage of the LaBattes is represented as a series of deceptions – she feeds him food mixed with her menstrual blood to "catch" him in marriage; he turns on her "with the strength of the weapon he carried between his legs, and he wore her out" (1996: 65) – so the couple use Xuela for their own ends: he for sex and she to acquire the baby she cannot carry herself. Xuela manages to escape this predicament, at great cost to herself, by arranging the termination of her pregnancy.

This abortion, which reduces her body to a "volcano of pain" (1996: 82), is life shaping: "I was a new person then, I knew things I had not known before, I knew things that you can only know if you have been through what I had just been through. I had carried my own life in my own hands" (1996: 83). Following this trauma, the narrator leaves the LaBattes and retreats into a regime of hard physical labour on the land, in which she eschews any sexual pleasure and assumes an androgynous identity: "not a man, not a woman, not anything . . ." (1996: 102). During this period she lists a variety of precise and cruel ways in which she might kill off the children she will never have: throwing them off cliffs, freezing them in the postures in which they were born, eating them whole – a series of images which powerfully and violently refuse to celebrate maternity as woman's "natural" role. The cruelty of such images is rendered poignant by the sense of bereftness which is seen to motivate such imaginings: "My life was beyond empty. I had never had a mother, I had just recently refused to become one, and I knew then that this refusal would be complete" (1996: 96–97).

This period of isolation ends with a return to the house of her father in Mahaut, but not before Xuela has reaffirmed her faith in herself, recognizing that her ability to "carry her life in her own hands" has given her an awesome authority and power:

> I could feel that I had become hard; I could feel that to love was beyond me, that I had gained such authority over my own ability to be that I could cause my own demise with complete calm . . . It was seeing my own face that comforted me. I began to worship myself . . . My own face was a comfort to me, and no matter how swept away I would become by anyone or anything, in the end I allowed nothing to replace my own being in my own mind. (1996: 99–100)

It is this hard-edged, hard-won independence which Xuela takes with her when she returns to her father's house and to the hostility which greets her there. However, her stay there is again truncated by the threat of sexual danger which her father foresees with the arrival of her stepsister's husband and Xuela is sent away (having already had sex with her sister's man) to other friends of her father – Philip, the doctor, and his wife.

It is in the relationship with Philip that Kincaid offers the most sustained exploration of the complex ways in which political and historical forces impact upon the personal and the sexual. Xuela first attracts his attention when he examines her chest because she has a persistent cough and she tells him about the sensation in her breasts: "I told him that my breasts were filled with an irritable sensation that I found pleasant because it could be relieved only by a sensation I found even more desirable, a man's mouth placed securely over them" (1996: 147). What is interesting in this quote is the matter-of-fact way in which the narrator conveys this desire without gesturing towards the rules of propriety which would censor such desire.

This narrative voice which asserts bluntly, "this is, simply, how things *are*", is one which Kincaid exploits to explore many unpalatable and/or taboo areas. Sex is not alluded to through a veil of metaphors, neither is it embedded in the familiar context of a "loving relationship", but it is described straightforwardly and in detail. As with Monsieur LaBatte, Xuela's first sexual encounter with Philip is preceded by a description of her masturbating:

> I had been sitting on the floor caressing in an absentminded way various parts of my body. I was wearing a nightgown made from a piece of nankeen my father had given me, and when Philip came in, one hand was underneath it and my fingers were trapped in the hair between my legs. When he came in I did not remove my hand hurriedly. (1996: 151)

The recurring image of Xuela absorbed in the pleasures of her own body signifies ambivalently, testifying to the restricted parameters of her world, to her loneliness *and* to her ability to transcend these limitations. Philip is English, "but by the time Philip was born, all the bad deeds had already been committed; he was an heir, generations of people had died and left him something" (1996: 146).

But the legacy of the cruelty committed by his ancestors is one which leaves its trace in Philip's need to capture/categorize Dominican insects and in his desire to control the landscape in his gardening enterprise ("for it is an act of conquest, benign though it may be" [1996: 143]). Xuela describes him as completely at sea in Roseau – "outposts of despair; for conqueror and conquered alike these places were the capitals of nothing but despair" (1996: 61). The fact of Philip's whiteness is frequently foregrounded:

> but I could not bear to see him naked, his skin in its almost skinness would remind me of the world that was outside the room which was the dark night, the world that was beyond the dark night, and so I closed my eyes and I turned around and removed his belt, and using my mouth I secured it tightly around my wrists and I raised my hands in the air, and with my face turned sideways, I placed my chest against a wall. I made him lie on top of me, my face beneath his; I made him lie on top of me, my back beneath his chest. (1996: 154)

This scene is rich with ambivalences: Philip's "whiteness" – his "almost skinness" – reminds Xuela of the power and privilege he commands beyond the bedroom, and her strategy for undermining this is to present him as repulsively "unfinished" and to actively play the role of sexual victim as a way of taking control of the situation. The passage continues with a list of the various sexual favours Xuela makes Philip do, and she describes the way in which she would force him to stop his endless talk of England: "and I would grow tired of it, and it would cause me to take offense, and I would put a stop to it by removing my clothes and stand before him and stretch my arms all the way up to the ceiling and order him to his knees to eat and there make him stay until I was completely satisfied" (1996: 145).

The vivid image here of Xuela using her body and sexual power to silence a patriarch in full flow about England and Englishness does not imply that Xuela can harness her sexuality to short-circuit the problems of the broader sociopolitical context, "the world that was outside the room"; rather, it highlights the limited ways in which it is possible for these two to communicate *because of* their respective – and mutually constitutive – histories. Xuela makes the decision to marry Philip, after his wife dies, fully aware of what is being traded in such a marriage. She marries him because it allows her to "make a romance of my life", and "Romance is the refuge of the defeated; the defeated need songs to soothe themselves" (1996: 216). He marries her because "[h]e thought I made him forget the past" (1996: 221); "He and I lived in this spell, the spell of history." Kincaid's *Autobiography* captures eloquently the strange and precarious mix of tenderness and exploitativeness which characterizes the relationship for *both* Philip and Xuela. The couple move away from Roseau to live high in the Dominica mountains: "It was a place to rest. We were weary; we were weary of being ourselves, weary of our own legacies" (1996: 221).

Before Xuela marries Philip, but while she is involved with him sexually, she also has an affair with a man called Roland. Indeed, he is introduced to the reader as the man she thinks about while having sex with Philip, when the pleasure of Philip's "thrusts and withdrawals waned" (1996: 163). He is described as "Philip's opposite" – a man without a country: "a small island is not a country" – and a man after whom no mountains or valleys were named; a stevedore, working in the holds of ships that sailed the seas but not sailing those seas himself: "And he did not have a history; he was a small event in somebody else's history, but he was a man" (p. 167).

Described as having a mouth that looked liked an island, lying in the twig-brown sea of his face, and a powerful body, Roland – a stevedore – and Xuela – a doctor's servant – appear to be perfectly matched, and his symbolic role as "island man" tantalizes the reader briefly with the possibility that *he* may be the route via which Xuela can be reconnected with her island. Their "love-at-first-sight" meeting is described with a lyricism that distinguishes it from the other relationships in the text: "so I had to call out my name again and again until he stopped, and by that time my name was like a chain around him, as the sight of his mouth was like a chain around me. And when our eyes met, we laughed because we were happy" (1996: 166).

The narrator declares: "I could feel myself full of happiness"; but the reader is not allowed to savour this romance for long, for the one area in which Roland *can* exercise any power – in the sexual arena, where proof of his prowess would be the fathering of children – is denied him by Xuela, whose own control of her sexuality and fertility becomes the grounds on which she asserts control of *him*:

> I felt much sorrow for him, for his life was reduced to a list of names that were not countries (that is, women's names), and to the number of times he brought the monthly flow of blood to a halt; his life was reduced to women . . . (1996: 175–76)

The end of her relationship with a man of whom the narrator says "I loved him so" is presented with a sense of inevitability and without embellishment of any kind; sitting on the steps of the jetty being fondled by Roland: "I looked out toward the horizon, which I could not see but knew was there all the same, and this was also true of the end of my love for Roland" (1996: 178).

If connection with an "island man" like Roland proves untenable despite the passion of their affair, then another avenue for solace or affirmation of identity for Xuela might have been with other women in the community. Relationships between women are certainly often presented as affirming and sustaining in the texts of other Caribbean women writers. However, in *The Autobiography,* the privileging of heterosexual relationships often results in the narrator being perceived as a source of danger and mistrust by other women. The first example of this rivalry (in this case, rivalry over the father) results in the stepmother attempting to poison the young Xuela; later, despite – or perhaps *because of* – Xuela's role in terminating her stepsister's unwanted pregnancy, the stepsister, too, turns against Xuela. But it is perhaps in the confrontations with the wives of Roland and Philip that any notion of sisterly solidarity is obliterated. When Roland's wife confronts Xuela in the street, calling her "a whore, a slut, a pig, a snake, a viper, a rat, a lowlife, a parasite, and an evil woman" (1996: 171), slapping her and tearing her dress, Kincaid uses the encounter to dramatize the humiliation and defeat attendant upon women for whom the possession of a husband becomes essential for their survival:

> And yet I was standing before a woman [Roland's wife] who found herself unable to keep her life's booty in its protective sack . . . I saw that her feet were without shoes. She did have a pair of shoes, though, which I had seen; they were white, they were plain, a round toe and flat laces, they took shoe polish well, she wore them only on Sundays and to church. I had many pairs of shoes, in colors meant to attract attention and dazzle the eye; they were uncomfortable, I wore them every day, I never went to church at all. (1996: 174–75)

While the relationship between Moira (Philip's wife) and Xuela is much less dramatically focused, Kincaid again uses the relationship between the two women to foreground the particular (confident bordering on flamboyant) kind of gendered identity Xuela has constructed for herself. Despite also having a "broken womb", Moira's insistence on maintaining an affected femininity which proclaims her class and cultural privilege makes any connection between the two women impossible:

> she was a lady, I was a woman, and this distinction for her was important; it allowed her to believe that I would not associate the ordinary, the everyday – a bowel movement, a cry of ecstasy – with her, and a small act of cruelty was elevated to a rite of civilization . . . a lady is a combination of elaborate fabrications, a collection of externals, facial arrangements, and body parts, distortions, lies and empty effort. *I was a woman and as that I had a brief description: two breasts, a small opening between my legs, one womb; it never varies and they are always in the same place.* (1996: 158–59; my emphasis)

In this image, Kincaid confronts the stark realities confronting the postcolonial woman in her attempts to construct a viable identity. Kincaid's texts repeatedly reject the distortions and fakery involved in Eurocentric versions of femininity – the ladyhood business – which Moira represents; instead she confronts the truncated version of female identity – *two breasts, a small opening between my legs, one womb* – on offer to the postcolonial woman, and points up the possibilities and limitations of such a model. In the absence of a viable, indigenous challenge to colonially inherited sexual mores, the battle for a more productive sexed identity for Caribbean women must be waged alone. Xuela's principled investment in her identity as sexually confident and active "woman" is achieved at great cost: she loses the attendant social privileges of ladyhood and is isolated from community. The novel ends with Xuela's assessment of the account of her life which comprises the novel and with an anticipation of her own death (having buried all her immediate family):

> In me is the voice I never heard, the face I never saw, the being I came from. In me are the voices that should have come out of me, the faces I never allowed to form, the eyes I never allowed to see me. This account is an account of the person who was never allowed to be and an account of the person I did not allow myself to become . . . Death is the only reality, for it is the only certainty, inevitable to all things. (1996: 227–28)

Conclusion

The kind of hybrid polyphony of voices associated with "noisy" texts such as Collins's *Angel* or Brodber's *Louisiana* are, strategically, not delivered in Kincaid's *Autobiography* but remain, as indicated in the quote above, as thwarted potential. This reluctance to deliver the speaking creole voice operates symbolically in the quote above but is there in another guise in the marked absence of any attempt to represent creole speech within her texts. So, for example, the narrator in *Annie John* tells us that the mother repeats the word "slut" in patois, but we are not told what the word in patois is. In *Autobiography,* there are several references to patois being used as exclusively indigenous means of communication, but it remains a secret for the reader because it is not represented on the page. In each of the three novels discussed above, despite their feistiness, a sense of the speaking voice of the protagonists is practically nonexistent; rather, their silence operates as a reminder of the isolation and loneliness of these subjects. *Muteness* operates as a powerful trope and is presented, implicitly, as the only sane response for the postcolonial female subject, relegated by colonial history to the margins.

Similarly, at the level of Kincaid's aesthetic choices, her texts are *not* marked by the kind of excess and plenitude associated with the literary representation of creole culture (and with *ecriture feminine*). Narrative voice in her texts is always measured and precise – almost "hyper-correct" – and marked by a definite preference for an even control and understatement rather than for hybridity and a multiplicity of narrative perspectives. The kind of verbal wit and anarchic humour associated with creole culture (and utilized so effectively by Hodge and Senior, for example) is also absent from Kincaid's text where, again, economy and understatement are preferred; for example, when Xuela is being abused by Roland's wife, the narrator says that she had "a face I had so little interest in that it would tire me to describe it . . ." (1996: 171). So, although Kincaid does signal that creole culture has positive value (indigenous ways of knowing are frequently cited as productive, in contrast to European versions), she is also at pains to foreground the ways in which this same culture forecloses on all kinds of possibilities for Caribbean women.

So, for Kincaid, unlike many other Caribbean women writers, the Caribbean female subject is presented as marooned in the islands, bereft of the structures (adequate parenting or supportive mother culture) which might allow her (at least partially) to transcend the limitations of being born into a postcolonial context. This state of "orphanhood" is not compensated for, in her novels, by effective surrogate mothers, sisterly networking or by the warm embrace of the creole mother culture. Instead, Kincaid presents a Caribbean culture which is so profoundly damaged by the impact of colonialism and the trauma of that initial loss of culture that any kind of love becomes an impossibility in such a brutalized context. Sex "stands in the place of love" as a bold assertion of acceptance of woman's individuality and her embodiment, the first step to self-validation in a hostile and conformist Caribbean. Kincaid's literary project stands as an elegant and spare lament for what might have been as vital a representation of the Caribbean as the more frequently invoked celebrations of creole culture.

References

Brodber, Erna. 1980. *Jane and Louisa Will Soon Come Home*. London: New Beacon.

_____. 1988. *Myal*. London: New Beacon.

_____. 1994. *Louisiana*. London: New Beacon.

Cooper, Carolyn. 1993. *Noises in the Blood: Orality, Gender and the "Vulgar" Body of Jamaican Popular Culture*. London: Macmillan.

Hodge, Merle. 1981. *Crick Crack Monkey*. London: Heinemann.

Kincaid, Jamaica. 1984. *At the Bottom of the River*. New York: Picador.

_____. 1985. *Annie John*. London: Picador.

_____. 1991. *Lucy*. New York: Plume.

_____. 1996. *The Autobiography of My Mother*. London: Vintage.

Mordecai, P., and E. Wilson, eds. 1989. *Her True-True Name*. London: Heinemann.

Morrison, Toni. 1990. *The Bluest Eye*. London: Picador.

Senior, Olive. 1986. *Summer Lightning*. London: Longman.

_____. 1989. *Arrival of the Snake Woman and Other Stories*. London: Longman.

Walcott, Derek. 1998. *What the Twilight Says*. London: Faber.

20 Gender as a Dynamic Concept in the Media

HILARY NICHOLSON

An essential and sometimes controversial component of the mass media is the depiction of women and men. It is apparent to any observer that the mass media portray women and men differently. To present these differences as polarized, female versus male, leads to stereotyping. The media tends to rely on stereotypes as short-cuts in order to elicit quick responses from us. These stereotypes limit our understanding of others, limit our perception of what is possible for us as women or men, and do not always reflect reality.

There is evidence from the late twentieth century that the situation has changed, not only in terms of representation but also in terms of how we respond to the media. Back in 1987 a public protest sparked by Sistren Theatre Collective (Jamaica) led to the withdrawal of a display appearing in the overseas press for Jamaica National Investment Promotion, featuring the silhouette of a female bottom and legs, with high-heeled shoes, under the copy "Your bottom line is beautiful when you make it in Jamaica." This promotion was geared to luring investors to Jamaica's free zone, with its largely female labour force. It was criticized as selling young working women as sex objects.

A few years after the contested Jamaica National Investment Promotion incident, the Jamaica Promotions Corporation, the new national promotion agency, displayed a message in the overseas press, again relying on the female bottom (this time without legs), clad in underwear with the words "a brief example of our work" on the buttocks. The copy mentioned, among other things, "low labour costs" when investing in Jamaica, presumably referring to a cheap female workforce in Jamaica's free zone garment factories.

On 14 March 1994, the front page article and photograph of the Jamaica *Daily Gleaner* dealt with the controversy surrounding the winning entry in the Jamaica Chamber of Commerce/Jamaica Tourist Board Tourism Poster Competition, which gave prominence to a woman's derriere protruding from shorts, with "I love Jamaica" emblazoned on the pocket. Between the thighs appeared the island of Jamaica. Print space, television and radio time were taken up as the public challenged the suitability of the poster to advertise a nation.

A common feature in the three messages described above is the use of the truncated female body, with no indication of what activity – if any – the "person" is engaged in or initiating. What happens to the female body when dismembered in this way? When we see body parts, without head and face, do we still respond to the picture as a woman, as someone with a personality and feelings? How often does the dismembered *female* form appear in the media, on posters and calendars, in movies and magazines, in ads for cosmetics and cars, in comic strips and cartoons? Does this not reinforce the notion of woman as an object rather than a person with thoughts and ideas?

The media stereotype women in another way, by referring to their physical appearance when this is irrelevant to the topic. For example, a newspaper article appearing in the *Gleaner* of 13 June 1995 under the title "Iron Lady of the Caribbean to Retire after 15 Years" began:

> Prime Minister Eugenia Charles answered the door of her third-floor walk-up in a house dress, a mustard-coloured scarf covering curlers in her hair, her feet tucked into green terrycloth slippers . . .

What is the effect of introducing the article in this way? Is the writer trying to humanize the "Iron Lady"? Or reminding us that though a prime minister, Charles is an (ordinary) woman? Is the writer creating a stereotyped image of an elderly retired person (the article informs us that Charles is soon to retire)? Is there an implication that ultimately a woman's role is in the home, rather than in politics?

In another example from the *Daily Gleaner,* under a photograph of three VIPs at a press conference (a university professor, a minister of government, a doctor of philosophy) the caption began: "a row of beauties . . .". Had the VIPs been male, might the caption have read "a row of debonair [studs] . . ."? Such tactics, conscious or not on the part of journalists, detract from the issue or trivialize an otherwise serious piece.

A very different portrayal of woman appears in a display advertisement by Mutual Life showing a woman smartly dressed, with handbag-cum-briefcase, striding out confidently, smiling, over this copy:

> The career woman: she wants to forge her independence . . . We want her to be a force to reckon with. Jamaican women are marching into the future, self-assured and aware. They are dreaming dreams and creating realities their mothers never knew. Mutual Life is proud of Jamaica's women . . .

The presentation of woman in this ad is extended to include her various roles: she is economically active, a mother, a visionary, a shaper-of-the-future – clearly, the message is that she contributes in an important way to society. This image contrasts sharply with the more frequent image of the dismembered female form. Caribbean women are not a homogenous category, thus one would expect a range of media images covering the many facets of their real lives – domestic, community, economic and political.

Not only women but also men and children are affected adversely by stereotypes in the media. In the late 1990s in the United States a multimillion-dollar advertising campaign for Calvin Klein jeans was withdrawn as a result of a public lobby which claimed that the ads promoted children as sex objects.

In June 1994, in Jamaica, there was public protest of the wording of a media message to promote condom usage: "If you want to see how fast he can run, tell him you're pregnant." The accompanying photograph showed a man in running shorts. While, unlike the earlier images of women described above, this illustration made it clear that the man was about to engage in some athletic activity, Fathers Incorporated[1] objected to the implication that men reject their responsibility as fathers. And, rightly so, various organizations and members of the public supported this criticism. Women's Media Watch[2] pointed out that the message reinforced the myth that there "are no good men out there", and that it placed the responsibility for contraception back on the woman, reinforcing the notion that the parenting role is a woman's concern. In addition, the sexual stereotyping included elements of race and colour: the condom package showed a nude woman with fair complexion and long hair.

The public debate and lobbying by the majority of Jamaican population around these images under representation resulted in a number of changes being made to the message.

The media also use violence to create ideas of what is acceptable for women and men. Stereotyped images of violence contribute to our present concept of what is "news", in sensational coverage of crime, war, disasters, rape and domestic abuse. Media violence contributes to our notion of what is "entertainment", by feeding us violent films and music videos and, specifically, sexual violence, which reaches as far as "snuff" movies. The media include popular music, with the gun lyrics of the dancehall genre, which produce lines such as "me haffi get yuh body even at gunpoint".[3] In such media, the majority of violence is perpetrated by a male stereotype (the sexually violent, mean, macho male) on a female. Violence is generally unchallenged and presented as heroic – as a role model. The victim is often a stereotype – certain sexual, ethnic and socioeconomic characteristics are repeatedly associated with victim images.

Public response is slow and mixed when it comes to questioning this diet of violence. It is estimated that by the age of eighteen, a youngster in today's United States will have seen eighteen thousand violent deaths[4] – it is worth noting that much of our region's television programming originates in the United States. The impact of television violence on audiences has been the subject of research for decades – sometimes with inconclusive findings. A special US Senate Judiciary Sub-Committee set up to address television violence concluded in 1993, however, that television violence does have an impact, and told top executives of major networks and cable giants "to tidy up their houses by the end of the year or the Congress would do it for them" (Segree 1993). Consumer lobbying in North America earlier in 1995 demanded – and obtained – the withdrawal of an advertisement for perfume on the grounds that the ad linked sex and violence. The ad featured a nude, dismembered female body viewed from behind, hands tied behind her back.

These media messages of violence carry strong messages of "acceptable" dominance and coercive power in the everyday relations between women and men. These messages need to be constantly looked at in order to understand their changing impact on audiences – audiences which differ according to age, sex, ethnicity, socioeconomic background, location (as for instance rural or urban). Whom do these messages serve and whom do they exploit?

Why the Media Matter

We are reminded of the potential of the media in shaping, not just reflecting, reality, when we consider that in 1993, $755 billion were spent around the world on advertising (Gallagher 1995b), on the assumption that media messages do alter our way of thinking. To put this figure in perspective Gallagher reminds us that "the combined GNP of the 43 least developed countries (as defined by the UN) is approximately $100 billion – just 13 percent of what the world currently spends on advertising". The advertising industry which feeds media production is immensely powerful.

The media occupy an increasingly central place in the lives of women and men all over the world. By 1991 the developing regions had increased their share of world radio sets to 36 percent, of world televisions to 29 percent, while in many Caribbean countries ownership of radios and televisions is well above the world average (Gallagher 1995b). In Jamaica nearly half the population now has access to home videotape players. Advances in information technology have facilitated the development of international media enterprises which transcend national boundaries, satellite dishes have mushroomed around our region, and Caribbean people have opened their living rooms to cable, as well as to some new local channels and stations. Print media, more locally owned throughout the region, has not expanded at the same rate as electronic media, although new tabloids appear on the scene from time to time Such tabloids often demonstrate a sexist, sensationalist slant, relying on headlines such as "Sex-Starved Youths on the Rampage" or "My Husband Beat Me then Raped Me" (*Star*).

Much of our knowledge of the world, as well as our notions of self, comes from the media, and our idea of who we are as female and male is influenced by value-laden messages from overseas. The media are not transparent technologies, they do not offer merely a "window on the world" (Graydon and Verrall 1994). In mediating events and issues, television, film, video games and other media are involved in *selecting, constructing and representing another reality*. In so doing the media tend to emphasize and reinforce the priorities and values of those who create the messages and own the means of dissemination. The media product presented is the result of commercial, political, racial, class and other cultural determinants. Inevitably the interests of the owners of the media prevail, and these interests frequently do not coincide with those of the working women and men who read, view or listen to the media. As a result, the views and experiences of other people are often left out or shown in biased ways.

What Is "News" Anyway?

Most of us are aware of a class bias in the news; we need to ask also whether there is a gender bias in what is considered newsworthy. Equally significant as what does appear is what does not appear. Much news material is omitted as a result of editorial process and policy. Noeleen Heyzer (1994) talks about "absences" – "the blanking out of areas of experience which never find their way into mainstream media – stories of rural people, of urban working class, of the elderly, of youth, of women coping with everyday experiences of sexual harassment at the workplace, violence in their domestic lives".

There is an urban, professional bias in much of Caribbean news media, as well as an ethnic bias. Information on indigenous peoples of the region does not appear. Some specific examples will be cited from the Jamaican experience: Protz's (1993) informal study of the *Gleaner*'s coverage of rural persons and their work – especially rural women – testifies to this: rural people appear in less than 3.5 percent of all pictures, rural women in less than 1.5 percent (Protz 1993 cited in de Bruin 1994: 17). This contrasts with the prominent role played by women in the cultivation, distribution and processing of food. The stereotyped image of a woman working in agriculture ignores the possibility that she might also be a religious leader in her community, active in politics, a leader in the local parent-teacher association, and so on. The Jamaican media's low valuing of the rural sector is reflected in the lack of interest shown by JBC TV in *Sweet Sugar Rage,* a homegrown video produced by Sistren Theatre Collective in 1985. The video reveals the conditions of work and life of women sugar workers in Clarendon. The video has never been broadcast in Jamaica, although it was selected for television screening in Canada, the United Kingdom, Germany and several Caribbean territories.

The underrepresentation of women in news media is a commonplace in research findings (see Gallagher 1981; Gallagher and Quindoza-Santiago 1994; Lindsey 1994). A casual observer will notice that to find women, one looks in the tabloids, in fashion, home and social sections (considered "soft" news), and in the entertainment programmes on television and radio – not in the so-called hard news of finance and business.

A UNESCO study in ten European countries found that 1.4 percent of television news items dealt with women's issues, and three-quarters of these were presented by men (UNESCO 1995). A similarly small proportion of news on gender and development in the Caribbean is reported in de Bruin (1994). When poor urban people – especially women – reach the news, it is often as victims (of dire circumstances, crime or disaster) or as troublemakers. An example in the Jamaican press is the coverage of female vendors/higglers (only) when they disrupt Metropolitan Parks and Markets, demonstrate against police or customs officials, or block the road. Their achievements rarely reach news, nor do the issues that concern their day-to-day entrepreneurial efforts attract analysis. The first regional conference of informal commercial importers (ICIs) which took place in the Eastern Caribbean in 1991, at which tariffs, quotas and customs regulations (among other things) were discussed, was a milestone that missed the news.

The media reproduce assumptions about the status of women, the role of women in society, the relations between women and men. The question is whether this is done in a manner that contributes to the advancement of women, or that transforms gender relations, rather than demeaning women. In the Caribbean as in Africa, the Pacific and the Middle East, the "lack of up-to-date documentation and recorded experience on most aspects of women's relationship with the media is still a tremendous limitation" (Gallagher 1994). Still, a number of small regional studies and observations have been mentioned here and appear below as the trends follow a pattern which becomes significant.

It becomes clear that while national and international media offer "the promise of greater interaction among people, rapid exchange of knowledge and accessible resources for education, they can also reinforce stereotypes, ignore or exploit people and perpetuate existing structures of domination and power imbalance" (International Women's Tribune Centre statement, February 1995). The reinforcement of gender stereotypes is one of the key elements transmitted in the media. These stereotypes must be challenged and transformed to ensure that they do not perpetuate power imbalances in society. We must understand how media function in this regard.

Gender as a Dynamic Concept

Gender refers to the way in which sexual differences linked to biology become arranged socially. Within each particular culture these differences are organized according to standards which dictate what is acceptable for women and for men. Gender refers to cultural norms and concepts of what is appropriate "femininity" or "masculinity', in terms of traits, attitudes, behaviour, occupational roles. Kate Young refers to "gendering" as a process by which "we acquire the social characteristics of masculinity or femininity . . . a highly complex set of processes which start almost at birth . . . acquiring an identity (masculine, feminine) which in part involves learning a set of differentiated behaviours and capacities appropriate to one's gender" (Young 1988: 98).

Gender is a dynamic concept, and the changing social relations between women and men are referred to as gender relations. Gender relations do not just refer to the day-to-day relations between a woman and a man, but rather as Kate Young puts it, "gender relations involve the structured set of social behaviours and relations to which we refer when we say men (as a social category) do this (and do not do that), women (as a social category) do that (and never do this)" (1988: 98).

Lise Ostergard extends the idea of gender to include the "qualitative and interdependent character of women's and men's position in society" (1992: 6). This interdependent nature of gender, of the relations between women and men, as well as *among* women and men, is reflected by media processes, which daily recreate "correct" concepts of gender relations. Thus the media create a stereotype of masculinity which results in men feeling they have to compete with or emulate other men, and women with other women, in order to be acceptably "masculine" or "feminine".

Gender changes over time and place, with some gender patterns shifting easily, others being deeply embedded. Gender is shaped by cultural and social variables which include historical, political, educational, religious, racial and ethnic considerations as well as biological and psychological determinants. Each of these variables can have an effect on when, where and how gender patterns shift.

Gender-appropriate dress offers an example of this kind of shift: consider the male student wearing a single earring. In 1995 it was acceptably masculine. Twenty years before this the single earring on a male symbolized homosexual masculinity. One incident that comes to mind took place in 1974 on a bus in Jamaica. A Guyanese student's single, left earring was interpreted as a sign of femininity by other males who threatened him with a machete and threw him off the bus.[5] Today, should a middle-aged farmer stop by a local rum bar in a rural Caribbean setting sporting an earring, he would hardly meet with the approval of his peer group. Yet the "macho" buccaneer of yesteryear is depicted wearing a single gold earring and lambada-style head tie.

The media obviously play a major role in shaping notions of acceptable, and *ideal,* physical femaleness and maleness, full as they are of fashion and beauty messages, many of which target women, telling them how to look and how to behave. These messages also tell men what women are supposed to look like. Ideals of beauty are particularly influenced by overseas standards, reflecting characteristics deemed to be desirable, such as long hair, slim figures, small breasts, flat stomachs, and thighs that must not bulge in French-cut underwear. These have little to do with the reality of motherhood, much less hard work, which defines the lives of most Caribbean women.

From Mills and Boon for young readers, through local *Flair* and imported *Cosmopolitan, Essence, The Young and the Restless* (all popular in the region), to locally produced soaps, women are persuaded to beautify themselves *for men* and to compete with other women. The *Jamaica Herald*'s *Today's Woman,* launched in March 1995, follows in the mould of other magazines and television shows which target career women yet focus on relationships with men and how to become beautiful. Is the message that career achievement is contingent on physical appearance, and if a woman does not match up to her duty to be beautiful, it must be *her* fault? We saw above that even the Caribbean's "Iron Lady" was scrutinized in relation to her physical appearance in a news piece which purported to be concerned with her as a leading Caribbean personality.

Prime-time entertainment television from overseas, popular throughout the region, shows women "regularly paraded as the mute and partly clothed background scenery against which speaking and fully clothed men take centre-stage" (Gallagher 1995b).

The dancehall medium produces lyrics which dissect women's physiques and identify body parts which have to be improved upon. DJs demand that women have a "healthy body", singing "mi nuh waan no lazy body". The male DJs tell women in the dancehall to "hol up yu han if yuh arm nuh frowzy".

Other lines are more graphic about female "private parts" and encourage women to compete with one another: "mate a rebel but tell her go to hell, dis year mek she know a de better hole tell" (Cobra).

Seen through a gender perspective, the subjection of women's bodies to analysis and evaluation by *men* is quite different from women's relationship to their own bodies – there is a persistent implication of male-female relations based on dominance and control.

Putting a Value on Women and Men

Traits are not rigidly attached to women and men, but become associated with them. A critical issue is that observed differences attributable to gender, and referred to as gender differences, are *hierarchically valued* or ranked. Different values are placed on gender-related traits, attitudes, behaviours and roles, or on women as a group, men as a group. Traits such as nurturing, independent, aggressive, for example, are valued differently, and those associated with men tend to be more highly valued. When traits or behaviours associated with women are present in men, they are valued negatively. In the Caribbean, a caring, nurturing man may be called soft, "mama man", unmanly; a man who is emotionally expressive may be called weak. The popular medium of calypso has for decades ridiculed the man who emotionally "succumbs" to a woman or helps with housework (Rohlehr 1988). A gender critique of the media requires us to challenge stereotypes and hierarchies and to recognize "difference" in relation to gender.

Hierarchical valuing creates an ideology of superordination/subordination. Within the social relations of gender "men as a social category relative to women as a social category are superordinate . . . though such relations are fragmented by other hierarchies, notably class and race" (Young 1988: 98). Lorna Gordon-Gofton describes a gender ideology as one which "accords male dominance over the values, processes, decisions which define how society should be organized, how it should function . . . [thus] the values of men predominate almost all areas of social living . . . the dominant cultural and institutional practices enshrine male experiences as absolute" (Gordon-Gofton et al. 1987: 4).

How the Media Reinforce the Idea of a Traditional Sexual Division of Labour

One of the most embedded gender concepts relates to child care, presumed throughout the Caribbean to be "woman's work" and of less value than "man's work". Yet even within the broad area of child care, there is a sexual division of labour, in which women are expected to do the nurturing and men the disciplining.

Let us look further at the way in which a different value has been placed on tasks traditionally performed by women, in the home, community and wider society, as compared to the value placed on tasks performed by men. Even among household chores, ranging from cooking, cleaning, sweeping, fetching water and so on, we find that tasks done by women and children have a lower status than those done by men, for example, fixing a leaking pipe. Disciplining children (associated with males) is accorded a higher status than the task of bathing or feeding children. As Lorna Gordon-Gofton points out, "women's inclination to nurture, which stems from their reproductive capacity, has been co-opted by gender ideology and used to justify the relegation of women to a subordinate, dependent and subservient existence to men . . . Caribbean societies boast the pervasive influence and moral authority of women, simultaneous with an adherence to norms of male dominance" (Gordon-Gofton et al. 1987: 4–6).

This sexual division of labour, and undervaluing domestic labour below all other labour, is reflected in occupational roles, and in the global marketplace where women who are skilled as domestic workers or sewing machine operators are considered unskilled and accorded low status. Nowadays many men learn to cook, and do so quite efficiently when on their own, but once a woman is around, cooking is seen as *her* job. At the same time this division of labour is being modified. We notice in the Caribbean that attitudes of fathers towards taking children to school, doing the shopping, are slowly changing. Streetside cooking of jerk chicken or soup is done by men – the same men might not cook at home. Knitting is an acceptable activity for Rastafarian men. The recent feminization of certain professions such as teaching and journalism in the United States, however, contributes to their decreased status in society.

Just as one can critique the way the media set up unrealistic ideals of beauty for women, the media's emphasis on male identity in terms of worker or breadwinner may pose a problem in the Caribbean of the 1990s, where unemployment is widespread. It sets up some unrealistic expectations (in women and men) and undermines a man's self-esteem when he fails to match up.

To what extent do the media reflect or challenge such traditional expectations? One reinforcement is by constantly referring to the marital status of women, and not to that of men, suggesting that to be complete, a woman must be the "wife of . . .". Eugenia Charles, for example, came in for some undeserved stereotyping in the *Gleaner* article mentioned above: "Charles, who never met anyone she wanted to marry, lived with her father . . .". A February 1995 *Gleaner* article spoke of Pauline Knight, incoming deputy director of the Planning Institute of Jamaica, as "wife of . . .". Yet the new director, Dr Wesley Hughes, was not described as "husband of . . .".

Some of the most established research findings worldwide are that the mass media consistently show women in the domestic arena and pay little attention to other spheres of women's activity, economic, political and cultural; whilst men rarely appear in a domestic role, they do appear in a wide range of occupational roles, portrayed as breadwinners, and in roles of leadership or authority, in control of situations (Lindsey 1994; Gallagher 1981; Gallagher and Quindoza-Santiago 1994; de Bruin 1994a, 1994b).

After twenty-five years of research into gender portrayal on television in the United States, the School of Communication, University of Pennsylvania, concluded in 1994 that "in the world as seen through the lens of the media, social and occupational roles are almost completely divided along gender lines". Similar findings are reported in a number of small surveys of media portrayal conducted in the Caribbean: women's roles are limited, focus is on the domestic arena, and women hardly feature in news stories; the exceptions are a few female politicians, beauty queens and the token "women achievers" (see Royale 1981; Charles and Fontenard 1992; WAND 1990). A survey of all *Gleaner* newspapers published during the months of October and November 1993 was commissioned by Women's Media Watch[6] and conducted by Andrea Graf. The survey involved a total of 3,510 articles in the news-oriented sections of the paper, excluding strictly entertainment and sports pages. Of the total number of articles, only 203 or 5.6 percent had women as a focus. When women did appear, the most usual theme was fashion and beauty, accounting for 39 percent of (the few) articles on women. The next most prominent theme where women were found was violence, accounting for 17 percent of the articles on women; this was followed by a broad category including VIPs and women honoured or elected (14 percent); business (9 percent); home and health (7 percent); development (7 percent); discrimination against women (3.5 percent); crime by women (3 percent).

Graf looked at articles on business: of 230 articles in the sample, only 7 percent were on women. Yet vast numbers of women in Jamaica, as throughout the Caribbean, are involved in small business and microenterprises. Of 162 articles on development (admittedly a small proportion of the total number of 3,510 articles) only 8.6 percent were on women.

An exception to the norm of male visibility in relation to business matters was the front page of the business and finance section of the *Sunday Herald,* 12 February 1995, which featured five women, with photographs, under the heading "Jamaica's Powerful Businesswomen". Interestingly, an unnamed interviewee in the article said, "There are a lot of 'powerful' women who are not visible and therefore the term 'powerful' would not usually be applied to them." Clearly, visibility is deemed a necessary ingredient of power – thus media coverage is a critical component in gaining status.

A birds-eye view of media content is found in the *Global Media Monitoring Project 1995* coordinated by Media Watch (Canada). This recent, extensive, international survey of the position of women in the news media monitored over forty-nine thousand data records in over fifteen thousand news stories from seventy-one countries during a Global Media Monitoring Day on 18 January 1995. The findings show that although worldwide the proportion of women workers in the news media has increased considerably since 1985,[7] the voice of women is not being heard significantly more: only 17 percent of interviewees in the Global Media Monitoring Project were women. Interviewees included all who were mentioned/quoted in print news stories or who spoke on radio/television news stories. Of all male interviewees, 51 percent were politicians or government spokespersons, compared to 19 percent of women.

In this same global monitoring project, 28 percent of the women interviewees were accorded no occupational role, whereas for only 9 percent of men was no occupation stated. The report suggests that this might be related to the fact that women appear as victims three times as often as men – and the occupation of victims (of crime, disaster, and so on) is often not recorded.

These are some of the ways in which the media reinforce the notion of unequal contributions of women and men in economic and productive activity, and of unequal gender relations of authority and power.

Photograph Analysis

Interestingly, in the Jamaica Media Watch survey, although only 5.6 percent of all articles had a focus on women, the analysis of photographs showed a different trend:

Photographs of women/woman   35 percent
Photographs of men/man   28 percent
Photographs of both   37 percent

Gender differences in the role or activity of the person in the photograph were marked. Over one-third (36 percent) of all males were politicians, while only 12 percent of females photographed were politicians. The activity of the politicians differed along gender lines: over 90 percent of males were signing contracts, donating money, discussing business or politics. Female politicians however, were making courtesy calls, doing social tasks, and a small number were donating money. For women in photographs, the most common occupation was "artist", accounting for 22 percent of all photographed women.

The focus on women's links to the domestic arena reinforces the view that man's place is outside the home, women's inside, and, most critical of all, that there is a division between the two and that the public sphere is of more significance.

Radio and television soaps, and advertisements in particular, both overseas and locally produced, show women in romanticized housewife roles, frantically caught up with the hygiene of their sinks and toilet bowls, their shiny floors or bouncy-soft laundry. Household chores are often performed with hair-dresser-fresh hairstyle, makeup and nails intact, attractive outfit (which the mop/broom/toilet brush never soil in error). Missing from this view of what domestic work involves: the planning, budgeting, organizing, scheduling, prioritizing of activities, training of others, deploying of personnel, monitoring of tasks – all the skills of coordination involved in household management which, when recognized in other occupations, accord them value and status. Also missing is the burden it places on women to be on duty all the time. For example, in a recent Vicks Vapo Rub ad appearing on Jamaican television, the sleeping husband is awakened during the night by the sounds of his child coughing. Lying in bed, he wakes up his wife next to him, then she gets up sleepily, goes for the Vicks, and tends to the child. (Presumably he has gone back to sleep.)

Another media image – the "superwoman" executive/homemaker/hostess – is a vehicle for consumerism (she stops at nothing to please her family through the purchase of products), and may create unrealistic expectations in women, men and families. The image is also class bound: there are very few working-class or rural "superwoman" images.

What is the impact of the way in which the media divides the world along gender lines? One impact is illustrated by research findings in many North American and European studies, that among male and female viewers of all age groups, heavy television viewing is strongly associated with an adherence to traditional gender views (Lindsey 1994: 305).

Shifts in Gender Portrayal

We have seen earlier that there is no single definition of what it is to be woman or man, that notions of gender fluctuate over time, from one cultural milieu to another. We should note therefore that the media's treatment of gender does reflect these shifts, so that changes can be observed in the manner in which the media depict women and men, girl children and boy children.

For example, interesting attempts at gender-role reversal have been seen in some Jamaican ads in the mid-1990s. In a Soflan detergent ad, the husband offers to do the baby's laundry. We realize this is not his normal routine because he is unfamiliar with Soflan. It then turns out that it is the couple's anniversary, and he is doing his wife a special favour "helping" with the laundry – implying that it is really her responsibility. A caring male image does appear in a Kentucky Fried Chicken series of ads on television, while a Foska Oats ad in the print media shows a boy carried on the shoulders of an adult male – they both look as though they are having fun.

A recent print ad for a corporate merchant bank also breaks with the traditional macho portrayal of men by showing a man relaxing, lying on a sofa cradling a sleeping baby on his chest. The copy says, "Don't take chances with what's precious to you." It goes on to promote a corporate investment scheme.

The double meaning – that both baby and funds are precious and need long-term investment – puts a high value on the nurturing role, emphasizing it as worthy of serious financial planning. (In a newspaper business section a more traditional portrayal might have been a figure in a suit and tie, with no reference to child care.) This newer image reflects a current debate in Caribbean society about men's participation in parenting, and about notions of "masculinity". This topic is now discussed at many different levels, on talk shows, in workshops and church groups, as well as in academia – and we now see another aspect of the male role appearing in the media. One example from entertainment media was the popularity of the film *Three Men and a Baby*, where single male parents have to learn to cope with child care.

Sexual Violence in the Media

A paper looking at gender in the media is incomplete without mentioning violence in the media, including sexual violence. In the first place, consider the way in which violence has become an integral part of "news" and packaged as entertainment.

The manner in which violence is reported in the news media often reflects the gender ideology that it is "manly" and thus desirable to perpetrate violence on women. Sensational styles trivialize the incident, minimize the crime, and make a laughing matter of something that is painful and traumatic to the abused. The language even puts blame on the person who suffers, as in this *Star* headline: "Hubby Digs Out Wife's Eye. She Was Accused of Having a Man."

The word "hubby" is usually used as an affectionate, endearing term – this contrasts with the hideous action, and softens our perception of the offender. The word "accused" turns the female spouse into the offender. And there is an implicit suggestion that the "crime" of which she is "accused" merits the action by the male spouse.

A familiar cartoon image is a woman with large breasts and bottom, often exposed by tight tops and short skirts, complaining of sexual harassment or rape while a male ogles her. The severity of sexual abuse is trivialized through the cartoon and the language used in the caption. Over the years, the subtext perpetuates the myth that by dressing in a particular manner she invites and deserves the abuse. Over time such attitudes become ingrained, normative even, so that men blame women for provoking the abuse, and women come to accept responsibility for abuse perpetrated against them.

Sex and violence are juxtaposed in the entertainment media, and sexually violent "heroes" often win women as a reward; perpetuating a myth that the two go together as a norm, that sex is a deserved reward for violence, that women enjoy rape and sexual violence. The linking of sex and violence can infiltrate media other than entertainment media.

Calculated decisions are made at every stage of construction of media violence. The negative consequences of sexual violence are minimized in entertainment media. Violence is made appealing, and it is often linked with power and pleasure (Graydon and Ferrall 1994; Gerbner 1998). As Linda Bloodworth-Thomas noted, "It's a crime to kill a man; it's sexy to kill a woman."[8] In 1985 Judy Flander wrote: "In the new television season, for most starlets, the only chance for a television role will be, quite literally, a one-shot appearance, since the majority of the roles for women are as victims of sadistic killers . . . Victims are very often 'sexy'-looking young women in sexy and/or morally dubious lines of work." In her article, Flander quotes an unnamed television scriptwriter as saying that victims "have to be people who don't matter, you don't have to explain why such a person could die". Thus, concludes Flander, "Women of easy virtue are easily disposable. And nobody seems to care" (1985: 13). Ten years later, in 1995, the video rental stores were full of titles which would suggest that women continue to be "easy targets".

The lack of concern for what happens to a female victim is exemplified also in recent popular dancehall and rap lyrics: "Me legal me have me sexing ticket / an' if me sex her an' she dead / notten nuh come outa it" (Powerman, a Jamaican DJ). An example from US gangsta rap is, "Her body's beautiful so I'm thinkin' rape / Shouldn't have had her curtains open so that's her fate . . . / Slit her throat and watched her shake" (from *Mind of a Lunatic,* quoted in Gooch 1995).

It is in relation to violence that men's sexuality is probably most exploited by the media, in a way that is harmful to men themselves. Deeply imbedded attitudes about maleness, reinforced by media images, make it very hard for a man to deviate from the concept of "Caribbean hegemonic masculinity" referred to by Linden Lewis, which would view the male as "powerful, exceedingly promiscuous, derelict in his parental responsibilities . . . with a propensity for female battering and alcohol consumption . . . and aggressively heterosexual" (Lewis 1994).

Asking New Questions

If we are to view gender as a dynamic concept in media, then a critique of the media from a gender perspective requires us to question what the media value, how the media construct notions of gender and gender relations, whether the media present a traditional sexual division of labour, whether the media perpetuate structures of dominance and power, or, in a more positive vein, whether the media suggest a transformation of roles towards more equitable gender relations.

We may be concerned with gender differences at several levels. The first has been touched on in this paper, that is, media content: the way women and men are represented in the media, and the coverage of the issues and priorities that women identify as newsworthy as well as those identified by men. The second level (which has not been addressed here) concerns the ways in which women and men are employed in the media industry: the sexual division of labour that is played out within the industry, so that women are often relegated to the "soft news beats", at the lower end of the ladder, and underrepresented at the point where editorial policy is shaped. A third level would involve exploring women's and men's access to media – gender differences among the media's audience. Especially in the so-called less developed world, data shows that women have less access to media information, and thereby less access to the power which access to information accords one.

As Heyzer notes, "the unasked question, the unexplored line of investigation . . . the way in which the issue is tackled – how it is researched, which aspects are singled out, which people are consulted as experts, what questions are asked, how they are framed – all these result in the 'story' which is finally packaged for us" (1994: 13).

The perspective taken on a news item results in either a gender bias or gender balance, and will result in fair or skewed media information. A gender perspective can offer, not a divisive way of seeing the world, but an integrating, analytical framework. To approximate some measure of reality we need to develop a gender "lens" in the media. We need media stories that reflect and shape balanced female and male experiences.

Acknowledgments

I wish to acknowledge the work of Women's Media Watch, Jamaica, on which I have drawn. Women's Media Watch is a nongovernmental organization involved in monitoring the media, public education, research in gender and media issues, and lobbying. Much of the work of Women's Media Watch is unpublished; some exists in visual displays and short reports. I would also like to thank Patricia Mohammed for her most helpful comments on the first draft.

Notes

1. Fathers Incorporated (Fathers Inc.) is a Jamaican nongovernmental organization involved in community development and advocacy, promoting responsible parenting; the members of Fathers Inc. are men from all sectors of society.
2. See acknowledgments.
3. Line from a song by DJ Buju Banton in the mid-1990s. Buju is now including "positive" lyrics in his work.
4. US National Coalition on TV Violence, 1991. Note that over 80 percent of Caribbean television programming originates overseas, and in some territories the percentage is higher.
5. Personal testimony related to the writer.
6. Women's Media Watch is a nongovernmental organization involved in monitoring the media, public education, training and research on gender and media issues. Women's Media Watch lobbies for gender sensitivity in communication policy.
7. Global Media Monitoring Findings: the proportion of women workers in the news media has increased to a world average of 36 percent to 64 percent men. The proportion of women in media in India is in fact much higher than this.
8. Linda Bloodworth-Thomas, co-executive producer of the ABC series "Lime Street", quoted in *Media Values* 33 (1985).

References

Charles, Janelle, and Tecla Fontenard. 1992. "Images of Women in Television Commercials in St Lucia". Paper presented at the conference Women in the Caribbean Media, St Lucia, March.

de Bruin, Marjan, ed. 1994a. *Women and the Caribbean Media.* Occasional Paper no. 3. Kingston, Jamaica: Caribbean Institute of Media and Communication, University of the West Indies.

_____. 1994b. *The Impact of Communication Technologies on Women.* UNESCO Report no. 108. Paris: UNESCO.

de Bruin, Marjan, Hilary Nicholson, and Gayatri Persaud. 1994. "Content". In *Women and the Caribbean Media,* edited by M. de Bruin. Occasional Paper no. 3. Kingston, Jamaica: Caribbean Institute of Media and Communication, University of the West Indies.

Flander, Judy. 1985. "Television Targets Women as Victims". *Media Values* 33.

Gallagher, Margaret. 1981. *Unequal Opportunities: The Case of Women and the Media.* Paris: UNESCO.

_____. 1995a. "Communication and Human Dignity: a Women's Rights Perspective". *Media Development* 42, no. 3.

_____. 1995b. "Women and the Media". In *Focus on Women.* New York: International Women's Tribune Centre, United Nations.

Gallagher, Margaret, and Lilia Quindoza-Santiago. 1994. *Women Empowering Communication: A Resource Book on Women and the Globalisation of Media.* London: WACC.

Gerbner, George. 1988. *Violence and Terror in the Mass Media.* UNESCO Report no. 102. Paris: UNESCO.

Gooch, Cheryl. 1995. "Gangsta Rap: Message Music or Mayhem for Profit?" *Media Development* 42, no. 3.

Gordon-Gofton, Lorna, et al. 1987. *Understanding Women's Agenda.* Kingston, Jamaica: Trade Union Education Institute.

Graf, Andrea. 1993. "Images of Women in the *Gleaner*". Research commissioned by Women's Media Watch (Jamaica). Typescript.

Heyzer, Noeleen. 1994. "Women, Communication and Development: Changing Dominant Structures". *Media Development* 41, no. 2.

Lewis, Linden. 1994. "Constructing the Masculine in the Context of the Caribbean". Paper presented at Nineteenth Caribbean Studies Conference, Merida, Mexico, May.

Lindsey, Linda. 1994. *Gender Roles: A Sociological Perspective.* Englewood Cliffs, NJ: Prentice Hall.

Ostergard, Lise, ed. 1992. *Gender and Development: A Practical Guide.* London: Routledge.

Protz, Maria. 1994. "Education and Training for Rural Women in Jamaica: the Role of Communications". In *Women and Caribbean Media,* edited by M. de

Bruin. Occassional Paper no. 3. Kingston, Jamaica: Caribbean Institute of Media and Communication, University of the West Indies.

Rohlehr, Gordon. 1988. "Images in of Men and Women in the 1930s Calypsoes". In *Gender in Caribbean Development,* edited by P. Mohammed and C. Shepherd. Kingston, Jamaica: Women and Development Studies Project, University of the West Indies.

Royale, Gloria. 1981. *Women and Media Decision-Making in the Caribbean Media.* Kingston, Jamaica: Caribbean Institute of Media and Communication/ UNESCO.

Segree, Clifton. 1993. "Effect of TV Violence on Society". *Gleaner,* 29 May.

UNESCO. 1995. "Raising Women's Profile in the Media". Paper prepared for Fourth UN Conference on Women, Beijing.

Women and Development Unit (WAND). 1990. "The Involvement of Caribbean Media in the Implementation of the Nairobi Forward-Looking Strategies for the Advancement of Women". Report of a study for UNESCO, March.

Young, Kate. 1988. "The Social Relations of Gender". In *Gender in Caribbean Development,* edited by P. Mohammed and C. Shepherd. St Augustine, Trinidad: Women and Development Studies Project, University of the West Indies.

21 The Presence of Women in Caribbean Media

MARJAN DE BRUIN

Before 1994 there was not much systematic documentation of the status of women in Caribbean media and communication. This reflected the field of communication in general, which was described in the late 1980s as a "latecomer to feminist scholarship" (Dervin 1987: 111). Most research on women and media had been conducted in first world countries and had been published through the larger, well-known distribution networks. A few locally produced texts were available but their distribution was very limited. It was often easier to get information on the region from foreign sources than from within the Caribbean. We are not the only region that struggles with this impediment. Complaints from women researchers in Africa, Asia, the Middle East, the Pacific and the Caribbean are similar: shortage of research and exploration, many small-scale studies and initiatives but no overall picture (Gallagher and Quindoza-Santiago 1994).

Things are changing: Caribbean journalists and researchers initiated various regional studies on women and communication (Women's Media Watch 1996; Graf 1994; Francis Brown 1995a, 1995b; de Bruin 1994b; de Bruin et al. 1994). Also, since 1994 some comprehensive global inventories on women and media/communication have been produced, in which the Caribbean has been included (Gallagher and Quindoza-Santiago 1994; Gallagher and von Euler 1995b; Jimenez-David 1996).

In this contribution I want to introduce the debate on women/gender and the media internationally, to sketch our position in the Caribbean and to share the first phases of a research project on women and decision making in (anglophone) Caribbean media. The first stage of this research was descriptive: I collected the facts on positions held by women in Caribbean media. The second stage, not here developed, will consist of qualitative research.

The sections of this paper comprise the following: background information on Caribbean mass media and women in the Caribbean media workforce, using recent research material; introducing media organizations as the context for media production from a gender perspective; and some of the research questions relevant for the Caribbean.

Rationale and Assumptions

For more than two decades the topic of women and/in the media has been on the agenda of various women's and researchers' groups. The Mexico City conference in 1975 for the first UN Decade for Women mentioned several areas that would grow into popular research topics: women's underrepresentation in the content of news and serious programming; trivialization and sex-role stereotyping in content; and underrepresentation in decision-making (gatekeeper) positions. Access to the media, increasing the creative participation of women, was seen as a major tool for change. The precise content and the purposes of this change varied. The subsequent stream of research studies and analyses shows a variety of purposes: opening up the media for women's participation as the consequence of a political principle – human rights and equal opportunities; gaining access for women for purposes of social-political activism; and the expectation that the presence of more women in the media would change the quality of media product.

As the consequence of a political principle – human rights and equal opportunities

An unequal distribution of men and women in the media labour force is seen as an obstacle to equal participation of women in every other field of work. So is the unbalanced representation of the sexes at management level, the discrimination in salaries and differences in working conditions. Opening up the media for women aims for equal rights for all.

In the 1994 UN Seminar on Media Development and Democracy in Latin America and the Caribbean held in Chile, "equal opportunities" were explicitly referred to: "according to a study carried out in six Latin American countries, it was noted that a high percentage of women were qualified in media-related fields. Thus, the central problem was no longer access to the media but equality of opportunity at work" (UNESCO 1994: 41).

For purposes of social-political activism

The media are seen as potentially powerful agents of social change, especially for the improvement of women's status. The assumption is that male-dominated media do not pay enough attention to women's issues. The solution is sought by establishing a greater presence of women and diminishing the male control of the media.

An example can be found in a UNESCO text, where it was "very obvious" (UNESCO 1980: 10) that one of the first explanations for biased and irrelevant images of women lay in the tiny place women held in all the audio-visual professions. An increased creative participation of women in the media would gradually change for the better the images which have given cause for concern. "The major concern is how to make these media work in women's interest". When the framework, constructed by men, "expands to admit women, the media can be seen to reflect this expansion . . ." (Gallagher 1981: 30). These approaches come close to the "equity" and "empowerment" approaches described by Sreberny-Mohammadi at the international symposium on Women and the Media (Sreberny-Mohammadi 1995: 3–4).

A third perspective on opening up media access for women
anticipates a change in the quality of media product

The assumption is that media access for women will not only counterbalance the gender-biased selection of information by males – which is believed at its best not to serve women's interests – but also result in a different output. A different quality will lead to "new perspectives and interpretations". Although Gallagher in 1981 admits that there is "little hard evidence to support the proposition that the portrayal of women differs when a woman is producing the images", it is "in the area of priorities and values", she writes fourteen years later, "that women's increasing numerical strength in the media could be expected to make an impact" (Gallagher and von Euler 1995a: 3).

This third perspective is the focus of my contribution and research: what is this different output believed to be? Is it desired and if so, why? Is the mere presence of women in media organizations a sufficient condition to bring about this change in quality? What are the nuances and dynamics of this process? What does research elsewhere show us? Are any of the findings applicable to further research in the Caribbean?

Mass Media in the English-Speaking Caribbean

Mass media content comes to us through radio, television and the press. Internet and online publishing will develop into important distribution channels, but at the moment in the Caribbean the major, most widely used channels of mass communication are still the traditional mass media operated by private and government-owned media organizations. Of the mass media in the Caribbean, radio is clearly the most popular medium. A number of factors account for radio's popularity. It is affordable; it taps directly into the Caribbean oral tradition; and in some countries, the low adult literacy rates make the appeal understandable.

In most English-speaking Caribbean countries, the government owns some of the major mass media, especially electronic media. Government ownership in some instances means policy discontinuity over time, as each new regime imports its own set of administrators – and sometimes even entire newsroom staffs. On the other hand, where the same party has ruled for a long time, positions within the media are very stable because they are tied into political loyalty.

Print has always been an area of mainly private ownership. The larger countries (Jamaica, Trinidad and Tobago, Barbados) have daily morning and/or evening newspapers – usually not more than two or three. In the smaller countries the press generally consists of one or two, sometimes three, weeklies or fortnightlies, often aimed at special communities.

Only recently has the private sector developed its own strongholds in radio and television. Several of the larger Caribbean countries have seen explosive growth in electronic media: Jamaica, with approximately 620,000 households and a population of 2.5 million, grew from three to eight radio stations, and from one to three television stations, within a period of six years. Trinidad and Tobago, with 300,000 households and a population of 1.2 million, went through a similar process: eleven new radio stations and two new (privately owned) television stations joined the media landscape between 1992 and 1997. In Guyana seventeen privately owned television stations mushroomed within a period of four years. In Belize, within ten years, thirteen broadcasting television stations and twelve private radio stations. Barbados, with about 50,000 households and a population of 260,000, has long supported two daily newspapers. There are two television stations on the island but viewers can receive television signals from neighbouring islands. Its number of radio stations increased from five to seven.

Satellite dishes, cable connections, VCRs and computers are breaking down traditional communication borders. In the Jamaican capital, Kingston, in 1995, 28 percent of households owned a dish and 21 percent owned a computer. Twenty miles away, in the rural neighbouring parish of St Thomas, the figures were 1 percent and 2 percent, respectively (Brown 1995). New technologies are affordable for the "happy few" and are increasing the information gap between the haves and the have-nots.

Over the years the overwhelming amount of foreign programming affecting media quality has been mentioned as a serious concern. In the 1980s, in a period of ten years (1976–86) the imported content of four large television stations in the region moved up from an average of 78.5 percent to 87 percent (Brown 1987). An analysis of print coverage of major social issues by some of the leading newspapers in Trinidad and Tobago and Jamaica shows similar trends. More than half of news and features originated abroad and were dealing with non-Caribbean territories, without any attempt to "localize" the information (de Bruin 1996).

It is much cheaper to buy foreign programming than to produce original content. For instance, thirty minutes of foreign television programming in Jamaica in 1998 cost a little under US$300. A relatively simple local television production (*Entertainment Report*, thirty minutes) at the same station cost J$200,000 which was then the equivalent of US$6,000 – or twenty times as much (M. Forbes, general manager, TVJ, personal communication, June 1998). Examples from Trinidad and Tobago show an even worse ratio: TT$1,400 for one episode of a foreign sitcom versus TT$77,000 for one episode of local origin (Davis 1998). For the cost of one episode of local origin the station could buy fifty-five episodes of foreign programming.

Most media organizations are commercial organizations and depend on market forces. This creates its own constraints and influences. The small market in English-speaking Caribbean countries has important implications for the financial basis of the media, especially the privately owned media. Advertising influence can be considerable; several cases are known of advertisers withdrawing support. Most Caribbean media houses have scarce resources and cannot afford to allocate time for staff to do serious investigative journalism, for example, or allow workers to specialize on "beats". There is a limited number of potential advertisers. The networks of influential companies and persons are narrow, and economic interests are very easily intertwined.

Women in the Caribbean Media Workforce

A survey in 1993/94 showed that in most Caribbean media organizations women formed between 34 percent and 45 percent of the total permanent staff. There were exceptions: some smaller media organizations consisted only of men, and one organization – National Broadcasting Service in Trinidad and Tobago – was 70 percent female (de Bruin 1994a). A new survey, four years later, shows increases in women's share in the total workforce, accompanied by increases in women's share of senior positions.

Some organizations were difficult to compare over time, because mergers had occurred and staff records were no longer kept for two different organizations. For instance, in Trinidad in 1994, women formed 34 percent of the total workforce in TTT Radio and Television; in NBS radio, at the same time, they formed 70 percent of the total workforce. Both organizations (total workforce 189) have come to work under the same management, and the new percentage of women working in the new organization in 1997/98 is 41 percent.

In Barbados, in the *Nation*, one of the leading newspapers, women formed 46 percent of the total workforce (of 173 employees) in 1993/94; four years later they formed 48 percent of the total workforce.

In 1993/94 women formed 34 percent of the total workforce (of 277 employees) of the Caribbean Broadcasting Corporation (CBC) in Barbados; in 1997/98 the proportion was 40 percent.

The Broadcasting Corporation of the Bahamas (257 employees) was not included in our earlier baseline study, but it is worth mentioning since it is one of the few larger organizations in the study and in the Caribbean. Women form 51 percent of the total workforce.

In Jamaica, the *Gleaner,* the largest daily newspaper, in 1993/94 counted 40 percent women in its total labour force. Four years later, women accounted for 43 percent of the total labour force.

For radio we had no baseline data in 1993/94, but in 1997 in three Jamaican national radio stations (RJR, Power 106 FM and Irie FM), women formed between 48 percent and 56 percent of the total workforce; between 43 percent and 53 percent of the editorial departments are women. In one of the three national television stations (CVM Television), 49 percent of the workforce is female; 22 percent works in the editorial department. A recently transformed television station is headed by a woman (who has ensured that her "old" new staff goes through a series of gender workshops).

Women's average share of jobs in the Jamaican media included in our study – 46 percent – is very close to the percentage of women in the total Jamaican labour force – 47 percent. Gallagher's 1995 study shows that in most of the forty-three countries women's share of jobs in media organizations is lower than in the labour force as a whole (Gallagher and von Euler 1995a).

Compared to recent global data on women's share in the media workforce, the Caribbean is not doing so badly. There are two sources which we can use for this comparison. Gallagher and von Euler (1995a: 12) looked at the percentage of women in the media workforce in forty-three countries world-wide, and Weaver (1998: 458) collected data from twenty-one countries in various regions of the world. Given the methodological differences, some of the data are contradictory. Gallagher's overview is commonly used as a reference, especially in gender studies, but is based on an unbalanced selection of media organizations. Weaver's compilation includes research based on probability samples and interviewing of journalists, and seems more reliable. In six Latin American countries women average 25 percent of media employees, according to Gallagher; according to Weaver (in four Latin America countries) the average of women among journalists is 33 percent. In southern Africa (average of ten countries) women represent 27 percent of workers in media organizations, says Gallagher. The data for Europe in Gallagher's report show percentages between 35 and 45, while Weaver's figures show a range between 25 and 49 percent. Gallagher says that in Canada women's share in media employment is 39 percent. Weaver says it is 28 percent of the total number of journalists. Surveys in the United States show that the proportion of women rose from 20 percent of journalists in 1971 to 34 percent in 1992 (Weaver 1997).

The number of women in Caribbean media, however, is not reflected proportionately in middle management (supervising positions) – and even less so in senior management (heads of departments). Fewer women than one would expect (from the percentage of women throughout the organization) are found in the editorial departments, and fewer women occupy leading or decision-making positions.

In Barbados, in the *Nation* newspaper in 1993/94, women occupied 30 percent of positions in senior management; four years later they occupied 44 percent of positions in senior management. In 1993/94, in the Caribbean Broadcasting Corporation in Barbados, 18 percent of senior management positions were occupied by women. Figures for 1997/98 show a different composition: women occupied 70 percent of the positions in senior management. The Caribbean Broadcasting Corporation also has a female general manager. In the Broadcasting Corporation of the Bahamas, women occupy 43 percent of the senior management positions; 59 percent of the rather large layer of middle management consists of women. In Trinidad and Tobago's 1993/94 figures, the – now merged – NBS Radio had 14 percent of its management positions taken up by women. The 1997/98 figures of the new organization showed 59 percent of the senior positions were taken up by women. In Grenada in 1993, only 12 to 15 percent of the senior management in broadcasting were female. Nowadays 20 percent is taken up by women.

In Jamaica, in 1993/94, in the *Gleaner* women counted for 10 percent of senior management positions. Four years later, women accounted for 30 percent of senior management positions.

For the Jamaican radio stations (RJR, Power 106 FM and Irie FM) not included in the earlier baseline study we cannot make a comparison, but women occupy between 37 percent and 50 percent of the senior management positions. In one of the three national television stations (CVM Television), 25 percent of the senior positions are occupied by women.

In some of the smallest Caribbean countries the major electronic media are headed by women (St Kitts and Nevis, St Vincent and the Grenadines,

Montserrat). Newspapers aligned with political or church organizations are very often owned and headed by men, who also occupy the leading positions in the editorial departments. Some of the much larger organizations (GBC in Guyana; BCB in the Bahamas) have female general managers. (In the 1980s, both the chairman and the general manager of the Jamaica Broadcasting Corporation were women.)

Here and there women begin to appear on boards of directors, occasionally forming the majority (CBC in Barbados: 56 percent). In most cases women occupy between 20 and 25 percent of the board memberships.

The underrepresentation of women in middle management, and especially in senior management, is only too familiar from research elsewhere over the last twenty-five years. Gallagher, in her latest worldwide overview of 239 organizations, finds women accounting for just 12 percent of jobs in the top three levels of management: "if the analysis is restricted to the highest management level only, women's share of jobs drop to 9 percent across the same organizations" (Gallagher and von Euler 1995a: 47). Fifteen years earlier the same author looked at women media managers and observed 5 percent and 7 percent in the United States and in Canada (Canadian Broadcasting Corporation), respectively. Large national broadcasting organizations or institutions in Australia, Italy, Finland, Norway, Ghana and Britain were reported by her, at that time, as having between 0 and 6 percent women at the managerial level (Gallagher 1981: 88).

Weaver and Wilhoit sketched a less pessimistic picture for American journalists, and observed that women journalists gained managerial responsibility and influence during the 1980s. This was especially true of weekly newspapers and magazines, where women were approaching parity with men in numbers by 1992 (1996: 181–82).

Media Organizations as a Context for Media Production

Mass media production takes place in the context of a media organization. There are freelance journalists working from home, although in the Caribbean they form a minority. Most media content produced locally has been produced in Caribbean media organizations by journalists on staff or by journalists as correspondents. Even when produced by correspondents, the content will have been screened, judged and approved by editors on staff in media organizations.

The products that media organizations turn out all bear some sign of the individual producer: the byline that indicates the author in print, the reporter's face that we see on the screen, the voice of the radio journalist. These glimpses of individuals give the impression that what is presented is written, filmed or taped by the people we can identify, whom we can see and hear. It suggests a direct and close connection between media worker and media product. But what we see, hear and read through television, radio and the press is the end product of a rather complicated process, subject to many influences and constraints which are usually invisible to the audience. Between the first step in the production process and the finished product ready for broadcasting or circulation many decisions need to be taken, each of them shaping the process and moulding the product.

The production starts with a story idea, the choice of a topic to be covered – sometimes the product of creative thinking, more often dictated by events and agendas. Epstein (1974), for instance, in his study on television news in the United States describes how decisions about the type of film pieces that were needed, the cities to be favoured, the visual content that would fit the mould of a news programme, the news makers to be given preference, the focus or perspective – all decisions taken in advance – would eventually determine which news stories were weeded out or selected.

Caribbean reporting of news seems to be event oriented, following the rhythm of the institutional world (the launching of a campaign, the publication of a study or survey, the opening of a debate) rather than the journalist's initiatives. Analysis of the Jamaican *Gleaner* on the topic of family planning and development between 1991 and 1995, for instance, shows that more than 92 percent of the news and feature stories appear to be responses to events, usually staged events – that is, media events (de Bruin 1995).

Whatever sparked the story, the journalist needs to follow up the story idea, whether hers or that of the supervising editor. She needs to develop a focus, choose and contact her sources, raise the right questions, select which information will be included in or excluded from the story to make it "newsworthy". She must structure it into a format of a prescribed length, and follow the conventional routines, which are partly determined by professional codes and the house style of her employer. In all of this her personal background plays a crucial role. This includes the way she thinks, feels and acts, shaped by her gender, race/ethnicity, class, age, sexual orientation and professional experiences. "News judgments are ways of knowing, and as such they are inescapably gendered" (Creedon 1993: 14).

Journalists can witness only a limited number of events personally. For the most part, news comes from external sources. A journalist's network of sources will reflect her (or his) personal preferences, likes and dislikes – in short, biases. Sources which appear to be convenient, reliable and efficient become easily part of the professional network; others are never considered or are rejected. Gans' research provides some useful insights into the mechanisms of source selection. His findings show how availability and proven suitability of sources in daily journalism practice are often more decisive factors in the selection of sources – and therefore of stories – than the perceived relevance of the event (Gans 1979). He does not mention gender as a factor in selection of topic or source, but (as I will describe in a later section), more recent research does. In most Caribbean countries, there are not many information sources available, neither is access to electronic sources always easy (yet). This makes the relationship between journalists and news sources intimate and extremely vulnerable. No research has been done in the Caribbean on the role that gender plays in this field, but every female journalist knows that she has to protect herself when she has to negotiate for information with a male source. In the United States a 1992 survey of job conditions reported that 60 percent of over one hundred female journalists said that they had been subjected to sexual harassment involving coworkers, sources or both (Allen 1994: 164).

At the organizational level, the journalist in the mass media is only one link in a bigger chain. If her material takes more space than is allocated for her text, it will be cut. If it comes in late it will not appear at all. A headline – usually produced by someone else – will give her story a certain emphasis; the placement in the paper, a matter not of her decision, will give the text more or less prominence. Her writing needs to fit the style of the medium. It will be polished and if necessary corrected by her subeditor to fit the media house. Thus, in an informal way the journalist learns what style is accepted and preferred by her colleagues: "That's how we do it here." She knows by experience the informal system of rewards (status, privileges, position) from senior colleagues.

Research traditions starting almost fifty years ago began to identify some of the organizational influences on the final media product. In 1950, David White applied Kurt Lewin's concept of the "gatekeeper". White wanted to examine the way one of the "gatekeepers" in communication channels operated his "gate". When he asked his "Mr Gates" why certain stories were selected and others weren't, a large proportion of the answers referred to "lack of space", poor writing or absence of journalistic interest. This was a clear indication that craft-oriented norms and technological limitations formed the main criteria of news selection. The study made no attempt to assess gender in Mr Gates's choices. A follow-up study was done seventeen years later (Snider 1967), showing consistency in the findings but still not including a focus on gender. Forty years later, "Ms Gates Takes Over". An updated version of the original gatekeepers study shows more or less the same tendencies: the same news categories accounted for 53 to 60 percent of the total output (human interest, international politics and national politics). Under Ms Gates's editorship, in 1989, 8.5 percent of the news during the study dealt with "women's news", but "no significant patterns could be related to the possible effects of a female gatekeeper" (Bleske 1991: 93). No research has been done yet on the possible differences of female gatekeepers in Caribbean media.

A few years after White's gatekeepers study, Walter Breed (1955) confirmed and refined White's findings. Breed, too, suggests that sociocultural dynamics of the newsroom explain more of the story selection than personal bias. Intrigued by how the publisher's/owner's policy came to be followed by newsroom practitioners, Breed studied the factors which control the behaviour of the newsroom workers and contribute to their conformity with company policy. Breed describes how senior staffers apply institutional authority and sanctions, such as ignoring a story, changing the story, cutting a story, and by withholding friendly comments, praise in public, getting a byline, or special privileges. Feelings of obligation and esteem for superiors may put pressure on the worker to conform to the corporate style and culture, while the desire for upward job mobility may suppress "deviant" behaviour such as being too political or too critical. Certainly in the English-speaking Caribbean vertical mobility, even if it is no more than moving from the lowest level to a less low level, is important. Horizontal mobility of media workers is not as great as in media-rich countries – there are simply not that many options.

Not only vertical mobility is at stake; conditions that are crucial to professional development can depend on the smooth relationship between workers and superiors. At the Caribbean Institute of Media and Communication (CARIMAC), the only regional training and educational institute and part of the University of the West Indies, few, if any, of the students applying for the one-year diploma programme will be granted study leave from their media houses. Most journalists have to take special leave without pay in order to get the necessary training; paid leave remains an exceptional favour.

In later research, which refined the gatekeeper metaphor, Berkowitz emphasized the need to look at decision making in the newsroom as a group process (Berkowitz 1990). Organizational routines form the written and unwritten rules of the media worker in her or his organization, and they structure individual judgements of what is news. Some schools of thought assume the influences of the organization to be so strong and all-determining that they have argued that radical changes in paradigm and orientation cannot be realized within the existing structures. In analysing Women's Feature Service as a case, Byerly suggests that "individual journalists have more power to reshape news codes in favour of marginalized groups when they operate in structures controlled by those groups" (Byerly 1995: 116), and she refers to the managing of the Women's Feature Service by women, working with women only. Suzanne Francis Brown, having worked at the Caribbean Women's Feature Service desk, describes the way in which, between mid-1988 and early 1992, this desk filed more than 150 feature stories originating in the Caribbean. "Editors considered them worthy of space and not necessarily on women's pages. Yet, in general, these editors are not getting such stories from their own staffs" (Francis Brown 1995a: 58–59).

Understanding news production and media output from an organizational view cannot be separated from the approach in which the focus is placed on the "cultural givens" in everyday interaction. The taken-for-granted values embodied in professional practice play a role in content as well as format: "the unquestioned and generally unnoticed background assumptions through which the news is gathered and within which it is framed" (Schudson 1997: 19).

Such cultural influences form the context in which people – also in media organizations – relate and communicate with each other. They substantiate a gendered substructure formed by "spatial and temporal arrangements of work, the rules prescribing workplace behaviour, and the relations linking work places to living places" (Halford, Savage and Witz 1997: 15).

One example of this gendered substructure is the gender division of labour: the division of labour into "male" and "female" work areas. Certain jobs are more often done by women than by men, or the other way around. In Caribbean media, sales and marketing, advertising, accounts, administration and personnel management are favourite departments for women: they are either headed by women or have a high concentration of women among their staff. In most media organizations the lower echelons – service and support – are also mainly staffed by women: telephone, typing, clerical work. The lowest concentration of women is usually in engineering and in operations. These data are not very different from recent global studies, which show that women in media organizations are more likely to be found in administration than in production/editorial departments, creative/art departments or technical departments.

Often, in editorial departments one can find another type of vertical segregation: women and men tend to be associated with different kinds of stories. However, the Global Media Monitoring Project showed, for the six Caribbean countries involved, "a surprising degree of parity between women and men. The most obvious gender difference was in sports, which accounted for 10 percent of all male journalists and less than 1 percent of females" (Gallagher and von Euler 1995b: 17). An analysis of front page stories of ten top United States dailies in 1992 over a period of twelve months shows that "men wrote on war, leisure activities, politics, technology and the economy. Women wrote on education, health and medicine, social issues and spot news. Women covered more than their share of local news; men more than their share on state stories" (Allen 1994: 164).

Media Organizations and Gender

By focusing on the organization, several theoretical perspectives are possible: a *structural explanation* considers the dynamics and effects of positions in organizational hierarchy and the ratio of sex as crucial for understanding the work environment. *Organizational policy* focuses on how employers and managers create gender divisions of labour; and a third approach, *organizational culture theory*, looks at the systems of shared meanings, symbols and understandings and how they inform people's behaviour (Alvesson and Billing 1997: 70).

There are also various political perspectives, each interpreting the organization differently. The organization can be seen as fundamentally gender-neutral and gendered patterns/processes as accidental: the position in the hierarchy, rather than gender, determines opportunity and behaviour. Thus power differences rather than gender differences provide the key to understanding. Another perspective looks at the organization as intrinsically tied to masculinity and patriarchy, "a fixed reflex of male characteristics", and as a consequence, women who are socialized into feminine ways of behaving and relating to others are necessarily muted in the masculinist setting (Halford, Savage and Witz 1997: 10). A third way of interpreting organizations sees the social relations of gender as embedded within the organization – part of the social fabric of the organization. An example is the corporate culture in media organizations which assumes that the news – and therefore work – never stops. Indeed, Caribbean female journalists report "institutional discrimination" in long hours which force them to neglect family responsibilities, often with no husband to keep the family and domestic side of life in order (de Bruin 1994b: 10).

Studies on the interaction of gender and organizational variables are only beginning to emerge, as are studies on the interaction between gender and media production. In the Caribbean both fields are still relatively untouched by research, though CARIMAC has initiated some. Research on organizational influences on media production elsewhere, as well as studies in the field of organizational culture, although not focusing on gender specifically, can offer insights that can help to understand the gender dynamics in media organizations and help to formulate relevant research questions for the Caribbean.

I would like to look at two important moments in the production process: story selection and use of sources. In choosing which events to cover, the individual journalist partly follows her or his own "hunch", but at the same time, this feeling for what constitutes news has been shaped by editorial tradition and institutional and organizational culture. Tuchman's research (1978) demonstrated, among other things, that the news organization must reduce all phenomena to known classifications that can fit into a system of routine processing and dissemination. Over time, these typifications become part of the reporter's professional knowledge and taken for granted as absolute truths. It is quite likely, at least until recently, that these classifications will have been developed by men – who used to dominate decision-making positions – based on their typical life experiences. What was supposed to be of interest to women was judged from a male perspective. Topics which traditionally do not engage men's interest will not easily have become part of such an institutional vocabulary.

The increased presence of women in the newsroom, however, must have become an influence in these institutional priorities, especially after women's presence reached a "critical mass". Mills (1997) describes interviews with US female senior editors and journalists who feel that "If there is just one woman in a story conference or editorial page meeting, you have to blend in. If there are two you compete for attention. When there are three women, you reach a critical mass" (Mills, in Norris 1997: 45).

Do women choose different stories from men? Does the female professional choose differently from her male colleagues? Some authors point out that media nowadays cover different kinds of topics than they did ten or twenty years ago. Thus Mills selects some headlines from 1995, taken from the *New York Times* and *Los Angeles Times,* which, she assumes, would not have been taken seriously by most editors two decades ago: "New Clues in Balancing the Risks of Hormone after Menopause", "Increasing Shift Work Challenges Child Care", "Sexism Still Alive in Sacramento" (Mills 1997: 45). A similar observation could be made of our own Caribbean press: for instance, "Thousands Choose Abortion" (*Gleaner,* 4 August 1996 [written by a female journalist]), "Domestic Violence and the Legal Protection of Women in Jamaica" (*Trinidad Express,* 15 July 1996), "Doctors Urge Africa to End Women's Genital Mutilation" (*Trinidad Express,* 15 July 1996), "Working Women Pick Leaders" (*Trinidad Express,* 15 July 1996). But does the prominence of these topics have anything to do with the presence of women?

In the Caribbean, research on this topic has just started and is still in progress. Some journalists indicate that a female at the helm leads to different story selection, but others express their disappointment that a female managing editor seems to make no difference.

Research conducted elsewhere on these questions appears to be contradictory. Although the media situation in the United States is in some aspects very different from the Caribbean media, it is interesting to note their research findings. A 1992 survey of managing editors of the hundred largest daily newspapers in the United States found that 84 percent of responding editors agreed that women have made a difference – both in defining the news and in expanding the range of newsworthy topics: women's health, family and child care, sexual harassment and discrimination, rape and battering, homeless mothers, quality of life and other social issues (Gallagher and Quindoza-Santiago 1994). Mills shows that in thirty years the percentage of front page stories in the *New York Times* written by female journalists increased from 2.7 percent in 1964 to 19 percent in 1994 (Mills 1997). At the same time the range of stories in 1994 that might be considered to be of special interest to women appeared to be much wider (fertility research, women's colleges, sex education for the young, and so on) than in 1964 when personalities and society news were standard. In the Caribbean we know that the number of female bylines on front page articles has increased (although we cannot compare a similar time frame in the Caribbean: the oldest "modern" newspaper in the Caribbean, the *Gleaner,* did not use bylines on its front page until not too long ago). When we compare more recent issues of the *Gleaner,* a growing percentage of female-authored stories are carried on the front page: in August 1990, 31 percent of the bylined front page stories were written by female journalists; in August 1996, this had risen to 39 percent. We do not know if the range of stories also has widened; this kind of comparative research has not yet been undertaken.

In data from large-scale surveys in the United States among journalists, Weaver found that "the ratings of general media priorities by men and women journalists were quite similar, except that women were considerably less likely to consider providing entertainment and relaxation as extremely important (as compared with a decade earlier, and to a lesser extent with men) and somewhat more likely to value getting information to the public quickly" (Weaver 1997: 33). More limited research showed that male and female writers selected different subjects. After analysing 180 stories Weaver found those written by women more likely to be concerned with social problems and protests, and less likely to emphasize timeliness (Weaver 1997: 39). (These findings have to be interpreted very carefully, Weaver notes, and cannot be generalized easily: journalists in mass media are not always in a position to determine the subject of their choice.)

In the late 1970s a similar question had been researched on topic selection by male versus female editors of a particular section of the paper: women's page/lifestyle editors. Findings then indicated that women editors of these pages were more likely than men editors to use stories about the women's movement, women's club and social events (Merritt and Gross 1978: 508). But other research during the same period showed a tendency among gate-keepers of both sexes to reject news items about women as less newsworthy (Whitlow 1977: 573). This suggests that women's presence in the newsroom does not make a difference.

Not only the newsroom "vocabulary" of newsworthy topics, but also traditional associations between certain topics and the gender of sources, seem to have become established newsroom practices. The choice of sources has an immediate effect on the content of the story and the portrayal of gender. The Global Media Monitoring Project found a connection between certain kinds of stories and the representation of gender: men appeared more in economic news, political stories, labour news, and stories on war and terrorism ("twice as likely"). Women were more likely than men to appear in stories on social issues and health/medicine (Gallagher and von Euler 1995b: 17). In crime stories women appeared more than three times as often than in any other single news category. A similar observation was made by Graf for the 1993 *Gleaner*: when women did appear, more than half the time the theme was either fashion and beauty or violence (Graf 1994: 25). Women appeared in only 7 percent of the articles on business (Graf 1994: 33). Overall of the 3,610 articles in the *Gleaner* published during the months of October and November 1993, Graf found that only 5.6 percent had women as a focus (1994: 25). Similarly, research on gender representation in American elite newspapers in the mid 1980s showed women featuring prominently and more often than men in crime or accident stories (Potter 1985: 640).

My own research on the *Gleaner* over a period of five years (1991–95) on coverage of family planning and development, a topic that is traditionally associated with women, showed women playing a prominent role as the main source of a story, but more so in the softer stories (features) than in news. Also, certain sources were more often male (government officials) while other sources were more often female (nongovernmental organization officials and professionals) (de Bruin 1995). In content analyses on HIV/AIDS coverage, Jamaican as well as Trinidadian data from 1992 show that men were cited as the most frequent sources of news as well as feature stories: in 80 percent and 58 percent of print news and features respectively (de Bruin 1994a, 1996). Three years later the difference is less: 71 percent and 50 percent. I also noticed that sources used in stories for background information and/or for giving the story expert authority were more likely to be men than women, even in cases where female experts were available. This corresponds with research elsewhere, for instance, some Canadian findings on social trends in CBC prime television from 1977 to 1992, where women were found to account for only 15 percent of all expert opinion interviews (Allen 1994: 165).

Analogous to what various authors describe as an imbalance between the representation of the already privileged on the one hand, and the already unprivileged on the other, when sources are limited to the privileged body of politicians and academics, a similar political effect arises when the voices of women are underrepresented. "Imbalance of access results in partiality, not only in *what* assertions and attitudes are reported – a matter of content – but also in *how* they are reported – a matter of style, and therefore . . . of ideological perspective" (Fowler 1991: 23). The pattern appears to support a 1977 finding that there is "a deep-rooted prejudice against women as newsmakers in society among gatekeepers" (Bleske 1991: 93). No systematic research has been done on whether female sources are likely to provide a different kind of information, to put different emphases, to highlight different aspects, compared to male sources.

If the selection of sources and topics seems to relate to gender, what about the individual journalist herself or himself? Is there a tendency for female journalists to look for female sources and for males to look for male sources? Here too, research shows contradictory findings. Weaver (1997: 39), reflecting on earlier research in the United States, found that "women journalists were somewhat more likely to include female sources in their news stories than were men, who were more likely to include male news sources . . . they may be stepping out of more conventional news systems and tapping ordinary people as sources more often". Other research confirms imbalances in the gender of sources – more men than women – but suggests that they may be *unrelated* to the gender of the journalist who wrote the story. The Global Media Monitoring Project, in looking at the regional data for the Caribbean, found "absolutely no association between the gender of journalists and the gender of news actors" (Gallagher and von Euler 1995b: 23).

Other Differences?

In the section above I have highlighted only two aspects of the production process in media organizations in which gender may play an influential role: story selection and source selection. But what about other possible differences?

It is "in the area of priorities and values", Gallagher writes in 1995, "that women's increasing numerical strength in the media could be expected to make an impact". A different quality will lead to "new perspectives and interpretations" (Gallagher and von Euler 1995a: 3). Women enlarge "the definition of news", they impact on the political coverage, they bring a new perspective to issues; they influence story decisions and editorial policy, according to Mills's interviewees, thirteen women occupying senior positions in US media, who were asked to identify the areas in which they think they produce differently (Mills 1997: 46, 50, 52). Caribbean research on this matter is in progress.

Other authors express disappointment: the greater presence and visibility of women in mass media hardly make a difference (Creedon 1993: 3). Yes, we see more women in news roles and more feminist interventions, yet we do not see a change in processes of gathering and defining the news. Reflecting on US mass media in the 1980s and 1990s, Creedon concludes that they are profit driven and commercial power is stronger than ideology; white males occupy the decision-making positions in news selection and in hiring and firing; and workplace routines and norms force reporters to conform to dominant values, rather than act on empowering values (Creedon 1993: 13). In Gallagher's global study (1994), the accounts of various women from different regions show uncertainty, sometimes hope, often disappointment.

Do men and women in journalism operate from different professional perspectives? There is no Caribbean research available on this aspect.

Weaver, comparing three large-scale surveys of United States journalists in news media, found only very few "detectable differences between men and women journalists in their perceptions of which news media roles were most and least important" (Weaver 1997: 37). Newsroom learning and family upbringing were the most cited sources of influence on ideas about journalism ethics for both women and men. His findings suggest "that newsroom and community interest are stronger influences on journalists' professional values (and probably on the kind of news content they produce) than is gender" (Weaver 1997: 37).

Earlier studies point in the same direction, that education explains most of the differences in professional values (Johnstone 1976). Others again (see Van Zoonen 1994: 55) show no significant differences at all, or contradictory findings.

Some studies indicate that women themselves believe they differ from men in their professional perspectives. Van Zoonen (1988) cites a study where women indicated a general belief that women journalists pay more attention to background information and are more willing to look for spokeswomen instead of spokesmen. They perceived a difference in approach but not in actual topics. They also perceived their organizational role and responsibilities as different from that of their male colleagues. American female journalists in 1992 were less likely than their male counterparts to think they had a great deal of influence on hiring and firing employees. On the other hand, women journalists surpassed men in the amount of editorial control they thought they had (Weaver 1997: 28, 30).

Reports on work conditions in media organizations in the Caribbean certainly indicate that women encounter some typical barriers. A major one is not being able to combine job pressures and working hours with family life. African female media workers similarly identify conflict between the taxing conditions of work and family responsibilities as one of the seventeen main problems mentioned by them (Adagala and Kiai 1994: 16). Among the other complaints are the cultural expectation that women should be subordinate and subservient; sexual harassment by colleagues and information sources; lack of opportunities for further training; male colleagues' doubting women's capabilities as journalists, and psychological pressure from male coworkers, especially when women are in decision-making positions.

This last point is a very common problem. Female media workers from regions as diverse as the United States, the Netherlands, India and Senegal all mention the attitudes of male colleagues and decision makers as the most important barrier within the organization (Van Zoonen 1994: 52–53).

Working towards a Research Agenda for the Caribbean

Many questions remain unanswered. For instance: If women produce a different kind of journalism does it add the kind of quality we are dearly waiting for? Do women respond differently to the organizational constraints of media organizations? If so, what is the price they – or we, the readers – pay? Do they perform differently as managers and leaders? If so, does a different kind of leadership lead to a better or more relevant product?

To expect "a greater diversification of images and messages" and "new perspectives and interpretations" assumes a direct link between the presence of women in media organizations and an improved product. But it seems that the mere presence of women in media organizations is not a sufficient condition to bring about this change in quality. What are the nuances and dynamics of this process? And where are all the female graduates in communication studies? If they have such a substantial share of media training, why do they not have a substantial share in the media labour force? What happens to them in the labour market? Do they get any chances to realize their potential? If not, why not?

The same perspective also assumes that a "gendered" media output is of more relevance to the audience. But who benefits from this "different quality", the professional producer, the commercial owner, the general audience, the female segment of the audience, the male segment of the audience? And how does this new quality relate to our national and regional priorities?

Although looking at women's presence in media has been a continuing focus of researchers and activists over the last decades, an analytical approach needs to go further. If the quality that we associate with women's presence is not necessarily embodied in women physically, but related to socially constructed sets of values and behaviour – and equally so with the qualities we associate with men's presence – we need to include in our analysis the masculinity and femininity – as forms of subjectivity – in the media organizations. Once we look at the complexity of this situation we would have to include other forms of subjectivity as well, such as ethnicity. If we want to look at the organization from an organizational cultural approach we need to look at the way this production of meaning is shared, opposed, bargained for. In all of this, different identities inform the production of subjectivity: identification with a profession, identification with a company, identification through gender, class and ethnicity.

If we choose gender as our perspective, we need to find out what in the professional and organizational communities is being described as masculine and feminine, and where and how these notions inspire or constrain people's behaviour.

None of these questions has been researched in the Caribbean. Some are included in current CARIMAC research and others are still on the research agenda. Some have been taken on elsewhere, either in formal research, or during the course of women sharing their experiences and describing their personal observations.

The search for adding new quality to Caribbean journalism products is not a matter of art for art's sake. Women's issues in the Caribbean have always been very strongly connected to national and regional development issues. Those mostly affected among the poor have been women, children and the elderly; the concerns of the majority of women in the Caribbean have to do with a concern for basic living conditions.

It is a search to bring our reality back in our media. Nan Peacocke, Caribbean writer and feminist, says this so clearly that I close with her words:

> The task, then, is to "revision" . . . the work of journalism, to embrace the narrative voice of many Caribbean social groups and interests . . . the kind of journalism which confronts the whole problem of cultural exclusion of ourselves from our media. This is journalism which takes up the Caribbean historic imperative; the demand for inclusion; a demand inherent in the struggle for emancipation, struggles against indentureship, struggles to organize labour, struggles to resist the culture of race and to reject destructive gender power relations. (Peacocke 1995: 49–50)

References

Adagala, Esther, and Wambui Kiai. 1994. "Folk, Interpersonal and Mass Media: The Experience of Women in Africa". In *Women Empowering Communication: A Resource Book on Women and the Globalisation of Media,* edited by M. Gallagher and L. Quindoza-Santiago. London: WACC.

Allen, Donna. 1994. "Women in Media, Women's Media: The Search for Linkages in North America". In *Women Empowering Communication: A Resource Book on Women and the Globalisation of Media,* edited by M. Gallagher and L. Quindoza-Santiago. London: WACC.

Alvesson, Mats, and Yvonne Due Billing. 1997. *Understanding Gender and Organizations.* London: Sage.

Balakrishnan, Vijayalakshmi. 1994. "Indigenous Social Norms and Women in Asian Media". In *Women Empowering Communication: A Resource Book on Women and the Globalisation of Media,* edited by M. Gallagher and L. Quindoza-Santiago. London: WACC.

Berkowitz, Dan. 1990. "Refining the Gatekeeper Metaphor for Local Television News". *Journal of Broadcasting and Electronic Media* 34.

Bleske, Glen L. 1991. "Ms Gates Takes Over: An Updated Version of a 1949 Case Study". *Newspaper Research Journal* 12.

Breed, W. 1995. "A Social Control in the Newsroom: A Functional Analysis". *Social Forces* 37.

Brown, Aggrey. 1987. *TV Programming Trends in the Anglophone Caribbean: The 1980s.* Occasional Paper no. 2. Kingston, Jamaica: Caribbean Institute of Media and Communication, University of the West Indies.

Brown, Hilary. 1995. "American Media Impact on Jamaican Youth: The Cultural Dependency Thesis". In *Globalization, Communications and Caribbean Identity,* edited by H.S. Dunn. Kingston, Jamaica: Ian Randle Publishers.

Byerly, Carolyn M. 1995. "News, Consciousness and Social Participation: The Role of Women's Feature Service in World News". In *Feminism, Multiculturalism, and the Media: Global Diversities,* edited by A.N. Valdivia. Thousand Oaks, Calif.: Sage.

Creedon, Pamela J. 1993. "The Challenge of Re-Visioning Gender Values". In *Women in Mass Communication,* edited by P.J. Creedon. Newbury Park, Calif.: Sage.

Davis, Geddes. 1998. Presentation at conference, Ownership and Control of the Caribbean Media Industries: Implications for Information Flow and Communication, CARIMAC/WACC, Kingston, Jamaica, 23–27 March.

de Bruin, Marjan. 1994a. "HIV/AIDS and Responsible Reporting: A Content Analysis in Three Caribbean Countries, Part 1, Jamaica". Paper presented at Eleventh Annual Intercultural/International Communication Conference, University of Miami School of Communication, 3–5 February.

———, ed. 1994b. *Women and Caribbean Media.* Occasional Paper no. 3. Kingston, Jamaica: Caribbean Institute of Media and Communication, University of the West Indies.

———. 1995. *Jamaican Print and Radio on Family Planning and Population Issues, Content Analysis 1991–1995.* Kingston, Jamaica: Caribbean Institute of Media and Communication/National Family Planning Board.

———. 1996. "How Do Caribbean Media Industries Treat HIV/AIDS: A Comparative Content Analysis of Major Newspapers in Two English-Speaking Caribbean Countries, Jamaica and Trinidad and Tobago, 1992–1995". Paper presented at Transmission 1996, University of Bradford, England.

de Bruin, Marjan, et al. 1994. "Mass Media in the English Caribbean". In *Women Empowering Communication: A Resource Book on Women and the Globalisation of Media,* edited by M. Gallagher and L. Quindoza-Santiago. London: WACC.

Dervin, Brenda. 1987. "The Potential Contribution of Feminist Scholarship to the Field of Communication". *Journal of Communication* (Autumn).

Dunn, Hopeton S., ed. 1995. *Globalization, Communications and Caribbean Identity.* Kingston, Jamaica: Ian Randle Publishers.

Epstein, Edward Jay. 1974. *News from Nowhere: Television and the News.* New York: Vintage Books.

Fowler, Roger. 1991. *Language in the News: Discourse and Ideology in the Press.* London: Routledge.

Francis Brown, Suzanne. 1995a. "Practising Gender: Aware Journalism". In *Media, Gender and Development: A Resource Book for Journalists,* edited by S. Francis Brown. Kingston, Jamaica: Caribbean Institute of Media and Communication, University of the West Indies.

———, ed. 1995b. *Media, Gender and Development: A Resource Book for Journalists.* Kingston, Jamaica: Caribbean Institute of Media and Communication, University of the West Indies.

Gallagher, Margaret. 1981. *Unequal Opportunities: The Case of Women and the Media.* Paris: UNESCO.

Gallagher, Margaret, and Lilia Quindoza-Santiago, eds. 1994. *Women Empowering Communication: A Resource Book on Women and the Globalisation of Media.* London: WACC.

Gallagher, Margaret, and My von Euler. 1995a. *An Unfinished Story: Gender Patterns in Media Employment*. Reports and Papers on Mass Communication, no. 110. Paris: UNESCO Publishing.

_____. 1995b. *Global Media Monitoring Project: Women's Participation in the News*. Toronto: Media Watch.

Gans, Herbert. 1979. *Deciding What's News*. New York: Vintage Books.

Graf, Andrea. 1994. "Images of Women in the *Gleaner*". Women's Media Watch. Typescript.

Halford, Susan, Mike Savage, and Anne Witz. 1997. *Gender, Careers and Organisations*. London: Macmillan.

Jimenez-David, Rina, ed. 1996. *Women's Experiences in the Media*. Manila: Isis International.

Johnstone, John W.C. 1976. "Organizational Constraints on Newswork". *Journalism Quarterly* (Spring).

Merritt, Sharyne, and Harriet Gross. 1978. "Women's Page/Lifestyle Editors: Does Sex Make a Difference?" *Journalism Quarterly* 55, no. 3.

Mills, Kay. 1997. "What Difference Do Women Journalists Make?" In *Women, Media, and Politics,* edited by P. Norris. New York: Oxford University Press.

Norris, Pippa, ed. 1997. *Women, Media, and Politics*. New York: Oxford University Press.

Peacocke, Nan. 1994. "Revisioning Journalism". In *Media, Gender and Development: A Resource Book for Journalists,* edited by S. Francis Brown. Kingston, Jamaica: Caribbean Institute of Media and Communication, University of the West Indies.

Potter, James W. 1985. "Gender Representation in Elite Newspapers". *Journalism Quarterly* 62.

Schudson, Michael. 1997. "The Sociology of News Production". In *The Social Meanings of News: A Text-Reader,* edited by D. Berkowitz. Thousand Oaks, Calif.: Sage.

Snider, Paul B. 1967. "Mr Gates' Revisited: A 1966 Version of the 1949 Case Study". In *Approaches to Media: A Reader,* edited by O. Boyd-Barrett and C. Newbold. London: Arnold.

Sreberny-Mohammadi, Annabelle. 1995. *Women, Media and Development in a Global Context*. Paper presented at the symposium Women and the Media: Access to Expression and Decision-Making, Toronto.

Tuchman, Gaye. 1978. *Making News: A Study in the Construction of Reality*. New York: Free Press.

UNESCO. 1980. *Women in the Media*. Paris: UNESCO.

_____. 1994. Seminar in Media Development and Democracy in Latin America and the Caribbean, Santiago, Chile, 2–6 May.

van Zoonen, Liesbet. 1988. "Rethinking Women and the News". *European Journal of Communication* 3, no. 1.

_____. 1994. *Feminist Media Studies*. London: Sage.

Weaver, David H. 1997. "Women as Journalists". In *Women, Media, and Politics,* edited by P. Norris. New York: Oxford University Press.

_____, ed. 1998. *The Global Journalist, News People Around the World.* Cresskill, NJ: Hampton Press.

Weaver, David H., and G. Cleveland Wilhoit. 1996. *The American Journalist in the 1990s: US News People at the End of an Era.* Mahway, NJ: Lawrence Erlbaum.

White, D.M. 1951. "The Gatekeeper: A Case Study in the Selection of News". *Journalism Quarterly* 7, no. 4.

Whitlow, S. Scott. 1977. "How Male and Female Gatekeepers Respond to News Stories of Women". *Journalism Quarterly* 54, no. 3.

Women's Media Watch. 1996. "A Revisioning the Jamaican Media 1987–1996". In *Women's Experiences in the Media,* edited by R. Jimenez-David. Manila: Isis International.

22   Saga of a Flagwoman

KIM NICHOLAS JOHNSON

The death of Yvonne Smith, known far and wide in Trinidad as "Bubulups", was sadly ignominious, starting with the onset of her illness on 1 January 1993 and ending when her abandoned corpse was finally laid to rest a year later, on 6 January 1994, at what used to be the paupers' cemetery in St James, Port of Spain, North Trinidad, after thirty-nine days of shuttling between funeral homes.

Bubulups always said that if she took to bed she wouldn't get up again, and it turned out to be true. When her companion for twenty-four years, Eugene "Tepoo" Bristo, a panman from Tokyo steelband, first took her to the General Hospital, she spilled out of a wheelchair and was unable to rise. Although she'd lost weight she wouldn't have displaced much less than two hundred and fifty pounds, and the hospital attendant laughed at this beached whale on the floor.

"In my day he woulda be crying", she fumed afterwards in impotent rage, for in her day she was the most notorious, most belligerent whore in Trinidad. But in 1993 all she could do was to return to her dilapidated two-room shack on Clifton Street, John John, where she remained bleeding from her vagina for several months, emerging from bed mainly for Tepoo to sponge her down in the front room. In October she spent two weeks in hospital but there was no one to donate blood: Tepoo was too old, and her friends were alcoholics.

On 29 November she died at home of "abdominal malignancy" and "anae-mia", according to the death certificate. She was sixty-nine years of age.

Born on 2 May 1924, Yvonne Smith grew up on Duncan Street in Port of Spain. As a child she attended a school on Duke Street. Her father, "Pinhead" Smith, was not wealthy, but the family was respectable enough. They had a parlour on St Vincent Street by the law courts, and there was a piano at home on which Yvonne played. "She was an ordinary girl but always miserable, always big and she didn't take nothing from nobody," recalls Wellington "Blues" Bostock, who went to school with her and later enjoyed the pleasures she sold on the streets.

A wilful and uncompromising child, she probably chafed against the taunts about her size. She had been separated from her mother, Ethel Charles, as a child and must have also resented that too. Whereas one half-brother, Selwyn Charles, rose to become a parliamentary representative, Bubulups found herself pushed towards a different eminence.

"Is I break she out in life," admits George Blackman. He used to ride his bicycle past her house every day and look in the window where she practised playing the piano. "She was about fourteen and I was about sixteen and we loved one another, so she jumped through the window and we went Carenage to sleep."

Unfortunately from that first liaison she became pregnant and fled or was chased away from her "respectable" family, just as happened to her younger friend, "Jean-in-town" Clarke, years later.

"I met her on Prince Street when I came out as a young girl on the street: I had a child and my father tell me where I catch my cold go and blow my nose. I had nobody to help me out," recalls Jean-in-town. "I stand up on George Street looking for friends the first night and both of us became friends".

Similarly, Bubulups had gone long before to live with "friends" on Charlotte Street when she was put out of her home. Blackman, then a stevedore, remained living at his home with his mother, who took her granddaughter, Hermia, away from Bubulups the day she was born. Hermia Blackman grew up a stranger to Bubulups, her mother, even after (through coincidence) they lived next door – much as Bubulups had grown up a stranger to her own mother. Hermia would also follow her mother into the *demi-monde*, and is at present facing trial for a murder in a rumshop.

Perhaps Bubulups, barely a teenager, felt she could not afford a child on her own; perhaps she knew a daughter would have no place in the life she was about to enter; but whatever means decent society used to compel Bubulups to surrender her baby must have wounded her to the bone. And she didn't take nothing from nobody.

"She went on the streets for company; she had a lot of young girlfriends, and young girls like money," says Blackman. He remained involved with Bubulups for several years after Hermia was born, although he did not attempt to pull her out of the world she had entered. Perhaps by then she would not have accepted his help. Instead she joined the world of steelband, badjohns and saga boys. For some time she hung out in the "Big Yard" on George Street where a devil band came out, and by the early 1940s she was wining and waving flag for Bar 20 steelband, leading them into battle like an enormous, brown Joan of Arc.

"Bubulups with a flag in she hand," goes one calypso, "beggin the police don't stop the band." Even the most fearless men, such as Carlton "Zigilee" Barrow from Bar 20, found it daunting to keep up with Bubulups when she led them into battle. "When she was in front with the flag your stones was cold but it was a woman in front so you had to go," he admits.

"When the police come, don't run," she told the band when they paraded the streets illegally after the funeral of Bar 20 skipper Ancil Boyce, and they went on to beat a handful of policemen and smash their squad car on Quarry Street. The subsequent police retaliation destroyed Bar 20.

At least twice she was sentenced to gaol, apart from the routine police harassment she experienced as a whore sitting by a gateway on George Street. "Police used to give we a hard time on the road," says her younger friend and colleague Jean-in-town, although eventually they left Bubulups alone. "Once they take all of we to court. The police say she was sitting on a box and Bups tell them they have to be explicit: 'Am I selling *chataigne*, *peewah* or *pommecythere?*' The whole court start to laugh and the magistrate dismiss the case."

On another occasion Jean-in-town told the magistrate, "I did now come out to work and as I pull down my panty to pee the police come with torchlight. I hold the police hand and say let we go drink two Guinness." Again the court laughed and the case was dismissed.

The police harassment made Jean-in-town move to the clubs along the "Gaza Strip" on Wrightson Road, west of Port of Spain. Perhaps her decision was influenced by her involvement with the Renegades captain, Stephen "Goldteeth" Nicholson, who was the bouncer at a club in the Strip. But Bubulups remained in town on George Street.

One term in gaol was for a licking she put on a policeman who had chucked her. After that, when reinforcements were brought to arrest her she had to be carried by several of them, screaming and kicking and naked because she had ripped off her clothes. That was down Carenage Bay at a St Peter's Day fête during the war, when she was still with Bar 20.

According to Clem Belloram, then a child living in the district, it started when the band went to the festival in honour of St Peter, patron saint of fishermen. As expected, the rum was flowing and Bubulups got into an argument with someone. She began to fight and it spread into an all-out battle between those supporting the whore and those supporting her opponent, until the police arrived and one officer named Alfred Gilkes attempted to tackle Bubulups. "She hit him some coconut and spread him out," recalls Belloram. "She drop him but you know Alfred Gilkes with he little boxing tactics can't handle Bubulups to get her in the van cause he had to hit her a punch. I think he hit her a punch in her breast and knock her down. That was the only way you coulda get her to carry. Yeah. She was heavy. All now she would have been still fighting. I'm telling you. You couldn't carry her nowhere. I could remember that as a little fella. It was during the war, yes, about 1945."

"Bubulups darling, why you beat the officer?" sang one calypsonian after the incident: "Six months hard labour."

Some time before she'd befriended a young calypsonian fresh out of the countryside, Aldwyn Roberts, better known as Lord Kitchener. By the time he sang about Zigilee and Bar 20 in "The Beat of the Steelband" in 1946, however, the band was dead and Bubulups had moved on. She was now flying flag for Red Army of Prince Street, a band of pimps if there ever was one. "She was one of the first flagwomen and all of them was *jamettes* [whores]," says Blues Bostock, a veteran of that band.

The liming spots in the wee hours were Tanti's Tea Shop on George Street and Luther's Tea Shop on Prince Street, where all-night bake and saltfish and coffee would be on sale. Kitchener, Spoiler and other calypsonians would be talking and trying out their latest songs. Bubulups remained friends with Kitchener until her death.

When Red Army, cleaning up its act, metamorphosed into the Merry Makers by shedding its more unsavoury members, and fell under the patronage of a different type of dancer – Beryl McBurnie, the founder of the Little Carib Theatre – Bubulups moved on to Trinidad All Stars where she met Mayfield Camps, a stripper and one of the greatest winers in the country. The two waved flag for All Stars.

Although many whores found acceptance in the world of the outcast steelband men, it was not an easy world. Once a panman broke Bubulups's arm with blows. He got eighteen months for that. As for Jean-in-town, she was disfigured for life when a man stabbed her.

"One night I was liming with some Renegades panmen with some of the other girls and we went in this place on Park Street to buy some food," recalls Jean-in-town. "This little boy who did just like to harass me come pushin money in my face. I spit in he face. Then when I comin out of the place later, somebody bawl 'Look out!' and I throw my hand to cover my face."

Until her death many years after she had left the streets, Bubulups remained close to Mayfield, as to all her friends of "her days", remarking often that one didn't find friends like them again. The hardship and promiscuous intimacy of their lives must have forged firm bonds of friendship. Although she gave up Hermia as a newborn to George Blackman's mother, she always advised Jean-in-town to save her money for her child, not for any man. To her friends, however, Bubulups was generous whenever she had money.

Despite Bubulups's complete immersion in the underworld, she maintained a very clear-cut code of ethics. She abhorred dishonesty and would never pick a client's pocket, as whores routinely did to supplement their meagre earnings. Jean-in-town admits, "I never really like sex and thing, you know. I used to more rob man."

Despite her many battles with them, Bubulups would not let a policeman be unfairly beaten. "She saved my life years ago," recalled former police commissioner, Randolph Burroughs. That was when he was a constable on the beat. "She used to sit and open she legs under Big Man club on Prince Street. Ruby Rab was there too, and I was pursuing a chap for pickpocketing," he continued.

The rogue darted into the Lucky Jordan club, a hangout for some of the country's worst criminals, and when the young Burroughs dashed in after him, someone locked the door behind them. "Bubulups knew the danger and she and Ruby Rab began pounding on the door, bawling 'Murder! They killing the man! Ring the police!' " Burroughs recounted. "Police didn't have revolvers, but I put my hand in my pocket and pretend I have a gun until reinforcements from Besson Street arrived."

Bubulups's formidable wilfulness – and, ironically, her self-respect – were what got her into the most despised profession. There, in the gutter, she defended her dignity with all the belligerence and moral rectitude she could summon. Later, after she had left the streets for good, she would exaggerate to her Clifton Street neighbour, Velma Denbow, that she had always earned a fair amount of money, always had nice clothes – as if to justify the life she had lived. According to Denbow, Bubulups would recall to her how good it felt to always have food in her kitchen and new clothes on her back, a rose-tinted memory at best. She also impressed upon Denbow how ladylike she always had been, even when on the streets, which was certainly a lie.

Social commentators, however, merely considered her the biggest whore in Trinidad, and she was scorned in calypsos by Lord Melody, Lord Blakie, Roaring Lion, Kitchener, all the way down to the Mighty Chalkdust's 1992 "Trinidad ent Change", in which he compares the prostitutes of yesteryear with contemporary hypocrites:

> Trinidad ent change
> Just re-arrange
> Prostitutes like Jean and Dinah
> Bubulups and Bengal Tiger
> They now Mrs Clarke
> And Mrs Doris Mark
> In Federation Park

Perhaps when Kitchener celebrated flagwomen in his calypso of the same name, this first flagwoman felt a surge of pride, but it is unlikely. By then she had already forsaken the streets and Carnival for good. More likely she felt stung on hearing, in 1946, Kitch's gloating "Ding Dong Dell" with its unspoken rhyme, "pussy in the well":

> Well the Yankee leave them sad
> All them girls in Trinidad
> And the course is getting hard
> Port of Spain to Fyzabad
> Ding Dong Dell

The girls in the town they catching hell
Ding Dong Dell
Starvation in town, they must rebel
Bubulups and Elaine Pow
Every night they making row
Well the thing is not the same
They gone in the poker game

Small and wiry, Tepoo Bristo was a butcher who played tenor for Tokyo when he met Bubulups one night in 1969 on George Street. "From the first night we liked one another," he says. "I told her I don't want her to make no fares again, I going to mind her." She moved in with him and became progressively reclusive. Once she went to look on at Carnival and tripped somewhere along Prince Street. She never left the neighbourhood again. Eventually she hardly left Tepoo's shack, not even to go to the nearby standpipe for water.

After she died, squabbling broke out between Tepoo and her estranged daughter Hermia, who lived a few steps away along a rocky dirt path. Hermia, surprisingly, stole the framed photograph Tepoo had of himself and Bubulups. The death certificate also disappeared and the corpse remained in Nella's Funeral Home for thirty-two days, after which it was returned to Tepoo, who slept with Bubulups for a last night on the same bed. The following day he tried to get the Co-operative Funeral Home to take her corpse, but did not have the money.

Eventually Yvonne "Bubulups" Smith was laid to rest on 6 January 1994, about two in the afternoon, after a funeral service sponsored by Clark and Battoo's Funeral Home. Her last rites were attended by a handful of mourners, none of whom included the steelband pioneers such as Blues Bostock, who worked next door to the funeral home in the Pan Trinbago office. Flowers were donated by La Tropicale Flower Shop. At the St James cemetery the coffin was lifted with great difficulty out of the hearse, because she had been a big woman; and George Blackman was the only man there to pay his last respects.

23   Woman of the Shadows

Kathy-Ann Waterman

Prologue

The three-storey red, green and gold house still broods over the neighbourhood, like an artefact of the last decade of gundeleros and drug thugs. Strangers live in it now. Survivors of the family who lived there have fled.

From this castle on the hill, a dreadlocked man, with a Bible in his hand, would emerge and make his way through this blighted fiefdom of waterless pipes and unschooled children, to preach a distorted Rastafarian message of deliverance. He stole drugs and minds.

He made school dropouts rich and powerful overnight by giving them guns and money. As drug turfs were being carved up along racial lines in the 1980s, he wore the image of the dreadlocked folk hero, challenging the light-skinned and straight-haired bosses of the underworld.

It was the kind of story told in the movie *Marked for Death* about twin Rastafarian brothers in the drug sewers of Jamaica and America. Until this dreadlocked man from the hills was shot dead by police in 1993, outside his castle, he spread his influence as easily as the hundred-dollar bills he gave away.

In the early 1980s, into this badland of drugs and crime came a family of four brothers and three sisters. They soon grew accustomed to the police raids and the booyaka-booyaka of firearms.

This is a story about one of those sisters, who was befriended by the drug baron on the hill and became his brother's woman. I call her Rudy. She's the "rude gyal", who seeks status and love from a ruling "bad boy".

A slim, full-hipped woman, she has a child's smile, flawed only by a shaved incisor, once covered by a $100 gold cap. She likes to wear lots of gold jewellery and white dusting powder on her neck and cleavage. Her favourite outfit is a velvet suit of sleeveless jacket and fringed shorts, that shows her navel and stops traffic.

Rudy, fourth among her siblings and the first person in her family to complete high school, was the "trophy" of the drug baron's brother – a younger, more brutal version of the drug baron himself. Her sister had a brief relationship with a third member of that doomed ruling family of the East-West corridor neighbourhood. When Rudy's relationship with the drug baron's brother ended, she moved on to another drug dealer, so that by age twenty-one, she had had two boyfriends who had been shot to death by their enemies – one at a party, the other in a drive-by "execution".

Darius Figueira describes the role of women in the East-West corridor drug culture. "The women hold the bail money and the guns when the men get arrested. They pay the lawyers. They handle the savings. They keep the secrets."

As the "childmothers", they are raising another vulnerable generation, who will either grow up in the "gundelero" life or shun it.

Rudy is now twenty-seven and the mother of two girls, aged five and one. Her high-flying days, when she was the woman of drug dealers, are over. "I done with all of that", she said. But the past continues to define her life. Her present live-in boyfriend used to belong to that gang that ruled from the castle on the hill.

Last year they moved out of her father's house, which is overlooked by the red, green and gold burglar-proofed fortress, into their own apartment a few streets away, in the same neighbourhood of cocaine and unemployment.

Her family lives nearby and shows no greater potential for escaping the past. Rudy's older brother has been to jail several times for larceny. He was acquitted on a robbery charge last year. Rudy pawned her children's gold bracelets and chains to pay a lawyer, although that brother used to steal from her. A younger brother has pending drug trafficking charges. Violence has been a recurring factor in her family's existence, and Rudy has hardened herself to it.

Her "cousin", a state witness in a murder trial, was shot dead near her own home, in daylight, in front of passers-by. Last month a man killed another of her relatives by plunging a knife into her chest. He gave himself up to the police afterwards. Rudy's older sister was chopped by an ex-boyfriend some years ago. The blood spattered on Rudy as she caught her sister's hand, which was almost severed in the attack.

Rudy agreed, with a shrug, to tell her story about the choices she had, the choices she made and the men she loved. Her cooperation, over a period of two months, provided an opportunity to go behind the stereotyped images of young, gold-toothed bandits and their women, to examine the interrelationships among poverty, drugs, violence, sex. Names have been changed and some details omitted to cover her family's identity.

I asked Rudy if she had one lesson out of her own life to teach her two girls, what would it be. She said, "I'll tell them, look, I know plenty. Badness do not pay."

Then, cynically, she added, "I cannot teach them to go and friend with a church man. He could be a bandit too. But whatever they ask, I'll tell them."

I

Wednesday, 17 January 1996

Rudy, in black spandex bra-top, was at her usual post. She was sitting on a neighbour's front step, finger-waving someone's hair with thick, pink gel. She enjoyed talking about her life. She liked the break in the monotony of housekeeping, chatting and skimping on money and food.

Michael, a twenty-one-year-old retired bandit, was a labourer who worked on a construction site, loading and unloading truckloads of bricks and bags of cement. He gave Rudy money for Christmas and she bought chairs with pink and blue flowered cushions for the rented one-bedroom house with a single electric lightbulb. They got the stove on hire-purchase and she kept cold drinks in a styrofoam ice box.

Rudy had no running water indoors but her linoleum-covered floors were spotless and her kitchen utensils hung evenly in a row from nails in the wall. Every afternoon she bathed and powdered the children and dressed them in matching outfits, before Michael came home from work. Michael was the father of her one-year-old, Teresa. The father of her five-year-old, Princess, was shot dead in 1992 at a party.

Sometimes Rudy lost her temper and smacked the children on their arms and bottoms for whining and wriggling when she combed their hair, or for being disobedient. Other times she would suddenly grab one of them onto her lap and cover the child with kisses. "You know Mummy love you bad, bad, bad?"

Rudy was proud of her domestic skills. "All that I do today," she said, pointing to rows of freshly washed clothes on the line in the backyard. She enjoyed baking and icing cakes for family and friends, for birthdays and christenings.

Michael, a dark, unsmiling man, had pasted photographs of the family on the walls and painted in black letters: "Ask and it shall be given unto you. Seek and you shall find."

Among the family pictures on the wall were blurred snapshots of one of his old drug-dealing friends – a lean, dreadlocked man, now in prison serving a five-year term for possession of counterfeit US dollars.

Rudy kept a bank account, and in a blue diary she wrote down how much money she collected and how much she spent, how much she owed and who owed her, with dates and times. It was a habit she had developed since she was a child and would cut a slot in a grapefruit tin and drop her coins in there. She talked about moving "for the sake of the children", but did not expect to find anywhere nice for $150 a month – what she paid now.

The area was a contrast of freshly painted houses and well-tended gardens lower down the street, and overcrowded, crumbling buildings at the barren, forgotten end, where Rudy lived, and where children and dogs were bathed at the standpipe. Women in batty-riders and cycle shorts rolled their hips up and down the rocky, unpaved road, to buy some ice or a $2 disposable diaper from the shop. Men, doing nothing under a "galvanize" shed, either ignored the performance or expressed their approval.

A broad-shouldered man was eating a plate of mixed rice one afternoon. Rudy called out to him, "See how you big? Your food coming to meet you."

"I not big," he called back. "Is she c—— I want. When I get that, I big."

Rudy looked embarrassed and said nothing.

The sexual energy crackles through the neighbourhood like a live electric wire. The teasing, the pursuit and the consummation, which takes place in tiny "galvanize" backyard bathrooms as well as on mattresses in the heat of the afternoon, fill the long, empty hours and distract from the purposelessness of every new morning.

II

"Is only now I know what it is to get up in the morning and not have milk for my children. Is only now," Rudy was saying one afternoon.

When she was the girlfriend of drug dealers, she had everything she wanted – money, clothes, gold jewellery, trips to other Caribbean islands, food on the table.

"I'm not stingy with food," she said. She used to keep her parents' cupboards stocked and helped pay their bills. She bought clothes and toys for her nephews and nieces. Her family still looks to her for relief.

Rudy and Dexter became a couple when she was about fifteen and he was a few years older. He used to breakdance for money when they first met – then came the drugs and the guns.

Dexter, a shortish, stocky man, was a thug. He was the younger brother of the dreadlocked gang leader, who controlled a drug turf a few miles outside Port of Spain.

Dexter's family ranked somewhere in the middle of the drug hierarchy. They were not as high as importers-exporters and they were more than pushers on the block. They built their empire by robbing other drug lords of cocaine and selling it on the streets through their "agents".

When the Jamaat-al-Muslimeen was muscling in on the cocaine blocks along the East-West corridor in the late 1980s, Dexter and his big brother Albert went down to the Muslimeen's mosque in Mucurapo and joined the organization. They "confiscated" cocaine from pushers on the block – and sold it again on the streets.

Dexter was shot in the neck by his enemies in 1993. His big brother Albert, wanted for attempted murder, was killed by police months later; he had been on the run for about two years. Charles, a third member of the family gang, went to prison for robbery, after being freed on a murder charge. The case was dropped after the witness was gunned down. Charles is now in prison for possession of counterfeit currency.

Rudy had known the family since she was in primary school, when her family moved into the neighbourhood. Her grandmother had invited the family to live with her so they would not have to pay rent elsewhere. As she became part of Dexter's family, it was not hard for Rudy to figure out what Dexter was doing for a living. "He come home with a set of money and tell me his brother give him. I ask his brother. I farse, you know. His brother say who me? Give him money?"

She showed me a picture of Dexter lying on the bedroom floor, talking on a cellular phone, with hundred-dollar bills strewn over the floor. I counted twenty of those bills.

He used to take her to the grocery with some neighbourhood girls. The girls would push the trolley. Rudy would point out what she wanted on the shelves and they would load the trolley. Dexter would pay for it all at the cash register.

"In all the years I know him, he never buy a snack box of chicken and bring for me. Is always a bucket or a five-piece . . . and I cannot eat five pieces of chicken," Rudy said.

One night he came to her balancing a tall bucket his head. It was filled with cash. She emptied it on the bed and called her relatives to help her count "until we could not count no more". She bought ten-speed bikes for her nephews and nieces and put the rest in the bank.

From time to time, police caught up with Dexter and when he was jailed for various drug-related offences, she was left in charge of his money and guns. She used to hide the guns in the ceiling. On her birthday and on New Year's Day, she would fire off a .38 into the air. Sometimes she carried it in her waist. She usually travelled with an entourage of Dexter's friends, whose job was to protect her. She escaped death one day when one of Dexter's enemies opened fire on the men who were supposed to be keeping her safe. They were in Barataria, to buy marijuana to smuggle to Dexter in prison. Her friend was "running and pelting shots behind him". He was wounded in the hand. She took him to hospital and admitted him under a fake name.

When Dexter got out of prison, he shot and wounded the gunman who had attacked Rudy and her friends.

III

Dexter was supposed to be Rudy's passport out of poverty. When she was attending junior secondary school, he used to help buy her schoolbooks. When she later enrolled in a technical school, Dexter's big brother, Albert, used to pay her tuition fees. Rudy became the first person in her family to complete secondary school and get CXC passes.

As a child, Rudy used to play doctor with her doll. She still likes to imagine herself as a doctor, and she claims knowledge of what bush to drink for "cooling" and infections.

Rudy was a prefect at Morvant Laventille Junior Secondary, and when she graduated she got book prizes and a study lamp for doing well in school. "My father cry. My mother too. They was proud!" She wears her school ring with the blue crest every day and has kept a faded photograph of her graduating class, taken outside the school. She was the thin girl in the back row, squinting in the sunlight.

Her days at Morvant Laventille Junior Secondary remain her favourite memories. She ran track and field and played netball for the school. One day her class visited a home for handicapped children and Rudy sang "We Are the World".

"My teacher kissed me right here!" She pointed to her forehead. She had taken on a little-girl voice, as if she were that spirited child in the schoolyard again.

An old schoolfriend dropped by one afternoon and Rudy urged her friend to "Tell them about me. Tell them how I was bright and quiet and thing." Her friend grinned. "She was not quiet but she was not wild. She was just nice. She used to do homework for shilling and thing."

Rudy's role model used to be her eldest brother, who "passed for college and thing". But then he went mad and drowned. "He used to cut his flesh with bottle and tell me this is only flesh, only flesh. I used to cry."

Another brother and a sister passed Common Entrance but dropped out of high school. She was disappointed in her father but she loved him. He used to work on the wharf and made good money but never seemed to save a cent of it. He drank and gambled. Her parents separated when Rudy was in junior secondary and her mother went to live a few houses away. Rudy and her six brothers and sisters remained with their father but saw their mother often.

Rudy could always get money off her father when he had it. Once he bought Bata sneakers for Rudy and her sister to wear to school. Rudy told him the other children laughed at her in school; she got in a fight with another girl in the bathroom over the teasing. The next day, her father bought Rudy and her sister Superstar sneakers. "He never give us Bata shoes again. We never even wear Bata in the yard."

The only other people Rudy looked up to were her teachers. "They encouraged me a lot. They made the difference, not my parents."

The former junior secondary she attended has since been converted to a single-shift, five-year school. No teacher there could remember Rudy or locate her records in the disorganized filing system. She was just one of thousands and thousands that had passed through the school gates. But the lessons Rudy had studied so well in the classrooms could not withstand the new realities of her adult world.

IV

At El Dorado Senior Comprehensive, Rudy wanted to study science but was told her grades were not good enough. She passed English, economics and history with credits. She had also written Spanish, mathematics and geography. Until last week, she said she did not know whether she had passed. She never collected her certificate. "I did not go graduation. My father did not have no money to send me." She hung her head. When I told her I had got the information from the school, she said she was disappointed she did not pass Spanish. She used to be good at it, she said.

Another day, when I asked her about Albert's drug trade, she mentioned that she had once acted as a decoy for him, speaking Spanish to some Venezuelan cocaine smugglers. She collected the cocaine, paid them the money and as she left, Albert waylaid them and robbed them of the money.

After two years at the senior comprehensive, Rudy was accepted at San Fernando Technical Institute where she signed up for science subjects. She went to stay with Dexter's family, who lived in the south. Dexter and his older brother, Albert, were still friends then. Rudy never got to write her examinations at the technical school. The money meant for her examination fees was spent by Dexter's family on new furniture.

Rudy packed up her dreams of becoming a doctor and went back home to her father's. She practised her cake baking, went to parties and bought pretty clothes with the money Dexter gave her.

V

When she got pregnant for Dexter, Rudy was not sure what to feel. She had not planned to be a mother just yet. On the other hand, she was glad she could have babies. "I thought I could not breed. All my sisters having babies. What happen to me?"

She had a miscarriage in her third month.

Dexter bought nightgowns and matching slippers for her when she was in hospital. "He was nice!" He cried over the loss of the baby.

"Everything does happen for the best. Today that child would be paying for his deeds," she said.

Dexter got it into his head that Rudy's mother, Helen, had done something to cause a miscarriage because he knew Helen disliked him. He pulled a gun on Helen, outside her apartment. And Rudy, just home from the hospital, stood there, speechless, pale and trembling.

After that, Rudy's feelings for Dexter began to drain away. He was also getting deeper into the underworld. He and Albert fell out and Dexter formed his own ruthless gang. Dexter was getting too dangerous to be around.

Regularly, when police raided her home in Laventille looking for weapons and drugs or Dexter himself, Rudy used to be arrested and detained for questioning by police. No one bothered her too much in the women's prison. She was respected by other prisoners as the woman of a major bandit. But she was getting fed up with spending her weekends behind bars.

When Dexter was charged with kidnapping and was sent to prison, awaiting trial, Rudy had already decided she was through with him. One afternoon Rudy grew angry at a teenage friend over her involvement with an older man. Rudy shouted at her, "I had love a man. His name was Dexter. I had anything I wanted when I was with him. And I leave him? I used to grieve for him, it used to hurt my heart when he come talking to me and I watching him just so. But I overcome that . . . Girl, you do not know nothing about life yet."

VI

"Bandits could ever change?" Rudy remarked. She was chopping vegetables in the kitchen. "Hear how it is with bandits. When they want to change, it does be too late and is then they does get kill."

Bobby, sweet-talking and suave-looking, was the father of her first baby, a girl they nicknamed Princess. Rudy is still known and respected in her neighbourhood as "Bobby's childmother".

He was shot dead at point-blank range at a public fête in 1992. His close friends, Curtis "Tooks" Greenidge and Steve Bulls Sandy, were found dead in shallow graves in Caroni three months later.

Police say it was an old quarrel between two friends that ended in Bobby's death, but were unclear whether drugs had anything to do with it. Rudy believes a ruptured marijuana deal was part of what went wrong that night, but something deeper, which she would not talk about for the record, led to Bobby's death.

"It was jealousy," Rudy said, making a face, as if she wanted to spit. "He could dress too bad!"

She pulled out a picture of him from a stack she kept in a zipped plastic bag, along with his death certificate. There was a young man of average size in a bronze silk shirt and a thick gold chain around his neck.

Hours before he was killed, Rudy told him, "You go dead!" He held her by her throat. Then, he smiled and said, "I real love you, yes, girl."

Rudy used to tell him it was time to get out of the drug dealing, that he would meet his death. He would laugh. "Like he had get to like the badness the longer he stayed in it," she said.

Bobby was not feeling well the night of the party; his friends came to his home and persuaded him to go with them. It was around three in the morning and the fête was still rocking. A man came up to Bobby and asked the time. Bobby looked at his wrist. Then there was the crack of gunfire, the pitching of blood and the scattering of a crowd. As Bobby lay dying, soca music blared. His last words were, "Oh God, nobody to mind Princess."

He was twenty-one. His death certificate listed his profession as "Nil". He sold cocaine and some marijuana through his "agents", who peddled it on the streets. Rudy did the same for about a year. It was casually one afternoon that she mentioned her own days as a drug dealer, right after reminding herself aloud to get some limes to clean the fish for dinner that evening.

When she was selling cocaine, she had not given it much thought. Bobby was doing it, his family was doing it. She did it too.

Two men were charged for Bobby's murder. The case was dismissed at magistrate's court, after the key witnesses did not show to give evidence.

Rudy was nineteen, maybe twenty, when she met Bobby, who was a few years younger. Dexter, her old gangster boyfriend, was in prison awaiting trial for a kidnapping charge. She was working then, at a club in Barataria. "Not any ordinary club and bar, you know. A decent, air-conditioned place."

Bobby met her after work and offered to drive her home. She knew he was a "fella who had gun" and was "doing wrong things". He knew she was the ex-girlfriend of a feared gang leader.

Bobby was not like Dexter, Rudy said. Bobby did not rob anybody. Bobby used to give other people the cocaine to sell for him. He was respectful to her parents, he never smoked in front of them. And they adored him. "He used to give them anything they wanted."

VII

Bobby had survived some close calls before that night at the party. Once when he went to buy cocaine on Nelson Street, Port of Spain, he was wounded in the leg by a bullet that almost caught his cousin in the back. Rudy was not scared when she heard Bobby was in hospital. "I did not used to think about that. I did not let that bother me."

Shortly before he was killed, Bobby was planning to move to the United States, to escape a motor-car manslaughter case. Police arrested him the day before he was supposed to fly out.

Bobby did not live long enough to be tried and convicted of anything. His police record included 1990 charges for firearm and ammunition possession and shooting with intent to do bodily harm.

Bobby adored his little girl, Princess, who was less than a year old when he died. He bought clothes and toys that she was too young to wear and play with. Rudy still has a suitcase of new baby clothes.

"Oh gosh, when he found out I was pregnant he just could not stop buying. He gave me $1,000 to buy baby things. I bought a pair of shoes, a Bally, instead." She giggled.

"He did not like me to use no cloth diaper. If she pee in the Pamper, he changing it, he checking to see. He did not used to buy Pampers by the pack, you know. By the bale. No one tin of milk. A whole case."

He gave Princess a gold chain with diamond studs and someone stole it off her neck right there in the yard. The last toy he bought for Princess was a red and white bear, as tall as the child, which was propped up on the new furniture. "He had real love me, eh. He had love me more than I love him," Rudy said. He would have done anything for her. Weeks before he died, he got his gang to tear down the house of a family that had crossed Rudy.

Her love for Bobby started to cool, not because of the drug dealing, but because of his running around with other women. She had heard about AIDS and she did not want to catch it.

Rudy got vexed one day and, taking Princess, she went home by her mother. Bobby found her and grabbed the sleeping baby. Rudy made a report to the police and got back her baby. "He tell me he would always do that and one day, I would not know where he gone with the child." So she moved back in with him "because of the child, but my love had start to go".

At Bobby's funeral, Princess kissed her daddy and grabbed at his clothes. Afterwards, she used to hide behind a chair and cry. Rudy has told her about Bobby. "She knows how he died. She says my daddy was killed by his friend."

Rudy was pregnant again at the time of Bobby's death. The baby was born prematurely several months later. It was a girl, who died when she was three months old from congenital heart failure and bronchopneumonia. "What's that? Like a cold or something?" Rudy asked.

She believes someone tried to work obeah on her and the lash caught the child instead. She remembers the baby "crying like a cat" and her fingers turning blue before an ambulance came to take her to hospital, where she died, surrounded by doctors and nurses, while Rudy was filling out medical forms.

Rudy had a picture of the baby in the coffin before she was buried. Only her tiny, perfect face was visible in the bed of pink satin.

VIII

Michael, Rudy's current boyfriend, shook her awake before daylight. "What we go do?" he asked her. They had no money. He told her to pawn her jewellery until he collected his pay the following week, but she believed that was bad luck.

"I ent feel to do it. I ent pawning my children jewellery again. That is jumbie thing," Rudy was saying later that morning.

One week when she was broke, she borrowed $2 from a friend to buy a disposable diaper. She felt ashamed. When she got home a neighbour, sensing her difficulty, surprised her with a pack of diapers. Rudy held on to her and wept.

"I never had no friend to do anything like that for me," she said. "My friends just for what they could get out of me." Rudy walked over to her mother's to borrow $5 for something to cook.

"I glad I break out knowing plenty money," she said, suddenly. "Nobody could fool me with money now. I know money. So much girls sexing they self all over the place because a man promise them something."

Her mother, Helen, was absorbed in Nikki's machinations to prevent her son's impending marriage to Victoria in *The Young and the Restless,* which was showing on a new remote control colour television her sister had given her.

Helen's little apartment with the lumpy, peeling walls was often populated by her grown children and their babies. Rudy and her sister Marcia came to wash clothes in the new washing machine. Then Helen would fret about how the children ransacked her place and would rush about, straightening up in their wake.

The soap opera over, Helen switched on the radio and soca music poured out of it. "Wine for me, Stinky," she urged Rudy's toddler, Teresa. Helen was thinking about the Carnival fêtes coming up. She went through her assortment of black spandex shorts. "This gives a better fit," she said, holding up a few inches of shiny black material.

Rudy asked her for money. Helen threw some picong[1] for her. "Rudy used to have money, plenty money. Now she do not have a cent."

Rudy: "I'm very happy . . . you have meat?" Helen shook her head. Helen's boyfriend had not given her any money yet to "make message". She roused herself to cut a triangle of pumpkin into a smaller triangle and tried to break half a carrot in two. The carrot would not break, so Rudy got all of it. A neighbour had promised Rudy some pigeon peas and she had a dry coconut. She could make a meal with that before Michael got home.

Some weeks later, Helen asked Rudy for $20. Rudy shouted back, "*I do not have any money*. I tell you that already."

IX

Rudy's mother Helen had grown up a "posh girl" with her grandmother and step-grandfather who had a Bosch refrigerator and she could take anything out of it to eat and drink. Her step-grandfather was a police inspector. Her parents had separated when she was a baby.

"I was real pretty. I tell Rudy she not pretty how I used to be pretty," she said.

When she got pregnant at sixteen, her grandfather was angry. She later met the man who became the father of her other children. Except for her first baby, "I had all my children for one man, you know." She had a baby almost every year until there were seven of them, and then she "adopted" an eighth.

Two of her three daughters, Marcia and Karen, were teenage mothers and now have six children between them. They are raising their families in the neighbourhood they grew up in. Marcia works as a babysitter, Karen as a security guard. Marcia's boyfriend recently lost his job for assaulting someone with a weapon. Marcia suggested that having babies early was normal. "If you lived here, you would have children by force, you know," she said jokingly one afternoon, as her toddlers and their friends played noisily nearby. "Everybody else does."

Helen made ends meet by accepting gifts of money from her sister, who works on the New York subway. It was her sister who had paid for the new television, fridge and washing machine for Helen for Christmas.

I asked Helen if she ever talked to Rudy about her underworld boyfriends. "Me? I do not tell my children who to choose. Let them choose for themselves. Just do not run in my place."

When Marcia was chopped by her ex-boyfriend and left for dead in the street, Helen ran outside from the bathroom naked, screaming. That boy had seemed so quiet.

When he was a teenager he had been to the Youth Training Centre, Golden Grove, for killing someone. But she had not told Marcia to stay away from him. It was not as if Marcia did not know his history, she said. She does not know where they got their ideas from. "I never had a bandit man yet," she whispered.

X

Michael, Rudy's current boyfriend, was a dark, sullen looking man with high cheekbones and dreadlocks. He had been out of work for a week, but in four days, he got another labouring job on a government project.

Rudy was at her mother's apartment, using the washing machine to do the laundry. Michael had come with her. He was sitting barebacked in the drawing room, leaning forward, his hands clasped between his knees. The front door swung shut, closing out the daylight, so that Michael's angular, dark profile was smudged by shadows, as if someone had made a life-sized impression of him in thick, black crayon on grey canvas and then rubbed their finger along the edges. Light leaked in from above the doorway and fell on the left side of his face, making it look as if he had one topaz eye.

Michael was fourteen when he got his first gun and his first robbery charge. He's had several charges for robbery, drug possession, car theft and firearm offences, but they were all dismissed for want of evidence or because witnesses did not show up.

The longest he ever spent in prison was six months, when he could not raise the $100,000 bail. He had been caught with an illegal gun while riding in a stolen car. He was released in 1993, after the firearm charges were dropped and bail was reduced. Months after that, he was held for a robbery in Chaguanas. Last year he was charged for rape. Rudy does not believe he committed the rape. The robbery and rape charges are pending in magistrate's court.

Michael said he had given up "the life" – for now. "Is only one thing could make me go back. Is one thing I will die for . . . and is only one thing I living for now." He pointed to his daughter, Teresa, a chubby one-year-old, who was playing on the couch next to him.

He wanted his daughter to grow up "in the right way" but could not specify what that meant. He said he had not made any clear plans, except to work hard.

Michael had lived with his mother and stepfather in Prizgar Lands, Laventille. He disliked his stepfather and his mother was strict. She wanted him to live "like a girl".

He was the only one who turned out "like this". He smiled. When Michael started attending a junior secondary school, he saw boys being bullied by bigger, tougher students. "I tell myself nobody going to advantage me. I tell myself I real bad."

He heard boys talking about guns and break-ins, money, and smoking weed. He wanted to find out more – and he did. He left home and moved to Malick.

After he was held for robbery, his mother told the court he was beyond parental control. He was sent to the Youth Training Centre, Golden Grove. Released, he never entered a classroom again. He then became a full-time member of the urban gang, led by its Rastafarian antihero.

Since Michael was in short pants he had known the family. He remembers Albert, the leader, giving him money.

"He would come to talk to you in a gown and preaching the Bible. He could get the youths to do anything for him," Michael said.

Asked how Albert reconciled Bible preaching and drug dealing, he repeated the hollow ideology of the drug culture – that people in collar and tie were dealing drugs too and besides, Albert helped send plenty people's children to school.

With Albert's death in 1993, Charles, the third brother, was left to run the show. But one by one, the members of the gang were killed or jailed, until Charles and Michael were left in control of a vastly reduced plundering and recycling drug business. Then Michael and Charles, gang leaders by default, fell out over Rudy.

When Rudy and Michael became close, Rudy's baby daughter, Princess, was about two years old. The child father's had been dead a year. Rudy was impressed when Michael tipped her off that a bracelet she was going to buy from Charles was not really gold.

Since the decimation of the gang, Michael was surviving on "small robbery". Rudy told him she could not love another bandit man. "I had get to like him and I did not want him to be a bandit," she said.

When Charles would send word for Michael to meet him in south Trinidad, Michael would ignore the message. Michael expected Charles to make a move soon. He expected Charles to kill Rudy.

One afternoon Charles stopped Rudy near her father's home and asked her for money. She cut him off short: "I minding you? All you is thief." She flung herself up the road, on her way home, not hearing Charles creeping up behind her. He struck her with a bamboo pole at the back of her head and left her lying there in the street, senseless. Michael was indoors and heard the wallop. He ran outside with his guns drawn but Charles had already disappeared. Rudy lay bleeding from a wound in her head. A friend took her to hospital, where she was stitched up and bandaged and sent home.

After that there were clashes between Charles's friends and Michael's friends. To escape the feuding, Michael and Rudy moved to Arima.

When Rudy became pregnant with Michael's baby, neither of them had a job. Rudy used to drink bush tea alone with nothing to eat some days. After Teresa was born, Rudy got a job in a gas station, cleaning windshields; then she was allowed to open and close the station and handle the money. It was a big step down for her. "It was embarrassing, eh. But what I go do? My child have to live."

Michael would bring the baby to the station for Rudy to breastfeed.

They were living in her father's house, with Rudy's brothers and sisters and their children. Rudy was the only breadwinner in the family. "When I buy a chicken, my sister would cut the leg into about ten smaller pieces."

Rudy was popular with the gas station customers, who tipped her generously. One man used to give her US dollars, which she saved up and hid at home. One day her brother crept through a bedroom window and stole it all.

The gas station closed down, and Rudy was again out of a job. Then Michael found work as a labourer and when he got his first pay packet, last year, he could not stop grinning.

He and Rudy moved out her father's house into their own apartment a few streets away. "I real happy with my boyfriend, yes, real happy," she said again. "I not sorry. True, it was fast money but it could be fast dying too."

XI

Michael missed the old days sometimes.

"You wake up and you seeing Mercedes Benz, Super Saloon. You spend $10,000 in the grocery. You pass through Chaguanas and people stopping to let you pass. Girls rushing to stop the car to get your autograph. I like plenty girls, that's what the life is all about. Plenty girls, fast cars, nice things."

I could not tell if he was exaggerating. His face was almost expressionless. He made no moral pronouncements on drug dealing and drug use, no recanting, no promises. He said his four or five years with the gang were "the best days of my life. Everything was free." The gang lived at Albert's base in the southland, hiding their guns in the cane fields. "It was something like the base at Teteron. You hardly get to go home. You in training, like soldiers." But life was cheap in the ghetto, he said. Youths would cut or shoot a man for no reason other than that it would earn them some stripes.

"Everybody feel they bad. Everybody want they rank. Girls looking at you as a bad man and I want my pips . . . Is you driving a nicer car than me. Is more girls talking to you than me."

He said he had tried telling youths in the neighbourhood that the fast life had its penalties too and that they were "living stupid and dying stupid" but they were too stubborn to listen. "It hurt me when I see fellas get kill, knowing I take them out their mother house and introduce them to the life and I get out. It does hurt me," Michael said.

Rudy had finished running the clothes through the dryer and had come inside to watch *The Young and the Restless* on television, to find out if Nathan got the results of his HIV test.

She reminded Michael that he was through with the banditry. "You would not go back to that, ent, Michael?" she asked, playfully locking an arm around his neck. "Ent, Michael? Ent?"

He smiled with one half of his mouth and said nothing.

XII

Rudy's younger brother, Douglas, was due in court in March, charged with possession of cocaine rocks for the purpose of trafficking. Douglas, twenty-one, said he had not sold any cocaine since the boss went to prison last year. "Not till he come back," he said. He was lolling barebacked in Rudy's apartment. He lived with his father but visited Rudy's street every day because his girlfriend lived there.

He asked Rudy what she was waiting on to cook. Rudy told him to get a job. "I have a job," he said, smirking. "What? Selling cocaine?" she snarled.

Rudy said she was tired trying to talk Douglas out of the life. She also told his girlfriend she was making a mistake getting involved with a drug dealer. "Is my brother, yes, but badness do not pay."

Rudy gave Douglas $200 to buy a pair of sneakers so he would stay away from the drug lord.

Douglas was arrested when police raided the drug lord's house. He had the rocks in his pocket. He had forgotten to bury them as he was supposed to. He started in the drug trade by working in the drug lord's bar and people would come in to buy "a beer and two coffee", meaning two rocks. Then he graduated to selling rocks on the streets.

The following week, he wanted to take back what he had said. "I was only kicking the other day," he said. The new version was that no one had given him rocks to sell; he had bought them himself from an acquaintance and he had no more interest in drug pushing.

Rudy told him to get out of her house because she hated people who lied. I asked Rudy if she would pay his legal fees, as she did when her older brother was charged with robbery. "Over my dead body," she exclaimed. Douglas giggled. Did anything Rudy had said to him make sense? He nodded. Rudy reminded him how many youths had lived fast, brief lives and were gunned down before they could enjoy old age. He shook his head. "I ai not deading now. I deading when I is three hundred years."

Rudy asked him how he would like it if his children smoked cocaine. "I would not like it," he replied meekly. "But if your daughter bring home a bandit man, you ca not tell she who to like."

"No," Rudy shot back. "I cannot tell she who to like but she cannot bring no bandit man in my house."

Epilogue

Nicholas and Sharon were getting married. Sharon wore a traditional white wedding gown, with delicate yellow flowers near the hem. Her maid of honour wore blue. Everyone looked beautiful. The wedding all *Young and the Restless* fans had been waiting for was taking place on the television screen.

Rudy was imagining herself in the wedding gown. "I wish I could get married like that, boy," she told me the next day. She was grating a carrot for a pasta and vegetable pie. She sighed. "The right man will come along." She liked to daydream about a different life. "I wish I could be better than how I am now."

Some of her friends lived in houses with carpets on the floors. She wanted to have a house of her own like that one day, with the bathroom inside and built-in glass cabinets in the kitchen. She often said what she did not get, her children would. But she got scared sometimes when she thought of their future. What if something happened to her? Who would feed them, send them to school, buy them pretty dresses and teach them about boys?

Her greatest fear was that they might be molested one day. She smiled when her girls drew away when adults tried to kiss them. She had taught the five-year-old that no one should touch her, and together they watched a television movie about child abuse.

When Rudy was growing up, she used to think of herself as posh, like white people. Those were the images fed to her by television. "I used to call myself white. If my mother tasted the sauce when she cooking and put back the spoon, I used to throw away the food . . . because you not supposed to do that."

When she built that dream house, she would "play white". She stuck her chin in the air.

Her boyfriend, Michael, a labourer, was never sure when he would be out of a job. Rudy signed up for some ten-days' work.

"I tell myself like I have to get a rich man," she said, wearily. She knew men with big jobs who were sweet on her but they just were not her type, she said. Men in her neighbourhood were either bandits or unemployed. Even the men she knew with legitimate jobs had come into her life through crime. One was a police officer, another a prison officer. She had met them both in magistrate's courts, which she used to visit often when she had drug-dealing boyfriends.

She believed Michael loved her, although he stabbed her in her back with a shoemaker's knife during a quarrel last year. Noticing his jealous eyes following her as she went to the shop to get two bottles of Chubby (soft drink), she said, "That ent love, eh? Tell me."

While she dreams of a better way, there remains a gap between what she says and what she does.

She does not want any more children but she will not use birth control, saying those devices and medicines were bad for a woman's body because "God say to multiply and fill the earth".

Rudy has acquired a conglomeration of religious practices and beliefs for the super-protection she thinks she needs. When she was a teenager, a schoolfriend invited her to an Adventist church. Rudy went there regularly, never connecting what she heard from the pulpit with what she was doing outside. Dexter, the drug dealer, was her boyfriend then. She was baptized recently in the Spiritual Baptist tradition, and believes if her sister had done that she might not have been chopped. Later this month, on a special day, she intends to light candles in nine different Catholic churches. She read certain psalms and prayed to St Michael, who she said had special powers to grant petitions. She said she prayed for protection, for her children to "grow in the right way", and for that dream house.

She talked about going "foreign" one day. She had lots of relatives in New York. She had some savings in the bank for her children. That was money she had stashed away when she was living with Bobby, who used to shower her with cash and gold, until he was shot dead.

Pressed for an answer on exactly how she was going to achieve all that she talked about, Rudy said, "The way I saving, I could make it. I will band my belly when I do not have anything to cook . . . Anything I pray for, I notice I does get it. I'll get out of here one day."

Acknowledgments

This story took place in 1996 and was first published in the *Trinidad Express*. What appears here is an edited version.

Note

1.   In Trinidad this refers to taunts.

Section

VII

Made in the Caribbean
Constructing Gender

24 Grandma's Estate

SISTREN WITH
HONOR FORD-SMITH

I am four years old: a child facing the southern horizon, standing back to the anger bouncing between the brown woman and the white man. The water is shallow enough to make bubbles that reflect like stars on the sand below. I am standing in the harbour with the blue mountains behind it.

The man is my father; the woman, my mother. He tried to take me away. He said we were going to Cuba on a sailboat. Mummy found out and came to the sea. She stopped the car. While they quarrelled, I paddled. Then she lifted me gently out of the water and we went home to Grandma's house.

He never came inside the house again after that. He came on Sundays only. We skipped over the wavy green tiles on the verandah or played in a sand pile under the mango tree. One day, he built a big castle out of the sand and told me he was going to London. He gave me '78 records – "Little Darling" and "Rip it Up". I kissed him on his prickly moustache and he went away and never came back.

The world it seemed was peopled by women. Grandma, aunts – like Belle (who they said was hiding there from her husband because he beat her) – Ivy, the cook and my mother, who it was plain to see, knew everything there was to know on earth. Every afternoon I waited for my mother to come home from work. Sometimes she didn't come till after dark. Sometimes she didn't come till the next day. I would stand on the verandah ledge, holding on to the green pole that held up the awning, and watch all the cars go past on Hope Road. I thought she ought to be a teacher instead of a doctor. She said she couldn't because she had no patience and too many patients to look after. Often she went out in the middle of the night. I woke when the phone rang or sometimes I slept till the door slammed. Then I put my foot down from the bed very carefully. Duppies and other nameless shapes lived under the bed. Even if the lights were on, you had to be very careful or suddenly a hand or a slapping claw might suck you, feet first, into another world. I was always too quick or I simply confronted them when they weren't expecting it. If I looked suddenly, under the bed, they would up and disappear. Holding my pillow, I tiptoed through the passage into Grandma's room, racing past the cupboard where Boogie Man and Ole Hige lived, climbing high up past the monster-size Ananse that lived between the mahogany legs of her old-time bed, and curled in the green blanket at the foot of her bed till morning.

If Mummy came home early, we sometimes went to London. It was the corner of the verandah and you got there by swing. Mummy said it rained all the time in London. The sun never shone. We didn't see Daddy so we came back by umbrella.

One night I dreamed I went to London. It was dark there. It was just like the corner of Hope Road where I lived. King's House was there and the Chinese shop. The men that sat on the fence at the corner were there too.

Grandma, who was the person I saw most often, lived propped up on five or six pillows in an ex-four poster bed which she had "improved" by chopping off the carved posts. Often she had a piece of sewing by her side and the *Daily Gleaner* folded in four by her stockinged feet. On her bedside table, she displayed a collection of religious tracts, a small flask of brandy and a range of pills, bottles and mixtures. She suffered from an illness she called "the bad feeling". If you asked, "How you feeling, Grandma?" she usually replied, "Ahh, me dear. One foot in the grave and one out. Ah feel mash up yuh see." No one believed her. She came from Westmoreland, a parish I was never allowed to visit, a place Mummy refused to go. When I asked why, Mummy only said, "Because I hate it."

So I would sit on Grandma's bed and try to get hold of the information I thought she must have. She preferred to talk about God or to leaf through the pages of her tattered backless Bible. If I timed my questions badly, her voice would change and she would deliver a long evangelical sermon and oblige me to pray to be more obedient each day.

One day a torn photograph fell from between the pages of the Bible.

"Look at that! Ah find di snap of Mammee at last."

"Give me," I said, for Mammee was her mother and I heard about her.

"Is di only one ah have. Yuh can only look at it. Come back here at once. Doan put yuh dirty finger marks on it."

I held up the picture to the sunlight by the big sash window. An old black woman sat in front of a tiny house cotched up on stones. Her mouth, without teeth, scooped inward like a closed cave. Her hair was wiry, with huge steps in it, each ridge carefully running uninterruptedly around the entire head, a long dress with a pattern of flowers, hands which hung empty and limp-wristed from the pair of old lace-up men's shoes.

"Was she a slave?"

"Don't be rude!" my grandmother said. "Give me that picture at once!"

"What happen, Grandma?"

"Look how long slavery over," she said, stitching and stitching the hem of my shirt. ("Take up a little bit of the top and a little bit of the bottom," she always said.) I looked at the picture; it seemed very old. She had no other pictures like this. She had in fact no pictures, except one large one of my uncle Dick and another of Jesus. It seem natural that I should connect the picture with the only bit of history I had learned.

"No," my grandmother was saying. "She was not a slave."

"Was her father a slave?"

"No, Ella."

"Was her mother a slave?"

"No."

"Was her father a slave?"

"No."

"Was her mother a slave?"

"No."

"How come, Gran?"

"They were poor, but they were not slaves, Ella."

"Why?"

"They were not slaves."

"What were they then?"

"Must Satan get into yuh dis morning," she said.

"Tell me, no man," I persisted – and finally . . .

"Her father was a freemason and an apothecary."

"A what?"

"Yuh see? Now ah tell yuh and yuh doan even understand." She turned over, sat up slowly in the bed and dangled her feet over the bed as if she was going to go.

"But what is it?" I followed her, my bare feet squeaking on the shining mahogany floor board. On the verandah she tried to escape me by lowering the large green awning against the evening sun.

"What is it?"

She dropped a phrase like a seed from the cracked brown pod of the leafless dry Women's Tongue tree.

"Something like a secret society."

"Oh."

"But his wife was fair," she added quickly. She never said white, black or coloured or Negro; always fair and dark. I followed her back to the bedroom. She decided to go on a little, not sure if she was doing the right thing.

"When she was to marry, Mammee said, everybody in the district wondered how come she could marry a man like that. His mother was a pure Negress."

"How come?"

"They were uncouth mountain people. He was not a slave," she said. "Now go take up your reading book."

Mountain people. Who were they? I had never heard of anybody called a mountain person before. Every week a higgler from the hill came selling vegetables. Her skirts were just like Mammee's in the picture. I imagined Mammee riding to town on the back of a mule or donkey, her feet trailing in the dirt.

I packed leaves of croton and pimento into a basket I found in the kitchen. I twisted a piece of cloth into a cotta and put it on my head. I placed the basket on top of it and practised walking while balancing it on my head. Then I stepped off down the pathway, arriving with my produce under Grandma's window. "Lady, Lady, yuh want anything to buy, maam?" I readjusted the basket, which proved difficult to control.

At first there was no answer, so I repeated, "Lady, Lady, yuh want anything to buy, maam?"

My grandmother pushed her head through the window.

"Ella! Come inside at once and put down that basket!"

I obeyed.

"What do you think you are doing, Miss?"

"Playing market woman, Grandma," I said, not sure what I had done wrong.

"Never let me see you doing that again."

"Why Grandma?" I asked. "What is wrong with market ladies?"

"Ladies? They are not ladies. They are women. Go and take a seat in your room."

I wondered what the difference was between a woman and a lady. I began to think of all the females I could and theorize as to whether they were a woman or a lady. I wondered whether my mother was a woman or a lady. I wondered if Ivy was a woman or a lady. I knew that Mammee clearly was not a lady, since she was a mountain person. So I wondered if ladylike qualities were born in you, or if you learned them. I meditated for a long time about this.

If higglers were women and women were not so good as ladies, perhaps women were bad ladies. I'd heard Grandma say Mummy had brought disgrace on the family by carrying on with my father. I supposed my mother was a woman. But I really didn't know. I wondered if it had anything to do with colour or the way you spoke.

Grandma used to speak of people having good hair and bad hair. One day I asked her what bad hair was. She said it was what the ordinary people had. "Oh," I said, "so good hair is what white people like you have."

She laughed.

"Poor me, I'm not white." She looked white to me. She was certainly whiter than Mummy, and her black hair was long and straight like Ivy's. "Uncle Dick is the only white one in the family. Your mother isn't white." (I thought, "How can that be, since Mummy and Uncle Dick have same mummy and same daddy?") "You must remember," she told me, "you are not white; you only look white."

I looked at myself in the mirror and scrutinized myself for a patch of dark skin under my arms or on the back of my legs. It was true that I had a lot of moles. Perhaps there had been an accident and the colour that should have been evenly spread out had condensed into little dots here and there. I peered at my nose – it was dead straight. My lips were thin. I compared my nose to other noses. I checked my hair – it was brown and long and soft. Yet I was not white. I concluded that white was not a colour.

In the photograph of my class clustered round the plump (bleached) blonde teacher from England, there are only three children with dark skin. It was a very old-fashioned school. The moment you entered the gates you knew something was wrong because it was filled with the uneasy silence of terrorized children. The classroom was in an open shed behind Miss Butler's house. After the bell rang, we rattled off "Our Father" and got down to the hours of spelling, dictation, addition, subtraction or multiplication. There was no poetry or stories. No music. No song and no games. We existed in fear of the possibility of a visit from Miss Butler. She was a tiny red-haired old lady with wire-rimmed spectacles and a thin red hairnet that almost matched her hair. She always appeared unexpectedly in order to chastise the condemned among us who had written what she called "bosh" in her books. This was very easy because the books had a vast quantity of lines in them. There were lines you couldn't write below, lines you wrote between and lines you had to touch with some letters but not others. When she visited, the bosh-filled exercise books came flying through the room like uncharted missiles. They usually hit the innocent.

It was easy to go wrong with the children too, at Miss Butler's. You could, for instance, be caught and tortured as a spy by the gangs of older children who roamed the yard in break time. Once a gang of boys captured Daniel, an English boy, who was "guilty of drawing pagodas and flowers", they said. They picked him up by his feet and his arms and swung him through a pile of dog mess one hundred times. Me and my friend Bridget Chang watched them from the back of the shed. We were angry, but we could only feel righteous for they were stronger in number and force than we were. We could do nothing about Daniel. After that, I hated Miss Butler's and missed my first school where the days had been filled with carnivals. Mummy and I had to stay there because everyone who did passed the scholarship.

One lunchtime I waited for hours by the school gate where they came to collect me. Nobody came. Bridget Chang's father came for her and then all the others gradually disappeared. Then there were three of us left. I watched nervously, praying that I wouldn't be last. About fifteen minutes later, I was the only one sitting under the lignum vitae tree with my lunch pan. I watched the cars pass without stopping. The trees around me stood tall and still with a cold silence different from the silence of the terrified children. I walked tentatively down towards the gate and peeped out to see if Mummy was coming, but there was no sign of her.

Groups of primary school children ran past laughing and chattering in their blue and white uniforms. I watched them disappear around the corner by the clock tower at Half Way Tree. I wished I could walk out on the road like them and take the big silver and green bus, but it was forbidden and I had no money for the fare. I had only been in the bus a few times, always accompanied by someone. I thought it a superior mode of transportation because from it, you looked down on the cars and the people. I didn't mind the long wait at the bus stop because the road was like a magic procession to me. At home, I still spent hours swinging from a steel bar on the verandah and watching from a distance as it passed. Cartmen passed riding on drays filled with coal or bottles. The bread van clopped past early in the morning drawn by mules. Cows mingled with the traffic on their way to the pasture opposite. The fish man came by shouting "Fee! Fee!" On Sundays, truckloads of Poco people passed beating tambourines and singing loudly. Sometimes I missed them, only running out on to the verandah as the music receded up Hope Road.

Now I watched the people on the road not knowing what to do. Grandma's house wasn't far away but I didn't know how to get there. The hours passed and still the world continued on the road, while I sat in the empty yard. I began to wonder if I was adopted.

I had thought this before and asked Mummy but she had denied it; maybe she was telling an untruth – she was so much darker than me. Perhaps I wasn't really hers and she had chosen this moment to abandon me. My stomach churned and my hands were clammy. It seemed to me the day would never end and I would sit in the empty garden alone beside the busy street forever.

Someone was clapping. I turned round and saw Miss Butler's helper calling me.

"Come, me love, come." I ran to her, crying now, and put my face in her damp apron. "What happen darling?" she said. "Dem figat yuh? Never mind." She took me into her kitchen smelling of kerosene oil and phoned my mother, who had been called away to the hospital. A nurse came to pick me up and I went home.

I was twelve years old when Jamaica gained independence. I knew nothing about the strike of 1938 or the birth of the political parties and trade unions. Our West Indian history consisted of Spaniards and slavery. Inside drawing rooms, I gained a vague impression from overheard conversations that Norman Manley was a man of integrity who couldn't communicate with the masses, that Busta his cousin was a ginnal, that politics was not something one immersed oneself in totally if one was a truly decent member of society. Something about power corrupts and encourages violence.

I watched the independence ceremony from the top of Beverly Hills, a new upper-middle-class suburb where my uncle now lived. We could hardly see the huge fireworks (one was called "the waterfall") because someone's mansion jutted out, obscuring the National Stadium, where the ceremony was held. It was thought to be better to watch from the hill, "away from the crowds".

To tell the truth, I wasn't much interested anyway. There was little incentive to be interested in the life around me. I had retreated from the splendid contradictions of my early childhood. At first, my fantasies were imitative of what I saw around me, but when this was permitted, they altered gradually to imitate the life of Canada and America that I read about and longed for. I used to come home from school and change. I could hardly wait for my grandmother to disappear so that I could begin constructing my personal world. I married Elvis Presley and Richard Chamberlain most frequently, although occasionally I also married Ricky Nelson. I went to live with them in America, flying there after publicly renouncing my career as a movie star. I played all the roles in my fantasies, imitating the voices of the actors in the Australian soap operas like *Portia Faces Life, Doctor Paul* or *Life Can Be Beautiful,* which daily were broadcast on the radio. I measured my speech against their accents. My way of speaking seemed flat and cumbersome and so, in my scenarios of eternal romance, I did my best to imitate the English of Portia or Dr Paul. It was clear to me that real life was to be in a future world where people spoke like them and not like Grandma or Ivy.

At St Andrew High School for Girls, my fantastic American future was balanced by a curriculum steeped in the British past. Looking back, I realize that our education attempted to inculcate in us the rationalism of the European intelligentsia. We were being equipped to become women who through intelligence and education have the right to take our place among the men who sit at the top of their professions. It was liberal in that it prepared us to become women with work that would earn us financial independence and thence emancipation. There was nothing in our education which confronted the needs of the private world. We never spoke about class or about relations between men and women or about the world of rearing children, the aged and the ill. It implied that those women who inhabited the inferior world of the home were, if not stupid, certainly beneath us. Only in drama club, after school, where we improvised emotional and physical situations, was anything connected to our real lives. Our education did not unravel the veiled irrationality which had entwined our past history with unmentionable contradictions. We learned, at least, equally from the things the school left unsaid and from the relations and organization of the school. Why else would all our seating arrangement be colour coded. The white girls sat together. So did the brown, the black middle class and the few black working-class girls that had filtered through the Common Entrance Exam.

In third form, they gave us *Jane Eyre* to read. It was the only piece of literature in which there was any mention of the Caribbean. It was also the only book by a woman which they had given us to read. We liked the bits about school, and then we came upon the mad heiress from Spanish Town locked up in the attic. At first we giggled, knowing that it was Jane we were supposed to identify with and her quest for independence and dignity. Then we got to the part where this masterpiece of English literature describes Bertha Mason as "inferior, blue skinned . . . etc.". Someone was reading it out loud in the class, as was the custom. Gradually the mumbling and whispering in the class room crescendoed into an open revolt with loud choruses of "It not fair, Miss!" Miss admitted it seemed unfair, but she went on to do nothing with that insight. I took the book home and finished it. It wasn't set for homework but I couldn't put it down. I skipped the part after the interrupted wedding scene, anxiously looking for a chapter, a paragraph or a sentence, that might redeem the insane animal inferiority of the Caribbean. It was a woman's novel and I had liked so much of the earlier part, but I couldn't stomach the way I had been relegated to the attic. I felt betrayed. Dimly, a few pages in the novel had spoken to my life in a way which most of the nonsense we wasted our lives on at school did not. I remembered the contradictory conversations with my grandmother. The conflicts began struggling to come to the surface of my subconscious and be resolved. Bertha Mason forced me away from my fantasies for a moment, and I vaguely glimpsed the possibility of a richer literature that revealed and illuminated the aspects of life that seemed covered forever in the unspoken.

"Why is it," I asked my mother at dinner, "so few Caribbean women have written books or painted pictures?" We were sitting round the mahogany table. Carmen had already served the vegetables from the left and had disappeared into the kitchen. You rang a silver bell or shouted (considered unladylike) if you wanted more. Mummy was quiet for a while, as if she couldn't think of an answer. She looked faintly embarrassed. Then she said, "Because they don't have time. Bringing up children takes all their time."

I couldn't see what bringing up children could have to do with it. I was fiercely proud of my mother, who everyone described as "clearly exceptional". She had been island scholar and seem to manage doctoring all right with the help of Ivy and Grandma and Carmen to look after the house. I couldn't imagine that writing was any harder than doctoring.

"It doesn't take up all your time."

"No," she said and paused. "But there were other things I wanted to do." Carmen came in with the tray. I helped myself to some more spinach.

"Like what?" I asked.

"Research. I wanted to do research."

"Why didn't you?"

"I started, but to finish would have meant going back to England. I'd have had to leave you with Grandma. I decided against it."

"What was it about?"

"Sickle cell anaemia."

"Why don't you do it now?"

"It's a bit late for that now, dear. Anyway I think bringing up children is just as creative as writing books and doing research." I swallowed my chicken and thought about it. As far as I could see, the rest of the world didn't agree with her that it was just as creative. I didn't know what sickle cell anaemia was, but I felt deeply disappointed, as if an opportunity had been lost for the world. Mummy had always seemed to me to know everything, to have infinite power and freedom, but now somehow like the woman in the attic it had been contained. She was limited and restricted too. I felt angry about it, but I wasn't sure who with. I couldn't work it out so I stopped thinking about it when Carmen came in again in silence with the tray to clear the food away.

In front of my eyes the city had begun to change. The familiar wooden houses were burned down or knocked down. Where large pastures had been, concrete hot-houses multiplied. Wherever there was a gully, squatters improvised houses from cardboard and zinc.

My mother became ill from overwork and so we went to live with my uncle in Beverly Hills. The houses there were big and concrete with lots of grillwork. My uncle's was big, concrete and white with lots of grillwork. Mummy and me lived in the flat in it. Everyday driving up the hill we passed a gully at the bottom where people lived, straddled by a huge billboard advertising Coca Cola. Now I overheard other conversations . . .

" . . . going to Miami for the weekend . . ."

" . . . building himself a private army . . ."

" . . . man to murder another . . . costs five shillings . . ."

" . . . raped in front of the children . . ."

" . . . guns . . ."

My uncle's house was guarded by several cross Alsatian dogs in case of a burglary. The house next door had been held up by masked gunmen and my aunt was afraid they would come to our house next. The men in the family began to carry guns. Once my cousin came to dinner and put his on the side plate. Nobody mentioned it and we went on eating as if it wasn't there or was a piece of salad and couldn't kill people.

People in Beverly Hills began to erect more huge and elaborate grills around their windows. At night, I listened for the inevitable squeak or bang that might herald the coming of a burglar. The rest of the time I lived in a world of *Seventeen* magazines, Mills and Boon romances, hair rollers and continued fantasies of my movie-star lovers.

My cousin Jennifer (three years older) and I were marooned at the top of the hill, absolutely dependent on our parents to take us to the few places we were allowed to go. I had been held up on the street, so we were not allowed to walk down the hill. Only Carmen walked up and down it. Our limited freedom of movement was even more tightly curtailed now, in an effort to prevent us from facing the scourge of rape or teenage pregnancy which had visited itself on the family, to the great shame of Grandma – who seemed to take it as a question of personal failure. I was bitterly resentful of my confinement.

I acquired a boyfriend at about fifteen. The relationship was carried on in lengthy telephone conversations in the afternoon before Mummy came home from work. Somebody at school smuggled notes to me from him. We danced at parties, caught glimpses of one another at a distance and met at the home of a friend who had a trusting mother. And we kissed.

Carmen was my confidante in this relationship. By now we were living in the old house with Grandma again and I was not even allowed to play music on the record player because it "confused her brain". Carmen was an ally who took messages from the boyfriend and told me about hers. She was the only working-class person I knew. I would sit on the concrete steps of her sand-dashed board outroom and she would tell me about her Saturday dates. She was fat and on Saturdays she always wore a wig and miniskirt and high heels to meet him. She was very young but she had children who lived in St James with her mother. She felt no obligation to her former baby-fathers and cussed them because they didn't support their children. I had been taught in church that having children outside of marriage was wrong. I couldn't see anything wrong with Carmen; in fact I envied her what I thought was her sexual freedom. Inevitably, our conversations were interrupted by my grandmother shouting "Carmen!"

"She no believe we should a get no time at all," Carmen grumbled to me. She quarrelled plenty with Grandma. "Don't hale at me, Maa! Doctor say I supposed to get some time before dinner." I was on Carmen's side on this issue. Her apparent sexual freedom was undercut by her position as a domestic helper and her total responsibility for her children. She earned about four pounds a week, and I wondered how she made it stretch.

These things were simply observed and stored. Nobody seemed to think they meant anything and so I thought my observations silly too. I absorbed the world around me like a sponge. I had no tools to make a pattern of my observations.

It was September and the first day of term after the O level exams, which I passed. I walked across the dusty school yard, late but laughing loudly – the privilege of a sixth former.

"We have a cute little guy teaching us history," my friend Sharon told me. "He's young and he wears corduroy pants and psychedelic ties." There was only one other male teacher in the school. So the addition of a second man – especially a young man – filled us with excitement. Mr Phillips was a "white" Jamaican with beady eyes, mousy hair and a tiny build. To tell the truth, his lectures on Tudor England were rather boring, but his comments before the lectures and at the end intrigued and sometimes shocked me. One he spoke of a Rasta friend of his who had given him a gift of a painting. A Rasta man? I thought, looking outside and away from the class. I had heard that they preached peace and love, but had no idea what that meant. Grandma was convinced that they were the souls of violence, and if she saw one passing on the road, she vacated the verandah and locked the front door of her house. But Mr Phillips had Rasta friends. I envied him his freedom and his common sense.

When I turned my attention back to the class Mr Phillips had been lured into a current affairs lesson on the subject of peace, love or justice. He was speaking about his experience in the peace movement in the United States, where he had been a student. He told us about the war in Vietnam and how the Americans had invaded on a pretext. He told us about the young people who had become conscientious objectors to the Vietnam War – and the importance of speaking up and demonstrating for what you wanted. He was a pacifist, he said, and justified it by quoting bits of Jesus' Sermon on the Mount. I had never met anyone who believed in something which was against the tacit acceptance of violence as part of a natural order of things – far less someone who was prepared to make personal sacrifices like going to jail for their ideas – as he said he had. The fact that he came from a similar background to mine suggested to me that there might be an alternative to the direction my life seemed fated to go in. Somebody passed the door of the classroom with a transistor radio. A rocksteady song cut through the old colonial wooden building. He leaned against the doorpost which framed the lignum vitae tree in the yard and asked, "Are they telling us anything about our society?" I thought about the music we danced so automatically to at the policed parties of middle-class children and ran the lyrics through my mind. "Going down the road / with yuh pistol in yuh clothes / Johnny yuh too bad / woo ooo . . ."

(gun crime) ". . . fifty-four / forty-six that's my number, pick it up Mr . . ." (jail/police brutality). The songs peeled back the bandages covering the diseased skin of the society. Then I remembered another set of songs, those that abused women for nagging or for not behaving according to the rules the men thought they ought to abide by. I wondered why lyrics that were so original and so immediate about one set of social injustices could be so blind to another. I mentioned this to Mr Phillips, but he changed the subject, adding that of course he thought girls ought to be concerned with more sterner stuff than home economics and the family.

A friend told me that Mr Phillips organized a kind of retreat for youth where there were discussions and debates about some of the things we had glimpses of in class. "You're not allowed to tell what happens, because it will spoil it," she said, looking as if she had some special knowledge. I wanted to go, badly. I could hardly wait to fill out the application.

On the Friday night, I went into a hostel with about forty other boys and girls from mixed-class backgrounds. For the next forty-eight hours we were bombarded with a theatrical arrangement of talks, film, song, discussions, meditation and masses. There was little time for sleep. No wonder we "changed" – though some of us only briefly.

At eleven o'clock on the Saturday night, Mr Phillips entered to give his speech. It was called "The Challenge". He had disappeared earlier so that his entrance through the little "inner" door at the top of the room was a surprise. He had dressed carefully in a pair of dark trousers, a white shirt and tie and dark glasses. I settled myself into a serious mood. This was the moment I'd heard so much about. I listened spellbound as his voice rose and fell with the design of a well-rehearsed monologue. Here he used the parallelism of the Bible, there imagery or rhetorical questions. Here abuse, there statistics. Now he coaxed us, peppering the message with personal experience – "One hundred thousand unemployed in Kingston alone – one quarter the population . . . A young fourteen-year-old girl living in a room with ten others . . . repeatedly raped by her stepfather . . . take up the challenge of life in the breach – a life of taking risks and personal sacrifice – Jesus," he said, "was a true revolutionary because he preached love and the rule of love means a reversal of injustice in society."

The preceding sixteen years of my life flashed through my tense conscious-ness as I listened. I was jerked suddenly from the pages of my *Seventeen* magazine, hair rollers and clandestine matinee meeting as I followed the others into the chapel to meditation in the silence which followed the loud climax of "The Challenge". There, in the chapel with the candles and the murmuring chorus of the community of youth, I thought I glimpsed an existence in which I was no longer at the mercy of imitation America.

As I stood there in the darkness listening to the soothing guitar strumming the hymns written in the languages of pop culture, I began to feel part of a process that I could interfere in and act upon. I only feared that imprisoned in my swimming pool existence I wouldn't be able to.

After that, I became filled with new-found glory. I cut myself off from my old bourgeois acquaintances. I had always found their parties and conversations tedious, but before I had tried desperately not to. Now there was no need to bother. I considered them trapped by shallow, "plastic" existence. Secretly, I think I was afraid that if I hung around with them I might be reabsorbed into their lives, so I steered clear of their parties and their friendship. I would only be friends with those who were also filled with new-found glory. With them I threw myself into what I thought were the superior activities of Christian social action.

I went with my new friends to a youth camp at a primary school high up and deep in the mountains, where a village spread out almost secretly in the crevices of the hills. We repaired the school and took a census of living conditions in the area. We walked up and down along the track covered with jagged stones, investigating the grim living conditions, like the size of people's houses (one or two rooms and wooden), the number of people that lived in them (more than five), the sanitary facilities, the protein content of "their" diet, and the level of ignorance about "basic needs". Later on we joined in the daily life of the community, going to ground, or helping each other with the work activities. I found that weeding with a machete on a steep slope was highly skilled work and much too hard for me to master. My hands were too soft; it pained me to squat over the ground for more than five minutes. We broke stone with women on the road side and I learned that the chips flew into your eyes or cut you if you weren't careful. After a day of that, my hands were blistered. The hands of the countrywomen were as strong and as rough as the bark of trees.

In the evenings, the farmers gathered to discuss the everlasting problems of marketing and land room and unemployment. The meeting were always contentious. The men of the district were articulate and adamant about their problems, but the women were quiet if they came out at all. Yet from what I could see, they were farmers too, as well as housekeepers and mothers. In fact, generally speaking, even the young women in our group didn't speak much during discussions. That included me too. On the other hand, I noticed that when we distributed flour and bulgar from the big bags marked "A Gift from the People of the United States of America", many women were quarrelsome about their share and militant about the manner in which the distribution took place. I couldn't understand this contradictory behaviour, so again I forgot about it.

I traipsed about to the people's church and nine-nights and forty-nights where we played and sang an inexhaustible range of games. In a favourite one, a ring was strung on a rope and smuggled round a circle of hands holding a rope. If you reached for the ring and missed, you got a beating with a belt from someone in the centre of the circle. The beating was very hard. It was an endurance test and an image of slavery in one. Sometimes people would pad themselves with newspaper to be able to "tek di hot licks". When they were discovered, they were ridiculed, the paper was taken away and (if the group could catch them, for they always fled) they were beaten again.

I never volunteered to play but I loved to watch the forty-nights, struck by the creativity and humour of the people which had all the time been there, but hidden by . . . by . . . I wasn't sure what.

I suppose that whole experience must have grown out of the first stirrings of so-called liberation theology. Looking back, it seems moralistic and saturated with paternalistic evangelism. Sex, for instance, was never discussed – neither the act nor the relations which it gave rise to, probably because many of the people who led the camp were priests and doubtless threatened by that whole area of life. Women who lacked confidence rarely overcame their insecurities. In true Christian style, we were taught to ascribe blame to people whose lives had been shaped by social structures they neither understood nor controlled. Instead of helping them to understand the material forces that created those structures, Christianity made them feel guilty. Religion glorified the poor because they had suffered and suffering was supposed to be Christian. It ignored what they really were and their struggles. Still, in the 1960s in our society, it gave me an important chance for some discussion, exposure and activity.

My mother didn't much approve of the whole thing, although she didn't stop me. Intellectually, she was liberal enough because of her professional exposure, but she was rigidly class bound and didn't care much for the idea of me wandering through the countryside with the peasantry and the working class. In addition, she seemed jealous of the activities which took me away from the dinner-time conversations with her. I had become as critical of my family as I was of my friends. As my grandmother grew older, my mother's domestic responsibilities as an only daughter increased. Her success in her work and her rationalism and intelligence cut no ice where this was concerned. It was "naturally" assumed to be her task. Her brothers gave money and advice. Her life became more and more restricted.

I was sitting beside my grandmother on her old double bed. She suddenly put down the *Gleaner* and said,

"Ah dream yuh married to a Bongo man."

"Here we go again," I thought, biting my fingernails and hoping I could find an excuse to escape soon.

"Ah doan like how yuh going on. Instead of looking up yuh looking down. If yuh marry to one of those boys yuh will go right back . . . right back . . ."

"Back to what?" I asked impatiently.

"All my life," she said, taking a tiny sip of the brandy she still kept in a small flask by the radio (it was supposed to ward off the "bad feeling" which, still undiagnosed, plagued her), "ah try my best to be a respectable person. A lady. Ah had ambition. Ah look up. Yuh doan know what I go through to reach where I am today . . . so nobody can't say ah not a respectable person. And now yuh come and yuh just want throw it away. I tell yuh ah could hardly sleep last night when ah see the people yuh come in with."

I shut up. It was useless to try to escape. I decided to sit out the lecture.

"That's why ah marry yuh grandfather. Not because ah love him. (Never tell a man yuh love him – he will walk right over yuh.) Ah married him for protection because ah never want what happen to Mammee to happen to me. Ah doan know how Mammee could do a thing like that. To this day ah hate di word. Ahh, Ella! Yuh doan know what ah go through."

"Do a thing like what?" I asked, confused. To my surprise, her body suddenly became convulsed in sobs. "Never mind Grandma." I felt sorry for her, though I didn't know the cause of her tears. "Never mind." I stroked her black hair but she cried all the more.

"That word . . . Ummngh . . .," she groaned.

"What word . . . ?"

"Give me the brandy and let me wet me tongue." She screwed up her seventy-five-year-old face into a twisted miserable scrowl. I was in great suspense. I knew I was about to hear what I should have heard ten years ago about Mammee . . . "Bastard!" She spat out, "Bastard!" I was afraid. I didn't want to bring on the bad feeling.

"Ah never knew my father." She was still crying.

"That's all right," I thought, "I didn't know mine either."

"At least ah only met him . . . once." Pause. "He was a planter. A white man. They always marry English women, but Mammee was his . . . house-keeper." (Gone the higgler fantasy.)

"It seems," my uncle at the dining room table was saying, "that Mammee married a drunk, the son of a Scottish missionary. According to her, he was so wicked he stole the wedding ring off her finger the first night they were married and pawned it to buy rum. Anyway, after a time, he trampled all over her crockery with his mule and . . ."

"He what . . . ?" I interrupted.

"He rode the mule into the house and smashed up her things and then he disappeared leaving Mammee with the children. I think she had three . . . (later one disappeared in one of those Latin American revolutions and nobody knew what happened to him). Anyway Mammee had to look after them. So she went up to the Great House to work for this man Morris, the planter. A few years later, the drunken husband– his name was Campbell – reappeared and found Mammee with this young baby. Well, Sav-la-Mar is a small town. It wasn't hard to find out who the father was." My uncle helped himself to more coffee.

"Now under British law at the time, a man could sue another man for damages to his property if he had committed adultery with his wife. So Campbell, of course, took the opportunity to make a little money out of the whole thing. He threatened Morris with a lawsuit. Morris had lots of illegiti-mate children. He didn't want a repeat and so he settled the whole thing out of court. I think it was about $3,000. A lot of money at the time anyway.

Campbell pocketed it then disappeared again. The next time Mammee went to Morris for help, he said he was sorry, he couldn't do anymore. He'd given all he could to her husband and that was that. Mammee was so ashamed, she became a bit of a recluse. She took out her teeth and withdrew into her home."

I handed her the brandy flask. "The headmaster was my father's nephew, but ah didn't know. Ah was filling out the exam form . . . and ah put my father's name . . . ah didn't use it. Never used it . . . but ah put it then because ah was little and foolish and exam form had to go away. Ah didn't know it was something wrong. And he came and took it and when he saw it . . . in front of the whole class . . . he said, 'This can't be your father!' And I said, 'Yes it is.' And he said, 'Are you saying that you're a bastard? We don't have bastards in this school.' "

My mother was saying, "I don't know what she knew or what she didn't know. Mammee kept her very sheltered because she was so ashamed. She must have told you the story of how she met him, the father. She's so proud of it. Her single act of rebellion. When she was getting married she arranged with the clerk at Morris's bank to hide her upstairs. He had passed the father a note asking him to meet her secretly upstairs. She hid, worrying he wouldn't come. Then finally she heard him coming up the stairs. He came in, took her on his knee and said, 'So you're getting married!' and gave her five pounds – then he left."

"That's all?"

"That's all."

"Never mind Grandma," I said again, uselessly.

"Ah couldn't go back after that. Ah never got to take the exam, ah never got to finish my schooling." Pause while she cried quietly and I patted her. Deep breath and . . .

"So, ah made up my mind ah would never let a thing like that happen to me. Never. And praise God it never has. Ah never knew my father but ah wanted him to be proud a me and ah never did a thing to make anybody say ah wasn't a respectable woman. But now yuh come and yuh want to go right back . . . Ah doan know how Mammee could have done a thing like that. Ah doan know . . ."

The sun was going down and the heavy cloud turning to magenta as I leaned against the iron railing on the balcony and looked out at the mountains. The phrase "How could Mammee have done a thing like that?" kept echoing in my mind. How could Grandma talk like that about her own birth? How could she blame all that had gone wrong on her mother? I wondered. The depth of her self-hatred shook me. She had spent her life struggling for the approval of her father and that of his class. There was something pathetic about a seventy-five-year-old woman sobbing hysterically over an incident which had taken place over sixty years ago; but there was something maddening about the way she had allowed it to wither her. The more I pieced together the bits of her history I had collected, I cursed my grandmother's inability to question the assumptions on which the actions of her mother and father were based.

Why hadn't she questioned the system which she must have seen was crumbling even at the turn of the century? I wondered. Her story had made me feel more keenly than a thousand books the vital role that the control of women played in the maintenance of power. I couldn't explain it, but it made me furious that my grandmother had accepted it. I was angry that it had never occurred to her to question her father's right to control the profits of his estate when the labour of her mother and others had built it up. She had learned all the rules of colonial social convention by heart. She had vowed never to break one and she never had – but at what cost. She had repressed her sexuality, her intellect, her imagination and the truth about her life. Hence the pills and the evangelism.

"Grandma, you miscalculated," I thought, for she had underestimated the power of the powerless. She had failed to bargain for change. It seemed to me she had been so busy preserving the past that the present had swept past her and she hadn't even noticed. I wondered how she thought my grandfather had managed to get the land he had owned, except by struggling against people like her father.

For both Grandma and me, the meaning of her experience was to heighten the relationship between race, class and sex in our history; but in sixty years or so between her birth and mine, history had given me the space to be angry about her subservience to an unjust system. Since her birth, women had won the right to vote, Marcus Garvey had challenged racism, the Russian Revolution had taken place, and the British Empire had fallen. Sitting on the balcony of my mother's house, I wasn't even aware that I reflected on nineteenth-century Jamaica through a vision that was the child of these things. How different it must have been in Sav-la-Mar of the 1890s. In those days, what were the options of the daughter of a "housekeeper"? Where would the courage to question, let alone to defy, have come from? There were no celebrated examples of courage of resistance. For Grandma, to challenge her teacher would have meant taking a dangerous step back toward the cane field.

So for me, leaning against the grill work, it was relatively easy to promise myself that I would challenge every social convention in which her world had tried to imprison me. I not only had history to draw on, I had my mother's life too as an independent working woman. She had fathered me and I owed no allegiance to any white father on the basis of blood. But I had seen how the love and loyalty of family had strained and restricted the questioning side of my mother's nature, when as single mother and elder daughter she had to turn again and again to them for emotional support on matters of the household. I didn't want that. As the sky darkened, I thought that in my future I would never be the victim of family duty. I wanted the right to love members of my family because of who they were, not because we happened to have the same genes. I knew my work must be connected to all this but I wasn't sure how. I also knew that having a career was not enough to place between the future and all I was afraid of. It had to be something more than just me, but I wasn't sure what. As the lights came on in the hills, I thought about the people I had met there and wondered how their strength and experience could overtake the contradictions which presently governed the world around me. I hoped it would someday, as sure as the era of my great-grandfather had passed. Then I would be released from the attic of my grandmother's subconscious by more than a fantasy.

25 Diary Pages 1980–1990

Petrine Archer-Straw

This paper looks at diary entries accompanying artwork created in 1980–90. Whereas the art work under discussion is irrevocable, the journal lends itself to reinterpretation. In this paper the journal entries are layered with readings guided by seminal feminist writings. These ideas could not have been articulated as clearly when the paintings were first made. Feminist discourse was then little known in Jamaica.

The paintings referred to in the entries are not consciously feminist, but their imagery is gendered. With patterned and decorative surfaces they fit easily into a feminist genre. Their central theme is about female patterns and life cycles, but no other methodology or guideline for interpreting them is obvious. To view this body of work from an entirely feminist perspective is, however, erroneous. They are the product of a complex set of social and personal factors.

The decade represented in the journal saw dramatic political and economic change in Jamaica. In the early 1980s, certainly, debates about democratic socialism versus capitalism, International Monetary Fund directives, foreign-exchange shortages, and especially pocketbook issues of rice, flour and salt-fish shortages – all had greater impact on the Jamaican public's consciousness than feminism.

Artists engaged with all these issues. Jamaica's young, male, so-called avant-garde artists, such as Robert Cookhorne alias Omari Ra, Douglas

Wallace and Stanford Watson, demonstrated their social awareness and tackled these realities through their painting. A loosely interpreted Marxism, black separatism and anti-Americanism held the greatest sway over the artistic imagination.

When women artists addressed social concerns in their paintings and sculptures, their imagery was less direct. Instead, it was allegorized and framed by nature. Their anxieties took the form of doorways (Merilee Drakulich, *View From the Study,* 1983), windows (Hope Brooks, *Window Series,* 1983), tunnels (Marguerite Stanigar, *Journeying,* 1985) and caverns (Laura Facey, *Hunters,* 1983) that seemed to provide escape routes into interior spaces, far from the cacophony of the outside world. The paintings discussed here fall within this genre of escapist imagery.

Since the excerpts are taken from a journal, the authorial voice, the subjective "I", dominates in a way that might not be so prevalent in other texts. That "I" represents a denial of "otherness", the possibility of visibility, of existence outside the male domain, or, for that matter, within it. Yet, it is not used in a combative sense to distinguish the self from other women. Feminist writer Julia Kristeva recognized the use of "I" . . .

> [i]n this weird feminine seesaw . . . swings "me" out of the unamenable community of women into single combat with another woman. It is perturbing to say "I". The languages of great civilizations that used to be matrilinear must avoid the use of personal pronouns: they leave it up to the context to distinguish the protagonists, and take refuge in tones of voice to recover submerged, transverbal correspondence of bodies. (Kristeva 1985)

Yet "I", written in the most intimate of settings – the female journal – might read more like "we" in the recognition that there is commonality within women's experiences. If the artworks appear shrouded in silence, however, it is because there was no clearly defined feminist movement in Jamaica during the 1980s. Then, feminism was a luxury and "female bonding" was not encouraged. That tacit code of silence that seems to be an inevitable aspect of middle-class morality also pervaded the arts. Perhaps one visible manifestation of this was the prevalence of textured and collaged surfaces, visual poetry, graffiti, and layered surfaces that obscured the viewer from a clear reading of a painting's content. This veiled imagery, though enigmatic, was often little more than a smoke screen for disquiet. Many could read beneath the troubled surfaces, but we kept each others' secrets safe.

Gayatri Chakravorty Spivak has exposed the existence of class and race concerns within gender discourse. She suggests that American women dominate feminist issues, and their concerns are removed from the postcolonial realities of "Third World women" (Spivak 1985). Certainly during the 1980s in Jamaica, any Jamaican female artist who indulged in feminist tendencies was seen to be following a marginalized fashion, imposed from outside rather than within our island politic. Feminism was read as being external to the more urgent needs that "structural adjustment" within the Jamaican economy required. Feminism was something one read about in magazines like *Cosmopolitan*: extraneous, frivolous, and alien to a Caribbean culture that still enjoyed a strong matriarchal focus.

Class also dictated visual concerns. During the 1980s, those women who managed to continue creating artwork despite economic hardships were usually from middle or upper-class backgrounds where their financial contribution to a household was not essential. Women who fell outside this privileged category but still continued to be productive, managed to stay afloat by diversifying their work, by making it more commercially appealing, by creating craft items or by moonlighting.

So text, context and class need to be considered when deconstructing the diary entries that follow. My "not-so-hidden" voice is that of a "thirty-something" woman, married, "mothered" and divorced within the decade. I was middle class, career led and, to a certain extent, privileged, since I continued to paint, despite certain hardships.

The following excerpts seem to follow a repeating pattern of death and rebirth. They begin within the shadow of marriage, at that time an unrecognized death.

March 1980: The Pattern

My interest in the pattern began whilst I was still a student. Then, I had both time and freedom to paint. I selected my motif, a small square containing circles and triangles, and went to work repeating it ten times, one hundred times, one thousand times in innumerable combinations of the three primary colours: red, yellow and blue.

> Essentially, I study the pattern as I paint it, from the small to the large, hence I begin with myself and move outward toward a more collective understanding. But

it must begin with me, it must relate to me, it must be part of my reality and understanding. Otherwise I'm drifting. So as my life changes, as my awareness changes and develops, so too the pattern, grows and becomes all embracing. I strive for an understanding of the pattern inside and outside.

My days are quiet, long, and uninterrupted, my work is intense, disciplined, well ordered and ambitious. I set myself a challenge and paint giant canvases covered with this tiny motif. Through working in this manner, I come to understand the other side of the spontaneous creative act, that which occurs at the end of a long and disciplined road, and I love it. I don't just love it, I thrive on it, because that pattern rests me, it orders me. I become it, I personify it. I am pattern, disciplined, orderly and ambitious.

And then life changed . . .

June 1981: Patchwork: The Female Pattern

Patches, memories, pencil, paper
Fabric dinner working being
Kodachrome clicking touring antique
vintage drawing together coffee
bacon, onions classroom spareribs
library loving staying hiding
striving wanting failing winning
Dinner knowing Canvas cabbage
corn beef wine pushing needing
Toast Ice cracking breaking
Friendship making Dying frying
sunsets, winning, wanting
cleaning sweeping brushstrokes
tightening intense Pattern motif
living patches . . .

The initial step was to move that little bit more outside of myself and understand the pattern not just as it applied to me but as it applied to all women. I was functioning as a married woman in a new domesticated lifestyle and I threw myself eagerly into the role of housewife. Slowly I came to see that the female pattern was essentially a patchwork, a piecing together of different facets of life in order to achieve a harmony, a balance.

Only then could I fully appreciate the peculiar nature of women's creativity and the way we develop forms from the small to the large. Previously, I had

Figure 25.1 *Patchwork: The Female Pattern* (mixed media on canvas, 1981)

observed this in my own pattern-making; eventually I came to see this process reflected in other "craft" forms: in the convenient piece of crochet, knitting or sewing taken out at odd moments, or at the end of a long and tedious day.

In my case, my canvases became smaller, drained of colour, pieced together gradually, falteringly, edging their way towards completion. Like a patchwork, it was disciplined work achieved stitch by stitch and for me, it had as much integrity as other art forms such as a still-life in oil paints or a watercolour landscape.

Patchworks, like so many other creative art forms, were traditionally derided. Yet these "crafts" gained my respect with the realization that the patch signified more than a fragment of fabric in a quilt; it was the product of a lifestyle. I found a quote that seemed to summarize all this and I wrote it in

Figure 25.2 *Repetition* (mixed media on canvas, 1983)

my diary: "My whole life is in that quilt. All my joys and all my sorrows are stitched into these little pieces. I tremble sometimes when I remember what that quilt knows about me" (5 March 1983).

A patchwork quilt out of a patchwork life. The patch work was taking place in reality. From waking in the morning, fixing breakfast, hurriedly preparing work, dabbing on cosmetics, jumping into clothes, working in the office. Or at home, preparing the baby, ferrying children to school, cleaning the house, washing clothes. Then, setting the table, preparing more food, scrubbing down the floor, shopping, studying, loving, tidying . . . all activities thrown together to form a patchwork life. I understood it well because I was living it.

I lived it and admired it and it was an achievement to accomplish so much in the course of one day, and visually my patchworks reflected that lifestyle. I was excited by them. Those scraps of material, the torn thought from a diary, clippings from newspapers, all neatly linked with thin black lines, the stitches, and the scratchings of a black ink pen. The act of repetition settled my mind. I was lost in this ordered world. I took comfort in my little patterns. I was content to humble myself to it.

But slowly the spell began to break. I wanted to give this female work its proper status, venerate it and expose it. Yet, as I worked with the pattern, I talked to people, I read, and I considered why the patchwork had to be so fragmented in its execution. I started to resent it. I began to hate it. I became angry. There were things I had not even touched on; the economic factor for instance: that this piecing together of fabric had come about essentially from the need for cheap covers; that patching together was done in an atmosphere of deprivation; that torn edges of fabric and the neatly controlling stitches were not to be considered aesthetically, but rather as the result of an unjust economic system.

There was the fact that the pattern differed according to the economic background of the person living it. There were the women who told me that they resented their patchwork lives, of never having time to pursue one goal or objective. And the other women who avoided the life altogether, for fear of being trapped in domestication and the inability to create at will. Most importantly, there was the woman who helped me see that there was not enough great about this patchwork pattern to venerate. It was so small scale, it was the imposition of a lifestyle, the stifling of human potential.

And although I could still see the worth of the pattern, I came to see the patchwork as a distorted form, an ugly perversion.

> I still stand for the pattern. I still understand the function of the therapy of the patchwork, but I am becoming disenchanted, coming to see it as a sign of bondage and confinement. Each stitch is like another brick placed on the walls of a female prison. How many would break out of that prison and realize their true potential . . . ?

November 1984: Frayed Edges

If I could die
I wish I could
die with
Passion
Not lying

Figure 25.3 *Disquiet* (mixed media on canvas, 1983)

Dying, not seeping
away
Not unravelling
Not fraying at the
edges
let me die from
the intensity
let me burst
let my head explode
I don't want
to fray at the edges
Unravelling
Dwindling
Slip sliding away

And I harboured the anger, shored it up, because I wanted to use it, wanted to make it visual, give it an outlet. And I patched and pieced and patched together, but I also talked and seethed, and mumbled and even plotted.

> And the patchwork for me was wearing thin. The energy beneath the surface of it was so intense that it would burst those seams. I was still tacking and stitching and patching and piecing, while my guts were spilling out quietly. The stuffing oozing out of corners where the stitching had broken loose. The threads were straining, the patchwork was living. Beneath the surface . . . life almost like a chameleon effecting change. The surface was cracking . . . life peeling away a new skin . . . new pattern waiting to be revealed.

Hélène Cixous has couched the female struggle in terms of violence, yet she also recognizes that this violence can be experienced introspectively, through the text which becomes an escape route. In this "anti-land", truth is the only imperative. She admits her anger and that she "has always been at war" (Cixous 1975).

> I called the work *Disquiet* 1983 but what I really wanted to call it was "don't fuck around" but that might have seemed gimmicky and most definitely out of character. But that is exactly what I meant and felt. It was a warning.
>
> And I wasn't just talking about female concerns, I was talking about the patchwork school that I taught in, or the patchwork economy with its patchwork cars on patchwork roads that we all functioned in. I could feel that we were living on the edge, that marginal concerns could become major ones, that the violence was right there, up front. *Disquiet* was both a warning and a threat.

In 1984, I became pregnant. In *Stabat Mater,* Julia Kristeva (1977) discusses the complex issues that exist around the maternal body. It is couched in terms of mystique, defies analogy, yet is the very space in which a new form of ethic "herethics" is nurtured. The sense of alterity I experienced during pregnancy directly affected my visual language; introspection and a sense of temporary invisibility smouldered in tinier and tinier triangles.

1984–1985: Meditation Mats

I don't know how and when the change was effected, but the evidence was there. Perhaps it was that period of nothingness that followed conception, when I created surfaces that just appeared to be ongoing. Those meaningless surfaces were filled with meaningless shapes. An action which became mechanical. Or perhaps it was as a result of the waiting – an essential nine-month wait before creation begins again. Looking back at these surfaces, I do not know how I did them, how I captured the mundane. Yet now I read them anew. I see in them a resolve, a synthesis, and perhaps a personal levelling. I call them "contained energy" – sometimes one work might appear volatile, but for the most part they are meditative.

> I am at the point in the "don't care" phase somehow detached from these strange works – curious myself about their "mat-like", "window-like" formations wishing for someone else to apply the interpretations – offer the concepts – strangely drained – is this how other women feel when their creativity has been sapped? When the children, the house, the career, have had it all, one becomes depersonalized, the product, the offspring becomes the focal point and the self strangely recedes into the background. I look at these works and wonder who did them, what motivated *the person* to do them? But in the final analysis, I'm too tired to care.

March 1986: Magic Carpets

It is difficult to pinpoint when the change came about and *Meditation Mats,* with door-like entries, suddenly gave way to *Magic Carpets* that I convinced myself could and would fly. The first was called *Sweetest Taboo* and I locked into it, a new-found freedom. The dispelling of myth, the idea that one could do "wrong", and that "wrong" was not always "wrong".

Sweetest Taboo came in a rush. It was direct, colourful with an uncharacteristic clarity. It began the series, but it was the only one of its kind. As I settled to my Jamaican realities, my carpets, that I so believed would fly, struggled for their power. I realized my flight was far from literal. My carpets provided for an inner journey – pure escapism – journeying to another country, another life in my head only. I became obsessed with the shape inside the shape, inside the shape, journeying to the heart, revealing a little of what might reside inside, passion, hate, love, God, whatever. The inward flight.

> I am as yet uncertain about what I have found, reluctant to really look at the imagery. I find that I have created an attractive surface – I suppose because in this fantasy world I have no need to acknowledge anger. Now I wait to show them and put them to the test. Will they fly for others as they have flown for me?

Painting, like writing, can invent new worlds. Much of feminist theory has been built on the deconstruction and reconstruction of new realities. Cixous

Figure 25.4   *Black Magic* (from the *Magic Carpet* series) (mixed media on canvas, 1986)

writes, "If all my desire is possible, it means the system is already letting something else through. All the poets know that: Whatever is thinkable is real, as William Blake suggests" (Cixous 1986).

In 1986 I left Jamaica to study abroad. *The Letters I Should Have Written* series came about as a direct response to the dislocation I experienced as a young, black, single parent in England. Interestingly, the diary entry from this sojourn in a so-called First World country smacks of realities that I had never experienced in Jamaica. At home, despite political and economic constraints, one could still feel "rooted" and "protected", by virtue of one's status. England's realities were harsher, my status was ambivalent, more migrant than middle class.

October 1988: Letters I Should Have Written

Painting? . . . For a long time I didn't . . . how could I? . . . painting is after all a luxury and for nearly three years there was no room for luxuries in my life . . . in fact I had died . . . no . . . my imagination had died . . . the rest of me still functioned, it had to. Those years were about survival, hand to mouth living. I vaguely attempted a series of monoprints called *Letters I Should Have Written,* and although the title was poetic enough, there was no room for poetry in my expression. The frames were filled with stilted, stifled imagery. They would have been surface and superficial were it not for the push and pull tensions emanating from the forms. They were cheap and practical, they wreaked of my hardships.

Cixous also talks about woman in terms of race; otherness is blackness and everything that is opposite to white. Woman has been conditioned to see herself as the dark continent where men lose themselves, explore, and act out their fantasies. Being black and female in a "white world" is a double negative that provides for self-consciousness. But recognition of one's otherness is just the first step; self-love is the second.

October 1990: View from My Skylight

Then perhaps a year later, I received a gift of time. Four months in another country, in a village, in a house, in a room with a window that opened onto a sky, a skylight . . . and when I looked through it, I recognized *that space* . . . Wasn't it the same space where my triangles had dissolved into nothingness. Night after night, I lay there wanting to paint that nothingness – knowing that therein lay my

Figure 25.5   *Diadem (The View from My Skylight* series)
                (monotype, 1990)

inner soul. Eventually, tentatively, I started monoprinting images that bore tedious resemblance to everything I'd done before – so scared of the internal longing, I laboured the outer trappings, the door, the window frame, hinges and glazings . . . but the more I lay there, night after night, the more I came to understand the inner sweetness, the intoxicating calm of nothingness, the very poetry of my being. And so slowly I let go . . .

Strangely, its not over now. For, although I could not take those "starry starry nights" back to London with me, since then in the rooms that I have slept, I have discovered my own skylight. Is it possible that somehow I have realized a dream?

Postmodern discourse has questioned the notion of the literary "happy ending". Certainly within feminist texts there has been a rejection of the fairy-tale ending where the princess is saved by a kiss. The journal's last entry in 1990 might suggest that self-discovery brings happiness, yet such a reading would be deceptive. What it provides is a new measure with which to critique one's actions. Although I still treasure the view I found from my skylight, I have not painted since.

References

Cixous, Hélène. 1986. "Sorties: Out and Out: Attacks/Ways Out/Forays". In *The Newly Born Woman*, translated by B. Wing. Minneapolis: University of Minnesota Press.

Kristeva, Julia. 1985. "Stabat Mater". In *The Female Body in Western Culture*, edited by S. Suleiman. Cambridge, Mass.: Harvard University Press.

Spivak, Gayatri Chakravorty. 1985. "Feminism and Critical Theory". In *For Alma Mater: Theory and Practice in Feminist Scholarship*, edited by P.A. Treichler, C. Kramarae, and B. Stafford. Urbana: University of Illinois Press.

26 "We Kind of Family"

MERLE HODGE

When we seek reasons for the sorry state a country is in, we pick, as our chief scapegoat, the family. However, much of the discussion of family that takes place shows that we are a long way from coming to terms with what family means in Trinidad and Tobago. The increase in juvenile delinquency, for example, is to do with some vacuum that has been created "now that women are going out to work". A little reflection will make us realize that this cliché, while it might apply to North America and England and other places that we see on television, becomes quite nonsensical when applied to Caribbean society.

In our region, the only women who might "now" be going out to work are perhaps the women in the upper regions of the society. The bulk of the population in the Caribbean was brought here from Africa and India *to provide labour* – man, woman and child. Women here have always gone to work – first as enslaved or indentured labourers, and after as small farmers, cane cutters, domestic workers, market vendors, seamstresses, washers and ironers, inter-island traders, childminders, sellers of food at the roadside. Later on, as education became more and more available to the labouring population, women began to take up jobs as schoolteachers, telephone operators, nurses, clerks and so forth. There was never a time in Caribbean society when women did not go out to work.

The second cliché is: "Now that we have so many single-parent families . . .", which, of course, is a euphemism, a nice way of saying: "Now that women are making so bold as to have children without getting married . . ." Here, again, we are labouring under delusion. Women in the Caribbean (Afro-Caribbean women, specifically) have always been a little sceptical about the benefits of legal marriage, and have never been altogether convinced that there is any obligatory connection between childbearing and marriage, despite centuries of pressure from various agencies. As for the usefulness of the term "single-parent", when we look at our actual family systems, we might discover that Caribbean children, even when their mothers are not married to their fathers, are seldom brought up by one person alone.

In the Caribbean, traditionally, a family has meant a network of people, not just two parents and their children. However, our traditional family systems have not been given any recognition or value, while the nuclear family has been strenuously promoted. As a result, that limited concept of family may well be taking over. If there is, indeed, any increase in single-parent families, one of the causes will be the trend away from the family network, towards the isolated nuclear family. When one parent is subtracted from a nuclear family (for any reason – death, separation, divorce, migration) what you have left is a single-parent family. On the other hand, a family network minus one parent is still a family network.

The third cliché is this one: "From time immemorial, the man has been the breadwinner . . ."

Once I witnessed a lesson in an infant class that was amusing but at the same time very sad. "Who is the head of your family?" Miss asked. There was silence: the children did not know what their teacher meant. So the question was rephrased. "Who goes out to work and gets money so you can buy food and clothes and everything that you need?" Immediately thirty or forty eager voices bellowed their answers, all at once, and it was like the Tower of Babel, for they were saying different things: "Mammy! Granny! Ma! Mama!"

"Wrong!" the teacher scolded. "It is your *Daddy* who goes out to work and gets money for the family to buy things. So tell me now, who goes out to work and gets money . . ." Now the infants, considerably subdued, answered obediently: "Daddy, Miss."

Wherever in the world it might be that traditionally the male is *the* breadwinner, in Caribbean tradition, breadwinners are both male and female.

The first step towards improving family life in the Caribbean must be to face the reality of family in our society, so that we can work with what *is*, rather than what some of us think should be. If our goal is to protect and promote the institution known as family, then we will have to address all the forms of family that exist in our milieu. If we are only willing to count as a family the group that consists of a married couple and their children, then we may be excluding the majority of people.

When we give pompous little speeches about "family values", we are not talking to those people. When we campaign for better family life, people who do not think that they live in a real family do not have to listen. All the guidelines for good family are aimed at making a good nuclear family. "The husband should do this," we say, and "The wife must not do that." What messages do we have for the other kinds of family that people live in? The message is that they are wrong, as the teacher said. They represent "the breakdown of the family structure", another of those misleading clichés. There is no one family structure, here or anywhere else in the world for that matter. There are many.

A family is an organization of people that provides for its members' material needs (food, clothing and shelter), and their emotional needs (approval, acceptance, solidarity and warmth), and socializes the young. There are different kinds of groupings that perform the functions of family. In the Caribbean, the term "family" could refer to one, or to all, of three organizations: a sexual union and its offspring; a household; or a network not confined to any one household.

Sexual Unions

The types of sexual unions to be found in the Caribbean setting are:

- the visiting relationship or nonresidential union in which a man and a woman may have a sustained, often permanent relationship without living together;
- the common-law union, or concubinage, in which a man and a woman live together without legal sanction;
- the legalized union, or marriage.

Often these unions represent three stages of person's life. A visiting relationship may lead to a common-law union, and then after years of concubinage a couple might decide, quite late in life, to hold a wedding – with all their grown children, and sometimes grandchildren, in attendance.

Households

A household is a group of people living under one roof and cooperating to perform the functions of family. In a Caribbean household may be found any one of the following organizations:

- A nuclear family, that is, a unit produced by a sexual union: parents and offspring, or one parent and offspring.
- A three-generation family, which comprises grandparents, their adult children and their grandchildren. The oldest generation may be represented by one grandparent (usually the grandmother) or both. The middle generation may include grown children who never left home, or who left and returned home after separation from a sexual union. The children may be the offspring of adults who live in the household, or their parents might live elsewhere, either abroad or simply in another sexual union into which they preferred not to take their children. Some of the children may be godchildren or informally adopted children. Adoption, usually not formalized by any legal process, is a traditional feature of Caribbean family life, even in the poorest families.
- The three-generation family tends to develop around family ownership of house and land. In the Caribbean there is not the pressure that is exerted in the Western setting for every individual, on reaching adulthood, to split off and form a new and separate family unit. It is quite acceptable for grown offspring to live in the family house or on the family landholding until death. This kind of family organization ensures that old people are not abandoned and that unemployed adults can engage in productive work, that is, housework and child care, towards their own upkeep. It also means that children whose biological parents have not set up house together are not the poor "single-parent orphans" we imagine them to be.
- In a *functional* three-generation family, children enjoy certain advantages over those who live with their two parents in an isolated unit. Yet we are pressured into thinking that the best possible form of family organization is the nuclear family. No positive focus is given to our tried and tested three-generation family.

- A household may consist of grandparents (often simply the grandmother) and grandchildren, with no representatives of the middle generation, neither parents nor uncles and aunts. Parents may be living and working elsewhere to support the household or may have entered new unions into which they choose not to bring their children.
- A "sibling household" may also emerge out of the joint occupation of family property. When the oldest generation dies or migrates, the result may be a household of grown siblings with or without children.

Networks

Neither the sexual union nor the household provides a complete definition of family in the Caribbean. The functions of family may be performed by a far-flung organization which includes people living down the street, or in another village, or up in Toronto. Such a network might include the following:

- relatives who have migrated from rural to urban areas or to a metropolitan country to support the household by sending money, clothes, food . . . the famous "barrel";
- nonresident fathers who give material and/or emotional support to their children: such a father may even exercise some authority; for example, he may have to be consulted on matters such as the choice of a school for the child;
- nonresident sexual partners: the visitor in a visiting relationship;
- godmothers who sponsor godchildren: in the Caribbean the godmother-godchild relationship is a special one and often includes an economic commitment;
- brothers and sisters, or other blood relatives who have close bonds with members of a household;
- *macommeres*: women friends who, for example, throw sou-sou[1] together, give each other emotional support, and help each other with child care; for example, hundreds of Caribbean women traders who move vegetables and other merchandise up and down the region depend upon networks of family and friends to ensure that their children receive uninterrupted care while they travel to carry out their work.

What do we know about these networks? What value do we attach to them?

Caribbean Family Values

There is the perception that with regard to family in the Caribbean, "anything goes". On the contrary, even though there is variety, the number of forms that we practise and accept is limited. There are certain arrangements that we would find unacceptable, for example residential polygamy or communal marriages. We may turn a blind eye to men having relationships with two or more women at the same time, so that we do not entirely condemn polygamy. However, we would find it distasteful for more than one woman to *move in* with a man. Similarly, we have no accepted tradition of men and women living together as interchangeable partners, meaning that anybody within the household can mate with anybody, and all the children are reared by everybody – a family form that has been part of human history.

Apart from rules governing the composition of households, we do also have a philosophy of family – our own "family values". The first time I was asked, in the United States, "Do you have a family?" I was a little taken aback, because I thought that everybody had a family. The question meant, of course, "Do you have a husband and children?" By the American definition, I do not have a family!

In the Caribbean, family is not necessarily organized around a mating couple, and this, perhaps, is the feature of Caribbean family life that has most exasperated those who put themselves in charge of our morals. We may keep our sex life quite separate from our family life: the two are not always associated. A woman with children may enter into a relationship with a man but he does not automatically become her children's stepfather. Her children are in a family – household and/or network – and her men-friends do not have to be incorporated into that family. On the other hand, a man living in a three-generation household or a sibling household might have children elsewhere whom he does not support or perhaps even acknowledge. Yet at home he showers love and attention on his sisters' children!

We have a greater sense of responsibility to our biological family – blood relations – than to the group formed by sexual union. A well-known calypso asks, "If your wife and your mother was drowning / Which one would you be saving?" The calypsonian's solution to the dilemma is that he would save his mother, of course, because: "I can always get another wife / But I can never get another mother in my life" (Lord Kitchener, "Wife and Mother", *c.*1953).

Since we do not see family as something produced by a mating couple, we feel confident that children may be successfully socialized whether or not their biological parents live together until death do them part. In the Caribbean the kinship group is a greater source of stability for children than the sexual union, which, perhaps, we recognize as too volatile a relationship to guarantee long-term security. In our culture the nuclear family, the family formed by sexual union, tends to be linked to a wider and more permanent family network. Children know and constantly interact with family members not living in their home.

Where the nuclear family is embedded in a larger family network, sweeping statements such as the following, made by a minister of social services of Trinidad and Tobago, are simply silly: "Children of single-headed households are at risk of having learning, emotional and social problems when compared with children in two-parent families" (*Trinidad Guardian*, 9 July 1993).

That finding came fresh out of research done in the United States or somewhere similar. When we do our own research on our own society, we will find large numbers of well-adjusted, bright and productive children not brought up in two-parent families. I have one in my house. Our children, however, are regularly exposed to public statements such as those of that minister, and the result may be that problems are created where none would otherwise exist: the self-fulfilling prophecy. Children who are growing up comfortable and content in families that cater adequately to all their needs may begin to develop feelings of embarrassment, a negative self-image and anger against their families when we suggest to them that there is something wrong with their situation and that they are doomed to failure.

Discussions of family tend to focus mainly on its role of socializing children, reflecting the tradition of the Western nuclear family as an organization designed primarily to cater for the needs of children and of husbands. A Caribbean family, on the other hand, is as much an organization for the support of adults as for the rearing of children. As mentioned before, older people, adolescents and unemployed or unattached adults traditionally were not cut loose to fend for themselves, and today Caribbean people, by and large, still feel a deep sense of responsibility for such family members. We are given no credit, however, for this family value.

Attitudes to Marriage

Attitudes to marriage offer another area for research. Among Caribbean people there is great ambivalence towards this institution. Marriage is regarded with a certain amount of reverence, and carries undoubted prestige. Yet many prefer to admire it from afar. To Caribbean women, in particular, its benefits seem dubious. There is a very strong tradition of female independence found even among the poorest and seemingly most powerless of women. Therefore, while on the one hand women may see legal marriage as an indicator of upward social mobility (as expressed in many a calypso, for example: "Call me Mrs Joseph / You got to put handle in mi name" [The Mighty Duke, "Visina", 1969]), they also see wifehood as a kind of handicap, and a wife as a diminished woman.

Another deterrent to legal marriage in the Caribbean may be our history of deeply troubled relations between men and women, long evident in the lyrics of calypso, and exploding in today's economic climate into drastic domestic violence. Yet what do we and our family life experts know for sure about the development of male-female relations in our society? What we are told is that our men are turning violent because they "no longer hold their traditional role of breadwinner", since, of course, "women are now going out to work" and eclipsing their men.

Today women's attitudes to marriage are affected by the worldwide women's movement, which has challenged the unequal relationship that existed within the traditional marriage. Moreover, with increasing access to higher education, women are gaining the economic independence that allows them to change the rules of marriage. They can rewrite the marriage contract, making the relationship a more egalitarian one. Marriage becomes a more attractive option for women when men and women can be equal partners. At the same time, women at all levels of Caribbean society continue to exercise the option not to marry, and so families headed by women remain part of our reality.

Female Headship

The widespread phenomenon of female-headed households is the focus of much negative attention. A characteristic of Caribbean families has always been that headship may be male or female, with women, perhaps, having the edge in actual practice. This is acknowledged in the expression "Yu mother house" (or, in the French Caribbean, *"Kaï maman-ou"*), used to refer to a person's home even when the mother in question has a resident male partner.

Some of the concern surrounding female-headed households is based on the notion that boys cannot be successfully socialized by women. We are warned that boys reared by women turn into wimps and homosexuals. If that were the case, then between one-third and one-half of our present male population would have to be classified as wimps and homosexuals, for, historically, that is the proportion of Caribbean households headed by women! We are told that women cannot discipline boys; but in a society where "discipline" tends to mean physical violence, this must be read as: women cannot manhandle boys. Unfortunately, however, the evidence is that Caribbean women are extremely competent at manhandling all their children, male and female. In addition to corporal punishment, however, "boy-children need strong male guidance". To say that women cannot provide adequate guidance to children is to subscribe to the view that women are morally weaker, a view that is implicit in some religious teachings. The statistics of criminality in our society (or in the world) would not seem to suggest any moral superiority in men.

The ultimate argument against women socializing boys is that these boys will not know how to be men. To express this view is to admit that behaviours seen as male roles and female roles are not, in fact, entirely "natural", and that they are roles that people *teach* children: a man does this and a woman does not do that. If there is anything about male or female behaviour that is natural and inborn, then there is nothing to fear: boys will automatically become men and girls will become women regardless of who socializes them, for their genes will prevail. The fear is, however, that if one does not tamper with human beings in their childhood, the imposed gender differences will begin to disappear, and men and women might turn out to have more in common than we like to think.

Does female headship of families in the Caribbean setting have an adverse effect on boys? Where is the research? There is far too much that we do not know about our family systems. We hear only about their malfunctioning, not about their successes. No human institution is perfect. All family forms are liable to malfunction, including the nuclear family.

Negative Trends

No specific form of family must be set upon a pedestal, and certainly, the intention is not to idealize the Caribbean family. There are cultural features of family life in the Caribbean which are not in our best interest and which we must change.

Attitudes to fertility, for example, need to be addressed. A woman is defined by childbearing, and to produce a large number of children, regardless of the consequences, is for many women a source of self-esteem. These attitudes tend to change when women have adequate access to education and employment and can develop other sources of self-esteem. Early childbearing has become a critical problem in our society, and it may be related, in part, to this traditional pressure on women to declare their womanhood by giving birth. Teenage pregnancy can never be accepted as a cultural trait. The choice of having children with or without marriage has to remain an option exercised by adult women, not little girls. Little girls must also know that one of the options open to them later in life will be *not* to have children at all. That option is not, at present, part of our family philosophy. We firmly believe that a woman must have children, much as a mango tree must bear mangoes!

A much-publicized problem of Caribbean family life is the low involvement of men in the upbringing of children whom they have fathered. This is partly an economic problem, aggravated in times of hardship such as the current period of structural adjustment. A man who has been unemployed for months and cannot even bring a sweet for his child will save himself much distress by simply hiding from the child and its mother. Never before have we heard of so many men being imprisoned for nonpayment of child maintenance.

The third feature of Caribbean family life that needs to be addressed is the use of verbal and physical violence as normal, everyday, accepted methods of childrearing. Only a minority of people expressed outrage when in 1993, in Trinidad and Tobago, a magistrate set some policemen to put a savage horsewhipping on a little boy brought before the court. The number of parents who came out in support of that act of adult violence against a child should give us an indication of the level of violence perpetrated against children in the home. This violence that we have always used as part of the socialization process, reinforced now by American television and the impact of structural adjustment, may well be coming home to roost in today's statistics of violent crime among the youth.

Impact of Structural Adjustment

In seeking to improve family life in our society, we must not throw out the baby with the bathwater. Instead of blaming every present-day evil on the family, we need to find out first of all what the family is and then find out how present-day conditions have affected the functioning of this family.

The women's movement in the Caribbean has sought to draw attention to the fact that structural adjustment is having the most drastic effect on women. Since women in the Caribbean play such a major role in the running of families, any factor that adversely affects women has serious consequences for family functioning. The women's movement is concerned about the female-headed household, not for moralistic reasons but for economic reasons. It sees female headship of families as a perfectly viable option. But women worldwide are the poorest of the poor, and much needs to be done to increase their economic power so that they can better carry out the role of family headship.

Today, however, women are getting poorer. The impoverishment of women is an outcome of structural adjustment, as acknowledged even by the International Monetary Fund and the World Bank. In addition to this, structural adjustment policies have undermined the social services which support women in their family role. Unemployment is also rampant among women, so that they have to turn either to the informal sector (for example, street vending), or to illegal methods of earning a living (such as a drug mule operation).

As previously indicated, the economic role of men in the family is being seriously affected. Men are also being affected psychologically by the economic situation, and this is a major cause of family breakdown and violence against women. It may be that differences in the upbringing of male and female children leave our men without the emotional and spiritual resources that women seem to have, for under the pressure of structural adjustment, it is men who are crumbling. So many of our men have become vagrants, drug addicts, bandits and psychopaths that no amount of lecturing on "family values" will produce the wonderful family life we are expected to display.

The quality of Caribbean family life will not be improved by self-righteous moralizing but by the creation of conditions in which good family life can flourish, in all kinds of family.

Acknowledgment

This paper was adapted from the Ninth Anniversary Lecture for Women Working for Social Progress, 26 February 1994, Port of Spain, Trinidad. We have remained faithful to the style of presentation.

Note

1.   Throw sou-sou: To participate in an informal group revolving-savings scheme.

27 Gender and Adult Sexuality

BARRY CHEVANNES

Qualifying the discussion of sexuality and gender by the term "adult" draws a distinction with adolescent sexuality. Adolescence is the period of transition from childhood to adulthood. From the physiological and psychological points of view it begins with puberty, that stage in life when hormonal changes very rapidly transform the organism into a new being, fecund and possessed of powerful sexual drives that remain throughout most of its adult, mature life. Adulthood, therefore, really begins in adolescence, and the actual passage is only a socially determined matter.

Another way to view the matter is this: as far as his or her power is concerned, the adolescent is different from the adult in one critical respect, namely a lack of experience. It is the garnering of experience which matures and turns an adolescent into a young adult and a man or a woman.

It is quite common in this society for even preadolescents to engage in "sexual intercourse", though, we can assume, it is not until after puberty that the feelings of satisfaction and well-being associated with sex are experienced. It is for such reasons that many men I have interviewed associate the knowledge of sex with the first experience of penetration and ejaculation. Before he had completed his fourteenth year the average male adolescent would have had his first experience of sex, and the average female adolescent, before she had completed her sixteenth year.

Thus it is quite normal for the expression of sexuality to begin sometime in the period we adults generally describe as adolescence. Not to have begun one's sexual life during adolescence is to appear abnormal.

Certain very strongly held values appear to be at work in the Caribbean with regard to sexuality:

Sexual intercourse should begin early. Note, however, that this does not mean that early sexual intercourse is legitimate. Indeed, it is not. Sexual intercourse before social maturity is called "nastiness". By "social maturity" I refer not so much to any inherent quality but to the recognition by society (one's parents, older siblings and the peers of both) of sexual activity. If this recognition is not granted, one is not socially mature. Granting recognition means (allowing one) to have a girlfriend or boyfriend. I suspect recognition is granted earlier in urban than in rural Jamaica. It may also be earlier among working-class than among middle-class Jamaicans. Until such recognition is granted, sexuality is expressed in clandestine ways.

One compelling reason for the early start of sexuality is the danger of ill-health which people feel may result from repression. One's mental and spiritual well-being should not be put at risk by excessive denial. Thus, asceticism is of no value in this culture, unlike in others such as India and medieval Europe. Except for the brief and symbolic excursion into celibacy by some Rastafari, which in any case is not a ritual prerequisite for membership, Jamaicans do not believe it either possible, desirable, or of any special worth to maintain a permanent condition of sexual abstinence. Hence their widespread scepticism towards the celibacy of the Roman Catholic priestly and convent life. On the contrary, they believe such abstinence to be quite harmful, antisocial and antinature. Which is to say, against the purposes of God. Note that the sexual drive is itself called "nature".

Sexuality is fundamentally heterosexual. There exists a great antipathy to homosexuality. For adolescents, too late an interest in heterosexual contact and intercourse is considered a sign of homosexual tendencies, the stigma of which is so onerous that many male adolescents are driven to initiate relationships with girls before they actually want to do so.

Homosexuality is considered primarily a male "disease". This is not to say that women cannot be homosexuals, but they are not referred to as such.

Female homosexuals are called "lesbians", and are the object of ridicule, rather than of the contempt and hostility reserved for males.

The severe displeasure which Jamaicans feel towards homosexuality is well known. In one of the Eastern Caribbean islands a publicly known homosexual once ruefully commented to me that he found Jamaica an extraordinary, beautiful country, but he could never risk living there, so publicly hostile were the people to homosexuality. Much has been made in the United States of reggae artiste Buju Banton's song "Boom, Bye-Bye", which homosexuals there claim is an incitement of violence towards them.

The hostility towards male homosexuality on one hand, and the tolerance of lesbianism on the other, is somewhat curious. One difference between the forms of homosexuality is that anal penetration is possible in male but not in female homosexuality, leaving one to infer that it is the act of penetration which is especially obnoxious. The name "battyman" used for a male homosexual would strengthen this view. However, it is to be noted that anal penetration appears to be a not uncommon practice in heterosexual intercourse. Therefore, one is led to believe that it is not so much the unnatural penetration of the anus as such which is the main source of the aversion, but the "unnatural" coupling of man and man.

As an anthropologist I would like to suggest a perspective which allows another, possibly better, interpretation of this issue of homosexuality – that is, from the angle of symbolic life. In Jamaica, among the symbols used to express the relative places of the genders are the sun for the male, and the moon for the female. These, if not universal, are widely found symbols. In European mythology the moon is always depicted as female, and the sun as male. According to Mbiti (1969: 52), for some African peoples, including Jamaicans (Chevannes 1994: 26, 81–87), the sun is regarded as a male principle, a source of strength and power, light and life. It rules the day. The moon, on the other hand, is the female principle, multiple phased and apparently ambiguous. It rules the night. Together they achieve the harmony of nature by fusing, through complementation, two distinct orders: day and night.

Heterosexual intercourse is likewise a fusion of day and night, the male and female opposites. The famous intuitive artist and Revival leader, Kapo, in an interview with Neville Willoughby, told of a vision he had as a teenager of seeing the moon falling until it touched the water. It was ten o'clock in the morning. When he told his mother and her friends who were all washing clothes by the river, the friends laughed and said, "Yu son want to marry" (Kapo 1977). A man's sexual counterpart is woman, as the sun's counterpart is the moon.

Homosexual intercourse, on the other hand, is "unnatural", without precedent in the natural order. However, so is lesbianism. Were unnaturalness the main or only consideration, hostility would be of equal intensity against female homosexuality, which, as I have said, it is not. As Sandra Bem (1993) explains, because women's activities attract lower valuation than men's activities, not even women's homosexuality is taken as seriously as men's homosexuality. From the symbolic perspective, the difference lies in the order to which they belong, the *order of day* versus *the order of night,* the *seen* or *visible* versus the *unseen* or *invisible,* the *public* versus the *private.* Men's sexuality is "seen", public; it belongs to the realm of the day. Women's sexuality is "unseen" and "private", belonging to the realm of night.

Speaking of heterosexuality in this differentiated way may seem to involve some contradiction. How can the same sexual contact be "public" from the male point of view, but "private" from the female point of view? Obviously, I am not here talking about the act of intercourse itself, which is private and hidden from view. What I am referring to is the social posturing of the sexes. In the Jamaican context, a man (married or unmarried – it makes little difference) who is sexually attracted to a woman may initiate the contact directly and publicly, within the full view of others, without attracting negative sanction, indeed possibly adding to his reputation (Wilson 1969). On the other hand, it is not normal for a woman to initiate public and direct contact with a man she is sexually attracted to. She may employ body language or seek the mediation of a friend, but in the end she must leave it to the man to act. In short, a man's heterosexual initiative may be public, but a woman's will be "private", in the sense of being discreet and subtle. Jamaican folk imagery reinforces this point – man "look" (that is, pursues) woman; but woman "kech" (traps) man. The pursuer tracks, the trapper lures and waits. Man is direct and forthright, woman is indirect and beguiling.

Female homosexuality, like female heterosexuality, belongs to the private domain and is thereby tolerated. The problem then which male homosexuality poses for heterosexual Jamaicans is its claim to belong to the public domain. As long as it remains "private", in the sense in which I have defined it, and therefore approximates female homosexuality, it merits little or no hostility.

That known homosexuals are able to live in heterosexual communities without harm is possible because they suppress the public expression of their sexuality.

The intensity of this aversion, which seems in the Caribbean to be greatest in Jamaica, would then imply a greater weight placed in that country on the public domain as an essential attribute of male identity than elsewhere in the region. But why should this be so? One possible answer could be that in Jamaica the public domain has become or is fast becoming the last or the most important line of a defence that has not already been breached. For example, the attribute of household headship and control over one's spouse is no longer guaranteed a large number of Jamaican men, because of high male unemployment, improvement in the labour-force participation of women, higher female qualification, and the incursion of new ideas. According to recent census data, the proportion of female single-headed households in Jamaica was possibly the highest in the Caribbean. For a large number of men, therefore, the public domain would remain the only major attribute left to sexuality. Public acceptance of homosexuality is thus taken as a threat to an identity under siege, as it were.

The expression of heterosexuality is guilt-free. There is generally little association of guilt with heterosexual intercourse, and this partially explains why intercourse begins early. Where guilt seems to be present is among those deeply influenced by American and European religions which preach against "fornication", that is, sexual intercourse outside of legal marriage, or "adultery". Yet, even here, many will "backslide" into cultural practice rather than "burn". Indeed, if rumour and gossip are to be believed, those who preach against these sins, themselves indulge. One thing is certain: the defrocking and fall from grace of American televangelists for fornication would be only remotely possible in Jamaican culture. It most definitely would lose no politician his candidacy for office and might in fact aid it.

The expression of sexuality favours the male over the female. This explains why men start sexual behaviour on average earlier by two years. Even freedom from guilt is gender related, insofar as it holds true absolutely for the male, but conditionally for the female. For her the condition is the avoidance of first pregnancy. If she becomes pregnant before being granted social recognition as a woman, the parturition itself acts as a *rite de passage* transforming her into a woman. Guilt thus gives way to positive feelings of fulfilment.

Human reproduction is a function of adult sexuality. Both womanhood and manhood are fully achieved not by the act of intercourse but by reproduction. For the woman, pregnancy and childbirth are the fulfilment of womanhood; for the man impregnation is the proof of manhood. Impregnation and childbirth take on compelling force. Women who postpone this in order to pursue careers generally consider it a sacrifice.

As social action, sexuality is subject to relations of power insofar as it takes place between unequal parties. Here I refer not so much to the use of sex to assert dominance, as in rape, but as an arena for playing out gender relations as relations of power. For example, in keeping with the imagery of hunting, male (especially young male) expressions of the act of intercourse are aggressive, as any survey of popular songs would confirm. But women, too, are not content with the role of victim. They are "employers of labour" and can dismiss men for not being able to "do the work". Men are particularly vulnerable in this respect, as such rumours and accusations strike at their self-image and the way they are perceived by others.

Weight is placed on mutual sexual knowledge as a prerequisite to a deeper, more stable and more lasting union of man and woman. It is after and through intimate, including sexual, relations that most people take the decision to "make life together", that is, to approach the world, its opportunities and risks as a single unit.

These values are only part of the wider system of values that shape adult sexuality, starting in adolescence when this system begins to be internalized and to determine behaviour. For most young men and women, the onset of adulthood is marked by distinct features: first, its tentativeness, testing and searching. Males are in search of women with whom they can live, who will not pose a threat to their male self-image or the image which others, mainly their peer group, have of them, but will actively reinforce their dominance. On the other hand, women are in search of men with whom they share mutual respect, freedom and fulfilment, who will honour obligations. Very few succeed at first try. One of the qualities of the Jamaican female which the young adult male is unable to cope with is her assertiveness. Assertiveness takes various forms: disobeying directives, forming parallel relations, fighting back.

In sociological terms, the result is a series of relationships we call "visiting". These relationships are unstable; they form and break by simple agreement of both parties or by the unilateral declaration of one party. Visiting relationships bestow a distinct advantage on the female, in that they allow her to retain her independence. Independence is prized by the Jamaican woman. As the mother of one of the Sistren[1] told her daughter in *Lionheart Gal: Lifestories of Jamaican Women,* there are two things a woman must always have: a wash basin and a bed – the basin, so that she never has to borrow one from another woman; the bed, so that she, not he, can pronounce the fateful words of separation, "kum aafa mi bed!" (Sistren with Ford-Smith 1986: 46).

The second feature in the sexuality of the young adult is the passion of its loving and the scarring of broken love. Both passion and scar remain for life, sometimes as traumatic memories, but more often as reinforcing lessons in gender socialization. The stereotypes held by men are developed and reinforced in this period of adult life.

Adult Sexuality Is Often Multiple Partnered

I turn now to consider a feature of adult sexuality which is only now receiving the attention it deserves, namely multiple partnerships: one man in sexual relationship with more than one woman; one woman in sexual relationship with more than one man.

First, it is important to draw a distinction between multiple partnership and casual relations, using the presence or absence of commitment as the distinguishing feature. Second, the two may be connected, in that some casual relationships may evolve into committed ones, or, in another words, many multiple partnerships begin as casual relations. Third, casual sexual relations, given the value placed on the naturalness of sex, are of little moment and probably occur in all forms of union formations.

This brings us to the "outside" concept. Under the superstructure of state and church, polygamy has been outlawed in Jamaica, but polygyny is not. Available data suggests that the "outside" woman is not as prevalent as the stereotype would have us believe, namely as a practice of all or most men

(Chevannes 1986). However, its highest distribution is found among younger men.

The intriguing concept "outside" applies more properly to the male. Yet it has been known for ages that women also engage in sex outside of the primary relationship. This is recognized in Jamaican folklore in proverbs such as "Uman an hud neba kwaril" (Women never quarrel with a penis), and in concepts like "bu'n" (burn) and "jacket".[2] But there is no "outside man". We could simply say there is no "outside man" because polyandry is not socially sanctioned, and it is not because of male chauvinism. That is a sociological answer. A cultural one may be just as fruitful. In the domestic role definition, women and men occupy different spheres: women the domestic, men the interface between the family and the society. This is similar to the notion of "outside" as a male domain noted above. The concept of "outside man" would challenge the definition of the male gender role, therefore it is suppressed. As in the case of lesbianism, it allows women to express their sexuality unseen, in private.

Conclusion

The focus of the discussion on adult sexuality and gender has centred on the value system. However, by way of conclusion, it is important to stress that gender roles are presently undergoing a crisis, which has already begun to have an impact on the value system and to change the expressions of sexuality.

One instance of the crisis is the pressure on men to meet the requirements of their families, which are met only if their spouses also work. Women have become increasingly upwardly mobile, at faster rates than men. The chancellor of the University of the West Indies revealed that two-thirds of the graduating class of 1991–92 were female. By 1997–98 this proportion had risen to 72 percent. Domestic roles are therefore being refashioned, as questions such as who will take the child for immunization, or health care, are settled on the basis not of gender roles but of the ability of either spouse. Such a refashioning of roles is bound to have repercussions on the way men and women perceive themselves and express their sexuality.

Acknowledgment

This paper is adapted from a presentation to the Third Annual Professional Seminar, Race, Class and Gender in Psychiatry in Jamaica, Connolly House, Kingston, 28 November 1992.

Notes

1. Sistren Theatre Collective is a cultural and educational women's collective in Jamaica which since 1977 has explored the life of Caribbean women, from which they create performances and publications.
2. One gives one's spouse a "bu'n" by having an outside sexual relationship. Either spouse, male or female, can give the other "bu'n". Only women, however, can give a "jacket"; that is, pass off the child of a lover as her spouse's. In some countries of the Eastern Caribbean it is called "ready-made".

References

Bem, Sandra. 1993. *The Lenses of Gender: Transforming the Debate on Sexual Equality*. New Haven: Yale University Press.

Chevannes, Barry. 1994. *Rastafari: Roots and Ideology*. Syracuse: Syracuse University Press.

_____. 1986. "Jamaican Male Sexual Beliefs and Attitudes". Report to the National Family Planning Board, Kingston, Jamaica.

Kapo. 1977. "Neville Willoughby Interviews Kapo". *Jamaican Intercom* 2, no. 1.

Mbiti, John S. 1989. *African Religions and Philosophy*. London: Heinemann.

Wilson, Peter J. 1969. "Reputation and Respectability: A Suggestion for Caribbean Ethnology". *Man* 4, no. 1.

28 Crowing Hens Are Not Aberrant

Gender, Culture and Performance Conversation –
A Jamaican Perspective

KATHRYN SHIELDS-BRODBER

Introduction: The Case for Revisiting Gendered Interaction and Turn-Taking

There can be no doubt that many axioms about gendered behaviour, like those associated with other cultural attributes, reflect norms and categories of measurement spawned by the metropolitan West, while much interesting variation which is significant to nonmainstream cultures either goes unremarked or gets short shrift. Comment about gendered linguistic behaviour is a case in point. On the one hand, it has provided a range of stereotypes which, on the surface, seem to hold for many cultures. Inherent gender differences, unequal power relations and social inequality between men and women, for example, have been attested in numerous studies, and form the basis for many assumptions about asymmetry in mixed-sex conversation (see Zimmerman and West 1975; Fishman 1980; O'Barr and Atkins 1980; Sattel 1983; Tannen 1990, 1993).

Classic studies in this area have analysed men's propensity to take charge as the catalyst for their preference for hierarchically organized exchanges, in which they attempt not only to determine the focus and nature of the conversations in which they participate, but also to assert dominance by constant interruption of others, and taking long turns (see Edelsky 1981; Goodwin and Goodwin 1992; West and Zimmerman 1983). Men are portrayed as managing and manipulating the floor to their benefit and to the detriment of women. Women are presented as reactors rather than initiators, ultimately cooperating rather than competing, not only among themselves, but even with a draconian male interlocutor. In fact, one is often left with the distinct impression that the women researched are willing collaborators (if not always conspirators) in creating a setting which provides them with some comfort during their interaction with oppressive men, in spite of its restrictive nature. Although there has been recognition in recent years of the sociocultural construction of gendered reality (Eckert and McConnell-Ginet 1992; Gal 1992; Phillips, Steele and Tanz 1992), many analyses still give credence to stereotypical difference and dominance explanations, and regard their underlying precepts as axiomatic.

When applied uncritically to "nondeveloped" or "developing" Western society, research which represents the metropolitan West as the norm generates many questions. In the first place, assumptions about male/female asymmetry in power, or in the will to wield it, do not necessarily hold for all subcultures within a community (see Stanback 1985) or across communities which may be identified, as well, as "Western". Shields-Brodber (1992a), for example, points to the focus on and power of women of all strata in a talk-centred society such as Jamaica, and to their dominance of public/formal speech events, such as phone-in talk shows, which are primary vehicles for society's articulation of ideas and opinions about local and international issues, and fill the airwaves for all but four hours per weekday. Women, who comprise the majority of daytime callers, are collectively instrumental not only in influencing public policy perspectives, but also in making or breaking the reputation of many an important figure with whom they disagree, or who does not live up to their expectations. A listener to mixed-sex conversations in this forum will gain the impression not only that there is parity rather than asymmetry in power between male and female participants, but also that, where there is an imbalance, it is women who dominate.

While on the one hand, in places such as Jamaica gender relations appear to defy analysis from a traditional Western perspective, on the other, a study of the conventions and structure of conversation unearths many aspects of divergence from accepted Western principles of turn-taking. Much of the literature on conversation, especially that which is conducted in the public domain, has subscribed to a notion of its being a highly organized construct governed by the adage: "Do not speak while another is speaking" (Sachs, Schegloff and Jefferson 1974). The assumption underlying the turn-taking procedures of this floor is that when someone interrupts, she or he violates the current speaker's right to complete a turn, and causes the inevitable silencing of that speaker (West and Zimmerman 1983).

It is not difficult to appreciate the value of a one-person-at-a-time floor, especially when transmission or explanation of complex ideas or abstract notions is the aim. It allows one speaker to fully clarify the information or emotions she or he might wish to impart without being sidetracked or silenced. In fact, there seems to be general agreement that, in some cultures, simultaneous speech is inimical to good public/formal conversation, presumably because it requires at least a sharing of the floor. However, some researchers have suggested that in female conversations, simultaneous speech is a normal discourse pattern which marks cooperation between participants, rather than a malfunctioning floor (Coates 1996).

A prerequisite for a balanced exchange of ideas – a conventionally, prototypically "polite conversation" – is that any participant is provided with opportunities for contributing to the process. However, it is not unusual to find speakers on the one-at-a-time floor taking advantage of its conventions to indulge in lengthy monologues which – while guaranteeing thorough ventilation of their point(s) – denies maximal interaction between speakers.

This limitation is addressed by a cooperative floor, which allows several speakers (usually identified in the literature as female) to collaborate on developing a theme simultaneously. The result is often a more "multi-layered development of topics" (Coates 1995: 23), with possibilities for early clarification of ambiguous or complicated points, without the animosity which might naturally arise when a person on a one-at-a-time floor feels short changed by one who attempts to share the limelight. However, one possible negative consequence is that participants may be encouraged to explore tangential leads, and never discuss what was originally the main point.

In primarily oral societies such as Jamaica, while sequential and collaborative floors are part of conversational organization, it is certainly arguable whether either of these floors is paramount, especially when the transmission or development of ideas is not the principal focus. Reisman (1974: 124) noted the tendency for informal Antiguan conversations to mirror musical counterpoint in "the lack of strong norms against interruption, the acceptance of two or more voices talking at the same time". This tendency characterizes discussion at varying levels of formality by men or women "of words" (Abrahams 1983) whose verbal acumen is often as important as the substance of their input: an intrinsic performance dimension. One speaker's challenge to another, by means of interruption and subsequent sustained simultaneous speech, presents an opportunity for them both to display and contest their verbal prowess in a bid to gain the attention and admiration of others in the interaction, without necessarily having to convince listeners of the accuracy or logic of their positions.

The performance floor, unlike the two conventional floors, is thus an occasion for participants to contend for prominence. It represents a shared space and embraces voices which, in a polyphonic mode, enter a conversation periodically and then proceed to develop themes simultaneously (Shields-Brodber 1996). Unlike sixteenth- and seventeenth-century polyphonic music, however, voices on the performance floor are not constrained either to enter a conversation at regular, predictable intervals, or to bear some direct relation to the keys already in operation. This means that an ignorant listener may be deceived into believing that what she or he hears is no more than, at best, dissonance, and at worst, confusion.[1]

Gendered Interaction and Performance Conversations

The data for this discussion were recorded from radio and television interviews, phone-in radio talk shows and advice programmes aired in Jamaica. They represent a range of public/formal contexts, all of which employ a host who is in charge of the interaction. A host is not merely a channel through which speakers either gain access in sequential order or are encouraged to collaborate, since it is not the intention for speakers to gain, by right, an equal– or even certain – chance of being heard. On the contrary, speakers are expected, in the face of a formidable challenge from others, to sustain themselves on the floor for which they compete.

The organization of a performance floor, does, at times, include one-at-a-time and/or collaborative interaction, though this is not a norm. In neither case, however, is it possible to differentiate between the conversational features used by men and women solely on the basis of applying stereotypical analyses to the voiceless text. The propensity for attempting to take long uninterrupted turns, for instance, is a feature of moderators in general – a seeming hazard of the role. At a particular time, for example, a moderator may decide to indulge in lengthy editorializing – not just at the beginning of a programme, where an extended editorial comment has become a convention, but also in sympathetic response to a caller who exposes a raw nerve, or promotes an atmosphere of sentimentality:

Example 1

Host: I went out in the country yesterday an' as I drove along – it was one of these days where God jus' get up an' wipe off the world clean – it pretty, it pretty, it pretty coming through Junction, Agualta Vale go through the thing to get down to Port Maria. The sea beautiful an' I am sayin' to somebody – an environmentalis' who agree with me, "What will Jamaica be like in fifty years from now?" You an' I won' be here. Fifty years from now, what will our children see when they drive along? Do we here, in the face of unpopularity an' an' an' all a dis t'ing have a right to say we have to preserve some o' this even if it means that we don' buy apples from Omaha? We have to begin to – or wherever them come from. Is – am I wrong to say that? But there are people who jump in a you ches' [an go on with]

Caller: [mh hm]

Host: a t'ing an' begin to t'ing about unu t'ing an t'ing. So then what is it for us then? What is it for us? Because if I go to the United States, I can' vote up there excep' I have taken citizenship; an' even if I take it I can't run for the President of the country, because it say you have to be born there. So what is wrong with me defending where I come from, an' wanting to see it become better, an' to see peace an' harmony an' decency an' fulfilment for everybody? What is wrong with that?

(BG 528/371A)

The women whom I have researched are no more immune than are men to lengthy interventions such as these; nor are they less prone than men to make assertive, self-congratulatory statements about themselves and their attitudes. Self-deprecation and submission to male dominance are not generally characteristic of contributions made by Jamaican females.

Asserting Dominance: Simultaneous Speech

Since challenge is the essence of successful entry to and survival on a performance floor, it is not surprising that interruption and simultaneous speech are inherent properties of its character. A current speaker, of whatever gender or status, neither expects that she or he will be allowed to proceed unchallenged for any stretch of discourse nor accepts many constraints on how challenges should be presented. The consequence can be long stretches of simultaneous speech, with any number of voices participating:

Example 2

1	A	But sir you not listening to me
2		[I say we have two arms
3	C	[What other agency would you require besides the
4		[Public Complaints Authority
5	B	[I am simply saying to you I am simply saying to you
6		that if you're talking about the internal investigations by police
7		I don't really treat them with any degree of [credence I don't
8	A	[no I object to that
9		you know sir because there are they are officers with impeccable records =
10	B	= I don't know that
11	A	[They are I am telling you that sir I am telling you as somebody
12	B	[I don't know that Ms [Ramsay I don't know that I don't know that
13	D	[No sah you know that there are people
14	A	[can you look at the number of police officers who've may I
15	B	[But hol' on what I am trying to say (.) I don't know that

16   D   [come on come on sir no no

17   E   [records are there you know

18   A   finish making the point please (.) jus' look at the amount of police
officers

19   who have been put before the court who have been charged disciplined

20   and convicted as a result of investigations of these officers

(CH524/090B)

In the preceding example, two senior superintendents of police and an attorney-at-law discuss methods of police control with two afternoon radio cohosts. Regular interruption and simultaneous speech occur, with as many as four participants (lines 14–17) speaking at once and, on many occasions, proceeding unruffled until each has made the point to his or her satisfaction. Apart from one female host (D) whose contribution in this excerpt is minimal, the senior superintendent (A), who is defending the police, is female. There is no evidence that she is unable to hold her own, or is daunted by challenges to her opinions posed by the three male participants; in fact, she is able to invoke the conventional one-person-at-a-time formula and engineer an (admittedly limited) breather in which to articulate her point.

The constant negotiation of verbal prowess, which is part of the character of a performance floor, often nullifies any personal advantage related to social power or authority with which a participant may enter the fray. In dyadic, interview-type situations, for instance, an interviewee, in spite of being an invited guest, cannot expect special treatment.

Example 3

1   B   Let me say this to you (.) whether it was normal practice or not

2   I cannot recall exactly (.) in 1994 why the delay (.)

3   but I DID and we have correspondence in which we asked them

4   to expedite the process for us

5   [what they could do the best that they could do

6   A   [okay I want to stay there no no I want to stay there

7   B   The best that they could do AT THAT TIME was to give
us a draft

8   and they gave [us a draft for ninety four

9   A   [No I am not goin' to let you go on that one sir

10   because you were very active in the market

11   you were somebody goin' both internally and externally

12   for funding you had a concept that was considered good by people

13   and in 1994 it would seem to me that it was in your interest

14   and the interest of all your depositors to have [had a quick

15   B   [I am in agree-

16   A   [audit

17   B   [ment with that I am in agreement with [that

18   A   [so something ca some

19   there was a reason [why

20   B   [but I am giving you the reason

21   [but you don't want to you don't find it acceptable (.)

22   A   [no sir (.)   no sir (.)   there is you are not giving me

23   [enough there is a reason why this thing was delayed

24   B   [no no please   no no please I am giving you the

25   reason (.) whether you fin' you are making a judgement [call

26   A   [why

27   B   [here   I am telling you

28   A   [was it delayed in excess of six months

                                              (AS522/060)

Since an interviewer may have a personal agenda, a point of view or analysis which she or he is determined to promote, she or he is unlikely to be averse to embarrassing or frustrating guests in order to achieve it. In this regard, two features are worthy of note in the example above. Speaker A's attempt to upstage and out-talk her guest results in her brief capture (lines 9–14) of an uncontested floor. However, she is unable to bully speaker B into submission: he stubbornly resists her attempt to force him to present an explanation consistent with her analysis (lines 19–27), employing simultaneous speech as a way of signalling his intention not to give in to her attempts to harass him.

Volume and Volubility

Another method of dominating a performance conversation is the engineering of sustained levels of high volume and speed in the delivery of words. This is potentially disconcerting for an opponent who may be unable to compete at the same volume or pace, or with equal perseverance, and may have to stop and inhale, thereby temporarily yielding the floor. In this context, a speaker may also make an effort to reduce the speed at which words are emitted, so that she or he can participate on a more equitable basis; if she or he is unable either to engineer a slowing of the pace or to sustain simultaneous speech, this becomes a tacit admission of inferior verbal dexterity.

There are many female callers and hosts who attempt to dominate the conversation and even maintain it as a monologue by using high volume, volubility and excessive speed of delivery – techniques recognized as being manipulated by men in order to dominate others.

Manipulating Silence as an Instrument of Control

In less structured exchanges, such as phone-in talk shows, there is an obvious platform for public competition between participants, who are not confined to those conversing, but include the wide audience of overhearers (Bell 1991) who will be the ultimate judges of a performance. A caller to a talk show, for example, may wish to articulate ideas to a wider public than that with which she or he would otherwise have easy contact, and from which she or he would normally gain feedback. Another caller may have no such agenda. By phoning in, she or he may simply be taking advantage of an opportunity to gain centre stage in public – to perform for an otherwise inaccessible audience.

The moderator and other participants become potential conspirators in what the unknowing may interpret as an adversarial role, but can really be a supportive one to the extent that it facilitates the performance and is integral to its success. The important factor is both speakers' willingness to engage in spirited *simultaneous dialogue,* manifested by their responding to and incorporating into their presentation the contribution of other parties.

If an exchange generates a monologue, it receives a negative evaluation. Withdrawal of speech is one technique which participants interested in winning the battle for dominance are likely to employ as a means of unnerving a current speaker.

Example 4

Caller: Now (.) the time that a government becomes a parent
            is when they become elected
            is that right or is that wrong

(Host does not respond)

Caller: Hello

Host: Go on talk nuh

Caller: OK (.) now if at the point of becoming a parent
            You don't trust you parent
            don't isn't there a problem

Host: (..) Go on taak maam yu doin di taakin yu nuo
            wi don taak yu a taak[2]
            You put [your point

Caller: [No no I would like your reaction

Host: Darling I am hearing you that's all I'm doing now
            because when I try to speak you interrupt [so proceed

Caller: [no I apologize

Host: No proceed mi dear you have a argument you have a position
            gwaan put it mek Jimiieka mek a disijian[3]

Caller: Okay (.) if you have a parent

(caller proceeds to present an uninterrupted, somewhat incoherent lengthy monologue)

            Second issue (.) you not goin' to reac' to that one

Host: gwaan taak no ma'am

                                        (AH 420/287A)

It is clear that the caller in the exchange above is destabilized by the moderator's withdrawal of speech, but is unable to manipulate her meaningful reengagement in the discourse. This is a result of her "hogging" the floor in the segment immediately preceding – a technique to which the notoriously vociferous and strident female moderator responds by withdrawing her challenge and resorting to silence in order to emphasize her caller's flouting of convention by her seeming unwillingness to engage a combatant.

Facilitation and Encouragement: Minimal Responses

Minimal responses have been found to signify a speaker's cooperation with and encouragement of a current speaker (Fishman 1980; Holmes 1995; Coates 1996). A plethora of minimal responses in too quick succession gives the impression that the listener is not listening, and is hurrying the speaker so as to (re)capture the floor; however, when they are used at intervals in which they provide support rather than discouragement for a speaker (Fishman 1983), minimal responses facilitate participation by all interlocutors:

Example 5[4]

Caller:	Yu nuo ol taim piipl se popi tek twelv deez opn dem ai yu nuo sa
Host:	Oh
Caller:	De ai opn (.) twenti wan die bifuo dem ai opn
Host:	Oh
Caller:	But yu nuo wat mii glad fa in a dis taim ina fi mi uol deez
Host:	Aha
Caller:	Di piipl av Jimieka (.) kyaa rialaiz se (.) wat a gwaan in a Tivoli Gyaadn iz tatiks bai di govament (.) yu hier sa
Host:	A si
Caller:	At dis taim (.) mi se mi lisn Mista A far mi de a yaad ya an (.) naa du notn (.) an mi lisn di piipl dem evri die an som a fi yu proogram =
Host:	mhm
Caller:	for mi kyan tel yu se sa Missa P woz duin a gud jab bot yu duin a beta jab dan HIM

[*section omitted*]

Host:	Aarait dadi wi a tek it de fi tide (.) Gud (.) tek kier

(PA 597/008A)

Example 5, in which both speakers are men, is a good illustration of a host's strategic placement of back channels at the end of a caller's phrases as a signal of his support. Minimal responses such as these are also an explicit indication of another speaker's active participation.

The speakers in the following exchange are men:

Example 6

A: Do you have people (.) you ever had a case of
        somebody who has come and you know
        ridden on your jet skis and then (.)
        come back every year after year and patronized you

B: Oh definitely (.) you have people who comes back
        and a mean you know year after year you have people

A: = An' they tell you one of the real things
        they like about Jamaica is is
        riding on the jet [skis and you know

B: [definitely among other things a mean you know
        Jamaica represent to them a level of freedom
        Jet ski is one of them

C: Because of course jet skis are banned
        where many of them come from

                                                    (XT525/90A)

Speaker B is a guest of three others, who, with speaker C as moderator, form a regular afternoon radio panel. On this occasion, speaker D, who is silent at this juncture, has called into question the credibility of their guest. Speaker A, in assuming the role of mediator, helps this guest to boost his self-confidence by leading him to present his business in a more positive light. Speaker C's observation, at the end of the process, contributes to a feeling of community, with no one person gaining prominence.

It is instructive to note the discrepancy between the Jamaican data presented here and the findings of many studies that, at least in public, one-at-a-time strategies are the prerogative of men, with collaboration and facilitation being the forte of women. Predictions that speakers who demonstrate adeptness at hogging the floor are likely to be male, while those who collaborate are likely to be female, are not generally corroborated in performance contexts.

In fact, the style of a speaker engaged in performance conversation, rather than being gender derived, is clearly role oriented. Designated moderators and self-assigned leaders of conversation, for example, will be vested with the authority to regulate the flow of a discussion. If they assume a didactic stance, they may present themselves as purveyors of wisdom, and may exercise this authority by hogging the floor, or may also actively construct frames which divert the focus from guests to themselves, by the use of phrases such as "from where I sit", "in my opinion", "you can't convince me" and so on. It is not uncommon for them thereafter to assume a cross-examination mode, in which they act as inquisitor. High levels of apparent animosity may be generated, with both parties trading below-the-belt punches, and neither gender demonstrating any difficulty assuming or maintaining the stance of antagonist; each is usually able to return as good a blow as she or he receives. If, on the other hand, they interpret their role as one of facilitation, they will employ minimal responses and other supportive devices as tools of an inductive approach which encourages self-expression of other participants, with limited input of their own.

The variable which seems most effective in influencing the style a moderator will adopt is the role which she or he has assumed for the moment. Thus it is not possible to decipher from the text itself, without recourse to the audio tape, the gender of the speakers involved – unless there is explicit reference to gender during the discussion. In other words, there is no gender stereotype which is automatically applicable to interlocutors on a performance floor. The truth is that Jamaican speakers, when in the public domain, exhibit great flexibility by assuming a variety of roles and positions, in keeping with the demands of their context. Gender is not an overriding variable as far as performance is concerned.

Interestingly, although participants on the performance floor often sound as if they are in combat, not all the exchanges which employ interruption and simultaneous speech are adversarial: there are some in which the conversants speak together in support of a mutually agreed point; there are others which sound contentious, but are not unfriendly, and there are still others which exhibit all the elements of war – including, for example, argument ad hominem/feminem and attacks against institutions – and end on an antagonistic note. Further, since being allowed to speak uninterrupted is usually an indicator of one's failure to engage the interest of others, and therefore to stimulate their active involvement, even agreement between participants does not negate the need for competition and simultaneous speech.

It is also worth noting that the examples included above are not restricted to informal village interaction, as were those from which Reisman's (1974) observations originated: instead, they characterize public on-air conversation, with participants including national and public figures in Jamaica.

Conclusion

In primarily oral communities like Jamaica, it is conversations like these which, apart from being considered entertaining and animated, are acknowledged to require advanced levels of verbal skill. The floor operates as a forum for performance talk; understandably, therefore, substance can find itself subordinated to form. It is not that the one-person-at-a-time floor does not operate successfully in contexts like these, but rather, that it is not highly favoured by those who seek to pit their verbal skills against each other. Cooperation becomes a disincentive to lively exchange, and, rather than marking a dysfunctional conversation, interruption and simultaneous speech signify conversants' ability to take advantage of an obvious opportunity to contest their verbal prowess.

In the confines of a performance floor, men and women are equally adept, not only at holding their own, but also at holding opponents of either gender at bay. It seems incontrovertible, therefore, that in a cultural milieu which includes performance floors, cocks and hens have equally to master the art of crowing.

Transcription Conventions

[	indicates	the beginning of overlap between utterances
(.)	indicates	pause of five seconds or less
=	indicates	lack of a discernible gap between utterances

The Cassidy–Le Page phonemic system is used to represent Jamaican creole utterances. Standard English translations are provided in footnotes.

Notes

1. Shields-Brodber (1996) presents an extended discussion of the analogy between counterpoint and performance conversations.
2. The Standard English translation of the Jamaican creole switch is as follows: "Go on talking, ma'am; you are doing the talking, you know; we have stopped talking. You are talking."
3. The Standard English translation is: "Continue to present it and allow Jamaica to decide".
4. Caller: "You know old time people say puppies – it takes twenty-one days for puppies to open their eyes; but you know what I am happy about in these days of my old age? The people of Jamaica can realize that what is happening in Tivoli Gardens is government tactics at this time. I listen, Mr A, for I am at home and not occupied, and I listen to the people every day, and some of your programmes; for I can tell you that Mr P was doing a good job, but you are doing a better job than he."

References

Abrahams, Roger. 1983. *The Man of Words in the West Indies*. Baltimore: Johns Hopkins University Press.

Bell, Allan. 1991. *The Language of the News Media*. Oxford: Blackwell.

Coates, Jennifer. 1993. *Women, Men and Language,* 2d ed. London: Longman.

_____. 1995. "Language, Gender and Career". In *Language and Gender: Interdisciplinary Perspectives,* edited by S. Mills. London: Longman.

_____. 1996. *Women Talk*. Oxford: Blackwell.

Eckert, Penelope, and Sally McConnell-Ginet. 1992. "Think Practically, and Look Locally: Language and Gender as Community-Based Practice". *Annual Review of Anthropology* 21.

Edelsky, Carole. 1981. "Who's Got the Floor?" *Language in Society* 10.

Fishman, Pamela. 1980. "Conversational Insecurity". In *Language: Social Psychological Perspectives,* edited by H. Giles, P. Robinson and P. Smith. Oxford: Pergamon Press.

_____. 1983. "Interaction: The Work Women Do". In *Language, Gender and Society,* edited by B. Thorne, C. Kramerae and N. Henley. Rowley, Mass.: Newbury House.

Gal, Susan. 1992. "Language, Gender and Power: An Anthropological View". In *Locating Power: Proceedings of the Second Berkeley Women and Language*

Conference 1, edited by K. Hall, M. Bucholtz and B. Moonwomon. Berkeley
    Women and Language Group. Berkeley: University of California Press.

Goodwin, Marjorie, and Charles Goodwin. 1992. "Children's Arguing". In
    Language, Gender and Sex in Comparative Perspective, edited by S. Phillips and C.
    Tanz. Cambridge: Cambridge University Press.

Holmes, Janet. 1995. *Women, Men and Politeness.* London: Longman.

O'Barr, William, and Bowman Atkins. 1980. "Women's Language or Powerless
    Language?" In *Women and Language in Literature and Society,* edited by S.
    McConnell-Ginet, et al. New York: Praegar.

Phillips, Susan, and Christine Tanz. 1992. *Language, Gender and Sex in
    Comparative Perspective.* Cambridge: Cambridge University Press.

Reisman, Karl. 1974. "Contrapuntal Conversation in an Antiguan Village". In
    Explorations in the Ethnography of Speaking, edited by R. Bauman and J.
    Scherzer. Cambridge: Cambridge University Press.

Sachs, Harvey, Emmanuel Schegloff, and Gail Jefferson. 1974. "A Simplest
    Systematics for the Organisation of Turn-Taking in Conversation".
    Language 50.

Sattel, Jack. 1983. "Men, Inexpressiveness and Power". In *Language, Gender and
    Society,* edited by B. Thorne, C. Kramerae and N. Henley. Rowley, Mass.: Newbury
    House.

Shields-Brodber, Kathryn. 1992a. "Hens Can Crow Too: The Female Voice of
    Authority on Air in Jamaica". Paper presented at Ninth Biennial Conference of
    the Society for Caribbean Linguistics, Barbados.

_____. 1992b. "Dynamism and Assertiveness in the Public Voice: Code-Switching
    and Turn Taking in Radio Talk Shows in Jamaica". *Pragmatics* 2, no. 4.

_____. 1996. "Are Interruptions and Simultaneous Speech Always Anathema?"
    Paper presented at Eleventh Biennial Conference of the Society for Caribbean
    Linguistics, St Maarten.

Stanback, Marsha. 1985. "Language and Black Woman's Place". In *For Alma
    Mater: Theory and Practice in Feminist Scholarship,* edited by P.A. Treichler, C.
    Kramarae, and B. Stafford. Urbana: University of Illinois Press.

Tannen, Deborah. 1990. *You Just Don't Understand: Women and Men in
    Conversation.* New York: Ballentine.

_____. 1993. *Gender and Conversational Interaction.* Oxford: Oxford University Press.

Thorne, Barrie, Cheris Kramerae, and Nancy Henley, eds. 1983. *Language, Gender
    and Society.* Rowley, Mass.: Newbury House.

West, Candace, and Don Zimmerman. 1983. "Small Insults: A Study of
    Interruptions in Cross-Sex Conversations between Unacquainted Persons".

1983. In *Language, Gender and Society,* edited by B. Thorne, C. Kramerae and
N. Henley. Rowley, Mass.: Newbury House.

Zimmerman, Don, and Candace West. 1975. "Sex Roles, Interruptions and
Silences in Conversation". In *Language and Sex: Difference and Dominance,* edited
by B. Thorne and N. Henley. Rowley, Mass.: Newbury House.

29 Envisioning a Politics of Change within Caribbean Gender Relations

LINDEN LEWIS

Introduction

The issue of social change is always fundamentally a political phenomenon. The necessity for change, the inclination to embrace it or resist it, are all politically charged elements which are ultimately contingent on the socioeconomic and political climate of a given historical conjuncture. By definition, therefore, social change presupposes some degree of concession and compromise, and it is very often accompanied by some notion – however articulated – of struggle and resistance.

The Caribbean is at a critical stage of its development. It is in the middle of a process of globalization which has been taking place for some time now, and which has profound implications for the socioeconomic configuration of these island states. In recent years the region has had to adjust to structural changes brought on by multilateral institutions, it has watched its slim advantages in the production and export of textiles diminish with the coming into being of the North American Free Trade Agreement, and it has had to brace itself against the effects of the removal of protective tariffs on bananas entering the European Union, inter alia. Many of these adjustments have had a destabilizing effect on civil society in the Caribbean. Not least of the problems brought on in part by such changes is the tension which currently exists in the relationship between men and women in the region.

We are at a crucial conjuncture with respect to the change in the way men and women relate to each other. The nature of these gender relations is being renegotiated. This change is made political by the general dislocation and anomie within Caribbean civil society. The concern here is not how any individual man relates to any individual woman. Such relationships are enormously important and this essay in no way seeks to minimize the significance of quotidian social experiences. This paper, however, is concerned with how men and women collectively relate to each other and among themselves. Once we begin to think about these relationships in more structural terms, we become cognizant of the asymmetry of power which inheres in the relationship between men and women with respect to access to resources, privilege, knowledge and status.

Given this imbalance of power in favour of men, it is fairly axiomatic that men ought to play a pivotal role in the reconfiguration of gender relations – since everywhere, at some level, we benefit from what R.W. Connell called the patriarchal dividend in society (Connell 1995). The suggestion that men play a central role in a proposed process of gendered change is not born of any patriarchal preoccupation with men's supposed divinely imbued capacity for leadership. Neither is this suggestion a critique of existing feminist struggles for gender change in the region. The point here is that given the power of men in society in general – and in the Caribbean in particular – the onus should be on men to recognize the need for change and to pursue this objective in earnest.

The relationship of men to power is not without limitation or contradiction. Not all men exercise the same level of patriarchal power. Patriarchal power is mediated by issues of race, class, sexual orientation, religion and other cultural considerations. Nevertheless, we all benefit in one way or another from patriarchal privilege. Examples of patriarchal privilege abound but have become so commonplace for us as men that we often fail to recognize it as such – this is a clear indication of the normalization and naturalization of male privilege. The ability to command service in a public restaurant or office, to be listened to in a public gathering, to obtain certain types of loan from a commercial bank, to attend social functions alone, to move around freely at night, to claim public spaces for oneself, are all activities men do without hardly thinking about the privilege of exercising these civil and individual rights. Women, with few exceptions, are more reflective about engaging in the above activities.

In recent years, we have become increasingly aware of the modalities of women's struggles against the strictures of the existing gender order. This essay's objective is to suggest the ways in which men could support the efforts of women to create change in the nature of gender relations. There is a tendency among some feminists in the Caribbean to employ the language and practices of human resource management, and to propose a win-win situation for men in a system of gendered change.[1] The truth of the matter is that there is no win-win strategy: the reality of the situation is that men will have to give up their privilege and their access to resources and apparatuses of power which have been facilitated by a dominant patriarchy and hegemonic masculinity. All substantive changes in history have meant that privileged groups have had to concede power or lose it outright in a process of struggle and resistance. To suggest a win-win path for gendered change in the Caribbean is to validate the status quo. Rather than delude men about the consequences of change, it is better to try to persuade them that living in a more equitable, more efficient society benefits all citizens rather than some.

Why should we envision a politics of gendered change at this time? First of all, the old order has clearly run its course. There is sufficient disturbance and interrogation of the present gender order by feminists and other groups of women, along with some sympathetic men, to rethink the existing gender regime. Second, fundamental social, political and economic changes are taking place globally. It would be foolhardy of us to think that gender relations would somehow be immune to changes of such magnitude.

Gender relations, like other social relations, are dynamic, constantly changing, shifting, evolving – sometimes even in contradictory ways. Some of the ways we relate to each other have already become outmoded and require us to rethink these behaviours. Examples of outmoded behaviours include the "male breadwinner", "male protector" and the exclusive "female nurturer" roles. In addition, globally and regionally, women have become more politicized and more organized and have been asserting themselves for decades – particularly in relation to the issue of gender equality.

It is useful, for conceptual clarity, to define "masculinity". Masculinity refers to that whole corpus of behaviours and practices with which men learn to identify in a system of gender relations and in the context of the wider society. As a set of practices, masculinity is extremely protean, yet not so alterable as to be unidentifiable. Masculinity is both plural and variable. Rather than being some very fragile abstraction, masculinity – particularly in its hegemonic form – is remarkably resilient. Perhaps at a more basic level we understand masculinity as it relates to femininity. Masculinity, however, is not only defined in opposition to femininity but as a complement to it. Masculinity is the cultural expression of men's understanding of themselves and their relations to women. Unmistakably, masculinity has much to do with the way men relate to other men – how they seek approval, recognition, respect and honour from each other. In short, masculinity refers to how men come to understand themselves as gendered subjects. In constructing their identities, men are mindful of the influence of other men, women and societal expectations on the way their gendered beings are configured.

Gender Performance

R.W. Connell suggests that we need to pay particular attention to what men actually do, and not to what society expects them to do or imagines that they do (1995: 138). Judith Butler also writes about gender as performance – recognizing, of course, that not all of gender is performed (see Butler 1990, 1995). She argues that it is not so much who we are but what we do that determines our gender identity. I would like to suggest that we need to unpack the issue of gender performance even further, proposing that there is often a dissonance between public performance and private practice. Both men and women at times perform their respective gendered roles and act out their gendered identities privately in ways that often contradict their public personae.

For example, some men have no problem privately performing tasks which are stereotypically defined as "feminine", but they would be highly embarrassed if another man were to discover them doing so. Some Caribbean men are good cooks and also wash dishes – but would never do so when guests visit their homes. Even though some may be willing to do the household laundry to "help out around the house", they are likely to balk at the sight of a man laundering ladies' or girls' undergarments. At the same time, it is perfectly acceptable for women to wash their husband's or boyfriend's underwear. Men who are seen by other men or women washing ladies' undergarments are vilified and considered stupid. More importantly, such men are regarded as completely bamboozled by their women. In such circumstances, therefore, not many men are eager to perform this simple domestic chore, because of its symbolic signification. Those who do so would hardly publicly admit it and may in fact be among the most vociferous of those condemning the practice. A friend of mine who had just taken a load of clothes out of the washing machine went into the yard to hang them out on the clothesline. Seeing him hanging panties, two repairmen working on a nearby utility pole began sniggering and pointing fingers. My friend silenced their derision by turning to them and stating loudly, "If you could pull them down, you could hang them up."

At another level, some women who inveigh against sexism and who are single parents of boys tend to overcompensate for the absence of a father in the household by taking their sons to the most rugged and macho sports, simply because they fear that the boys might become too "soft". In addition, there are women who publicly define themselves as ardent feminists but who in their personal relationships tend to date or marry some of the least gender-sensitive men. These practices are not merely contradictions within gender conventions. They represent ways in which men and women satisfy public expectations of gendered behaviours which may or may not be compatible with their private views. We need, therefore, to understand the implications of these private practices for envisioning a politics of gendered change. In so doing we might be able to free both men and women of some of the burdens of rigidly defined constructions of gender identity which inhibit the process of gender transformation.

Modalities of Change

A politics of change should be articulated as part of a wide programme of engendering democracy. We should not want to change because of some vague moral consternation, or because we think it is the politically correct thing to do. Men should approach the matter of change because we are persuaded that gender equality is an important and fundamental part of true democracy. It is indeed mind-boggling how progressive and liberal men could claim to democratize all manner of social processes but completely ignore the gender order. In fact, gender equality is not generally a part of the consciousness of men in the vanguard of social change. A politics of change with an emphasis on engendering democracy would require us to rethink many practices, particularly organizational hierarchies.

> In so far as the organization is in some ways, a microcosm of the wider society, it is reasonable to assume that given the status of men in society, they are much more likely to benefit from a hierarchical arrangement at work, than would women. Very often organizational hierarchies separate the men from the women and are based on a number of social networks that may extend outside of the workplace. These social networks nevertheless exert considerable influence on the workplace, on available opportunities, promotions, advanced training or other important contacts. Women and minorities are usually excluded from such networks, severely restricting their career movements and limiting their potential. Gender sensitivity at this level may actually function to improve the organization in so far as it may benefit from tapping the potential of all its available human resources. Moreover, much of the literature and thinking on issues relating to management now seem to be suggesting that productivity and organizational commitment could be enhanced by abandoning the practice of hierarchy in the workplace. (Lewis 1998: 19)

In short, democracy should be envisioned as a societal project designed to extend the benefits of full citizenship to women and nonhegemonic men who are normally excluded from the apparatuses of power. This is one way in which civil society could really be strengthened.

Another important dimension of the process of gendered change is that of interrogating the areas of culture and religion. It should be noted that not all religions and religious practices are oppressive. Indeed, liberation theology has taught us that – quite apart from transforming our moral being – religion could minister to the material conditions of our existence. In envisioning a politics of change, however, we should seriously interrogate those religious and cultural practices which promote the subordination of women. Much resistance to change by many Caribbean men is rooted in the comforting normalization and naturalization of the subordination of women on the basis of religious authority. We should also be fully cognizant of the fact that culture (religion as part of culture) is a very powerful tool for reproducing patriarchy in ways that transcend race, class and age. Connell also counsels: "Further, masculinity exists impersonally in culture as a subject position in the process of representation, in the structure of language and other symbol systems"

(1996: 163). Gendered change may involve a process of unlearning some habits and practices which are fundamental to the national and regional cultural imaginary. We must come to terms with the notion that culture, like nature, is historically constructed. Culture is not some static phenomenon; it is a dynamic process within which gendered change can be negotiated.

Gender and Power

A politics of change has to be able to appreciate fully the relationship between the practices within gender relations and the structure of power within production. It is within the sphere of production that the principal source of power resides. From this site, other locations of power are largely determined. The social relations of gender are fundamentally tied to the social relations of production in society.

> The social relations of production correspond to the historical development of society and its mode of production. In this site, the link between the social relations of production and gender can be established. The social relations of production have historically been mediated by such issues as race and gender, particularly in the context of colonial and imperialist expansion. In many ways, the social relations of production establish the general parameters for all other social relations, even though those other relations may assume autonomy in different conjunctures. (Lewis 1998: 18)

Gender relations do not exist outside of class relations. This is not to say that all power can be reduced to class power. Rather, social class considerations lie at the heart of any understanding of the workings of power.

The phenomenon of power is also manifest in the state and state relations. In envisioning a politics of gendered change in the Caribbean, we should also be mindful of the relationship between gender and the state. The postcolonial Caribbean state is not only masculinist in its personnel but also in its orientation and policy formulation. Of course, this is not unusual: R.W. Connell surmises that "the state is a gendered institution, marked by its internal gender regime. It is typical of modern state structures that the major centres of state power are heavily masculinized" (1996: 165). However, not all men have equal access to the state. Class membership, race, ethnicity and, in some cases, religion may mediate some men's access to state apparatuses and resources. Hence, one may argue that although men predominate in the administration of the state, ruling-class men and hegemonic masculinity have the most access to the state.

In terms of gender transformation, the concern in the Caribbean revolves around the issue of the degree of access women and marginalized men have to the apparatuses of state power. How are women's voices interpreted at the level of the state and how are their concerns addressed?

> This treatment of the female as an invisible presence – that is, made absent when she is most present – is a continuing factor in the political and intellectual backwardness of our institutions. The female presence in political office, or in the leadership of the Party and the Trade Union Movement is not only rare, but she is often there as a result of male patronage, and not through the attainment and exercise of power in her own right. (Lamming 1995: 38)

In societies such as the Caribbean, with underdeveloped private sectors dominated by merchant capital, access to the resources of the state becomes crucial to the reproduction of certain sections of the society. Moreover, we should not lose sight of the relationship between gender and capitalism, gender and the economy and gender and labour in the Caribbean. George Lamming presciently comments:

> For it must be clear to the most alert . . . that the dysfunctional nature of man/woman relations cannot be trapped in a crusade about gender since the liberation of women is not possible without the liberation of the total society. It is in the Caribbean woman's struggle for her liberation that the complexities of race and ethnic antagonisms are most likely to collapse. (1995: 39)

Lamming's appeal here is not to disregard or de-emphasize gender as an important category in the consideration of change, but rather to treat it as part of a whole complex totality.

Men, Women, Violence and Change

One of the areas in critical need of change among men in the Caribbean and in the rest of the world is our resort to violence as a technique of conflict resolution or control maintenance. Men are the main perpetrators of violence against each other and against women. Socialized into a generally accepted warriorhood in defence of honour, nation, country and God, we find it difficult to seek other ways to negotiate autonomy, difference and change. It is in such a broad context that one must place the question of violence in society.

Caribbean colonial society was forged in the crucible of violence. European occupation, the destruction of the indigenous peoples of the region and the enslavement of millions of African men and women are all fundamentally acts of violence perpetrated on the minds and bodies of people. Fanon first drew our attention to the broader context within which we should assess the concept of violence. His project extended to include the implications of violence for the process of decolonization (see Fanon 1963). In this sense, therefore, violence is endemic to the system we have inherited and seek to reproduce. It is manifested in the nature and operations of the state. Violence is, however, not reducible to the physical, emotional or verbal. Violence also has to do with the deprivation of rights. Exclusion of women and marginalized men from participation in the major decision-making processes – political and corporate – of the society is also a form of violence. At another level, however, participation in one's own oppression and domination is tantamount to what Gayatri Spivak described as "epistemic violence" (Spivak 1997). Ignorance of the weight of history on the nature of the relationships and institutions which are created in the postcolonial context is, in part, the result of the legacy of violence of the colonial project. The issue of violence of men (and in some cases of women) should not be divorced from these historical, sociological and structural factors which help to shape behaviour.

Men in the Caribbean must begin to mobilize against verbal and physical violence meted out to women, as well as to marginalized or nonhegemonic men and children. Every major report on the status of women in the Caribbean in the last five years has pointed to an increase in the level of violence against them. This situation of violence against women is acute in places such as Haiti, Guyana, Trinidad and Jamaica. In other islands, although the situation may be less severe, the problem nevertheless persists. In my work on men in the Caribbean, I have noted that no one takes responsibility for such unsavoury conduct. In interviews men are quick to condemn the action of violence against women. However, despite their protestations, violence against women continues. Part of the problem is society's ambivalence towards aggressive manhood. In some public arenas, violence against women is firmly condemned as a cowardly act. In other public fora, the ability to "rule things" (to discipline one's woman) and to establish oneself as a man – "to let her know who is boss" – is tacitly condoned by many more men in the Caribbean than we might care to acknowledge. An article on domestic violence published in *IDB América,* the newsletter of the Inter-American Development Bank, explores the possibility of measuring the public costs of domestic violence in such areas as health, social services, justice and loss of productivity:

> Domestic violence also has a serious impact on the health of pregnant women and their unborn babies. Physical and psychological abuse cause higher rates of prenatal and infant mortality and leads to health problems that shorten women's working lives. (IDB 1997a: 2)

Here, too, it must be pointed out that social class issues often mediate circumstances of domestic abuse. Mayra Buvinic, chief of the Women and Development Program Unit of the Inter-American Development Bank, suggested that "poverty is a significant risk factor for domestic violence" (IDB 1997a: 2). The evidence from Chile, for example, indicates so far that lower income women are at greater risk of domestic violence; in Nicaragua poorer women are overrepresented among the physically abused (see IDB 1997a: 2). Research into this issue is therefore critical, given the increasing levels of violence against women.

Men need to start helping other men to break the cycle of destruction. A useful place to start is to adopt a method that has proved to be successful in certain parts of Latin America. The idea is to create a dialogue between men who are abusers and those who are not on the issue of violence in general and, more specifically, violence against women. Other types of intervention are clearly necessary here, but it seems to me that men can start taking responsibility for ending this way of dealing with conflict, and can also begin to develop some initiatives in this direction. The work of Men Against Violence Against Women in Trinidad is therefore to be encouraged, as this group grapples with the issue of resocializing some men away from the brutality of domestic and other forms of violence against women. Whereas violence against women has received much popular attention, the violence of men toward other men is normalized, and therefore not considered particularly worthy of attention. Moreover, violence directed at homosexual men is not even considered really problematic. Violence against homosexuals in the Caribbean is often rationalized by both men and women on religious grounds or by appeals to nature. We cannot afford to condone violence against people who may not share our sexual orientation while condemning the same action when directed against women. We need to be more vocal in our condemnation of the physical and verbal abuse of others, irrespective of gender or sexual orientation. Failure to recognize all forms of violation is tantamount to being disingenuous.

Public Harassment

Public harassment in the Caribbean is generally considered a taken-for-granted widespread public ritual. At best, it is considered a minor annoyance by people who are not subject to it. Public harassment, however, is more than verbal abuse. Carol Brooks Gargner defined public harassment as

> that group of abuses, harryings, and annoyances characteristic of public places and uniquely facilitated by communication in public. Public harassment includes pinching, slapping, hitting, shouted remarks, vulgarity, insults, sly innuendo, ogling, and stalking. Public harassment is on a continuum of possible events, beginning when customary civility among strangers is abrogated and ending with the transition to violent crime: assault, rape, or murder. (1995: 4)

In the context of the Caribbean, public harassment rarely gets beyond the point of shouted remarks, including vulgarities and insults. Many view this behaviour as relatively innocuous. Public harassment in the Caribbean, as in other parts of the world, is usually directed towards women. As a result some women decide not to travel certain routes, not to frequent some public places, not to travel alone. That women have to adjust their ways of doing things in public is some indication of how the domain of the public sphere is highly masculinized. "In short, the public harassment of women is pertinent to feminist concerns with the reification of the public/private split. Public harassment also suggests ways in which a different environment has affected women's sense of self in society" (Gardner 1995: 12–13).

Two more points should be addressed at this stage. First, though women are more often the subject of public harassment, they themselves participate in this activity – though less often and certainly with less intensity. For most heterosexual men who are subject to public harassment by women, be it taunting or teasing, it does not usually create discomfort. Given the dynamic interplay of power and sexuality in patriarchal cultures such as those in the Caribbean, for men such harassment is a minor embarrassment or a form of flattery. Women should consider, however, the extent to which such actions validate heterosexual machismo and underscore hegemonic masculinity, perhaps, in some ways, much to their detriment.

Second, women are not without agency in the matter of public harassment. Over the years, women in the Caribbean have developed a battery of responses and put downs. Often, their responses are enough to stop some men dead in their tracks. On other occasions, however, women's responses simply occasion a new round of abuses and verbal insults from the men or boys. Irrespective of women's verbal skills at countering harassment, the point remains that they should not be forced to defend themselves against such verbal attacks.

When asked about their behaviour towards women in public some men responded by first apportioning blame to the women. One young man in St Lucia summed it up this way: "Some girls, the things they wear, they just walking around asking for comments. A little skirt which they can't even bend over with and you see everything. I mean if she bends over, you can see her ovaries or something like that" (focus group session, conducted by the author, 1997). A Grenadian man echoed the sentiments of his younger counterpart from St Lucia, indicating that such behaviour may in fact be self-affirming for some women:

> Some women don't want it but a lot of women does dress in a way for men to interfere with them. And a lot of women ah know does feel let down and does feel less if they walk the street and nobody ain't harass them. They does feel like they not looking good. Sometimes the molestation does go a bit too far, that depend on the individual but women does like it in that kinda way. (Focus group session 1997)

Some men rationalize public harassment of women in other ways, as does this young man in St Lucia: "Yes though I agree that women shouldn't be harassed in public, it is just that sometimes men are just really bored and they just sit there with nothing to do. A woman passes by and they make a comment. It is not like they really want to do it. It is an excuse to find something to do" (focus group session 1997).

Another St Lucian man tried to make a case for public harassment as a form of ego retrieval:

> Some fellas on the road, eh, they build up a negative attitude, right. And everybody know them as being harsh and crude and all that, they calling a woman, saying things and the woman don't take them on, and don't say anything . . . they [the

fellas] start calling them names because they feel that they lose their pride. So it takes to them that they have to insult her or say something [negative]. Some fellas see that as an advantage to abuse them. So I wouldn't really classify them as men. (Focus group session 1997)

What should not be overlooked in this analysis is that though women are principally affected by public harassment, this abuse is also experienced by gay and transvestite men. Though it is safe to argue that the public sphere is the principal arena of operation of men in the Caribbean, it is not so for marginalized men. In short, public harassment is essentially reserved for women and "feminized" men in the Caribbean. The difference in the nature of the harassment is that directed towards women it is characterized by some notion of sexual desire, whereas harassment of gay men is marked by derision, hostility and sometimes violence. If the terrain of gendered practices is to be transformed, then men need to recognize that public harassment is not only unacceptable behaviour but also a violation of individual rights. Women, too, would do well to analyse their own collusion with men in the public ridicule of marginalized men.

In addition to the public harassment of homosexual men, there is also the public abuse of lesbian women. Women who are known as or perceived by the community to be lesbian are the subject of much public derision. The lesbian woman in the Caribbean faces the double burden of public harassment as female and as one whose sexual preference is openly disparaged by both men and women. Moreover, the use of anti-lesbian invective is not limited to lesbians but can be used as a form of social control over heterosexual women and/or feminists who are perceived to be too assertive or ambitious. Many female political aspirants in the Caribbean have been stigmatized as lesbian. It is clear, therefore, that we should be moving to some understanding of the public arena as a sphere which ought to be free of personal abuse and oppression. Here is another meaningful way in which we could begin to rethink the organization and everyday reproduction of civil society in the Caribbean. It is important that community-based organizations expand their focus to include some emphasis on transforming the political culture of the public sphere in the Caribbean.[2]

Sexual Harassment at the Workplace

In the Caribbean, sexual harassment at the workplace is common. It transcends race, ethnicity, class and age. Like public harassment, it is so much a part of the gendered landscape of the region that some men are unaware that it is a violation. Sexual harassment at the workplace refers generally to unwelcome advances, inappropriate touching and speech, sexual advances, sexual innuendo which create thereby a hostile or poisoned work environment. Sexual harassment can take place between coworkers or between a worker and a supervisor or employer. Sexual harassment usually occurs when the unwelcome behaviour is repeated, but the initial act could be sufficiently egregious to constitute harassment without repetition. Fondling of women's breasts or behinds or groping of the male or female genitals would qualify as flagrant acts which need not be repeated in order to constitute sexual harassment. Women are the main victims of sexual harassment at the workplace; however men can also be victimized in this way, as recent examples in the United States have shown. As the legal drafters in the Caribbean begin to write their specific legislation against sexual harassment at the workplace they should define conduct in such a way that it may be equally applicable to men and women in the region. Same-sex sexual harassment is equally inappropriate and indictable, as recent Supreme Court decisions in the United States have proven. Men are rarely the victims of sexual harassment at the workplace, but the fact remains that on the occasion that it does occur, men should have some legal redress to protect their rights. Some men argue that the Caribbean has succumbed to foreign propaganda on this matter: "This whole sexual harassment thing, I think that thing is overblown, eh. Especially because of the US and the television thing. I don't think that is a problem in our society" (Grenadian respondent).

Others demonstrate a basic ignorance about what constitutes sexual harassment at the workplace:

> By a coworker is not a problem. If you can talk yuh way through and you and the lady organize a little thing for later, I don't have a problem with that. I don't even have a problem with the boss doing a little touching, but the problem I have is if the boss use the touching to employ her. In other words, she could get the work she must lie down with him. I have a problem with that. But if by working, she reach the boss standard, he could do with a touch, he is human too. (Grenadian respondent)

Among the younger men of St Lucia, opinions about sexual harassment at the workplace ranged from understanding to confusion. One respondent viewed the matter both sensibly and perceptively when he related sexual harassment to gender and power: "I think it is kind of the equivalent of rape. It is showing dominance over the female. You are showing that you have more power than she does and you are demonstrating it by forcing her to do something she does not want to do or may not want to do."

Sexual harassment has to do with the fundamental asymmetry of power between individuals at work. It usually occurs between an employer and employee, or supervisor and employee, or it can, in other ways, reflect hierarchical differences between the harasser and the one being harassed. In such situations the junior person (usually a woman) has to become concerned with job loss, lack of promotion, failure to obtain the more prestigious assignments, inter alia, because of noncompliance with someone's sexual advances. In the Caribbean, this burden of vulnerability falls mostly on working-class women, who have so many economic obligations that resistance to sexual advances may come at a tremendous personal cost. Professional and other middle-class women are often better able to ward off such advances.

Another St Lucian young man voiced his opposition to sexual harassment, suggesting that it may be the fault of the woman as temptress, combined with the sexual vulnerabilities of the male:

> I do not support sexual harassment per se, but at the same time, one must recognize that men are human beings. And some of the women, the way they dress, they dress very suggestively. And naturally, the man would be attracted by that, so you should expect a certain response to the way you dress. Everyone has the right to dress in a certain way but however you dress makes a statement and you must expect an answer to the statement. (St Lucian respondent)

Another respondent viewed sexual harassment as the result of men being out of control: "Well, I am against that [sexual harassment] and personally it shows weakness in a man." Here sexual harassment becomes a trope about the failure to possess the steely will and control of a "real man". The issue of control as a manly characteristic is again valorized by another respondent:

> I don't agree with that thing about how they dress. I mean, a woman should be allowed to dress how she wishes, how she feels. The same way a man can walk on the street with his short pants and his chest out. Not because a woman is dressed with a short skirt means that she has to be harassed, that means that she want to

go out with you and all these sort of things. A man should be able to show some kind of control. That is part of being a man, control yourself. (St Lucian respondent)

In the following comment, however, this young man raises the spectre of harassment against men as a reaction to what he perceives as the progress of women in terms of legal protection. Finally, he anchors his concerns over sexual harassment in the familiar allegation about female temptation mentioned above:

But at the same time, I think that men do get harassed as well. The women feel empowered with the new laws and so on to go ahead and touch a man. Cause if a man reports sexual harassment, he is looked on as weak, gay, a pappy show. And I will go further and say that the short skirts, and I mean some of these skirts are really, really short, is also a form of visual sexual harassment. And I don't care how strong the man is, the man is still a man. And even if he doesn't do anything about it in the workplace, it is still in his head. (St Lucian respondent)

In the Caribbean at the moment, only the Bahamas has adopted any legislation which addresses the issue of sexual harassment in the workplace. According to a relatively recent Caribbean report which examined this legislation, "It is important to note here that the law does not deal with the subject of sexual harassment as a criminal matter but seeks to provide solutions through mediation and conciliation" (ILO/CARICOM 1995: 21).

In the other Caribbean countries there is no legal redress for sexual harassment at the workplace, except in a tangential way through sexual battery laws that are inadequate to address this phenomenon in any meaningful way. Moreover, there is no redress for a hostile environment, which may be created without inappropriate speech or touching. Women in the Caribbean have to depend on moral suasion to deal with this problem.

Envisioning a politics of gendered change in the Caribbean necessitates a major rethinking of the way men and women relate to each other in general, but particularly in the workplace. If men are to play an important role in facilitating such a change then we have to be sensitized about what is and what is not appropriate behaviour in the workplace. Governments in the Caribbean must begin to police these boundaries at the workplace more diligently. There is therefore an urgent need to create specific legislation to deal with the issue. Such legislation would not eliminate the problem, but it would certainly send an important message to everyone that inappropriate behaviour at the workplace will not be tolerated and that there are consequences attendant to such behaviour. Furthermore, legislation would not only name the behaviour but would also give remedy; that is, it would allow the aggrieved person to retain his or her job while the matter is being investigated.

Public harassment is much more intractable. Here resocialization and moral suasion are the only hope. Public harassment does not lend itself to policing quite easily. Men have to begin to understand how to respect women and marginalized men, and their right to conduct their affairs in public free of harassment. The more open, honest and serious our dialogues around this issue, the sooner all our consciences will be raised.

Growing Men's Awareness

Last of all, given the struggles for equality of Caribbean women and the impact of gender and economic changes taking place globally, men in the region have become more aware about certain gender issues than they have ever been before. Not all of the awareness has been positive or progressive. There are many Caribbean men who resent the changes which are taking place in the relations between themselves and women. Considerable work is required at this level by progressive men and women to allay their fears, placate their frustrations and assist them in this transition to a new era of gender equality.

There are, however, other men in the region who embrace a different brand of change which is largely influenced by the mythopoetic men's movements of North America, in conjunction with homespun religious fundamentalism and evangelism. I am referring here to those men who believe that God and nature ordained gender roles, and that these roles are not historically or culturally specific but transcendent. Many of these men believe that they need to find themselves and rekindle ideas of male bonding and becoming more in tune with their emotional selves (often described as the "feminine side"). I call this the politics of an interior journey. I have no problem with men working on their foibles, be they psychological or social. However, I am concerned that such desires to discover the real or true self or to fathom the need for atonement sometimes lead to "retreatism" and to the belief that the problem can be solved at the level of the individual, disregarding other dimensions of gender relations, which require a more structural and collective response. The danger of this response is that quite often working on one's self becomes an end in itself, truncating the possibility for transformation. Change is something which should not be undertaken in isolation.

Conclusion

Caribbean gender relations are best described at this historical stage as tense. The growing economic independence of some women, the advancement and achievement of the feminist movement in the region, the economic decline of the area, the problems in civil society, the loss of jobs of some men, have all had their impact on gender relations, creating different and new roles for men and women in the Caribbean. We cannot ignore the threat that all this represents for some men in the region. What is abundantly clear is that however we imagined the past to have been, we cannot expect the present or the future to be exactly the same. Gender change in the Caribbean is not only inevitable but necessary. What is urgently required are ways of continuously negotiating these changes, a massive process of gender resocialization, the creation of an environment for dialogue between men and women, and the development of creative strategies for intervention in the ongoing process of gender negotiation and accommodation. Initially, men behaved as though issues relating to gender had nothing to do with them. Part of the explanation of this response is that in reality gender was articulated in the region as a woman's issue. Fortunately, this approach is gradually shifting, and more men are beginning to think through what it means to be a man in the Caribbean and to map the terrain of masculinity in contemporary society. This development is to be encouraged. Rather than face the future with trepidation or resentment, men can demonstrate more willingness to become actively involved in constructing new processes of interaction, and can contribute to the creation of a society based on mutual respect and equality in the sphere of gender relations.

Acknowledgment

This paper has benefited from a presentation at the Twenty-second Annual Society for Caribbean Studies Conference, University of Warwick, Coventry, England, 7–9 July 1998.

The author would like to thank Vivette Glen Lewis for her comments on this paper.

Notes

1.   See, for example, Brown 1997. Other feminists in management departments at the University of the West Indies have expressed similar sentiments.
2.   The work of the Sistren Collective in Jamaica is to be commended in this regard.

References

Brown, Janet. 1997. "Young Men: Resolving the Clashes Between Old and New Images of Masculinity". Paper presented at the conference Gender, Families and Sexual Health: A Spotlight on Men, Barbados, 1–3 September.

Butler, Judith. 1995. "Melancholy Gender/Refused Identification". In *Constructing Masculinity*, edited by M. Berger, B. Wallis and S. Watson. New York: Routledge.

_____. 1990. *Gender Trouble: Feminism and the Subversion of Identity*. New York: Routledge.

Connell, R.W. 1996. "New Directions in Gender Theory, Masculinity Research, and Gender Politics". *Ethnos* 61, nos. 3 and 4.

_____. 1995. "Politics of Changing Men". *Socialist Review* 25, no. 1.

Fanon, Frantz. 1963. *The Wretched of the Earth*. New York: Grove Weidenfeld.

Inter-American Development Bank (IDB). 1997a. "Domestic Violence: Private Pain, Public Issue". *IDB América* (October).

_____. 1997b. "The Cost of Violence". *IDB América* (October).

International Labour Organization (ILO) and CARICOM. 1995. *Women, Labour and the Law: A Caribbean Perspective*. Geneva: ILO/CARICOM.

Gardner, Carol Brooks. 1995. *Passing By: Gender and Public Harassment*. Berkeley: University of California Press.

Lamming, George. 1995. *Coming, Coming Home: Conversations II*. St Martin: House of Nehesi.

Lewis, Linden. 1998. "The Social Relations of Gender and Work". *Caribbean Perspectives* (January).

Rousseau, Jean-Jacques. 1997. *Émile*. London: Everyman Library.

Spivak, Gayatri. 1987. *In Other Worlds: Essays in Cultural Politics*. New York: Methuen.

Contributors

Patricia Mohammed is Senior Lecturer and Head of the Mona Unit, Centre for Gender and Development Studies, University of the West Indies, Mona, Jamaica. She has published and written extensively in the fields of women's and gender studies for over twenty years. Her major publications include *Gender Negotiations among Indians in Trinidad* (Macmillan, 2001); *Caribbean Women at the Crossroads: The Dilemma of Decision-Making among Women of Barbados, St Lucia and Dominica,* co-authored with Althea Perkins (The Press, University of the West Indies, 1999); and the volume co-edited with Catherine Shepherd, *Gender in Caribbean Development* (1988; reprint, The Press, University of the West Indies, 1998).

Petrine Archer-Straw is a Jamaican lecturer and curator who works in both the Caribbean and the United Kingdom. She has taught at the Courtauld Institute of Art, University of London, and she has curated a number of exhibitions for both Caribbean and British audiences, including New World Imagery: Contemporary Jamaican Art (1995) and Photos and Phantasms: Harry Johnston's Photographs of the Caribbean (1998). She is co-author, with Kim Robinson, of *Jamaican Art* (Kingston Publishers, 1990) and the author of *Negrophilia: Avant-Garde Paris and Black Culture in the 1920s* (Thames and Hudson, 2000). She is currently consultant curator for the National Art Gallery of The Bahamas.

Barbara Bailey is Senior Lecturer at the University of the West Indies, Mona, Jamaica, and has been the regional coordinator of the Centre for Gender and Development Studies, University of the West Indies, Mona, since 1996. She has published and written extensively in the area of gender and education and co-edited two major Caribbean books on gender and development studies.

Anne Maria Bankay is Lecturer in the Department of Educational Studies University of the West Indies, Mona, Jamaica. Her research interests include methodology for the teaching of Spanish language and Hispanic literature. She has published articles on Spanish American and Caribbean writers, translated stories and poems from Spanish into English and recently published a book used in Caribbean high schools to prepare students for the examinations set by the Caribbean Examination Council.

Eudine Barriteau is Senior Lecturer and Head of the Centre for Gender and Development Studies, University of the West Indies, Cave Hill, Barbados. She has written widely on gender issues in economics, macroeconomics and structural adjustment. Her two recent publications are *The Political Economy of Gender in the Twentieth Century* (Palgrave International, 2001) and the collection co-edited with Alan Cobley, *Stronger, Surer, Bolder: Ruth Nita Barrow – Social Change and International Development* (University of the West Indies Press, 2001).

Bridget Brereton is Professor of History and Deputy Principal, University of the West Indies, St Augustine, Trinidad. She has written extensively in the areas of gender and women's studies in history. She is the author of *Race Relations in Colonial Trinidad* (Cambridge University Press, 1979); *A History of Modern Trinidad* (Heinemann, 1991); and *Law, Justice and Empire: The Colonial Career of John Gorrie* (The Press, University of the West Indies, 1997); the editor of *The Caribbean in the Twentieth Century,* volume 5 of the *UNESCO General History of the Caribbean* (Macmillan, 2000); and co-editor, with Verene Shepherd and Barbara Bailey, of *Engendering History: Caribbean Women in Historical Perspective* (Ian Randle Publishers, 1995).

Barry Chevannes is Professor of Social Anthropology and Dean of the Faculty of Social Sciences (Mona). Among his publications are *Rastafari: Roots and Ideology* (Syracuse University Press, 1995); the edited collection

Rastafari and other African-Caribbean Worldviews (Macmillan, 1994; reprint, Rutgers 1998); and *Learning to Be a Man: Culture, Socialization and Male Identity in Five Caribbean Communities* (University of the West Indies Press, 2001).

Richard L.W. Clarke is Lecturer in Literary and Cultural Theory, Department of Language, Linguistics and Literatures, University of the West Indies, Cave Hill, Barbados. He has published several articles on various aspects of cultural theory and criticism in general and on postcolonial theory in particular.

Marjan de Bruin is Senior Lecturer, Caribbean Institute of Media and Communication, University of the West Indies, Mona, Jamaica. Between 1996 and 2000 she was president of the Gender and Communication section of the International Association of Media and Communication Research. Her research interests include professional socialization of media workers, gender and media, and health communication, on which she has published regularly.

Denise de Caires Narain is Lecturer in English and Sub-Dean of Student Affairs, School of African and Asian Studies, University of Sussex. She has taught English at the University of the West Indies, Cave Hill, Barbados, and at the Open University in the United Kingdom. Her teaching and research interests are in the fields of Caribbean, postcolonial and gender studies. She is the author of *Contemporary Caribbean Women's Poetry: Making Style* (Routledge, 2002) and has also been awarded a Leverhulme Research Fellowship to work on a book on contemporary postcolonial women's writing.

Honor Ford-Smith is a teacher, performer and writer and presently lectures in cultural pluralism and the arts and women's studies at the University of Toronto. Her current research is "Performing the Nation: The Politics and Pedagogy of Jamaican Drama". Her publications include *My Mother's Last Dance* (Sister Vision Press, 1997), a collection of poems about family, death and colonial racism in Jamaica; and, with SISTREN, *Lionheart Gal: Life Stories of Jamaican Women* (Women's Press, 1986), a collection of oral and written autobiographies. She was the founding artistic director of the Jamaica feminist theatre SISTREN and with them wrote, directed and produced several plays.

Merle Hodge is Lecturer in the Department of Liberal Arts, University of the West Indies, St Augustine, Trinidad, and a founding member of the Trinidadian organization Women Working for Social Progress. Her publications include a teaching text, *The Knots in English: A Manual for Caribbean*

Users (Calaloux, 1997), and two novels, *For the Life of Laetitia* (Farrar, Straus and Giroux, 1993) and *Crick Crack Monkey* (Deutsch, 1970).

Kim Nicholas Johnson is a journalist at the Trinidadian newspaper the *Sunday Express* and has published extensively on Trinidad.

Elsa Leo-Rhynie is Professor of Women's Studies and Deputy Principal, University of the West Indies, Mona, Jamaica. She has published extensively on education, training and gender concerns and edited a number of publications including, with Barbara Bailey and Christine Barrow, *Gender: A Caribbean Multi-Disciplinary Perspective* (Ian Randle Publishers, 1996). In 2000 she received the Order of Distinction, Commander Class, from the Government of Jamaica for her contribution to the field of education.

Linden Lewis is Associate Professor of Sociology, Bucknell University, Pennsylvania. He has written and published extensively on the political economy of the Caribbean, with specific reference to global economic restructuring and its impact on labour, race, class and gender. He recently completed editing an anthology on the culture of gender and sexuality in the Caribbean and is working on a book on the social construction of masculinity in the Caribbean.

Keisha Lindsay is a graduate of the Consortium Graduate School of the Social Sciences, University of the West Indies, Mona. Her research interests include gender politics and popular culture in the Caribbean. She is a doctoral candidate in political science at the University of Chicago.

Janet Momsen is Professor of Geography, Department of Human and Community Development, University of California, Davis. She is author of *Women and Development in the Third World* (Routledge, 1991) and co-author of *A Geography of Brazilian Development* (Bell, 1974) and *Geography of Gender in the Third World* (Hutchinson, 1987). She is also the editor of *Women and Change in the Caribbean* (Ian Randle Publishers, 1993) and *Gender, Migration and Domestic Service* (Routledge, 1999). She is the co-editor of a series on international studies of women and place for Routledge.

Hilary Nicholson is Programme Coordinator of Women's Media Watch, a "small but tallawah" women's group involved in training, research and advocacy around gender-based violence and sexism and violence in the media. She is also co-founder of Video for Change, a two-woman team that has produced some twenty-five documentary videos on topics from social issues to legendary women in Jamaica. Prior to this she worked with the University of the West Indies Women's Group and the Centre for Gender and Development Studies from 1992 to 1997.

Odette Parry is Senior Research Fellow, Research Unit of Health, Behaviour and Change, University of Edinburgh. Between 1993 and 1996 she was a research fellow at the Institute of Social and Economic Research, University of the West Indies, Mona, Jamaica. Her research on Caribbean male educational underachievement has been the basis for regional and international publications. Her most recent publication from this Caribbean research is *Male Underachievement in High School Education in Jamaica, Barbados, and St Vincent and the Grenadines* (Canoe Press, University of the West Indies, 2000).

Carmen Pencle is Senior Lecturer, Faculty of Education and Liberal Studies, University of Technology, Jamaica. She is also head of the education division in the School of Technical and Vocational Education. She has an ongoing interest in gender socialization, particularly in the preparation of women for work in nontraditional roles.

Paulette A. Ramsay has taught in the Department of Modern Languages and Literature and in the Department of Language, Linguistics and Philosophy, University of the West Indies, Mona, Jamaica. She has published articles in *Afro-Hispanic Review, Caribbean Quarterly, Langston Hughes Review* and *PALARA*. She has co-authored two Spanish texts for the Caribbean Examination Council's secondary school examinations. Her translations of poems and short stories have been published both locally and in international journals.

Joan M. Rawlins is Senior Lecturer in Sociology and Health, Public Health and Primary Care Unit, Faculty of Medical Sciences, University of the West Indies, St Augustine, Trinidad. She has worked as a research fellow in the Institute of Social and Economic Research, University of the West Indies, Mona, Jamaica, and earlier as a health sociologist in the Department of Social and Preventive Medicine (Mona). Her publications include articles on teenage pregnancy, family, antenatal health, midlife and older women, and the elderly.

Michelle Rowley is a doctoral candidate in the women's studies programme at Clark University, Worcester, Massachusetts. She is a recipient of a Woodrow Wilson Dissertation Fellowship (2001) and a Fulbright/LASPAN Fellowship (1998). She is currently completing research in Trinidad for her dissertation, "The Politics of (M)Othering: Matrifocality of Afro-Trinidadian Women's Identity".

Verene A. Shepherd is Professor of History, Department of History University of the West Indies, Mona, Jamaica. She has published widely on Asians in the Caribbean, slavery and gender issues. She is editor/compiler of *Women in Caribbean History* (Ian Randle Publishers, 1999); co-editor, with Bridget Brereton and Barbara Bailey, of *Engendering History: Caribbean Women in Historical Perspective* (Ian Randle Publishers, 1995); and author of *Transients to Settlers: The Experience of Indians in Jamaica, 1845–1950* (University of Warwick, 1994).

Kathryn Shields-Brodber is Lecturer in Linguistics, Department of Language, Linguistics and Philosophy, University of the West Indies, Mona, Jamaica. She has written widely on issues of language and linguistics in the Jamaican society.

Alissa Trotz is Assistant Professor, Institute of Women's Studies and Gender Studies/Sociology and Equity Studies, Ontario Institute for Studies in Education, University of Toronto. Her research is on gender, "race" and class in the Caribbean context, and she is co-author, with Linda Peake, of *Gender, Ethnicity and Place: Guyanese Women's Identities* (Routledge, 1999). She is a member of Red Thread Women's Development Programme, Guyana.

Kathy-Ann Waterman is an attorney-at-law in the Office of the Director of Public Prosecutions in Trinidad. She has worked as a journalist at the *Express,* Trinidad. In 1996 she was voted most outstanding journalist in her country by a panel of judges in an annual media competition.

Peter Whiteley is Director, Quality Assurance Unit, University of the West Indies, Mona, Jamaica. He has taught science education in the Department of Educational Studies, University of the West Indies, Mona, and has published for many years in the field of education and made numerous professional presentations throughout the Caribbean.

Saskia Wieringa is Associate Professor of Women's Studies at the Institute of Social Studies, The Hague, The Netherlands. She has published widely on issues of feminist theory, gender and development, and sexual politics.

David Williams is Lecturer, Department of Literatures in English, University of the West Indies, Mona, Jamaica.